Critical Acclaim for *User Interface Design and Evaluation!*

User Interface Design and Evaluation *is comprehensive and clear. It's an amazing achievement — a textbook in plain English that works both for the classroom and for practitioners learning on their own. It covers the entire user-centered design process with details on the steps and techniques for requirements gathering, design, and evaluation. It includes great stories and case studies as well as engaging exercises. This is a superb book that puts all the pieces together.*
—Ginny Redish, Redish & Associates, Inc.

What makes this book unique is its blend of traditional HCI concepts and contemporary guidelines as well as its inclusion of practical pointers for acceptance of user-centered design. Unlike other HCI books, this text is generally succinct and to the point. Yet beyond being an excellent reference, it also includes very good practical examples, e.g., design of GUI, Web, and embedded systems are especially useful. The book's coverage of traditional HCI notions (e.g., visibility, affordance, feedback, metaphors, mental models, and the like), combined with practical guidelines to contemporary designs (e.g., GUIs, Web) ranks this work among the best in the field, particularly well suited as a textbook for students in a HCI class.
—Andrew Duchowski, Clemson University

The entire UI design process is presented in this text with an effective blend of theory and practice. The authors do a fine job of presenting "classic" HCI foundations and current trends in UI design. The authors have a keen knack for using interesting and practical demonstrations, examples, and exercises to reinforce key concepts. The strength of this text is the step-by-step "how-to-do-usability" guidance provided throughout the text. This book will motivate the reader to want to immediately "jump on the UI design bandwagon" and to get started on the business of attending to users in UI design.
—Laurie P. Dringus, Nova Southeastern University

This text provides a solid introduction to current thought and practices in User Interface Design and Evaluation. The authors provide a logical structure for the highly iterative work of UI Design, and the book is organized to support classroom presentation and discussion. This text can be a valuable resource for students of UI Design and Evaluation, as well as for technical and management professionals interested in an introduction to the field.
—Karl Steiner, Karl Steiner, Ph.D. Usability Manager, UGS

While reading the review copy of this book, I actually felt guilty about having taught so many HCI courses with the existing well-known textbooks. This book offers much more of the sort of material that students yearn for but find too little of in existing textbooks: extensive, concrete, and realistic advice and examples about how to proceed while designing and evaluating user interfaces. With a steady stream of brief examples and some longer case studies; with "how-to-do-it" advice and worked-out solutions to problems, the student is constantly confronted with — and guided through — the multifaceted real world of user interface design. The book also contains the material that we are accustomed to finding in HCI textbooks: presentation of well-known HCI concepts, principles, results, and methods.

This material is woven together with the more concrete, practical information in a creative way that enhances the appreciation of both types of content.
—Anthony Jameson, Professor, International University in Germany and principal researcher at DFKI, the German Research Center for Artificial Intelligence.

This book provides the computing professional with a solid base in interface design and evaluation. It continually reinforces the role of the user by integrating the discussion of the guidelines and practices of effective interface design with thoughtful and appropriate examples, exercises and case studies. The authors follow a life-cycle approach in the discussion of the topics, which are treated in enough depth to be useful to the practitioner. Of particular note is the discussion of the design issues for GUIs as well as for the web, embedded computer systems and small devices. The treatment of usability evaluations and their outcomes rounds out the topics. Overall, I consider this book to be one of the best in this area.
—Evelyn P. Rozanski, Rochester Institute of Technology

User Interface Design and Evaluation

The Morgan Kaufmann Series in Interactive Technologies

Series Editors:
- Stuart Card, PARC
- Jonathan Grudin, Microsoft
- Jakob Nielsen, Nielsen Norman Group

User Interface Design and Evaluation
Debbie Stone, Caroline Jarrett, Mark Woodroffe, Shailey Minocha

Cost-Justifying Usability
Edited by Randolph Bias and Deborah Mayhew

Personas and User Archetypes
John Pruitt and Tamara Adlin

Rapid Contextual Design
Karen Holtzblatt, Jessamyn Burns Wendell and Shelley Wood

Voice Interaction Design: Crafting the New Conversational Speech Systems
Randy Allen Harris

Understanding Users: A Practical Guide to User Requirements Methods, Tools, and Techniques
Catherine Courage and Kathy Baxter

The Web Application Design Handbook: Best Practices for Web-Based Software
Susan Fowler and Victor Stanwick

The Mobile Connection: The Cell Phone's Impact on Society
Richard Ling

Information Visualization: Perception for Design, 2nd Edition
Colin Ware

Interaction Design for Complex Problem Solving: Developing Useful and Usable Software
Barbara Mirel

The Craft of Information Visualization: Readings and Reflections
Written and edited by Ben Bederson and Ben Shneiderman

HCI Models, Theories, and Frameworks: Towards a Multidisciplinary Science
Edited by John M. Carroll

Web Bloopers: 60 Common Web Design Mistakes, and How to Avoid Them
Jeff Johnson

Observing the User Experience: A Practitioner's Guide to User Research
Mike Kuniavsky

Paper Prototyping: The Fast and Easy Way to Design and Refine User Interfaces
Carolyn Snyder

Persuasive Technology: Using Computers to Change What We Think and Do
B. J. Fogg

Coordinating User Interfaces for Consistency
Edited by Jakob Nielsen

User Interface Design and Evaluation

DEBBIE STONE
The Open University, UK

CAROLINE JARRETT
Effortmark Limited

MARK WOODROFFE
The Open University, UK

SHAILEY MINOCHA
The Open University, UK

AMSTERDAM • BOSTON • HEIDELBERG • LONDON
NEW YORK • OXFORD • PARIS • SAN DIEGO
SAN FRANCISCO • SINGAPORTE • SYDNEY • TOKYO

Morgan Kaufmann Publishers is an imprint of Elsevier.

MORGAN KAUFMANN PUBLISHERS

Publishing Director	Diane D. Cerra
Publishing Services Manager	Simon Crump
Editorial Coordinator	Mona Buehler
Editorial Assistant	Asma Stephan
Project Manager	Daniel Stone
Cover Design	Shawn Girsberger
Cover Image	© 2005 Artist Rights Society (ARS), New York/ADAGP, Paris. Courtesy of SuperStock, Inc.
Composition	SNP Best-Set Typesetter Ltd., Hong Kong
Technical Illustration	Dartmouth Publishing
Copyeditor	Karen Carriere
Proofreader	Phyllis Coyne Proofreading Services
Indexer	Gerry Lynn Messner
Interior Printer	RR Donnelly
Cover Print	Phoenix

Morgan Kaufmann Publishers is an imprint of Elsevier.
500 Sansome Street, Suite 400, San Francisco, CA 94111

This book is printed on acid-free paper.

Library of Congress Control Number:

Library of Congress Cataloging-in-Publication Data
User interface design and evaluation / Debbie Stone . . . [et al.].
    p. cm. - (Morgan Kaufmann series in interactive technologies)
    ISBN-13: 978–0–12–088436–0   ISBN-10: 0–12–088436–4
    1. User interfaces (Computer systems) I. Stone, Deborarh L. II. Series.

[QA76.9.U835 2005]
005.4'37-dc22

                                                        2004061900

ISBN-13: 978–0–12–088436–0
ISBN-10: 0–12–088436–4

For information on all Morgan Kaufmann publications, visit our website at *www.mkp.com.*

Printed in China
07 08 09   5 4 3

Contents

Contents

Contents

Contents

Figure Credits

Figures 1.5 and 1.6 Picture © Copyright Steve Krug 2004. Used with permission.

Figures 4.6 and 4.7 © Copyright London Transport Museum. Used with permission. Registered user no. 05/4288.

Figures 5.5 and 5.8 © Copyright 1951 by the Board of Trustees of the University of Illinois, American Journal of Psychology. Used with permission of the University of Illinois Press.

Figure 5.7 © Copyright Bernards Ltd. Used with permission.

Figures 7.1, 12.7, 12.16, 12.20, 14.3, 19.1, 19.2, 19.6, 21.4, 22.2, 22.3, 23.4, 25.1, 26.1, 28.1, 28.3, 29.1 Reprinted by permission of Open University.

Figure 12.1 and Dilbert Cartoon reprinted by permission of United Feature Syndicate, Inc.

Figures 12.3, 12.4, 12.9, 12.10 © Copyright Keytools Ltd. (UK) www.keytools.com. Used with permission.

Figure 12.6 © Copyright PalmOne Inc.

Figure 12.17 © courtesy of Sony Entertainment.

Figure 12.18 © Copyright Iridian Tech. Used with permission.

Figure 12.19 Copyright © 2004, PalmSource, Inc. The Grafitti 2 character stroke images are the copyrighted materials of PalmSource, Inc. PalmSource and Graffiti are registered trademarks of PalmSource, Inc. or its affiliates in the United States, France, Germany, Japan, the United Kingdom, and other countries. All rights reserved.

Figure 12.22 © Copyright Paul Forster. Used with permission.

Figure 13.3 Reprinted by permission, Envisioning Information, Edward Tufte, Graphics Press, Cheshire, CT, 1990.

Figure 18.6 © Copyright Interaction Design Inc.

Figures 22.4, 25.6 courtesy of Caroline Jarrett.

Figure 23.1 Ovo Studios Copyright © 2004 Scott A. Butler.

Figure 23.5 © Copyright Tobii Technology. Used with permission.

Preface

1   An Introduction to User Interface Design and Evaluation

How many of us can say that all the technology we encounter is easy to use and easy to learn? Do you find some software packages more difficult to use than others? Have you ever watched someone struggling to program their video recorder or set the clock on their microwave oven? How often does your computer behave in a manner that you do not understand? The cause of most of these problems is a poorly designed user interface (UI).

The UI is a vital part of almost all computer systems. Numerous accidents and disasters have been blamed on the design of the UI. Every day, poor UIs result in increased error rates, higher training costs, and reduced throughput. This costs businesses money and causes stress for those interacting with the UIs — the users.

By studying this book, you will learn the theory behind good UI design and develop the skills needed to design and evaluate your own UIs. Throughout the book, we emphasize the importance of the user in developing UIs. You will learn that attending to the users and to how they behave in practice is the key to the development of usable UIs. We will teach you the skills needed for getting to know the users and

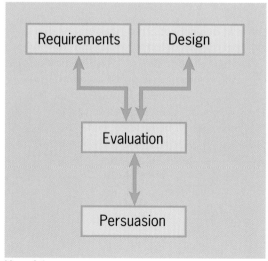

Map of the parts

addressing their needs when you are designing a UI. We will also show you how to evaluate a UI. After acting on the results of the evaluation, you can have confidence that the UI is as usable as possible.

The book is divided into five parts:

1. Introduction — Using examples, we illustrate the importance of good UI design, and the costs related to poor UI design.

2. Requirements — To create a good UI, you need to ensure that you know who will use it and for what purpose.

3. Design — The design part takes you through conceptual design, choosing interaction devices and software components, and then integrating these components within specific design areas.

4. Evaluation — Finding out whether your UI works is an intrinsic part of developing it. This part will tell you how to do this.

5. Persuasion — Many of us work, or plan to work in the future, in organizations. It is as important to convince your colleagues of the need to make changes to the UI as to decide what those changes might be. This final part is about the challenges of winning and maintaining support for the changes you wish to make.

2 | The Viewpoint of This Book

We have a particular viewpoint, or philosophy, that permeates this book:

- UI development should be user-centered. This means that an understanding of the users, the tasks that they wish to carry out, and the environments in which they will be working must be central to the development process.
- Developing a UI should be an iterative process, requiring repeated prototyping and evaluation, and close collaboration with users and other stakeholders. This means that the precise activities and the order in which they are undertaken is likely to be different each time a UI is developed.
- A UI is an ensemble of elements. It is necessary to look at the relationship between these elements in order to understand the whole.
- Designing usable UIs draws on a range of disciplines, including computer science, cognitive psychology, and graphic design.

The aim of the book is to communicate this viewpoint by showing how it can result in the development of usable UIs. This is achieved by explaining the theory underpinning the design and evaluation of UIs and helping you develop a range of relevant professional, cognitive, and key skills.

3 | What This Book Aims to Achieve

The overall learning outcomes of this book are

3.1 Practical and Professional Skills

After studying this book, you will

- Have an awareness of the role of the UI in the development of software
- Be able to promote user-centered UI development within your organization
- Be able to design and evaluate UIs

3.2 Knowledge and Understanding

After studying this book, you will have an understanding of

- The importance of user-centered UI design and evaluation
- The relevant aspects of related academic disciplines, including computer science, cognitive psychology, and graphic design
- The concepts, principles, and techniques associated with usability requirements gathering
- The concepts, principles, and techniques associated with designing UIs
- The concepts, principles, and techniques associated with evaluating UIs

3.3 Cognitive Skills

After studying this book, you will be able to

- Develop a UI in a flexible, iterative manner, working in close collaboration with the users
- Specify the profile of the users, the tasks they wish to carry out, and the environments in which they will be working
- Design a UI that better supports the users as they carry out their tasks
- Represent the underlying organization and structure of the UI
- Apply design principles and guidelines
- Choose appropriate input and output devices
- Make effective use of text, color, sound, images, moving images, and layout
- Design UIs for graphical UIs and web sites
- Develop an evaluation strategy and plan
- Undertake user observations and inspections to evaluate UI designs
- Make use of your findings from an evaluation to improve a UI

3.4 Key Skills

After studying this book, you will be able to

- Communicate effectively about UI design and evaluation
- Provide appropriate, effective documentation for the design and evaluation process

4   What We Have Not Covered in This Book

Because this book is aimed at people who are going to start designing interfaces immediately, we have omitted some topics that are important for people undertaking research in user interface design and evaluation but that we considered are less immediately useful for day-to-day practitioners. The topics that we have omitted include:

- The history of the field of human–computer interaction
- The analysis techniques Goals, Operators, Methods, and Selection Rules (GOMS) and Hierarchical Task Analysis (HTA)
- Unified Modeling Language (UML)
- The design of formal or controlled experiments
- Computer supported cooperative work (CSCW)
- Specific implementation technologies such as GUI toolkits or Javascript

Some other topics are touched on only lightly, if at all. These include:

- Fitt's Law and reaction times
- The psychology of human–computer interaction
- Virtual reality (VR)
- Statistical analysis methods
- Translation, internationalization, localization, and the development of multilingual interfaces

We apologize if we have left out something that is important to you, but we hope that this book will inspire you to want to read more deeply into the subject, including the topics that we have omitted. To assist you, we have included many suggestions for web sites and books where you can find out more. If you find that we have covered something in too much depth — well, we rely on you to use your judgment about when to skip.

5   Exercises and Discussions

When we read technical books, we like to have occasional points where the authors challenge us to try it out, so we have included various exercises. If you prefer not to stop reading to try the exercise, then by all means just continue to the discussion.

6   Acknowledgments

6.1 Case Studies

The book includes two case studies: Tokairo (in Chapters 7 and 15) and NATS (Chapter 19). We would particularly like to acknowledge the help and support of Treve Wearne, Tim Cowell, and Paul Booker from Tokairo, and Hugh Rowntree and Rachel

Darley from Tankfreight. Treve in particular spent a great deal of time with us, arranging visits to both Tankfreight and Shell Haven and providing a great deal of support and background information. We are very appreciative of all their help.

We would like to convey our sincere thanks to Alyson Evans, leader of the HCI Team at NATS ATMDC, who kindly offered to provide information about FAST. She arranged meetings with her team members, who included Colin Smith, Margaret McKeever, and Richard Harrison. We are very grateful to them, both for their help and for the time they spent with us.

6.2 Open University Course

This book is based on materials that were first published as the Open University course M873 User Interface Design and Evaluation. We would like to acknowledge the contributions of

- Felicity Head (Course Manager) and Denise Whitelock (author)
- Stephen Draper (University of Glasgow) and Geoffrey Inett (BT) (external assessors)
- The production team: Jenny Chalmers, Debbie Crouch, Paul Forster, Henryk Krajinski, Callum Lester, Michael Peet, Daniel Seamans, Stephen Webb, and Andy Whitehead

6.3 The Authors

Debbie Stone is a lecturer in the faculty of mathematics and computing at the Open University. She has attained a B.A. (Hons) in psychology and a master's degree in intelligent systems. Her Ph.D. was completed at the Open University and was based on empirical studies of designers performing design activities early in the HCI design life cycle. These studies were undertaken with a view of making recommendations as to how designers may be supported in their early HCI design tasks. Stone has been involved in the teaching of HCI via distance learning since 1993, as a course author, a course tutor, and an exam marker. More recently, she has been undertaking consultancy work for practical usability evaluation.

Caroline Jarrett is an independent usability consultant. After 13 years as a project manager of computer systems integration projects, she founded Effortmark Limited in order to concentrate on what systems are for instead of how the system is put together. Through her work with the United Kingdom tax authorities, she became fascinated with forms and now specializes in evaluation and design of paper and web forms, and effective implementation of business process that includes forms. She is author of a forthcoming book on forms design (Morgan Kaufmann, 2005) and has taught tutorials on form design and usability engineering for UPA, STC, and the Nielsen/Norman group. You can get her advice by reading her column on www.usabilitynews.com, *Caroline's Corner*. She regularly teaches and consults in the U.K., the U.S.A., and Australia. Her web site is at www.effortmark.co.uk.

Mark Woodroffe is a staff tutor, senior lecturer, and deputy head of the computing department at the Open University. He completed his Ph.D. in artificial intelligence at the University of Essex, United Kingdom, and has taught both undergraduate and postgraduate computing students for the past 16 years. Woodroffe chaired the production of the Open University course on which this book was based.

Shailey Minocha is a senior lecturer in human–computer interaction in the faculty of mathematics and computing at the Open University, where she leads a research program in customer relationship management and service quality of e-commerce environments. Her other research interests include the design and evaluation of e-learning environments for usability and learnability, the internationalization of products and systems, and the evaluation of interactive systems by eye-tracking analysis. She also teaches and provides consultancy and training in the usability of interactive systems. Minocha has a Ph.D. in digital signal processing, and she did her postdoctoral work in adaptive user interfaces at the Technical University, Braunschweig, Germany. Details of her research projects and teaching activities are available at http://mcs.open.ac.uk/sm577.

1

Introducing
User Interface Design

1

Introduction

1 Why the User Interface Matters

Human–computer interaction (**HCI**) is the study of how humans interact with computer systems. Many disciplines contribute to HCI, including computer science, psychology, ergonomics, engineering, and graphic design. HCI is a broad term that covers all aspects of the way in which people interact with computers. In their daily lives, people are coming into contact with an increasing number of computer-based technologies. Some of these computer systems, such as personal computers, we use directly. We come into contact with other systems less directly — for example, we have all seen cashiers use laser scanners and digital cash registers when we shop. And, as we are all too aware, some systems are easier to use than others.

When users interact with a computer system, they do so via a **user interface (UI)**. This book explores how to design good user interfaces — interfaces that are easy to use and easy to understand, that meet the needs of the intended users, and that support users in the tasks they wish to undertake. In this part of the book, we introduce you to user interface design and evaluation. In particular, we explain why good user interface design is important and highlight the consequences of poor or bad user interface design. More important, we will get you to start thinking about users — and why and how to involve them in the design and evaluation of the user interface.

2 Computers Are Ubiquitous

Technology has advanced so much that computer systems are used on an everyday basis by almost everyone. A **computer system** (or an **interactive computer system** or just a **system**) is the combination of hardware and software components that receive input from, and communicate output to, a user in order to support his or her performance of a task (see Figure 1.1). Computer systems may be used directly, as in the case of personal computers (PCs) in use at work or at home. Often, though, we use **embedded computer systems** where the technology is invisible to us. For

Figure 1.1 The interface is the part of the computer system with which the user interacts in order to use the system and achieve his or her goal.

example, computer-based microchip technology can be found embedded in personal goods such as digital watches and mobile phones, in domestic appliances such as microwave ovens, washing machines, and video recorders, and in the instrument panels of cars. Again, but less directly, computers are used when we shop; many stores use laser scanners that "swipe" the bar codes on goods to record both the goods we purchase and total the amounts we spend. Behind the scenes, the scanning of goods assists with automated stock control and stock reordering. When we take money from our bank accounts using an automated teller machine (ATM) or when we use ATM debit cards to buy goods electronically, our bank details are accessed via the bank's computer system. The list of everyday ways in which we use computer-based systems seems endless.

Whether we are aware of it or not, computers pervade our life. Computer applications are used either by us, or for us, in some way almost every day. The user interface (or just **interface**) is that part of the computer system with which a user interacts in order to undertake his or her tasks and achieve his or her goals.

The user interface and the ways of interacting with computer-based systems are different for each system. For example, digital watches generally have buttons that users press to set the time or use the stopwatch facility. Microwave ovens might have dials to turn or a digital display and a touchpad of buttons to set the cooking time. PCs have a screen, a keyboard, and a mouse (or sometimes a trackball or a joystick) that enable **interaction** to take place. So each user interface is different. Depending on the design of the interface, each of these systems will either be usable — that is, easy to learn and easy to use — or problematic for users.

Earlier we described a computer system as the combination of hardware and software components that receive input from, and communicate output to, a user to support his or her performance of a task. Although the user interface is simply the part of the computer system that enables interaction and serves as a bridge between users and the system, to users the interface often *is* the system (Constantine and Lockwood, 1999). The user's view of a computer system is often limited to and based solely on his or her experience of the user interface (see Figure 1.2).

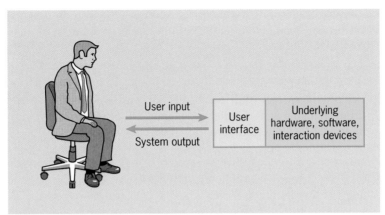

Figure 1.2 To the user, the interface *is* the computer system. (From Constantine and Lockwood, 1999.)

The design of controls, and the selection of interaction devices for input and output, will be discussed further in Chapters 12 through 14.

For example, when you use the controls on the panel of a washing machine, the controls form the interface between you and the machine — you are not concerned with the underlying technology or the software of the washing machine itself. What is important to you is that the controls and their settings are intuitive and easy to understand and use so that you will achieve your goal of laundering clothes. Similarly, when you surf the Internet, the pages of a web site displayed on your PC's monitor form the interface between you and the site. The web page UI may contain controls like scroll bars, clickable hot spots, or links in the form of text or images. These items are all part of the interface.

<table>
<tr><td>3</td><td></td></tr>
</table>

The Importance of Good User Interface Design

You will learn more about command-line interfaces and other interaction styles in Chapter 11.

Good **user interface design** is important because, as we have discussed, computer use permeates everyday life. Early computer systems were expensive and were developed mainly for particular tasks, like advanced number-crunching; as such, these systems were employed only by specialist computer users. Often the systems had command-line interfaces, with obscure commands known only by these specialist users. Thus, the user had to adapt to the system, and learning how to use the system required much effort.

Computing systems, however, are no longer the province of the specialist user. As the price of PCs and computer-based technologies has fallen, the ownership of these types of goods by nonspecialists has widened. In August 2000, 51% of households in the United States had access to one or more home computers, and 42% of households had access to the Internet (U.S. Census Bureau, 2001). In 2002, 54% of households in the United Kingdom had access to some form of home computer, and 44% had access to the Internet (National Statistics, 2004). Therefore, the need for the design and development of user interfaces that support the tasks people want to do and that can be used easily by a variety of people with varying abilities has become an important issue. Users are more comfortable with computer systems that are easy to use, easy to understand, and enable them to attain their goals with minimum frustration.

One way of demonstrating the importance of good user interface design is by showing tangible benefits that can be discussed in cash terms. For businesses, good user interfaces can lead to benefits such as higher staff productivity, lower staff turnover, higher staff morale, and higher job satisfaction. Economically, these benefits should translate into lower operating costs. In addition, computer systems that are easy to use and easy to understand require less training, again saving employers money. Bad user interfaces, on the other hand, may result in stress and unhappiness among staff, leading to high staff turnover, reduced productivity, and, consequently, financial losses for the business. As you will see later, it is easy to give examples of the effects of bad design, but showing the financial benefits of good user interface design can be more difficult. Invariably, many factors are involved and this makes it difficult to attribute success directly to good user interface design.

3.1 What Is a Good User Interface Design?

A good user interface design encourages an easy, natural, and engaging interaction between a user and a system, and it allows users to carry out their required tasks. With a good user interface, the user can forget that he or she is using a computer and get on with what he or she wants to do. Just as knowledge of the transmission mechanism of a car is of little concern to most motorists, knowledge of the internal workings of a computer system should be of little consequence to its users.

Although we have used the adjectives "good," "poor," and "bad" to describe user interfaces, it is worth noting that each of these terms is subjective: they have different meanings for different people and their use to rate various aspects of a user interface will vary. You may have used the terms "good" or "bad" to describe, for example, the colors used in an interface, the pictures on the icons, or how attractive or eye-catching the interface was. These attributes describe the overall look or aesthetics of the UI. Nevertheless, they are only a part of our focus in this book. Our real concern is whether a user interface is good, bad, or poor in relation to its **usability**.

▶ What Is Usability?

Usability is defined in Part 11 of the **ISO 9241** standard (BSI, 1998) as "the extent to which a product can be used by specified users to achieve specified goals with effectiveness, efficiency and satisfaction in a specified context of use." *Effectiveness* is the accuracy and completeness with which specified users can achieve specified goals in particular environments. *Efficiency* is defined as the resources expended in relation to the accuracy and completeness of the goals achieved. *Satisfaction* is the comfort and acceptability of the work system to its users and other people affected by its use.

We discuss some alternative definitions of usability in Chapter 6.

Note two key aspects of this definition of usability. First, to be usable an interface should be perceived as being usable by the *specified* users — users for whom the system has been designed and developed. Next, the scope of focus for the design of

You will learn more about domains, tasks, and environments in Chapter 4.

the interface is extended by looking beyond the users' immediate work environment and looking at the wider *context* or situation within which the system is expected to operate (i.e., the domain, tasks, and the environment that make up an organization). Thus, usability is concerned with the extent to which users of an application are able to work effectively, efficiently, and with satisfaction in their particular contexts.

A computer system that is usable in one context may be unusable in another. As a user interface designer, it is important to consider the context in which the system will be used. A UI that users find pleasurable is likely to be more acceptable than one that annoys them. Users are more likely to use a computer system that they enjoy than one that irritates them. Contented users are likely to be more productive, so usability is clearly related to user satisfaction (Constantine and Lockwood, 1999).

3.2 The Problems of Poor or Bad User Interfaces

▶ User Frustration and Dissatisfaction

Problems for users and the public in general arise as a result of poorly designed user interfaces. The term "computer rage" was coined in 1999 following a Market & Opinion Research International (MORI) poll conducted on behalf of Compaq Computer Limited, UK and Ireland. The study, *Rage against the Machine* (Compaq, 1999), (www.mori.com/polls/2002/bthomecomputing.shtml) found that, for one reason or another, stress and frustration levels with workplace technology are rising. Workers, it reports, have started to become both verbally and physically abusive toward the information technology (IT) in use (see Figure 1.3 and Box 1.1). Concerning monetary matters, the study indicates that

> *[t]he cost to business of this increase in stress levels of employees is not only based on sick days or under-performance, but also the working time lost through waiting for IT problems to be solved. Confederation of British Industry (CBI) statistics currently evaluate this at a staggering £25,000 ($40,000) per person in lost business each year (based on one hour a day being spent sorting out IT problems). (p. 4)*

In October 2002, research for British Telecom (BT) Home Computing, (www.mori.com/polls/2002/bthome-topline.shtml) again conducted by MORI, found that 70% of personal computer users suffered from "PC rage" — that is, the users surveyed admitted to shouting, swearing, or being violent to their computers when problems like crashing or virus infections arise.

Figure 1.3 Computer rage: Workers have started to become physically (and verbally) abusive toward IT.

| Box 1.1 | **Man Shoots Laptop** |

A 48-year-old man, George Doughty, was allegedly so frustrated by his laptop crashing that he took a handgun and shot it four times. According to police he apparently hung the destroyed laptop on a wall as if it were a "hunting trophy." Lafayette police officer Rick Bashor told local newspapers, "It's sort of funny, because everybody always threatens their computers, [but] it's the first time someone shot a computer because he was upset with it." The man admitted to police that he should not have shot his laptop, but that it seemed appropriate to at the time.

From http://news.bbc.co.uk/1/hi/world/americas/2826587.stm,
reported March 6, 2003, downloaded June 1, 2004

| Box 1.2 | **Survey Highlights Computer Rage** |

One in five Scots suffers from "Internet rage" and some feel like hurling their computers through a window, according to a survey undertaken in February 2004. Around 1000 Scots were asked to tick a box with several options about their pet hates in everyday life for the survey this month. Some 45% of those polled blamed sluggish Internet connections for making their blood boil. This was more than twice the number of people (20%) who said watching their favourite soccer team get beaten drove them mad. . . . One in 10 surfers confessed they sometimes felt like punching their keyboard, whacking the monitor with a hammer and even throwing their PCs out the window. A third of people quizzed said they had to walk away to cool down. Additionally, one fifth of Scots feel that slow Internet connections at work make them lose up to an hour a day.

From Jude Sheerin, PA News, as reported at news.scotland.com,
http://news.scotsman.com/latest.cfm?id=2522311, February 12, 2004.

Despite more than two decades of HCI research, it remains an unfortunate fact that many computer systems do not do what users want them to do. Users often describe their difficulties in system use as "computer problems," which is nonspecific as to the source of the problems. There could be several explanations. For example, the problems could be related to buggy software or to the use of older, less efficient hardware or technology that slows the processing of information. Or maybe there was no clear understanding about the work environments in which the new computer systems were expected to operate. Box 1.3 looks at problems that occurred when the UK Passport Agency introduced a new computer system.

Equally, a poorly designed user interface could have contributed to the problems. While there is no direct evidence in any of the news reports to suggest that poor user

Box 1.3	**Passport Agency Delays**

In May 1999 the UK Passport Agency hit the headlines as the waiting time for a passport applied for by post lengthened from a target time of two weeks to between seven and ten weeks. While this increase in waiting times was partly due to a larger than expected increase in passport applications (because of a new requirement for children to have their own passports), a second reason cited was "computer problems" caused by the introduction of new computer systems at two of the Passport Agency's offices. Applicants anxious to ensure that they would have their passports in time to holiday abroad queued by the hundreds in Glasgow, Liverpool, and London.

Drawn from the BBC News web site,
June 15, June 24, June 28, and June 29, 1999.

interface design was to blame, it is likely that user interface problems contributed to the difficulties that users had with these systems.

EXERCISE 1.1 (Allow 10 minutes)

Think for a moment about the situation outlined in Box 1.3. Suggest what the consequences of the Passport Agency's computer problems may have been for the following groups of people:

- The general public
- The workers at the Passport Agency

DISCUSSION

The consequences to the general public were enormous. People had great difficulty getting their passports in time for their vacations. People waiting for passports may have suffered from stress and anxiety related to the possibility that they may not be able to go away. Some may have lost money as a result of being unable to travel. Business travelers would have been affected too. Both groups probably felt anger and frustration with what they would have perceived as computers being in control and staffed by unorganized, incompetent government administrators. Furthermore, many people had to take time off work to line up for hours at passport offices. The passport agency workers, too, suffered consequences. They would have been under great stress to meet the demands of the public, and they would have felt anger and frustration because the system did not enable them to do their jobs of processing passport applications and issuing passports.

▶ Loss of Productivity, Efficiency, and Money

Computer systems with poor user interfaces can have a financial cost. Take the crisis at the Passport Agency. It was reported that the cost of this fiasco was $20 million

(£12.6 million), which included nine million dollars (six million pounds) on staff overtime and at least $242,000 (£161,000) in compensation to the hundreds of people who missed their vacations as a result of not receiving their passports on time. The Passport Agency also spent $24,000 (£16,000) on umbrellas for people who had to wait outside of passport offices in the rain to get their passports over the counter. Subsequently the price of a passport was increased. The supplier of the computer system had agreed to pay $3.7 million (£2.45 million) of the costs, leaving the remainder to be paid by the taxpayer. In these days of payment for productivity and efficiency, wages may have been lost if agency workers' earnings were linked to a level of productivity they were unable to meet because the computer system was unfit for its purpose.

3.3 Safety and the User Interface

So far we have considered the problems of poor user interfaces in terms of user frustration and dissatisfaction, and the loss of productivity and efficiency to business. There is another important aspect to consider: the issue of safety, both for computer systems users and the general public.

Systems in which human or environmental safety is of paramount concern are referred to as safety-critical systems. These systems include aircraft, aircraft flight decks, air traffic control consoles, nuclear power plants, control systems, and medical devices. The Three Mile Island nuclear power plant disaster (see Figure 1.4 and Box 1.4) illustrated that safety can be severely compromised by poor user interface design, with potentially serious consequences.

Box 1.4	**The Three Mile Island Nuclear Power Plant Disaster**

One of the most discussed issues during the early 1980s was the Three Mile Island nuclear power plant disaster. The incident nearly resulted in a meltdown of the nuclear reactor. The cause of the incident was never conclusively determined, but experts, official bodies, and the media all blamed a combination of operator error and bad interface design. In particular, much media attention and several official reports focused on the design of the control panels in the process plant. The incident could have been prevented if the control panels had been designed to provide the operators with the necessary information to enable them to perform their tasks efficiently and correctly. The following are just some of the interface problems that were identified:

- A light indicated that a valve had been closed when in fact it had not.
- The light indicator was obscured by a caution tag attached to another valve controller.

Figure 1.4 The Three Mile Island nuclear power plant.

- The control room alarm system provided audible and visual indication for more than 1500 alarm conditions. Evidently this number of alarms was intended to facilitate control of the entire plant during normal operating conditions. However, the layout and grouping of controls on the control panel had not been well thought out and so enhanced, rather than minimized, operator error (Brookes, 1982; cited in Leveson, 1995).
- A single "acknowledge" button silenced *all* the alarms at the same time, but it was not used because the operators knew they would lose information if they silenced some of the alarms. There was simply no way for the operators to cancel the less important signals so that they could attend to the important ones.

The root of the problem, therefore, seemed to be that the control panels did not support the task of serious error and incident recovery. The control panels misinformed the operators. They did not indicate to the operators the true state of affairs in the reactor plant, and they did not provide the necessary information in a form that the operators could understand and use to rectify the situation.

3.4 Elections and the User Interface

In November 2000, the topic of user interface design suddenly became international news when the outcome of the U.S. presidential election hung on the results of one county in Florida. In this election, an apparently minor aspect of equipment design turned out to have major consequences. Many voters in Palm Beach County felt that their vote went to the wrong person (see Box 1.5).

State law in Florida limited the time in the voting booth (Figure 1.5) to five minutes. The design of the ballot (Figure 1.6) was considered by some to be difficult to understand. After the election, some voters said that they wanted to vote

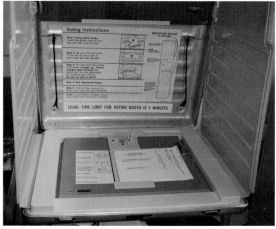

Figure 1.5 The type of ballot booth used in Palm Beach County. © Steve Krug 2004, used with permission.

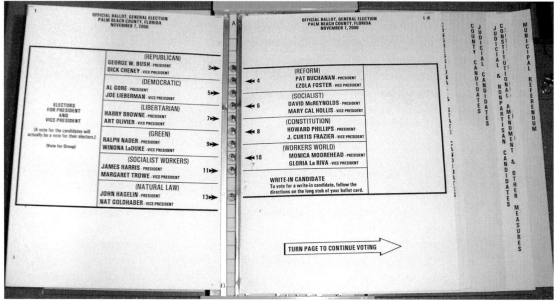

Figure 1.6 The problematic page of the ballot in the booth. © Steve Krug 2004, used with permission.

Box 1.5	**A Palm Beach Voter Comments on the Disputed Ballot**

Tuesday at the polls, the ballot information was very confusing if one was voting for the Democrat. It was hard to know whom I was voting for, the way the ballot was printed. I did not know whether I was voting for my choice, Al Gore, or for Pat Buchanan.

That was very scary and upsetting. I had to take the ballot out a couple of times and place it back again to be sure that the arrows pointed to the right hole; even after the third try, I was not sure whom I was voting for, and that makes me very mad. Many other citizens have complained regarding this situation. I am sure this was extremely confusing for senior citizens especially.

Delia Pinto-Houbrick

From the Palm Beach Post, *letters to the editor, November 10, 2000,*
www.palmbeachpost.com, visited July 8, 2003.

for Gore (which required them to punch the third hole) but they mistakenly punched the second hole down because Gore was listed second on the left.

▶ **Small Irritations Are Also a Problem**

If you have found it difficult to relate to the "catastrophic" examples we have discussed so far, there are many less disastrous but still problematic examples that may be more familiar to you. Take, for instance, the process of shutting down your computer from Microsoft Windows. To do this, you have to press the Start button on the task bar, and find the command Shut Down on the **menu**. Intuitively, is that where you would expect the Shut Down command to be? What other domestic appliance, or any other type of device, is stopped by starting it? Although the Start button may not have been the obvious place to look for the Shut Down command when you first used Windows, once you have used Windows for some time you adapt to what it makes you do to shut down your computer and you just do it.

EXERCISE 1.2 (Allow five minutes)

Think about your use of the different software applications provided in the Microsoft Office Suite or in another suite of office applications that you use (e.g., StarOffice from Sun). Choose one application, and think about a particular feature that you find confusing when you use it.

DISCUSSION

Debbie writes: The application I use most often from the Microsoft Office Suite is Word. For me, a confusing feature in more recent versions of Word is tabbed

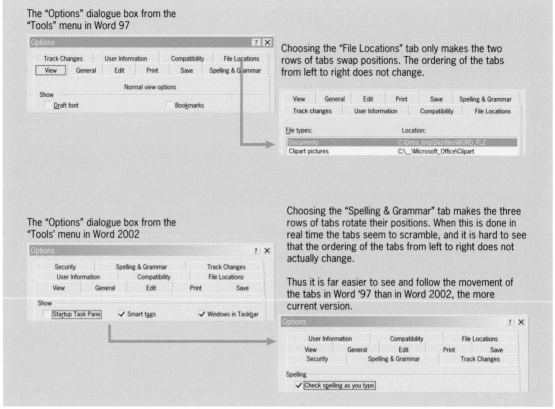

Figure 1.7 A comparison of tabbed dialog boxes for Word 97 / Word 2002.

dialogs. Specifying document settings is done via the Options tabbed dialog box, which is accessed from the Tools menu.

Before my work computer was upgraded, I had been using Word 97 for a number of years. In Word 97, there are only two rows of tabs for setting document options. As there are more tabs in one row than in the other, it is easier to see and understand how the tabs move when a tab is clicked on.

With greater word processing functionality, the Options dialog box became more complex in Word 2002; there are eleven tabs in the Options dialog box arranged in three rows of tabs. Clicking on any tab causes a puzzling rearrangement of the tabs. In fact, each row of tabs moves as a whole; only the row positions are changed rather than the positions of the tabs themselves, so there is some reason to it (see Figure 1.7).

4 Designing for Users

With the more widespread use of computers, the knowledge, skills, and experience of computer users have become very broad. A good user interface caters to end users and supports them in the tasks they wish to undertake. A computer system that is developed without a good knowledge of the users and what they want to do with the system may be usable in that it can be used to do *something*, but it may not do what the users want to do in order to achieve their goals. The system will be *usable*, but not necessarily *useful*. This is not to say that all computer systems have to be designed to accommodate everyone. Computer systems should be designed for the needs and capabilities of the users for whom they are intended. Ultimately, a user should not have to think unnecessarily about the intricacies of how to use a computer unless, of course, that itself is the user's task.

4.1 User-Centered Design

User-centered design (UCD) is an approach to user interface design and development that involves users throughout the design and development process. User-centered design not only focuses on understanding the users of a computer system under development but also requires an understanding of the tasks that users will perform with the system and of the **environment** (organizational, social, and physical) in which they will use the system. Taking a user-centered design approach should optimize a computer system's usability.

Earlier we provided the ISO 9241:11 definition of usability. ISO 13407, *Human-Centered Design Processes for Interactive Systems* (ISO, 1997), provides guidance on and lists the main principles and essential activities for human (user)-centered design, for achieving usability in systems. Briefly, the four main principles of human-centered design are (ISO, 1997 p. 7):

1.	The active involvement of users
2.	An appropriate allocation of function between user and system
3.	The iteration of design solutions
4.	Multidisciplinary design teams

The four essential human-centered design activities are (ISO, 1997 p. 10):

1.	Understand and specify the context of use
2.	Specify the user and organizational requirements
3.	Produce design solutions (prototypes)
4.	Evaluate designs with users against requirements

Adopting the approach prescribed by ISO 13407 ensures that the users' perspectives form part of the HCI design and development process, which will positively influence the usability of the final product.

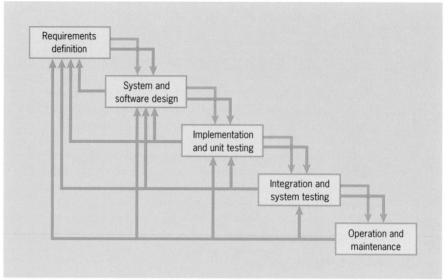

Figure 1.8 The classic life cycle. (From Sommerville, 1995.)

4.2 The Classic Life Cycle

User-centered design and traditional software engineering take very different approaches to computer system design. Traditionally, software developers have treated each phase of the software design life cycle as an independent part of software development, which must be completely satisfied before moving on to the next phase. This is particularly so in relation to the **classic life cycle** (also known as the waterfall model, so named because of the cascade from one phase to another; see Figure 1.8). It prescribes a predominantly sequential transition between the successive software life cycle phases, where each phase is completely satisfied before the next begins (this is represented in Figure 1.8 by the red arrows).

This view is, of course, simplistic. Software engineers readily accept that although the design is guided and regulated by this top-down somewhat linear model, in practice there are many iterations up and down between stages. Sommerville (1992), for example, has the following to say on the matter:

> In practice, however, the development stages overlap and feed information to each other. During design, problems with requirements are identified; during coding, design problems are found; and so on. The software process is not a simple linear model but involves a sequence of iterations of the development activities. (p. 7)

Therefore, within the software design life cycle there is a need for the phases to feed information to each other, and for iteration, rather than the development proceeding from start to finish in a simple linear fashion. This iteration is represented in Figure 1.8 by the blue arrows. The essential difference between the classic life cycle

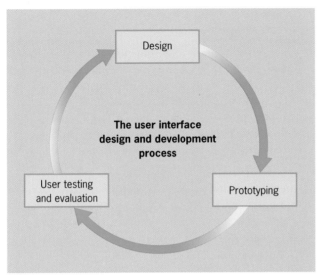

Figure 1.9 The iterative user interface design and evaluation process. (From Greenberg, 1996.)

and user-centered interface design is that user interface design and development is based on the premise that users should be involved throughout the design life cycle. Additionally, the process should be highly iterative, so that the design can be tested (or evaluated) with users to make sure it meets the users' requirements. Unlike this **iterative design** process, the waterfall life cycle generally leaves evaluation to the end. Let us look at these aspects further. Figure 1.9 illustrates the iterative user interface design and development process.

4.3 Involving Users

The way to be user-centered is to involve users and to pay attention to their views. This can include a variety of approaches, from simply observing users' working practices as part of collecting system requirements, to using psychologically based user-modeling techniques, to including user representatives on the design team. More important, users should be involved in the testing and evaluation of the system during its design and development. But who are the users?

▶ Who Are the Users?

In a user interface design project, developers generally refer to several types of people as users:

- Customers, who pay for and perhaps specify the computer system under development
- Other people within the users' organizations who have an interest in the development of the system
- Users or end users — the people who actually use the system directly to undertake tasks and achieve goals

To avoid confusion, from this point on we will reserve the term "users" for the end users of a computer system.

The difficulty in having so many different people involved is that everyone works from his or her own perspective and has a particular agenda. For example, managers will want to ensure that their organization's effectiveness is not impaired by the introduction of a new system. They will want to be sure that the final solution is cost-effective, does not threaten efficiency, and is safe and reliable. Professional bodies or trade unions will want to ensure that working agreements are not broken and that workers' rights in relation to employment and IT-related health and safety issues are protected.

Additionally, there is the design team, which potentially includes, as well as users, design team managers, marketing personnel, software engineers and designers, programmers, graphic designers, systems analysts, HCI specialists, and other research and development staff. Again, each works from his or her own perspective. A software engineer, for example, may provide advice about optimal configurations of computer system architecture and the performance of the software. A graphic designer will focus on the visual appeal of the UI and may wish to establish whether graphics are appropriate to all application areas or whether there are any potential problems in selecting iconic representations for certain situations. Marketing people want to sell products on time and as cost-effectively as possible and want the right image for the application. Users need to feel confident that the computer system will offer the right facilities to ensure that their work is carried out at least as effectively as with previous methods or computer systems.

You will learn more about constraints and trade-offs in Part 2.

You will learn more about persuading others to make changes in Chapters 28 and 29.

It can be difficult to reconcile all the views, and there will be constraints and trade-offs related to decisions made for the final design.

EXERCISE 1.3 (Allow 10 minutes)

Think about a recent project you have been involved with at work or an important meeting that you have attended (for example, a meeting at a club you belong to or a local community meeting). Various people were there, all expressing their own views. In the project or at the meeting, was it easy/necessary/appropriate to accommodate all the views expressed when arriving at a decision?

DISCUSSION

Many people have been involved in the development of this book. The following is a partial list:

- The academic members of the editorial team
- The authors and others involved in the Open University course that this book has been drawn from
- Academic and professional reviewers
- Our publisher and its editing staff

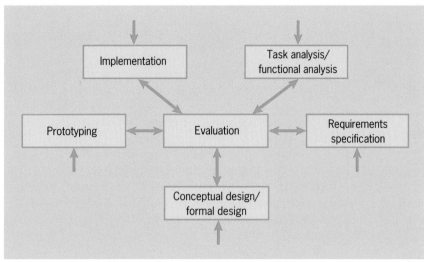

Figure 1.10 The star life cycle. (From Hix and Hartson, 1993.)

> It has sometimes been challenging to work as a team as we are scattered across different time zones and some people have moved on to other work since they made their original contributions.

4.4 Making the Design Process Iterative

Making the user interface design and development process iterative is a way of ensuring that users can get involved in design and that different kinds of knowledge and expertise related to the computer system can be brought into play as needed. We shall use an approach adapted from a model proposed by Hix and Hartson (1993). It is known as the star life cycle for obvious reasons, as you can see from its appearance in Figure 1.10.

The star life cycle encourages iteration. First, you will notice that the central point of the star is **evaluation**, which is viewed as being relevant at all stages in the life cycle and not just at the end of product development as the classic life cycle tends to suggest. Evaluation is concerned with gathering data about the usability of a design or product by a specified group of users for a particular activity within a specified environment or work context. Not surprisingly, a host of different evaluation techniques are needed to support the different stages of design and to reflect the design needs of different kinds of products. These include **interviews** with users and others, observing users in their workplace, and getting users' opinions from questionnaires or other types of surveys. Second, the star life cycle is "intended to be equally supportive of both top-down and bottom-up development, plus inside-out and outside-in development" (Hix and Hartson, 1993, p. 101). Thus, a design can start with any process in the star life cycle.

You will learn more about evaluation in Part 4.

▶ When and How to Involve Users

Users should be involved in every part of the user interface design and development life cycle.

- *Early in the design process when the requirements are being specified.* Users could help in defining the requirements for the system by contributing a specification or by testing early mockups. Users can get involved by allowing themselves to be observed and giving feedback about the problems of the current system.
- *During prototyping, to test designs and options.* Users could test versions of the interface to provide feedback and make suggestions to the designers.
- *Just before delivery of the product.* Users again could test the product by using it or completing surveys about the various features. At this point, however, only minimal changes would be allowable.
- *During training/after delivery of the system.* Again, users would use the product and give their opinions and detail any problems. Revisions at this stage would be included in the next version.

EXERCISE 1.4 (Allow 10 minutes)

Think about the approach you take to software development at work. If this is not applicable to you, think about how you might approach a task like preparing a meal for friends. Think about where you would involve users and where you might work iteratively (that is, where you might repeat steps).

DISCUSSION

If I were to prepare a meal for friends, I would certainly involve them by first asking when they could come — there's no point in cooking a great meal and then asking them whether they are available! I would also consult them in advance over particular food likes and dislikes or perhaps what they would want on the menu. In cooking, there are dozens of things you do repeatedly (or iteratively): lots of tasting goes on, and we tinker with ingredients until the taste is how we want it. My grandmother owned a restaurant and my father was a chef, so when I make, for example, a sauce for spaghetti or lasagne, it's an all-day affair. I start with tomatoes and vegetable stock, I add some spices, and then let it simmer (stirring occasionally) before tasting it. Usually it will need more salt or more stock, and once this is added I let it simmer a while longer. Somewhere along the way I add vegetables and meat (if there are no vegetarians dining with us). The sauce is usually just right about five hours later, after lots of iterations to the cooking sauce! Essentially, my approach is no different to that in Figure 1.10 — I *design* the sauce from my recipe, I test *prototypes* of the sauce as it simmers, and then I *evaluate* how good (or not!) it is.

5   The Two Types of Knowledge Needed for UI Design

You will look at the information-gathering activities in Part 2 and the UI design knowledge in Part 3.

In addition to the need for knowing about the intended users of a system and for designing iteratively, there is other information you need to know about and take into account when designing a user interface. This information comes from two sources:

- Information-gathering activities and analyses that form part of the user interface design and development process
- User interface design knowledge — for example, design principles and design rules.

6   Evaluation

This book is text based. The limitation of it being a static text-based volume of work is that the knowledge we are trying to impart can only be presented sequentially: chapter by chapter, topic by topic, in a given order. However, while you are studying this book, it is important to keep in mind the star model and to remember that there is no one single-user interface design approach or life cycle: it can start with any of the processes detailed in the star life cycle, and it should be highly iterative. Iterative design provides the opportunity for evaluation and user testing, the reviewing of the results of user testing, and the consideration of how that feeds into the cycle. In addition, it allows you to consider what design alternatives would improve the user interface design.

Don't be intimidated by the thought of *doing* evaluation. For most of us, evaluation is something we actually already do, but without formally saying, "I'll just do an evaluation here." We undertake evaluation every day, in many ways. For example, we shop, we buy different foods, we eat them, and then we decide whether they are good enough to buy again. If you drive a car, then you may be thinking about things like how many miles per gallon you are getting from your car or how well it is running. And if your car is running badly, then you may be skeptical about how well the mechanic has done his job — you are evaluating the mechanic's skill in servicing your car in relation to how well the car is performing. When we buy consumer goods, we may go into a retail outlet and play with (or evaluate) several different manufacturer's models of the item we are interested in purchasing; we press buttons, turn knobs or dials, and generally try to decide which model seems to do best what we want to purchase the item for.

> **EXERCISE 1.5 (Allow 10 minutes)**
>
> Think about a recent purchase you have made. It might be a new PC, a new car, or a domestic appliance for the home; or perhaps you were involved in making the decision about buying some equipment at work. Think about how you made the decision. Did you buy the first item you saw, or did you look for specific features to judge alternatives by and to guide your choice?

DISCUSSION

There is no right or wrong answer here, as decisions in relation to purchases are often personal to the individual and specific to the item being purchased. For example, I recently bought a microwave oven. I was looking for an oven without a turntable. This feature was important to me, as my previous model had a rotating microwave antenna under the floor of the oven (rather than an internal turntable). I had become used to being able to put any size or shape of cookware into my now defunct 15-plus-year-old model without worrying about cookware getting wedged, as often happens in ovens with turntables. Although there were other features to consider, like cost, color, design style, power levels, cooking programs, and the type of controls (dials and knobs versus touchpad and digital display), these were less important to me personally. In the end, as I was unable to find a microwave oven without a turntable, I evaluated the dozen or so models available on the other features before deciding which model to purchase.

Although I didn't find the microwave oven I wanted, in the end I made an okay choice: the oven looks good, it is only one-third the size of my old oven (which freed up some worktop space), and it was reasonably priced. However, the biggest flaw in my decision making was that I did not (or rather could not) assess (evaluate) how usable it was. It is a limitation that you cannot test certain domestic appliances in showrooms before you buy them. Now I own a microwave where I need to have the manual in front of me to set a cooking program, as the sequence of button presses is complicated and there are no reminders anywhere on the interface to tell me what the steps are (i.e., the visibility is poor).

At one meeting we discussed how each of us decided which washing machine to buy. One person was clear that he would only buy from a particular manufacturer. Another person's concern was style, another person's was spin rpm. Not one person mentioned the interface, interface controls, or usability as a prime determiner in their choice. The point here is that choices are made for many reasons, which often have nothing to do with the actual interface. Nevertheless, in designing your interfaces you should ensure that you follow an iterative user-centered design process both to increase the usability of your interfaces and to make it less of a gamble for the users.

Consciously or unconsciously we "do evaluation" in everyday life. We gather information, compare alternatives, reflect on outcomes, and make choices based on the information gathered and how well our requirements could be met. Evaluation undertaken for UI design is no different in essence. What differs is when the evaluation is done, and how the information (or knowledge) gathered is used to inform the design and development process.

6.1 When and How Do You Evaluate?

Evaluation is a way of finding out whether your systems work, and it is an ongoing activity throughout the life cycle. You can look for as many problems as possible (**diagnostic evaluation**) or you can try to measure the performance of the system (**measurement evaluation**). The role of the evaluation is always to inform the design and to improve it at all stages. Measurement evaluation frequently contributes to subsequent versions of a product. Different kinds of evaluation may be carried out at different design stages and for different reasons.

▶ Evaluation Early in the Life Cycle

Evaluation during the early design stages is undertaken to validate the users' requirements, predict the usability of the product or the usability of an aspect of the product, and to assess how well the interface meets the users' needs.

The earliest user evaluations may be best done using paper-based prototypes and mockups. These are very low cost but can yield a great amount of information and feedback about a design. Findings from early evaluations can be taken on board and fed back into the design process before the design is set.

▶ Evaluation Later in the Life Cycle

Evaluation later in the design cycle is also undertaken to assess how well the user interface meets the users' needs. It is carried out to check the usability of the nearly completed system and to ensure that the system meets the specified usability requirements. At this point, findings are unlikely to be fed into the UI design and development process, as generally by this point the system is more or less ready. These findings might be used for the next version or release of a system rather than for changing the near-finished product.

▶ How Do You Evaluate?

Choosing what to do will depend not only on the questions that you want to answer but also on logistical factors, such as the time available to do the evaluation, the availability of suitable expertise and equipment, access to users, and so on. Often the choice comes down to money: How much will it cost and how will we benefit from doing it?

There are many different techniques for evaluation. Here are just a few to get you started. The first two will be discussed further in Chapter 2, while the process of evaluation will be covered in depth in Part 4.

- *Observing the organization and how people work.* Several kinds of evaluation depend on some form of observation or monitoring of the way in which users interact with a product or **prototype**. The observation may take place informally in the field or in a laboratory as part of more formal usability testing.
- *Interviewing, talking, and asking questions.* As well as examining users' performance, it is important to find out what they think about using the technology. No matter how good users' performance scores are when using technology, if for some reason they do not like using it, then it will not be used. Surveys using questionnaires and interviews provide ways of collecting users' attitudes to the system.

- *Making predictions.* The aim of this kind of evaluation is to predict the types of problems that users will encounter without actually testing the system with them.

As a general rule, any kind of user testing is better than none. You will learn something valuable from even the most informal evaluations — watching a single user interacting with a UI under design will provide interesting and informative feedback about the design.

7 Summary

In this chapter, we introduced you to user interface design, discussed why it is important, and explored what can happen when UIs are badly designed. We then introduced you to user-centered design, emphasized the importance of user involvement throughout design and development, and stressed the need for an iterative approach to design and frequent evaluations of the design in progress. We then discussed when to evaluate user interface designs and provided a short introduction to evaluation techniques.

2

Requirements

1 Overview

Good user interface (UI) design involves understanding, so far as possible, the requirements for the system under development. Whether you are redesigning an existing computer-based system or designing a system that will computerize tasks currently being performed manually, you will find it a lot easier if you gather the necessary information in order to gain an understanding of the requirements.

Part 2 of this book concentrates on **requirements**. We will consider the following questions:

- What area of expertise, or domain, will the application be developed for?
- Who are the users?
- What do they want to do with the system?
- Where will it be used?

We then help you to analyze and make sense of the information for your UI design.

2 What You Will Find in the Chapters

Chapter 2 describes some techniques to use for finding out the requirements for the system. We introduce you to several techniques — observation, interviews, and questionnaires/surveys — that you can use in your requirements-gathering activities. Chapter 3 gets more specific. We detail the investigative activities for finding out about the the users of the system and the domain for the system. Chapter 4 explores the work or other tasks the users will perform with the system and the environments within which they will work.

In Chapter 5, we ask you to think about the information you might have gathered and how to analyze it. Analysis involves looking at the information gathered and deciding how it can inform the design of your UI. This will prepare you for the discussion of conceptual design that takes place in Part 3.

Chapter 6 describes creating usability requirements, the section of the overall requirements that specifically relates to the usability of the interface. We discuss constraints and trade-offs in creating requirements, and we describe prototyping and consider how it can be used for requirements gathering and for working toward an effective design with users and stakeholders. Prototyping is an important part of the iterative, user-centered design life cycle. You will meet it again throughout the course as you learn about designing the UI and about user evaluation of UI designs under development.

Finally, in Chapter 7, we take a break from theoretical material to look at a practical example. The first part of our case study illustrates how requirements were gathered in practice by Tokairo, UK, for the design and development of a system to collect worksheet information from truck drivers distributing oil-based products.

3 | Learning Outcomes

After studying Part 2, you will be able to:

- Employ several techniques that can be used to gather the requirements for the design of a UI
- Describe the activities involved in gathering the requirements for the design of a UI
- Understand the role of prototyping in requirements gathering

4 | Theoretical Influences

The chapters on requirements-gathering techniques, domain, users, tasks, and mental models draw from the fields of psychology and cognitive psychology. The section on environments draws from psychology and social/organizational psychology. The chapter on prototyping draws from computer science/software engineering.

2

How to gather requirements: some techniques to use

1 Introduction

There are many techniques you can use to find out about the application domain, the users, their tasks, and the environment within which the system will be used. These techniques include observing users, interviewing users, and obtaining information from users via questionnaires or surveys. Our discussion here focuses on the use of these techniques for **requirements gathering**, but you will meet these techniques again later, when we discuss how they can be employed to evaluate user interfaces (UIs).

2 Observing Your Users

Going to observe users in their natural setting — observing them while they are doing real work in their real working environment or using a home system in their homes — is an essential part of user-centered design. In addition to finding out what users do, you can also discover what aspects of the current system they like and dislike. Observation of users in their workplace or home can be either direct or indirect.

2.1 Direct Observation

Direct observation is a straightforward activity and will rapidly provide you with an insight into the users, their tasks, and the environment for a computer system. Direct observation can be undertaken in many ways, but generally direct observation studies are classified as either field studies or controlled studies. Field studies directly observe users in their usual work or home environment, doing their normal work or home tasks, with the observer making notes about interesting behaviors. Controlled studies directly observe users in a place other than their normal environment (for example, in a usability laboratory), performing specially devised tasks, with the observer recording their performance in some way, such as by timing tasks or particular sequences of actions.

You will learn more about field studies and controlled studies in Part 4.

Direct observation is always worth doing, as it is an easy activity to undertake and always yields interesting data, but it does have some limitations. For example, it only allows a single pass at the information gathering (or data collection), and although the observer may take notes, it is hard to get a full record of user activity in one observation session. The observer has to make decisions about what is important to record, and there is no opportunity to review that decision and look at alternative data later on. Furthermore, direct observation is considered to be obtrusive and can alter a user's behavior and performance.

EXERCISE 2.1 (Allow 10 minutes)

Suppose you have been asked to go into a school where a prototype of a new multimedia teaching application is being tried out by groups of 10-year-olds for the first time. The developers have asked you not to interfere with the children's activities, but to note the kinds of things they do and what difficulties they encounter. What problems might you experience using direct observation?

DISCUSSION

A lot will be going on: children talking at once, getting excited, changing groups, and maybe taking turns using the keyboard. Some children may not have listened to the instructions and may be more interested in disrupting the activities of others than in joining in the lesson. You will not be able to write down everything you see or hear. You will have to decide what is important and focus on that, which may mean that you miss some interesting interactions. You may also get distracted yourself and thus miss things. When you try to make sense of your notes later, you may not understand your own cryptic comments or you may not be able to read your own writing. However, despite these problems, having gone into the school you will undoubtedly have a better idea of how the teaching application can be used. So even this kind of observation is better than none at all.

Direct observation is useful early in the life cycle as part of gathering the requirements for a computer system. If you want a permanent record of your observations, then some sort of recording equipment (such as video, audio, or interaction logging) should be used.

2.2 Indirect Observation: Video Recording

Video recording on its own is an alternative to direct observation as it provides a permanent record of the observation session. Sometimes video recording may be used with software that automatically logs users' keystrokes or interactions. Although collecting several kinds of information can be beneficial, it means that there is more data to analyze, which can be time consuming. Because indirect observation creates more distance between observers and users, it is considered to be more objective than direct observation. Although specially mounted recording equipment (the facilities typically found in a usability lab, for example) is extremely useful, you may be surprised by just how much valuable data you can collect using ordinary consumer video equipment, especially now that small digital video recorders are available at a reasonable price. However, there are some important issues to consider. You need to plan the observation, which means thinking about what you want to find out and what kind of data you need. For example, in a study of the way that people use a UI in the context of their own workplace, it may be useful to record samples of them using the UI every day over a period of several days or weeks. These interaction samples could then be analyzed; categorizing the activities, for example, will tell you what the UI is used for, what work it helps the users to do, or how often a particular task is done. A study with quite a different and much finer focus might involve an in-depth examination of two users interacting with the UI over a period of just five minutes.

There can be practical problems associated with setting up video equipment. For instance, no matter how unobtrusive you try to be, users are likely to be aware that they are being filmed. One way of reducing the impact that the equipment has on their behavior is to leave it in place for several days before recording starts, so that the users grow accustomed to it. You will also need to decide how and when you will start and stop your recording, how you will label the recording so that you can catalog it, who will change the cassette, where the equipment will be physically located, and so on.

2.3 Points to Consider in Relation to Observation

Both direct and indirect observation will require you to make trade-offs. If you record data using video or logging software, then you can go back and look at it later. However, you may end up with an overwhelming amount of data to analyze, which can be a problem unless you have a clear idea of what you are looking for and what you want to find out. It takes many times longer to fully analyze video than it does to film it in the first place. If you record those things of interest by hand, however, your recording will probably be incomplete because you will miss things. You will thus have a less complete picture to review later.

Direct observation is the cheapest and most straightforward way of recording observations. Automatic indirect recording provides a permanent record that you can return to later and as often as necessary. The two techniques are not mutually exclusive, since you may use direct observation to initially plan your automatic recording.

EXERCISE 2.2 (Allow 10 minutes)

Figure 2.1 shows a machine for purchasing tickets to travel on the Prague underground. It is a standard UI, much like the machines you might use to purchase travel tickets for train journeys in other countries. But do you notice anything unusual?

Figure 2.1 A Prague ticket machine.

DISCUSSION

As noted previously, the UI shown in Figure 2.1 is pretty much what you would expect of a machine that lets you purchase travel tickets. However, did you notice the areas on the right-hand sides of the machines, near the coin slots, where the paint had been scraped off? This wear on the machines was caused by users who thought that the coins would drop more effectively if they were rubbed against the machine before being pushed into the slot. The reasons for this particular wear pattern on the machines would have remained unknown if someone had not gone out and observed the ticket machine being used by real commuters.

What may not be immediately apparent is how this informs the design of the UI. Basically it implies that the finish on these machines needs to be more robust. These machines are already vulnerable, as they are situated in an outside environment and exposed to all types of weather and extremes of temperature. Any damage to their finish, beyond expected wear and tear, will shorten the working life of the machine.

3 Interviewing Your Users

Interviewing involves talking to or questioning users. It enables the gathering of information in a fast and friendly way. You will need to plan interviews carefully, deciding in advance who to interview, what questions to ask to gather the relevant information, and how long the interviews should be. There are two main kinds of interview: structured and unstructured (flexible). A **structured interview** has predetermined questions that are asked in a set way; there is little, if any, scope for exploring additional topics that might arise during the interview. In contrast, a **flexible interview** generally has some set topics for discussion and exploration, but no set sequence: the interviewer is free to follow up the interviewees' replies, and to find out more about anything that is said.

A flexible interview is less formal than a structured interview and is very useful early in the design process for gathering requirements and gauging users' opinions about a particular idea. If you intend to undertake a flexible interview, however, you will find it useful to have a rough plan of the topics you want to cover, particularly if you are inexperienced at interviewing. This rough plan can be either in your head or discreetly written on paper and kept out of view. As you gain experience, you will find that interviewing becomes easier. Another factor you will need to consider is how to make the interviewee feel comfortable so that rapport is established between you. This is particularly important if you are trying to gain information that the interviewee may feel embarrassed or concerned about telling you. For example, some people feel embarrassed about criticizing a system, particularly if it involves describing their own difficulties in using it. In general, people who lack confidence tend to assume that the mistakes they make are due to their own stupidity rather than to poor design. Alternatively, they may think that their opinions are trivial and of no interest to you, or that what they say is of no importance. If you want to obtain this kind of information, then you will need to create a friendly, unthreatening atmosphere by being casual yourself while keeping sufficient control to direct and channel the discussion so that you obtain the information you want. This requires practice and experience.

3.1 Points to Consider in Relation to Interviewing

In general, the more structured the interview, the easier it is for the interviewer (Welbank, 1990). The less structured the interview, the more scope there is for picking up relevant issues, but the harder it is for the interviewer. You will need to make a judgment about the right balance to strike. Another issue to consider is how you intend to avoid asking leading questions that provoke a particular response. You will gain a lot from doing a small pilot study: either try out your interview questions and practice your interviewing skills on one or two users who will not take part in the real study, or, if you have too few users, try it out on colleagues. Data analysis is, of course, more difficult with flexible or less structured interviews, but in general such interviews provide much richer information. It is standard practice to record interviews with users; you should seek permission to record, and users rarely object. As with video logging, the advantage of audio recording is that you have a permanent record. Audio recordings of interviews should be transcribed so that you can examine what has been said in detail. Subtle comments can be easily missed if you rely solely on notes taken during the interview, as your notes are likely to be incomplete. A disadvantage to audio or video recording interviews is that initially the technique may change users' behavior.

4   Questionnaires and Surveys

Questionnaires and surveys take a different approach to interviews for the purpose of gathering information. The focus shifts from the flexible and friendly approach provided by interviewing to the preparation of unambiguous questions and statements for the gathering of more precise information.

4.1 Types of Question Structure

Broadly speaking, there are two question structures for questionnaires: closed questions and open questions.

► **Closed Questions**

A **closed question** asks the respondent to select an answer from a choice of alternative replies. Closed questions may require just "yes" or "no" responses, or they may have some form of rating scale associated with them. Which type you use will depend on whether you need simple or detailed information, as you will see from the examples below. The simplest rating scales are just checklists consisting of basic alternative responses to a very specific question. For example, a three-point scale that allows respondents to choose "yes," "no," or "don't know" is often used (see Figure 2.2). These questions are easy to analyze because all you need to do is to count the number of responses in each category.

More complex rating scales increase the number of points (or responses) to produce a multipoint rating scale called a **semantic differential**. The meanings of just the end points are given, as shown in Figure 2.3. Users are asked to select the point along the scale that most closely matches their feelings or opinion about what is being rated.

Can you use the following text editing commands?

	Yes	No	Don't know
COPY			
PASTE			

Figure 2.2 An example of a simple checklist.

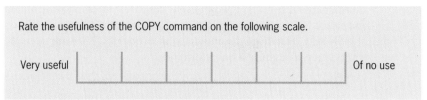

Figure 2.3 An example of a semantic differential.

For more information on questionnaire design and attitude measurement, see Oppenheim (1999), a much easier book to read and use than its initial appearance would suggest.

You can explore a variety of views about the system such as whether the users think it is easy or hard to do certain tasks or whether it makes them feel good or bad.

Semantic differentials are often created with seven points, but five-point or even three-point scales can be just as effective and are quicker to analyze. You will get better results from semantic differentials if you make sure that the two adjectives at the end points are definitely opposed and are meaningful for each of the aspects that you are asking the users to rate. A series of specifically designed pairs of adjectives will often give you better results than asking users to rate a variety of aspects of the system from "poor" to "excellent."

A **Likert scale** is a selection of statements, each similar to a semantic differential, that when analyzed together portray a user's attitude. The construction of Likert scales requires statistical analysis that is outside the scope of this book.

Once a semantic differential has been completed by the selected population of users, then you can get a feel for the strength of opinion in the respondents by counting up the number of responses at each point in the scale. Although it is tempting to try to calculate a numeric value by adding up the plus and minus points score and dividing by the number of respondents, this can be misleading as some people rarely or never choose the outside values in the scale even though they have strong opinions, while others will choose extreme values to represent milder opinions.

▶ **Open Questions**

An **open question** allows respondents to say whatever they like in response, and they are used where there are no predetermined answers. Open questions typically start with phrases such as "What do you . . . ," "How do you . . . ," or "What ways . . . ." Limiting the amount of space on the form for the answer can encourage respondents to prioritize their points (Rubin, 1994). Open questions provide richer data than do closed questions, although the responses will be more time consuming to analyze as you you need to read each one and decide on some way of grouping and classifying them. If you have a fairly small sample, say up to 100 respondents, it may be quicker and just as effective to create a simple list of all the responses to each open question.

4.2 Points to Consider When Designing Questionnaires

Potentially, questionnaires can reach a large number of people, so it is important to ensure that they are well designed. A boring questionnaire that asks impertinent or complicated questions will get a low response rate and may alienate your users. On the other hand, a carefully designed questionnaire that you have piloted can be a speedy way of getting data from a lot of users. There are several points to keep in mind when designing a questionnaire:

- Make the process easy for the person who is answering by keeping the questions simple, and ask as few questions as possible; unless absolutely necessary, aim for no more than two sides of letter paper or A4 paper (an ISO standard size of paper slightly longer and slightly less wide than letter paper).
- Make sure the questions are clear and unambiguous, as you will not be there to address any difficulties that the people completing the questionnaire may have.
- Make sure the questions will gather the information you need.
- Provide oppportunities for your respondents to offer information that you may not have thought about; for example, you might include some open questions or an "any other comments" box.

As with interviews, it is important to test your questionnaire by doing a pilot study, either with a small sample of users who will not be part of the survey or with some work colleagues.

If you need to survey a large number of users — to find out about their opinions and difficulties in relation to a system being redesigned, say — then closed questions will enable a large amount of information to be collected and analyzed relatively easily. Open questions provide a rich source of data, but making sense of this data requires more time. Generally, effective questionnaires contain a mix of both closed and open questions.

If you think you will need a more complex statistical analysis, then we advise you to consult a statistician while planning your survey. Many statistical packages are available to support data analysis; a good example is the Statistics Package for Social Sciences (SPSS). If you choose to consult a statistician, make sure you do so before designing your questionnaire. Many inexperienced evaluators fall into the trap of collecting data and then trying to decide what statistics they should apply after the fact.

5   Summary

This chapter explored several investigative techniques: observation, interviews, and questionnaires/surveys. Any or all of these techniques can be used in the requirements-gathering phase of UI design. Complementary investigative techniques are often used in combination; for example, you might use a questionnaire and also undertake some interviews, or you might use a questionnaire and also undertake some observation studies. This enables the strengths and weaknesses of the various techniques to be balanced.

3

Finding out about the users and the domain

1   Introduction

In gathering requirements you will be trying to collect particular sorts of information for your UI design. Whether you are redesigning the user interface (UI) to an existing system or designing the UI for a new system that will computerize tasks currently being performed manually, the investigations involved in requirements gathering are the same. (Though, of course, the design of a completely new computer system, which happens quite rarely, may require more in-depth investigations and the collection of more detailed information.) In either case, the starting point for your investigations should be to determine what the users are currently doing, how they are working, and where they are working. You can then use these findings to guide the UI design, so that the new or redesigned system enables users to perform their tasks. Although this sounds simple, in reality there is a lot you need to find out and make sense of before you begin the actual activity of designing the UI. Table 3.1 gives an overview of the main areas of investigation and the information gathered for UI design. We'll discuss the users, and characteristics of the users and the domain in this chapter. The tasks and environment are discussed in Chapter 4. Qualitative usability aspects, quantitative usability goals, constraints, and trade-offs are discussed in Chapter 6.

Traditionally, the classic software design life cycle focuses on the system's requirements rather than the users' requirements. As we emphasized in Chapter 1, a user-centered design approach focuses instead on the importance of the user. In Chapter 2 we discussed some suitable techniques for gathering requirements. Keeping the user uppermost in your mind, you should undertake the following activities in gathering the requirements:

- *Observe* users — *real* users — doing real work, where the application is to be used.
- *Observe* and talk to *real* users. Many people will have information to offer or will have something to say about the system. But you must also remember to observe and talk to *real* users — the people who will actually use the system.

Table 3.1 Areas of Investigation and Information Gathered for UI Design

Focus of investigation	Information gathered
The domain	Wider specialist knowledge Specific knowledge for a computer system
The users	Who they are; focuses on the *real* (primary) users, but also considers other stakeholders (secondary users)
Characteristics of the users	Age, sex, culture, physical abilities and physical disabilities, educational background, computer/IT experience, motivation, attitude, enjoyment, satisfaction
Characteristics of the tasks	Are the tasks easy, complex, novel, variable, repetitive, frequent or infrequent, single tasks or multitasking, time critical, requiring individual or collaborative working? Are there safety issues in relation to the work?
Physical environment	Noise, stress, comfort, dirt, dust, heating, lighting, ventilation, furniture, working space, individual offices, open-plan areas, equipment layout, hazards in the workplace
Social environment	Pressure of work, individual or collaborative working, individual offices or open-plan areas
Organizational environment	Organizational mission and aims, organizational attitude to IT, organizational policies, job design, and roles
User support environment	Availability of training, availability of colleagues/experts, availability of manuals or online help
Qualitative usability aspects	General, often unquantifiable goals, such as easy to learn, UI intuitiveness
Quantitative usability goals	Measurable goals, such as usability metrics
Constraints	Costs, timescales, budgets, technology hardware and software
Trade-offs	Conflicting/contradictory requirements

- *Observe*, talk to, and involve *real* users throughout the design process and its activities.

The real users are those people who use the application on an everyday basis for their work. For example, you may frequently visit your local library to borrow books or CDs. Although you are a user in the sense that the library computer system keeps a record of who you are and the items you have borrowed, you are a secondary user of the library system. The primary users of the library computer system are the librarians. They interact directly with the system as part of their job; they perform all the loan and return functions on your behalf. The process of booking a vacation provides a similar example. Most travel agencies employ a computer system to check the availability of flights or hotels (among other functions). The travel agents are the primary users of the system. Customers interact with the system indirectly, through the travel agent, when trying to achieve their goal of booking a holiday. Thus, the customers are secondary users. Although they interact with the system only indirectly, customers will be affected as much as the agents if the computer system has any usability problems. At best, the process may take more time than anticipated; at worst, the customer may miss a bargain.

We hope the point has been made as to how important primary users are in ensuring the development of a good UI design. Secondary users are important too, and they will have views that need to be taken on board; but your focus must be on the *primary* users who are and will be using the user interface.

2 Users: Finding Out Who They Are

In UI design it is imperative to know who the application is being designed for and what the users believe they want from an application. People or groups of people in an organization who use the application directly are referred to as the **primary users**. **Secondary users** are people or groups of people who are not primary users but who are affected or influenced in some way by the computer system or who affect or influence its development. Together the primary users and secondary users are known as **stakeholders**.

The intended primary users — or just **users** — of the system should be involved first and foremost in the system development, and they should continue to be involved throughout the UI design and development life cycle.

2.1 Describing the Users: Users Have "Characteristics" That Are Relevant to UI Design

An important part of UI design is ensuring that the UI matches the attributes, or *characteristics,* of the intended real users. We are aware from our everyday experiences that people differ in many ways (see Box 3.1). In UI design, users or user groups are described in relation to their characteristics. In other words, a profile of the real users of the application is created that describes the users in terms of their

Box 3.1	**User Characteristics**

The idea that people possess *characteristics* has caused difficulty for some students in the past. However, on an everyday level we all make assessments of people by their attributes or characteristics. For example, suppose you are introduced to someone who is very tall. You would not say to yourself, "That person has the characteristic of being tall." But you *would* unconsciously attribute the feature of being tall to that person. We all see a number of physical characteristics when we look at people, and we may unconsciously use those characteristics to classify them. For example, we may classify someone as short, stocky, slim, or robust.

particular attributes, such as age, sex, and physical abilities and disabilities (Mayhew, 1999). In addition to physical characteristics, it is also necessary to know about the educational background of the users and how much IT experience they possess. Users' psychological characteristics are also important. For example, when designing a computer system, you will need to be aware of the users' levels of motivation and their attitudes toward computer use or computerization of their work. It has been found that no matter how good or effective an application is, acceptance or nonacceptance of the application often hinges on the users' attitudes to the use of computers in their work. A user's cultural background will also have a bearing on particular aspects of UI design. For example, icons that are easily recognized by Westerners may be less easily recognized by users from Eastern societies. Table 3.2 lists the user characteristics that are relevant to UI design.

2.2 Designing for Physical Limitations

One of the characteristics listed in Table 3.2 is "physical abilities and disabilities." Many countries now have legislation that makes it unlawful to discriminate against disabled people in the provision of goods or services.

The United Nations collects the statistics on disability that are available from all its member nations. As the organization points out:

Many countries collect data on disability but the prevalence rates derived from these data vary greatly for a variety of reasons including:

- *conceptual issues — disability is the result of an interaction between the person with the disability and their particular environment. Disability is, therefore, a complex phenomenon with no static state; it can be conceptualized in many ways, including at the level of the body, the person, or the society.*
- *measurement issues — the questions used, their structure and wording, and how they are understood and interpreted by the respondents all affect the identification of the persons with disabilities in data collection.*

Table 3.2 User Characteristics Relevant to UI Design

Age
Sex
Culture
Physical abilities and disabilities
Educational background
Computer/IT experience
Motivation
Attitude

For these reasons, the observed differences among countries in the rates (or percentages) reflect conceptual and measurement differences, to varying degrees, as well as "true" differences.

United Nations Satistics Division
http://unstats.un.org/unsd/disability/introduction.asp
Visited July 8, 2004

Broadly, countries in the "developed" world (such as the United States, Canada, Australia, New Zealand, and the European Union) ask questions in their censuses and surveys that mostly concentrate on whether or not people can perform everyday tasks, and they rely on the person's own view of their abilities or disabilities. For example, the New Zealand census asked the two questions in Figure 3.1.

Generally, these countries report that between 15% and 35% of the population as a whole has some sort of impairment or disability that interferes with everyday activities. These are important figures for us as interface designers. We do not need to know what condition might cause an impairment or difficulty in using a computer; we simply need to know how many people might have such a difficulty.

One particularly important group for user interface design is people who are blind or visually impaired. In the United States, at least 1.5 million blind and visually

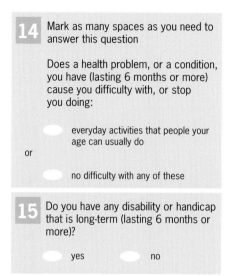

14 Mark as many spaces as you need to answer this question

Does a health problem, or a condition, you have (lasting 6 months or more) cause you difficulty with, or stop you doing:

everyday activities that people your age can usually do

or

no difficulty with any of these

15 Do you have any disability or handicap that is long-term (lasting 6 months or more)?

yes   no

Figure 3.1 Questions on illness and disability from the New Zealand 1996 census. (Taken from www.stats.govt.nz, visted July 9, 2004.)

You can get a simulation of what an image or web page might look like to a color-blind person by going to www.vischeck.com/vischeck.

impaired people use computers (American Foundation for the Blind, www.afb.org, visited July 9, 2004). Our prediction is that this number will rise as computer usage rises among older people, many of whom find that their vision deteriorates as they age.

An additional consideration for design is that about eight percent of the male population and one percent of the female population suffers from color blindness (Dix *et al.*, 2004). There are three forms of color blindness:

- Deuteranopia, where red/green are difficult to distinguish
- Protanopia, another type that affects the ability to distinguish red/green
- Tritanopia, a rare problem that affects the ability to distinguish blue/yellow

Figure 3.2 shows how a web site might be viewed by someone who with full color vision, someone with deuteranopia, and someone with tritanopia.

Thinking about and designing for users' physical limitations is important. It is not only beneficial to those individuals with a limitation, there is often a benefit to people in general. For example, while signs using large, clear print are enabling for the partially sighted, they are also easier for the public in general to read. Public conveniences are another often-cited example: larger toilet cubicles enable the disabled (particularly wheelchair users) but also make the use of public conveniences easier for everyone.

2.3 User Profiling: Describing Your Users and Their Characteristics

There are two main ways to find out about your users so that you can create a user profile. First, if you know who your real users are (that is, if you know who will actually be using the interface), then you can ask them to complete a questionnaire. Remember when developing your own questionnaire that you will need to pilot it before you distribute it to ensure that it gathers the information you are interested in. Second, if you are unsure about who your real users are, then you will need to talk to or interview knowledgeable people in the organization — domain experts, managers, work supervisors, personnel managers, and product development managers — to find out about the users.

Table 3.2 lists the characteristics of users that are considered relevant for UI design. Suppose we need to produce a user profile of customers for an ATM. Using the list in Table 3.2, we might produce the user profile shown in Table 3.3.

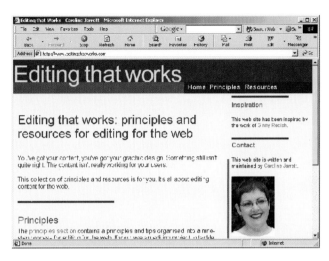

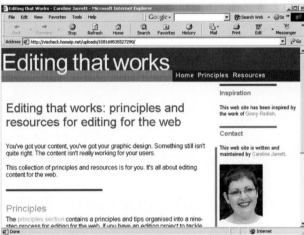

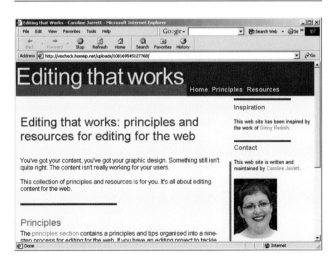

Figure 3.2 The same web site as seen by (top) a person with no problems, (middle) a deuteranope, (bottom) a tritanope. Simulation by www.vischeck.com.

Table 3.3 User Profile of ATM Customers (from Chapanis, 1996)

User characteristics	ATM customer characteristics
Age	Will range in age from about 12 to 80+
Sex	Both male and female
Physical limitations	May be fully able-bodied or may have some physical limitations in relation to hearing, sight, mobility, use of hands, or wheelchair use Will be of varying heights
Educational background	May have only minimal education qualifications and possess limited literacy and numeracy skills
Computer/IT use	May have little or no prior experience of computer or IT use
Motivation	May be very motivated to use the ATM, particularly if they can do their banking quickly and avoid waiting in long lines at the bank
Attitude	Attitudes to use may vary, depending on the services the ATM offers, the reliability of the technology itself, and the attitude of users toward computers

2.4 Smaller User Groups Are Easier to Design For

Table 3.3 reflects a true user profile in that it describes the whole user interface population in terms of the attributes or characteristics relevant to the design of the UI (Mayhew, 1999). However, as it stands, it gets us only part of the way to describing our users. Now we need to break up this large bunch of users into smaller groups. We will have a greater chance of arriving at a successful design if we focus on who the users of the system are than if we just try to accommodate a large band of users and their different patterns of ATM use. You, as a user, probably use an ATM in a different way than your parents do, and they will use an ATM in a different way than children or teenagers might. Let's have another pass through and try to really identify the users in this situation.

EXERCISE 3.1 (Allow 20 minutes)

Look at the user profile for ATM customers presented in Table 3.4. Based on people you know (family members, friends, or work colleagues), split the collection of customers in Table 3.4 into two or more different groups.

Table 3.4 ATM User Groups (adapted from Stone, 2001)

User characteristic	ATM customer characteristics, by group		
	Teens/young adults	**Young adults to middle age**	**Middle age to senior citizens**
Age	12 to 25.	25 to 50.	50 to 80+.
Sex	Both male and female.	Both male and female.	Both male and female.
Physical limitations	May be fully able-bodied or may have some physical limitations in relation to, for example, hearing or sight. Will be of varying heights.	May be fully able-bodied or may have some physical limitations in relation to, for example, hearing or sight. Will be of varying heights.	May be fully able-bodied or may have some physical limitations in relation to, for example, hearing or sight, mobility, or use of hands. Will be of varying heights.
Educational background	May have minimal or no educational qualifications.	May have only minimal educational qualifications.	May have only minimal educational qualifications.
Computer/IT use	Probably have some prior experience of computer or IT use.	May have little or no prior experience of computer or IT use.	May have little or no prior experience of computer or IT use.
Motivation	Probably very motivated to use the ATM, especially in relation to their banking habits.	Could be very motivated to use the ATM, especially if they can do their banking quickly and avoid standing in line at the bank.	Could be very motivated to use the ATM, but would probably prefer to stand in a line in the bank.
Attitude	Attitudes to use may vary, depending on the services the ATM offers and the reliability of the technology itself.	Attitudes to use may vary, depending on the services the ATM offers and the reliability of the technology itself.	Attitudes to use may vary, depending on the services the ATM offers and the reliability of the technology itself.

DISCUSSION

Debbie writes: I am a member of a large, extended family. Based on my knowledge of how various members of my family use ATMs, I split the collection into three smaller groups and profiled each as shown in Table 3.4. This is not the only way in which you could split the initial grouping into smaller groups. Depending on whom you modeled your groups, you may only have two groups or you may even have identified four groups.

The teens in my family generally use their account only once a week — to deposit their allowance (or to make a withdrawal if they have saved enough for a particular purchase). There are also occasions, such as Christmas and birthdays, where extra money, received as presents, is deposited. For the teens, and the young teens especially, using a card machine is "cool" and grown up, and it means they won't have to wait in line on a Friday afternoon or a Saturday morning when the banks and savings institutions are already busy. The young adults in my family use ATM facilities like a wallet. They withdraw small amounts of money frequently — maybe even several times a day — as and when they need it, rather than withdrawing a great wad of cash that they may spend recklessly.

The family members between the ages of 25 and 50 are generally busy, working people. Banking is a necessary part of life, but the quicker it can be done, the better. Waiting in bank lines is something to be avoided, and they prefer to withdraw enough money from an ATM to last several days.

The older members of my family bank even less often. They tend to make a single weekly cash withdrawal to cover the week's expenses, although where possible they prefer to get their money from a person rather than a machine.

Having drawn up your groups, now is the time to discover how accurate your "commonsense" categories are. The obvious way to do this is to observe and even talk to ATM users. You will have to do this with great care and discretion, or someone might become suspicious and call the police! Alternatively — again with care — you might want to observe the customers who are standing in line waiting to perform their transactions with a human teller. Observation of either user group will give you information about users' age ranges, physical limitations, and sex. But to uncover information that is not apparent upon observation, like educational qualifications, computer/IT experience, or attitude and motivation, you will need to either interview the users directly or ask them to complete a questionnaire. This type of information could be gathered without the need for them to divulge personal information, like names and addresses. Then, based on the information gathered from observing and talking to real users, you would revise the descriptions of your user groups.

Having iterated to an accurate description of your user groups, the next step is **analysis**. Analysis is the process of taking the information you have gathered, examining it closely, and drawing conclusions about what it tells you. You would then translate your conclusions into requirements for the design of the UI to the application, as shown in Table 3.5.

Table 3.5 Translating User Characteristics into UI Design Requirements (middle age to senior citizen group)

User characteristics	ATM UI requirements
Age range from 12 to 80+	ATM screen height needs to accommodate users of varying height.
May be fully able-bodied or may have some physical limitations	ATM screen height needs to accommodate able-bodied users as well as users with walking sticks or those who use wheelchairs. Arthritis of the hands could be a problem, so any controls used should accommodate this.
May have some physical limitations in relation to hearing	All user inputs should have both visual and auditory feedback.
May have some physical limitations in relation to sight	Screen text should be of a reasonably large font, in order to be read by both the visually impaired and unimpaired.
May have some physical limitations in relation to use of hands	Touchscreens, if used, should have target areas that are large enough to locate with limited manual dexterity. Touchscreens, if used, should be sensitive enough to respond to users with decreased strength in fingers or hands.
Little or no experience of computer/IT use	The application should be easy to use (i.e., the tasks users want to undertake should be simple to perform). The application should be easy to learn (i.e., the user should be able to use the system without help, training, or instruction).

Chapter 12 will step you through the decision-making processes involved in choosing input and output devices for users and the tasks they want to undertake with an application.

Note that although we have presented the conclusions of our analysis in a table, nothing is yet set in stone. For example, we indicated that a touchscreen could be used for the ATM interface, but this is not the only choice you could make. Further on in your development, after undertaking other investigations, you may refine your ideas about what users really want. For example, suppose the bank manager told you that there were an unusually large number of senior citizens with accounts at her bank. Based on this, touchscreens might be unfeasible. Users with physical limitations (arthritis, perhaps, or diminished strength in their limbs) may be unable to place their fingers accurately enough on the screen to make a correct selection, plus there is no tactile feedback to help them know that a selection (right or wrong) has been made. A more appropriate choice for the unusually high number of senior citizens might be a UI that uses a keypad with larger than normal keys. This would make the selection of options easier, and tactile feedback could be included. Large text labels and even Braille markings on the keys might be appropriate for these users and their banking tasks. This information would then be fed back into the development cycle, and the table revised. In doing this, you would have demonstrated that you were taking an iterative approach to design: the replacement of the choice of touchscreen with a keypad means you are revisiting an activity already completed and making better choices for the interface based on additional acquired information.

2.5 Personas: Another Way to Describe Your Users

More recently, Cooper (1999) has proposed the use of **personas** as an effective way of designing for a broad population. A persona is a precise description of a user and what he or she wishes to do when using a system. Personas are not real; rather, they are imaginary examples of the real users they represent. In defining personas, Cooper recommends that you be as specific as possible about the "madeup" details and also that you give the persona a name, as "[a] persona without a name is simply not useful" (p. 128). Then during the design process, the persona is referred to by name rather than as "the user." He gives each persona an image, whether it is a stock photograph (from a photo library) or a sketched caricature. All these details serve to make that persona a concrete person in the designer's mind and in the minds of the design team. Pruitt and Grudin (2003) suggest that personas are of great value in providing a shared basis for communication, enabling a broader range of information to be conveyed to all the project participants and stakeholders.

Cooper suggests that a unique set of personas be defined for each individual project, which he refers to as the project's "cast of characters." Within a cast you may also find it useful to have some personas that have been defined only as people whom you are *not* designing for. Every cast, though, should have at least one primary persona who is the main focus of your design. Box 3.2 shows an example of the use of personas in a design situation.

Pruitt and Adlin (in press) point out that although your personas are more likely to be robust and helpful for design if they are based firmly on data, there is also value in personas based on assumptions:

> It's impossible to ignore the impact of assumptions . . . [everyone] in your organization has assumptions about the target users . . . [some] so strong that they seem woven into the very fabric of your organization. . . . At the very least, [you] will make all of your organization's assumptions about target users very explicit, and this can be a painful but valuable outcome.

EXERCISE 3.2 (Allow 30 minutes)

Create a persona for each of the three groups profiled in Table 3.4. The discussion for Exercise 3.2 may help you get started.

| Box 3.2 | **The Use of Personas in Developing the Roll-aboard Suitcase** |

The roll-aboard suitcase makes a good example of how powerful designing for one person can be. This small suitcase with the built-in wheels and retractable handle revolutionized the entire luggage industry, yet it wasn't designed for the general public — it was originally designed just for airline flight crews, a very narrowly defined target user group. The personas used may have included, for example, Gerd, a senior captain flying 747s from Vancouver to Frankfurt for Lufthansa; or Francine, a newly minted flight attendant on Reno Air. Gerd flies long distance flights, while Francine flies the length of California three times a day, serving drinks and handing out peanuts. Gerd and Francine are dramatically different personas, flying on different types of flights and schedules, but their suitcase goals and needs are equivalent.

The design purity of the roll-aboard suitcase pleased airline flight crews enormously. The rest of the travelling public soon saw that it solved their luggage problems, too. Carrying it through crowded airports was as easy as maneuvering it down airliner aisles, or stowing it aboard planes.

After the roll-aboard succeeded in its target segment, it was launched into other markets. Now, you can buy double-sized roll-aboards, designer roll-aboards, armoured equipment roll-aboards, and kid's roll-aboards. Today, purchasing luggage without built-in wheels and a retractable handle is difficult.

From Cooper, 1999, pp. 126, 130.

DISCUSSION

Felix: Persona for the user group "teens/young adults"

Felix is 13 years old. He gets an allowance every week, but spends it while out with his friends, and there usually is not anything left over to bank. He often gets money from his grandparents and uncles for his birthday and at Christmas, and this money is always deposited into his bank account. He saves this for more expensive or extravagant purchases; for example, he has a game console and likes to have the newest games. Plus he likes to be trendy and have the newest jeans and trainers. Felix's account allows him to withdraw small amounts of money from ATMs.

Sandra: Persona for the user group "young adults to middle age"

Sandra is 30 years old. She is married to Jason, and they have two children: Todd, age six, and Carly, age 18 months. When Carly was born the family moved into one of the newly built housing areas in the town; local amenities such as shops, bars, or a bank have yet to be built. This means that any shopping or banking must be done in the town center, which is a six-mile round-trip from the family home. Jason uses the car for work, and he works long hours — he is often gone from 6:45 a.m. to 8 p.m. Sandra is partially sighted, so she does not drive and depends on public transportation to get anywhere. She tries to do any errands, like shopping and banking, during Todd's school hours, as handling one child by public transportation can be difficult (especially with a stroller), but it is far easier than trying to cope with two. More often than not she needs to make two shopping trips on two separate days to get everything she needs. Sandra likes the ATM for depositing and withdrawing money and for checking her bank balance because she can see the screen if she gets near enough to it, and she has learned the menu sequence. The ATM is in the front wall of the bank, and there is no canopy to protect customers from poor weather conditions.

Grandpa Maurice: Persona for user group "middle age to senior citizens"

Grandpa Maurice is 68 years old. His pension is automatically credited to his bank account once a month. Every week he goes into the bank to withdraw enough cash for the week as he prefers to pay for his groceries and other day-to-day expenses with cash. While standing in line is a bit difficult (Grandpa Maurice has arthritis in his hip), he does it because he prefers to get his money from a person. Also, as he is not very comfortable with technology, he does not have an ATM card.

2.6 Other Stakeholders

We have said that together the primary users and secondary users are known as **stakeholders**. We have discussed the profiling of primary users of a system, using either profiles or personas. While knowledge of the real, direct end users of a system is of the greatest importance, in the information gathering process there will also be secondary users — that is, other stakeholders — who will have an interest or "stake" in the development of an application.

It can be difficult to determine the identity of all the stakeholders in an application development. Besides primary users, these secondary users can include, among others, senior managers, business analysts, system analysts, project managers, application developers, interface designers, marketing and sales representatives, trainers, and customer support staff (Hackos and Redish, 1998).

Identifying stakeholders and gathering their requirements will often identify missed, conflicting, ambiguous, overlapping, and unrealistic requirements (Kotonya and Sommerville, 1998). As each stakeholder or stakeholder group will come to the application development with their own set of issues and their own view of what is important, it can be difficult to reconcile the various views of all involved to specify the requirements for an application. In addition, sometimes what is seen as a benefit by one stakeholder may be seen as a cost by another (Wilson *et al.*, 1996). For example, managers might view an increase in productivity due to computerization as a benefit, while users might view the increased productivity as a cost if it leads to workers being made redundant. Requirements negotiation will be necessary to resolve any conflicts, overlaps, or ambiguities in requirements, and the final requirements specification will inevitably be a compromise, as you cannot produce a system that will satisfy everyone.

> **EXERCISE 3.3 (Allow five minutes)**
>
> Earlier in this chapter, we discussed the users of a computer system for a lending library. Who might the stakeholders be for this type of application?
>
> **DISCUSSION**
>
> In addition to the primary users (the librarians), the various stakeholders would include library users, library counter staff who handle the lending and return of library items, and acquisitions staff who, in conjunction with the librarians and resource managers, choose and order items for the library stock. There will also be system administrators and project managers; if it is a new computer system, then there may also be cataloging and data entry clerks. The council or educational institution funding the library will also be a stakeholder.

Once created, your user profiles or personas and details of the other stakeholders involved will be included in the requirements specification and used to inform your design decisions.

3   Users' Needs: Finding Out What Users Want

After identifying the real users of a system, you can then start to discover what they want the system to do — simply by talking to them in order to identify their needs. This sounds straightforward, but one of the problems with trying to identify the requirements for a computer system is that users often do not know what they want, or else their work has become so second nature to them they are unable to tell you what work they do. When they are able to tell you, users will in general describe what they want from an application in terms of two types of need: **felt needs** and **expressed needs**.

Felt needs, in many cases, are hidden or slow in being identified, as users may not know or understand what a system may be able to offer them or how it could make the accomplishment of their goals easier; so they do not realize that they have a need in the first place. You might identify felt needs by questioning individuals or, on a wider basis, by using surveys.

Expressed needs, on the other hand, are what people say they want. For example, users may have grumbled for years about the lack of a particular feature in a computer system without ever doing anything about it; yet when they are consulted, this missing feature may be one of the first things they identify as an essential requirement.

Based on our previous experience as professionals, we will often describe a **normative need**. That is, we will possess a professional view about the nature of the problem and what may be needed. There may be considerable discrepancies or conflicts between the professional normative needs and the felt/expressed needs of users and stakeholders. In addition, felt and expressed needs from users may be excessive or in conflict with each other and we will be in the situation of having to negotiate trade-offs to reconcile needs. It is important, though, that we do not simply impose our opinion as to what is needed upon users. We must listen to what users say, as they will certainly know more about their tasks and their domain than we will.

The output from discovering the users' needs will provide a starting point for the specification of the functional requirements of the computer system — that is, *what* the system must do and the functionality it must have to support users in their tasks.

4 The Domain: What Expert Knowledge Is Relevant to the Application?

In UI design, the term **domain** refers to the area of expertise and specialist knowledge — for example, financial applications or process control systems — for which an application may be developed. A domain may be described using particular concepts that highlight important aspects (Dix *et al.*, 2004). For example, the domain-specific concepts for a financial application would include credits, debits, accounts, and interest rates. Also included in the description of a domain is any specialized knowledge needed to perform tasks and accomplish goals. (We will talk more about goals and tasks in the next chapter.) For example, if you want to accomplish the goal of paying a bill by credit card, you will need to have a general idea about how credit cards operate. You will need to know that you require a credit card that is valid, that you must have enough credit available on your account, and that you will need to repay some or all of your account balance each month.

4.1 Understanding the Domain

The activity of gathering information about a domain is known as **domain analysis**. This involves talking to, observing, and interviewing domain experts, people who are knowledgeable and skilled in the domain area you are investigating. You will also want to look at any existing relevant documentation. For example, if a system already exists, then you can look at any user or training manuals. If this is a completely new UI design, then you will want to look at procedure manuals, job descriptions and forms, or other paperwork used in relation to the job.

Depending on the application area, the identity of the experts will vary. In a financial application, the bank manager might be the initial expert that comes to mind; but bank tellers as well as bank managers will be experts — each will be expert in that part of the financial domain where they have the most experience. This is an important point. To gain a broad view of the domain for which an application is being developed and to understand the important concepts of a domain that tasks will be based on, several domain experts should be consulted — *including users*. A lack of understanding of, or lack of knowledge about, the computer system domain will lead to errors in specifying the requirements for the application and will result in a UI design that fails to meet the users' needs. This may happen if you interview only one domain expert. However, you should also be aware that different domain experts may contradict each other, and further investigations may be needed to reconcile opinions.

Bear in mind that domain experts are often unable to articulate their knowledge, either because they are poor at talking about what they do and what they know or because their knowledge has become so implicit or second nature to them (that is, *tacit*) that they really cannot say what they do or what they know. Much of the knowledge used by domain experts in relation to their performance of particular activities is acquired informally, without intention to learn, and without awareness that it has been learned (Sternberg and Horvath, 1999). Though unarticulated, personal knowledge and experience is an important part of the way in which individuals undertake their work. For example, in the area of law, knowledge of the law is only a small part of legal expertise. The understanding, interpretation, and application of legal rules to a particular situation is dependent on implicit knowledge gained through experience of having applied law, through the observation of the legal system in action, and through analogy with similar cases. Lawyers, when asked, will recall that learning has taken place in courtroom observation; but when asked specifically what they learned, they are unable to describe it satisfactorily (Marchant and Robinson, 1999).

As well as the problem of trying to elicit implicit tacit knowledge, you may also find yourself in the situation where domain experts are deliberately uncooperative because they are resistant to the idea of a new application being developed and implemented (Bell and Hardiman, 1989). They may feel threatened by what they perceive as negative implications of new technology, such as job losses or changes in work practices leading to decreased job satisfaction. In both cases, therefore, information from other sources, such as any available system documentation, textbooks, or training materials, should also be examined. An iterative cycle of observation and interviews, analysis, and further observations and interviews in the work environment will be necessary if you intend to gain a good understanding of a domain.

In the course of your interviews with domain experts, you are likely to gather unsolicited information about the users, their tasks, and the environments within which the system will be used. This information will provide a starting point for the further requirements-gathering investigations that need to be undertaken in relation to the users, their tasks, and their work environments (Kotonya and Sommerville, 1998). We will discuss this later in the book.

4.2 Representing the Domain

The outputs you arrive at upon completion of a domain analysis are **domain models**, which describe the domain information and concepts relevant to the particular system under development. These domain models contain a subset of the total expert knowledge of the whole domain (i.e., they contain the information relevant to the area of the computer system under development). Consider the financial application once again. If an automated teller machine (ATM) is being developed, then the relevant domain information and concepts would be related to account transactions, such as depositing and withdrawing money, checking an account balance, or ordering a bank statement. There would be no need to model, say, information about bank loans, mortgages, or life insurance in the computer system. Although these concepts are related to finance and banking, they would be beyond the scope of the system under development. Figure 3.3 shows ATM domain knowledge as a subset of banking domain knowledge.

Domain models can simply be textual descriptions of the relevant domain information, as shown (very briefly) in Figure 3.3, but often graphical notations from systems analysis are used to model the domain. These include, for instance, the **dataflow diagram**, the **entity–relationship diagram**, and the **state transition diagram**. Once created, your domain models — whether textual or graphical — will form part of the **requirements specification** document.

EXERCISE 3.4 (Allow 20 minutes)

Think about your last visit to a library (either physical or online). If you were developing an application for use by librarians, what domain knowledge would be required for the system? Describe the domain knowledge needed. This is an opportunity to consider the skills of direct observation. How easy is it to identify the information you are seeking?

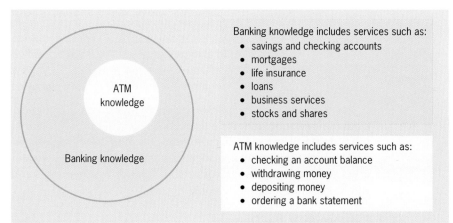

Figure 3.3 ATM Domain Knowledge Is a Subset of Total Banking Domain Knowledge. (From Stone, 2001.)

DISCUSSION

Here are our suggestions for some of the domain knowledge for a library:

- Different categories of books are available. The library can loan some of the books, while others are only for reference or use within the library.
- Different types of media are available: books, audiotapes, CDs, maps, and microfiche.
- Various classification schemes are used for numbering and ordering the items.
- Different types of readers use the library (e.g., children and adults).
- Some readers want to read at the library; others want to borrow or check out items.
- Librarians need to keep track of items in the library.
- Librarians issue loans to users with library accounts.
- Librarians issue overdue notices to users and collect fines from those who return items late.

Many more items could be included here. Did your list of items differ from our list? Most of the items on this list came from our own experiences as library users; confirming that this is an accurate view and gathering any other information required for the domain model would be obtained by interviewing and more detailed observation of librarians at work.

5   Summary

In this chapter we discovered the importance of understanding the characteristics of our users, particularly any physical limiations, and creating user profiles to document the range of users that we are designing for. We described personas, a technique that helps the sometimes bald facts in the user profiles to come alive.

We then mentioned the importance of finding out what users need, and that there may be a difference between what they say they need, what they feel they need but cannot easily express, and what we consider would be most helpful for them.

One especially important aspect of understanding users is establishing how much they know about the domain of the user interface, the area of specialist or expert knowledge that is relevant to this system. This chapter closed with a discussion of how to find out about and represent the domain.

In the next chapter, we continue our investigation of users and their needs by looking at the tasks or work that users will be doing with the system.

4

Finding out about tasks and work

1   Introduction: Describing Users' Work

To design a computer system that meets the needs of users, you must understand the aims or goals that users may have when they use the system. Therefore, after identifying the users of the system, the next step in the requirements-gathering process is to discover what the system will be used for. **Task analysis** is the activity system designers use to gain an understanding of what a computer system must do and the functionality that the system must provide if it is to support users in their goals and tasks. In this chapter we discuss users' work: their goals and tasks, the characteristics of the tasks, and techniques for examining and describing work in closer detail.

1.1   Goals, Tasks, and Actions

Before we discuss techniques for examining users' work, it will be helpful to explain the terminology. In describing users' work, we talk in terms of goals, tasks, and actions. A **goal** is an end result to be achieved. For example, a person might want to communicate with a friend in writing, enjoy a meal, see a movie, put together a new computer desk, and so on. A goal must be described at a high level of abstraction, indicating *what* is to be achieved. The specific details of *how* the goal is to be achieved are not stated.

Typically, a goal can be accomplished in numerous ways by undertaking or performing a particular set of tasks. A **task** is a structured set of related activities that are undertaken in some sequence. Tasks are what a person has to do (or thinks she or he has to do) in order to accomplish a goal. At some point, in order to perform the tasks that accomplish the goal, a person will need to physically interact with a device by performing actions. An **action** is defined as an individual operation or step that needs to be undertaken as part of the task.

For example, the goal of communicating with a friend in writing can be achieved in several ways, such as through a handwritten letter or card, using a typewriter or a word processor, sending a text message, or by e-mail. Each method will involve a different set of tasks and actions.

The tasks involved in writing a letter by hand might include the following:

- Obtaining some writing paper and a pen or pencil
- Finding a flat surface upon which to write and a place to sit
- Using the pen or pencil to write words on the paper to convey a particular meaning

The actions would involve writing the individual letters of the alphabet to form the appropriate words.

The tasks involved in sending a handwritten card are similar, using a greeting card rather than plain paper (some people find it easier to convey a particular meaning by choosing an appropriate card than by composing their own message). Sending a text message by cell/mobile phone or e-mail shares the aspect of the task of writing words (that is, keying them in) to convey a particular meaning, but the other two tasks — the need for a flat surface and writing instrument — are irrelevant to communicating via these means.

Figure 4.1 shows the relationship between a goal, a task, and an action. Although we have shown only one level of task, there may be more than one: some tasks are decomposable into subtasks before the action level is reached.

Goals, tasks, and actions will be different for different people, depending on their previous experience and knowledge. Actions, in particular, may be different for experts and novices. Users iterate between forming a goal and then determining the tasks and actions they need to take to accomplish the goal. This iteration describes a decomposition of goals into tasks, and tasks into subtasks or actions, as the user

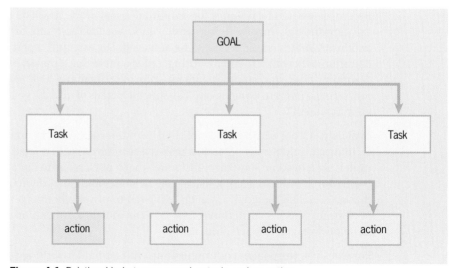

Figure 4.1 Relationship between a goal, a task, and an action.

moves downward through the hierarchy shown in Figure 4.1. For example, an "edit" task can be decomposed through the subtasks of "locate the text to change," "make the changes," "verify that the change was successful," and so on until the level of an action is reached — "move the cursor one character forward," "type the letter *j*," and so on.

Therefore, in order to design a system that supports users in the goals they wish to accomplish, it is necessary to understand the users' goals in their work. Focusing your attention on users' goals and how the goals break down into tasks and actions will help you to design UIs that more accurately reflect what the users want to do.

▶ Task Characteristics: The Nature of the Work

We have discussed how users have attributes or characteristics. Tasks, too, have characteristics that we need to take into consideration when designing the UI. These are listed in Table 4.1. You will be able to gather information about the characteristics of the tasks by interviewing users, observing them working in their work environment, and consulting any relevant documentation.

As with user characteristics, task characteristics are important because they influence the decisions made in relation to the UI design and the choice of devices used. For instance, warehouse workers who check goods in and out may need to wear

Table 4.1 Characteristics of Tasks

The extent to which tasks vary from one occasion to another
Whether tasks will be carried out regularly, infrequently, or only once
The knowledge and kinds of skill required to perform tasks
How much the work is affected by changes in the environment
Whether time is critical for the work
Whether there are safety hazards
Whether the user will do the work alone or with others
Whether the user will normally be switching between several tasks

heavy gloves to help them grip items and to protect their hands. The gloves would make it difficult for them to use a standard keyboard and mouse to keep track of stock, and having to remove them for every computer transaction would quickly become irritating. This would need to be kept in mind when choosing the technology for these workers. Let's consider some more examples. In a café with a limited food and drinks menu, where tasks are repetitive, you would want to provide simple and straightforward methods of input, such as having one or two key presses to record and total orders. Long messages about how orders should be input would be unnecessary and, in fact, annoying for the users. More open-ended work, such as document creation, would require a flexible application with good context-sensitive help facilities that can assist a user who may not have carried out a particular task for some time. In cases such as air traffic control work, where users must carry out several tasks simultaneously and safely, carefully designed screen displays are required that take account of cognitive issues (such as getting users to focus their attention on critical information).

Chapter 12 will step you through the decision-making processes involved in choosing input and output devices for users and the tasks they want to undertake with an application.

Once you have described the tasks' characteristics, they would be included in the requirements specification document and be used to inform your design decisions.

EXERCISE 4.1 (Allow 15 minutes)

Using the list in Table 4.1, describe the characteristics of the tasks undertaken when using an ATM to withdraw money.

DISCUSSION

Table 4.2 describes the task characteristics for withdrawing money from an ATM.

▶ **Task Sequences: There May Be More Than One Way to Do a Task**

Often there can be differences in the way that tasks are undertaken. You will need to know about them and ensure that the UI supports them. Take, for example, the goal of sending a letter. Table 4.3 shows the processes used by two different people when sending a letter.

While the set of tasks is the same for both, the sequence in which they perform those tasks is different. (You may perform the tasks in yet another sequence, such as write the letter, get an envelope, address the envelope, put the finished letter in the envelope, and then put a stamp on the envelope.) Therefore, in addition to knowing what tasks are undertaken, it is important to observe and gather information about the sequences in which tasks are performed. Your UI must be flexible enough to accommodate these different ways of working. You should not force users to work in one set way unless there are overriding safety considerations that require them to do so.

1.2 Task Analysis

Task analysis is the process of examining the way in which people perform their tasks. It involves taking an in-depth look at the tasks and actions a person undertakes, along

Table 4.2 Task Characteristics for Withdrawing Money from an ATM

Does the task vary from one occasion to the next?	No.
How frequently is the task carried out?	May be daily, weekly, or less frequently.
What kinds of skills or knowledge are needed?	Must remember PIN to access machine.
Is the task affected by the environment?	Weather conditions could affect use of machine (e.g., the user may be wearing gloves in winter, it may be raining, bright sunlight may make reading the display difficult).
Is the task time critical?	Users may be in a hurry when using the ATM, since ATMs are often used for their speed and convenience.
Are there any safety or security hazards?	There are no safety hazards in the use of the ATM itself. However, the users' personal safety in relation to onlookers and the safeguarding of their PINs and the cash withdrawn are considerations.
Will the work be done alone or with others?	The work will be done alone.
Will the users normally be switching between several tasks?	Many users will check their balance before withdrawing money. The users will not switch between tasks when withdrawing money, but external factors (like children) may divert their attention.

with the knowledge they need to perform those tasks and reach a goal. By understanding how users work, you will be better able to design an application that supports the tasks they need to undertake in order to reach their goals, in the way they want to do them, in their particular domain. You will be able to gather information about users' tasks by interviewing users, by observing them in their work environment, and by consulting any relevant documentation.

To understand your users' work, there are several levels of detail (often referred to as *granularity*) that you could look at when performing your task analysis. For example, to gain a good level of understanding of how work is done in a business, you need to

Table 4.3 Different Task Sequences for Sending a Letter

How Bill Smith sends a letter	How Brenda Jones sends a letter
Write the letter.	Get an envelope.
Get an envelope.	Address the envelope.
Address the envelope.	Write the letter.
Put a stamp on the envelope.	Put the finished letter in the envelope.
Put the finished letter in the envelope.	Put a stamp on the envelope.

look at how overall work goals are achieved. For many work goals, several people will work together. Thus, you would focus on aspects such as how workers communicate and how they coordinate their work to get the job done. This is referred to as **work-flow analysis** (see Figure 4.2). Looking at high-level work flows will enable you either to confirm that you have identified all the relevant users or to identify those that you may have missed in your user analysis (see Chapter 3).

At a lower level of detail, you would look at individual workers with different responsibilities and examine what they do in their jobs on a daily or weekly basis. This is referred to as **job analysis**, and it will help you to identify the work that your UI will need to support. It is important to see for yourself what workers do. For example, from your everyday experience you might think that all the data clerk in Figure 4.2 does is enter data into spreadsheets and databases. You might disregard the need for a job analysis, but you would be wrong. In one example, we observed a data clerk who did indeed enter data, but also:

• Answered the telephone

• Booked staff for marketing activities

• Packed parcels with briefing and marketing materials for dispatch by courier

• Prepared marketing reports for feeding back information to clients

• Was also in charge of making cups of tea for the staff

Hackos and Redish (1998) refer to workflow analysis as a horizontal picture of how work moves across people and job analysis as a vertical picture of all the types of work performed by particular individuals as part of their role. An overall task analysis will

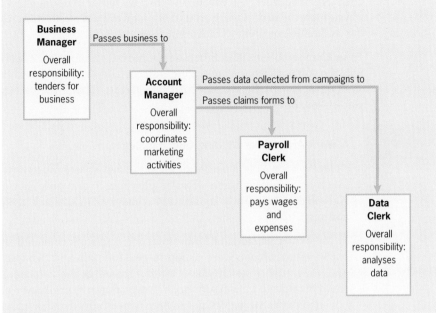

Figure 4.2 Workflow analysis — how work moves across workers.

include both types of analysis. To undertake workflow and job analyses, you will want to spend time in the workplace, observing, talking to, and interviewing users and domain experts. Here you will not only see what the users do, but you will also discover the characteristics of their tasks. Information about users' work may also come from work-related documentation, such as company procedure manuals, job descriptions, or training manuals (Dix *et al.*, 2004).

▶ **Clues for Improving Design: Problems and Difficulties with the Current UI**

Users often have problems or difficulties with their current system, and you will want to investigate and explore these concerns. For example, users may make frequent errors or they may repeat the same error. You need to observe and question users about this, to try and discover why the errors are occurring so that the problem can be rectified in your new design. Reasons for errors could include the task sequence being in a different order to that expected by users, or perhaps a command name does not reflect what the command actually does. One error we have noticed is that when using Word, we often select the Spelling and Grammar . . . option from the Tools menu, rather than the Language option, when we want to use Word's thesaurus. For some reason, we do not associate the use of a thesaurus with the word "Language"; in our mind, looking for similar or alternative words to use is part of grammar. In cases where users have had problems achieving their goals, they may have devised or found "work arounds" that enable them to perform certain tasks to achieve those goals. A work around is a way that users have found of doing a task when the UI does not support the task. A work around often involves very complex task sequences, and it is an inefficient method of working (see Box 4.1).

To spot any problems and difficulties in current system use, observe your users carefully. Do you notice them conferring with each other in any way about aspects of their work or the use of the system? Also, take a close look at the users' environment. Do you see any of the following?

| Box 4.1 | **A Work Around for Missing Functionality** |

Debbie writes: When I use PowerPoint, I like to create my figures very precisely, in order to make them visually pleasing. I am obsessive about making sure objects are evenly spaced and consistent in size and appearance where appropriate.

In the earlier versions of PowerPoint, the supports provided for the accurate placement of objects were a snap-to-grid function and two visible gridlines — one horizontal, one vertical — which crossed at the zero but each of which could be moved. I always found, however, that two gridlines were not enough; I needed many more gridlines to help me with my drawing tasks. For example, when aligning objects vertically on both sides of the zero point, I need more than one vertical gridline. This goes for horizontal alignment too. So each time I would use PowerPoint, which was infrequently, the first thing I found myself doing was drawing lots of vertical and horizontal lines, and spacing them one or two inches apart using the ruler. Only then would I feel that I could be precise in the placement of various shapes. Yes, the snap-to-grid and snap-to-shape facilities were there, but their behavior seemed less predictable, and they could not do for me what a visible grid in the background could. My preference for drawing like this stemmed from using early computer-aided drawing (CAD) packages in which I could turn the grid on or off and set the spacing of the gridlines.

I carried on using PowerPoint like this, and I even eventually made a template slide with the gridlines predrawn. I never thought twice about my self-created gridlines until I was producing some PowerPoint slides for my brother-in-law. While I was creating the slides he asked me what all the lines were for. Not knowing about my work around, he was worried that they would be included in the finished slides!

Drawing lines to create a grid was a work around for what, for me, was a missing function in PowerPoint — a function that was a part of previous drawing packages I had used. And it must have been a missing function for more than just me. I now use both PowerPoint 2002 and PowerPoint 2003, and both have the facility to display a grid on the screen. The gridlines can also be set either very close together or really far apart.

- Notes, cheat sheets, or other job aids on scraps of paper adjacent to the computer
- Sticky notes adorning the monitor
- Reference manuals that look well used, with marked pages
- Manuals that the users have created themselves
- Annotated pages from reports or manuals
- Paper forms that are perhaps being used as memory aids in performing particular activities

Each of these items is an **artifact** — an object or aid used in the performance of a task (Hackos and Redish, 1998). Wherever possible you should try to collect samples of these artifacts, as they are useful for understanding how work is done, where difficulties lie (e.g., where there may be too much to remember), and where functionality may be missing. They can provide pointers to areas for the redesign, such as where tasks need to be simplified in the future system.

It is worth questioning the users further about the work arounds and artifacts they use. Work arounds, especially, are the sort of knowledge that becomes implicit over time, and, unless prompted by questions, your users may not even realize that they are using work arounds (see Box 4.2).

Box 4.2	**Artifact Use to Supplement Poor Form Design**

A police department decided to make the change from handwritten or typed reports to word processed forms that would be stored in electronic form. As part of the work process, we observed how confiscated property and evidence were logged using paper forms. The task involved not just one form, but a set of forms, which were very complex to complete. We observed infrequent users of the forms struggling to complete them, then we watched how frequent users handled the forms. What we found was that the frequent users mostly ignored the paper forms initially and made notes about the property they were logging using a format different from that required by the forms — that is, they had devised an artifact that assisted them in their logging task. Once their notes were complete, they would then transcribe the information from their notes onto the forms.

It was apparent from this observation and subsequent interviews with the frequent users that how the form was structured for the recording of required property information did not support how the users' would actually do the task. This led to the design of better online forms for property logging.

This is another example of what a system developer can miss by not observing the real users in their workplace — information that only comes to light when explored further with users.

From Mayhew (1999, p. 80).

> **EXERCISE 4.2 (Allow 10 minutes)**
>
> Artifacts are objects or aids used in the performance of tasks. Look around your work or home environment. What kinds of artifacts do you see there?
>
> **DISCUSSION**
>
> *Debbie writes:* I can identify many artifacts in my work and home environments. Here are just a few.
>
> I spend a lot of time using Word. As an *aide memoire*, I have stuck on the wall — immediately above my monitor and in my line of sight — a list of shortcut keys for text formatting, which I printed out from Word's online help.
>
> On my monitor, I have an array of sticky notes reminding me of different things:
>
> - The label product number to use when printing mailing labels within Word
> - My daughter's mobile telephone number
> - Odd centimeter-to-inch conversions (e.g., 0.63 cm = 0.25 inch; 1.90 cm = 0.75 inch)
> - The serial number for installing MS Office
> - Different pieces of information that I need to remember to include in this chapter
>
> I also have a sticky note on my monitor, left over from when I used Word for Windows 2.0, which says, "CTRL-SHIFT-F7 to update source file (put cursor within field name)." This was a function related to working with master documents in Word for Windows 2.0. It is no longer needed for current versions of Word, yet it is still stuck there.
>
> On my printer there is a sticky note telling me that, if I want to print on both sides of the paper, the paper must go in the tray printed-side-up in order to print on the reverse. In the kitchen, a bit of scrap paper on the fridge door reminds me that my French classes are on Wednesday evenings at 6:30 (the day and time changed recently). There is always a sticky note there that I use as a shopping list — I add items when it becomes apparent that I will have to buy them on the next shopping trip. Near the washing machine, a sticky note tells my husband and daughter which wash cycles to use when they do their own wash.
>
> There are more I could mention. The point here is to show that we all use artifacts, for one reason or another. Artifacts related to the work may provide valuable cues for the improvement of your UI design.

▶ Techniques for Task Analysis

There are many techniques for task analysis. Deciding which technique to use depends on the type of information and the level of detail about tasks that you want to collect. One way of classifying task analysis techniques is to group them as follows:

A review of task analysis techniques for human–computer interaction was published in 1998 in the journal *Ergonomics*, Volume Forty-one, Number Eleven.

- Techniques that aim solely to describe the steps required to complete a task (these techniques describe what is to be done).
- Techniques that attempt to capture some representation of the knowledge that people have or need to have in order to complete the task (these techniques describe how a user does the task).

Next we discuss techniques from each category that you can use for your task analysis activities. When undertaking a task analysis it is impractical to study every task. You should start by focusing on the most important or key tasks that a computer system is used for.

▶ **Describing How to Do It: Scenarios and Use Cases**

Scenarios and use cases are stories about the use of a computer system, and at a general level they are very similar. Through the stories they tell, scenarios and use cases will encourage you to consider the range of users who will use the system, the range of activities for which the system is used, the environments within which users work, and more.

As you observe users at work, compile a list of tasks that you see them doing. Then describe the tasks by writing scenarios and use cases, focusing on the key or important tasks rather than trying to be exhaustive.

Scenarios and use cases can be short or long, abstract or detailed. The process of writing scenarios and use cases will help you in your attempts to understand the users and their tasks. As with all aspects of computer system design, you are unlikely to get a scenario right on the first try, but once you have created your scenarios and use cases, you can check whether your understanding is correct by running through (or testing) them with users. Scenarios and use cases are developed and refined over time and become more detailed during requirements gathering. Later in the UI design process, the scenarios and use cases you have created can be employed for evaluation and **usability testing** of the system being developed.

There are many variants of scenarios and use cases, having different and often confusing names. Typically where they differ is in the level of detail at which they describe tasks and the way in which they present the information. For the purposes of this course, we will focus on the following types of scenarios and use cases: task scenarios, concrete use cases, essential use cases, and use scenarios. These are explained next.

A **task scenario** is a narrative description of a task; it describes the *current* use of a computer system (Hackos and Redish, 1998). Task scenarios are usually personalized and describe a specific instance and situation of use. As such, task scenarios are very detailed and they describe, step by step, the procedures that a user followed in order to get a task done, as well as the features and behavior of the system with which the user interacted while performing the task. Any problems and difficulties that the user may have had with the current system will also be included in the description. An example of a task scenario is shown in Box 4.3.

| Box 4.3 | **Currency Exchange ATM Task Scenario** |

Emily Adams has just arrived at Kuala Lumpur airport en route to a large conference. Looking around for a bank in order to get some local currency, she sees a foreign currency exchange ATM that seems similar to the one she uses at home.

She parks her suitcase, takes out a credit card, and inserts it into the slot. A message is displayed on the screen:

```
Enter your PIN.
```

Emily thinks for a few moments and then types a four-digit number on the numerical pad, listening to the reassuring beep that follows each key press. The machine pauses for a few seconds and then displays:

```
Select currency required.
```

Emily pauses again. What is the currency in Malaysia? Fortunately the machine offers a default of "Ringgit," so she guesses that must be the local currency and presses the key. The machine displays the message:

```
Exchange rate is 3.75 Ringgit to one dollar U.S.

Enter amount required in Ringgit in units of [10].

Press (Proceed).
```

Emily enters 380 and presses ⟨Proceed⟩. There is a whirring noise and a few other indeterminate clunks and clicks. Her credit card is returned from the card entry slot and the money is deposited in the delivery slot, along with a printout of the transaction.

A **concrete use case** is similar to a task scenario in that it is also a detailed description of a task (Constantine and Lockwood, 1999). However, the two differ in that concrete use cases, unlike task scenarios, are not personalized and so describe the use of a system at a slightly more generic level. To turn the task scenario from Box 4.3 into a concrete use case, we would need to strip out personal details. For example, we would need to remove "Emily Adams," "Kuala Lumpur Airport," "Malaysian," and "Ringgit" and talk about the currency exchange task in general terms.

While concrete use cases can be written as textual narratives, in this book we shall divide them into two columns, as this highlights the way in which tasks performed are shared between the user and the computer system. Using the foreign currency exchange ATM as an example, a concrete use case for obtaining foreign currency is shown in Figure 4.3.

Note that the interaction in the concrete use case is described in terms of the detailed features and behavior of the user interface (Constantine and Lockwood, 1999).

In contrast, an **essential use case** describes a task at a high level of abstraction (Constantine and Lockwood, 1999). It is a simple and general description of a task that

User action	System response
User inserts credit card into the slot.	System requests PIN.
User types in 4-digit PIN number using the keypad.	System verifies user's identity. System requests foreign currency required, to be selected using menu keys.
User presses the key corresponding to the required currency.	System displays the exchange rate. System requests the user to enter the amount of foreign currency required using the keypad. The unit of currency is also displayed, as the system only deals with banknotes.
User enters amount required using the keypad.	System returns the credit card via the slot. System dispenses the currency via the currency delivery slot. System delivers a printout of the transaction via the receipt slot.

Figure 4.3 Concrete use case for obtaining foreign currency.

contains no assumptions about the type of UI or technology to be used. It focuses more on *what* a user would like to do (the user's intentions or purpose when using a computer system), and what the system's responsibilities need to be, than on how this will be achieved.

Figure 4.4 illustrates the essential use case for the foreign currency ATM example. We will not discuss the details of essential use cases any further in this unit, but note that Figure 4.4 demonstrates how an essential use case differs from a concrete use case.

A **use scenario** is also a narrative description of a task, again at a very detailed level (Hackos and Redish, 1998). It differs from a task scenario in that it describes the antic-

Get foreign currency	
User's purpose	System responsibility
Identify self.	Validate user's identity. Display currencies available.
Select currency required.	Display exchange rate.
Enter amount of foreign currency required.	Calculate amount multiplied by exchange rate.
Confirm amount.	Request initiation of payment. Obtain authorization for amount. Give money.
Take money and go.	

Figure 4.4 Essential use case for currency conversion ATM.

Concrete use cases, essential use cases and use scenarios will be dealt with in more detail when you learn about conceptual design in Chapter 8.

ipated use of the computer system. Use scenarios are based on the specified requirements, and are used to envision what the *future* system will be like for the user.

Task scenarios and concrete use cases are used as part of requirements gathering for examining and modeling tasks. They will help you analyze the issues in a user-centered way. Concrete use cases, essential use cases, and use scenarios are used in the design phase.

▶ **Cognitive Task Analysis: Moving from Scenarios and Use Cases to Cognitive Walkthrough**

Once you have determined what users do (that is, the existing tasks), examined their characteristics, and constructed your task scenarios, you will want to build models of *how* people perform their tasks. In the previous section, we mainly concentrated on the steps that are undertaken in doing a task, but here we are concerned with finding out what decisions are made and what type of knowledge might be needed or employed in performing a task.

Tasks are accomplished by performing actions in some order, using a suitable device. **Cognitive task analysis** recognizes that some of these actions are physical (such as pressing buttons, moving pointers, or speaking), but some of them are internal mental, or cognitive, operations. Undertakings such as deciding which button to press, where to place a pointer, recalling previously stored knowledge from memory, or comparing two objects are cognitive rather than physical operations.

To find out what cognitive operations are involved in system use, you can employ a method known as **cognitive walkthrough** (Wharton *et al.*, 1993). A cognitive walkthrough evaluates the steps required to perform a task and attempts to uncover mismatches between how the users think about a task and how the UI designer thinks about the task. For requirements gathering, you will be "walking" your users through your view of their tasks, which you have described using task scenarios and concrete use cases. Or you may have developed a low-fidelity paper prototype for the cognitive walkthrough.

Low-fidelity prototypes, including paper prototypes, are discussed in Chapter 6.

The cognitive walkthrough method is easy to apply and involves the following steps:

Step Zero: The user selects a task to be performed and writes down all the steps (actions) in the task.

Then, for each action in the task:

Step One: The user explores the artifact, prototype, or task scenario, looking for the action that might enable him or her to perform the selected task.

Step Two: The user selects the action that appears to match most closely what he or she is trying to do.

Step Three: The user interprets the system's response and assesses if any progress has been made toward completing the task.

For each action of the task in step zero, the evaluators try to answer the following questions as the user explores the prototype or task scenarios:

Question One: In relation to step 1, how does the user know what to do next? Is the correct action sufficiently evident to the user (i.e., the user can recognize it) or does the user have to recall what to do from memory?

Question Two: In relation to step two, will the user connect the description of the correct action with what he or she is trying to do?

Question Three: In relation to step three, on the basis of the system's response to the chosen action, will the user know if he or she has made a right or wrong choice?

It can take several iterations to get a cognitive analysis well worked out. It is important to document the cognitive walkthrough, recording what parts of the design are good and what parts of the design need improvement. In general, "no" answers to the questions indicate problems with the UI. If possible, an assessment should be made and recorded of how severe the problem is (see Box 4.4).

Box 4.4	**Cognitive Walkthrough for Setting a Video Using a Remote Control Handset**

Imagine that you are involved in designing a remote control handset for a video cassette recorder (VCR). A specific function of the device is to allow the user to set the machine ahead of time in order to record one or more programs (referred to here as timed recording). A cognitive walkthrough can be performed with no more than the requirements specification document or a paper-based prototype (**low-fidelity prototyping** techniques — of which paper-based prototyping is a common example — will be explained in Chapter 6). Here, though, we have a current remote control handset (see Figure 4.5) that we will use for the cognitive walkthrough. An equally valid approach for gathering requirements is to take a close look at any current devices that are similar to the one you are designing. You may not only discover problems that you will certainly want to avoid in your own design, but you might also find good points that you would like to include.

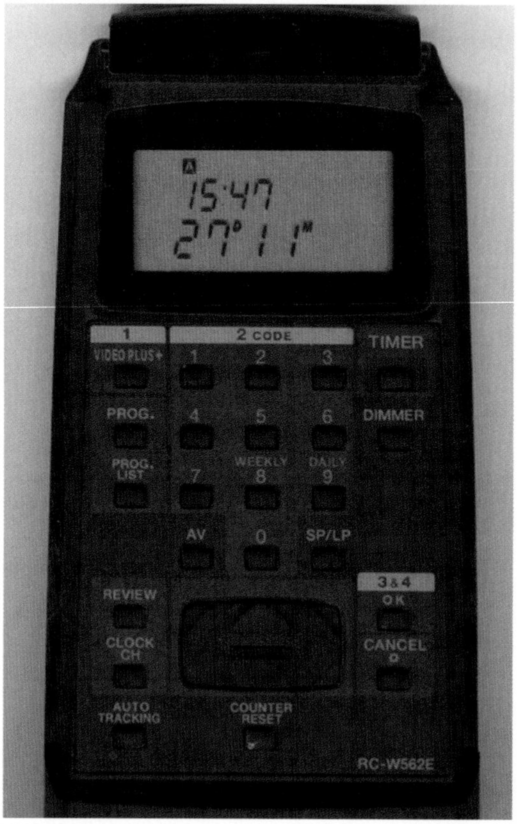

Figure 4.5 Remote control handset for cognitive walkthrough.

We will now undertake a cognitive walkthrough on our current device to assess how well the design supports the task. Notice that we're British and so we have to enter our times using the 24-hour clock — even though many of us prefer to think in terms of a.m. and p.m.

Step 0: Select a task, and write down all the steps (actions) in the task.

Our selected task is as follows. We want to set the VCR for a timed recording of a program starting at 21:00 and finishing at 22:30 on Channel 4 on August 18, 2005. Although we enter the information using controls on the handset, the information display is located on the VCR itself. The information is transmitted from the handset to the VCR via an infrared link. When switched on, the VCR in its resting state displays the number of the channel it last used. When switched off, the VCR displays a digital clock. To set it for timed recordings, the VCR must be switched on.

Once the actions for the task have been identified, they are specified in terms of what the user does (user action) and how the system responds to the user's action (system response). Although we could have simply listed the actions one after another, we have presented the actions as a concrete use case, which structures the actions of the task in two columns. This makes it easy to see what a user does and how the system responds in relation to that action.

User actions (UA)		System responses (SR)	
UA1	Press the PROG button on the handset.	SR1	VCR display shows a form fill-in for setting the start and stop times. These times are divided into separate sections for the hour and minute, separated by a colon. The cursor is flashing on the hour section of the start time.
UA2	Press the up arrow until the number 21 is showing.	SR2	21 is showing in the hour section of the start time.
UA3	Press the right arrow once to move the cursor to the minute section of the start time.	SR3	00 is showing and flashing in the minute section of the start time. This defaulted to 00 on selection of 21 in the hour section.
UA4	00 in the minute section of the start time is what is wanted. Press the right arrow once to move the cursor to the hour section of the finish time.	SR4	The cursor is flashing in the hour section of the finish time.
UA5	Press the up arrow until the number 22 is showing.	SR5	22 is showing in the hour section of the finish time.
UA6	Press the right arrow once to move the cursor to the minute section of the finish time.	SR6	00 is showing and flashing in the minute portion of the finish time. This defaulted to 00 on selection of 22 in the hour section.

User actions (UA)		System responses (SR)	
UA7	Press the up arrow until the number 30 is showing.	SR7	30 is showing in the minute section of the finish time.
UA8	Press the right arrow once to move the cursor to the day section of the date field.	SR8	On the display, the full date has now defaulted to the current date. The cursor is flashing in the day section of the date.
UA9	Press the up arrow until the number 18 is showing.	SR9	18 is showing in the day section of the date field.
UA10	Press the right arrow once to move the cursor to the month section of the date field.	SR10	The cursor is flashing in the month section of the date field.
UA11	Press the up arrow until the number 8 is showing.	SR11	18 is showing in the day section of the date field, and 8 is showing in the month section of the date field.
UA12	Press the right arrow once to move the cursor to the year section of the date field.	SR12	The cursor is flashing in the year section of the date field.
UA13	Press the up arrow until the number 04 is showing.	SR13	18 is showing in the day section of the date field, 8 is showing in the month section of the date field, and 04 is showing in the year section of the date field.
UA14	Press the right arrow once to move the cursor to select the channel to record.	SR14	The cursor is flashing in the channel field.
UA15	Press the up arrow until the number 4 is showing.	SR15	4 is showing as the channel to record from.
UA16	Press the right arrow once so the system accepts the setting.	SR16	The clock returns to the display. A small 1 is displayed on the left side of the clock, which indicates one timed recording has been set.

User actions (UA)	System responses (SR)
UA17 Press the TIMER button to initiate timed recording mode.	SR17 Video switches itself off and into timed recording mode. A small red clock is displayed in the upper right-hand corner of the display to indicate that the video is set for timed recording.

Having compiled our list of actions for the task of setting the video for a timed recording, we can now perform the walkthrough using the handset shown in Figure 4.5. For each user action (UA1, UA2, etc.), we must answer the following questions:

- How does the user know what to do next? Is the correct action sufficiently evident to the user (i.e., can the user recognize it) or does he or she have to recall what to do from memory?
- Will the user connect the description of the correct action with what he or she is trying to do?
- On the basis of the system's response to the chosen action, will the user know if he or she has made a right or wrong choice?

Remember, "no" answers to the questions generally indicate problems with the UI.

For the first user action, we now have the following:

UA1	Press the prog button on the handset.
Question One	*Is the correct action sufficiently evident to the user?* Neither the handset nor the VCR display give any indication that the user needs to press the PROG button to do a timed recording.
Question Two	*Will the user connect the description of the correct action with what he or she is trying to do?* Experienced users might associate timed recording with setting or programming (prog) the VCR. However, this is probably not the case for novice users.
Question Three	*Will the user know if he or she has made a right or wrong choice on the basis of the system's response to the chosen action?* Once the PROG button is pressed, the VCR display changes to a form fill-in that guides the user in entering the information (although the display on the handset does not change). Any user who notices the VCR display, or remembers where the form fill-in appears, will know that he or she has made a right choice.

For the second user action, we have the following:

UA2	Press the up arrow until the number 21 is showing in the hour section of the start time.
Question One	*Is the correct action sufficiently evident to the user?* No. It is not evident that to set the time one can use only the four unlabeled arrow keys. In fact, the handset is confusing for the user because there is a number pad above the four arrow keys. The user might assume that he or she can use the number pad to enter the time values into the form in much the same way as one would enter numbers into a calculator. This would be wrong, as the number pad is used solely for programming the VCR using VideoPlus+ codes. The number pad is labeled CODE, but this may not prevent the user from making the wrong assumption.
Question Two	*Will the user connect the description of the correct action with what he or she is trying to do?* No. There are no markings on the arrows themselves, nor anywhere near them, that might indicate that they are to be used for entering information into the programming form fill-in.
Question Three	*Will the user know if he has made a right or wrong choice on the basis of the system's response to the chosen action?* If the user is lucky enough to discover that the arrow buttons change the times and channel, then there will be feedback on the VCR display as the form gets filled in. However, this could easily be missed if the user stops looking at the VCR display — perhaps because he or she is so engrossed (and irritated) in trying to make the handset work.

Although we walked through only two actions from our list of 17, we found several usability problems with this remote control handset, indicating that this is not a good design. If we were designing a VCR handset, these findings would certainly be fed back into the requirements specification as design faults that we would want to avoid in our own design.

EXERCISE 4.3 (Allow 10 minutes)

Perform a cognitive walkthrough for UA17.

DISCUSSION

For user action 17 on our list, we have the following:

UA17	**Press the TIMER button to initiate timed recording mode.**
Question One	*Is the correct action sufficiently evident to the user?* There is a separate button labeled TIMER on the handset.
Question Two	*Will the user connect the description of the correct action with what he or she is trying to do?* Only if the user connects the label TIMER with the concept of a timed recording.
Question Three	*Will the user know if he or she has made a right or wrong choice on the basis of the system's response to the chosen action?* Yes. The video will switch itself off and a small red clock will become visible on the VCR display. This sound of the video switching off and the red clock give feedback that the VCR has been set for a timed recording.

At the end of the task analysis activities, you should have a thorough understanding of the work that users do and the tasks that the system will need to support. You should obtain four outputs from task analysis:

- Any work arounds used
- Any artifacts used
- The task scenarios and concrete use cases that describe users' work
- The results from the cognitive walkthrough

These outputs would form part of the requirements specification document.

1.3 Mental Models

When faced with an unfamiliar system, users do not come to the system completely devoid of capability. It has been suggested that we all go around with a model of the world in our heads that enables us to negotiate unfamiliar situations (Norman, 1988). Such a model is known as a **mental model**. While it is difficult to provide a definitive description of a mental model, a well-known definition in the context of UI design is provided by Norman (1988, p. 17):

> *They are . . . the models people have of themselves, others, the environment and the things with which they interact. People form mental models through experience, training and instruction.*

Mental models enable users to reason about a system, to apply already held experience and knowledge about the world to system use. So when users approach an unfamiliar system, they subconsciously refer to their mental model, or **user's model**. If the domain of the system or its possible use is already contained within their model, then they will have an idea of how to interact with the system (Rieman *et al.*, 1994). If the domain is new and unfamiliar, their model will be of less help. Roberts *et al.* (1997, p. 51) suggest that when the differences between what is encountered in an unfamiliar system and existing knowledge are small, then "the new situation is easy to manage or 'intuitive'; however, if the differences are large, the situation becomes difficult."

We usually construct a mental model when we are required to make an inference or prediction in a particular situation. In constructing a mental model, a conscious mental simulation may be run from which conclusions about the particular situation can be deduced. It is likely that most of us can recall using a form of mental simulation at some time or another. An example often cited is when we use what we know about simple arithmetic (for example, the steps involved in addition or subtraction) to perform calculations with a pocket calculator.

Perhaps the best way of understanding the dynamical aspect of a mental model is for you to construct one yourself.

EXERCISE 4.4 (Allow five minutes)

Without looking, calculate how many external windows there are in a house that you know well. If you find this exercise too easy, try doing the same for a larger building, such as the one where you work or one you visit. Then check whether you were right.

DISCUSSION

You might be surprised to find that you miscounted the windows. It is unlikely that you have any specific stored knowledge about the number of windows in your house. What you probably did was imagine going through all of the rooms and counting the number of windows in each room or imagine yourself walking around the outside and looking. This is a simple example of running a mental model.

Based on his own observations, Norman has made several general observations about mental models (see Box 4.5).

EXERCISE 4.5 (Allow five minutes)

Can you think of any examples of inappropriate mental models that you, or someone you know, have developed when using a computer system?

DISCUSSION

An example of a computer system that often elicits an incorrect mental model is voicemail (Erikson, 1990). A typical voicemail system provides each user with

Box 4.5	**Characteristics of Mental Models**

- Mental models are incomplete, as the user will not have a full understanding of the workings of the system.
- People's ability to run their models is severely limited.
- Mental models are unstable: people forget the details of the system they are using, especially when those details (or the whole system) have not been used for some period.
- Mental models do not have firm boundaries: similar devices and operations get confused with one another.
- Mental models are unscientific: people maintain superstitious behavior patterns, even when they know these superstitions are unneeded, because they cost little in physical effort and save mental effort.
- Mental models are parsimonious: often people do extra physical operations rather than the mental planning that would allow them to avoid these actions; they are willing to trade off extra physical action for reduced mental complexity. This is especially true where the extra actions allow one simplified rule to apply to a variety of devices, thus minimizing the chances for confusion.

From Norman (1987, p. 241).

a mailbox where messages can be left. When callers reach the voicemail system, a recorded message tells them that the person they are trying to contact is unavailable and invites them to leave a message. The system then passes on any message that is left for that person. If the system is busy, it can take up to half an hour for the message to reach its destination. The problem is that most people's mental model of voicemail is based on a model of a conventional answering machine. Hence, they assume that messages are recorded directly on the phone machine that sits on each person's desk, in the same way that an answering machine works. However, this is not the case, since all messages are recorded on a central machine and then delivered to individual mailboxes. When the system is busy, a queuing mechanism operates, whereby messages must wait their turn before being sent to their destination. This system works well provided that the message left on the system does not need immediate attention. However, a problem can arise when someone leaves a message on a colleague's machine saying, "See you in my office in five minutes" and assumes that the person has popped out of her office for a moment and will receive the message when she returns. While the person may indeed return to her office after a couple of minutes, if the system is busy she may not receive the message very quickly and so miss the appointment.

Erikson (1990) notes how most people do not understand how voicemail works, and even those who do still present the wrong model. A more appropriate model would be one based on an answering or reception service model, where messages are left with an intermediary whose job it is to forward them and where it is known that there may be a delay if the receptionist is busy or cannot reach the person for whom the message is intended.

In the early 1980s, two main types of mental models were identified that users employ when interacting with devices: the **structural model** and the **functional model**.

▶ Structural Models

Structural models assume that the user has internalized, in memory, the structure of how a particular device or system works. Consider the London Underground map shown in Figure 4.6, which represents the station locations and the lines that connect them. The schematic form used provides a structure that regular travelers learn, internalize, and remember. They then use their internal representation as the basis from which to work out how to get from A to B.

▶ Functional Models

Functional models assume that the user has internalized procedural knowledge about how to use the device or system. Functional models develop from past knowledge of a similar domain and *not* — unlike structural models — from a model of how the device works.

Look at Figure 4.6 again. While this figure is useful at showing the structure of the underground system and for promoting a structural model, it is much less useful at

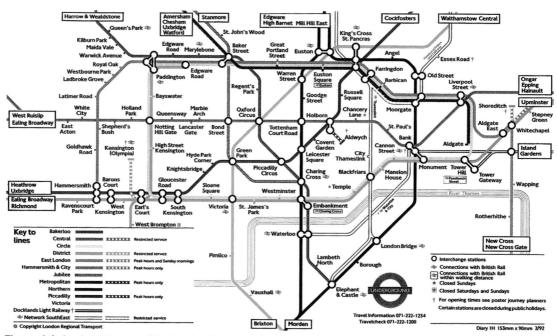

Figure 4.6 A schematic map of the London Underground.

promoting a functional model of how to use the underground system. The figure, for example, does not reveal how to get the correct sort of ticket from an automatic ticket machine, what to do with the ticket, how to get on and off trains, and so on — the type of information that would be held in a functional model. This would have been developed through using prior knowledge of underground train systems, observing others, and employing generally held knowledge about how to use different modes of public transport. London Underground uses a variant of the map to help promote part of the functional model, Figure 4.7, which has the six fare zones superimposed in an attempt to help customers who use the underground to purchase the right sort of ticket.

▶ Structural versus Functional Models

A simple distinction between the two models is to consider a structural model as a model of how-it-works and a functional model as a model of how-to-use-it. Taking another more everyday example, we know that most people use a calculator in the same way as they learned to do math at school (i.e., they use a functional model).

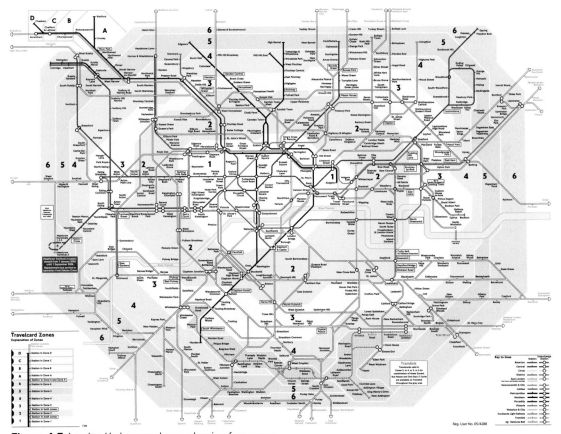

Figure 4.7 London Underground map showing fare zones.

With a calculator, it is rarely the case that anyone would develop a structural how-it-works model unless they have read the manual explaining the underlying mechanism of the device.

Another major difference between structural models and functional models is that structural models enable users to answer unexpected questions and make predictions, whereas functional models are centered on a set of tasks. Furthermore, functional models are context dependent, whereas structural models are largely context free. The advantage of a context-dependent model is that it is easier to use. On the other hand, the advantage of a context-free model is that it is easier to extend and integrate with other knowledge.

A key question is to determine whether users actually develop these kinds of models, and if so, the extent to which the models help them understand and make predictions about a device or system. In general, it is assumed that structural models are highly limited in their applicability because they do not account for how the users are going to perform their actions (this is what the functional models are assumed to do). Their advantage is that by explaining how a device works, they allow a user to predict the effects of any possible sequence of actions and hence to work out (eventually) how to achieve most tasks possible with the device. Their disadvantage is that constructing a structural model in one's mind often requires a great deal of effort, both in learning the model and in using it to work out what to do.

Structural models may be most useful when a device breaks down and you have to work out how to mend it. In certain domains, like electronics and engineering, the use of such models may also be essential for understanding how things like circuits work. Various types of instructional material have been developed with the aim of instilling an appropriate mental model in the user. However, in the everyday world of technological devices, people seem to get by without using structural models. Most of us quite happily operate the telephone, the television, and the microwave oven without ever thinking about the insides of these appliances and how they might work.

▶ The Utility of Mental Models in HCI

Numerous studies have been carried out in an attempt to discover whether people actually have and use mental models when interacting with devices and systems (Rogers *et al.*, 1992). The general assumption is that people use some type of model, but that it is often incomplete and vague. To achieve a good design, it is important for the designer to take advantage of the mental models held by users and to be aware of how users employ them.

Here we will focus on how to capture your users' mental models in the first place. Unfortunately, as the UI designer, you cannot simply ask all the potential users of a product to describe or draw pictures of their models, because (1) you will not have access to all the different users and (2) most users are unaware that they have a model. Even users who are aware that they have expectations about a situation typically cannot provide the insight needed to enable a designer to construct the mental models they hold. To develop the users' mental models, information must be gathered by observing users in their work situations and by surveying and interviewing primary and secondary users. You should listen carefully to how the users talk about their jobs, their tasks, and the tools they use, and focus on any problems they have doing tasks with their current systems or with other technology they currently interact with. These observations and conversations, when analyzed, will help you to understand users' expectations in system use, and how they apply their prior knowledge and experience to the tasks they perform. Because each user's mental model is influenced by different experiences, no two users' models are exactly alike. But by observing and talking to primary and secondary users, you should be able to pull together a fairly complete picture of the models of a cross section of users.

Investigating the users' mental models of their tasks and the problems they face with the current technology will help you discover the design strategies that you can employ to make a new system accessible and easily understandable.

EXERCISE 4.6 (Allow 15 minutes)

Imagine you have designed a new version of a microwave oven that is intended to replace an existing version. The oven is budget priced to be affordable by people on low incomes, such as students, or couples in their first house or with young families. Formulate a plan for finding out whether your system, as designed, matches the mental models of these user groups. What questions will you ask in your interviews with the users?

DISCUSSION

Debbie writes: For my study I would choose at least one user from each of these target groups. If they could be identified, I would also choose some users of the existing version of the microwave oven.

I would ask all users about the cooking tasks they might want to be able to do with the oven. I would then ask them to use the current version of the microwave oven for some small cooking tasks (e.g., making scrambled eggs or baking a cake). While they are doing these tasks, I would ask them to verbally describe what they think they should do with the oven control panel to do these cooking tasks. I would ask them about any problems they had, or if the microwave made them set the cooking cycles in a way that differed from what they had expected.

2 Environmental Considerations: Where Is This Work Done?

Just as knowing about your user and task characteristics will influence your decision making in relation to the UI design, you also need to consider factors related to the environment within which the application will be situated. The best way to find out about the working area is to make a site visit. As noted previously, you should be doing this anyway — you should be talking to the real users of the application and observing what they do, observing how they undertake their work, and observing the conditions under which they work. Again it must be stressed that it is necessary to observe the users, rather than just talk to them, if you want to understand what it is they do, how they do it, and the environment in which they work.

In Chapter 2 we used the example of the Prague ticket machine to show how some information only comes to light by going to where users are using the system and then observing them. Here is another example, which came from a recent television documentary about air traffic controllers. It has been widely publicized that air travel has increased, and that controllers work under great pressure directing the ever-crowded sky traffic. We had pictured the controllers sitting at individual consoles, concentrating on their radar screen, and talking to the pilots via headgear. In fact, the documentary showed that air traffic controllers, when working and concentrating hard, often stand and pace in front of their consoles, looking back and forth between their radar displays and the skies when directing air traffic and communicating with the pilots. In their work, controllers also use *flight progress strips*. These strips contain information about the individual flights, such as flight number, aircraft identification number, and originating and destination airports. In extended observations of air traffic controllers with a view to computerizing their work, Bentley *et al.* (1992) found that the manual manipulation of flight strips to control and direct air traffic was part of the working style of air traffic controllers. It focused the controllers' attention on their air traffic control tasks. The implications of these observations for system design are that individual, sit-at consoles with computer displays of information are not suitable for all controllers. If this design approach were taken, the chances are high that it would be unsuitable or that it could make some controllers work in a different way than they are used to. This important information is again something that could only have been discovered by observing real users in their working environment.

Several aspects of the working environment influence the design of the UI, as detailed next.

2.1 The Physical Environment: Is This a Pleasant Place to Be?

In addition to knowing about the users and their tasks, you will also need to look at the **physical environment** and the physical conditions within which the tasks are undertaken. There are many questions you might want to consider:

- Is the lighting sufficient for what they want to do?
- Is the temperature of the area comfortable, or are there specialized conditions (for example, stocktaking in an area that requires a low temperature, such as a freezer center)?
- What are the noise levels like? (For example, is it a noisy factory or a busy family kitchen, or is the noise level low, as you might find in a library?)
- Is the environment dirty or dusty?

The physical design and layout are also important.

- How is the area laid out? How much space is dedicated to the computer system?
- How many people are there in the given space? Is there generous space, adequate space, or are people tightly packed together in a limited area?

2.2 The Safety Environment: Is This a Safe Place to Be?

Are there any hazards or health and safety issues?

- Does the user need special clothing, such as gloves?
- Is it a safety critical system, where stress levels tend to be high and distractions need to be kept to a minimum?
- Are there any pollution or other environmental hazards that users must contend with?

2.3 The Social Environment: Do People Help Each Other?

How users interact, or are prevented from interacting, is also a consideration.

- Are the users under pressure, for example, from deadlines or production targets?
- Do users cooperate and share information, or do they work alone? Are they reluctant to cooperate?
- Do users share tasks or depend on each other?
- Do users help each other to learn, or do they distract each other? Does one person take responsibility for certain types of help such as setting up the technology?
- Is there a social hierarchy? If it is a workplace, are there individual offices, open-plan cubicles, or a factory floor? If it is a home, is there a separate computer table in a quiet corner or part of a busy family area? This not only can affect the use of the system itself, but it can also contribute to a good or a bad social environment.

2.4 The Organizational Environment: Does Management Support This Work?

Organizations come in all shapes and sizes. For the purposes of this chapter, they include families, groups of friends, and other social groups. They are highly complex, ambiguous entities consisting of a multitude of interacting factors. For computer systems to be useful, they need to be integrated within the existing networks of humans and technological artifacts. If little or no attention is paid to the organizational structure, the working practices, or the culture of the organization, then it is likely that any new computing system introduced will be used suboptimally or at worst discarded.

Organizational factors influencing the design of the UI include the following:

- The organizational mission and aims, or the purpose of the group.
- Structural working factors (working hours, group working, job function, work practices, assistance with work, any interruptions to work, management and communications structure, remuneration)

- Attitudes and cultural factors (policy on computers and IT, organizational aims, and industrial relations)
- Flexibility, performance monitoring and feedback, pacing, autonomy, and discretion
- Within a home or nonwork environment, the overall culture of the group and its attitudes and expectations

2.5 The User Support Environment

The implementation of computers also depends on what types of user support are provided to the users of the application. These would include the provision of assistive devices if required by the user, offering manuals for reference, providing or making training available, ensuring that colleagues are available for assistance, or ensuring that experts are available to guide novice users.

2.6 Consideration of Environmental Aspects and How They Affect Design

Each of these environmental aspects will affect choices in the design of the UI. Table 4.4 gives a few examples of how particular environmental characteristics might affect your design. As you collect information about the environments for which you are

Table 4.4 How Environmental Characteristics Affect Design for Interfaces in a Workplace

Environmental characteristic	How it affects the design
The environment is noisy.	The use of sound for alerting users to problems may not be effective.
The environment is dusty or dirty.	Equipment might require some type of protective covering (e.g., a keyboard might need a membranous cover).
Users wear protective clothing such as gloves.	Input devices will need to accommodate this.
The work is highly pressured and subject to frequent interruptions.	The application must allow the user to stop his or her work and restart it later, preferably from the point where the user left off.
There is a need for workers to share information, or the work is designed so that they work in groups rather than in isolation.	The workplace will need to be laid out carefully to take this factor into consideration.

developing a UI, you should record your observations (perhaps in table form) for inclusion in the requirements specification document.

3   Summary

This chapter has introduced you to task analysis and environmental analysis. These build on the user analysis detailed in Chapter 3.

The following are the key points of this chapter:

- User-centered system design focuses on people, their work, their work environments, and how technology can best be deployed and designed to support them.
- Requirements gathering is a central part of computer systems development.

5

Requirements gathering: knowledge of user interface design

Introduction: The Two Types of Knowledge Needed for User Interface Design

We have emphasized that for effective user interface design, the designer needs to know about the intended users of a system and must design iteratively. In addition, you need to know about and take other information into account. This information comes from two sources:

- Information-gathering activities and analyses that form part of the user interface design and development process.
- User interface design knowledge, which comes partly from theory, such as the field of cognitive psychology, and partly from experience, such as studying designs that are currently working well for users.

We looked at the first type, knowledge of the intended users of the system, their work, and their domains of work, in Chapters 2 and 3. This chapter looks at the second type: user interface design knowledge.

Undertaking a user interface design requires the utilization of specific and specialized knowledge. **Design principles**, derived from experience, are abstract, high-level guides for design which, because of their generality, are difficult to apply. To help make them easier to apply, they are often translated into **design rules**, which are low-level, highly specific instructions that the designer can follow with a minimum of interpretation. We will give some examples of working from principles to rules later in this chapter, but first we discuss some principles in more depth.

If you want to learn more about the theoretical context, then you should read Johnson (1992).

We could devote most of this book to theoretical knowledge that informs user interface design, but instead we have chosen four particularly useful insights from psychology for you to think about as you are designing your UI. As our approach is selective, you may disagree with our conclusions or feel that we have oversimplified the issues. As with all principles and guidelines, you should apply these with care, taking into account the needs of your users, the tasks they are carrying out, and the environment in which they are working.

2 Four Psychological Principles

Figure 5.1 illustrates some of the ways in which users can get confused when they interact with a UI.

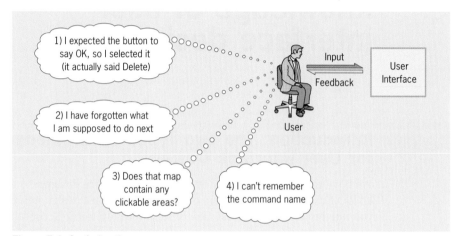

Figure 5.1 Confusing the user.

Do any of the situations illustrated in Figure 5.1 sound familiar? They arise partly because UIs often disregard the following principles:

1. *Users see what they expect to see.* If the OK button is usually on the left of the Delete button and a new screen swaps these around, users may think they see the OK button on the left and erroneously press the Delete button.
2. *Users have difficulty focusing on more than one activity at a time.* A user who is working in a busy environment may be distracted, so the UI should remind the user what he or she needs to do next.
3. *It is easier to perceive a structured layout.* It is difficult to perceive a button if the screen does not give you any clues, such as lines or shadow encompassing a clickable area.
4. *It is easier to recognize something than to recall it.* Some UIs expect the user to recall esoteric information such as command names. This can be difficult, particularly for a novice user. It is often better to make the information visible in the form of a menu or a button.

2.1 Users See What They Expect to See

Consider Exercise 5.1. It demonstrates the effects of context.

Exercise 5.1 (Allow two minutes)

Look at Figure 5.2 and read what it says. Do you notice anything strange about the middle letter of each word?

THE CAT

Figure 5.2 The effect of context. (From Selfridge 1955, ©1955 IEEE.)

DISCUSSION

The letters in Figure 5.2 are usually read as the words "the cat." The middle letter is the same in both words although it is seen as an *H* in the first word and an *A* in the second.

We interpret the letters as two meaningful words that go together ("the cat") rather than two meaningless syllables ("tae cht"). The context of the other characters, together with our prior knowledge, enables us to interpret the middle letter as two different characters. Thus, our prior knowledge of the world helps us to make sense of it and we see what we expect to see. This means that we are not very good at handling unexpected situations (what if we were supposed to read the words as "tae cht"?). The same applies to information displayed on computer screens.

The implications of this for the UI designer are twofold:

- *The principle of consistency.* As users find it difficult to handle the unexpected, it is important to be consistent throughout the UI. For example, you should use colors in a consistent manner. If you use red to indicate danger, then always use red, rather than red sometimes and green at other times. The same applies to screen layout, such as the positioning of buttons, and to all aspects of UI design.
- *The principle of exploiting prior knowledge.* As users perceive the screen using their prior knowledge, this provides the opportunity to draw on their experience. A screen metaphor, such as the calculator that comes with the Microsoft Windows operating system, does this by presenting users with a familiar image that allows them to apply their prior knowledge and experience of a physical calculator to the Windows version.

2.2 Users Have Difficulty Focusing on More Than One Activity at a Time

Computer users often need to divide their attention between several activities at the same time. For example, a travel agent may be talking to a customer while looking up information on the computer screen. We are quite good at dividing our attention, as Box 5.1 illustrates. However, some people are better at this than others and the UI should provide support if this situation is likely to arise.

Box 5.1	**The Cocktail Party Effect**

Do you remember the last time you were at a party or in a crowd and you were surrounded by a sea of faces and a babble of voices? How long was it before you found yourself turning your attention to one specific conversation? What happened to the other voices and faces? Did they simply become a blur? While being involved in the one conversation, did you find yourself overhearing anyone else's conversation? Perhaps it was a piece of gossip, which you could not resist listening to. What happened when you tuned in to this other conversation? Were you able to carry on with your conversation or did you become distracted?

This everyday experience of focusing on one particular activity while switching between others has become known as the **cocktail party phenomenon** (Cherry, 1953). You probably found that, after the initial impression of chaos, you found yourself attracted to one group and one conversation, and the others faded. But, for example, if you heard your own or a familiar name mentioned elsewhere in the room, you may have found that your attention switched in this new direction and that you then lost the thread of the former conversation.

Thus, to focus attention you should adhere to the following principles:

- *The principle of perceptual organization.* If you group things together that go together, it is easier for the user to pay attention to the appropriate group. For example, the screens in Figure 5.3 both represent the same information. However, part (a) has been grouped into categories and part (b) has not. The lack of structure in part (b) makes it difficult to find information.
- *The principle of importance.* If something is important for the user, it should be placed in a prominent position. For example, alarm and warning messages are often placed in the center of the screen, blocking the work that the user is carrying out.

When we say principle of importance, we mean something a big bigger than other features but not ridiculously so. If something is excessively large, then it may be seen as separate from the rest of the material on the screen rather than as more important than other material on the screen. For example, Benway and Lane (1998) found that an especially large and prominent box was completely missed by users.

2.3 It Is Easier to Perceive a Structured Layout

As we noticed in Figure 5.3, it is easier to perceive that things go together if they are arranged so that they look like they go together. According to **Gestalt psychology**, a number of laws determine the way in which we perceive the world. The psychologists who first described these laws (see, for example, Koffka, 1935, or Köhler, 1947) believed that our ability to interpret the meaning of scenes and objects was based on innate laws of organization. These laws help us to see whole figures standing out from a background, and particular groupings of the objects as well. Figure 5.4 shows examples of the following Gestalt laws of perceptual organization and grouping.

Destination	Flight	Carrier	Depart	Arrive	Rates Business	Standard
Aberdeen	4171	BA	0845	0945	£155	£102
Dublin	664	FR	1035	1135	£149	£100
Toulouse	8064	AF	1110	1410	£307	£182
Frankfurt	4618	LH	1115	1355	£222	£152
Amsterdam	2045	UK	1130	1335	£222	£152
Copenhagen	8363	BA	1145	1445	£315	£187
Paris-CDG	1803	BA	1150	1400	£248	£165
Exeter	446	JY	1205	1305	£155	£102
Glasgow	1903	BA	1210	1310	£155	£102
Munich	4526	LH	1225	1525	£301	£179
Geneva	8413	BA	1235	1420	£222	£152
Aberdeen	4172	BA	1245	1345	£155	£102

(a)

Dest: Aberdeen (BA4171) Dep: 0845; Arr: 0945
(B/S: £155/102)
Dest: Dublin (FR664) Dep: 1035; Arr: 1135
(B/S: £149/100)
Dest: Toulouse (AF8064) Dep: 1110; Arr: 1410
(B/S: £307/182)
Dest: Frankfurt (LH4618) Dep: 1115; Arr: 1355
(B/S: £222/152)
Dest: Amsterdam (UK2045) Dep: 1130; Arr: 1335
(B/S: £222/152)
Dest: Copenhagen (BA8363) Dep: 1145; Arr: 1445
(B/S: £315/187)
Dest: Paris-CDG (BA1803) Dep: 1150; Arr: 1400
(B/S: £248/165)
Dest: Exeter (JY446) Dep: 1205; Arr: 1305
(B/S: £155/102)
Dest: Glasgow (BA1903) Dep: 1210; Arr: 1310
(B/S: £155/102)
Dest: Munich (LH4526) Dep: 1225; Arr: 1525
(B/S: £301/179)
Dest: Geneva (BA8413) Dep: 1235; Arr: 1420
(B/S: £222/152)
Dest: Aberdeen (BA4172) Dep: 1245; Arr: 1345
(B/S: £155/102)

(b)

Figure 5.3 The structuring of text. (From Tullis, 1988.)

- *The law of **proximity***. Elements that are close together appear as groups rather than as random elements.
- *The law of **similarity***. Elements of the same shape or color appear to belong together.
- *The law of **closure***. Where possible, we see an incomplete element as complete — we fill in the gap.
- *The law of **continuity***. We see this figure as two lines of dots crossing each other, rather than as a random set of dots.
- *The law of **symmetry***. We tend to perceive regions bounded by symmetrical borders as coherent figures.

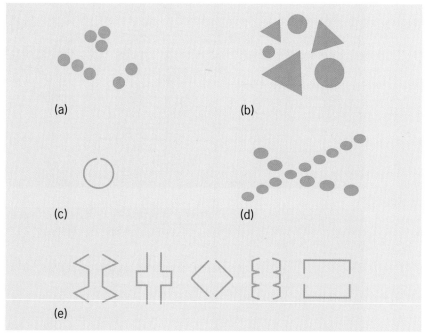

Figure 5.4 The Gestalt principles of perceptual organization: (a) proximity, (b) similarity, (c) closure, (d) continuity, and (e) symmetry.

While we see particular groupings of objects, we also see objects against a ground. That is, when a figure has two or more distinct areas, we can usually see part of it as a figure, and the rest of it as background — especially where edges are present or there is the existence of boundaries between areas in relation to brightness, color, or texture. This characteristic of perception is referred to as **figure-ground segregation**.

Look at Figure 5.5. Unless you have seen this figure before, it will probably look like nothing more than just black and white areas within a frame. However, look carefully; there is a picture of *something* concealed within these areas of black and white.

If you've taken time to look at the figure, and still can't see what it is, look at Figure 5.8 on page 101, and then look back at Figure 5.5 again. You should now be able to see the "something" that has been disguised in the figure.

To help the user, we should design UIs that anticipate these laws. For example, reading of information is easier if it is grouped in columns that are grouped spatially, as shown in Figure 5.3. This would be an application of the law of proximity. Adequate contrast between figure and ground will ensure that the object requiring the focus of attention is distinguishable from the background.

95

Part 2

Pagendarm and Schaumburg (2001) have an interesting review of the research, as well as the results of an investigation showing that banner blindness is more common when users are on a directed search than when they are browsing aimlessly.

One phenomenon that we consider may be caused by figure/ground perception is banner blindness, reported by several authors. The banner advertisement, frequently a large and colorful feature of the web page if viewed in terms of the amount of the page it takes up, is actually ignored by users to the point that they are unlikely to recall ever having seen it. We think this may be because the banner is regarded as "ground" and ignored by users looking at the text as "figure."

Figure 5.5 What is it? (From Dallenbach, 1951.)

These laws apply to both the hardware and the software components of a UI. Thus, they are relevant to the layout of buttons on a telephone just as much as to the layout of information on a screen.

EXERCISE 5.2 (Allow five minutes)

Figure 5.6 is an illustration of the home page for the Learner's Guide web site, one of the British Open University's web sites. How well does it support the principles of proximity, similarity, closure, and continuity?

DISCUSSION

The four main choices available (course choice, services for disabled students, career planning, and learning skills) are similar visually and placed together, so they look like a coherent group of choices. However, the four descriptions are placed closer to each other than they are to the main choice that they support, so it is not immediately obvious that they relate to the choices rather than to each other.

The principle of closure is illustrated in the design of the arrow logo, where we see an arrow even though it's really a white space in the colored button.

2.4 It Is Easier to Recognize Something Than to Recall It

One of the findings in memory research is that it is easier to recognize information than to recall it. Thus, it is easier to take a shopping list with you to the supermarket than to try to recall everything you want to buy.

In UI design, Norman (1988) has developed the notion of recognition and recall in terms of **knowledge in the head** and **knowledge in the world**. The basic idea is that

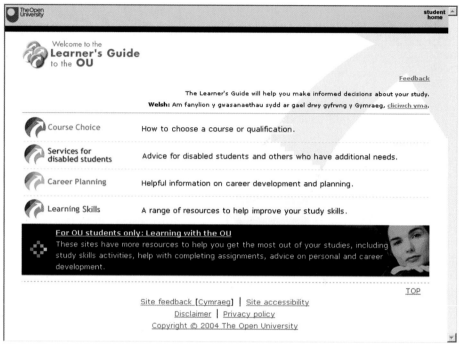

Figure 5.6 The Open University Learner's Guide, visited July 26, 2004.

For more information on icon design, see Chapter 13. For more information on metaphors, see Chapter 10.

when we carry out everyday tasks, we combine information that is stored in memory with information we locate in the world.

As a designer, you should try to put the information that the user needs in the world (that is, in the UI). This may take the form of menus, icons, and screen metaphors.

This gives us the *principle of recognition*: where possible, allow users to recognize what they want rather than making them recall it. Thus, instead of having to recall a name or a particular combination of keys to perform an operation, the user only has to scan through a menu or click the appropriate button. This is one of the reasons why direct-manipulation UIs are so successful.

As with all principles, there are exceptions. For example, experienced users often prefer key combinations because key combinations are faster. The effort of learning and recalling is worth it for the extra speed. Similarly, users who operate a computer system all day will be irritated by having to read the same information repeatedly. Identifying such exceptions requires a good understanding of the users, their tasks, and the environment in which they are working.

3 Three Principles from Experience: Visibility, Affordance, and Feedback

If you think about the complexity of most computer systems, you can see that the potential for poorly designed user interfaces is high; more functionality needs more controls, and unless great care is taken it is easy to get things wrong. Norman (1988, 1993) has cataloged many examples of everyday objects that are hard to use because the way they look is not in harmony with the way they work. He first started thinking about these principles during a visit to the United Kingdom, where as an American he found many things were different from the way he expected them to be. On his return to the United States, he realized that the same lack of logic and ease of use applied to other objects–he just had not noticed before.

From Norman's work we have drawn three key principles to help ensure a good human–computer interaction: the principles of **visibility**, **affordance**, and **feedback**. These are examples of design knowledge drawn from experience. But we should also note that Norman is a distinguished psychologist: an example of the overlap between theory and experience.

3.1 The Principle of Visibility: It Should Be Obvious What a Control Is Used For

In considering visibility, it is often useful to start from the goal you wish to achieve. For example, if you want to play a tape in a cassette player, can you see how to do it? Are the controls for playing the tape obvious? Are the controls for turning the player on/off or for adjusting the volume obvious?

3.2 The Principle of Affordance: It Should Be Obvious How a Control Is Used

Linked to the visibility of controls is the affordance of controls. To have the property of affordance, the design of the control should suggest (that is, afford) how it is to be operated. For example, buttons afford pressing. Norman defines affordance as "strong clues to the operations of things. . . . When affordances are taken advantage of, the user knows what to do just by looking: no picture, label, or instruction is required" (Norman, 1988, p. 9). When the affordances of an object or device are obvious, it is easy for us to know how to interact with it. Affordances play a large part in the design of objects, but what is important is perceived affordance — what a person thinks can be done with the object. Using the example of a cassette player again, what kind of controls are used? If buttons are used, do they afford pushing? If sliders are used, do they afford sliding? If knobs or dials are used, do they afford turning? Unfortunately, practicality sometimes conflicts with good affordance and the appearance of the object takes precedence over its use.

We were perplexed by the mixed affordance and text of the middle doorhandle in Figure 5.7, so we asked the distributors why they carried such a strange device. They replied:

Figure 5.7 Door handles. The one on the left affords pulling. The one on the right affords levering. What about the one in the middle?

A door which is only to be pushed could have a push plate or finger plate fitted.

There is of course no reason why a pull style handle cannot be used to push a door open, and, because such a door will almost certainly have a door closer fitted, the pull handle would probably be more convenient for holding the door open. Such doors are also likely to be fitted in public buildings where there is a fair chance that the door is held open by an electromagnetic hold open device (used for fire alarm reasons) or another type of hold open device. When the door is in the open position, it would need to be pulled from the device to close it, hence the need for a pull handle. There are also situations where the doors swing in both directions, glazing panels or signs help to stop doors being pushed into individuals on the other side.

Another factor to consider with door furniture is that aesthetics are sometimes put above practicality. A bit like fashion? Why do we wear a tight collar and tie or shoes with high heels? Are they really practical?

Alistair Boyd, Bernards Ltd, personal communication used with permission.

3.3 The Principle of Feedback: It Should Be Obvious When a Control Has Been Used

Feedback is information that is sent back to the user about what action has been accomplished upon the use of a control. Again, this principle is linked to visibility and affordance. Taking our example of a cassette player, if the controls are visible, then pressing, say, the play button would play the cassette; the feedback would be seeing the tape turning in the machine and hearing what was recorded on the tape.

Box 5.2 contains more information about visibility, affordance, and feedback.

<table>
<tr><td>

Box 5.2

</td><td>

Visibility, Affordance, and Feedback

The controls on newer VCRs are generally more visible than on older models. There are good mappings between the controls and their effects — that is, the functions provided by the VCR interface map onto or are related to the user's goals and needs. Controls often have just one function; for example, there may be several push buttons that do only one thing, like an on/off button that simply turns the VCR on or off. There is affordance, as the buttons make it obvious how they are operated (i.e., they afford pressing). There is feedback on the display, and the system is generally understandable. In general, the relationships between the user's goals, the required actions, and the results are sensible, meaningful, and not arbitrary.

</td></tr>
</table>

The principles of visibility, affordance, and feedback are very important in user interface design. As design principles, they form part of the knowledge needed and the knowledge that should be used to guide your UI designs.

4 Design Principles and Design Rules: Knowledge for User Interface Design

Because design principles are abstract and at a high level, they are not always easy to apply directly as they must first be interpreted. Take, for example, the principle of feedback. You could interpret this as providing feedback that is visual (a message), audible (a happy tune), or tactile (the button bounces back up). Or you could employ a butler to enter the room and announce to everyone: "Command successful." Not all of these will be equally desirable or practical. So we develop design rules that describe how the principle will be interpreted and applied in specific circumstances.

EXERCISE 5.3 (Allow five minutes)

Look at two or more applications in the Microsoft Office Suite or any other suite of office applications that you use. Describe how and where the principle of feedback has been applied.

DISCUSSION

Debbie writes: If, like me, you are a PC user, then you will probably use Windows, and you may have used Word, Access, Excel, or PowerPoint. When you open (or run) these applications, they are similar.

• There is usually a "menu bar" across the top. When you click on one of the menus, it gives feedback by dropping down a list of menu commands.

- They usually start with a blank area in the middle of the screen. If you type in this blank area, the words or numbers that you type appear on screen.
- There may be a scroll bar on the right of the screen. If you click and drag the bar, the document moves up or down depending on the direction you dragged it.

An interesting thing to note here is that we began by talking about general design principles, and we have finished with a few design rules in Exercise 5.3. Design rules are low-level, highly specific instructions that can be followed with minimum interpretation or translation by the designer. That is, by looking at Microsoft's own user interface designs, we have started to become aware of what consistency across Microsoft applications means, and in turn we have arrived at a few design rules that tell the designer fairly precisely how to design consistently for Microsoft Windows applications.

You will learn more about design principles and design rules in Part 3.

A point to be aware of here is that although design rules are specific, they are only applicable in relation to a particular system platform. This type of design knowledge (design rules) would mainly be found in platform-specific **commercial style guides**. In addition to design rules, commercial style guides also contain design principles, which are very general and require translation and interpretation if they are to be helpful to the user interface designer.

5 Summary

In this chapter we reviewed some crucial principles for user interface design.

These were four psychological principles:

- Users see what they expect to see.
- Users have difficulty focusing on more than one activity at a time.
- It is easier to perceive a structured layout.
- It is easier to recognize something than to recall it.

And there were three principles from experience:

- The principle of visibility: It should be obvious what a control is used for.
- The principle of affordance: It should be obvious how a control is used.
- The principle of feedback: It should be obvious when a control has been used.

Understanding and applying these seven principles is cruicial for user interface design, and they may be the most important part of this whole book.

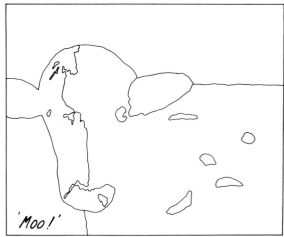

Figure 5.8 It's a cow! (From Pickering, 1981.)

6

Thinking about requirements and describing them

1 Introduction

If you want to get more information on developing overall requirements, we suggest (Kotonya and Somerville, 1998)

The full set of requirements for your user interface will include all the technical requirements for the system as well as the specific requirements that will ensure the user interface is easy to use. In this book, we are going to concentrate on the **usability requirements**, the desired qualitiative or quantitiatve usability goals for a system.

When you have found out as much as you can about the users and their tasks, the next step is to think about what you have found out and describe it as usability requirements. In this chapter, we start with a more detailed description of what usability requirements are. Generally, establishing usability requirements is a process of compromise between different constraints and tradeoffs, so we will spend some time in this chapter on them and then on some typical problems that you may encounter in the requirements-gathering process.

The result of your work will be a requirements specification. Unless your user interface is particularly simple, you will find that the list of requirements rapidly becomes large and possibly hard to grasp as an overall vision of the user interface. This brings us to the final section of this chapter: **prototyping**, where you check your ideas about the user interface with users and other stakeholders.

2 Usability Requirements

Usability requirements are gathered using techniques such as interviewing, surveying, and observation. They are of two types: qualitative usability requirements and quantitative usability requirements.

Qualitative usability requirements are concerned with the desired usability goals for a computer system; for example, "the system should be easy to use" or "there should be user satisfaction." Qualitative usability requirements can be subjective and are not always easy to measure or quantify.

Quantitative usability requirements may be expressed in terms of specific performance measures, referred to as **usability metrics**. Examples of metrics used to assess performance can include the completion time for specified tasks by a specified set of users, the number of errors per task, and the time spent using documentation.

The criteria for assessing and defining the usability of a system has evolved as computers have come to be used more extensively.

2.1 Early Views of Usability

One of the main criticisms leveled at information systems design and software engineering is that they focus too much on the system and not enough on the users. To address these limitations, requirements gathering must also explicitly focus on the usability of the application.

In the early days of computing, the notion of usability, was described by Gould and Lewis (1985) as

> *any application designed for people to use should be easy to learn (and remember), useful, that is, contain functions people really need in their work, and be easy and pleasant to use. (p. 300)*

Around the same time, Bennett (1984) identified particular aspects of usability, which he expressed in terms of the following concepts:

- **Learnability**: The time and effort required to reach a specified level of use performance (also described as ease of learning).
- **Throughput**: The tasks accomplished by experienced users, the speed of task execution and the errors made (also described as ease of use).
- **Flexibility**: The extent to which the system can accommodate changes to the tasks and environments beyond those first specified.
- **Attitude**: The positive attitude engendered in users by the application.

These concepts were later made operational by Shackel (1990), so that they could be testable aspects of a system's usability.

Also with a focus on quantitative measurability, Tyldesley (1988) indicated that many factors could — and should — be considered in assessing the usability of a system. He compiled a list of 22 possible measurement criteria that could be used for developing usability metrics for testing the usability of a system. These are shown in Table 6.1.

An example of a detailed metric specification, as it would be included in the requirements specification document, is shown in Table 6.2. In this example, the task of concern is the installability of an application for a system. The measure used to evaluate this aspect of the application is the amount of time taken to carry out its installation. The worst case is specified as one day; the best case as one hour.

In the mid-1990s, ISO standards in relation to systems were developed, most notably ISO 9241 and ISO 13407. ISO 9241 is mainly concerned with definitions and has

Table 6.1 Possible Measurement Criteria (from Tyldesley, 1988)

1. Time to complete task.

2. Percentage of task completed.

3. Percentage of task completed per unit time (speed metric).

4. Ratio of successes to failures.

5. Time spent on errors.

6. Percentage or number of errors.

7. Percentage or number of competitors that do this better than current product.

8. Number of commands used.

9. Frequency of help or documentation use.

10. Time spent using help or documentation.

11. Percentage of favorable to unfavorable user commands.

12. Number of repetitions of failed commands.

13. Number of runs of successes and of failures.

14. Number of times the interface misleads the user.

15. Number of good and bad features recalled by users.

16. Number of available commands not invoked.

Table 6.1 Possible Measurement Criteria (from Tyldesley, 1988)—cont'd

17. Number of regressive behaviors.

18. Number of users preferring your system.

19. Number of times users need to work around a problem.

20. Number of times the user is disrupted from a work task.

21. Number of times the user loses control of the system.

22. Number of times the user expresses frustration or satisfaction.

Table 6.2 A Sample Row from a Usability Specification (from Whiteside *et al.*, 1988)

Attribute	Measuring method	Worst case	Planned level	Best case	Now level
Installability	Time to install	1 day with media	1 hour without media	10 minutes with media	Many cannot install

extensive checklists for various aspects of the user interface, such as for keyboards. It recommends the inclusion of usability metrics in the requirements specification. Some example usability metrics from ISO 9241 are shown in Table 6.3. ISO 13407 is tiny compared to the 17 parts of ISO 9241. That's because it concentrates on process, taking the view that a usable system will be the result of a user-centered design process. Both have their value.

For usability metrics, the selection of the most appropriate metrics is dependent on the type of system application being tested. For example, with information-retrieval applications, search time would be a key design criterion, whereas for a word processing application, the efficiency and effectiveness of producing a document would be of importance. However, an overall measure of usability for an entire system may also be devised if this is considered to be important.

Table 6.3 Examples of Usability Metrics from ISO 9241 (British Standards Institution, 1998)

Usability objective measures	Effectiveness measures	Efficiency measures	Satisfaction
Overall usability	Percentage of goals achieved	Time to complete a task	Rating scale for satisfaction
Meets needs of trained users	Percentage of relevant functions used	Relative efficiency compared with an expert user	Rating scale for satisfaction with power features
Learnability	Percentage of users who managed to learn	Relative efficiency while learning to criterion	Rating scale for ease of learning
Error tolerance	Percentage of errors corrected or reported by the system	Time spent on correcting errors	Rating scale for error handling

EXERCISE 6.1 (Allow 10 minutes)

Think of some usability metrics that may be appropriate for laser bar code scanning systems. These systems could be for grocery store use, perhaps, or for use by clothing retailers, DIY/home improvement stores, or electrical goods outlets.

DISCUSSION

There might be metrics such as the following:

- The system should be learnable by cashiers with not more than one hour of training. (This amount of training may seem excessive, but cashiers will also need to know what to do in cases where codes will *not* scan or where codes show the wrong price.)
- The system should be relearnable after a period of up to one year in less than 10 minutes.
- The system should provide a response to a scanned item in not more than two seconds.
- Scanning devices should be able to scan bar codes even if they are not absolutely aligned to the bar code.

2.2 The Modern-Day View of Usability

Although users' attitude was one of Bennett's usability concepts, if you look closely at the early views of usability you will see that there was a primary focus on the utility of systems — that is, the things a system could do for people's work. Usability was described more often in terms of quantitative performance metrics than in terms of subjective or qualitative usability goals such as user enjoyment. At that point in time, there was a great expectation for computers to be useful for supporting humans in their work, for lightening their workload, or even perhaps, in some cases, for computers to replace human workers for certain tasks.

However, systems have moved beyond being just work based. As described in Chapter 1, computer-based systems are everywhere. In Chapter 1 we noted that there is over 50% ownership of home computers in both the United States and the United Kingdom. The focus for usability has moved beyond just the usability of work-based systems to the usability of all computer-based systems with which a human interacts. Whereas there is still a focus on measurable outcomes such as effectiveness and efficiency, the user's experience in interacting with a system has taken on a great level of importance.

In Chapter 1, we presented the ISO 9241:11 definition of usability. To establish the connection between usability and the user experience, Quesenbery (2003) has proposed a framework for usability comprised of five dimensions, referred to as *the five Es*. These dimensions — effective, efficient, engaging, error tolerant, and easy to learn — each describe an aspect of the user experience. The five Es build on ISO 9241's three characteristics of usability (efficient, effective, and satisfying, which becomes engaging in Quesenbery's framework), plus two other dimensions of error tolerant and easy to learn.

Quesenbery describes these dimensions as follows:

- *Effective*. The completeness and accuracy with which users achieve their goals.
- *Efficient*. The speed (and accuracy) with which users can complete their tasks.
- *Engaging*. The degree to which the tone and style of the interface makes the product pleasant or satisfying to use.
- *Error tolerant*. How well the design prevents errors or helps with recovery from those that do occur.
- *Easy to learn*. How well the product supports both initial orientation and deepening understanding of its capabilities.

The five Es can also be useful for planning evaluations, and we will return to them in Chapter 21.

The five Es can be used in a number of ways to arrive at a successful system. They can be used to set priorities for design, as they can be used to identify users' needs for a product, and they can suggest design approaches (see Table 6.4). They can be useful for creating usability goals.

It is important, when working with the five Es, to consider them all together, as they are interdependent. It is also important to keep the focus on each of the dimensions in balance; where one dimension takes on a greater significance (for example, the

Table 6.4 Design Approaches to Meet Key Usability Requirements (from Quesenbery, 2003)

Dimension	Key needs	Design tactics
Effective	Accuracy	Consider how many places in the interface are opportunities for error, and protect against them. Look for opportunities to provide feedback and confirmations.
Efficient	Operational speed	Place only the most important information in front of the user. Work on navigation that moves as directly as possible through a task. Be sure the interaction style minimizes the actions required.
Engaging	Draw users in	Consider what aspects of the product are most attractive and incorporate them into the design.
Easy to learn	Just-in-time instruction	Create step-by-step interfaces to help users navigate through complex tasks. Look for opportunities to provide small chunks of training.
Error tolerant	Validation	Look for places where selection can replace data entry. Look for places where calculators can support data entry. Make error messages include opportunities to correct problems.

"engaging" dimension in a game), it can be easy to lose sight of the other four dimensions which may impact negatively on your final design.

Usability requirements are targets to work toward for a usable UI and a pleasing user experience. Once gathered, the usability requirements and metrics are compiled into a **usability specification**, which also forms part of the requirements specification.

3   Constraints and Trade-offs in Relation to Requirements Gathering

So far, the requirements-gathering activities have been based around what the system should do — that is, on the functional requirements. During the design and development of the computer system, there will probably be a number of **constraints** or trade-offs that affect what you are able to deliver. These are sometimes referred to as nonfunctional requirements and are related to several considerations:

You will meet more about the choices of interaction styles and interaction devices for work in Chapters 11 and 12.

- Costs/budgets/timescales
- The technology available and its interoperability with other hardware and software
- The agenda of individual stakeholders
- Contradictory requirements
- Organizational policies

In order to gather the relevant information about constraints and trade-offs, you will need to talk to the users and other stakeholders. In the case of technical requirements or constraints, you should also look at any existing system documentation for information.

3.1 Costs/Budgets/Timescales

Most projects will have a fixed budget with which to develop a system. This will certainly constrain what you do during the life cycle and could have an impact on the final design.

3.2 Technical Constraints

In the design of a computer system, the available technology is also a consideration. For example, an existing application may be running on a particular system configuration using a particular platform. The decision may have been taken to keep the existing hardware systems in use, or management may have budgeted to upgrade the hardware in line with what is required for the new system. Either way, this decision will affect your system development. For instance, you may be constrained if the existing technology is not upgraded. Or you may be in the position to develop something more creative or novel if the technology can be upgraded and recommendations for other newer devices that are appropriate to the work can then be included in your requirements specification.

In addition to the technology that may be needed, you will also need to consider any other equipment that is in use, which may need to interface with the system under development. For example, a Web server may be being used to take information into the company via Web forms. The information received may then have to be transferred, either manually or automatically, to another system for some type of action — to inform a production control system, for instance, about the level of goods that will have to be manufactured. Or perhaps the information needs to be imported into a spreadsheet to be used in the production of sales reports or into a database for the recording of purchases and the dispatching of goods. Technically, this could all be done via a network of PCs, but it would not be uncommon for there to be, within a single company, several different systems of varying ages and capabilities, doing several different things.

3.3 Trade-Offs

As you consider how the information you gather will inform your design, you will inevitably be faced with numerous conflicts and you will have to make trade-offs. An example of a trade-off would be to decide not to include a particular feature in a UI that would be useful for only a limited number of users. Trade-offs should not be undertaken randomly; rather, each trade-off must be evaluated in terms of its impact on the users' ability to use the system effectively. As noted previously, sometimes what is seen as a benefit by one stakeholder may be seen as a cost by another (Wilson *et al.*, 1996). As far as possible, trade-offs should be negotiated and agreed on with the users and other stakeholders. This may not be easy: outspoken people on will make their opinions (right or wrong) heard, therefore individual stakeholder personalities can often overly influence the design decisions. Any constraints and trade-offs identified should be recorded and entered into the requirements specification document, as should any negotiations or decisions made for dealing with them.

4   Problems with Requirements Gathering

We may have given the impression that gathering the requirements for a computer system is relatively straightforward, but many problems can arise when eliciting and analyzing the requirements.

The list of problems is long, but forewarned is forearmed. There may be no way of preventing some of these problems, but if you are aware that they could occur then you may be able to plan your requirements-gathering activities strategically to ensure that you do the best job possible in discovering what users want. This will enable you to make appropriate decisions to design the UI appropriately.

Here is a list of potential problems:

- Not enough user/stakeholder involvement in the **requirements-elicitation** process may cause the requirements to be incomplete.
- Lack of requirements management — that is, changes to requirements as a result of feedback and negotiation are not tracked properly or not properly recorded. As a result, the requirements are inaccurate.
- Related to the above, if the requirements-gathering efforts are not properly co-ordinated, some activities may not be carried out. Once again, the requirements will be incomplete or inaccurate.
- Communication problems related to different stakeholders with different levels of understanding can be problematic for sharing understanding of the requirements between all groups.
- Capturing the relevant application domain-related information can be difficult, as the knowledge exists in a variety of places: textbooks, operating manuals, and in the heads of the people working in the area.
- People who *do* understand the problem may be heavily constrained by their workload and time, or they may be convinced that a new system is not necessary and be reluctant to participate or cooperate with those gathering the requirements.
- Organizational and political factors may influence the specification of the requirements, and these views may not tally with the end users. Related to this

We have more discussion of the differing goals and motivations of stakeholders in Chapter 28.

problem are the agendas of different stakeholders, which may make eliciting and negotiating requirements difficult.

- Some stakeholders will not know what they want from the computer system except in the most general terms, while others will be verbally forceful and detailed about what they want. Getting a balanced view can be problematic, as noted previously under constraints.
- Economic and business environments within organizations are ever-changing, as are employee roles within organizations. This, inevitably, changes the elicitation process, because stakeholders will change over the duration of the design and development of the application.

5 Requirements Specification

The requirements specification is produced by analyzing the information gained from the requirements-gathering activities — that is, after the information is gathered (for example, stated requirements, observations of users, tasks, and environments), it is examined closely, and conclusions are drawn for the design of the system. These conclusions are translated into requirements for the design of the system, which are then recorded in a requirements specification. The focus here is on what the system should provide, rather than how the system works (which is a design consideration). This is not as easy as it may sound. Describing the requirements for a system comprehensibly and precisely is practically impossible, as requirements are inherently incomplete, are rarely ever completely understood, or they change during the design and development life cycle (Berry and Lawrence, 1998).

There is no standard way of writing the requirements for a system. Rather than set information in a standard format, the requirements specification document will contain different types of requirements, including, but not limited to, the following:

- Requirements related to user characteristics.
- Requirements related to tasks and task characteristics.
- Requirements related to the various environmental factors.
- Usability requirements.
- Statements of constraints and trade-offs and any requirements negotiations.

Organizational practices may influence or even dictate the way that the requirements specification document is produced and presented. Requirements are generally written in natural language rather than executable languages for software (Dix *et al.*, 2004), as natural language is easily understood by all readers, and the document is likely to be read by various people, each with different motives and intentions in relation to the system. One drawback of natural language requirements is that they can be misleading or ambiguous, and they may be interpreted differently by different people. This can lead to disagreements among users and stakeholders (McGown *et al.*, 1998). Figure 6.1 gives some guidelines for writing requirements.

Guideline	Description
Define standard templates for describing requirements.	You should define a set of standard formats for different types of requirements and always express requirements using that format. This makes it less likely that important information will be missed out and makes it easier for the reader to understand the different parts of the requirement.
Use language simply, consistently, and concisely.	Do not write requirements using convoluted language, but follow good writing practice such as short sentences and paragraphs, using lists and tables and avoiding jargon wherever possible.
Use diagrams appropriately.	You should not develop complex diagrams but should use diagrams to present broad overviews and to show relationships between entities.
Supplement natural language with other descriptions of requirements.	Do not try to write everything in natural language. If readers of the requirements document are likely to be familiar with other types of notation (e.g., equations), you should not hesitate to use these notations.
Specify requirements quantitatively.	Wherever possible, you should specify your requirements quantitatively. This is often possible when you are specifying the properties of a system such as reliability, usability, or performance.

Figure 6.1 Guidelines for writing requirements. (From Kotonya and Sommerville, 1998, p. 21.)

Designers read and use the requirements specification document to assist them with the design of the UI. This makes it essential to specify the requirements as accurately as possible, even though they are likely to change as the requirements become better understood. Errors in specifying the requirements will result in errors in the UI design, and poorly specified requirements will lead to a design that does not meet the users' needs.

Any conflicts, overlaps, or ambiguities in requirements need to be resolved through negotiation with the users and stakeholders. As requirements will be viewed with differing levels of importance by the users and other stakeholders, an important part of this negotiation process is prioritizing the requirements. Agreement will need to be reached as to which requirements are critical, which are a high priority, which are of normal priority, and which are of low priority. This will help to focus the development and ensure that the highest priority requirements are addressed first (Young, 2003). Inevitably, the final requirements specification document will be a compromise, as a computer system cannot be produced that will satisfy everyone.

6 Prototyping

You have gathered the requirements, written some documentation, thought about the users, their tasks, the domain, and the environment for the application you are developing, and you think you know what the computer system should do and what it should look like. You've written a thorough requirements document that explains all of this. You are now ready to get down to the UI design and start programming it.

Or are you?

Copyright ⓓ 1999 United Feature Syndicate, Inc.
Redistribution in whole or in part prohibited.

The example shown in the cartoon may seem rather silly, but in reality it is easy to get the requirements wrong. Comprehensive requirements gathering produces a lot of data, not necessarily neatly related to each other. Instead of guessing what the forbiddingly large requirements specification document is about, and before spending a lot of time designing and developing a system which, based on your speculations, could be quite wrong, you should check your ideas with the users. Ensure that what you have interpreted as needed is what the users feel they need. The best way to do this is by having users test prototypes.

A prototype, which is an experimental, usually incomplete design, can be used in two ways.

- Early in the design process it can be used to communicate and share ideas between the UI designer and the users and stakeholders, so that requirements can be clarified.
- Later in the design process it can be used for exploring and demonstrating interaction and design consistency.

6.1 Purposes of Prototyping: Why Bother Trying Out Your Ideas?

The purposes of prototyping are as follows:

- To check the feasibility of ideas with users
- To check the usefulness of the application
- To allow users to contribute to the design of the application
- To allow users to test ideas
- To validate the requirements (i.e., to reveal inconsistent or incomplete requirements)
- To negotiate requirements

To test ideas, you can take a purely creative approach to the UI design and produce something completely original; or you can start with a previous system (bespoke or commercial) to generate some ideas, and then work toward the UI for the system currently under development. Either way, your initial designs will be subjective, as there is no set way to design a UI.

Broadly speaking, prototypes fall into two categories: low-fidelity prototypes based on paper prototypes and high-fidelity prototypes based on software prototypes. You will probably want to use both during the UI design life cycle.

6.2 Low-Fidelity Prototypes

Low-fidelity prototypes are generally paper based and include sketches, screen mockups, and storyboards. They can be created by hand, but they can also be created using a drawing package like Paint or PowerPoint and then printed out for testing with users.

Low-fidelity prototypes are useful in the requirements-gathering phase of UI design. They can be used as a communication medium between you and the users and stakeholders. Low-fidelity prototypes also help users and stakeholders to articulate what they want and need from a system, as they will find it easier to talk about something visual and concrete as opposed to conceptual (or abstract mental) ideas, which can be harder to share.

Low-fidelity prototypes can be used to illustrate design ideas, screen layouts, and design alternatives. While they can give users some indication of the **look and feel** of the UI, they provide only limited detail of how the UI will function, or how tasks might be undertaken.

▶ Sketching

Sketching has many uses in the UI design process. Initially it can be used as a way of helping you, the designer, determine what is wanted and needed in a system. Look at Figure 6.2. The designer who made this sketch, Andy, was trying to make sense of a UI design specification for controlling the production of steel tubes. After reading the specification, he sketched his interpretation of what he thought the specification called for, in the presence of the client commissioning the new computer system. Initially Andy used this sketch to communicate with the client and to check that they were both thinking about the system in the same way.

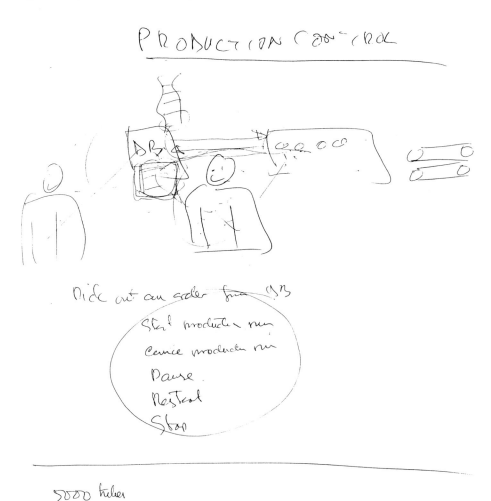

Figure 6.2 Initial high-level sketch of a UI for production control. (From Stone, 2001.)

As the sketch progressed, Andy used it to validate the requirements. He thought that the control system needed two separate UIs: one for data entry and one for monitoring and controlling the orders. In the sketch, the figure on the left is a data entry clerk who enters the orders into the system (marked in the figure as DB for database). The figure on the right is the person who is overseeing the production run.

Andy also used the sketch to emphasize certain essential pieces of information contained within the UI design specification. For instance, the requirements specification document said that the production control operator should, for many valid reasons, be able to start, cancel, pause, restart, and stop a run. Andy wrote this on the lower part of the sketch and circled it. The requirements specification document said that the maximum quantity of tubes that can be produced at any one time is 5000. Andy wrote (at the bottom-left corner of the sketch) that this is the maximum quantity that can be produced at any time. The cylindrical items on the right-hand side of the sketch represent the steel tubes that have been produced as the output of the production run.

Figure 6.2 shows one use of sketching as part of requirements gathering — to help the designer formulate his or her own ideas. A sketch can be used to facilitate communication between you and your users and stakeholders, which will assist with gathering requirements. Requirements can be refined and revised once there is something visual for you and the users and stakeholders to see and discuss. The sketch can be passed between you and users so that developing the image becomes a joint iterative process.

Sketching techniques are also useful for exploring early design ideas and are essential for crystallizing ideas in the early stages of design (Suwa and Tversky, 1996). Design alternatives can also be explored using sketches. After you have produced some initial sketches, you can further develop the best ideas by constructing cardboard mockups of the designs or generating storyboards that you can discuss with users.

Some UI designers find it difficult to sketch, as they do not have confidence in their sketching abilities. Try Exercise 6.2 to see what your sketching skills are.

EXERCISE 6.2 (Allow five minutes)

Sketch a familiar user interface.

DISCUSSION

From your sketch, is it possible to see how the interface works? What problems did you encounter? For example, how easy did you find it to represent the dynamics of the interface (for example, menus, dialog boxes)? What graphic techniques did you use (for example, arrows, lines)? If you had any problems (other than not being able to remember as much about the familiar interface as you thought you should), you might like to practice sketching, starting with individual UI components and then working up to full screen designs.

▶ **Screen Mockups**

Screen mockups can be easily produced using flipcharts, whiteboards, or overhead transparencies and an assortment of different colored pens. You can do this alone, or you can produce your mockups collaboratively with users. Another useful approach to screen mockups is to use not only different colored pens on a flipchart or whiteboard but sticky notes in different colors and differing shapes to represent **widgets** like buttons and menus. The advantage of using sticky notes as widgets is that you can easily move and change them in response to feedback from the users who are testing your ideas.

▶ **Storyboards**

Storyboards are sequences of sketches or screen layouts that focus on the main actions and interactions in a possible situation. Storyboards take textual descriptions of task flows (such as scenarios) and turn them into visual illustrations of interactions.

For example, a workflow analysis storyboard to describe the process of mail merging for a bulk mailing to advertise a product may look something like Figure 6.3.

The level of detail contained in a storyboard is related to when in the life cycle it is used. If it is used to model tasks and task flows during requirements gathering, then it will contain more detail than if it is used at the conceptual design stage, where the concern will be with what the system needs to do but not how the system will do it.

The greatest advantage of low-fidelity prototypes is that they are cheap, fast to produce, and can be easily changed. Any problems discovered early in the design process can then be rectified before the design has proceeded too far in the development to allow essential changes to be made. Although it used to be thought that low-fidelity prototypes cannot be "run" in the way that high-fidelity prototypes can, Snyder's (2003) book explains how to get users to use paper prototypes with the evaluator or facilitator updating it as and when the user's actions require a change of state.

Table 6.5 summarizes the advantages and disadvantages of low-fidelity prototypes. Don't forget to update your requirements document to reflect what you learned after prototyping for requirements.

Table 6.5 Advantages and Disadvantages of Low-Fidelity Prototypes (from Rudd *et al.*, 1996, and Snyder, 2003.)

Advantages	Disadvantages
They are cheap to produce.	Their ability to check errors in design is limited.
They can evaluate design ideas and design alternatives.	The specification is less detailed so it may be more difficult for programmers to code.
They promote rapid, iterative development.	
They are useful for facilitating communication between users and stakeholders and the UI designer.	A human facilitator is needed to simulate how the UI will work (e.g., by manipulating how different prototypes in response to users actions).
	Paper may seem less compelling.
They can show the look and feel and layout of screens.	They are useful for gathering requirements but are generally thrown away once the requirements have been established.

Action	Illustration
1. Margaret is an account manager for a marketing company. One of the accounts she oversees is for *Great Groceries!* which is a large foodstore chain. The *Great Groceries!*, supermarket in Premiumville has recently been extended and now includes a home appliance section. The supermarket manager wants everyone in Premiumville to know that *Great Groceries!* is having a Grand Re-Opening Day, and that there will be lots of bargains. Margaret has created a colorful flyer to be sent out that contains all the details. She gives this to Susan, who is creating the address list.	
2. Susan is Margaret's secretary. She is helping Margaret to organize the *Great Groceries!* marketing campaign. Using *Hey-Presto* a software database containing names and addresses, Susan does a postcode search and compiles a list of all the street addresses in Premiumville. She gives this list to Amy, who will do the mail merge.	
3. Amy is responsible solely for mail merging. She is expert at her job, but takes great care as the software is often unreliable. Because of the expense, the company frowns on wasting marketing materials due to mail merging errors. No matter how long the list, Amy generally runs her merged documents in small batches. This is time consuming, and fiddly, but Amy can put up with this inconvenience if in the end she gets an accurate result with few spoiled documents. She then gives the documents to Linda.	
4. Linda is responsible for quality control. She collects the mail merged documents from the printer and inspects a certain percentage of them for quality and accuracy. She then prepares the documents/flyers for feeding into a computer-controlled machine that folds them and inserts them into windowed envelopes. Finally, Linda collects them and has them sent to the mailroom at the appropriate point in the campaign.	

Figure 6.3 Storyboard describing the workflows in mail merging a bulk mail shot. (From Stone, 2001.)

6.3 High-Fidelity Prototypes: Using Software Tools to Try Out Your Ideas

Paper-based prototypes are quick and inexpensive, and they can provide valuable insights. But they do not demonstrate functionality. For this, we need to turn to **high-fidelity prototyping**. High-fidelity prototypes, which are based on software, provide a functional version of the system that users can interact with. As such, they show the UI layout and its navigation. If the user selects a menu command, such as opening a window or calling a dialog box, he or she will see the command executed; messages, such as error messages, will be displayed as appropriate. The user can experience the look and feel of the final system. Usability testing can be undertaken. In essence, a high-fidelity prototype looks and behaves as if it is the final product and can be used as a tool for marketing the final product.

Formerly, high-fidelity prototypes were expensive and time consuming to construct; however, this is no longer the case. Software applications like Microsoft PowerPoint and languages like Visual Basic and HTML have made it easier to produce high-fidelity prototypes cheaply and quickly. Table 6.6 summarizes the advantages and disadvantages of high-fidelity prototypes.

Ensuring that a proposed system has the necessary functionality for the tasks that users want to do is an important part of requirements gathering and task analysis. If feasible, high-fidelity prototyping can fulfill an important role in testing designs with users and in validating requirements. For instance, missing functionality may be discovered, task sequences can be tested, and the meaningfulness of icons can be assessed. Usability metrics can also be tested with a working prototype.

Table 6.6 Advantages and Disadvantages of High-Fidelity Prototypes (adapted from Rudd *et al.*, 1996, and Snyder, 2003)

Advantages	Disadvantages
They can show complete functionality.	They are more time consuming to create than low-fidelity prototypes.
They can show the look and feel, layout, and behavior of the final product.	They are not as effective as low-fidelity prototypes for requirements gathering, because they cannot easily be changed during testing.
They are fully interactive, and can be useful as a marketing tool (demo).	They can look so professional and finished that users are less willing to comment. This may mean that the prototype gets built irrespective of its merits and loses its throw-away benefits.

6.4 Cautions about Prototyping

Just as we warned you earlier about some of the problems you might meet with requirements gathering, here are some possible difficulties you may encounter in relation to prototyping.

Prototyping, while advantageous and necessary, may take time and therefore incur costs. Additional development time will need to be catered for in the project schedule. The type of prototype constructed also influences costs. Low-fidelity prototypes are quick and cheap to produce and are easily changeable. High-fidelity prototypes, which are based on software, may be more time consuming to produce, although they take less time if newer software applications like Microsoft PowerPoint or languages like Visual Basic or HTML are used.

Despite these cautions, prototyping is an essential part of user-centered design and development and a necessary part of user-centered, iterative design, whether it be for gathering requirements, trying out UI designs and UI design details, or for usability testing.

> **EXERCISE 6.3 (Allow 10 minutes)**
>
> We have talked about the advantages of prototyping for the users. But why might it be beneficial for members of the development team to see a design prototype?
>
> **DISCUSSION**
>
> If design is being carried out by a team, it is important for the team members to communicate effectively, and a prototype can help to facilitate communication.
>
> Also, designers need to simulate their designs-in-progress as an aid in making design decisions. Although it may be possible for designers to perform such simulations in their heads, it is not necessarily desirable: humans have a limit to their cognitive capacity, it is tiring, and people are prone to forget or to make errors that they may not realize or remember later on. It may therefore help the designers to see a prototyped version of their design.

7 Summary

We once again emphasize that design should involve the users and be iterative. Typically, requirements gathering collects some information, which is analyzed, and negotiated with the users and other stakeholders. Then another round of requirements gathering takes place. This cycle of requirements-gathering–prototyping–negotiation continues until schedule pressures force the development of the application to begin (this is the normal terminating condition) or until all the stakeholders are satisfied with the requirements (Kotonya and Sommerville, 1998).

Designing for usability, therefore, places a strong emphasis on iteration, starting with the testing of early design representations (paper-based and simple software prototypes) with users, undertaking further design or redesign and then testing with users again until the requirements have been agreed. This test with users, redesign, and test again cycle should carry on through to the testing of a **full prototype** or early version of the system (Wilson and Clarke, 1993).

A user-centered, iterative approach attempts to ensure a continuity of testing with users, undertaking further design or redesign and then testing with users again until the requirements are agreed upon.

7

Case study on requirements: Tokairo, part 1

1   Introduction

In previous chapters in this part, we emphasized the typical characteristics of good UI development. In particular, we mentioned flexibility, iterative evaluation, and the need for collaboration with users and other stakeholders. But are these features important in the real world?

To give you some insights into how professionals develop UIs, this final chapter in the Requirements part is the first segment of a case study. As you will see, the case study did not always proceed quite as we suggested in the previous chapters, but the developers responded positively to their circumstances and succeeded in producing an extremely effective UI.

But how did they do it? It can be difficult for experts to explain how they do something, because the process becomes automated and they stop thinking about it. Try explaining to someone how you cook dinner or fix your car. If you do either of these jobs regularly, you would probably use phrases like "I just add a bit of this and a bit of that" or "I just listen to the engine running and know what's wrong." Unfortunately this is not very informative.

We have tackled this problem by interviewing industrial practitioners, transcribing what they said, and then adding our own commentary.

2   The System

In this case study, we investigate the design of the UI for a kiosk and worksheet that enables oil tanker drivers to record the details of their deliveries. A typical tanker is shown in Figure 7.1.

The original system was a paper worksheet that the drivers completed and passed to the administrative staff for processing. This worksheet is illustrated in Figure 7.2. The plan was for the new design to have two main components: a worksheet that the

Figure 7.1 A typical tanker outside the oil refinery.

driver completes as he is making his deliveries and a kiosk (an embedded computer system) into which he scans the worksheet when he completes his shift. The kiosk looks similar to an ATM and includes a touchscreen, scanner, and printer. For ease we refer to the worksheet and the kiosk together as the *drivers' system*. The drivers' system was designed by Tokairo software house, in collaboration with Exel Tankfreight (referred to throughout as Tankfreight). The first kiosk was installed at the Shell Haven oil refinery in Essex in the late 1990s. It enables drivers to record the deliveries of bitumen they take from Shell Haven to various sites in the United Kingdom.

As part of the research for this industrial case study, we visited Tokairo, Tankfreight, and Shell Haven.

3 Background Information

3.1 The Companies Involved in the Project

Three companies were involved in the project, each with a different role: Tokairo, Tankfreight, and Shell. The relationship between these companies is illustrated in Figure 7.3.

Shell owns a number of oil refineries. Each of them requires a fleet of tankers to distribute the various oil-based products around the country. This task has been sub-

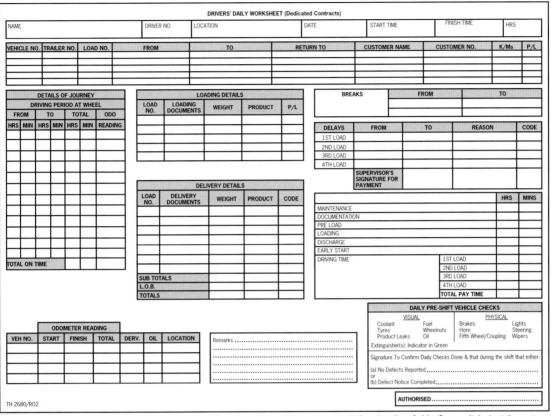

DRIVERS' DAILY WORKSHEET (Dedicated Contracts)

NAME		DRIVER NO	LOCATION		DATE	START TIME	FINISH TIME		HRS

VEHICLE NO.	TRAILER NO.	LOAD NO.	FROM	TO	RETURN TO	CUSTOMER NAME	CUSTOMER NO.	K/Ms	P/L

DETAILS OF JOURNEY

DRIVING PERIOD AT WHEEL

FROM		TO		TOTAL		ODO
HRS	MIN	HRS	MIN	HRS	MIN	READING

TOTAL ON TIME

LOADING DETAILS

LOAD NO.	LOADING DOCUMENTS	WEIGHT	PRODUCT	P/L

DELIVERY DETAILS

LOAD NO.	DELIVERY DOCUMENTS	WEIGHT	PRODUCT	CODE

SUB TOTALS

L.O.B.

TOTALS

BREAKS	FROM	TO

DELAYS	FROM	TO	REASON	CODE
1ST LOAD				
2ND LOAD				
3RD LOAD				
4TH LOAD				

SUPERVISOR'S SIGNATURE FOR PAYMENT

	HRS	MINS
MAINTENANCE		
DOCUMENTATION		
PRE LOAD		
LOADING		
DISCHARGE		
EARLY START		
DRIVING TIME		

1ST LOAD		
2ND LOAD		
3RD LOAD		
4TH LOAD		
TOTAL PAY TIME		

ODOMETER READING

VEH NO.	START	FINISH	TOTAL	DERV.	OIL	LOCATION

Remarks ....
....
....
....
....

DAILY PRE-SHIFT VEHICLE CHECKS

VISUAL — PHYSICAL

Coolant	Fuel	Brakes	Lights
Tyres	Wheelnuts	Horn	Steering
Product Leaks	Oil	Fifth Wheel/Coupling	Wipers

Extinguisher(s): Indicator in Green

Signature To Confirm Daily Checks Done & that during the shift that either:

(a) No Defects Reported ....
or
(b) Defect Notice Completed..

AUTHORISED..

TH 2680/R02

Figure 7.2 A copy of the original worksheet. (You do not need to understand the details of this figure. It is just here to give you a general impression of the original worksheet.)

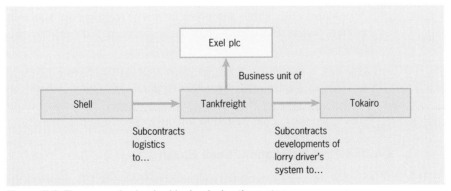

Figure 7.3 The companies involved in developing the system.

contracted to Tankfreight. Tankfreight needed a computer system to help with this distribution process (known as logistics), so the company subcontracted Tokairo to develop it.

In this context, logistics is the process of moving people and commodities around a country. Logistics is an important area for, for example, supermarket chains, who need to ensure the shelves of all their stores are full.

3.2 The Software House: Tokairo

Tokairo is a software house based in the United Kingdom and the United States. Tokairo originated within Epson (the IT manufacturer), where the founding members developed skills in imaging and recognition. These skills were not central to Epson's business objectives, and by mutual agreement these members left Epson to create Tokairo. Tokairo started as a separate company in 1996.

The people who work for Tokairo aspire to be innovative and creative, bridging the gap between business problems and technical solutions; they provide high-quality, cost-effective solutions. They do not claim to have any specialist expertise in designing UIs, but they still manage to do it very successfully. Tokairo specializes in developing computer systems to support logistics. Within logistics it focuses on those aspects that require expertise in imaging, recognition, and document management.

3.3 The Client: Tankfreight

Exel plc is a global logistics company with more than 50,000 employees operating in 1300 locations around the world. It is one of the world's largest international logistics companies, with a turnover in excess of five billion pounds (eight billion dollars U.S.). It manages the flow of information and customers' products, from raw materials, through manufacture and sales, to the point of consumption, for all sectors of industry.

Tankfreight is a business unit of Exel. It specializes in transporting chemical, petroleum, and edible products. It has a turnover of 100 million pounds (150 million dollars U.S.), and operates more than 1000 vehicles from more than 40 locations.

Logistics is an extremely competitive field, and it is essential for a company to keep its costs to a minimum. An effective computer system could mean the difference between success and failure. This put Tokairo and Tankfreight under significant pressure when they collaborated in the development of the system.

3.4 The First Installation: Shell Haven

Shell Haven, in Essex on the east coast of the United Kingdom, is the smaller of Shell's two oil refineries. It processes four million tonnes of crude oil each year. Tankfreight uses Shell Haven's facilities to load its tankers, as illustrated in Figure 7.4. The

Figure 7.4 Loading the tankers with bitumen. Shell Haven also provides Tankfreight with an office, a reception area, and a common room for its drivers.

bitumen is contained in the holding tanks. The driver then puts the load into the tanker. You can see the driver standing on top of the tanks in Figure 7.4.

4 User Requirements Gathering

4.1 The Characteristics of the Users, Tasks, and Environment

We interviewed Rachel Darley and Hugh Rowntree. Hugh is the systems manager for Tankfreight, and Rachel is an analyst with the company. Both have worked extensively with the drivers employed by Tankfreight. Rachel helped train the drivers to use the system.

The following is only a subset of the information Tokairo would need to have collated to develop the system. We have been deliberately brief and informal, as we are more interested in the process of requirements gathering than in the requirements themselves. We have included this to enable you to understand more fully the issues that Tokairo needed to address. When you carry out requirements gathering, you will probably need to be more comprehensive.

▶ **Domain Analysis**

The domain is logistics for the oil industry. We have already briefly described this in the section on the client.

▶ **The Drivers**

All the drivers are male. As you can see from Figure 7.4, some aspects of the job require considerable strength and fitness. Some of them have particularly large hands, a characteristic that will influence the choice of input device(s). They all have good eyesight.

The drivers tend to be nonacademic. However, their reading skills are perfectly adequate, so this is not an issue for the design. Some of the drivers are very keen on computers, but others are less confident and reluctant to use them.

Most of the drivers enjoy driving, and the job is well paid, so they are well motivated.

Payment is linked to the deliveries the drivers make, so they are motivated to submit the relevant information quickly and accurately.

Many of the drivers are in unions. Some of the unions are cautious about innovations, aiming to protect their members' interests.

▶ **The Tasks the Drivers Carry Out**

The tanker drivers have to perform a variety of tasks. They include the essential aspects of the job, such as making safety checks, loading the tankers, driving, and making the deliveries. The drivers also need to complete worksheets, which record the details of deliveries. In the previous system, at the end of a shift a driver would hand his worksheet to administrative staff, who entered the information onto the computer system.

Most shifts start between midnight and 5 a.m. They typically last about 12 hours.

Loading and unloading times are reasonably predictable, but the journey between the two places varies according to the time of day. This influences how much time a driver has to complete his worksheet. If he is in a particular hurry he may even forget to do so, in which case completing it later in the day will be difficult if he has not recorded the mileage from his odometer. Thus, the worksheet needs to be easy to complete quickly.

Completing the worksheet is a routine activity. This is particularly true of sections that need to be completed every day, such as safety checks. This can be a problem, because it is easy to tick a box thoughtlessly without thinking to complete the check.

When completing the worksheet, a driver may well be distracted, perhaps by a potentially dangerous situation, such as a problem with the loading or unloading. It is important that he can clearly see what he needs to do next when he returns from an interruption.

▶ The Environment the Drivers Work In

A driver spends a great deal of time in a badly lit, noisy, and confined cab. This environment is likely to make it difficult for him to complete his worksheets clearly. The writing implement that is immediately at hand may not be the best choice for completing the worksheet, as there can be a problem with pencils puncturing the worksheet and fiber-tip pens soaking through. Their hands are likely to be dirty and greasy.

When the drivers return to the refinery, the Tankfreight reception area is a busy working environment with restricted space. As this is the site for the kiosk, the kiosk will need to be robust.

4.2 How Tokairo Gathered the User Requirements

To understand how Tokairo had approached the requirements-gathering process, we interviewed three key members of staff: Treve Wearne, the sales and marketing director, Tim Cowell, the technical director, and Paul Booker, the senior software engineer. All three were directly involved with the development of the drivers' system, but each had a different role in it. Figure 7.5 shows Treve, Tim, and Paul. Caroline Jarrett, one of our authors, asked the questions.

▶ Understanding the Users, the Tasks, and the Environment

Some time before the kiosk was developed, Tokairo and Tankfreight had started work on a separate project, which had been canceled. This earlier work meant that Tokairo was in the fortunate position of knowing a lot about the drivers, the work they carry out, and their working environment before this project even started.

Figure 7.5 The Tokairo team.

> *Treve: We had access to the users before the project started. . . . We had meetings with the driver foremen before the project began, so we knew a lot about the Tankfreight business and the people in it before we actually started on this project. We had already visited a number of their depots and oil terminals. So we already had an appreciation of the mentality, the environments they were working in, what sort of intellectual skills they had.*

You need to be analytical when you carry out your observations. Treve looks for "pockets" (his term for what we call "groups") of users.

> *Treve: The rule is . . . to understand what those pockets are and where those pockets exist. The best way to identify [them] is [by] . . . functions. So you will have, for example, drivers, and they will all group together as a logical group; you will have foremen, who will all group together as a logical group; and managers. . . . There is a unity there, and they will feel one of a group. Drivers will congregate together and they will communicate together, and therefore views will manifest themselves within that group; foremen likewise; managers likewise; senior managers, etc.*

For more information on identifying user groups and user characteristics, see Chapter 3.

These groupings enable you to identify common characteristics for the different groups, so you can tailor the UI accordingly.

▶ The Site and System Audit

Tokairo also has a more formal approach to gathering the requirements.

> *Treve: We run a methodology. The first stage in that is what we call "the site and system audit."* . . . *The whole objective there is to understand the requirements* . . . *and the objectives.* . . . *The whole objective for ourselves within the site and system audit is [first] to identify those groups and then individually address each, because their requirements [and] their problems will be different between each group. But more importantly, if you just talk with the managers, they will interpret what they want you to hear and you will therefore have a skewed view of the world.* . . . *If you don't address the true requirements right up front, when you implement that system, you will have a lot of surprises. And that's something we can guarantee.*

According to Tokairo documentation, the site and system audit involves analyzing the functions within the organization and linking these to the various documents involved. The documents are analyzed according to recipient, value added, the environment in which they are handled, the political environment, and so on. The document and data flows are also analyzed.

There is no explicit reference to the UI in the audit, but information relevant to an understanding of the users, tasks, and environment is implicit. As you can see from Treve's description of the audit, they are looking at much more than the business processes and documents.

The audit involved a variety of stakeholders from Tokairo, Tankfreight, and Shell.

> *Tim: Treve actually went initially to the oil terminals and depots. Treve met the drivers and the driver foremen, and I was involved at the various meetings with Tankfreight at their head office. And Hugh Rowntree, who's the head honcho up there — he's got a very open structure, very similar to ourselves — he got everyone at his end involved. He appointed a lady called Rachel Darley to project manage it from his end.* . . . *Rachel had already done a number of installation projects, IT projects at the depot side of things, so she already had a very good understanding of how the depots work and how drivers work* . . . *so that everyone who needed an input was present including [people] like account managers. So* . . . *the Tankfreight/Shell account manager, the person responsible for the Shell business, and the driver foremen representatives [all] got involved in the early project meetings.*

Representatives of the drivers' and driver foremen's unions were also included in the meetings at Tankfreight headquarters. This helped to ensure that their needs were taken into account. Including user representatives in early project meetings can be an important element of user-centered requirements gathering.

For more information on techniques for gathering requirements, see Chapter 2.

User-centered development can be difficult to achieve when you are working with people in a client organization, as they may not be used to working in this way. Treve was very keen to emphasize to us the importance of having a good project manager within the client organization. Ideally, the project manager has authority within the organization; he or she is the person who makes things happen, understands the environment, and is in touch with what is happening. Hugh Rowntree took this role.

▶ **Communicating with the Programmers**

Once the requirements have been gathered, they need to be communicated to the members of staff responsible for their implementation. In this case, this meant Tim and Treve communicating with Paul.

> *Paul: Well, my involvement started once the spec was produced, which Tim passed to me, and having talks with Tim regarding . . . who was using the system and the sort of thing that was required.*

The Tokairo office is mainly open plan. This meant that informal talks of this type could happen spontaneously. This is the ideal, but it may not be attainable if you are working in a large organization or you are part of a work group that is distributed around the country. Communication breakdowns can cause serious problems.

> *Caroline: So the sort of information about who the users were, what they were like, what their needs were in terms of their nonfunctional type of things, do you write all that down or do you communicate that by talking about it?*

> *Paul: It was just talking about it. It wasn't documented. . . .*

> *Caroline: . . . so, you really immerse yourself in the needs and discuss them amongst [yourselves]. Does that sound similar to [your] approach?*

> *[General agreement.]*

> *Treve: Now we know what we do [laughter].*

Even though Tokairo did not write down the user requirements, we recommend that you do so, because not all companies communicate as well as Tokairo. In addition, like software requirements, they are a reference point for the implementation phase. This could be important if a new member joins a project team.

▶ **The Benefits of Conscientious Requirements Gathering**

It is tempting to hurry through the requirements gathering, but taking care at this stage can have long-term benefits.

> *Tim: We had a meeting, the first proper project meeting, for the Shell Tankfreight project . . . on the sixth of January and we wrote the first functional spec on the seventh of January, and I [have just] read that first functional spec and it's 90% accurate on what was actually developed. Which is . . . pretty good [for] most projects. Most projects are completely different by the time you reach the end.*

> *Caroline: And you'd attribute that to the early work you'd done, really understanding [the users]?*

> *Treve: [Agreement.] And the client.*

> *Tim: Normally you produce a specification and issue it to the client and then they'll suddenly realize that they've missed a whole section of things, and it'll go through*

two or three revisions before they think they've got it right, and then while you're working to a specification, other things will come out of the woodwork. But with Tankfreight, that's . . . not so much the case; it's more we put in the thing [the work-sheet] we originally specified, and then [minor] additions came to it, because the client realized [that] if we could capture this we could capture a bit more informa-tion; the form got more and more complicated as it aged.

Conscientious requirements gathering can save time and money.

We'll return to the Tokairo case study in Chapter 15, where you'll see how they moved from requirements gathering through to design.

EXERCISE 7.1 (Allow 10 minutes)

From your knowledge of the area, what techniques were available to Tokairo for gathering the user requirements? Briefly describe how the company could have used each of these in this context. What difficulties might Tokairo have experienced with each? You may find it useful to look quickly through the section in Chapter 2 on the techniques you can use for requirements gathering.

DISCUSSION

Many techniques are available for requirements gathering, such as observing the drivers, interviewing the drivers and driver foremen, and administering questionnaires.

Direct observation. They could have shadowed a driver for a single shift, observing all the activities he carried out and making notes. These notes could have included timings of the various activities, the problems that arose, and so on. The driver might have found the presence of an observer stressful, possibly worrying about being criticized to his manager and about future threats to his livelihood.

Interviewing. A number of interviews could have been carried out with just the drivers and driver foremen. At each, one or more drivers could have been asked a series of questions. The interview could have been structured or unstructured. This approach would probably have been less controversial than direct obser-vation, but it would have been difficult to arrange the interviews, as the drivers were unlikely to want to arrive early before their shifts or stay afterward, when they would be tired.

Questionnaires. Some drivers and driver foremen could have been given ques-tionnaires to complete. This would have been easier to organize, as they could have taken the questionnaires with them to complete at leisure. However, designing questionnaires can be difficult. How do you know what the right questions are? How do you avoid ambiguity? It would have been necessary to include open questions to compensate for any omissions. In addition, some drivers might not have wanted to commit their thoughts to paper.

5 Summary

In this chapter, we have heard about requirements gathering for a specific user interface. We will return to Tokairo in Chapter 15 to find out about how the company did the design based on what its management found.

3

Design

1 Introduction

In Part 2, you saw the importance of taking a user-centered approach to developing a user interface (UI). This approach requires an understanding of users and their requirements, and involves them in the design and evaluation of UIs.

Part 3 of this book has these main aims:

- To introduce you to conceptual design and, in particular, to show you how to create a content diagram.
- To explain the various sources of design advice and introduce four more key design principles.
- To explain the use of metaphor in UI design and the different interaction styles that are available.
- To provide you with the necessary skills for choosing suitable input and output devices and for using text, color, images, moving images, and sound effectively; to show you how to combine these to create a usable UI.
- To give you practice in designing different types of user interface. In particular, we look at three different approaches to combining the design components to create a UI. We start by looking in detail at graphical user interfaces (GUIs) and web sites. For both of these, we present a range of design issues, rules, principles, and guidelines to help you create usable designs. We then look more briefly at generic aspects of embedded systems.

1.1 Overview

In Part 2, you learned how to analyze an existing UI and hence gather the requirements for a new UI. The next step, work reengineering, is introduced in Chapter 8. Work reengineering involves identifying how a new UI can best support users' work. An important aspect of work reengineering is task allocation, in which you decide how the various tasks will be shared between the user and the computer system. We then move on to conceptual design and to creating a content diagram. A content diagram represents the underlying organization and structure of the new UI, and it can be used to inform the physical design of the UI. We demonstrate work reengineering and conceptual design through the example of a digital library system for use within a university department.

Designing UIs is a complex process, so in Chapter 9 we explore the different sources of design advice, in particular user interface standards and commercial style guides. We suggest managing all this advice by creating a customized style guide for your UI. A customized style guide can also form the basis for your design rationale, or justifications for the design decisions you make. Building on the principles of affordance, visibility, and feedback from Chapter 5, four more important design principles are presented and explained: simplicity, structure, consistency, and tolerance.

To ensure your UI is usable, you must understand the interaction process. In Chapter 10, we start by considering a model of interaction known as the human action cycle.

This model highlights the various problems that can arise when a user interacts with a computer system. We also consider the importance of the user having an accurate mental model of the system, and the use of metaphors to help users develop accurate mental models.

In Chapter 11, we use the human action cycle to help you choose between the available interaction styles, including command-line, form-fill, menu selection, direct manipulation, and anthropomorphic. We also briefly revisit the psychological principles for design set out in Chapter 5.

The main components that make up the UI can be divided into hardware components and software components. Chapter 12 looks at the hardware components — that is, the input and output devices. You may feel that you have little control over the devices you use, but using the correct device can make all the difference. A supermarket that chose not to use bar code readers/scanners would probably soon be out of business. We show you how to choose the most suitable hardware components.

Chapter 13 discusses the software components: text, color, images, moving images, and sound. These combine to provide users with feedback from the system, and we show you how to use these to best effect. You can make a lot of difference to a UI simply by changing some of the colors or the type size.

In Chapter 14, we show you how to combine the software and hardware components into a usable UI that meets the needs of your users, allowing them to carry out their tasks within their environment.

Chapter 15 illustrates how design was undertaken by Tokairo, UK, for the design and development of a worksheet system for its truck drivers.

UIs can be classified according to the way in which their various components are combined. We refer to these groupings as design areas. In Chapters 16 through 18, we identify three such design areas, and we consider the design issues that relate to each. We concentrate on GUIs and web sites, as these are the types of UI that you are most likely to be able to influence in your workplace.

Chapter 16 is about how to design usable graphical user interfaces (GUIs). In particular, we explain how to choose the most appropriate widgets, how to use each of these effectively, and how to combine them to best effect. We do this by looking in detail at an extended example based on a GUI for booking facilities at a sports center.

In Chapter 17, we show you how to design good web sites. In particular, we consider the structure of a site, the design of individual pages, and how to write the content. We do this by looking in detail at an example based on a web site for a hotel room reservation system.

Chapter 18 looks at embedded systems and small devices such as mobile phones. We consider safety-critical systems to be a type of embedded system. No new information on safety-critical systems is given, but we do provide an exercise that reinforces the relevance of the design issues, principles, and guidelines introduced in Chapters

8 through 15. We also consider a type of embedded system known as the information appliance. Chapter 18 finishes by looking in more detail at generic aspects of embedded systems, considering the issues of portability, general purpose versus specialized devices, connectivity, and the commercial environment.

Chapter 19 illustrates how the requirements were gathered and the design and evaluation of the UI for the Final Approach Spacing Tool (FAST) were undertaken by the research and development group at National Air Traffic Services (NATS). The system was developed to support air traffic controllers in their task of managing air traffic safely, efficiently, and effectively.

1.2 Learning Outcomes

After studying Part 3, you will be able to:

- Reflect upon how a new UI can better support the users' work
- Allocate tasks to either the user or the computer system for a new UI
- Create a content diagram that represents the underlying organization and structure of a new UI
- Critically evaluate a UI against the design principles of simplicity, structure, consistency, and tolerance
- Choose appropriate metaphor(s) for a UI, taking into account the potential difficulties associated with the use of metaphors
- Identify the most appropriate way for the user and computer to interact from a range of possible interaction styles
- Choose one or more input and output devices that match the requirements and constraints of the particular task, user group, and environment
- Design a UI that makes effective use of text, color, images, moving images, and sound
- Design a usable UI that combines input and output devices, text, color, images, moving images, and sound, as appropriate
- Design a GUI
- Design a web site
- Explain some considerations in the design of embedded systems

1.3 Theoretical Influences

Part 3 draws from:

- Cognitive psychology in the chapters on the human–action cycle, communicating the designer's understanding of the system, and how to use design components effectively
- Object-oriented software engineering in explaining the conceptual design process
- Graphic design and multimedia theory in the chapter on choosing text and color, sound, images, and moving images
- The experience of practitioners in creating designs

8

Work reengineering and conceptual design

1 Introduction

This chapter describes an approach to bridging the gap between gathering the requirements and creating the **physical design** of a user interface (UI). When you start planning the design of a UI, you want to improve on the design of the existing system if there is one. To maximize the benefits of developing a new UI, it is important to consider the issue of **work reengineering**. With the new UI, it may be necessary for people to work differently if they are to work effectively. This will require sensitive handling, which is another reason for involving the users in the whole of the development process: if the suggestions you make are likely to be unpopular or are really unreasonable, the users will soon tell you.

According to Mayhew (1999), the process of work reengineering has three goals:

> *Realizing the power and efficiency that automation makes possible.*
>
> *Re-engineering the work to more effectively support business goals.*
>
> *Minimizing retraining by having the new product tap as much as possible into the users' existing task knowledge, and maximizing efficiency and effectiveness by accommodating human cognitive constraints and capabilities within the context of their actual tasks. (p. 172)*

We shall focus on one particular aspect of work reengineering: task allocation. One of the most important decisions to be taken during the development of a UI is to allocate the tasks to the user or to the computer. The designer needs to establish who (or what) will provide the data or knowledge necessary to accomplish a task and who (or what) will physically accomplish the task.

It is important to maximize the strengths of both the user and the computer. For example, in the UI for a bank ATM, it is difficult to imagine how the computer could provide the PIN. This must be a user action in order to meet security criteria. Similarly, you would not expect a user to have a precise knowledge of her or his bank balance before deciding whether to make a withdrawal. The computer should

| Box 8.1 | **The Equivalent of "Work" When the UI Is for Home or Leisure** |

This chapter concentrates on the introduction of a new UI for a system that is used in a workplace. There are equivalent concepts for a system that is used for leisure. The "work" is whatever the users want to do with the system — for example, play a game or purchase a product. It is just as important to consider the reactions of the users, as this story illustrates:

"A few years ago, when eBay designers opted to change the background color of every page from yellow to white, they actually changed the shade of the pages in almost imperceptible increments daily for months, until the pages were finally white. 'If they'd flipped a switch and gone from yellow to white, everyone would have screamed,' said eBay senior usability engineer Laura Borns. 'But no one had any complaints about it, because it was so gradual.'"

From Mathew Schwartz, "Grow Your
Site, Keep Your Users," Computerworld, June 4, 2001,
www.computerworld.com/developmenttopics/websitemgmt/story/
0,10801,60997,00.html, visited July 8, 2004.

provide this information. Essential use cases can be a useful tool for thinking about the task allocation process.

1.1 Introduction to the Digital Library

A university department has academic and research staff and research students, all with various teaching and research activities. All staff and research students maintain personal libraries of books, CD-ROMs, videos, and journals related to their particular research interests. As they are all in the same department, they often find that someone else in the department has interests that overlap with their own.

To make the personal libraries of the department's members accessible, the department has decided to design and develop an online digital library. It will keep track of the personal resources of each member of the department. As in an ordinary library, borrowers will be able to search its database for items of interest. Unlike in an ordinary library, items are not owned by the library but by individuals, who may need constant access to them. Therefore, for each request the owner of an item will need to agree to lend it to the borrower.

A member should be able to search the digital library for the item he or she needs. The system will therefore need to keep details of each resource, such that its owner can be contacted easily. The system will also need to be regularly updated, as members acquire new resources, join or leave the department, or change their contact details. It is the responsibility of individual members to keep their details up to date. The library will run on the department's intranet.

We shall go step-by-step through a simple example of work reengineering and task allocation, using the digital library as detailed. This involves use scenarios and essential use cases. In Chapter 4, we said that use scenarios are similar to task scenarios, but that they describe the anticipated use of the new UI rather than the use of the current UI. We start by showing how the use scenarios are likely to be quite different from the task scenarios, drawing out the impact on the working practices of the members of the computing department. We then show how to elicit essential use cases from the use scenarios, and we consider how these useful tools can help us think about the task allocation. Finally, we derive some concrete use cases from the essential use cases. These will act as a bridge to the conceptual design section, which follows.

2 | Work Reengineering for the Digital Library

Figure 8.1 contains some task scenarios for the present situation within the computing department. There are likely to be many more. As you can see, the situation is rather unsatisfactory.

Task scenario. Search and request resource
Julia, a lecturer in the department, is looking for a particular CD-ROM containing examples and exercises on Object Oriented Analysis and Design. She knows that Tom, another lecturer, mainly teaches Object Oriented Analysis and Design so she knocks on his door. Unfortunately he is not there, so she leaves a note on his door. Later he returns and searches for her, finding her in the coffee bar. He tells Julia that Geoff has the CD-ROM. Unfortunately Geoff is on leave, so Julia telephones him and he promises to post it to her.

Task scenario. View updates and request resource
Mark has recently returned from six months of study leave and wants to find out what books other members of the department have bought since he left. To do this he telephones everyone in the department and arranges an appointment. He has to do this because everyone is at the university at different times. He then meets everyone individually and checks through their bookcases, asking to borrow books that interest him. He only asks for one book at a time, as he is a slow reader!

Figure 8.1 Task scenarios for the digital library.

As part of the redesign, we have drafted some use scenarios in Figure 8.2 to illustrate how the digital library might operate. Notice that there are no details about the

> **Use scenario. Search and request resource**
> Julia is looking for a particular CD-ROM containing examples and exercises on
> Object Oriented Analysis and Design. She accesses the digital library from home
> and types in the key phrase 'Object Oriented Analysis'. The system retrieves one
> result. Geoff owns the appropriate CD-ROM. Julia then sends an e-mail to
> Geoff, asking to borrow the CD-ROM.
>
> **Use scenario. View updates and request resource**
> Mark has recently returned from study leave and wants to find out what are the
> latest additions to the digital library. He selects 'check updates', identifies the
> books he is interested in, and sends an e-mail to the owner of the one
> that interests him most.

Figure 8.2 Use scenarios for the digital library.

technology that will be used, because the focus is on the users and how they will carry out their tasks. In reality, we would develop more use scenarios than this, analyzing their particular strengths and weaknesses in terms of their implication for the users.

EXERCISE 8.1 (Allow five minutes)

In what respects will the digital library be better than the present arrangements for Julia and Mark? In what respects will it be worse? What disadvantages will there be for all the members of staff who are members of the digital library?

DISCUSSION

For Julia. *Advantages:* She will not be dependent on other lecturers being in their offices, as the digital library will be available all the time. She will know for sure who has a particular resource, rather than having to guess. She can find all the information she needs and request the resource from her desk. *Disadvantages:* She will not have an excuse for a chat, and maybe coffee, with her colleagues. This may seem trivial, but important work-related discussions can occur in this sort of spontaneous manner. Such social contact can also be important if staff members are to avoid becoming isolated.

For Mark. *Advantages:* The digital library will save the huge amount of time currently spent meeting other staff members. Other staff members will not need to go through their shelves to help them remember what they have purchased in the previous 6 months. *Disadvantages:* Again, there will be a loss of social contact with other members of the department. Also, Mark will lose the opportunity to find out what others think of a particular resource (this could be an option with the digital library, but people tend to be more honest face-to-face).

Generally. All the members of the digital library will need to enter the details of the resources they purchase. This will take time, and keeping the library up to date will take a lot of effort. Also, members may not add all their purchases to the library, particularly those they find useful. In this case, the library may be sparse and contain only the resources that no one wants.

3 Task Allocation for the Digital Library

Once we have decided on some use scenarios, we need to agree how to share the different tasks between the user and the computer. This is referred to as **task allocation**. We can specify the task allocation using essential use cases. An essential use case corresponding to the "Search and request resource" use scenarios is shown in Figure 8.3. As you can see, this does not contain any specific details, such as the technology used. For example, the search parameters could be entered using a keyboard or by voice recognition. In addition, it does not include the details of the task. For example, the essential use cases do not indicate the types of resources available or the details of the search parameters. Instead, they concentrate on showing how the tasks will be shared between the user and the system.

In this example, we have presented the use scenarios before the essential use cases, but in reality you will probably develop both in parallel. As you can see, the "Search and request resource" essential use case maps very simply onto the corresponding use scenario. This is because as we were developing the use scenarios we had an increasing sense of the form the essential use case would take. Similarly, your understanding of the tasks typically carried out by the user or system will influence the wording of the use scenarios. As with all aspects of UI development, the different activities are closely linked, and there is no single approach that will work in all

User's purpose	System responsibility
Enter search parameters	Show results
Select a resource	Show the contact details of the owner of the selected resource
Send an e-mail	Confirm the send

Figure 8.3 "Search and request resource" essential use case.

situations. The answer is always to involve the users and be prepared to keep modifying your ideas until you identify the best solution.

> **EXERCISE 8.2 (Allow five minutes)**
>
> Draw the essential use case for the "View updates and request resource" use scenario.
>
> **DISCUSSION**
>
> The "View updates and request resource" essential use case is illustrated in Figure 8.4. As you can see, there is a close correlation with the use scenario.

User's purpose	System responsibility
Request latest updates	Show results
Select a resource	Show the contact details of the owner of the selected resource
Send an e-mail	Confirm the send

Figure 8.4 "View updates and request resource" essential use case.

4 Conceptual Design

Conceptual design is the process of establishing the underlying organization and structure of a UI. This is an important activity, as it makes little sense to design screen layouts before you have decided what functions the screen should support. This information is represented in a content diagram. A **content diagram** is a low-fidelity prototype that represents the organization and structure of the user interface from the designer's perspective.

The network comprises nodes, referred to as **containers**, and links. Each container is an abstract representation of a part of the user's work and the functions that are required to do that part of the work. For example, a container in the digital library system may correspond to entering the search criteria for a book. The links represent how the user will navigate between the functional areas within the UI, thus showing how the functional areas need to be structured. Figure 8.5 illustrates the simplified outline of a typical content diagram.

The relation between the content diagram and the final UI will vary. In a web site, for example, each container may become a screen, and the links may become navigation elements such as hypertext links, selectable areas, or menus. Alternatively, in a

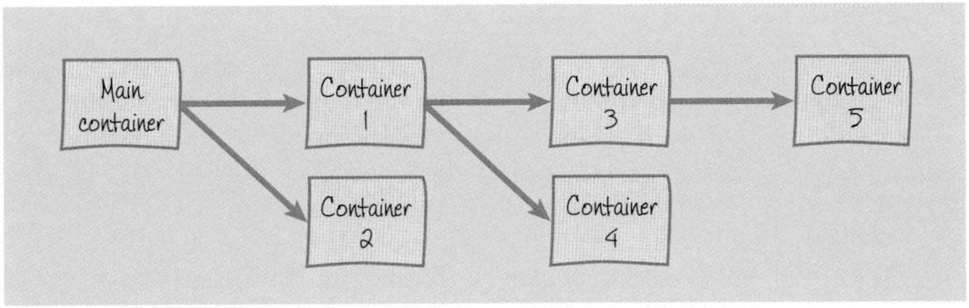

Figure 8.5 Simplified outline of a typical content diagram

graphical user interface (GUI), the containers may become windows, dialog boxes, or message boxes, and the links may become buttons and menu items. However, if you were designing a purely sound-based system, such as a voice messaging system, then the containers would become clusters of menus and their associated responses.

In some cases, the relation between the structure of a content diagram and the structure of the UI may appear less close. For example, the navigation around the UI may be slightly different, or several containers may be combined to form a single screen. The Lovely Rooms Hotel group example in Chapter 17 illustrates the former. Figure 8.20, later in this section, illustrates the latter. Thus, you should not allow the content diagram to limit your creativity when you are designing a UI.

A content diagram is based on both the findings of the requirements gathering and the concrete use cases derived from the essential use cases used during task allocation. As it is unlikely that you will have identified all the possible concrete use cases, the content diagram will probably be incomplete. However, it is still valuable for identifying the main functional areas in a UI and the essential relations between them.

To produce a content diagram, you need to do four things:

1. Derive the concrete use cases from the essential use cases.
2. Identify the primary task objects, attributes, and actions.
3. Identify the different containers and the task objects that go into each one.
4. Link the containers to show the navigation flow.

Experienced UI designers may not complete these activities in order and may omit some activities completely. Others may use less formal approaches that involve discussing diagrams drawn on flipcharts or whiteboards. As you are new to UI design, however, we recommend that you attempt the activities we describe here: they will make you aware of the issues you need to consider when creating a conceptual design.

Completing these activities is a creative process, and developing the best solution is a process of informed trial and error. To help you with this, we suggest you use some low-fidelity prototyping tools, such as sticky notes on flipchart paper. These can be useful for the following reasons:

- Sticky notes are flexible. They can be moved around easily and discarded if necessary. This makes them ideal for experimenting with designs that may change.
- The very fact that a sticky note does not look like a UI control is a constant visual reminder that the representations generated during conceptual design are abstract. This will help you to focus on the structure of the user interface rather than on its visual appearance.
- A sheet of flipchart paper can be attached to the wall. This means that if you are working with other people, everyone in the team can see the design.

We have formulated this approach to conceptual design from a number of sources, in particular Weinschenk *et al.* (1997) and Constantine and Lockwood (1999). There is no single universally accepted approach to conceptual design. We believe the one we present here draws together many of the best features of the alternatives available.

4.1 Deriving Concrete Use Cases from Essential Use Cases

Figure 8.6 illustrates a concrete use case derived from the "Search and request resource" essential use case illustrated in Figure 8.3. This is just one of many alternatives. For example, we could have had an academic searching for a book, a

User action	System response
The academic enters one or more of the search parameters for the CD-ROM: title, year and platform	The system displays the search results
The academic selects a search result	The system displays the full details of the CD-ROM and the contact sdetails for its ownerm who is a research student
The academic chooses the e-mail address	The system displays a message area
The academic writes and sends the e-mail request	The system confirms the sending of the request

Figure 8.6 Concrete use case: "Search and request CD-ROM."

researcher searching for a journal, and so on. You should be able to see that we have added detail to the essential use case and altered the column headings, showing that we are moving toward the final design. The level of detail will vary between concrete use cases, but we suggest that you avoid any implementation details, such as references to screen elements or particular types of hardware or screen layouts. This is not necessary for conceptual design and may limit your creativity later in the process.

EXERCISE 8.3 (Allow 10 minutes)

Illustrate a concrete use case corresponding to the "View updates and request resource" essential use case illustrated in Figure 8.4.

DISCUSSION

Our solution is illustrated in Figure 8.7. Yours may contain a few differences; perhaps you included an academic rather than a research student or had the member choose a CD-ROM rather than a book. These alternatives are all correct.

4.2 Identifying Task Objects, Attributes, and Actions

See Macaulay (1995) for more about an object-oriented approach to UI design.

The next step is to identify the **task objects**, their attributes, and the actions the user will perform on them. These details will influence what goes into each of the containers in the content diagram and the links needed between the containers. We do not teach object-oriented design in detail, but the information in this section should provide you with sufficient understanding to get started.

User action	System response
The research student requests recent updates in the digital library	The system displays the availability of the latest books, CD-ROMs, videos and journals
The student selects this year's book by her favourite author: J. Nielsen	The system displays the full details of the book and contact details, including name, for the owner, who is an academic
The student chooses the e-mail address	The system displays a message area
The student writes and sends the e-mail request for the book	The system confirms the sending of the request

Figure 8.7 Concrete use case: "View updates and request book."

We start by explaining what task objects, attributes, and actions are. We then show you how to identify each from a concrete use case, and finally we discuss how to prototype your ideas.

▶ Task Objects

Primary task objects are the units of information or data with which the users interact to carry out their tasks. They are high-level objects, central to the tasks the users will be carrying out. Typically there are only a few primary task objects, and they are easy to identify. For example, if you were designing a UI for a hotel registration system, there would probably be only two primary task objects: one corresponding to the customer, the other to the room. For brevity, from now on we shall refer to primary task objects as task objects.

When you are identifying the task objects, it can be helpful to check the requirements documentation and concrete use cases for the new UI. In particular, you should check for units of information that are searched through or modified in some way. These may include artifacts, such as forms, documents, papers, and lists.

These task objects will typically be translated onto your UI design as combinations of user interface objects, such as screens, windows, dialog boxes, pull-down menus, icons, combo boxes, and so on, as you will see in Chapter 16. In embedded systems, such as mobile telephones, these may take the form of physical buttons and other simple input devices, plus output on the screen.

> ### EXERCISE 8.4 (Allow five minutes)
>
> List the task objects for the digital library. You will need to check the description in the introduction to the digital library presented earlier in this chapter.
>
> ### DISCUSSION
>
> The task objects we identified were book, CD-ROM, video, journal, academic staff, research staff, and research student.

It is sometimes possible to group task objects into classes. In the digital library, resource is a **class**, containing book, CD-ROM, video, and journal. Resource is an abstraction of the resource types. In other words, it contains the common elements of those types. In particular, this means the attributes that are common to all the resource types, such as keywords, title, and author.

Classes are a type of task object, because users can interact with them. For example, in the digital library, the member may want to search through all the resources. Identifying classes can help guide the decisions you make when you are designing a UI. The member could search all the resources in the digital library, using separate search screens for book, CD-ROM, video, and journal. This would be repetitive, but it would allow searches on all the attributes. A simpler solution may be to have a single screen that corresponds to the resource task object. This would contain just the common attributes. This solution would be less powerful, but it may well be sufficient to meet the needs of the member. It may be possible to group classes into higher-level classes, thus creating a hierarchy.

> **EXERCISE 8.5 (Allow two minutes)**
>
> Identify a second class of task objects within the digital library. List the members of this class.
>
> **DISCUSSION**
>
> Member is a class containing academic, researcher, and research student.

▶ Attributes

A task object must have attributes. If a task object does not have any attributes, it is not an object in its own right but rather the attribute of another task object. For example, for the hotel registration system the number of people who can occupy a hotel room is an attribute of the room object rather than an object in its own right. There are two kinds of attributes:

- *Properties*. For example, in the digital library title and author are properties of the book task object.
- *Child objects*. These are task objects in their own right. For example, an attribute could indicate who owns a CD-ROM. The owner could be an academic, making the academic task object a child object of the CD-ROM task object. It is a task object in its own right because it has its own attributes, such as the name of the academic, his e-mail address, and so on.

This relation can influence the design process, as visual containment results when an attribute is a child object. In user interface design, this means that when the task object is displayed on a screen, the child object will also be displayed on the same screen. Depending on the implementation, either the whole object will be displayed or only a summary. An example of the latter would be if the screen that displays the details of a book has a line indicating the name of the person who owns it. Double-clicking on this may display another screen containing the person's details.

▶ Actions

When users carry out their tasks, they perform various actions on the task objects. For example, in the hotel registration system, the receptionist will want to allocate guests to rooms. This means the room task object will need to have a corresponding allocation action.

You can identify these actions by reviewing the concrete use cases. In addition, you should consider standard actions such as view, create, delete, copy, save, edit, and print.

4.3 Marking Up the Concrete Use Cases to Identify Task Objects, Their Attributes, and Actions

A useful technique for identifying task objects and their attributes is to mark up the concrete use cases. We suggest the following markup convention:

- Single-underline nouns that you think may correspond to task objects.
- Double-underline the attributes of these task objects.

Verbs in use cases often correspond to actions. We do not suggest marking these up as the relationships are often less direct. However, identifying the verbs can still be useful.

By way of illustration, we have marked up the "Search and request CD-ROM" concrete use case. The result is shown in Figure 8.8.

You can see from the markup that we have identified the academic, research student, and CD-ROM task objects. In addition, by implication we have identified e-mail, a further task object. This is not mentioned explicitly, but two of its attributes are e-mail address and message area. We have also identified the title, year, and platform attributes of the CD-ROM task object.

You are unlikely to identify all the task objects and attributes in this way, unless the situation is particularly simple or you use a great many concrete use cases, but it should give you most of them.

User action	System response
Academic enters one or more of the search parameters for the CD-ROM: title, year and platform	The system displays the search results
The academic selects a search result	The system displays the full details of the CD-ROM and the contact details for its owner, who is a research student
The academic chooses the e-mail address	The system displays a message area
The academic writes and sends the e-mail request	The system confirms the sending of the request

Figure 8.8 Marked-up concrete use case: "Search and request CD-ROM."

EXERCISE 8.6 (Allow five minutes)

Identify the task objects and attributes for the "View updates and request book" concrete use case in Figure 8.7.

DISCUSSION

We have illustrated our solution in Figure 8.9. As you can see, we have identified the research student, academic, book, CD-ROM, video, and journal objects, plus a number of their attributes.

Once you have identified the task objects and attributes, it is helpful to compile them, along with the actions, into a single object–action–attribute table. Table 8.1 contains the CD-ROM task object from the digital library. As you can see, some of the attributes come directly from the concrete use cases, but others come from the domain analysis. The "owned by" attribute corresponds to the academic, researcher, and research student child objects.

The actions are the standard actions, plus the reserve action, which allows the member to indicate that the CD-ROM has been reserved. You should note that the actions relate to the CD-ROM details in the digital library system, rather than to the CD-ROM itself. Thus, the table indicates that it is possible to edit these details, but it does not say it is possible to alter the CD-ROM itself.

User actions	System responses
The research student requests recent updates in the digital library	The system displays the availability of the latest books, CD-ROMS, videos and journals
The student selects this year's book by her favourite author: J. Nielsen	The system displays the full details of the book and the contact details, including name, for the owner, who is an acedemic
The student chooses the e-mail address	The system displays a message area
The student writes and sends the e-mail request for the book	The system confirms the sending of the request

Figure 8.9 Marked-up concrete use case: "View updates and request book."

Table 8.1 Object–Attribute–Action Table CD-ROM Task Object

Task object	Attributes	Actions
CD-ROM	Keywords	View
	Title	Add
	Author	Print
	Year	Delete
	Platform	Save
	Owned by (academic, researcher, or research student)	Reserve
		Edit

Table 8.2 Object–Attribute–Action Table: Academic Task Object

Task object	Attributes	Actions
Academic	Name	View
	Phone number	Add
	Office number	Edit
	E-mail address	Print
		Save
		Delete

EXERCISE 8.7 (Allow 10 minutes)

Draw an object–attribute–action table for the academic task object. You will need to make some assumptions, as not all the necessary information is in the concrete use cases. Explain how you identified the attributes and actions.

DISCUSSION

Table 8.2 shows the table we developed. The name and e-mail address attributes have come from the "View updates and request book" concrete use case in Figure 8.9. There are no child objects, as academic is a child object of the various resource type objects: book, CD-ROM, video, and journal. They are all standard actions.

4.4 Prototyping Task Objects, Attributes, and Actions

Marking up the concrete use cases is one approach to identifying task objects and attributes, but this should only act as a starting point. As you saw earlier, some of the task objects, attributes, and their actions may not necessarily come from the con-

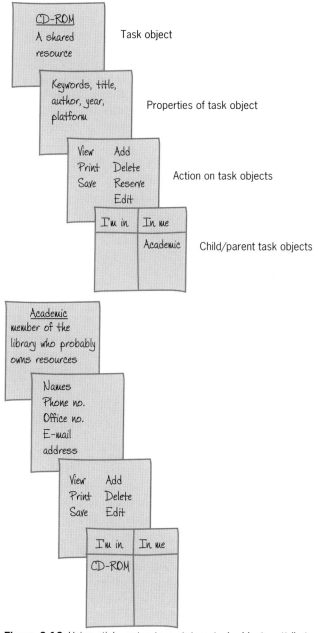

Figure 8.10 Using sticky notes to prototype task objects, attributes, and actions.

crete use cases but rather from the users' knowledge of the domain or from your own domain analysis. Consequently, the best approach is to prototype your ideas, working alongside potential users of the system.

One approach is to use sticky notes. Write a one-sentence definition of the task object on one sticky note, the task object's properties on another, and the actions that can be applied to it on a third. We have discussed two kinds of attributes: child objects and properties. Divide a fourth sticky note into two columns, one headed "In me" and the other headed "I'm in"; write any child objects under the column "In me" and any parent objects under "I'm in." Once you have done this for each task object, you can stick these on a sheet of flipchart paper. Figure 8.10 illustrates some sticky notes developed as part of the conceptual design process for the digital library system.

You can check the completeness and correctness of the paper prototype by walking through a selection of concrete use cases with the users and verifying that the identified task objects, attributes, and actions will satisfy the tasks they plan to carry out.

4.5 Creating the Content Diagram

The content diagram represents the underlying organization and structure of the UI. It is a network made up of containers and links. The next step is to identify the containers that are needed for the content diagram. Each container collects functions and task objects into a coherent place in the system to support a part of the user's work. Typically, these become screens, windows, dialog boxes, or message boxes in the UI. We also need to identify the links between the containers. These indicate the navigation around the UI.

▶ Template for Containers

Figure 8.11 shows a template for containers.

As you can see, each container has the following elements:

Name	The name you choose for this container
Purpose	A phrase indicating its purpose in supporting the user's task.
Functions	• Indicates functions that are invoked by the user to perform the work.
	▪ Indicates functions that are automatically invoked by the system.
Links	The links with other containers, indicating the name of the container linked to and its purpose. There are two types of **link**.

Single links ▶ A **single link** indicates that the user moves to another container and then that new container becomes the focus of the user's activities. For example, when you login to your PC, you get a login dialog box. After you enter your login name and password, the system validates it and then shows the main desktop window.

Double links ▶▶ A **double link** indicates that the work done in a second container needs the context of the first container and that the user will switch back and forth between the two; an example is

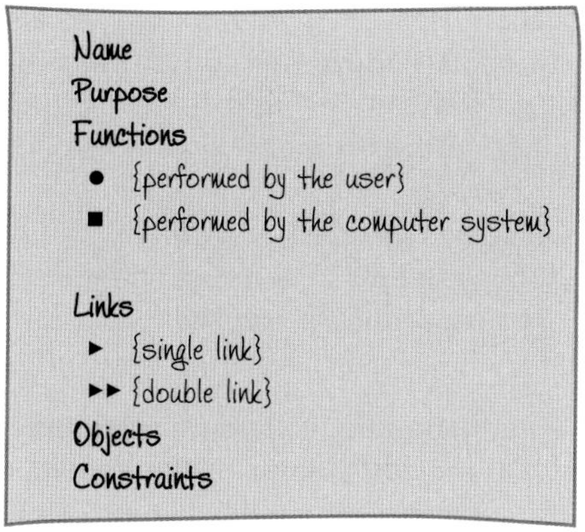

Name
Purpose
Functions
  • {performed by the user}
  ■ {performed by the computer system}

Links
  ▶ {single link}
  ▶▶ {double link}
Objects
Constraints

Figure 8.11 Template for containers.

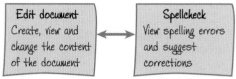

Figure 8.12 An example of a double link between containers.

when you are working in a Word document and you invoke the spell checker. This is a double navigation link because the focus keeps moving between the two windows when you perform the task. Figure 8.12 illustrates this situation. The containers are illustrated in outline form.

- **Objects** The task objects whose attributes and actions are required for the users to complete their tasks.
- **Constraints** Any constraints for that container, such as speed, reliability, and availability.

▶ The Main Container

To find out more about launch pad windows, see Chapter 16.

The first container we need to specify is the **main container**. This represents the first thing the users encounter and will be central to their work. In a GUI, this might be a launch pad window containing icons corresponding to the main tasks that can be carried out.

When you are designing the main container, you will typically include links to the following:

- *Vital tasks.* The user must perform these tasks quickly, even under stress. An example would be a network supervisor who continually monitors the traffic on a network. If something goes wrong (for example, if someone cuts a cable), it is important that the supervisor is able to assess the situation quickly and reroute the traffic.

- *Frequent tasks.* Those tasks that users spend the majority of their time performing must be fast to access. For example, the software used by the telephone operators who deal with emergency calls needs to offer good support for the limited number of tasks that the operators perform during each call.
- *Navigational aids.* The users need to understand quickly and easily what the application is capable of doing and how to accomplish their tasks. For example, information kiosks need to be easy to learn and use without written instructions. This might be achieved using a map or some other metaphor.

Typically the section of the UI corresponding to the main container will not perform any of these tasks. Instead, it will provide links to the containers that do. The main container for the digital library system is illustrated in Figure 8.13. This container lists functions that correspond to the most frequent tasks, as elicited by the requirements gathering:

- To search for a resource, identify who owns it, and send an e-mail to that person.
- To identify the current updates to the digital library, choose a recently added resource, and e-mail the owner.
- To contact the system support team.

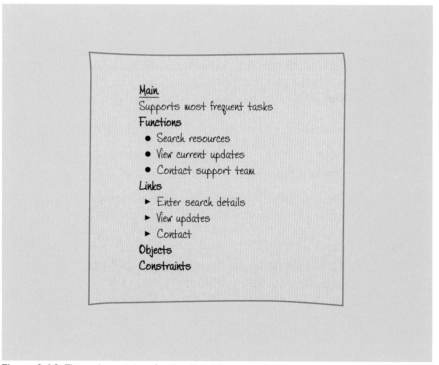

Figure 8.13 The main container for the digital library system.

There is a corresponding link for each of these functions. As the purpose of the main container is to access other containers, it does not contain any of the functionality or the details relating to any of the task objects. There are no constraints, apart from the obvious ones, such as reliability and availability. We have not included these, as they apply to all the containers.

This container does not represent all the information needed to start developing the physical design of the screen, but it does represent the essential elements and helps us to focus our thinking on the other containers that will be needed.

▶ Other Containers

Other containers are usually derived from the concrete use cases. Each concrete use case shows the sequence of steps needed to accomplish a particular task. The functionality needed to support these steps can be divided between one or more containers.

Consider the "Search and request CD-ROM" concrete use case in Figure 8.6. The first user action is to enter the search criteria. Rather than have separate search screens for each of the different resource types, we decided to have a single search screen allowing the user to search through all the resource types. The corresponding "Enter search criteria" container for the digital library system is illustrated in Figure 8.14.

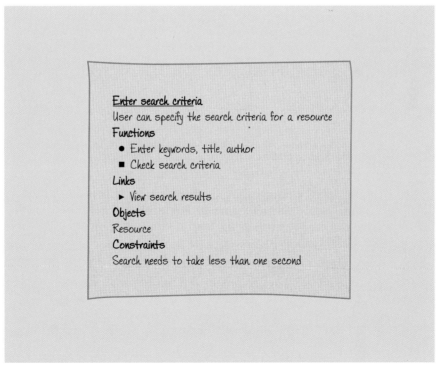

Figure 8.14 The "Enter search criteria" container for the digital library system.

The purpose of this container is to allow users to specify the search criteria. From the functions, we can see that the UI is responsible for checking that the search criteria are syntactically correct. There is only one link: this is to the container that displays the results of the search. Unlike the main container, "Enter search criteria" relates to a task object: the resource object. In the UI, the attributes common to all the resource types will form the search criteria. For example, the corresponding screen might be as illustrated in Figure 8.15.

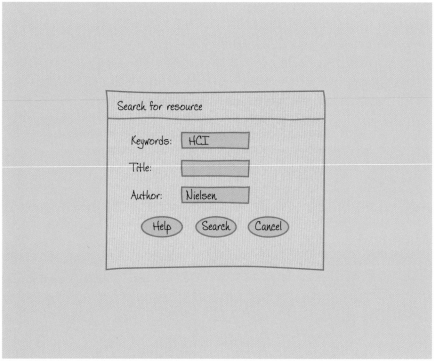

Figure 8.15 A possible screen design for the "Enter search criteria" container.

This is a very limited implementation. It may have been better to have included additional fields corresponding to the attributes that are particular to the different resource types, such as the length of the video or the platform needed for the CD-ROM (Mac or PC).

Ideally you should not anticipate the more detailed aspects of your UI design during the conceptual design phase, as it can constrain your thinking; nevertheless, it can help you if you are inexperienced.

EXERCISE 8.8 (Allow 10 minutes)

Illustrate the "View search results" container, identifying the functions, links, and associated task object(s). Explain the decisions you have made and draw a simple screen mockup, showing how the screen might look. How would you implement the container for an audio output UI, such as a telephone menu system?

DISCUSSION

Figure 8.16(a) illustrates the container we designed. In our design, the "View search results" container shows the results of the search, allows users to select the one they want, and then allows them to move on to the next container, so that they can view the contact details. The resource object is associated with this container because the attributes will occupy most of the screen, as Figure 8.16(b) illustrates. The screen is simpler than it will be in the final design, because it does not contain information such as the resource type for each title.

If this container were to be implemented using an audio-output UI, each result would need to be read out, with an associated number. Users would then choose the number of the result for which they require the contact details and either speak the number or press the appropriate key on the telephone keypad.

▶ Links

Once we have identified the containers we need to link them together to reflect the navigation flow, the way in which the users will move through the UI to achieve their goals. We refer to the resulting diagram as the content diagram; it is the outcome of the conceptual design process. For clarity, we have presented the steps of identifying and linking the containers as separate stages, but in reality you would develop the two in parallel.

When you are drawing the content diagram, draw single links as single-headed arrows ▸ and double links as double-headed arrows ▸▸. These arrows correspond to the links each container indicates are necessary. If any conditions determine the navigation flow to a particular container, label the arrow. Such labels are known as **conditions of interaction**. These links and the conditions of interaction in the content diagram will help you determine whether the user interface architecture supports the users' tasks as they navigate from one container to another.

Identifying the links should not be too difficult, as they will reflect the order of the actions in the concrete use cases. However, producing the content diagram for a complex UI is not a trivial task, as it will probably involve combining a large number of concrete use cases into a complex network of containers and links.

Figure 8.17 illustrates the whole of the relevant section of the content diagram corresponding to the "Search and request CD-ROM" concrete use case in Figure 8.6. As you can see, there is a condition of interaction between View details and Write e-mail message. This is necessary because the user may choose to telephone the owner or to knock on the owner's office door rather than to send an e-mail.

▶ Prototyping Containers and Links

Because of the potential complexity of the task, it is important to prototype your ideas when you are developing the content diagram. As with the prototyping of

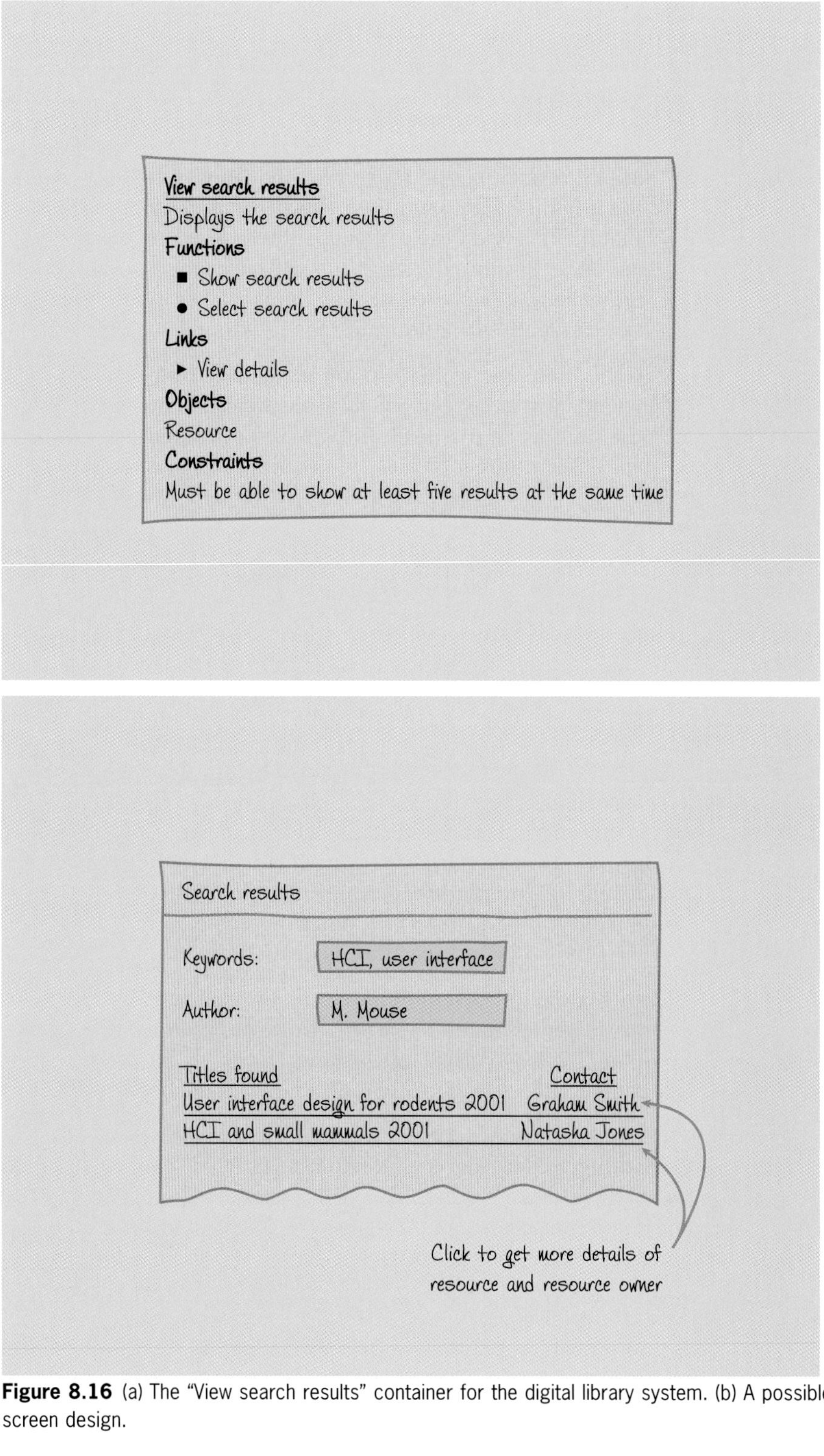

View search results
Displays the search results
Functions
- Show search results
- Select search results

Links
▶ View details

Objects
Resource

Constraints
Must be able to show at least five results at the same time

Search results

Keywords: HCI, user interface

Author: M. Mouse

Titles found   Contact
User interface design for rodents 2001   Graham Smith
HCI and small mammals 2001   Natasha Jones

Click to get more details of
resource and resource owner

Figure 8.16 (a) The "View search results" container for the digital library system. (b) A possible screen design.

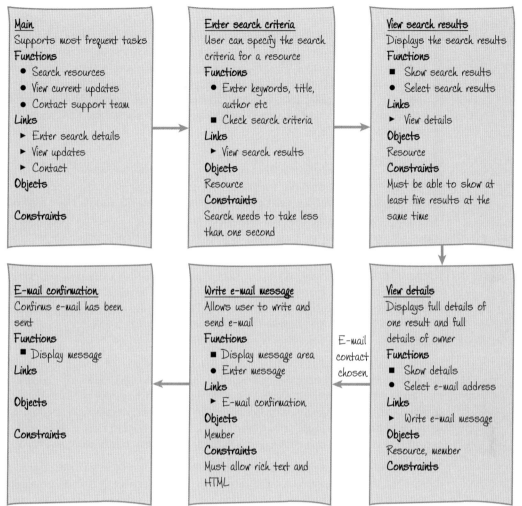

Main
Supports most frequent tasks
Functions
- Search resources
- View current updates
- Contact support team
Links
▸ Enter search details
▸ View updates
▸ Contact
Objects

Constraints

Enter search criteria
User can specify the search criteria for a resource
Functions
- Enter keywords, title, author etc
■ Check search criteria
Links
▸ View search results
Objects
Resource
Constraints
Search needs to take less than one second

View search results
Displays the search results
Functions
■ Show search results
- Select search results
Links
▸ View details
Objects
Resource
Constraints
Must be able to show at least five results at the same time

E-mail confirmation
Confirms e-mail has been sent
Functions
■ Display message
Links

Objects

Constraints

Write e-mail message
Allows user to write and send e-mail
Functions
■ Display message area
- Enter message
Links
▸ E-mail confirmation
Objects
Member
Constraints
Must allow rich text and HTML

E-mail contact chosen

View details
Displays full details of one result and full details of owner
Functions
■ Show details
- Select e-mail address
Links
▸ Write e-mail message
Objects
Resource, member
Constraints

Figure 8.17 Section of the content diagram corresponding to the "Search and request CD-ROM" concrete use case.

task objects, attributes, and actions, one way of doing this is to put sticky notes on a flipchart sheet. Each sticky note should represent a container or a link. You do not need to add all the details for the containers at this stage; just the name and purpose will be sufficient. You can then move the sticky notes around, adding and removing containers and links as appropriate. This representation can help you discuss matters with the users. In particular, you can step through some of the concrete use cases to ensure that the containers represent the necessary functionality and that the links allow for all the sequences of actions needed to carry out the users' tasks.

> **EXERCISE 8.9 (Allow 10 minutes)**
>
> Draw the section of the content diagram corresponding to the "View updates and request book" concrete use case in Figure 8.7. You should base the content of the containers upon the task objects, attributes, and actions you identified earlier. As for the content diagram corresponding to the "Search and request CD-ROM" concrete use case, assume that the implementation will be at resource level rather than having separate update screens for books, CDs, videos, and journals.
>
> **DISCUSSION**
>
> Figure 8.18 illustrates the section of the content diagram corresponding to the "View updates and request book" concrete use case. As you can see, four of the containers are the same as those in Figure 8.17.

▶ Final Thoughts on Conceptual Design

Figure 8.19 illustrates the whole content diagram based on the two concrete use cases. For brevity, we have given only the titles of the containers. We have combined the containers common to the two content diagrams illustrated in Figures 8.17 and 8.18. You can see how the network of containers is starting to evolve.

Transforming the content diagram into a user interface is a creative activity. There are no strict mappings from the content diagram onto the UI design, but for GUIs and web sites, most containers will translate into screens, windows, or dialog boxes. The task objects and their attributes will become UI controls such as list boxes, combo boxes, radio buttons, data fields, and so on, and the actions will become menu items or items on the tool bar in the windows. The navigation from one container to another will typically be achieved by selecting a link, tool bar button, and so on.

The navigation flow, as represented by the links, will underlie any corresponding UI, but the relation may not be as straightforward as you expect. It is sometimes possible to have a one-to-one relation, but that may not be ideal. For example, Figure 8.20 illustrates a web page that corresponds to three containers: the main container, the "Enter search criteria" container, and the "View updates" container. Thus, we have translated three containers into a single screen while maintaining the same navigation flow. Similarly, a single container may correspond to several screens.

In Chapters 16 and 17, this process of transformation is demonstrated for graphical user interfaces and web user interfaces. As you will see, the content diagram informs the UI design, but there are still numerous design decisions to make.

5 Summary

In this chapter, we discussed work reengineering and conceptual design. Work reengineering involves deciding how a UI will help users carry out their tasks. An

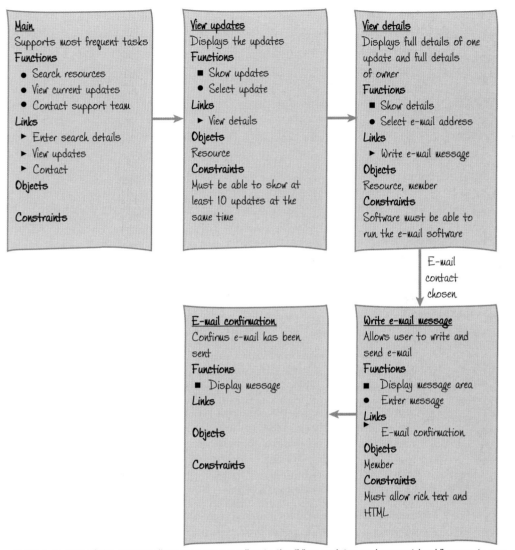

Figure 8.18 A section of the content diagram corresponding to the "View updates and request book" concrete use case.

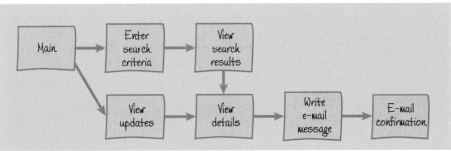

Figure 8.19 The content diagram for the digital library.

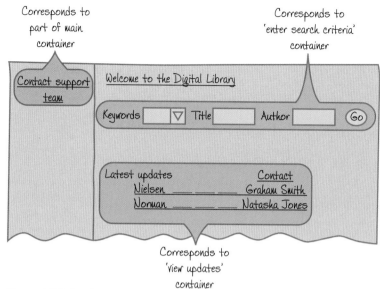

Figure 8.20 A web page corresponding to part of the content diagram.

important part of this process is task allocation, by which the various activities are shared between the user and the computer system. We have shown how use scenarios and essential use cases can help us think about work reengineering.

We then discussed the process of conceptual design. Conceptual design results in a content diagram, which represents the underlying structure and organization of the UI. We showed you how to develop the content diagram; first the essential use cases are translated into concrete use cases; then the task objects, attributes, and actions are identified from the concrete use cases; and finally the containers and links for the content diagram are identified.

Work reengineering and conceptual design are demanding but important tasks. For these reasons it is important to prototype and check your ideas with the users.

In Chapter 10, we begin to discuss the physical design of the user interface.

9

Design guidance and design rationale

1   Introduction

In the previous chapter, we used the requirements to help us create a conceptual design. The next step is to move from conceptual design to a physical design (see Box 9.1).

Architects do not design in a vacuum but instead follow principles and guidelines, both structural and aesthetic. Similarly, you will create a better physical design if you are aware of principles and guidelines for good UI design.

In this chapter, we consider the different sources of design guidance: standards, guidelines, and style guides; and we discuss four important design principles: simplicity, structure, consistency, and tolerance. These principles are in addition to the three design principles introduced in Chapter 5: visibility, affordance, and feedback. We also discuss designing for **accessibility**, or designing UIs so as not to exclude people with visual, physical, or hearing disabilities. We end by discussing the different ways of keeping a record of your design decisions, which we call **design rationale**.

Box 9.1   **Quotations on User Interface Design**

More usable software comes from thinking about the user interface, from trying it out, and from successive refinement. It's not rocket science.

Great user interface design is like great architecture. It fits beautifully with its environment and its purpose, with room for creative flavour and artistry.

From Constantine and Lockwood (1999).

2 Sources of Design Guidance

In Chapter 5, we introduced design principles and design rules as one of two types of knowledge needed for UI design. Additional sources of guidance for UI design are standards, guidelines, and style guides. A **user interface standard** is a set of internationally agreed design principles, or approaches, focusing on particular areas such as human-centered (in our terms, user-centered) design and the design of multimedia user interfaces. **Design guidelines** are somewhere between design principles and design rules in terms of detail. A **style guide** is a collection of design rules, frequently augmented with some design guidelines; commercial style guides apply to a particular product or family of products such as Microsoft Office. These different forms of guidance have been developed from both academic research and the experience of usability practitioners.

Whether you choose to adhere to particular user interface standards or a specific style guide depends on your particular circumstances, but the design principles will always be applicable.

2.1 User Interface Standards

Standards are official, publicly available documents that define standards for user interface design. One organization developing such standards is the International Organization for Standardization (ISO), a worldwide federation of national standards bodies (ISO member bodies) that are involved in the preparation of international standards through various technical committees. There are several ISO standards for human–computer interaction (HCI) and usability:

- The most elaborate is ISO 9241: *Ergonomic requirements for office work with visual display terminals (VDTs)*. It contains guidelines for the software and hardware ergonomics aspects of the use of VDTs. It covers issues such as the requirements for displays, guidance on the working environment, and the use of icons and menus.
- ISO 14915: *Software ergonomics for multimedia user interfaces* provides guidelines for the design of multimedia user interfaces.
- ISO 13407: *Human-centered design processes for interactive systems* provides guidance on human-centered design activities through the development life cycle of computer-based interactive systems. It is aimed at those managing design processes and provides guidance on sources of information and standards relevant to the human-centered approach. Box 9.2 gives more details of ISO 13407, listing the benefits its developers claim for human-centered design purposes and the four essential elements they believe are necessary for human-centered design. As you can see, ISO 13407 underpins the philosophy of this book.
- ISO/CD 20282: *Ease of operation of everyday products* is a four-part standard being defined to provide guidance on how to design products to ensure that they can be used in the way consumers expect them to be used. The standard

Box 9.2	**ISO 13407 Human-Centered Design Processes for Interactive Systems**

The idea behind this international standard is that by following the human-centered process described within it, a design team can ensure that the computer system it is developing will be effective, efficient, and satisfying for its users. The standard lists the benefits of adopting a human-centered approach:

- Systems are easier to understand and use, thus reducing training and support costs.
- Discomfort and stress are reduced, and user satisfaction is improved.
- The productivity of users and the operational efficiency of organizations is improved.
- Product quality, aesthetics, and impact are improved, and a competitive advantage can be achieved.

The standard describes four essential elements of human-centered design:

- The active involvement of users and a clear understanding of them, their tasks, and their requirements.
- An appropriate allocation of functions between users and technology, specifying which functions can be carried out by users.
- An iteration of design solutions in which feedback from users becomes a critical source of information.
- A multidisciplinary design perspective that requires a variety of skills, so multidisciplinary design teams should be involved in the human-centered design process. The teams should consist of end users, purchasers, business analysts, application domain specialists, systems analysts, programmers, and marketing and sales personnel.

167
Part 3

Details of how to purchase these standards and other ISO standards in the areas of ergonomics, HCI, and usability are available on the ISO's web site www.iso.ch/iso/ en/ISOOnline. frontpage. They are also available from some countries' national standards organizations such as the American National Standards Institute (ANSI) http://webstore. ansi.org/ ansidocstore/ default.asp.

also focuses on ensuring that the needs of a wide range of users, including those with disabilities, are addressed through better product usability. As of the summer of 2004, two of the four parts of the standard had been produced to ISO draft standard Part 1: *Context of use and user characteristics*, and Part 2: *Test method*.

If you are considering using one of these standards, you will need to start by identifying an appropriate one and then interpreting it according to your particular circumstances.

EXERCISE 9.1 (Allow five minutes)

List three circumstances under which your organization, or one that you are familiar with, might choose to apply the ISO standards in the areas of ergonomics and HCI.

DISCUSSION

We thought of the following circumstances:

- The organization makes a strategic decision to apply the standards, so it can be publicized to potential customers that they have been used.
- The organization does not have a great deal of in-house knowledge of ergonomics and HCI, and the standards provide a starting point for development.
- The organization is developing a system for a government agency, an overseas customer, or some other client who requires that the system's user interface should conform to these standards.

2.2 Style Guides

A style guide can provide the basic conventions for a specific product or for a family of products. A guide typically includes the following:

- A description of the required interaction styles and user interface controls, covering both the required look (appearance) and feel (behavior).
- Guidance on when and how to use the various interaction styles or user interface controls.
- Illustrations of the various interaction styles and user interface controls.
- Screen templates to show how screens should look.

There are two types of style guides: commercial style guides and customized style guides.

▶ **Commercial Style Guides**

Commercial style guides are usually produced by a single organization or vendor and are made commercially available. They are composed of design rules: highly specific instructions that can be followed with the minimum of interpretation or translation by the designer. Because commercial style guides are so specific, they are only applicable in relation to a particular system platform or class of system. Here are several popular examples:

- Apple Human Interface Guidelines for the Macintosh, http://developer.apple.com/documentation/UserExperience/Conceptual/OSXHIGuidelines.
- Microsoft Windows XP User Interface Guidelines, http://www.microsoft.com/whdc/hwdev/windowsxp/downloads/default.mspx.
- IBM's Common User Access (CUA) guidelines were developed in the late 1980s, and thus are only available in print form (IBM Systems, 1991). Online IBM hosts its *Ease of use* web site, which covers many fundamental aspects of UI design at www-3.ibm.com/ibm/easy/eou_ext.nsf/publish/558. The *Design* section lists design guidelines for following a user-centered process for product development.

- Motif formed the basis for Sun Microsystems' GUIs in the early 1990s. The early Motif Style Guide can be found at http://w3ppl.gov/misc/motif/MotifStyleGuide/en_US/TOC.html. More recently, Motif, as CDE 2.1 / Motif 2.1 is used for the Common Desktop Environment (CDE) of Unix-based systems. The style guide is not freely available but can be purchased at www.opengroup.org/public/pubs/catalog/m027.htm.
- Sun Microsystems' Java Look and Feel Design Guidelines, http://java.sun.com/products/jlf/ed2/book/HIGTitle.html.

Some informal organizations also publish or maintain style guides, such as the one for K Desktop Environment, "a powerful free software graphical desktop environment for Linux and Unix workstations," available at http://developer.kde.org/documentation/standards/kde/style/basics.

▶ Customized Style Guides

It can be useful to draw together all the design principles, guidelines, and rules that are relevant to the user interface you are designing. These may come from user interface standards, other style guides, and design principles and guidelines developed by academic researchers and usability practitioners (it is likely there will be a lot of overlap between these sources). They can then act as a **customized style guide** for your UI. A customized style guide was used by National Air traffic Services for the development of the Final Approach Spacing Tool (FAST; see Chapter 19).

Using a customized style guide has a number of advantages.

- It helps you (and the rest of the design team, if there is one) focus on design issues early in the development process.
- Developing a customized style guide early in the development cycle will enable you to use the principles and guidelines to influence the requirements gathering. For example, one design principle might be that color should be used carefully if the users are mostly male (as color blindness is more prevalent in men). This principle can then be used during requirements gathering to prompt you to check the gender balance in the users.
- The customized style guide can steer decision making throughout the design process. It can also serve as a record of the design decisions that have been taken and of the design constraints that have been identified, so that the design team can refer back to them.
- The customized style guide will help ensure consistency across the user interface. This should help improve the usability of the UI.
- One can check against the customized style guide during the evaluation.
- If it is used across the organization, it will help to give a corporate look to all the UIs.

In Chapter 26 you will see how to evaluate UI designs against principles and guidelines.

The content of the customized style guide will vary according to circumstances, as it needs to take into account the characteristics of the users, their tasks, and the environment in which they will be working. For example, if you were designing a

UI for users who are working on mobile devices in harsh environments, you will need to take into account the particular challenges they are facing.

For many organizations and in many countries, you may be required by law to take into account the special needs of people who have a disability. Even if this is not a legal requirement, it is good practice. We will discuss this issue further in the section titled "Accessibility."

It is important not to be too rigid about your style guide. If you develop your UI in a genuinely user-centered way, it is likely that the users will identify problems with your style guide, and it will probably remain a work in progress for most of the development cycle.

EXERCISE 9.2 (Allow five minutes)

List four circumstances under which your organization, or one that you are familiar with, might choose to use a style guide.

DISCUSSION

We thought of the following circumstances:

- The organization has found that its target users are familiar with UIs that use the particular style guide, and the organization wants to make it easy for users to transfer to the software its developers are writing.
- The organization makes a strategic decision that all its UIs should follow a particular style guide. This will ensure that its users can move between its products relatively easily.
- The organization has a particular hardware/software platform and wants to associate itself with the relevant family of products.
- The organization has no in-house knowledge of UI design, and a style guide provides detailed guidance. In this situation, a style guide may be more useful than standards because it requires no interpretation, but it can also be misleading because it may fail to emphasize the importance of understanding users.

3   Design Principles: Simplicity, Structure, Consistency, and Tolerance

This section describes four important design principles: simplicity, structure, consistency, and tolerance. These principles complement the principles introduced in Chapter 5: the Gestalt principles of proximity, similarity, continuity, and symmetry, and visibility, affordance, and feedback, three principles from experience.

3.1 Simplicity

Simplicity is a design principle which emphasizes the importance of keeping the UI as simple as possible. The user interface should be communicated clearly and simply

If you would like to find out more about these design principles, see Chapter 3 of Constantine and Lockwood (1999).

in the users' own language. To keep the UI simple, the UI designer should employ actions, icons, words, and user interface controls that are natural to the users. Complex tasks should be broken into simpler subtasks, to keep the behavior and the user interface appearance as natural as possible for the user. Keeping things simple for the users is a difficult challenge for UI designers.

Figure 9.1 shows the home page for the National Park Service in the United States. We found the front page simple, uncluttered, and well structured. The graphic at the top reflects the theme of the site, and it refreshes to show a view of a different park

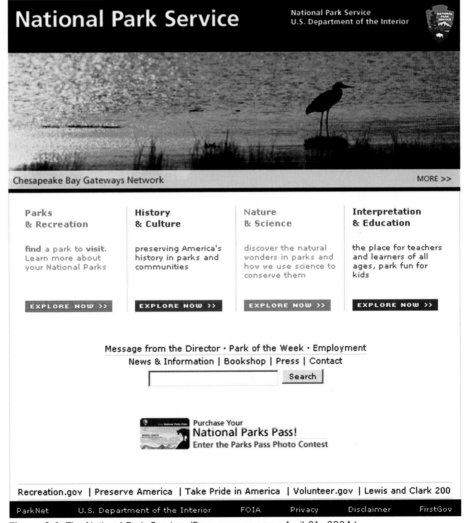

Figure 9.1 The National Park Service. (From www.nps.gov, April 21, 2004.)

each time you visit. The various navigation **links** from the home page (Explore Now, Message from the Director, Park of the Week, NPS Digest, Bookshop, News, etc.) are mostly worded in such a way that they are simple to understand and easily differentiable.

EXERCISE 9.3 (Allow five minutes)

Review the links on the National Parks Service home page in Figure 9.1. Do you think that the most important links are simple to understand? Are there any that you find confusing?

DISCUSSION

You might wonder whether the "Explore Now" links are a little too simple: each of the four areas has the same graphic and the same title to the link, and if they all had the same "alt" text then a person using a screen reader would hear the same link four times.

(Alt text provides an alternate message to your viewers who cannot see your graphics. Without alt text, images on a web site are meaningless to these users.)

In fact, each alt text is differentiated so that the one below "Parks and Recreation" says "Explore Parks and Recreation" instead of "Explore Now."

We weren't sure about the difference between "NPS Digest" and "News." At the time we visited the site, "NPS Digest" was a newsletter for supporters of the park, whereas "News" contained press releases about topics such as forest fires, but this isn't at all obvious from the home page.

From our point of view, "FOIA," "FirstGov," and "Lewis and Clark 200" are all somewhat obscure. Did you share our difficulties?

3.2 Structure

If you would like to find out more about the design principle of structure, see Hix and Hartson (1993).

Structure is a design principle that emphasizes the importance of organizing the UI in a meaningful and useful way. Features that users think of as related should appear together on the user interface, or at least they should be clearly and closely associated. Those features that are unrelated either in terms of work or in the minds of the users should be separated or distinguished on the user interface. Thus, the structure of the user interface should reflect the users' understanding of the domain and their expectations about how the UI should be structured.

Consider the dialog box in Figure 9.2. The layout of the dialog box's window shows how related information can be grouped into frames, for example **Printer**, **Page range**, and **Copies**. This grouping of information helps the users to anticipate that a particular **frame** will contain all the controls needed for a set of related tasks.

Using Visual Basic, we drew a screen that was designed without regard for order or organization. It is illustrated in Figure 9.3 and relates to the digital library example

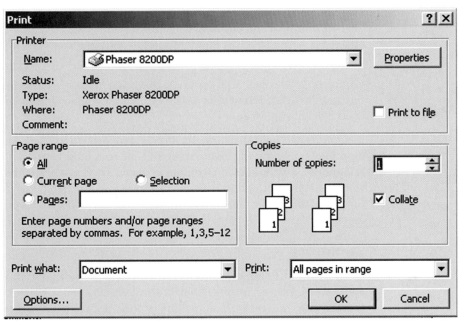

Figure 9.2 Print dialog in Word 97.

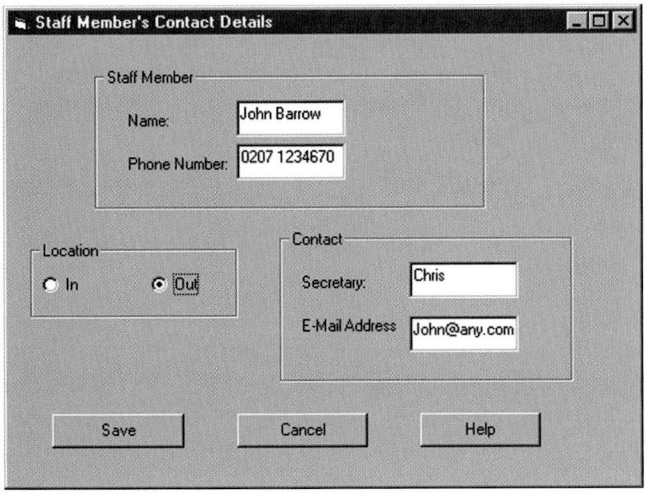

Figure 9.3 A sample screen demonstrating poor structure.

that we discussed in Chapter 8. As you can see, the staff member's contact details appear in the frame called "Staff member" and the e-mail details are given in the frame called "Contact," along with the name of the member's secretary. This would mean that the user has to search the screen for the e-mail address and may miss it. The "Contact" frame is not even directly underneath the "Staff member" frame to help with the search. To improve this design, the user interface controls should be aligned, grouped, and positioned in a way that helps the users to obtain information effectively and efficiently. The information resulting from the task analysis should influence this process.

Completing the conceptual design stage conscientiously should also help ensure that the underlying structure of your UI is clear and enables the users to carry out their tasks quickly and easily.

Metaphors can help structure the interface in a way that users easily recognize. For example, if you have the task of designing the user interface for an information kiosk at a tourist spot, an obvious approach would be to use a site map metaphor. This would enable information seekers to feel situated and help to relate their location to the rest of the tourist area. Interaction with the metaphor could provide information about places of interest and directions to reach that place.

> The use of metaphors in UI design will be discussed in Chapter 10.

3.3 Consistency

Consistency is a design principle that emphasizes the importance of uniformity in appearance, placement, and behavior within the user interface to make a system easy to learn and remember. If something is done or presented in a certain way on the user interface, users expect it to be the same throughout. This is because they develop a mental model of the user interface and then use the model to predict how subsequent screens will appear and how the user interface will behave.

Consistency significantly affects usability. Users expect certain aspects of the interface to behave in certain ways, and when that does not happen it can be very confusing. This is true not only for a single computer system, but across all the systems in an organization.

Consider the Microsoft Office suite — PowerPoint, Word, Excel, Access, and so on. They all have a similar look and feel, and the arrangement and labels of most of the menu items are similar. Consistent user interface design across applications helps users to switch easily from one application to another.

A customized style guide helps to achieve consistency by ensuring that the same design principles and guidelines are used through the interface. The other way to ensure consistency is through reuse. The reuse of GUI controls and design strategies within and between systems can be advantageous to users because they will have fewer things to learn and remember. Also, the interface will be more predictable and understandable. Building user interfaces from reusable components such as GUI controls and the underlying structure of the interface ensures consistency not only in appearance but also in behavior. What users have learned before — about this system or from others similarly designed — is more likely to be applicable when they see familiar appearances and behaviors. By reusing designs, you can create not only a more consistent user interface but also a less expensive system.

Figure 9.4 shows an example of inconsistent appearance. The buttons have been placed in two different positions in different dialog boxes associated with the same

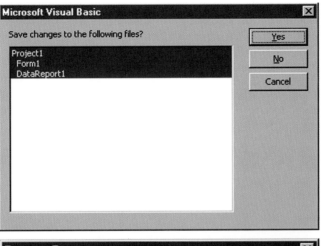

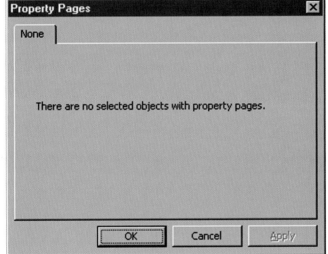

Figure 9.4 An example of inconsistency.

application — Microsoft Visual Basic. In part (a), the buttons are vertically aligned on the right-hand side, whereas in part (b), the buttons are aligned horizontally.

EXERCISE 9.4 (Allow five minutes)

From your own experience, can you identify inconsistency in an application?

DISCUSSION

Mark writes: The application I found to be inconsistent is Microsoft Outlook, the desktop information management system. I mainly use Outlook for sending and receiving e-mail. I wanted to re-send a message, so I highlighted the relevant message in the appropriate folder and started looking for a re-send option. I first checked the pop-up menu (activated by clicking the right-hand mouse button) and then the Tools menu item on the menu bar, but neither allowed me to re-send the message.

I then opened the selected message and checked the pop-up menu and Tools menu item again. To my surprise, the **Tools** menu had changed and it now contained a re-send option. This lack of consistency (the menu item appearing in one context but not in another) confused me, and I suspect that as I only re-send occasionally I may not remember how to do it next time.

It is not uncommon to experience inconsistency of this sort.

3.4 Tolerance

Tolerance is a design principle that emphasizes the importance of designing the user interface to prevent users from making errors. However, errors are not always due to poor user interface design. They could be due to poor task or domain knowledge, stress, or poor communication between colleagues. There are a variety of environmental, organizational, and technological reasons why users make errors. Here we focus on how the user interface should be designed to reduce the number of user errors and facilitate recovery from them.

Many user interfaces help the users to avoid mistakes by making wrong choices unavailable. Graying out menu choices or buttons when they are not available is a good example. However, this can lead to frustration for users who do not know why the desired choice is not available. Displaying a help message if a user attempts to choose a grayed item can solve this.

Some user interfaces provide examples to show the type of information that is required. For instance, entering a date in an invalid format is a common error. An input field for a date ideally should accept any format a user enters, but often they do not. If an example appears near the data entry field, informing the user how the date should be inserted, the number of errors can be reduced. Good feedback through audio or visual cues, either textual or graphic, can also help users avoid making errors.

If users do make mistakes, you should design a tolerant user interface, which helps them to recover. **Recoverability** is how easy it is for users to recover from their mistakes in their interaction with a system and hence accomplish their goals. There are two types of recovery: forward error recovery and backward error recovery.

- In forward error recovery, the system accepts the error and then helps the user to accomplish his or her goal. Therefore, although the users may not be able to undo their actions, the system provides an alternative route to enable them to recover.

- Backward error recovery involves undoing the effects of the previous interaction in order to return to a prior state. An example of this is the Undo feature in Microsoft Word.

To help users recover from their mistakes, it is also important to display error messages that provide the information necessary for recovery. Good error messages can have a great impact on a user's performance with the system. Here are some guidelines for providing positive, constructive, informative, and user-centered messages:

- Explain errors to help the user correct them.
- If the user requests it, provide additional explanation during error correction.
- Use language that the user will understand.
- Use positive, nonthreatening language.
- Use specific, constructive terms.
- Make sure that the system takes the blame for the errors.

Error messages should clearly highlight the problem immediately after an error occurs and make it easy to correct. There are some web sites in which, if an error is detected after the completion and submission of a form, users are taken back to the top of the form and have to complete it all again. They may not even be told where the error is. Ideally, the system should validate each field as the information is entered, so that it can be corrected immediately.

4   Accessibility

The use of technology is becoming more widespread. We saw in Chapter 1 that over 50% of the households in both the United Kingdom and the United States have one or more home computers. With this has come a greater need to consider designing systems for those with disabilities. As a result, a number of accessibility guidelines have been developed. The emphasis is not only to enable the disabled, but also to make the use of systems easier for all users.

4.1 The Principles of Universal Design

Ron Mace, from the Center for Universal Design at North Carolina State University, defines universal design as

> . . . *the design of products and environments to be usable by all people, to the greatest extent possible, without the need for adaptation or specialized design.*

To this end, the center has developed seven principles of universal design to support accessibility. They are listed in Table 9.1.

A poster giving further description and examples of the application of the guidelines can be obtained from www.design.ncsu.edu:8120/cud/univ_design/poster.pdf.

Table 9.1 The Principles of Universal Design
(from www.design.ncsu.edu:8120/cud/univ_design/ poster.pdf)

Principle	Description
Equitable use	The design is useful and marketable to people with diverse abilities.
Flexibility in use	The design accommodates a wide range of individual preferences and abilities.
Simple and intuitive use	Use of the design is easy to understand, regardless of the user's experience, knowledge, language skills, or current concentration level.
Perceptible information	The design communicates necessary information effectively to the user, regardless of ambient conditions or the user's sensory abilities.
Tolerance for error	The design minimizes hazards and the adverse consequences of accidental or unintended actions.
Low physical effort	The design can be used efficiently and comfortably with a minimum of fatigue.
Size and space for approach and use	Appropriate size and space is provided for approach, reach, manipulation, and use regardless of user's body size, posture, or mobility.

4.2 W3C Web Content Accessibility Guidelines

The World Wide Web Consortium (W3C) has around 350 member organizations worldwide. It was established to lead the World Wide Web to its full potential. One of its long-term goals is universal access, which it describes as follows:

To make the Web accessible to all by promoting technologies that take into account the vast differences in culture, languages, education, ability, material resources, access devices, and physical limitations of users on all continents.

(W3C goal from www.w3.org/Consortium)

To this end, the W3C has developed a set of guidelines — the Web Content Accessibility Guidelines — which explain how to make web content accessible to people with disabilities. Again, the emphasis is not only to promote accessibility for the disabled, but also to make web content more accessible for all users.

The Web Content Accessibility Guidelines (WCAG) are composed of 14 general principles of accessible design. These are listed in Table 9.2.

Table 9.2 The W3C's 14 General Principles of Accessible Design
(from www.w3.org/TR/WAI-WEBCONTENT)

Guideline 1:	Provide equivalent alternatives to auditory and visual content.	Provide content that, when presented to the user, conveys essentially the same function or purpose as auditory or visual content.
Guideline 2:	Don't rely on color alone.	Ensure that text and graphics are understandable when viewed without color.
Guideline 3:	Use markup and style sheets and do so properly.	Mark up documents with the proper structural elements. Control presentation with style sheets rather than with presentation elements and attributes.
Guideline 4:	Clarify natural language usage.	Use markup that facilitates pronunciation or interpretation of abbreviated or foreign text.
Guideline 5:	Create tables that transform gracefully.	Ensure that tables have necessary markup to be transformed by accessible browsers and other user agents.
Guideline 6:	Ensure that pages featuring new technologies transform gracefully.	Ensure that pages are accessible even when newer technologies are not supported or are turned off.
Guideline 7:	Ensure user control of time-sensitive content changes.	Ensure that moving, blinking, scrolling, or auto-updating objects or pages may be paused or stopped.

Table 9.2 The W3C's 14 General Principles of Accessible Design (from www.w3.org/TR/WAI-WEBCONTENT)—cont'd

Guideline 8:	Ensure direct accessibility of embedded user interfaces.	Ensure that the user interface follows principles of accessible design: device-independent access to functionality, keyboard operability, self-voicing, etc.
Guideline 9:	Design for device-independence.	Use features that enable activation of page elements via a variety of input devices.
Guideline 10:	Use interim solutions.	Use interim accessibility solutions so that assistive technologies and older browsers will operate correctly.
Guideline 11:	Use W3C technologies and guidelines.	Use W3C technologies (according to specification) and follow accessibility guidelines. Where it is not possible to use a W3C technology, or doing so results in material that does not transform gracefully, provide an alternative version of the content that is accessible.
Guideline 12:	Provide context and or entation information.	Provide context and orientation information to help users understand complex pages or elements.
Guideline 13:	Provide clear navigation mechanisms.	Provide clear and consistent navigation mechanisms — orientation information, navigation bars, a site map, etc. — to increase the likelihood that a person will find what they are looking for at a site.
Guideline 14:	Ensure that documents are clear and simple.	Ensure that documents are clear and simple so they may be more easily understood.

4.3 Section 508

The Section 508 Standards are a U.S. directive. It states that electronic and information technology that is developed, procured, maintained, and/or used by federal departments and agencies must be accessible and usable by federal employees and members of the public with disabilities — unless it is an undue burden to do so.

The Section 508 Standards are divided into four subparts; subpart B describes the technical standards for the range of systems/products that the standards pertain to:

- §1194.21: Software applications and operating systems
- §1194.22: Web-based Intranet and Internet information and applications
- §1194.23: Telecommunications products
- §1194.24: Video and multimedia products
- §1194.25: Self-contained, closed products (for example, copiers)
- §1194.26: Desktop and portable computers

As a government document, Section 508 is expressed in very formal terms (see www.section508.gov), and, in comparison to the W3C Web Content Guidelines, it is also lacking in detail in relation to the practical application of the guidelines.

Table 9.3 lists the standards that U.S. federal agencies must follow when they produce web pages.

A number of web sites have been created to augment the information in Section 508 to help designers apply these standards. For example, the Access Board's web site, at www.access-board.gov/sec508/guide/1194.22.htm, lists the standards in Table 9.3 and provides further explanation of each standard, why it is necessary (the rationale for the standard), how a web page can be designed to comply with the standard, and, for some standards, example HTML code and web sites are provided.

At www.jimthatcher.com/sidebyside.htm, there is a side-by-side comparison of the WCAG and the Section 508 Standards, which shows the similarities and differences.

4.4 The Limitations of Guidelines

Although following guidelines will help you to create better interfaces, guidelines are not sufficient on their own. For example, look at (o), navigation links, in Table 9.3: "A method shall be provided that permits users to skip repetitive navigation links." Clearly, wading through lots of navigation links is likely to be tedious, especially if you are using a screenreader that lists them all before you can get to the content of the page. So implementing a way to skip the links is a good idea.

However, having such a thing does not necessarily mean that users will be able to take advantage of it. For example, Theofanos and Redish (2003) tested web sites with blind and partially sighted users. They reported the following:

> *Many Web sites include a Skip Navigation link at the beginning of each Web page. Clicking on that link bypasses the global navigation at the top (and left — depending on where the developer has ended the skip navigation). Our participants des-*

Table 9.3 Section 508 Standards for Web Page Development by Federal Agencies (amalgamated from www.section508.gov and www.access-board.gov/sec508/guide/1194.22.htm)

(a) Text tags	A text equivalent for every nontext element shall be provided (e.g., via "alt," "longdesc," or in element content).
(b) Multimedia presentations	Equivalent alternatives for any multimedia presentation shall be synchronized with the presentation.
(c) Color	Web pages shall be designed so that all information conveyed with color is also available without color — for example, from context or markup.
(d) Readability	Documents shall be organized so they are readable without requiring an associated style sheet.
(e) Server-side image maps	Redundant text links shall be provided for each active region of a server-side image map.
(f) Client-side image maps	Client-side image maps shall be provided instead of server-side image maps except where the regions cannot be defined with an available geometric shape.
(g) and (h) Data table	Row and column headers shall be identified for data tables. Markup shall be used to associate data cells and header cells for data tables that have two or more logical levels of row or column headers.
(i) Frames	Frames shall be titled with text that facilitates frame identification and navigation.
(j) Flicker rate	Pages shall be designed to avoid causing the screen to flicker with a frequency greater than 2 Hz and lower than 55 Hz.

Table 9.3 Section 508 Standards for Web Page Development by Federal Agencies (amalgamated from www.section508.gov and www.access-board.gov/sec508/guide/1194.22.htm)—cont'd

(k) Text-only alternative	A text-only page, with equivalent information or functionality, shall be provided to make a web site comply with the provisions of these standards, when compliance cannot be accomplished in any other way. The content of the text-only page shall be updated whenever the primary page changes.
(l) Scripts	Frames shall be titled with text that facilitates frame identification and navigation.
(m) Applets and plug-ins	When a web page requires that an applet, plug-in, or other application be present on the client system to interpret page content, the page must provide a link to a plug-in or applet that complies with §1194.21(a) through (l).
(n) Electronic forms	When electronic forms are designed to be completed online, the form shall allow people using assistive technology to access the information, field elements, and functionality required for completion and submission of the form, including all directions and cues.
(o) Navigation links	A method shall be provided that permits users to skip repetitive navigation links.
(p) Time delays	When a timed response is required, the user shall be alerted and given sufficient time to indicate more time is required.

perately wanted to not listen to the navigation each time they got to a page. They wanted to get right to the content. But only half of our participants knew what "skip navigation" means. Some ranted to us about the problem of having to listen to the same "stuff" on each page, but they did not choose "skip navigation." Some jumped to the bottom of each page and scanned back up the pages to avoid the "stuff" at the top. If we think about that, it's not surprising. "Navigation" in this context is Web jargon. In fact, the half that knew "skip navigation" were the 508 consultants, the software engineer, and the highly sophisticated computer users. (pp. 43–44)

Part 4 of this book explains how to evaluate user interfaces.

Similar problems apply for users without any difficulties or disabilities. For example, *legible* text is not necessarily *meaningful*. So as well as following the guidelines or style guide, you must also test your product with users.

5 Design Rationale

Designing UIs is about choice and making design decisions. A customized style guide can help you make these decisions, but you still need to find a way to record when you made your decisions and the reasons why you made them. This is referred to as the design rationale.

5.1 The Benefits of Recording Design Decisions

Record keeping is always time consuming and can be rather uninteresting, but it is necessary for a number of reasons.

First, you may need to reconsider the decisions you have made in light of changed circumstances, and it is very likely that after some time you will have forgotten why you made them. This can be frustrating and result in wasted time. In addition, you will probably benefit from an explicit representation of the design rationale while you are designing a UI, as it will encourage you to approach the process in a more systematic and principled way. It will also provide you with the information you need to justify the design decisions you make.

Second, various people — trainers, marketing personnel, or even, in case you leave the project, other UI designers — may need to understand your decisions. New staff joining the development team may also need to understand why certain design decisions have been made. The users, too, may benefit from understanding why you designed the system the way you did.

EXERCISE 9.5 (Allow five minutes)

Why is it helpful for other UI designers, trainers, and marketing personnel to have a written design rationale for the UI? Suggest one reason for each category.

DISCUSSION

- *UI designers.* Another UI designer may need to reconsider the decisions you made if you move on from the project. If there is no coherent record of the options you considered and your reasons for rejecting them, the whole issue may need to be discussed again, thus wasting time.

- *Trainers.* The people training the users need to understand why certain functions behave the way they do, so that they can help the users to build a suitable understanding of the system.
- *Marketing.* Marketing personnel need to sell the system to potential customers. In the course of marketing the system, they are likely to be asked why the system does certain things and why it does not do other things. Understanding the rationale for the system's design will help them to answer these questions appropriately.

Another advantage of having a design rationale is that it will facilitate the reuse of parts of the UI, thus possibly saving development effort.

5.2 How to Record Design Decisions

Recording design decisions is not a trivial problem, as the following quotation from Kerry, a designer, shows. She was designing a UI to control the production of steel tubes. Here, as quoted in Stone (2001), she explains why she probably would not want to use side menus (more commonly referred to as cascading menus):

> *I think current opinion is moving away from having these side menus. They are a little bit difficult to operate; I'm surprised how difficult some users find [it] to use a mouse. These would be regular users, but I guess they would have new members of staff sometimes. It's just slightly slower . . . if you have a disabled member of staff. . . . I think trying to make the accuracy with which you have to position the mouse, the carefulness with which you have to use it . . . I would try not to make that too difficult for our disabled users, and many people are not that good with their hands. I'd probably do prototypes of both [menu options] and ask the [production control] operators what they thought. I wouldn't necessarily do what they wanted — that would depend on things like whether they have a high staff turnover; if they did I would probably give less weight to their views. (p. 246)*

Kerry gives the rationale for her decision not to use cascading menus. As this type of menu is in common use, this is the type of information that needs to be recorded so that it is clear why the interface has been designed as it has.

Unfortunately, if every design decision and every blind alley were documented in detail, the documentation would quickly become unwieldy. It is therefore practical to document only key decisions — those that were particularly contentious, difficult to make, or before which an exploration of alternatives was important.

One of the main questions associated with design rationale is how to document it. One approach might be to produce a table of some sort, with a date, the alternatives considered, the reasons for choosing one solution rather than others, and so on. This would be better than narrative text, which in turn is better than a transcript of the meeting or meetings at which decisions were made. It is always a good idea to keep such documentation brief, using illustrations where possible.

However, none of these approaches would make the information particularly easy to use. Imagine, for example, trying to identify at the maintenance phase the reasons for a decision made at the beginning of a project. If information were categorized by date, you might have an idea where to find it, but many decisions are made at the beginning of a project, and it would take time to find the specific point you need.

6 Summary

Designing UIs is a complex process that requires you to complete a range of contrasting activities in a flexible and iterative manner. However, a lot of advice is available to lead you through this process, in particular user interface standards, commercial style guides, and design principles and guidelines developed by academic researchers and usability practitioners. Guidelines for accessibility also have been developed, and a discussion of these guidelines has been included here.

One approach to controlling this quantity of information is to produce a customized style guide to lead you through the design process. This can then act as the basis for your design rationale, which enables you to justify the decisions you have made.

10
Interaction design

1   Introduction

To create a physical UI design, you need to understand how users interact with computer systems. In this chapter, we consider a model of the interaction process known as the **human action cycle**. This builds on the concept of tasks, actions, and goals introduced in Chapter 4. We then consider the model that a designer has of the computer system and how the UI can communicate it to facilitate interaction. Based on this understanding, we then discuss the use of metaphors in UI design.

2   The Human Action Cycle

Users tend to be goal oriented when they use a computer system. In other words, they have something particular they want to achieve by using it. The human action cycle (Norman, 1988) is a psychological model that describes the steps users take when they interact with computer systems. In particular, the cycle shows the way users perform actions and tasks to achieve their goals. We have adapted the human action cycle proposed by Norman and shall discuss its significance for understanding the interaction process.

2.1   The Details of the Human Action Cycle

The flow of the activities in the human action cycle is illustrated in Figure 10.1. This shows that the user:

- Forms a goal
- Creates and executes actions that move toward that goal
- Perceives and interprets the outcome of executing the actions to see whether the goal will be achieved as anticipated
- Recognizes that if the goal cannot be achieved, it may have to be reformulated and the cycle repeated

Thus, the human action cycle involves both cognitive and physical activities.

There are three main stages in the cycle:

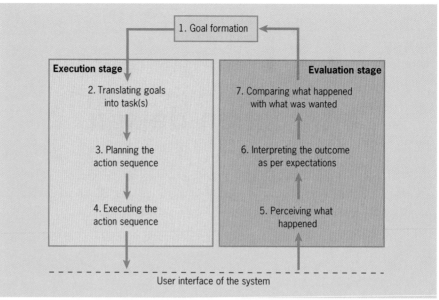

Figure 10.1 The human action cycle.

1. *Goal formation.* This constitutes step one, which is a cognitive activity. Users need to be able to form appropriate goal(s) to use the UI effectively.
2. *Execution stage.* This constitutes steps two, three, and four. During the execution stage, the users perform both cognitive and physical activities. Cognitive activities include translating the goals into tasks and planning the action sequences, whereas physical activities involve executing the sequences of actions.
3. *Evaluation stage.* This constitutes steps five, six, and seven. These are all cognitive activities involving checking what has happened and comparing it with the desired outcome (the goal(s) that were formed in step one).

In some cases, the complete cycle will last only a few seconds, and in others it may last hours. For example, if you want to type in a word, you will probably achieve this goal in a few seconds, whereas typing a report will take much longer. As you can see from this example, there will be a hierarchy of goals — for entering letters, words, paragraphs, and so on. Each of these will have associated tasks and actions. This illustrates why task analysis can be such a complex process.

Another interesting aspect of the human action cycle is the flexibility in the execution stage. Once a user has formed his or her goals, there may well be a range of different tasks and task sequences that will enable the user to achieve these goals, and for each of these tasks there may be a range of different possible actions. For example, the user can print from Word by selecting an icon, choosing a menu item, or by using a keyboard shortcut. A user chooses according to his or her knowledge of the UI and whether he or she wants to alter the print settings.

EXERCISE 10.1 (Allow 10 minutes)

Give an example of each of the seven stages of the human action cycle for sending a parcel at a post office.

DISCUSSION

Table 10.1 lists the steps that Jane, for example, would need to take. In reality, the situation may not be this simple. For example, the post office may be closed, in which case Jane would be unable to achieve her goal. In this situation, the goals may have to be reformulated (she may decide to send the parcel via a courier service) or discarded (she may decide not to send the parcel at all).

Table 10.1 The Human–Action Cycle — An Example

The seven steps of the human–action cycle	Example
1. Jane forms a goal.	Post a parcel.
2. Jane formulates the tasks.	Some of the tasks would be Prepare the parcel. Walk to the post office to send the parcel.
3. Jane specifies the actions.	Some of the actions would be Pick up the parcel. Walk to the front door. Open the front door. Lock the front door behind her.
4. Jane does the actions.	Jane hands over the parcel to the counter assistant. The counter assistant weighs the parcel. The counter assistant affixes the required postage stamps. Jane pays for the postage.
5. Jane perceives the outcome.	Jane observes that the counter assistant has deposited the parcel in the mailbag.
6. Jane interprets the outcome.	The parcel is now in the mailbag, ready for the journey to its destination.
7. Jane evaluates the outcome.	The goal of sending the parcel has been achieved.

EXERCISE 10.2 (Allow 10 minutes)

In Chapter 4, we explained how you should use the following three questions to carry out a cognitive walkthrough, as part of the task analysis process:

1. Is the correct action sufficiently evident to the user?
2. Will the user connect the description of the correct action with what she or he is trying to do?
3. Will the user know if she or he has made a right or wrong choice on the basis of the system's response to the chosen action?

How does the human action cycle justify asking these questions?

DISCUSSION

The first and second questions relate to step four in the human action cycle: executing the action sequence. It is possible to execute the action sequence only if the necessary actions are sufficiently evident to the user and the user can connect the description of the correct action with what she or he is trying to do.

The second question also relates to step three: planning the action sequence. The user's understanding of the actions that are available will influence the planning process. Thus, the single-headed arrow linking steps three and four in Figure 10.1 is a simplification.

The third question relates to steps five, six, and seven: perceiving what happened, interpreting the outcomes, and evaluating what happened. The quality of the feedback will influence whether steps five, six, and seven can be carried out successfully. Confusing or limited feedback may mean that the user cannot perceive or interpret what has happened.

As you can see, the human action cycle helps to explain why the three questions asked during cognitive walkthroughs are so powerful.

2.2 Using the Human Action Cycle to Influence the Design Process

You can see from the human action cycle how important it is to design a UI that helps the users achieve their goals. One way to critically evaluate this aspect of a UI prototype is to walk through the prototype, checking to see if it satisfies the requirements of a use scenario and asking questions based on the human action cycle. Answering these questions can provide you with various types of information:

*   You may be able to predict difficulties that the users may face with the design and suggest modifications.
*   You may be able to suggest suitable changes in the users' environment and the system's technology.
*   You may be able to suggest necessary skills for the users when they work with the UI, or identify training needs.

This section was strongly influenced by Newman and Lamming (1995) and Hackos and Redish (1998).

In addition, you may come up with new requirements for the UI design or changes to the existing requirements. As we have emphasized throughout, developing UIs is an iterative process, so when you are designing, you may well have to go back to the requirements-gathering stage and make some changes. Table 10.2 lists some of the questions you could ask when walking through a prototype.

In Table 10.3 we suggest some solutions that you should consider when you encounter difficulties in the walkthrough and where in the book to look for further help. This list of possible remedies is not comprehensive. It is only indicative and should encourage you to come up with your own remedies, depending on your particular users, the tasks they are carrying out, and the environment in which they are working.

We shall introduce further design issues, principles, and guidelines in the remainder of Part 3, which you could apply depending on your particular circumstances. These include the choice of metaphor and interaction style; the choice of interaction devices; the effective use of text, color, sound, and moving images; and good GUI and web page design. All of these have an impact on a system's usability.

> ### EXERCISE 10.3 (Allow five minutes)
>
> Look at the TV remote control handset in Figure 10.2. Use the human action cycle to step through lowering the volume. Which stage in the cycle highlights the confusing nature of the design? How would you improve the design?
>
> ### DISCUSSION
>
> When you plan the action sequence, it becomes apparent that the labeling of the increase and decrease volume buttons is unclear. The danger is that a user will push the button indicated by the arrow. This will increase the volume. In Figure 10.2, the letter *V* for volume is on the two volume-control buttons. Although the buttons are shaped like up and down arrows for increasing and decreasing the volume, the letter *V* suggests a down arrow. When users scan the remote control for a down arrow, they perceive the *V* as a down arrow and press it. Unfortunately, the first *V* visible is on the up arrow button.
>
> Instead of the large *V* on the volume-control buttons, "vol" in smaller letters could be used as a label. In general, a control's features — such as placement, labeling, size, and color — need to work together to show how to use the control. In this example, the shape and the label convey conflicting information.

3   Communicating the Designer's Understanding of the System

In Chapter 4, we considered the user's understanding of the UI. We referred to this as a mental model or, more briefly, as a model. We all develop these models, albeit unconsciously, from our day-to-day experiences. We then apply these models to

Table 10.2 Questions to Ask According to the Stage in the Human–Action Cycle

Step in the goal formation and execution stages	Questions
1. Forming a goal.	Do the users have sufficient domain and task knowledge and sufficient understanding of their work to form goals? Does the UI help the users form these goals?
2. Translating the goal into a task or a set of tasks.	Do the users have sufficient domain and task knowledge and sufficient understanding of their work to formulate the tasks? Does the UI help the users formulate these tasks?
3. Planning an action sequence.	Do the users have sufficient domain and task knowledge and sufficient understanding of their work to formulate the action sequence? Does the UI help the users formulate the action sequence?
4. Executing the action sequence.	Can typical users easily learn and use the UI? Do the actions provided by the system match those required by the users? Are the affordance and visibility of the actions good? Do the users have an accurate mental model of the system? Does the system support the development of an accurate mental model?
5. Perceiving what happened.	Can the users perceive the system's state? Does the UI provide the users with sufficient feedback about the effects of their actions?
6. Interpreting the outcome according to the users' expectations.	Are the users able to make sense of the feedback? This depends on both the users and the UI. If the task is complex and the users have not been trained, they may be unable to interpret the outcome of their actions. Does the UI provide enough feedback for this interpretation?
7. Evaluating what happened against what was wanted.	Can the users compare what happened with what they were hoping to achieve? This depends on their domain and task knowledge and their understanding of their work, as well as the feedback from the UI.

Table 10.3 Solutions to Problems That May Arise When Walking through the Human Action Cycle

Problem	Cause	Solution	Where to look for help
The user cannot form the goal or formulate the tasks and action sequence needed to achieve it.	Users have insufficient domain or task knowledge, or do not documentation or the skills required for the work.	Provide additional documentation or training in the domain.	
	The UI does not provide the necessary support for the users.	Redesign the UI so that it suggests possible goals, tasks, and actions.	Chapter 11 for interaction styles.
The users are unable to execute the desired action sequence for the task.	The users find the UI difficult to use.	Provide additional documentation or training in the use of the UI.	Chapter 5 for an explanation of visibility, affordance, and feedback.
		Ensure the UI is well designed and uses all the appropriate design principles and guidelines.	Chapter 9 for an explanation of design guidances, design principles, and acessibility guidelines.
	The UI does not support the necessary actions.	Redesign the UI so it supports the actions that users are likely to need.	Chapter 8 for conceptual design. Also, Chapter 4 on task analysis.
	The users have an incorrect mental model of the system.	Redesign the UI so that it supports the users' mental models.	The discussion of mental models and metaphors later in this chapter.
The users are unable to perceive the system's state.	The UI provides insufficient or inappropriate feedback about the effect of the users' actions and the current system state.	Redesign the UI so that it provides adequate feedback.	Chapter 5 for an explanation of feedback. Chapter 9 for design principles.
The users are unable to interpret the outcome or compare the outcome with their goals.	Users have insufficient domain or task knowledge or do not have the skills required for the work.	Provide additional documentation or training in the domain.	

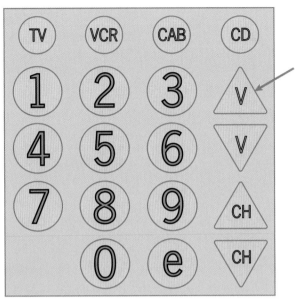

Figure 10.2 Lowering the volume on a television.

similar situations in order to predict outcomes. To interact effectively with a UI, we need an accurate model of its behavior. Here we consider a view developed by Norman and Draper (1986). It is illustrated in Figure 10.3.

Norman and Draper described the three elements in Figure 10.3 as follows:

- *The designer's model.* This is the designer's understanding of a system. It includes both the structural and functional aspects of the system — both how it works and how to operate it. The designer's model is usually complete and correct.
- *The user's model.* This is the user's understanding of the system. Typically it contains mainly functional information, possibly incomplete and incorrect.
- *The system image.* This includes the UI, supporting documentation, training, and so on. The purpose of the system image is to communicate enough of the designer's model to the users so that they can create an accurate mental model of the system. The design of the system image should also take into account the users' existing knowledge of the area.

Let's look at each of these elements briefly, considering how the system image can promote a more accurate user model and hence improve the interaction between the user and the computer system.

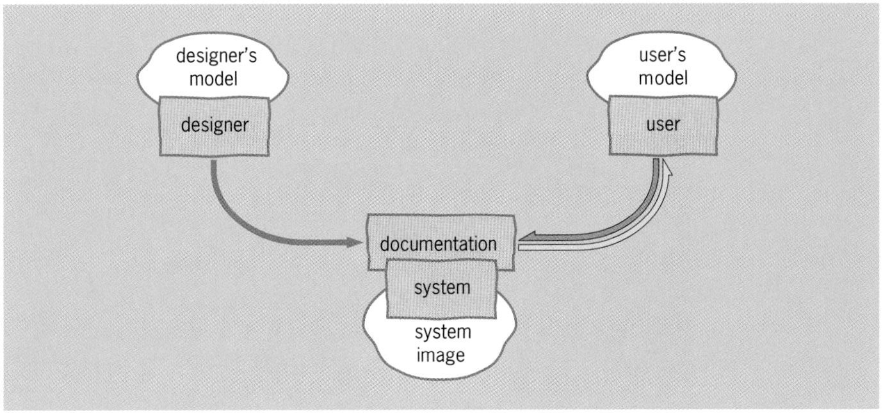

Figure 10.3 The designer's model, the user's model, and the system image. (From Norman and Draper, 1986.)

3.1 Designer's Model

The **designer's model** is an explicit and consciously developed model, derived from:

- The structure and organization of the UI, as represented by the content diagram (for more detail on the content diagram and conceptual design, see Chapter 8)
- An understanding of the domain and the system's purpose and functionality
- An understanding of users' requirements, their characteristics, tasks, and expectations of the new system
- The system's technology and the environment
- Any hardware platform or implementation constraints or any trade-offs

For example, the designer's model of a car might include a knowledge of the way the engine, brakes, steering, and other parts operate; a knowledge of the design of other cars; and a knowledge of how to drive a car. The designer's model is typically not the same as the user's model, as it contains much more detail than the user would normally require. As cars become increasingly reliable, most drivers just need to know how to drive the car.

This list indicates that the requirements-gathering activity of the life cycle is important to the development of the designer's model. It is during this stage that the designer meets the users, observes them, and talks to them.

3.2 System Image

The **system image** is the means by which the functionality and state of a system is presented to the user, and this can be through a variety of channels: the UI, training, documentation including instruction manuals, and online help.

The users acquire their knowledge of the system from the system image. The most important part of the system image is the UI since, through interaction with it, users build up their own mental model of the system and how it works. Users do not always read instruction documents, use the help function, or receive training. Therefore, the maximum burden of influencing the user's mental model is on the UI.

Norman and Draper (1986) noted:

> *[I]n many ways, the primary task of the designer is to construct an appropriate System Image, realising that everything the user interacts with helps to form that image: the physical knobs, dials, keyboards, and displays, and the documentation, including instruction manuals, help facilities, text input and output, and error messages.*

They go on to discuss the implications for the system designer:

> *If one hopes for the user to understand the system, to use it properly, and to enjoy using it, then it is up to the designer to make the system image explicit, intelligible, and consistent. And this goes for everything associated with the system.*

Because it is the system image and largely the UI that influence the users' mental models, the designers needs to translate their knowledge of users' mental models onto the design of the UI. For an effective, efficient, and satisfying user–computer system interaction, it is important for you, as a designer, to understand the users' mental models.

EXERCISE 10.4 (Allow five minutes)

Choose a system that you use either at home or at your workplace. List the constituents of its system image. How well does the system image communicate the designer's model? You might like to consider, say, a toaster.

DISCUSSION

Caroline writes: The system image of the toaster in my kitchen comprises the following:

- Written instructions on the box that the toaster came in and in a small leaflet in the box (both long since discarded)
- A small rotary dial with some markings
- Two extra buttons, one marked RESET and another with a snowflake symbol
- A slot across the top long enough and wide enough for a slice of bread
- A lever-knob on the side that lowers the bread into the slot
- Feedback from the system — a clicking noise while the bread is being toasted, the sound of the bread being popped up, the appearance of the freshly cooked toast, and the smell of toast (or, sometimes, of burning bread)

> Usually I rely on the putting the bread in the slot and pushing down on the lever knob. Sometimes I recall that RESET will pop up the toast if I press it. I often forget to press the snowflake button (the snowflake is a symbol for frozen bread), so I have to toast the bread twice (two loops around the human action cycle) to get the desired level of doneness. Sometimes this goes wrong, and I end up with burnt toast. The two extra buttons accurately communicate that two further functions are available, but they are less satisfactory as reminders of what the functions are or when the functions might be needed. The written instructions are no longer any use at all because I have thrown them away.

For brevity, we concentrate on the UI, but as a designer you should consider all the system image elements.

3.3 How the User Interface Enables the User to Develop an Accurate Mental Model

As Figure 10.3 illustrates, the UI needs to take the following points into account:

1. *The existing user model.* The users will have expectations of the UI, and if these are not met they may experience difficulties.
2. *The designer's model.* The UI needs to communicate effectively the relevant parts of the designer's model, in particular the functional aspects — how the users need to operate the UI in order to achieve their goals.

In this section, we concentrate on taking the existing user model into account when designing a UI. Communicating the designer's model through the UI is a matter of good design.

When confronted with a new computer system, users — often unconsciously — "run" their existing mental model to interpret the new situation, explain it, and make predictions about the outcome of their interaction with the system. The mental model helps the users to answer questions such as "What am I now seeing?" "What did the system just do?" and "What have I done to make it do that?"

> **EXERCISE 10.5 (Allow five minutes)**
>
> Consider the process of buying a train ticket from a railway clerk. You probably have a mental model of this process. How would this mental model help you purchase a ticket from an automatic ticket machine?
>
> **DISCUSSION**
>
> Your mental model probably includes telling the clerk where you are going, specifying the type of fare (single, return, off peak, etc.), and paying. You probably then expect the clerk to give you the ticket and a receipt. Therefore, in your head, you know what is involved in buying a ticket. You have a mental model of the process.

Suppose you want to buy a train ticket from a self-service ticket machine. From your original mental model, you probably know what you must do to get the ticket. You might anticipate the following: pressing various buttons to enter the information that you would have said to the railway clerk, inserting the money or a credit card into a slot and taking the ticket and receipt from other slots in the machine. In this way you are able to apply your old mental model of buying a ticket from a railway clerk to this situation of interacting with a machine.

This may work perfectly well, or it may cause problems if the automated machine wants information in a different order such as requiring ticket type before destination.

When users interact with a new computer system, they apply their old (existing) mental models and expect the new system to work in a way that their mental models suggest. For this reason, it is important to take into account the users' prior knowledge and experience when designing a new UI. Users may become uncertain if their existing mental models do not explain how to use a new system (unless they can develop a new model quickly). They may proceed hesitantly and become frustrated, perhaps abandoning the new system entirely because it is unfamiliar.

EXERCISE 10.6 (Allow 10 minutes)

How might an inaccurate mental model of a television and video recorder create problems for users? Relate these problems to each stage in the human action cycle.

DISCUSSION

Problems may arise as follows:

- *Forming a goal.* The users may not know what is a reasonable goal. For example, they may want to surf the Web on a television that is not equipped for this.
- *Translating the goal into a task or a set of tasks.* Users may not have a clear view of the tasks needed. For example, with some video recorders it is possible to record television programs by entering a code; others will require entry of the date, start time, end time, and channel.
- *Planning the action sequence.* The method for carrying out a particular task may be unexpected. For example, programming the time to record a television program may involve stepping through the times using arrow keys on the remote control, which may be a surprise to a user who is used to typing in the times using buttons on the remote control.
- *Executing the action sequence.* The UI may not appear to support the actions required. For example, the user may expect the volume control on a handset to be represented by two buttons, one with a ∧ for louder, the other with a ∨ for quieter. In reality, these may be represented by two buttons, with a + and –, respectively.

- *Perceiving what happened.* No problems resulting from an incorrect mental model should arise here.
- *Interpreting what happened.* If the feedback does not match the users' expectations, they will probably misinterpret it. For example, suppose you expect a red light to flash when an error has occurred when you are programming a video recorder, but on this particular video recorder the light flashes when it is programmed successfully. You might assume that you have failed and keep on trying.
- *Comparing (evaluating) what happened with what was wanted (the goal).* A user who has incorrectly interpreted the feedback may not be sure whether she or he has satisfied the goal. In the previous example, the user is unsure whether he or she has successfully programmed the video recorder.

To take into account the user's model, you need to consider a number of design issues:

- *Matching the users' expectations.* As a designer, if you are aware of the users' expectations, then you will be able to create a UI design that is more immediately understandable and easier to learn. It may not always be possible for you to exactly match the UI to the users' expectations, either because of technological constraints or because the system requirements are different, but it is always worth trying.
- *Shaping the user's model.* A user may find a system daunting if it includes a lot of functions. One way to overcome this is to organize the UI so that the familiar functions are easy to pick out. This means the user can gain confidence in using these functions before moving on to the unfamiliar functions. For example, on a cell phone it should be immediately apparent how to dial a number, so users can try this before experimenting with more advanced features such as changing the ringing tone.
- *Flexibility.* Typically, the user's model is not static but grows through interaction with the UI. A user slowly develops a picture of what is in the system, what it is capable of doing, and how it responds to various actions. Since user's models change with time, the designer should create a flexible UI — for example, providing different ways of accomplishing the same tasks to suit both novices and experts.

In conclusion, the designer's aim is to create a UI that effectively communicates his or her model while reflecting an awareness of the user's existing mental model.

4 **Using Metaphors to Develop Accurate Mental Models**

In the previous section, we emphasized the importance of designing a UI that matches the users' mental models or supports the adaptation of the users' mental models toward the one desired. In this section, we show you how metaphors can help users develop accurate mental models.

4.1 The Benefits of Metaphor

Hackos and Redish (1998) and Neale and Carroll (1997) strongly influenced the content of this section.

Webster's Third New International Dictionary defines **metaphor** as follows:

A figure of speech in which a word or phrase denoting one kind of object or action is used in place of another to suggest a likeness or analogy between them.

There is a sense in which everything generated by a computer is metaphorical. Even the text on the screen could be seen as a metaphor for text on paper, and the command line interaction style, which will be described in Chapter 11, could be seen as a metaphor for a conversation between the computer and the user. All UIs are artificial environments created by the computer, which we can understand only because of our experience of the physical world.

In this context, we use the word metaphor in a more restricted way, to refer to the metaphorical use of the following elements. These elements are often combined to create an integrated environment. Probably the best-known example of this is Microsoft Windows:

- Words on the screen, such as screen titles and labels (for example, the use of the word "shop" in an e-commerce web site)
- Static images and icons, such as the printer icon in Word
- Interactive graphics, such as the calculator that comes with Windows

These elements are metaphorical when the designer deliberately draws on the users' existing knowledge to enable the user to formulate an accurate mental model of the UI.

Metaphors are often used to unify UIs. Consider the example of e-shopping. The experience of shopping online — selecting goods, proceeding to the checkout, and entering details of your credit card and delivery address — is very different from the shopping experience in a physical store. To help bridge this gap, many e-shopping (or e-commerce) sites present a shopping metaphor by using terminology, icons, and graphics that are analogous to shopping in the real world. For example, Figure 10.4 shows a page from the Amazon web site. In this, the shopping basket acts as a metaphor. Shoppers are familiar with putting items to be purchased into a basket when they shop in a store. When they are shopping on the Amazon web site, it is possible to put the selected items into the virtual basket. The content of the basket is then displayed before the consumers purchase the items. The shopping metaphor is further reinforced by the use of metaphorical language, such as "shop" and "store."

EXERCISE 10.7 (Allow five minutes)

Explain why the following are being used metaphorically and how this enables the user to develop a more accurate mental model of the UI.

- The word "shop" in an e-commerce web site
- The printer icon in Word
- The calculator that comes with Windows XP

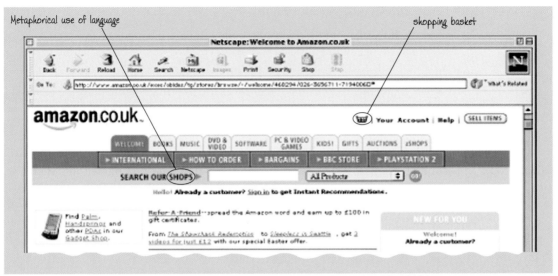

Figure 10.4 A shopping basket metaphor. (From www. amazon.co.uk, December 18, 2000.)

DISCUSSION

- Most people who are likely to use the web are also likely to have visited an ordinary non-web shop. They know what to do in a shop: for example wandering around to see what is for sale, picking up the items they want, and going to the checkout to pay. All this is brought to mind when the word "shop" is used in an e-commerce site, so the users know what to expect when they are using the site.
- The printer icon illustrates a printer, probably not exactly like the user's printer but near enough to be recognizable. As the most common use for a printer is printing, it is likely that the user will assume that selecting this icon will cause a document to be printed.
- The calculator looks very much like a conventional handheld calculator. Thus, users who are familiar with handheld calculators will assume that it operates in an analogous manner, which it does. This makes it extremely easy to use. It also presents an integrated and consistent UI.

4.2 Problems with Metaphor

As you can see, metaphors can be extremely powerful, and it would be easy to conclude that they are the solution to all UI problems. Unfortunately, it is not that simple. The following sections describe two important classes of problem that can arise when using metaphors.

▶ Metaphors That Do Not Match the Users' Experience of the World

When you choose a metaphor, you deliberately choose one that will exploit the users' existing knowledge of the physical analogue. This knowledge brings with it expectations about how to interact with the metaphor.

However, many metaphors do not behave as the user might anticipate. For example, the Windows calculator can be changed from a conventional calculator to a scientific calculator. Although this is unexpected, it is extremely useful. Thus, metaphors are often developed beyond what occurs in the physical world, taking advantage of the power of the computer. This means that the metaphor is more useful, but it risks becoming less usable. For example, the researcher who first named the Microsoft graphical UI "window" may have considered it a metaphor, from windows in a house. When you open a window, a new view emerges, just as when you open the curtains in a house. However, the metaphor starts to break down quickly, because you cannot reduce the windows in a house to icons or move them around the walls.

Adhering to a metaphor too rigidly can be just as problematic, possibly requiring the inefficient use of the system. For example, pressing the printer icon in Word is a slow operation, as in most cases it requires you to move your hand from the keyboard to the mouse, move the mouse pointer, and click a button. For experienced users, a faster way to achieve the same thing is to press ⟨ctrl⟩ p, but this bypasses the metaphor.

As a designer, you need to decide how consistent a metaphor is going to be with the physical analogue and whether the similarities or differences are going to significantly decrease the usability of the UI. If they are, you should consider alternative approaches.

Box 10.1	**The Apple Trash Can**

The trash can on the Apple desktop is a classic example of a designer's metaphor that confounded users' expectations. The trash can is illustrated in Figure 10.5. Apple designers worked with two rules for the design of desktop objects: that each object has only one function and that they minimize the number of objects on the desktop. When they created the desktop metaphor, they chose to compromise between creating a minimum number of desktop objects and keeping one function per object. They gave the trash can two functions: to delete files and folders from the desktop and to eject floppy disks. This confused the users. The trash can being associated with deleting files and folders is understandable, and users had no trouble with that. However, they could not associate it with ejecting a disk. Some users thought that they would lose the contents of the disk if they used the trash can.

Figure 10.5
The Apple trash can.

▶ **Metaphors That Relate to Objects or Concepts That Are Outside the User's Experience**

There is no point in using a metaphor if the physical analogue is outside the user's experience. For example, many dialog boxes in Windows contain "radio buttons." This metaphor comes from early radios that used mechanical buttons for selecting wavelengths. The physical design meant that only one of these could be depressed at a time. However, most buttons on radios are now electronic and do not have this built-in limitation, so increasingly users will not encounter buttons of this type. Thus, the metaphor is becoming dated. This is probably why radio buttons are increasingly referred to as "option buttons."

There are many reasons why your users may be unfamiliar with a particular metaphor, including, for instance, cultural differences or age differences. These differences should become apparent during requirements gathering.

When users are unfamiliar with a metaphor, it may not mean that they are unable to use it; rather they will have to learn it, just like any other UI. How many users are able to use the scroll bar because it is like a scroll of paper? Not many, we suspect. Users are either taught or work it out through a process of trial and error. If too many of your users are doing this, it calls into question whether it is worth using the metaphor at all.

4.3 Choosing a Suitable Metaphor or Set of Metaphors

As with other activities in the design of UIs, the approach to the choice of metaphors should be iterative and user centered. You may come up with several to start with, then retain some and reject others. During requirements gathering, the analysis of users, tasks, and environment may provide ideas for metaphors that could be used in the UI design. In particular, the task scenarios and use cases are often a good source of metaphors. Conversations during requirements gathering may also give you an insight into the metaphors that users tend to employ.

> **EXERCISE 10.8 (Allow five minutes)**
>
> Imagine you are designing a web site for a supermarket. The web site allows users to select items they would like to purchase and have them delivered to their homes. Suggest a possible interactive metaphor based on graphics, and identify two possible problems with its use.
>
> **DISCUSSION**
>
> One metaphor would be an interactive image of the supermarket's layout that allows users to focus on particular aisles and shelves within the aisles. Users then choose their purchases. This would work well for customers who know the store well, but it could be confusing for those who do not — how would they know where to look? This approach could also be slow, as it would probably mean

downloading several web pages to make the purchases. It might be better to have an alphabetical list of the categories of products available. After all, most customers are likely to know the names of items and can just search the list.

When you are designing a metaphor, it is a good idea to walk through some use scenarios with the users. You do not have to draw the UI design in detail to get useful feedback; the idea is just to get a feel for how the metaphor may be presented. You can *then* make appropriate changes. In particular, you are looking to find out how easily those who are unfamiliar with the physical analogue can learn the metaphor.

We look at more examples of metaphor in Chapter 16.

Though metaphors are popular with many designers, you should not feel compelled to use one. Good UI design does not always start with a suitable metaphor. The important issue is not whether there is a metaphor or even a whole set of metaphors incorporated into a UI, but whether the interface is usable.

5 Summary

In this chapter, we have considered a model of the interaction process known as the human action cycle, and we have discussed the use of mental models and metaphors for UI design. In the next chapter, we turn our attention to interaction styles, which are the different ways by which a user and computer system can interact.

11
Interaction styles

1 Introduction

To create a physical UI design, you need to understand how users interact with computer systems. In the previous chapter, we discussed the human action cycle and the role of mental models and metaphor in UI design. In this chapter, we will look at the different interaction styles available to designers for facilitating communication between a user and a computer system.

2 Interaction Styles

There are different ways a user can communicate with a computer system and a computer system can communicate with a user. These are called **interaction styles.**

The content of this section was strongly influenced by Dix *et al.* (2004) and Shneiderman (1995, 1998).

An interaction style is a collection of user interface controls and their associated behavior. The interaction style provides both the look (appearance) and feel (behavior) of the user interface components, indicating the way a user will communicate with the system.

There are several interaction styles from which a designer can choose. In this chapter, we present five interaction styles in detail:

- Command line
- Menu selection
- Form-fill
- Direct manipulation
- Anthropomorphic

In Chapter 12, you will learn about the relation between the interaction styles and the interaction devices that support them.

We discuss these interaction styles and the factors that help designers choose between them. We also show how the different interaction styles can be combined. These explanations should help you to choose one or more interaction styles to meet the needs of your users and their tasks.

The choice of interaction style will also depend on the choice of interaction devices (both input and output devices), and vice versa.

2.1 Command Line

The **command line** interface was the first interactive dialog style to be commonly used. It provides a means of directly instructing the system, using function keys on a keyboard (F1, F8, etc.), single characters, abbreviations, or whole-word commands. As the user types characters onto the screen, they appear as a line across the screen, hence the term "command line."

Command line interfaces are powerful because they offer access to system functionality. They are also flexible: the command often has a number of options or parameters that will vary its behavior in some way, and it can be applied to many objects at once, making it useful for repetitive tasks. However, this flexibility and power, as we will discuss, is difficult to learn to use.

Consider the Command Prompt window in Figure 11.1. At the top of the screen you can see that initially the default drive for receiving commands was C, indicated by the prompt C:\>. The command dir at the C prompt has given a listing of the folders and files stored on the C drive. The command A: has set the current drive to A, and the command copy report.doc C:\Public\ has copied a file from the A drive into the directory called Public on the C drive.

Toward the bottom of the screen, the command C: has reset the current drive to C. The > symbol indicates that the system is waiting to receive a command; the line after

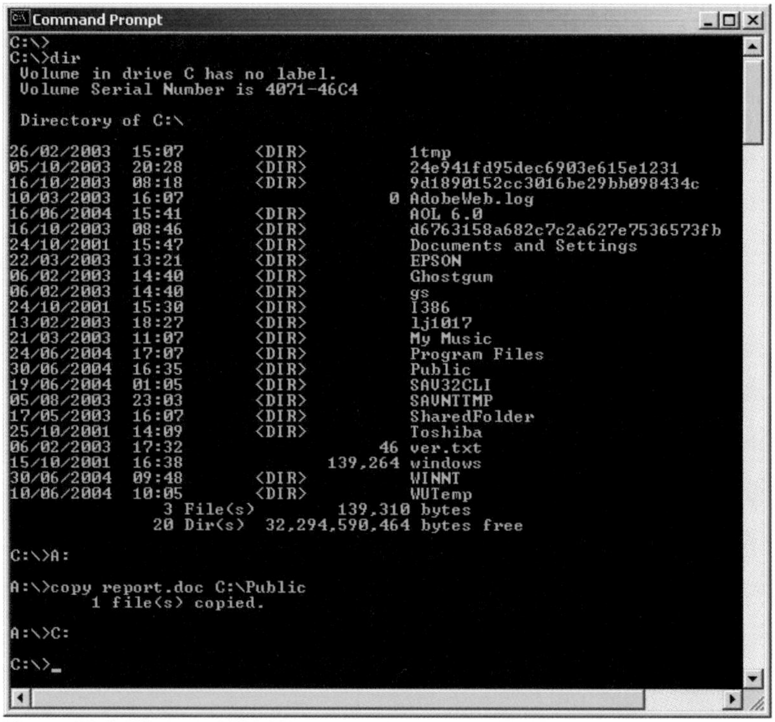

Figure 11.1 Windows 2000/XP command prompt window.

the > is the cursor, which, in real time, will be blinking or flashing to indicate where a command should be entered.

One limitation of command line UIs is that the commands need to be remembered, as no cue is provided to indicate which commands are available. So users have to remember command sequences, which are often cryptic with complex syntax. Commands are often obscure and vary between systems, causing the users to become confused and making commands difficult to learn. Users' frustration with command line interfaces often occurs because of the memory and typing demands and the low tolerance of errors shown by this type of interface — a confusing error message is often the consequence of a single typing mistake in a long command. The use of consistent and meaningful commands and abbreviations can help alleviate this problem.

Box 11.1 provides a set of guidelines for designing command line interfaces. The guidelines in this table, and those for the other interaction styles, are by no means exhaustive. They are listed here to guide your thinking so that you can come up with suitable design strategies relevant to the system that you are designing and for the interaction style that you have chosen. The seven design principles we have taught so far (affordance, visibility, feedback, simplicity, structure, consistency, and tolerance) apply to all interaction styles.

Command line interfaces are better for expert users than for novices. For expert users, command languages provide a sense of being in control. Users learn the syntax and can express complex possibilities rapidly, without having to read distracting prompts. However, error rates are typically high, training is necessary, and retention may be poor. Error messages and online assistance are hard to provide because of the diverse possibilities and the complexity of mapping from tasks to interface (command) concepts and syntax.

Box 11.1	**Guidelines for Designing Command Line Interfaces**

- Choose meaningful commands — use specific and distinctive names.
- Follow consistent syntax (grammatical structure) for all commands.
- Support consistent rules for abbreviation.
- Give commands a representative (inherent) meaning; for example, use commands such as add, plot, and print.
- Make commands as short as possible to help prevent entry errors and to facilitate the detection and correction of errors.
- If commands or responses to commands can be abbreviated, use common abbreviations, for example *Y* for yes and *N* for no.
- Limit the number of commands and ways of accomplishing a task.
- Offer frequent users the capability to create macros. A **macro** is a set of commands that can be called by a name to be executed in one step; they are useful for combining commands that are to be performed in a strict sequence. The use of macros saves typing effort and means that the user does not have to memorize long command sequences.

EXERCISE 11.1 (Allow five minutes)

Use the human–action cycle to critique the command line interaction style.

DISCUSSION

- *Forming a goal.* A novice user may not know what is a reasonable goal with the particular computer system, and the system provides no guidance — just a prompt.
- *Translating the goal into a task or set of tasks.* The user may not know what tasks are needed, and the UI does not provide any guidance.
- *Planning the action sequence.* This needs to be done from memory — the user needs to remember all the necessary commands and syntax.
- *Executing the action sequence.* Typically this involves using a keyboard and accurate typing. Mistakes usually result in error messages.
- *Perceiving what happened.* The feedback is often limited, sometimes nonexistent. For example, when copying a file, a user may find that there is no confirmation that the operation has been carried out successfully.
- *Interpreting what happened.* Interpreting such limited feedback can be difficult, and, if so, it is difficult for the user to develop an accurate mental model.
- *Comparing (evaluating) what happened with what was wanted (the goal).* Again this is difficult if the feedback is limited.

2.2 Menu Selection

Menu selection avoids many of the problems associated with command line interfaces. A menu is a set of options from which the user must choose. Typically, the interface displays the options as menu items or icons and the user indicates a choice with a pointing device or keystroke, receiving feedback that indicates which option he or she has chosen, and the outcome of the command being executed. Menu selection does not have to be visual. When you telephone a bank, for example, it is common to have speech interfaces, which require you to choose between several options.

Menus are effective because they offer cues for user recognition rather than forcing the users to recall the syntax of a command from memory. If the items are meaningful to the users, then menu selection can be rapid and accurate. If the items are hard to understand or appear similar to each other, users can become confused and make errors. This means that if menus are to be effective, their names or icons should be self-explanatory.

Menu selection can be advantageous, as it decomposes a complex interaction into a series of smaller steps and provides a structure for decision making. Menu selection is particularly effective when users have little training, use a system intermittently, are unfamiliar with the terminology, or need help to structure their decision-making process. On the other hand, the same decomposition process can be too rigid for some users, and it may slow the knowledgeable frequent user. With the careful design of complex menus and techniques such as shortcuts, menu selection can become appealing even for expert users.

EXERCISE 11.2 (Allow five minutes)

Assume that you are designing the user interface for a public information kiosk in a railway station. The system should enable the user to plan a bus route between two places in the area surrounding the station. Consider how to design this interface, first using a menu selection system, then using a command line system.

DISCUSSION

One possible menu design could provide the names of places as menu items on a screen for the user to indicate where the journey starts and where it ends. The user could press a "full route" button to see the bus route along with the timings presented on the screen.

If the same interface were designed using a command line interface, it would require users to recall and enter the command for finding the bus route. How would the users know which commands to use? Public information systems such as these have no help or documentation facility. If we assume that the users know the commands, they would have to enter the full names or abbreviated names of the places. Typing mistakes might occur. Users would also have to make many input keystrokes rather than just indicate the options from the menus. Most users would prefer a menu selection interface to a command line interface.

To design effective menu selection interfaces, you should consider menu structure, the sequence and phrasing of menu items, shortcuts through the menus for frequent users, menu layout, graphic menu features, and selection mechanisms. Box 11.2 provides some basic guidelines for designing effective menu selection interfaces. For

Box 11.2	**Guidelines for Designing Menu Selection Interfaces**

- Use task semantics (flow of tasks and interaction) to organize menus.
- Give menu items titles that reflect their functions.
- Group items meaningfully.
- Avoid lengthy menus.
- Order menu items meaningfully.
- Use short names for menu items.
- Use names that reflect the menu items' functions.
- Use consistent grammar, layout, and terminology.
- Provide online context-sensitive help.
- Consider the screen's size when deciding the number of menu items.

designers, menu selection systems require careful task analysis to ensure that all the functions are supported conveniently and that the terminology is chosen carefully and used consistently.

> **EXERCISE 11.3 (Allow five minutes)**
>
> Use the human–action cycle to critique the menu selection interaction style.
>
> **DISCUSSION**
>
> - *Forming a goal.* The UI does not give any real guidance as to the goals that can be achieved, but the menu items may bring some possible goals to mind.
> - *Translating the goal into a task or set of tasks.* The menu items should provide some guidance on how the goal can be achieved.
> - *Planning an action sequence.* Identifying the appropriate actions depends on how well the menu hierarchy has been structured. Ideally, a user should be able to guess where in the hierarchy a particular menu item is. In addition, the menu titles need to be self-explanatory.
> - *Executing the action sequence.* Again, this depends on the menu structure. If it is necessary to keep moving around the hierarchy to complete a task, this can be time consuming and irritating.
> - *Perceiving what happened.* The quality of the feedback varies according to the system. However, menu selection systems are typically more visual than a command line, so this is likely to be better. Also, when a user selects a menu item, there is usually some form of visual confirmation, so at least the user is reassured that he or she has chosen the correct command. The system also needs to show clearly whether the command has been successfully executed and any changes in the system state.
> - *Interpreting what happened.* This depends on the quality of the feedback.
> - *Comparing.* This depends on the quality of the feedback.

2.3 Form-Fill

If your interface has to gather a lot of information from the user, then it often helps if you provide a form to fill in. An example is the web page in Figure 11.2, which collects complaint information about Internet content from Internet users.

The users work through the form, entering appropriate values. Most **form-fill** interfaces allow for easy movement around the form and for some fields to be left blank. Most also include correction facilities, as users may change their minds or make a mistake about the value that belongs in each field.

However, just because it is possible for a users to jump between fields on the form, you should not necessarily allow them do so. For example, if a user is repeatedly entering data from paper forms or another source of information that has a predictable order, then it will help if you mimic this order to ensure the information is always entered into the correct field.

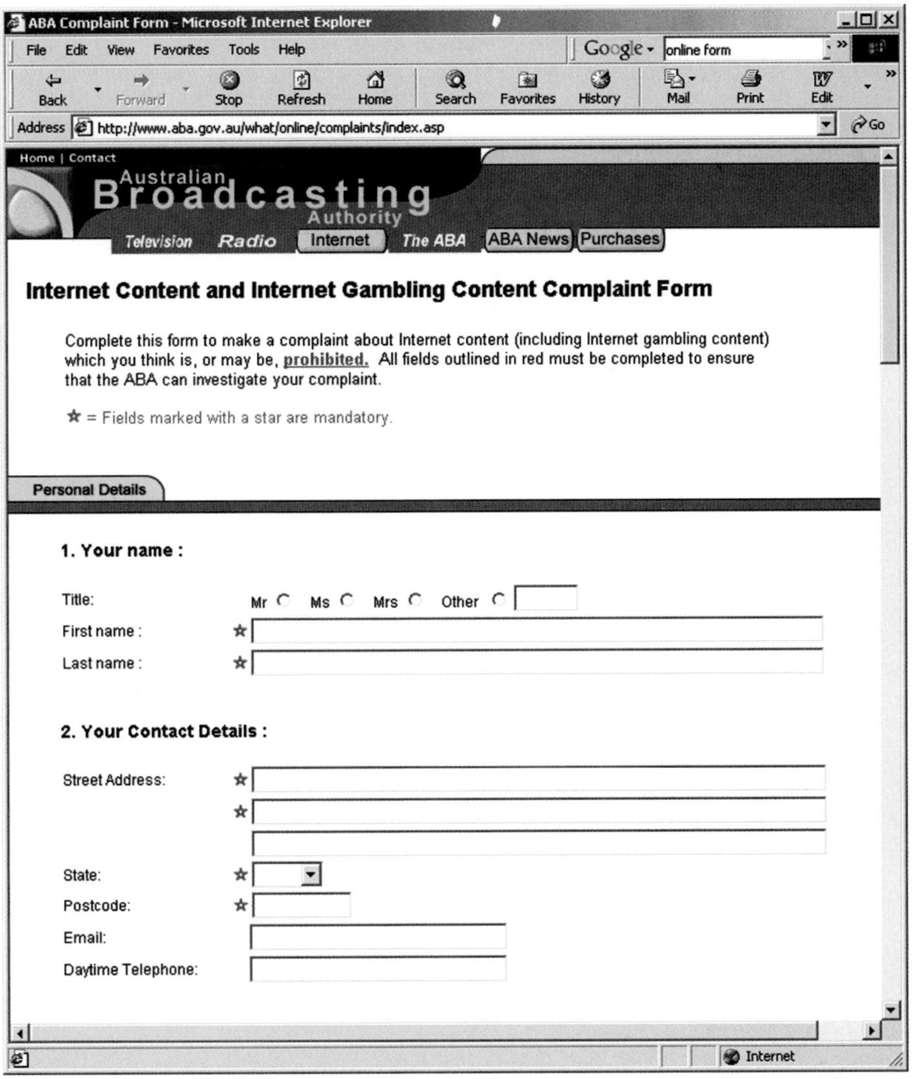

Figure 11.2 Form-fill on the Australian Broadcasting Authority's web site. (Retrieved May 15, 2004.)

There is more information on designing usable forms at www. formsthatwork. com.

The form on the screen is a metaphor for a paper form. A well-designed form-fill interface should help the user to construct an accurate mental model quickly, as most users are familiar with completing forms. This should make using such computer-based forms relatively straightforward.

Box 11.3 provides some guidelines for designing form-fill interfaces.

Box 11.3	**Guidelines for Designing Form-Fill Interfaces**

- Give meaningful titles or labels to the fields.
- Give familiar field labels (use the users' language).
- Provide comprehensible instructions.
- Incorporate a logical grouping and sequencing of the fields.
- Present a visually appealing layout for the form.
- Use consistent terminology and abbreviations.
- Provide white space and boundaries.
- Restrict the characters that can be entered or provide default values.
- Allow for convenient cursor movement.
- Provide error correction for individual characters and entire fields.
- Provide error messages for unacceptable values and error indicators as soon as possible (prompt error messages should identify the field the error occurred in and why).
- Indicate required fields.
- Provide explanatory messages for the fields.

EXERCISE 11.4 (Allow five minutes)

Use the human–action cycle to critique the form-fill interaction style.

DISCUSSION

- *Forming a goal.* Completing a form is usually the only task necessary for the achievement of a goal. The goal will depend on the system. For example, it may be to complain to the Australian Broadcasting Authority about illegal Internet content.
- *Translating the goal into a task or set of tasks.* The task will be completing the form.
- *Planning an action sequence.* The boxes (fields) on the form indicate the necessary actions. This is much easier than for command line or menu selection interfaces.
- *Executing the action sequence.* This depends on the implementation, but it involves moving to each field and entering the data, either by typing or by selecting from a drop-down list box. The latter is an example of a designer blending different interaction styles: form-fill and menu selection.
- *Perceiving what happened.* The quality of the feedback is one of the real strengths of form-fill — you can immediately see what you have entered.
- *Interpreting what happened.* You can check to see whether you have entered the data correctly.
- *Comparing.* If you have entered the data correctly, you are closer to having completed the task and achieving your goal.

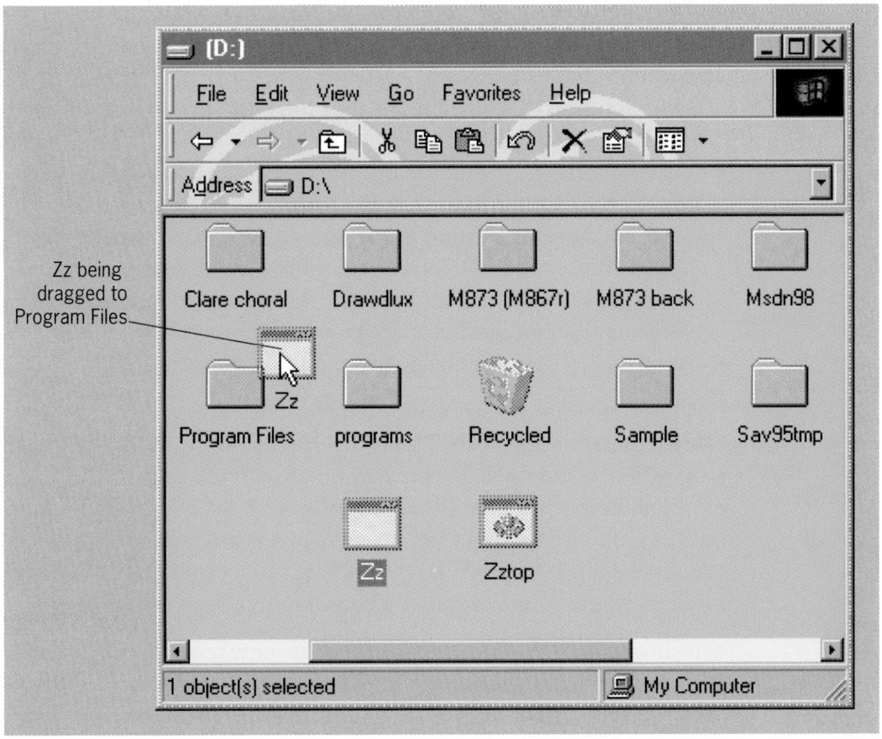

Figure 11.3 Dragging a file from one folder to another in Microsoft Explorer.

2.4 Direct Manipulation

For more
information on
continuous input
devices, see
Chapter 12.

Direct manipulation (DM) interfaces allow users to interact directly with the UI objects — for example, dragging a file from one folder and dropping it into another in Microsoft Explorer, as illustrated in Figure 11.3. In DM interfaces, the keyboard entry of commands or menu choices is replaced by manipulating a visible set of objects and actions. This is usually achieved by using a continuous input device, such as a mouse, pen, or joystick.

DM interfaces exist in many application areas, including word processing, desktop publishing, computer-aided design (CAD), flight simulation, virtual reality systems, and video games. Most word processors are DM interfaces, also called WYSIWYG (what you see is what you get) word processors. These word processors display a document as it will appear when printed, allowing users to make changes directly to it and to view the changes instantly.

Well-designed DM interfaces typically have a number of characteristics:

- There is a visible and continuous representation of the task objects and their actions. Consequently, there is little syntax to remember.
- The task objects are manipulated by physical actions, such as clicking or dragging, rather than by entering complex syntax.

- Operations are rapid, incremental, and reversible; their effects on task objects are immediately visible. Thus, users can instantly see if their actions are furthering their goals and, if they are not, can simply change the direction of their activity. This also means that there are fewer error messages and that the stress on the users is less.
- While interacting with DM interfaces, users feel as if they are interacting with the domain rather than with the interface, so they focus on the task rather than on the technology. There is a feeling of direct involvement with a world of task objects rather than of communication with an intermediary. This means that users gain confidence and mastery because they initiate an action, feel in control, and can predict the system's responses.
- Novices can learn the basic functionality quickly.

DM interfaces often use icons and metaphors to enable the users to develop an accurate mental model quickly. This is true, for example, for dragging a file from one folder to another, as most users will be familiar with the physical analogue that the images on the screen represent. Thus, DM interfaces are based on the idea that users should be allowed to manipulate UIs in a way that is analogous to the way they interact with task objects in everyday life. In this way, they represent a more natural and familiar mode of interacting with the representation of the task objects.

You should note that most embedded systems use a much more literal form of direct manipulation, in which the user presses physical buttons and turns physical dials. In these systems, there is no need for metaphors as the user has the real thing. This sounds ideal, but these systems are less flexible: with a DM interface, it is possible to move buttons around, change their appearance, and so on. Many embedded systems use a combination of physical input devices and software-generated buttons.

Box 11.4 provides a few guidelines for designing DM interfaces. There are some other issues we have not mentioned yet. For example, DM interfaces tend to take up a lot of screen space, which might be a problem with a small screen. In addition, what seems intuitive to the designer may not be intuitive to the user. The message is that you should check your design with the users; it is just as easy to design a bad DM interface as any other type of UI.

Box 11.4	Guidelines for Designing Direct Manipulation Interfaces

- Choose any metaphors carefully to ensure that they promote the rapid development of an accurate mental model.
- Create visual representations of the users' tasks.
- Provide rapid, incremental, and reversible actions.
- Replace typing with pointing/selecting.
- Present a visually appealing layout.
- Make the results of actions immediately visible — provide quick visual or auditory feedback.

EXERCISE 11.5 (Allow five minutes)

Use the human–action cycle to critique the DM interaction style.

DISCUSSION

- *Forming a goal.* The different actions suggested by the UI should give some guidance on the various goals that can be achieved.
- *Translating the goal into a task or set of tasks.* Again, the actions available should provide some guidance.
- *Planning an action sequence.* As the possible actions are visible, this should be straightforward.
- *Executing the action sequence.* This is achieved by directly manipulating the task objects.
- *Perceiving what happened.* The effect of the action is immediately visible.
- *Interpreting what happened.* There should be no problem with interpreting the feedback, as the screen should represent the present state.
- *Comparing.* It should be obvious from the visual representation whether or not the goal has been achieved.
- Thus, a well-designed DM interface should help you avoid many of the problems that can arise in the human–action cycle. This is one of the main reasons why DM interfaces are so popular and successful.

2.5 Anthropomorphic

Anthropomorphic interfaces aim to interact with users in the same way that humans interact with each other. Natural language interfaces and interfaces that recognize gestures, facial expressions, or eye movements all belong to this category. The design and development of anthropomorphic interfaces requires an understanding not only of hardware and software, but also of how humans communicate with each other through language, gestures facial expression, and eye contact. Signal must be separated from noise, and meaning must be identified from ambiguous messages.

The design and development of anthropomorphic interfaces represents one of the frontiers of user interface research. Natural language interaction uses a familiar natural language (such as English) to give instructions and receive responses. Research has been carried out over a long period because the use of language as a means of communicating with a computer has been considered highly desirable owing to its naturalness. There are three main ways of entering natural language: speech, handwriting, and typing. For all three, a system needs to be able to cope with vagueness, ambiguity, and ungrammatical constructions. Handwriting and typing overcome the problems associated with speech, such as accent and intonation, but introduce the problem of incorrect spelling. Also, handwriting has the additional problem of illegibility and typing has the problem of keying errors.

In spite of limited success so far, the hope that computers will respond properly to arbitrary natural language phrases or sentences engages many researchers. Typically, natural language interaction provides little context for issuing the next command, frequently requires clarification dialogue, and may be slower and more cumbersome than the other interaction styles. For example, entering natural language using a keyboard can be very time consuming. For users who are novices with the keyboard, it can be quicker to use a menu selection system. For expert computer users, a command language that requires minimum key-pressing may be even quicker.

While it is not yet possible to develop systems that can understand natural language as it is typed, several expert systems and intelligent tutoring systems have been created that use some form of structured subset of a natural language. In these, users are required to learn how to use such a subset language unambiguously and to phrase sentences in a way that the target system can understand.

Although natural language promises flexible and easy communication with computers, most natural language systems developed in the foreseeable future will be restricted to well-defined domains with limited vocabularies.

2.6 Blending Interaction Styles

Most modern UIs blend more than one interaction style. This is true of Windows and most other GUIs. Blending several interaction styles is particularly appropriate when the UI will be used for a wide range of tasks and the experience of the users is varied.

This blending can occur in a variety of ways. For example, commands can lead the user to form-fill where data entry is required, or menus can be used to control an otherwise DM environment when a suitable visualization of actions cannot be found. As we showed earlier, list boxes can supplement form-fill for less knowledgeable users. Similarly, for such users, command line interfaces can be supplemented by a form-fill or a menu selection strategy.

When combining different interaction styles you, as a designer, will have to work from your own experience and intuition. This is in addition to following a user-centered design approach, validating your designs by evaluating them with users. You will learn about conducting evaluations in Part 4.

2.7 Choosing the Most Appropriate Interaction Style

Choosing the most appropriate interaction style is crucial to the success of a UI. Table 11.1 presents a summary of the advantages and disadvantages of the five interaction styles we have discussed in this section.

We omitted any reference to anthropomorphic interfaces in Tables 11.2 and 11.3, as you are unlikely to be in a position to choose one of these. The choice of interaction style may well be different if the users have particular characteristics, as Box 11.5 illustrates.

Table 11.1 The Advantages and Disadvantages of the Five Primary Interaction Styles

Interaction style	Advantages	Disadvantages
Command line	Is versatile and flexible Appeals to expert users Supports users' initiative by allowing them to define macros and shortcuts	Requires substantial training and memorization of commands
Menu selection	Is easy to learn Involves fewer keystrokes than command line Structures decision making by breaking down the functionality into a set of menu items Is good for learners and infrequent users	Presents the danger of creating too many menus and complex menu hierarchies May slow frequent users who would prefer to use commands or shortcuts Consumes screen space
Form-fill	Simplifies data entry May require modest training Assists users by providing defaults (that is, examples of the inputs expected)	Consumes screen space
Direct manipulation	Presents the task concepts visually — the user can see the task objects and act on them directly Is easy to learn Is easy to remember how to use Avoids errors and allows easy recovery from errors if they occur Encourages exploration	Requires graphic displays and continuous input devices Presents the danger that icons and metaphors may have different meanings for different user groups
Anthropomorphic interfaces	Can relieve the burden of learning the syntax for the interaction with the system	Can be unpredictable Difficult to implement

Table 11.2 The Relation between Task Characteristics and Interaction Style

Task characteristics	Interaction style
A large amount of data entry is required	Form-fill or command line
A paper form exists that must be computerized	Form-fill
Familiar notation exists	Command line
A natural visual representation exists, or a modest number of task objects and actions can represent the task domain	Direct manipulation
Multiple decisions or selections from a large range of unfamiliar options are required	Menu selection or direct manipulation
Exploration is anticipated	Direct manipulation

Table 11.2 lists some of the aspects of the task domain that influence the selection of interaction style. The designer needs to have a good understanding of the kinds of task the users will be performing. Similarly, Table 11.3 lists aspects of user characteristics that may infuence the choice of interaction style.

| Box 11.5 | **Computer Technology and the Older Adult** |

The number of older people in the population has been growing and will continue to rise in the next decade, so the issue of aging and computer use is an important area of HCI. We need to understand the implications of age-related changes in functional abilities for the design and implementation of computer systems.

Relatively little research has been done to examine the impact of interface design on the performance of older computer users. Given that there are age-related changes in cognitive processes, such as working memory and selective attention, it is likely that interaction style will have a significant influence on the performance of older people.

One study evaluated the ability of older people to learn a word processing application as a function of the interaction style. The participants interacted with the application using one of three styles: onscreen menus, pull-down menus, and function keys. Those using the pull-down menus performed the word processing tasks more quickly and made fewer errors. They also executed a greater number of successful editorial changes. The researcher hypothesized that the pull-down menu reduced the memory demands of the task, as users did not have to remember editing procedures. Although the onscreen menu provided memory cues, the names of the menu items did not reflect the contents; the user thus had to remember which items were contained in which menu. The names of the pull-down menus were indicative of menu contents.

Another study found that older people had less difficulty with a display editor than with a command-based line editor. The line editor required the user to remember command language and produce complicated syntax. Changes were made with the display editor by positioning a cursor at the required location and using labeled function keys. Thus, there were fewer memory demands associated with the display editor.

Further research examined the differential effect of a command-line interface, a menu interface, and a menu plus icon interface on word processing skill acquisition among a sample of older people. The menu and menu plus icon interfaces produced better performance. The menus provided more environmental support and were associated with fewer memory demands.

Adapted from Czaja (1997).

Table 11.3 Relation between a User's Characteristics and Interaction Style

User's characteristics	Interaction style
Novice	Direct manipulation or menu selection
Modest knowledge of task domain with some computer skills	Form-fill, direct manipulation, or menu selection
Occasional user, knowledgeable	Menu selection, direct manipulation, form-fill, command line with online help, or natural language
Frequent user	Command line with macros, direct manipulation with adequate shortcuts, or form-fill with as much on each screen as possible

3 | Summary

In this chapter, we considered interaction styles, especially command line, menu selection, form-fill, and direct manipulation. To assess how well each interaction style helps users to achieve their goals, we critiqued these interaction styles using the human–action cycle, which was presented in Chapter 10. We also considered, to a lesser degree, anthropomorphic interfaces, as they are less commonly available.

In Chapter 12 we will be looking at hardware design components, such as input and output devices (collectively known as interaction devices), and the issues involved in choosing the most appropriate input and output devices to help users carry out their tasks with the UI.

12

Choosing interaction devices: hardware components

1 Introduction

As we explained in the introduction to Part 3, every UI consists of a mixture of **design components**.

- *Hardware components*. The hardware components are usually referred to as the input/output devices, or **interaction devices**. These may include a keyboard, mouse, joystick, screen, and so on.
- *Software components*. The software components are the aspects of the UI that are generated by the underlying computer program, such as the image on the screen and the sounds from the speakers. Thus, these include the layout of the screen, use of color, images, text, animation, sound, and video clips.

In this chapter, we will be thinking about choosing hardware components. We will discuss software components in Chapter 13.

2 Choosing Interaction Devices

2.1 Interaction Devices as Tools

When you are hanging shelves on the wall in a house, you need to make a number of decisions about the tools to use. For example, you might choose the size of a screwdriver. This depends on the size of screw you are using, which in turn depends on the way in which you will use the shelf. If you are going to put a set of printed encyclopedias on the shelf, then those screws need to be stronger and more firmly fixed in the wall than if you intend to display some light ornaments. Thus, the choice of tool depends on the precise nature of the task being carried out.

What would happen if you have weak arms? Maybe you would use an electric screwdriver, which would require less physical strength. What if you are working in a small bedroom and have a respiratory complaint, like asthma? You would probably use a face mask to limit the dust inhaled. Thus, the choice of tool also depends on the characteristics of the user and the environment in which the user is working.

In a similar way, when we use a computer we want to achieve something. For example, we may want to enter text, draw a picture, access information, or fly an airplane. Our choice of interaction devices is crucial to how well we can achieve these goals (see Figure 12.1). Thus, writing a manual using a mouse is likely to be slow and frustrating, and drawing plans for an aircraft using a keyboard could be virtually impossible.

To choose between interaction devices, you need to ask the right questions. Some of these questions are driven by the constraints of the technology and others by the uses to which the technology will be put. In the two sections that follow, we consider some of the key questions that you should ask when choosing input and output devices. These questions are only a subset of those that you will need to ask, as every situation depends on the user's goals, the characteristics of the task, the types of user, and the environment in which the devices are being used. These factors are given in the requirements specification.

Figure 12.1 "Darn these hooves! I hit the wrong switch again! Who designs these instrument panels, racoons?"

Box 12.1	**Why Choosing Interaction Devices Matters**

There are circumstances in which choosing the correct device is essential. Users may have particular requirements, so it is important to understand the users of the system and the way in which they use the technology. For example, the messaging company Pitney Bowes carried out a survey of office workers in North America, Britain, and Germany. One of the findings was that Europeans use communications technology very differently from the way North Americans do. In particular, Europeans prefer direct contact using a mobile telephone rather than leaving voicemail messages. The opposite is true for North Americans. The same difference is reinforced by the use of pagers: 20 percent of North Americans use pagers compared with about five percent of Europeans. The implications of these cultural differences are that the technology that a company purchases needs to take into account the way in which the employees will use it. Thus, a European company may prefer to employ a secretary, so that its clients can speak directly to a person; but for North Americans, a voicemail system might suffice.

Or the task may have particular requirements. For example, in a large warehouse, if the boxes were not bar coded, then the employees would need to type in all the details every time a box arrived or was dispatched. With a large warehouse having thousands of these transactions every day, doing this would be time consuming and prone to error.

For more information, see Partridge (1999).

2.2 Why Study Interaction Devices?

You may work for a company that uses a limited range of interaction devices and is unwilling to change them. For example, the purchasing department of the company may always buy a particular make of PC with a screen, keyboard, and mouse. Why? There are probably several good reasons:

- The company may be able to buy the systems more cheaply in bulk.
- Maintaining the PCs will be easier, as technical support will only need to know about one type of system.
- The organization will contain a considerable amount of expertise on the system. For example, it could cost a great deal of money to retrain all the users to operate a different keyboard.
- It is easier to continue with a solution that you are comfortable with than to take the risk of changing.

If this describes your situation, then you may be wondering: what is the point of studying interaction devices when you are unlikely to be able to change them?

Think about the first computer you used. What was it like? Did you have a one-, two- or multiple button mouse? What about a scrolling wheel? If you're older, you may even recall the days before mice, perhaps even the use of paper tape for input and a slow, poor-quality dot-matrix printer. We have moved on from there. A quick glance through any computer hardware catalog will show you that there are printers, mice, and keyboards for all sorts of specialist needs: mobile users, people with large or small hands, people doing presentations. The right technology can give you the edge in a competitive marketplace. This may be true for your company as well.

Box 12.1 gives two examples where using the right technology was particularly important.

3   Input Devices

The distinction between input and output devices is not as clear-cut as we have suggested. It is unusual to encounter a device that is purely one or the other. The keyboard is a good example: when you press a key, you receive tactile and audio feedback when the key clicks. Thus, the keyboard is acting as both an input and output device. Keyboards are predominantly input devices, but this confirmatory feedback is a feature of good design as it confirms that the user has done what she or he intended.

In this section we look at two categories of input device:

1. *Keyboards, keypads, and buttons.* There are a variety of keyboards and keypads. Individual buttons are also used extensively, particularly in embedded computer systems.
2. *Pointing devices.* We divide this category into indirect pointing devices, such as the mouse and joystick, and direct pointing devices, such as the touchscreen and stylus-based systems.

For both categories we consider what the particular devices can best be used for and how to choose between them. We finish by considering some of the more advanced input devices.

3.1 Keyboards, Keypads, and Buttons

Keyboards, keypads, and buttons are all **discrete input devices**. Discrete input devices can be used to enter individual items of information, such as letters and numbers or commands. Thus, a keyboard is good for typing documents and the "on" key on your mobile telephone is good for executing the "switch on telephone" command. None of these devices are ideally suited to continuous tasks such as dragging icons across the screen.

The most sophisticated form of discrete input device is the keyboard. The vast majority of keyboards for use in English-speaking countries have the QWERTY layout, the name being taken from the six keys in the top row of letters, starting from the left-hand side. The keyboard on your computer will almost certainly have this kind of layout. The QWERTY keyboard became an international standard in 1967. It has an interesting past, as Box 12.2 describes.

Box 12.2	**An Early Keyboard**

The keyboard is based on the typewriter, which was first envisaged in 1711 by James Ranson, who proposed a design for a machine with keys, rather like those on a harpsichord. Thus, using a typewriter was initially likened to playing a twin-keyboard harpsichord. One of the first actual keyboards was built in 1868 by Scholes, Gidden, and Soulé to help overcome the forgery of handwritten railway tickets.

For more information, see Baber (1997) and Tepper (1993).

Keyboards for other languages have different layouts, sometimes simply adding characters with accents (e.g., é in French, þ in Icelandic) or more extensive changes to allow easier entry of other scripts, as in the Russian keyboard shown in Figure 12.2.

One of the disadvantages of many keyboards is that they can be over-elaborate, containing a range of keys that are rarely, if ever, used. If this is the case, it might be possible to develop a variation of the standard arrangement. For example, BigKeys makes a range of keyboards with much larger keys. They find the extra room to enlarge the keys by removing keys that are unnecessary for the applications the keyboard is intended for. There is one aimed at young children that includes cheery pictures as well as letters on each key, as you can see in Figure 12.3. You can gauge the size of the keys from Figure 12.4, where some children are using it. Other keyboards in the BigKeys range are popular with people with special needs, such as vision problems or hand tremor, who find really large keys useful.

It is possible to move away from the QWERTY keyboard completely. Box 12.3 describes a different type of keyboard that you may come across.

225
Part 3

Figure 12.2 The Russian keyboard layout makes it easier to enter Cyrillic script. (From www-306.ibm.com/software/globalization/topics/keyboards/KBD443.jsp, retrieved May 17, 2004.)

Figure 12.3 The early learning version of the BigKeys keyboard.

Figure 12.4 Children using the early learning version of the BigKeys keyboard.

Box 12.3	**The Chord Keyboard**

An alternative to the QWERTY keyboard is the chord keyboard, on which several keys are pressed at once in order to enter a single character. This is similar to playing a flute, where several keys must be pressed to produce a single note. Because many combinations can be produced with a small number of keys, few keys are required; so chord keyboards can be very small. Many chord keyboards can be operated with just one hand. Training is required to learn the finger combinations needed to use a chord keyboard. They can be useful where space is limited or where one hand is involved in some other task. Chord keyboards are also used for mail sorting and for recording transcripts of proceedings in law courts. A chord keyboard is shown in Figure 12.5. Note that this is a left-handed keyboard layout (the thumb goes on one of the three colored buttons), which would be unsuitable for right-handed users.

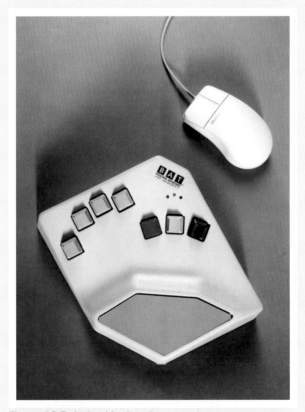

Figure 12.5 A chord keyboard.

If you do not need the full range of alphanumeric keys, a keypad may be more appropriate. Many everyday devices, such as calculators and telephones, use keypads successfully. An even simpler approach is to use individual buttons, as on burglar alarms and central heating controllers.

▶ **Choosing the Correct Keyboard, Keypad, and Buttons**

In Chapter 11, we described the interaction styles: command line, form-fill, and menu selection. All of these require keyboard input. When you are choosing the most appropriate keyboard, consider the following questions:

- *What size do the keys need to be?* Keyboards are available with every size of key from the huge keys of the BigKeys keyboard series (Figure 12.3) down to the tiny keys used to achieve functionality with maximum portability on mobile devices (Figure 12.6).
- *What shape should the keyboard be?* If you decide to use a QWERTY keyboard, then there are some alternatives to consider. For example, Figure 12.7 illustrates a split keyboard designed to combat repetitive strain injury (RSI). It does this by allowing the hands to rest in a more natural position than a traditional keyboard allows.
- *How robust does the keyboard need to be?* In difficult environments, such as factories, ordinary keyboards can clog up with dirt and liquids. Membrane

Figure 12.6 Keyboards for mobile or portable devices can be tiny. (Adapted from www.palmone.com.)

Figure 12.7 An alternative shape of keyboard.

keyboards solve this problem, as they are sealed. Unfortunately, they are flat, so they do not provide the same tactile and audio feedback. Software needs to compensate for this. Often such keyboards have software that detects if a key has accidentally been pressed more than once under unlikely circumstances and discards the repetitions.

The size and robustness of the keys (or buttons) also need to be considered if you decide to use a keypad or individual buttons. In addition, you need to decide which keys (or buttons) are required and how these should be labeled. If you own a scientific calculator or a graphics calculator, you will appreciate that these can be complex tasks.

3.2 Pointing Devices

Pointing devices are **continuous input devices**. This means they are particularly good at tasks that cannot be split easily into a number of discrete steps, such as dragging icons across the screen or drawing informal sketches. The standard configuration of input devices for many computer systems is the keyboard and mouse. This works well, as the keyboard is a discrete input device and the mouse is a continuous input device.

There are two types of pointing devices: indirect and direct. **Indirect pointing devices** require the user to move a screen cursor using a secondary device; **direct pointing devices** allow the user to point directly at the relevant position on the screen.

▶ **Different Types of Indirect Pointing Devices**

A flick through any online or offline computer equipment catalog will show you a range of pointing devices. You are probably familiar with some of them, but we shall briefly describe each before considering how to choose the best one for your partic-

Figure 12.8 Computer mice available in custom shapes as promotional items from www.subzeropromotions.com/ article.asp?id=96. (Viewed July 26, 2004.)

ular users. (We assume that you are familiar with the ordinary computer mouse, now available to suit all tastes, as shown in Figure 12.8.)

Other pointing devices that are often seen are:

- *Joystick.* A **joystick** is a lever mounted in a fixed base. There are various types of joysticks, including displacement and isometric joysticks. In **displacement joysticks**, the lever can be moved in two dimensions. Moving the lever in a particular direction causes the cursor to move and to continue moving in that direction. **Isometric joysticks** work in a similar way, but the lever is rigid and the pressure on the lever is translated into the necessary movement. UI designers often incorporate joysticks into game consoles, where they are used to control moving objects such as racing cars. Small joysticks are sometimes built into the keyboards of notebook computers (sometimes called "nipple" or "eraser head" joysticks due to the small size and shape). Figure 12.9 shows a joystick particularly designed for disabled users.
- *Trackball.* A **trackball** is an inverted mouse: the user rotates the ball and the case is fixed. These are often incorporated into game consoles. Some people with limited finger movement find it easier to move a trackball than a mouse. Like mice, trackballs are available in a huge variety of sizes and shapes to suit varying user needs. One example is in Figure 12.10.
- *Graphics tablet (or tablet).* A **graphics tablet** (see Figure 12.11) is a flat panel. The cursor moves as the user moves a stylus or finger across the tablet. Graphics

Figure 12.9 This especially tough joystick is helpful for people with disabilities. If gripping the joystick is awkward, the user can choose instead to screw the yellow spongeball or the T-Bar onto the joystick spindle. (Courtesy of Keytools ergonomics.)

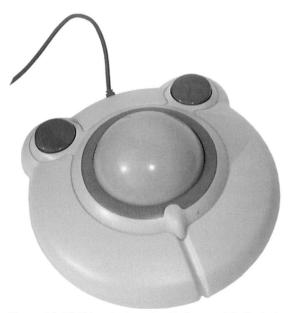

Figure 12.10 This extra-large trackball was originally designed for children, but it is also popular with people who have disabilities that affect their fingers. (Courtesy of Keytools ergonomics.)

Figure 12.11 A graphics tablet with stylus.

tablets are often used for creating drawings, as using them feels similar to creating a conventional drawing using a pencil and paper. Some portable computers have a small graphics tablet called a touch tablet (or touchpad). You roll your finger on this to move the cursor; to select an object, you tap on the tablet or press a button. Learning to use these devices requires more practice than a conventional mouse does, and users with limited dexterity often find them difficult to operate compared to using a mouse.

There is a great deal of variety in each of these devices. Almost every month a new variation comes out, so you might like to look in some of the recent computer magazines to find out what is happening now.

▶ Different Types of Direct Pointing Device

- *Touchscreen.* A **touchscreen** allows the user to input information and commands into the computer by touching buttons on the screen. For example, a system giving directions to visitors at a large exhibition may first present an overview of the exhibition layout in the form of a general map. Users touch the hall they wish to visit and the system presents a more detailed map of the chosen hall. Touchscreens on kiosks (as in Figure 12.12) are set up with big targets and used by pointing with your finger.

- *Pen system.* A **pen system** uses a touchscreen but is set up for using a stylus (a pen) rather than a finger. Because the stylus is much smaller, pen systems can have much smaller targets and they are therefore seen frequently on **personal digital assistants** (PDAs). Pen systems are also seen at checkouts in some stores, where the customer can sign on the screen using a stylus rather than using pen on paper (see Figure 12.13).

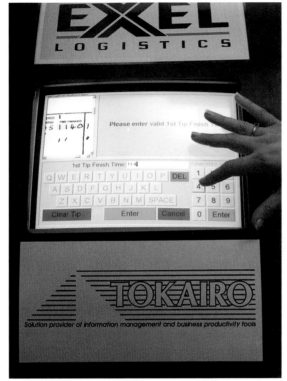

Figure 12.12 A touchscreen used on a kiosk.

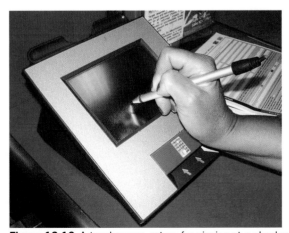

Figure 12.13 A touchscreen set up for signing at a checkout aisle.

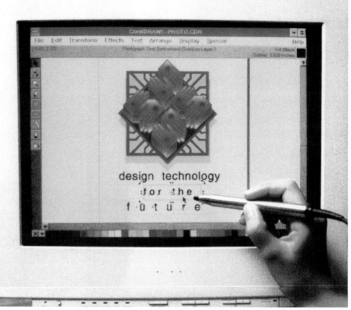

Figure 12.14 A light pen.

- *Light pen.* A **light pen** (see Figure 12.14) is a stylus that contains a photo receptor. As the user points at a cathode ray tube (CRT) screen, the light pen works out where it is being pointed by detecting the tiny variations in intensity of the light emitted by a CRT screen as the electron beam tracks horizontally and vertically across the screen. Light pens used to be quite common but have been overtaken by touchscreens and pen systems.

▶ **Choosing the Right Pointing Device**

When you are choosing a pointing device (indeed any input device) you need to ensure you understand the context of use fully. As Barber (1997) noted:

[I]n a hospital, the image from an ultrasound-scanner was being manipulated using cross-hairs and cursor which were used to select part of the scan for enlargement. The cursor was controlled by a joystick, much to the frustration of the midwife, who kept overshooting the point of interest. Eventually, the joystick was replaced by a trackball. The overshoot persisted.

This example, in which one interaction device was replaced by another, illustrates one response to these problems: to identify a specific symptom and to attempt to treat that. One might ask why a trackball was chosen. The principal reason is space. The interaction device is used on a piece of equipment mounted on a trolley, and there is a limited amount of space for the device to be positioned. However, the interaction device (whether joystick or trackball) is positioned behind the screen, to the left of the trolley. Given a right-handed midwife, operating the interaction device implies a reach across the screen, thus blocking the image, or an operation from behind the screen. In either case, there is a chance of overshooting the object of interest. (pp. 3–4)

In this example, the development team thought the joystick itself was the cause of the overshoot, whereas the actual problem was that the midwife obstructed the screen when reaching across to operate the joystick. In this situation, a pen system might have been better, as it would have allowed the midwife to touch the point of interest on the screen with great accuracy without obscuring the image or moving awkwardly.

The direction manipulation interaction style is much easier for the user with a pointing device, and many people use pointing devices extensively when using the form-fill and menu interaction styles. When you are choosing the most appropriate pointing device, consider the following questions:

Larger targets are easier to hit. See www.asktog.com/columns/022DesignedTo GiveFitts.html for an entertaining introduction to Fitt's Laws, the principle that applies here.

- *How easy to learn does the device need to be?* Direct pointing devices, like a stylus, tend to be intuitive to use, as touching and pointing come naturally in a way that using an indirect pointing device, like a mouse, does not. Therefore, they are ideal in situations where a particular user may only operate the system once or twice and cannot be expected to spend time learning to use it. This ease of use may be undermined if the software requires unnatural actions such as double-tapping.
- *How accurate does the device need to be?* The pointing device should reflect the degree of accuracy needed to carry out the task. Touchscreens are generally inaccurate; this is made worse if there is a buildup of dirt on the surface. Joysticks are also fairly inaccurate. When a device is inherently inaccurate, it is necessary to increase the size of the screen elements with which the user interacts. For example, buttons need to be larger. This can result in less room for text and graphics.
- *How much time will the user spend on the system?* Using a touchscreen for long periods can be tiring, as it requires the user to repeatedly lift an arm. This can be alleviated if the screen is horizontal or angled. Graphics tablets can be less tiring, as it is not necessary to keep lifting the hand. Also, the hand does not obscure the display. Joysticks require a wrist rest if they are used for lengthy periods. In contrast, the trackball is relatively comfortable to use, as the forearm can be rested on the table and the ball spun with the fingers.
- *How much space is there?* The trackball, joystick, and touch tablet require very little room. At one time, some notebook computers came with miniature trackballs, but these have now been largely abandoned in favor of nipple-style miniature joysticks and touch tables. Despite their small size, or possibly because of it, many users dislike them and carry a separate mouse.
- *How robust does the device need to be?* Touchscreens are often used for public-access systems, as they are easy to use and can be robust if sufficiently well built. Pen systems are not as good in these situations, as the stylus could be broken or stolen.

- *How manually dextrous is the user?* Some users, such as children and people with disabilities such as hand tremor, may find it difficult to use devices that require a high degree of accuracy. Therefore, such users may find a touchscreen easier to use than a mouse.

As you can see from this discussion, choosing pointing devices is an inexact science, as the appropriateness of a device is entirely dependent on the circumstances in which it will be used. There is also a lot of disagreement in the research literature. This makes drawing any general conclusions about these devices extremely difficult.

We have included Figure 12.15 as a summary of the research findings on accuracy, speed, and user preference. We have already considered accuracy; speed refers to cursor movement and data entry; user preference is self-explanatory. Unfortunately, the original experiments did not control all the relevant variables, such as the type of task being completed or the experience of the users. Consequently, you should only treat this chart as an indicator. The *y*-axis reflects the ranking of the device, with "1" being the best and "7" the worst. Pen systems are omitted, but it seems likely that pen systems and light pens have similar characteristics.

EXERCISE 12.1 (Allow 20 minutes)

A computer firm wants to design the UI for a computer system based in a tourist information center. The system will provide information about accommodation and events in the town and will be used by visitors of all ages. It will be located in the wall outside the tourist information center so that it can be accessed from the pavement when the center is closed.

Consider the merits of each of the following pointing devices as a means of interacting with this system:

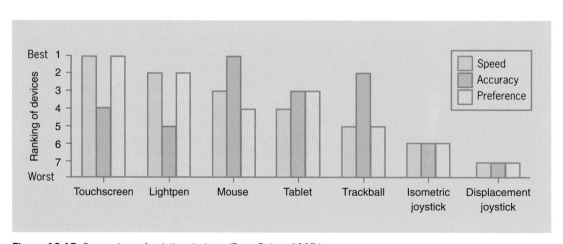

Figure 12.15 Comparison of pointing devices. (From Baber, 1997.)

- Touchscreen
- Trackball
- Mouse

Refer to the users, the tasks they will need to carry out, and the environment in which they will be using the computer system, as appropriate. In particular, consider the following points:

Users

- User attitude to the device (preference)
- How easy the device is to learn to use

Task

- The accuracy needed
- The speed needed
- The total amount of time spent on the system

Environment

- The robustness of the device
- The amount of space available

DISCUSSION

Touchscreen. It is easy to learn to use touchscreens, and the user attitude toward them is good: these are both advantages for use in a public-access system. However, they are not very accurate, so the screen buttons will need to be large. This will restrict the amount of information on the screen and could result in a large number of screens (for example, one for each hotel or guest house). This should be acceptable, so long as there are not too many or there is a good search facility. Speed is important because the user may well be in a hurry, particularly if the computer system is not under cover and it is raining. The total time spent on the system will be short, so arm ache should not be a problem for most users; however, it could cause difficulties for those with muscular problems. Touchscreens are robust, which is necessary for a damp and dirty environment. Space is probably not an issue, but touchscreens are very compact.

Trackball. Trackballs are robust and take up very little space. Young people are familiar with trackballs on games machines, so they may find these more intuitive than do people who are not games players. Other users tend to have a less positive attitude to trackballs. They are slower to use — moving to the precise position on the screen can be laborious — but they are more accurate than touchscreens. Thus, there is a trade-off between large screen buttons increasing the speed of use and smaller screen buttons increasing the amount of information that can be represented on the screen.

Mouse. Many users will be familiar with the mouse as it so widely used. It is more accurate than both the touchscreen and the trackball. This means that more information could be represented on the screen. However, the mouse would not be suitable for outdoor use because it is not robust and could be stolen.

3.3 Alternative Approaches to Entering Information

There is a lot of exciting research work in the area of input devices. As an example, Box 12.4 describes an eye-tracking system.

A few of the other important areas are described next. Computer systems with anthropomorphic interaction styles often require these alternative devices.

▶ Gesture

Gesture is widely used in communication between people. We gesticulate, shake hands, and move objects around. Gestural interfaces moved from the laboratory into the home with the launch of the Sony Playstation Eye Toy in the summer of 2003. The Eye Toy is a small camera that sits above or below the player's television, and then allows the player to be part of the game and use gestures to control it (see Figure 12.17).

▶ Iris and Fingerprint Recognition

Security is an important issue when carrying out activities such as withdrawing cash from an ATM or entering a building containing military secrets. One approach is to have a computer system that can recognize people based on their fingerprints or their irises (the colored part of the eye) (see Figure 12.18).

(a)

(b)

Figure 12.17 (a) The Sony Playstation Eye Toy camera. (b) The player in the middle of the screen uses gestures to control the game. (From www.us.playstation.com/Content/games/scus-97319/ogs, retrieved on June 6, 2004.)

Box 12.4	**Eye Tracking**

How could you operate a computer if you could only move your eyes? The answer is to use eye-tracking technology. Figure 12.16(a) illustrates one possible configuration for this technology. In this configuration, the camera is focused on the pupil of one eye and the software analyzes the direction in which the eye is pointing. To do this, an infrared light emitting diode (LED) in the center of the camera shines into the eye, creating the bright pupil effect shown in Figure 12.16(b). The reflection is then analyzed. Eyes vary in shape and size, so the user has to calibrate the system by looking at a series of dots that appear on the screen.

The user moves a cursor by simply looking at the place that is of interest. If it is a button, either blinking or looking at the button for a prolonged period can press it. This technology has to overcome several problems, including the following:

- Infrared light from other sources, such as the sun, may shine into the eye.
- The user wearing glasses or contact lenses can affect the technology.
- The image could be blocked if the user moves a hand between the camera and the eye.
- The calibration of these systems is often difficult.
- Considerable user concentration is required to use the system effectively.

For more information, see LC Technologies (2000).

We will return to the topic of eye tracking in Chapter 23, when we look at it as a way of finding out where a user is looking on a screen rather than as an input technology.

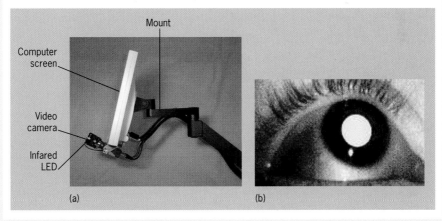

Figure 12.16 Eye-tracking technology.

Figure 12.18 Iris recognition equipment deployed at Amsterdam Schipol International Airport. (From Iridian Technologies.)

Figure 12.19 The letter forms for Graffiti. (Courtesy of PalmSource, Inc.)

▶ Handwriting Recognition

The popularity of handheld computers based on pen systems has meant that handwriting recognition has become an important approach to entering data. The recognition process is complex, as each person has different handwriting. In addition, when we join letters together, we shape the letters differently according to the letters that come before and after. For this reason, the majority of recognition systems insist that the user print the letters or use a specific alphabet such as that used by the Graffiti® system illustrated in Figure 12.19. This can make writing rather slow. Furthermore, the system must be trained to recognize a user's handwriting, so this approach is most appropriate for single-user systems.

▶ Speech Recognition

Speech recognition packages have been developing rapidly. It is now common to have telephone answering systems that respond to voice input. As with handwriting recognition, a number of problems need to be overcome. These include different regional accents, pauses, and meaningless words such as "err" and "umm," the vast range of possible words, and our tendency to use words incorrectly. For these reasons, the error rate for such systems is quite high. However, they do have their benefits, particularly for constrained situations where only a limited selection of words is required, such as some telephone voice response systems or as dictation systems for people who find it difficult or painful to use a keyboard.

4   Output Devices

In this section we look at four categories of output devices:

- *Screens*. Screens are excellent for displaying complex visual data. They are the most common category of output devices.
- *Loudspeakers*. These are needed for the more sophisticated inclusion of sound, such as music or speech.
- *Simple output devices*. Most computer systems have a selection of lights, dials, and buzzers, often indicating the status of the system.
- *Refreshable Braille displays*. These are used by blind people who are familiar with Braille. They display one line of Braille at a time, using small pins that push up to create the dots of Braille.

We finish by looking briefly at more advanced technologies, such as head-up displays, head-mounted displays, and stereoscopic displays.

4.1 Screens

Screens can represent a wide variety of visual elements. Even people with visual impairments generally prefer to read from a screen if they can, frequently using magnifying devices or magnifying software such as ZoomText to help them do so.

Two main types of screen technology are commonly available: the **cathode ray tube** and the **liquid crystal display**.

- *The raster-scan cathode ray tube (CRT)*. This technology is similar to that used for the television and is traditionally applied to desktop computers. At one time, CRTs were prone to flickering, but advances in technology have made the CRT the device of choice for a cheap-and-cheerful computer system and for applications where very large screens with accurate color rendition are essential (such as high-end graphics workstations).
- *The liquid crystal display (LCD)*. LCDs are much smaller, thinner, and lighter than CRTs with the same visible area. They also consume less power. At first, they were mostly used in portable devices, but advantages in technology have made them affordable for ordinary desktop use.

▶ **Choosing the Right Screen**

As with most computer technology, the quality of screens is constantly improving. However, several issues must be taken into account, such as the following:

- *How detailed does the image need to be?* The **resolution** indicates the amount of detail that can be represented on the screen. Resolution is defined in terms of the number of **pixels** (picture elements) per unit area. Thus, a screen may have 600 dots per inch (dpi). The higher this figure, the higher the resolution — and the smaller the pixels on the screen. So although high resolution may be essential, for example, if you manipulate photographs or representations of electronic circuits, it may not always be desirable, for example, if you work mainly with text and prefer larger letter sizes. Screen resolution is often lower than the resolution of paper (depending on your printer), so if the screen resolution is too low, you may find your users printing out the screen content.
- *How many colors are needed?* The number of colors available can vary from two (black and white) to millions. Although black and white can be very successful — for example earlier versions of the Palm Pilot or most mobile phones — the trend is generally to move to color as soon as it is affordable.
- *How large does the screen need to be?* By convention, screens have been measured across the diagonal, with common sizes for desktop monitors being 17 inches, 19 inches, and 21 inches. As the price of screens falls, users are tending to opt for larger displays. Larger displays have many advantages, as more visual information can be displayed. Larger text can also be displayed, which is an advantage for the visually impaired. Such equipment has been standard for many years for graphic designers. There is also a large market for smaller screens. In particular, these are used for small, portable devices, such as handheld computers. These always use LCDs, as it is difficult to make small, portable CRTs.
- *Does the screen need to be portable?* CRTs need an electrical supply and are very heavy. Thus, CRTs cannot be used for portable devices. LCDs are battery operated and lightweight. Also the batteries last a reasonable length of time. Thus, they are suitable for portable devices.
- *How much space is there?* Increasingly, LCDs are used instead of CRTs for desktop PCs as they take up less space. This can be important in a crowded office environment.

4.2 Loudspeakers

The use of sound is becoming increasingly sophisticated as technology improves. In the 1980s, many computers were able to beep, but that was all. Now many computers have sound output, and good-quality speakers are available. These can be used to reproduce speech, music, and sound effects. Many computers also have microphones that allow sound to be entered into the computer.

When you are choosing loudspeakers, you should consider how the user is going to use them. For example, if you are designing a UI for a composer who wants to create an intricate piece of music, then the quality of the loudspeakers needs to be high. In contrast, if the user is only using them for the sound effects generated by Windows, then the speakers can be of a lower quality. Surprisingly, the quality of speakers is often unrelated to their price, especially at smaller sizes. If you possibly can, arrange to try them in the environment where they will be used.

4.3 Simple Output Devices

There are a variety of simple output devices that can be used in the UI design in addition to (or instead of) a screen and loudspeakers. The most common of these devices are lights, dials, and buzzers. These devices are cheap, but they are extremely useful.

Lights often indicate the status of computer systems. The computer you are using probably has a light that indicates when the power is on. Lights can also be used in a more sophisticated manner. For example, some mobile telephones have a light emitting diode (LED) that is red when the telephone is charging and green when charging is complete (this can be a problem for those users who are color blind). It is also quite common for mobile telephones to have a flashing LED, indicating that the telephone is switched on.

Some UIs use seven-segment displays made up of LEDs, such as the answer phone illustrated in Figure 12.20. Different combinations of the LEDs are used to display different numbers and letters.

Dials and gauges are widely used to indicate levels. Examples include the speedometer dial in a car or the battery-level gauge on a handheld computer.

Simple sound output, such as the buzzer, is often used to attract the attention of the user. For example, some bread makers indicate the next stage in a cycle with a beep, so the cook does not need to keep checking for the right time to add the next lot of ingredients.

Some devices combine gauges, lights, and sound. Many microwave ovens indicate that they have completed an operation by using a buzzer, switching off the internal light, and displaying a digital clock. Users are thus given multiple outputs to tell them

Figure 12.20 Seven-segment display button and LED.

that the process is finished. Figure 12.21 shows an ambitious use of lights, dials, gauges, and buzzers.

One issue that you need to consider when choosing between lights, dials, and gauges is whether the data can be represented more effectively in analogue or digital form. A single light is effective for representing **digital data**. Thus, a single light can be used to indicate if a computer is on or off. In contrast, a dial or gauge is better for representing **analogue data** that can have a large number of different states. An example of this is the analogue display on some digital watches.

In addition, lights have a number of characteristics:

- *Color.* You may need a light that is a particular color or is able to change colors.
- *Frequency of flashing.* Flashing lights can be useful for attracting the attention of the user. A light that can flash at different frequencies may be useful. However, flashing lights can be a visual irritant.
- *Brightness.* It may be necessary to alter the brightness of the light. For example, a dashboard light needs to be adjusted as night falls.

Buzzers can be particularly effective if users are looking away from the UI. For example, the choice of a buzzer that sounds when a driver opens a car door with the headlights still on is a good one, because the user will not be looking at the dashboard. Buzzers are also used as an additional form of feedback. For example, selecting a button on a touchscreen gives no tactile feedback, so the UI often beeps instead.

Figure 12.21 An aircraft cockpit.

4.4 Alternative Approaches to Outputting Information

As with input devices, there is research into alternatives to the existing output devices. The following are a few of the other important areas. Computer systems with anthropomorphic interaction styles often require these types of devices.

Head-up displays are used in some aircraft. They use similar technology to conventional projectors. However, instead of showing the image on a screen, they project it onto the front window of the airplane. This means that the pilot does not need to keep looking down at the cockpit control system when she or he is concentrating on flying.

A **head-mounted display (HMD)** is a helmet that contains one or more screens that are positioned in front of the eyes. These allow the users to feel much more part of the **virtual world** created by the software. Often these are programmed so the view of the world changes when the user moves her or his head. HMDs are increasingly used in **virtual reality systems**. There are also military uses for this technology. An HMD is illustrated in Figure 12.22.

Stereoscopic displays create a three-dimensional effect by using two screens, one in front of each eye. The two images represent slightly different perspectives on the object, and together they create the illusion of three dimensions. These screens are usually found in an HMD. Box 12.5 describes a virtual reality system that uses a variety of unusual input and output devices, including stereoscopic displays.

Figure 12.22 A virtual reality headset.

| Box 12.5 | **Training Firefighters Using Virtual Reality** |

In collaboration with the Atlanta Fire Department, Georgia Tech (Georgia Institute of Technology) is developing a virtual reality system to train firefighters.

When directing the fighting of a real fire, a commanding officer will issue instructions to the firefighting team in the attempt to extinguish the fire. The *Firefighter Command Training Virtual Environment* simulates the incidence and events of a house fire. Through the use of a head-mounted display, or a computer screen, the commanding officer is able to view the virtual house fire. The officer can see the fire from different angles and navigate the fire scene as the fire is in progress. Virtual smoke and flames are seen, as well as a team of animated firefighters who respond to the commanding officer's instructions. The environment will respond to the events for fighting a fire in a realistic way. For example, if a door is opened, which causes a gust of wind, then the smoke and fire will change accordingly. If a firefighter sprays water on a fire, then it should die down, but more smoke would be created.

In the environment, if the correct sequence of commands has been issued, then the fire will be extinguished with the least amount of danger to the firefighting team and minimal damage to the house.

For more information, see St. Julien and Shaw (2003) and
www.gvu.gatech.edu/gvu/virtual/fire/index.html (viewed July 9, 2004).

5   Summary

The standard interaction devices (screen, keyboard, and mouse) are so familiar that we often take them for granted. A huge range of these devices is available, both for special needs of users (such as keyboards with extra-large keys for people with mobility problems) and for special applications (such as head-mounted displays for virtual reality applications). By thinking about who will use the device and for what, we can make better choices of interaction devices.

13

Choosing interaction elements: software components

Introduction

In the previous chapter, we discussed how to choose the hardware, the interaction devices. Now we need to consider how to use them effectively. We have relatively little control over the appearance or use of the input devices, so in this chapter we concentrate on the design of the cues to action, and feedback after action, provided by the output devices. In particular, we concentrate on the following software components:

- *Text*. How can we ensure that the text is legible? Which font should we use? How long should the lines be?
- *Color*. Which colors go well together? How should color be used to communicate information more effectively? How can we ensure that the colors we use have the correct connotations?
- *Images*. What are the different types of images? How do you choose the right one?
- *Moving images*. When is it useful to animate images? When can video clips be used to good effect?
- *Sound*. When can sound be useful? What are the different categories of sound and when should each be used?

These software components are usually relatively easy and cheap to change, but applying them in a consistent and thoughtful manner can make a big difference to the usability of the UI.

It is important to be clear what you are trying to achieve when you use these components. We are assuming that you want to communicate information and functionality in a simple but effective manner. This complements the role of a graphic designer, whose priority may be to create a design that is fresh and innovative. Overall, we are aiming for UIs that are easy to use and also look attractive.

2 | Text

Text is the dominant component in most education and training software and on many web sites. It also plays a central role in standard software applications such as word processors and spreadsheets. It is a flexible and powerful means of communication.

Text has a number of technical advantages:

- *Text files are small.* Images, sound, animation, and video all produce large computer files, even when compressed. These files can be slow to load from CD-ROM or to transmit via the Internet; this can reduce the usability of the UI. Text files are much smaller.
- *Text can be manipulated very easily.* For example, it is possible to search for words. If you are visiting a web site, this facility can save a huge amount of time. This is difficult to achieve with other media.
- *Text is less ambiguous.* Although it is possible to put more than one interpretation on text, that is a minor level of ambiguity compared to the many possible interpretations of a single picture or icon or of a musical tune.

It is probably society's reliance on text-based materials that maintains the central role of text in Western cultures, especially English-speaking ones. Nevertheless, although certain sectors of society spend much of their time reading and writing, this is not true for all sectors. As a UI designer you should explore the attitude of your user group to text. For example, you might like to find out their average reading age and the newspapers they read.

2.1 How to Ensure That Your Text Is Legible

Legibility is a product of a blend of factors, the most important of which are listed in Table 13.1. This is a complex area and it is hard to develop guidelines that apply in all circumstances, so you should apply these with care, always taking into account the needs of your particular users. Do not forget that your users may have poor eyesight.

The term "font" is used widely in this context. A particular **font** is made up of two components: the **typeface**, such as Trebuchet or *Comic Sans*, and the type size, which may be within a range such as 8 point to 72 point. There is some inconsistency in the literature concerning the definitions of font and typeface, but we feel these definitions are clear and useful. Figure 13.1 has a selection of different typefaces.

2.2 How to Ensure That Your Text Makes Sense

There is more information on the use of text in web sites in Chapter 17.

Even if your text is beautifully legible, that does not guarantee that it makes sense to your users. Try to choose words and expressions that are familiar to your users and that convey concepts clearly. UIs frequently use small amounts of abbreviated text, so checking that it still makes sense to your users is especially important.

Table 13.1 Factors That Affect the Legibility of Text (Adapted from Götz, 1998, Hartley, 1994, and Rivlin *et al.*, 1990)

Typeface	Serif or sans serif Familiar or unfamiliar	A serif is the finishing stroke at the end of a letter. See Figure 13.1. Sans serif typefaces are more suitable than serif typefaces for use on a screen: the resolution on screen is likely to be poorer than on paper, and the details of serif typefaces may be lost. Familiar typefaces such as Times or Arial are easier to read; unfamiliar ones, such as weisd are more difficult.
Type size	Too small is harder to read Too big is also hard	Most screens have around 72 dots per inch; ordinary office printers have around 300 dots per inch; high-quality printing (such as this book) typically has 1200 dots per inch. The lower the resolution, the larger the type size required for comfortable reading. For text for continuous reading, 11- to 14-point type is a good range to work with. Headings will stand out better if they are 3 to 5 point sizes larger. It is possible to use smaller type sizes for areas of the screen that are read episodically, rather than continuously, such as menu bars or captions for icons.
Letter spacing	Letters too close together are hard to read L e t t e r s t o o f a r a p a r t a r e h a r d t o r e a d	Well-designed type faces have a pleasant amount of space between the letters. Too little or too much and legibility is affected.
Line spacing (leading)	If you have small type sizes, then you can increase legibility by increasing the leading. This text is at the default leading If you have small type sizes, then you can increase legibility by increasing the leading. This text has extra leading.	The legibility of smaller type size can be improved by increasing the line spacing. The longer the line, the wider the line spacing should be (and the wider the line spacing, the longer the line can be). However, if the line spacing is too wide, then the lines may not be perceived as being related to each other (see the Gestalt laws of perceptual organization in Chapter 5).

Table 13.1 Factors That Affect the Legibility of Text (Adapted from Götz, 1998, Hartley, 1994, and Rivlin *et al.*, 1990)—cont'd

Line length	The maximum line length on a screen should be around 60 characters (or eight to twelve words). This allows a meaningful unit of text to appear in most lines. You should avoid very short lines, as they fragment the text and it is more difficult to construct the meaning.
Justification	Fully justified text (left- and right-justified) can create uneven gaps between the words on a page. It is usually best to left-justify blocks of text, as this gives a predictable place for the eyes to start from when they jump back to the beginning of the next line. On screen the right margin is best kept unjustified (ragged). If you are placing very short pieces of text next to other items on the screen (for example, putting captions on buttons or under icons), then you need to consider the relationship of the text to the item it belongs with. For instance, text on buttons usually looks neater if it is centered.
Line endings	Very short lines are easier to read if the line endings coincide with grammatical boundaries. Very short lines are harder to read if the line endings come at any arbitrary place. If you are using short line lengths — for example, in tightly-packed screen designs — it is easier for the reader to understand a line if it has a distinct thought in it, so, where possible, line endings should coincide with grammatical boundaries.

Figure 13.1 Blue on red can cause flickering.

3 Color

We can use color for a variety of reasons:

- *To draw attention.* You will often find that important buttons or areas of the screen are a different color. For example, warning signs are often in bright colors, such as yellow or red. Your eyes are drawn to these colors.
- *To show status.* As the status becomes more critical, the color might change. An example of this is a traffic light changing from yellow to red.

- *To make the information on the display clearer.* Color can be used to organize the screen or to show perspective.
- *To make the display more attractive.* This book concentrates on usability rather than aesthetics, but it is important to ensure that the combination of colors is visually appealing.

In this section, we concentrate on the meaning of different colors, how to use colors together, and how to use color to represent information.

3.1 The Characteristics of Color

Screens can only display a subset of the colors visible to the human eye. This limits the accuracy of color reproduction. There is also variation between computers, so a web page on a PC may look different when viewed on a Macintosh. There are similar problems with color printers. These issues can cause problems for some sectors, such as the fashion industry.

There are also differences in the way we perceive color from a screen compared to the way we perceive color from paper. This means that the screen versions of colors can appear pale and unreal when compared with the equivalent paper versions. It also increases the likelihood of flickering for color combinations such as red and blue, as shown in Figure 13.1.

3.2 Choosing Colors with the Right Connotations

When you use a color, you should think about what it is likely to mean to the people who look at it, as colors can have different connotations. These connotations are partly cultural, so you may find they do not ring true for you if you are from a non-Western culture, such as Chinese or Indian. For example, in Western culture, red is often used as a warning color, but in China it is a joyful or lucky color. However, connotations can be learned, and our society is increasingly international, so these differences are gradually becoming less of an issue. As communications improve, it is increasingly the case that the employees of multinational firms can have more in common with each other than with people living in their home towns.

Even connotations widely accepted in Western culture, such as red for danger, need to be used with care. For example, a car may have a red light that indicates when the handbrake is on. This correctly warns that you could damage the car if you drive with the handbrake on. However, it also effectively indicates that it is safe to take your foot off the brake pedal when the car is on a hill. This mixed message is confusing, and it might have been better to use another color. The situation is simpler for domains where established color conventions already exist. For example, in British politics, red is associated with the Labour Party and blue with the Conservative Party. This type of color coding can be applied more easily.

The **color saturation** can also be significant. Colors aimed at young people tend to be pure and bright, whereas colors evoking the natural world are relatively subdued, and colors aimed at older people are deeper.

Fashion also plays an important role in the choice of colors, particularly for young people. For example, the color of fashionable clothes changes regularly, as does the color of home décor. Thus, you should not use bright orange if it is thought to look dated. If you can, try to involve a graphic designer in your choices.

Make sure that you apply the colors consistently, always taking into account the characteristics of the users, the tasks they are carrying out, and the environment in which they will be using the computer system. It is good practice to evaluate your choices with users in order to inform your decisions.

EXERCISE 13.1 (Allow 5 minutes)

Look at the color chips in Figure 13.2 for a moment, and then write down a positive connotation and a negative connotation for each one. Don't agonize about this exercise: pick the first thing that you think of, and if nothing comes easily then move on to the next one.

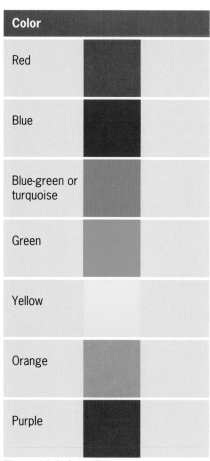

Color
Red
Blue
Blue-green or turquoise
Green
Yellow
Orange
Purple

Figure 13.2 Color Chips

DISCUSSION

Reactions to colors are

- Partly personal, due to associations that we have each created from childhood.
- Partly cultural, due to the way that colors are used in our surroundings.
- Partly contextual, inherited from the way the color is used in a specific object.

Table 13.2 has a selection of different connotations, partly drawn from a similar table by Götz (1998) and including some other connotations that we thought of.

Table 13.2 Connotations of Different Colors (partly from Götz, 1998)

Color		Positive connotations	Negative connotations
Red		Active, invigorating, exciting, powerful, strong, energetic, attractive, dominating	Aggressive, alarming
Blue		Controlled, abstinent, mysterious, intellectual, harmonious, deep, dreamy, faithful, rational, sensible	Aggressive, introverted, cold, melancholic
Blue-green or turquoise		Refreshing	Aloof, self-willed, unemotional, cold, sterile
Green		Refreshing, harmonious, optimistic, close to nature, calm, gentle, conciliatory, strong-willed	Jealous, envious, inexperienced
Yellow		Colorful, extroverted, cheerful, youthful, lively, full of fun, light	Superficial, exaggerated, vain
Orange		Exciting, direct, joyful, alive, communicative, warm	Intimate, vigorous, possessive, cheap
Purple		Serious, royal, luxurious	Sad

3.3 How to Use Color Effectively

The effective use of color is a complex and technical area. Table 13.3 lists some general guidelines.

An important factor when you use several colors is the **intrinsic brightness** of each. Table 13.5 gives the brightness of a variety of pure colors. The brightness of mixed colors depends on the brightness of each color in the mixture and the relative quantities of each. For example, mixing dark blue with white results in light blue. Light blue is a brighter color than dark blue.

Intrinsic brightness has some important implications.

- For legible text, there needs to be sufficient contrast between the brightness of the background and foreground colors. For example, white text on a yellow background would be difficult to read, but white on black would not, as Figure 13.3 demonstrates.

An example of the vibrating effect can be found at www.wcb.ab.ca/pdfs/ergobk.pdf, in a book titled *Office Ergonomics: Remembering the Basics*, published by the Worker's Compensation Board — Alberta.

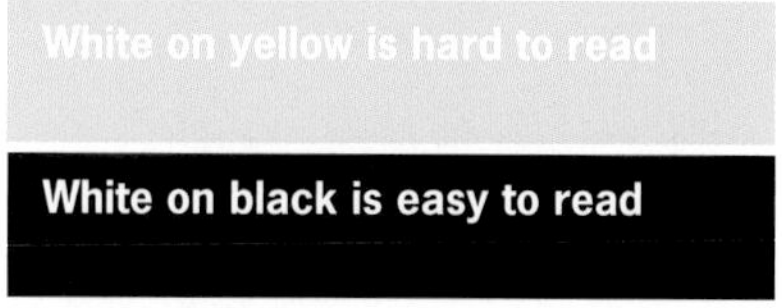

- You should be careful when using bright colors, such as white or bright yellow, for large areas of the screen because they can become tiring to look at. Although black text on a white background is easy to read, it would be better to tone down the white if your users are reading from the screen all day. Pale gray, cream, or magnolia can be good alternatives.
- Contrasts in the brightness should not be too extreme, as this may lead to a visual vibrating effect. A vibrating effect is caused by the eyes being unable to focus properly when two complementary saturated colors are used together (for example, a combination of red and blue). Figure 13.4 shows a variety of color combinations, many of which you will probably find difficult to read, and some of which vibrate. If you want to use complementary colors, make sure one of them is less bright than the other.

As color perception is so personal, it is good practice to allow your users to modify the color scheme.

Figure 13.3 Poor contrast is hard to read (Adapted from Götz, 1998)

Figure 13.4 Some color combinations are hard to read (Adapted from Götz, 1998)

Table 13.3 Making Effective Use of Color

Number of colors	If you are using colors to organize the screen, then it is better to limit their number: too many colors can be confusing and unpleasant to look at. Some guidelines recommend no more than six colors, in addition to black and white, for any one screen, and fewer is often better. Some experimental evidence suggests that using many colors arbitrarily can result in users suffering eyestrain, fatigue, and disorientation.
Design for monochrome	Designing in black and white first can help to focus attention on the layout of the UI. Also, there may still be some users who don't have color screens. Do not forget that monochrome displays can be extremely effective, like the display in a railway station that indicates when the next train is about to arrive.
Color perception	Color perception varies greatly. About eight percent of the male population is color blind. Red, orange, and green are often confused, as are purple, blue, and magenta, and white, gray, and cyan.
Color for reinforcement	Color should not be used in isolation. For example, speed limit signs on UK roads have a red border, but they also have black text on a white background stating the maximum speed allowed.

Table 13.4 Intrinsic Brightness (adapted from Götz, 1998)

Achromatic colors	Colors		Intrinsic brightness
White			Very high
	Yellow, yellow–green		High
	Orange		High to medium
Medium gray	Red	Green	Medium
	Violet		Medium to low
	Blue		Low
Black			None

3.4 Using Color to Represent Information

All UIs need to communicate information. Color can be particularly effective for this. Table 13.5 summarizes some of the techniques that are available.

Table 13.5 Using Color to Represent Information

Technique	Description	Example
Color for emphasis	Color can be used to emphasize the important areas of the screen or the key parts of a diagram.	Figure 13.5 shows two contrasting representations of marshaling signals. The one that uses color to emphasize the lights is much easier to understand than the one in black and white. Box 13.1 shows the use of color to emphasize oceanic features.
Color for grouping	Color can be used to organize the screen.	Areas of the screen containing different types of information may have a different background color.
Color coding	Color can be used to represent a particular object or status; this is known as color coding.	In an accounts package, the overdue accounts could be indicated by a red symbol.
Perspective	Color can be used to reinforce perspective on the screen.	You should use dark or dim colors for the background and brighter colors for the foreground. Thus, the title bar of an active window is usually a brighter color than that of an inactive window.
Layering	Related to the use of perspective is the use of color to represent different layers within a diagram.	In an air traffic control system, high-flying planes could be a different color from low-flying planes. The colors should be naturally related to each other, such as different shades of blue.

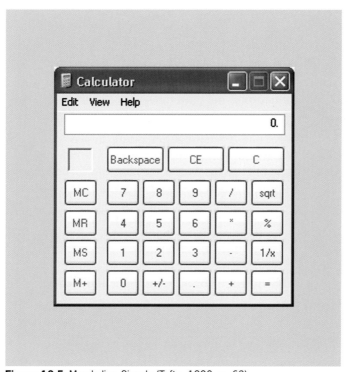

Figure 13.5 Marshaling Signals (Tufte, 1990, p. 63).

EXERCISE 13.2 (Allow 10 minutes)

How effectively is color used in Figure 13.5? Take into account the following points:

1. Number of colors
2. Color perception
3. Color for reinforcement
4. Intrinsic brightness
5. Color for emphasis
6. Color for grouping
7. Perspective

DISCUSSION

Number of colors. The space to type into is white. The foreground and background of the buttons are all in standard Microsoft shades of gray. The button titles are in two colors: red and blue. The colors appear to have been chosen arbitrarily. Each color is used to help identify a group of buttons.

Color perception. The color combination is acceptable for most users with impaired color vision.

Box 13.1	**Color in the General Bathymetric Chart of the Oceans**

Figure 13.4 is part of the General Bathymetric Chart of the Oceans (International Hydrographic Organization, Ottawa, Canada, 5th edition, 1984, 5.06). The map shows the ocean trenches of the western Pacific and Japan Sea. It uses color in an interesting and powerful way.

There are two distinct color groups: different shades of green/brown and different shades of blue. We naturally associate these colors with land and sea, so there is no need to memorize their meaning. The colors are graded according to height (or depth), so the deeper the blue, the deeper the sea.

The colors are not used in isolation, as the contour lines also indicate the gradations.

The colors have been chosen so that they are clear to color-blind users.

None of the colors are bright.

The contrast between the background color and the text color is good, so the text is legible.

Thus, each point on the map signals four variables: latitude, longitude, sea/land, and depth/altitude measured in meters. This would be very difficult to achieve without the use of color.

Adapted from Tufte (1990, p. 91).

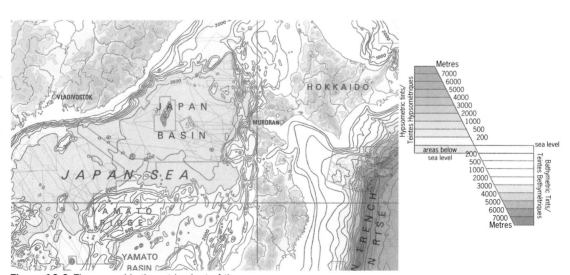

Figure 13.6 The general bathymetric chart of the ocean.

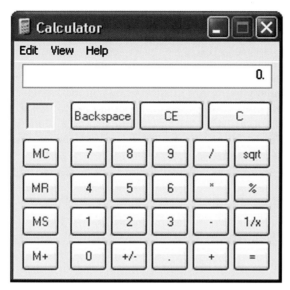

Figure 13.7 The Windows XP calculator.

Color for reinforcement. Color is used to help identify different groups of buttons. This grouping is reinforced by the numbers and letters on the buttons. Thus color is not used in isolation.

Intrinsic brightness and color for emphasis. The red and blue are both bright mixtures of the color and this makes them stand out even though the letters used on the buttons are very thin. The gray of the buttons is pale, so flickering is not a problem.

Color for grouping. In the main block of buttons, red is used to distinguish the most frequently used arithmetic functions (/, *, −, +, =) from the less frequently used functions (sqrt, %, 1/x).

Perspective. The effect is subtle, but we can just see that the buttons are bordered with darker gray to make them look as though they are raised from the screen and afford pressing.

It is important to consult users about their color preferences from the start of the UI development process. Many designers will seek views at the first meeting with users, often employing colored sketches to gain ideas, opinions, and suggestions. They will then continue to evaluate the colors during each iteration of the design. Many systems give users the option to change colors to meet their personal tastes, and this is especially important for users who are color blind or who have visual impairments.

4 Images

We can use images in several ways:

- *To motivate, to attract the attention of the user, to amuse, and to persuade.* These uses are particularly important in advertising and marketing.
- *To communicate information, especially spatial information.* This is often exploited in computer-based learning materials.
- *To help overcome language barriers.* This approach is widely used in instruction manuals for consumer items.
- *To support interaction.* Examples include screen metaphors and icons.

In this section, we concentrate on communicating information.

4.1 Using Images Effectively

The following are the main types of images:

Some books classify maps as charts. We have chosen not to do this.

- *Pictures.* These include photographs, drawings, and cartoons.
- *Diagrams.* These include maps and other representations of relationships between objects, such as family trees and Venn diagrams.
- *Graphs and charts.* These are visual representations of numbers. Thus, they include pie charts, histograms, line charts, and bar charts.

Each of these represents different types of information.

Pictures can provide information that would be difficult to describe in words. Figure 13.8 shows an illustration of the Museum Willet-Holthuysen in Amsterdam, a 17th-century building that was once a family house. The illustration contains a large amount of detail about the size, shape, and relative position of the various rooms in the house.

Diagrams take advantage of the two-dimensional layout of the screen to illustrate relationships and processes. For example, it would be possible to show flow of blood around the body or the relationship between parts of a space rocket. At work you may use software to generate dataflow diagrams and entity models.

There are a variety of graphs and charts that can be used for displaying numeric information. Figure 13.9 shows a selection of these images. It is important to choose the appropriate type according to the data you want to represent. For example, a histogram can be used to show month-by-month changes, while a pie chart shows the relative amounts of the different elements that make up the total.

It is common to incorporate some form of functionality into images. For example, you may be using a web page to search for information about hotels in a particular part of Asia. Such web pages often contain maps that allow you to click on the relevant country in order to find the necessary information.

Figure 13.8 The Museum Willet-Holthuysen. (From Eyewitness Travel Guide, 2004.)

When you are considering using an image, you should remember the following points:

- *Choose the most appropriate type of image* (picture, diagram, or graph/chart), according to the information you need to convey and the impact you wish to make.
- *Design the image so that it meets the requirements of the task* as closely as possible. Unnecessary or inappropriate diagrams can be distracting for the user.
- *Follow any relevant conventions*, to ensure consistency with other images of that type. For example, if you include dataflow diagrams, they should use the appropriate symbols.

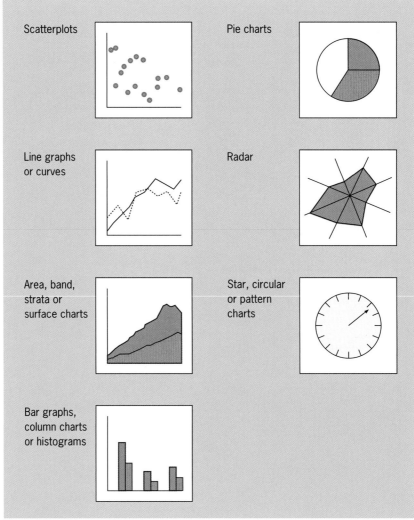

Figure 13.9 Charts and graphs.

- *Combining text and images can be particularly effective.* Images are often enhanced by relating them to text.
- *Take the user's screen resolution into account,* otherwise the details of the image could be lost.
- *Images, particularly photographs, can result in very large files and long download times for web sites,* so they should provide significant benefits for the users carrying out their task.

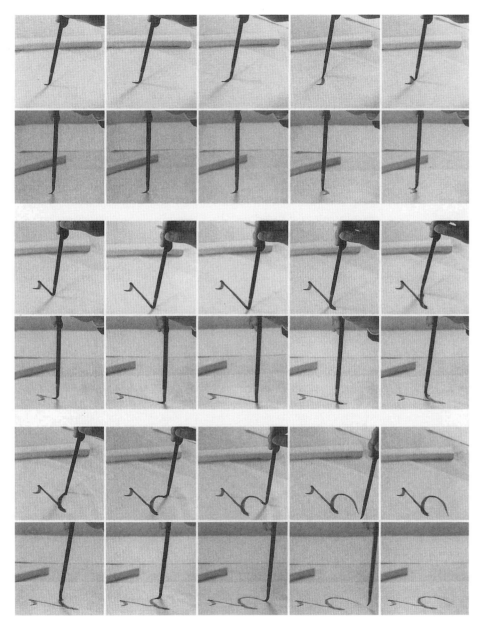

Figure 13.10 Techniques of calligraphy. (From Tufte, 1990, p. 68.)

5 | Moving Images

On paper, you can show movement by a series of diagrams each with a very small change. Figure 13.10 illustrates such a scenario. This has its uses, as it allows the process to be studied very carefully.

You can achieve actual movement on the computer screen through animation or the use of video clips. To create an animation, you need to understand the principles of animation and be able to use the relevant software. With video, in addition to having a video camera, you need to have editing software and a means of transferring the video from the camera to the computer. For both you need a lot of time and expertise, so only develop these components yourself if you are certain of their value to the user and it is not possible to buy them elsewhere.

Some moving images are clearly part of the UI, and others are part of the content of the software. For example, an animation showing files flying from one folder to another would be part of the UI, but an animated advertisement on a web page would be part of the content of the page. Unfortunately, in many cases, it is difficult to make a clear distinction of this sort. In addition, at present, most moving images are used in an unsophisticated way that requires little interaction from the user. For these reasons, we struggled to identify sufficient examples for the next two sections that are clearly only part of the UI and are not content. However, the principles remain the same. As technology improves, the use of moving images is likely to become more sophisticated.

When incorporating moving images into the UI, you should be conscious of the fact that people are used to seeing high-quality moving images on their television screens for several hours each day. They are therefore likely to expect similar quality on their UIs. Images that fail to meet this standard are unlikely to motivate users about the product. The cost of producing broadcast-quality video is high, so it must serve a key purpose and not simply be expensive wallpaper. You should also be aware that some people with disabilities find moving images problematic. For example:

- Flickering images can trigger some types of epilepsy.
- Moving images can be distracting for people with attention deficits.
- Rapid changes to images can make it harder for people with visual impairments but some sight to focus on the images.

If you decide to use moving images, then make sure you provide a way for the user to stop and start them easily and, preferably, control the speed of change.

5.1 Using Animation Effectively

You can use animation for the following purposes:

- *To illustrate movement.* An example of this would be an educational program that teaches about the muscles a horse uses when it runs.
- *To provide dynamic feedback.* For example, in some operating systems when you are copying a number of files, an animation appears that illustrates files flying from one folder to another. This is dynamic feedback, confirming that something is happening.
- *To attract attention.* For example, an advertisement on a web page may include some movement in order to attract the user's attention. This can become a visual irritant.

- *To show that the computer system is operating.* Dynamic screen savers are the most obvious example of this technique. Some kiosks simulate a user operating the system. This draws the attention of potential users and shows some of the functionality of the system.

Thus, animation is important and useful, but you should only use it when absolutely necessary.

EXERCISE 13.3 (Allow 10 minutes)

It takes a few seconds for cell phones to connect to the network. This causes some users to become anxious, as they think the cell phone is not working. Draw an animation to be used on the screen that indicates that the cell phone is trying to establish the connection.

DISCUSSION

Mark writes: I found this exercise quite difficult, as the screen is likely to be small and the concept is abstract. However, the time taken to connect can be disconcertingly long, so an animation could be reassuring. Figure 13.11 shows a sketch of a cell phone and an aerial, with arrows moving between them. This will only be effective if users can recognize the images.

5.2 Using Video Clips Effectively

You can use video clips in many of the situations where you could use animation. However, video has the following additional uses:

- *To convey human behavior and emotions.* For example, a training package teaching customer care for a bank may show a clip of an angry customer coming into a bank. Being able to see his facial expressions and body language would provide a lot of additional information.
- *To show events that users cannot see directly.* For example, video could be used to show the inside of a nuclear reactor or a recent historical event.

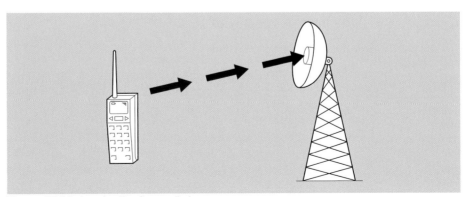

Figure 13.11 An animation for a cell phone.

- *To motivate.* For example, seeing a clip of the users of your software struggling with the UI should motivate you to improve it!
- *To provide additional contextual information.* Animations tend to focus on the particular sequence of events, whereas video usually also provides information about the location, the clothes people are wearing, and so on. This makes it essential to update video regularly, or the age of the application soon becomes apparent to users.

As technology continues to develop, it is likely that the use of video clips will increase. They have already been used extensively in computer-based training and multimedia educational packages.

6 Sound

Sound is especially useful as an output when people cannot easily see a visual prompt, such as:

- *Applications where the eyes and attention are required to be away from the screen.* Relevant examples include flight decks, medical applications, industrial machinery, and transport. If you are a runner, you may have a heart rate monitor that allows you to monitor how fast your heart is beating. This is often indicated by an auditory beep, which speeds up as your heart rate increases. In some monitors, the beep stops when your heart rate is within the target range. This can be extremely off-putting as it is ambiguous: either you are within the target range or your heart has stopped beating altogether!
- *Applications involving process control.* In some process control applications, alarms must be dealt with, or continuous monitoring is required. In these situations, the sound indicates a system change, which the user may need to attend to. For example, some print managers speak relevant phrases when problems occur, such as "out of paper" or "printer jam."
- *Applications addressing the needs of visually impaired users.* Screen readers are particularly important for visually impaired users. These read out the content of the screen.

6.1 Different Types of Sound

Sounds come in these categories:

- *Ambient sounds and sound effects.* Ambient sounds appear naturally as the by-product of something else happening. When thinking about computer systems, the computer itself makes a variety of noises as it works. For example, the clicks of the CD-ROM and hard disk drives confirm that it is operating correctly. So important are these ambient sounds that, in some systems, they have been recreated where they do not occur naturally. For example, in some handheld computers, the software generates a clicking sound when the user presses a key on the keyboard. Many UIs contain a range of warning beeps and reassuring sounds confirming that operations have been completed. These can include naturalistic sounds, such as the sound of a piece of screwed-up paper dropping into a wastepaper basket.

- *Music.* Many musicians use computer systems to compose or explore music, and programs such as games make extensive use of music. Short sequences of musical notes are also used in devices such as car alarms.
- *Speech.* This is the most demanding of the categories, as speech recognition and speech generation are technically complex.

We look at these categories next, concentrating on the information they can communicate to the user.

6.2 Making Good Use of Sound Effects

Sound effects can communicate information in a variety of ways. In particular, they can do the following:

- *Reinforce the visual component of the UI.* For example, turning a page on the screen could be accompanied by an appropriate sound. This could be taken even further in a children's program about animals, which could, say, include sounds of lions roaring and elephants trumpeting.
- *Confirm the successful completion of an operation.* For example, when my cell phone succeeds in connecting to the network, it beeps.
- *Attract attention.* For example, a warning sound might be used to draw the user's attention to an error message displayed on the screen.

As these examples suggest, sound effects usually reinforce other types of output.

6.3 Using Music Effectively

Music in UIs is relatively undeveloped, except in games and specialist packages designed for composers and musicians.

Copyright laws vary between countries, but be aware that in many countries it is illegal to use music composed by someone other than yourself unless you obtain the owner's express permission to do so.

Some operating systems have a signature tune that automatically plays when they are loaded. This informs the user that the operating system has loaded correctly and creates a sense of identity, but these tunes can be annoying to users if they have to listen to them repeatedly. A development on this use might be to signpost different parts of the program using musical clips.

The use of music can be evocative. In most films, the atmosphere is created and the viewer drawn in by music. For example, romantic music by Tchaikovsky or Rachmaninoff may accompany a melancholy section in a film. Music could be used in this way in a computer-based presentation, possibly at the climax of a talk. However, you would need to take care, otherwise it could seem manipulative. That encouraging or amusing music at the start of an application might become irritating or distasteful if the user has heard it ten times before.

6.4 Using Speech Effectively

Speech output is a powerful way of communicating information. It has particular benefits for the visually impaired. For those whose eyesight is good, talking elevators may seem a novelty, but they provide useful information and reassurance for the visually impaired. Some applications of the technology have less obvious benefits, such as supermarket checkouts that read out the product and prices. These were found to breach the customer's sense of privacy and to be noisy. Again, good design depends on a good understanding of the users and the environment in which the technology is going to be used. Box 13.2 describes an interesting speech-based system, but how many customers would want their financial details broadcast to everyone on a busy street?

One of the benefits of good-quality speech output over text is that it communicates tone of voice, pace, and accent. In this way it provides more information and helps to make the speaker seem more real to the user. The tone of voice can differ according to the content of the message: a warning message could sound urgent and an information message could sound reassuring.

Michaelis and Wiggins (1982) have suggested that speech output is most effective when the following conditions are met:

- The message is simple.
- The message is short.
- The message will not be referred to later.

Box 13.2   **Advanced Automatic Teller Machines (ATMs)**

For more than 30 years, bank ATMs have transformed the way we carry out banking transactions. However, the basic interaction technology has remained unchanged, using a numeric keypad and some buttons arranged around a small monochrome screen. More recently, this has been augmented by sound output indicating when an action needs to be taken, such as removing the card from the machine.

This approach has worked very successfully, but there have been ongoing problems with security. In particular, stolen cards can be used in the machines if the PIN is known. One way around this is the use of iris recognition. In such systems, the user is required to look into a camera. The camera then takes a photograph of the iris, the colored area around the pupil, and analyzes the complex patterns. These patterns are unique to an individual and hence allow the system to identify the user.

A system known as STELLA has been piloted by NCR in Canada. In addition to allowing for iris recognition, this system also allows for speech recognition and generation. Thus, the user walks up to the machine and stands on a pressure-sensitive mat that indicates her or his presence. Having carried out the iris recognition, the user speaks to the system, and the system provides the information available. Thus, there is no keypad or screen.

Drawn from NCR Press Release, June 21, 1999.

- The message deals with events in time.
- The message requires an immediate response.
- Visual channels are overloaded.
- The environment is too brightly lit, too poorly lit, subject to severe vibration, or otherwise unsuitable for transmission of visual information.
- The user is free to roam around.

Shneiderman (1998)

These guidelines assume that the output is digitized human speech or playbacks of tape recordings.

6.5 Problems with the Use of Sound

Prerecorded digitized speech can be included in a UI relatively easily, but generating speech is harder. One of the methods for synthesizing speech is called **concatenation**. The idea behind concatenation is that the computer stores sentences, phrases, or word segments of real human speech. New sentences are constructed by arranging words in the right order. For example, with current telephone directory inquiry systems in many countries, after having made an inquiry of a human operator, a voice says something like "the number you require is 273148." The phrase "the number you require is" is smooth and flowing (having been recorded in full by a human speaker). The number itself is rather jerky and stilted, as recordings of the individual digits are played back one after another.

Unlike the other media we have considered, sound has the potential to intrude on the environment. This can be overcome with the use of headphones, but not all users choose to use headphones, and they are inadvisable in some hazardous environments. It is often a good principle to allow users to change the volume or switch it off altogether if necessary.

Sound is not good at conveying detailed information unless accompanied by thext, video or still images, and information communicated solely by sound is often difficult to remember precisely. To maximize its effects, it is often best to combine sound with other media.

269
Part 3

> **EXERCISE 13.4 (Allow 15 minutes)**
>
> Imagine that you are designing a multimedia information kiosk for a sports hall. The kiosk is intended to give information about the different facilities available and to provide lists of times and prices. Give two different ways in which you could use each of the following media: video clips, animation, images, and sound. Explain the advantages of each.
>
> **DISCUSSION**
>
> - *Video clips.* A talking head of the manager could be used to welcome users to the leisure center. This would hopefully inspire them to use the facilities.

Short clips could also be shown of the swimming pool, gymnasium, and other facilities. These would give a real sense of what the facilities are like.

- *Animation.* Animation could be used to attract the attention of passersby — there could be a rolling animation that shows that the system is operating. Many of the users will be using the kiosk for the first time, so it may be helpful to have animations, indicating what to do. Thus, a button that users must press in order to proceed may have an arrow that repeatedly moves toward it.

- *Images.* Photographs of staff members could be used, as could illustrations of the facilities. These would help the leisure center to seem more attractive and friendly.

- *Sound.* Music could be used in combination with the animation intended to attract passersby. Recordings from the different facilities could also be used. For example, the description of the swimming pool could be accompanied by sounds recorded nearby the pool. This could make the pool sound like a happy and interesting place to be.

7 Summary

In this chapter, we looked at a variety of guidelines for using text, color, images and moving images, and sound. So far, we have considered them in isolation: text separately from color, images separately from sound. In the next chapter, we will consider how to combine design components to produce an overall interface.

14

Moving from choosing components into design areas

1 Introduction

In the previous two chapters, we looked at interaction from the point of view of interaction devices (hardware) and software components. We are now going to start to put these together into an overall UI.

This chapter starts with some design exercises that bring together hardware and software components. These give you the freedom to start a design from scratch. Mostly, however, we get a better design by working within the conventions that users expect to find. We have grouped these into **design areas** (sometimes called "paradigms"). This chapter explains the concept of design areas, and three further chapters look in more detail at creating UIs for specific design areas.

2 Combining Interaction Devices and Software Components

In the complete UI, you aim to combine interaction devices and software components into a single seamless whole. If you choose too many competing components, the result can be confusing. Many of us have had the experience of installing a new piece of software and being overwhelmed by the array of icons, menus, and windows.

The key is simplicity. In many cases, less can be more. You need to ask yourself: Does that software component really need to be there? Does this database system really need an animation highlighting the search button, when most users should already know where it is? Is it really necessary for users to hear that piece of music every time they run the program?

In some cases, a high level of complexity is unavoidable because the task or the level of experience of the users demands it. For example, it would be difficult to imagine a simple helicopter cockpit. However, helicopter pilots are experienced users, trained on the equipment, who need to have all the controls at hand in order to fly safely.

There are always conflicting requirements when you are designing a UI. For example, when we explained the human–action cycle in Chapter 10, we described the activities users carry out when they are using computer systems. One of these was planning a set of actions (action sequence) to accomplish the task. It is easier for a user to do this if the way to do it is visible in the interface. That is why, on many systems, frequent tasks, such as switching a device on or off, have their own buttons. The disadvantage to this is that the number of controls can increase rapidly, resulting in a UI that appears very complicated. Thus, there is a trade-off between visual and functional simplicity. In reality, only the simplest of UIs can have one control for every task.

EXERCISE 14.1 (Allow 10 minutes)

Design a remote control for a television that will be used by an elderly technophobe relative. The television does not pick up cable or satellite channels, so only a few channels are available. It should be as simple as possible. Include as few buttons as you can. Assume the current channel number is displayed on the television screen and that the brightness and contrast are already set correctly.

DISCUSSION

We came up with the sketch shown in Figure 14.1. This allows your relative to switch the television on and off and move between channels. We have also made it possible to change the volume in case your relative is hard of hearing. This device should be easy to use, as there is a clear and simple mapping between the tasks the user wishes to carry out and the controls.

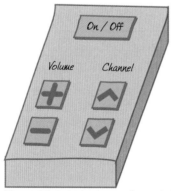

Figure 14.1 A simple remote control for a television.

3 | Principles of Good Layout

To create a usable UI, you need to combine the various components so that the users can achieve their goals quickly and easily. This requires good layout. Both the software components and the interaction devices need to be well laid out. For the former, this usually relates to the screen display; for the latter, it relates to the design of the keypad or the layout of buttons.

3.1 Create Natural Groupings

First, you need to think about the natural structure of the information. For example, in a personnel database you could divide the employee record screen into separate areas: one for home contact details, another for their employment record, and another for their pay details. The way you define these areas will vary: you could use different background colors, separating lines, white space, different fonts, or a group of consistently sized or shaped buttons. Whichever approach you choose, you should think about the Gestalt laws of perceptual organization discussed in Chapter 5.

The same principle relates to grouping controls. Thus, when you are designing a graphical user interface, you will probably want to group together all the menus or all the icons that relate to a particular concept such as drawing or formatting.

3.2 Separate the Currently Active Components

It is important to emphasize what the user is currently doing. This means that if they get distracted, they can carry on where they left off relatively easily. It also enables them to focus their attention on the matter in hand. This takes into account the psychological principle that users have difficulty focusing on more than one activity at a time.

The Windows operating system demonstrates one approach to this. The active window is placed in a prominent position on top of the other windows, and the color of the title bar is altered. The new color is brighter, whereas the title bars of the other windows are duller. Thus, the current activity stands out from the others.

3.3 Emphasize Important Components

It is important to emphasize the components that really matter. That is why panic buttons are usually red (unless the environment contains a lot of red). You need to start by identifying what needs to be emphasized; if you emphasize everything, it just gets confusing. Color, type size, positioning on the screen, and animation can all be used for emphasis. It is good practice to combine these components to reinforce the effect. For example, a car alarm may sound an alarm and flash the headlights.

3.4 Use White Space Effectively

When you are designing a UI, the **white space** is extremely important. White space refers to areas of the screen that do not contain any other software components — they are blank. White space is also important for embedded systems where it can be used to emphasize the grouping of physical buttons. White space is often more effective than lines for clarifying the layout of the UI.

Thus, it is important to include spaces and gaps. This may mean dividing the information between several screens, but this can be preferable to an over-complex screen. The same principle applies to controls: rather than have all the possible controls available, it may be better to have a menu hierarchy, which the user searches through to find the command he needs. This means that you should choose the information and controls that you place on the screen carefully, ensuring that the most important information is immediately available.

3.5 Make the Controls Visible

For a control to have good visibility, its function needs to be obvious. This complements the psychological principle that it is easier to recognize something than to recall it. Thus, the controls we include explicitly on the screen should suggest what their functions are, taking advantage of the users' knowledge of other computer systems and of the world in general.

3.6 Balance Aesthetics and Usability

The appearance of the UI is becoming increasingly important. This is particularly true in areas such as design and fashion, where UIs are often eye-catching and attractive. The introduction of the colored range of Apple Macintosh computers changed users' expectations of computers: suddenly they were not satisfied with gray boxes. Since then, various other devices have been redesigned to make them more attractive. For example, there are colored mobile telephones aimed at teenagers and preteens.

However, there can be a trade-off between the aesthetics of the UI and its usability. For example, a vivid background may look stunning, but it could be tiring for the eyes. You need to ask yourself which is more important. You may have some arguments with your marketing manager over this point.

EXERCISE 14.2 (Allow 15 minutes)

Sketch a web page for selling computer printers. This page is aimed at computer enthusiasts browsing on their home PCs. The users are interested in the price and functionality of printers. The screen should show details of several printers, along with prices and photographs.

Explain how you have achieved the following:

- Created natural groupings
- Emphasized important components
- Used white space effectively
- Made the controls visible
- Balanced aesthetics and usability

DISCUSSION

We came up with the design shown in Figure 14.2.

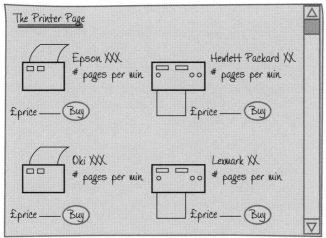

Figure 14.2 A web page selling computer printers.

- *Natural groupings.* It seemed natural to group together all of the information associated with a particular printer. The disadvantage is that the user may have to scroll down the web page, which will make comparing prices and specifications more difficult. It might help to include additional tables grouping together the printers by price and specification. This would better reflect user requirements.

- *Emphasizing components.* We identified the prices and buy buttons as the most important elements. We emphasized the prices by including a bright red, bold £ sign by each one (we are British, after all, so we assumed that our purchasers would like to see British £). We decided against flashing graphics or animations, as these can become a visual irritant. We emphasized the buy buttons by shaded borders, which make them look raised and hence afford pressing.

- *White space.* We separated the printer descriptions using white space rather than lines because we felt it looked less cluttered. This space helps to emphasize the groupings. The text, images, and button within each group are all in close proximity to ensure that they are perceived as a group.

- *Visibility.* The button has the word "Buy" on it. This is good visibility, as it suggests that clicking the button will enable you to buy the associated printer.

- *Aesthetics and usability.* The page layout is very simple. It could be made more elaborate and (arguably) more attractive by using a patterned background and more elaborate graphics. We felt that doing this would reduce the usability, and we think that people who access such pages are more interested in the product than in the look of the page. To be sure, we would need to carry out some market research. However, with web page design developing so quickly, it is important to be aware of these issues because a page that looks old-fashioned will give a bad impression of the company.

EXERCISE 14.3 (Allow 30 minutes)

Give a critique of the graphic calculator illustrated in Figure 14.3. This calculator is used by students who are studying mathematics at university level. Alternative arrangements are made for students with physical disabilities.

The following features of the calculator cannot be identified from the figure: the screen is not backlit, the screen is not a touchscreen, and there is no pen input — there is only keyboard input.

Comment on each of the following areas, and suggest how the design could be improved:

- Whether the psychological principles for the UI designer have been taken into account

Figure 14.3 A TI-83 Plus graphics calculator.

- The choice of input and output devices
- The use of text
- The use of color
- The use of images
- Simplicity of design, taking into account the task–action mapping
- Whether the principles of layout have been applied

DISCUSSION

- *Psychological principles.* The layout of the keypad is similar to that of a conventional calculator, so there is a degree of consistency. If the user gets distracted when entering a calculation, the screen shows what has been entered and the flashing black cursor indicates where the next number or operator will be displayed. The structure of the keypad is quite complex. We consider this in more detail later. One of the reasons that the calculator appears so difficult to use is that most of the buttons can be used for at least two different functions, and each of these functions is written either on or beside the relevant button. This means that the student can recognize these, rather than recall them, which is good, but the overall effect is overwhelming. We will suggest possible solutions.
- *Choice of input device.* There is a keypad containing a large number of buttons and an LCD screen. The buttons are reasonably large, allowing the user to press them quite easily. This is particularly important, as the device is portable and will usually only be operated by one hand. The arrow buttons are a different shape and are configured in a square. This makes it easy to distinguish them and to guess the direction in which the cursor will move on the screen as each button is pressed. The keypad is not sealed, so it would not be suitable for a dirty environment, but it should work well in the environment in which most students study. If a large touchscreen with a pen had been used, it would have been possible to use only screen buttons, which might have made the device more flexible.
- *Choice of output device.* The screen is an LCD, which is appropriate for a portable device. The screen is large for a calculator, but not too large — there is a trade-off between screen size and keeping the calculator small. The resolution is not very good (the lines are rather lumpy). This could be a problem if detailed readings were needed, but it is sufficient to give the general idea. The screen is not backlit, so it will be of little use if the lighting is poor or the student has poor eyesight. A backlit screen might be an improvement.
- *The use of text.* A sans serif typeface has been used for the buttons and a serif typeface on the screen. The latter is a surprising choice, and to our eyes the screen is slightly less readable than the buttons. However, the type size is large, which helps, and only a limited range of text and numbers is displayed.
- *The use of color.* The screen can only display black on a gray background. This is sufficient for displaying text and graphs. The background color of the

button section is black, the buttons are five different colors, and the text on and around the buttons is in four different colors. Thus, there are a lot of colors. It is difficult to know how the designers could have used fewer colors, given the complexity of the device. The brightest button is the second button, which is orangey yellow. This is suitable because it is frequently used. However, the On button is black, which may mean that new users struggle to find it. Color is used for grouping purposes, grouping together the number buttons, the basic function buttons, and so on. The contrast between the background color and the text colors is generally good.

- *The use of images.* Various types of graphs can be displayed on the screen. This visualization of data gives this type of calculator a great advantage over other calculators.

- *Simplicity of design.* The screen layout is simple. This is necessary because it is so small. However, the layout of the buttons is rather complex. A simpler approach might have been to put the buttons intended only for advanced users under a movable cover. Alternatively, an onscreen menu hierarchy could have been included, with the more advanced commands embedded in the hierarchy. The task–action mapping is generally quite direct — that is why there are so many buttons. The mapping for switching the calculator off is not as clear and direct as it might be because it requires two key presses (the second button followed by the On button). This is surprising, as it is such a frequent operation. A simpler solution would have been to make the On button work as a toggle between on and off.

- *Principles of layout.* Considerable effort has been put into grouping the buttons by color. They are also grouped by position (the basic function keys are in a column and the number keys are in a square). The buttons used for manipulating the graphs are physically separate from the other buttons, being grouped in a line underneath the screen. This seems intuitive. Color is also used to emphasize the important buttons. As there are so many buttons, there is very little white space. The space around the arrow buttons and beneath the top row of buttons is used effectively. Most of the buttons are well labeled, the label indicating the purpose of the button.

4 What Is a Design Area?

Question: How is a web site like a mobile telephone?

Answer: In some ways they are quite different, but there are similarities: they both use color and text, they are both laid out for ease of use (or should be), and they both respond when you select a button.

As we saw in the previous design exercises, there are various approaches to combining hardware and software components. We refer to each of these as a **design area**, which is defined by a set of design issues and design guidelines. We will investigate two design areas in detail and consider one area briefly.

- *Graphical user interfaces (GUIs)*. It is easy to believe that all GUIs are good GUIs because they are so widely used, but this is not the case. In Chapter 16 we consider how to choose and combine the correct widgets. We do this by providing design guidelines and a variety of examples of poor GUI design. There is also a set of progressive exercises that result in the design of a GUI for a sports center.
- *Web pages*. The Web is one of the most important developments in computer technology in recent years. Designing a web site is a challenge, as it may be accessed by a huge number of users from a wide range of cultural backgrounds, all using a different specification of computer. Unfortunately, many sites have been developed by people who are unfamiliar with the principles of good design. In Chapter 17, we consider three areas: how to structure the site, how to design web pages, and how to write the content. We do this by providing design guidelines and a variety of examples from actual web sites. There is also a set of progressive exercises that result in the design of a web site for a hotel booking service.
- *Embedded systems, such as handheld devices*. In the previous chapters, we have made regular reference to embedded systems. We consider this design area more briefly in Chapter 18, as you are less likely to be required to design UIs for these. However, they are still extremely important. We will ensure that you are familiar with the relevant concepts introduced in the earlier chapters by presenting a variety of examples and exercises that will act as reinforcement. These should help you recognize well-designed embedded systems.

This separation into design areas is not a neat one. The three areas overlap in complex ways. For example, web pages often include GUI widgets, and handheld devices can be used to access the Web. This merging of different design areas is known as **technological convergence**.

As the Web is increasingly a focus for the design areas that interest us, we could have concentrated exclusively on the design of web sites. We chose not to do this, because each design area groups a set of related issues. In addition, many UIs only draw from a single design area. For example, a spreadsheet package will probably draw only from the GUI design area.

In time, new design areas will develop. This is already happening, with research progressing into embedding computers into many of our household devices, our clothes, and maybe even into our bodies. These computers will communicate with one another, helping to control our homes and other aspects of our lives. This area is known as **ubiquitous computing**.

4.1 Design Components and Design Areas

When you design a UI, you need to perform the following tasks:

1. Identify the relevant design area, and think about the specific principles, guidelines, and issues for that design area.

2. Consider the conceptual design that you created in response to your requirements-gathering activities.
3. Combine the design components taking into account the demands of the design area and what you want to happen in the UI to meet the requirements.

Each design area has its own particular characteristics. For example, web sites are useful when your users are distributed around the world. However, it is difficult to ensure that the screen you have designed appears precisely as you want it to on user screens, as the browser settings may override the typeface or link colors. The ability of the user to specify the appearance of web sites can provide significant advantages, particularly for those with visual impairments. These characteristics will become apparent in the following chapters. You should consider them when you choose the design area for your particular UI.

UI design is developing extremely quickly and in a very fluid manner. As a consequence, existing design areas are in a permanent state of change. For example, the number and appearance of GUI widgets increases every time a new version of Microsoft Windows is released, and web site functionality increases every time the technology improves. So we cannot show you every single widget or every feature that you might come across in a GUI or on a web page. Instead, we aim to equip you with generic skills that will enable you to understand the main design issues and to apply the relevant guidelines in a thoughtful and critical way to meet the needs of your users, the tasks they are carrying out, and the environment in which they work.

5 Summary

In this chapter, we introduced the concept of design area. In the next chapter, we will look at how Tokairo designed the driver's system. This will be followed by three chapters that look at specific design areas in more detail.

15

Case study on design: Tokairo, part 2

1 Introduction

Now that we have done some of the design activities for our UI, we thought it was a good time to return to our first case study, Tokairo, to find out how the company approached the design of the new worksheet and kiosk. First of all, we describe the final system, then we explain how Tokairo went about designing it.

2 The Driver's Worksheet

Figure 15.1 illustrates the original worksheet, and Figure 15.2(a) shows the redesigned worksheet. As you can see, the designs are quite different:

- The original form requires the user to enter text and numbers only once. The new form requires the user to write a number in the box at the top of each column of numbers and to cross through the same number in the column. The latter overcomes the problem of bad handwriting and facilitates the recognition process. Thus, the truck drivers' work has been reengineered.
- The layout of the forms is very different. Both contain elements in groups. In the original form, each main element (such as Loading Details) is in a separate table surrounded by a solid line and white space. However, the details of any one trip are spread between the boxes, which makes it less clear. It is also necessary to enter the load number repeatedly. This repetition has been removed in the new form. The use of pale red on the new form also helps to emphasize the groupings and allows for the use of some white space.

Filling in numbered bubbles is quite a common technique in forms. You may have used it in when taking computer-scored tests at high school, such as the SATs.

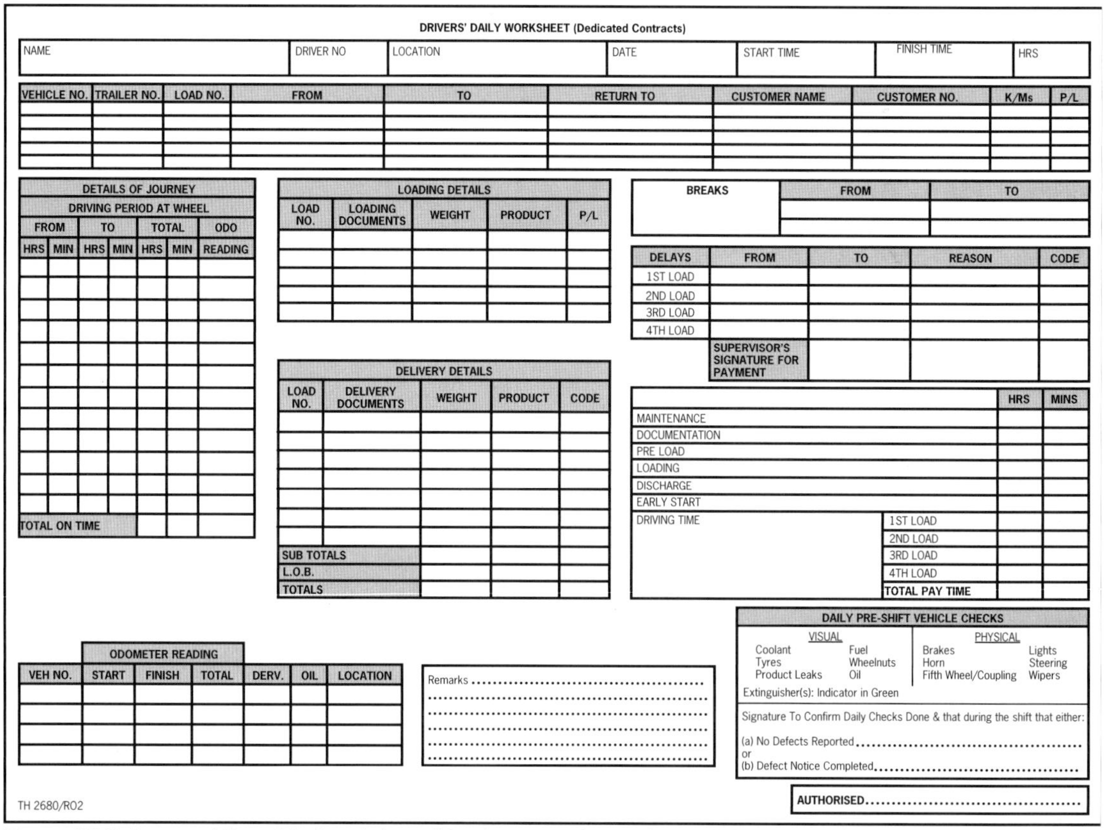

DRIVERS' DAILY WORKSHEET (Dedicated Contracts)

NAME	DRIVER NO	LOCATION	DATE	START TIME	FINISH TIME	HRS

VEHICLE NO.	TRAILER NO.	LOAD NO.	FROM	TO	RETURN TO	CUSTOMER NAME	CUSTOMER NO.	K/Ms	P/L

DETAILS OF JOURNEY

DRIVING PERIOD AT WHEEL						
FROM		TO		TOTAL		ODO
HRS	MIN	HRS	MIN	HRS	MIN	READING
TOTAL ON TIME						

LOADING DETAILS

LOAD NO.	LOADING DOCUMENTS	WEIGHT	PRODUCT	P/L

DELIVERY DETAILS

LOAD NO.	DELIVERY DOCUMENTS	WEIGHT	PRODUCT	CODE
SUB TOTALS				
L.O.B.				
TOTALS				

BREAKS	FROM	TO

DELAYS	FROM	TO	REASON	CODE
1ST LOAD				
2ND LOAD				
3RD LOAD				
4TH LOAD				
	SUPERVISOR'S SIGNATURE FOR PAYMENT			

		HRS	MINS
MAINTENANCE			
DOCUMENTATION			
PRE LOAD			
LOADING			
DISCHARGE			
EARLY START			
DRIVING TIME	1ST LOAD		
	2ND LOAD		
	3RD LOAD		
	4TH LOAD		
	TOTAL PAY TIME		

DAILY PRE-SHIFT VEHICLE CHECKS

VISUAL: Coolant, Fuel, Tyres, Wheelnuts, Product Leaks, Oil

PHYSICAL: Brakes, Lights, Horn, Steering, Fifth Wheel/Coupling, Wipers

Extinguisher(s): Indicator in Green

Signature To Confirm Daily Checks Done & that during the shift that either:

(a) No Defects Reported……………

or

(b) Defect Notice Completed……………

VEH NO.	ODOMETER READING: START	FINISH	TOTAL	DERV.	OIL	LOCATION

Remarks……………

AUTHORISED……………

TH 2680/RO2

Figure 15.1 A copy of the original worksheet. (You do not need to understand the details of this figure. It is just here to give you a general impression of the original worksheet.)

3 The Kiosk

Tokairo and Tankfreight worked together to design the kiosk from scratch, as the previous system did not include a computer system operated by the truck drivers.

The truck drivers' work has been reengineered — the way in which they carry out their jobs has been altered by the introduction of the kiosks. When the drivers return to the depot, they go to the kiosk that contains a scanner, touchscreen, and printer. To operate the kiosk, the driver enters his personal identification number (PIN) and scans in his worksheet. Figure 15.2(b) illustrates a worksheet being fed into the kiosk. The system then reads the data on the worksheet and checks for errors; if there are any mistakes, they can be corrected by using the touchscreen. A few seconds later, the worksheet reappears through the slot below the Tankfreight logo, and a receipt comes through the slot in front of the driver's right hand.

To design these kiosks, Tokairo needed to make a number of decisions about the input and output devices, the design principles and guidelines to apply, the layout, the use of color, the choice of font, and so on.

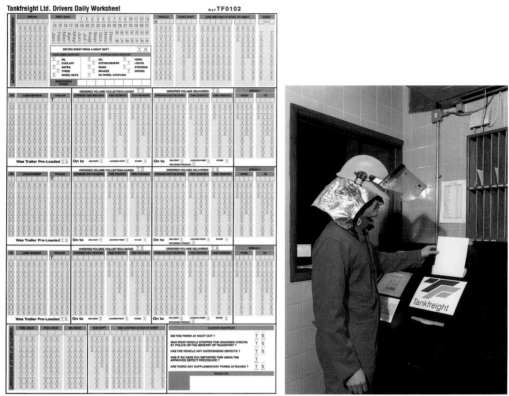

Figure 15.2 The drivers' system: (a) the worksheet and (b) the kiosk.

EXERCISE 15.1 (Allow 10 minutes)

Think about the users of this system and decide what choices you would make if you were Tokairo. Sketch a screen that asks for the driver's PIN.

DISCUSSION

The most important guideline for these users is simplicity. They are busy, not especially computer literate, and do not want any complication in a task to be done at the end of the day.

Also, the kiosk has a touchscreen that will be operated by drivers with big hands, possibly wearing gloves, so it is important that the buttons are large and easy to touch.

You need to take into account the connotations of the colors, the number of colors, users' color perceptions (particularly red/green color blindness), and the relative brightness of the colors.

In designing the screen layout, you need to create natural groupings, separate the currently active components, emphasize important components, use white

283

Part 3

■ space effectively, make the controls visible, and keep a balance between aesthetics and usability.

You can see typical results of Tokairo's design choices in Figure 15.3: part (a) illustrates the login screen, and part (b) illustrates one of the errors that can be identified by the system. As you can see, the screen highlights the section of the worksheet that contains the error.

4   How Tokairo Designed the UI

This section explains how Tokairo created the designs for the new worksheet and for the kiosk. The following is the second part of the interview with Treve, Tim, and Paul.

4.1   Establishing the Ground Rules: Simplicity and Flexibility

It can be difficult to know where to start when you are creating a design. Establishing some basic principles is always useful.

As embedded systems are often designed to carry out a single task, they tend to need only a single window. For other characteristics of embedded systems, see Chapter 18.

> *Caroline: When you got your spec, what did you do? Maybe you could talk us through that a bit.*
>
> *Paul: Right, well, I received the spec from Tim, which was quite detailed in the functional aspects of the system, and inserted some ideas [about] the user interface . . . the main point of the user interface just being simplicity, because the user base that's going to be using it is not necessarily computer literate.*

It is not enough just to be aware of design principles; they also need to be applied.

> *Paul: With discussions with Tim, and again considering the users involved, we decided to have a single window rather than [a] traditional multiwindow-type interface, so we wouldn't have the layering of windows and window management.*

Treve, Tim, and Paul also identified the need for flexibility.

> *Treve: This system might go into Europe, because Exel operates across Europe. They operate across the world, therefore you need a flexible user interface. The structure stays the same, but all the communication, the media will change.*
>
> *Caroline: How did you know to do this?*
>
> *Paul: It was experience with other projects.*

The theme of flexibility came through at a number of stages during the discussion. They programmed the kiosk so that Tankfreight could configure most of the software design components: fonts, colors, language used, and so on. This meant that the software could be modified to meet local needs.

4.2   Choosing the Technology: Simplicity and Familiarity

Tokairo and Tankfreight decided on the hardware components, the input and output devices, early in the project.

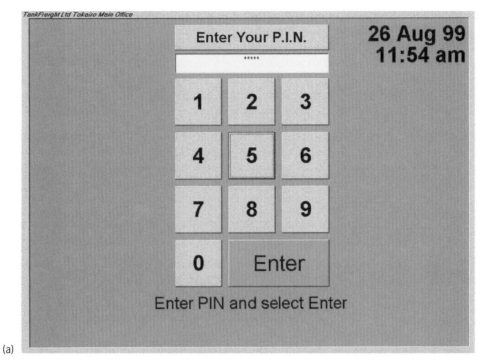

(a)

(b)

Figure 15.3 Two of the screens displayed on the kiosk.

Treve: Generally you need to know . . . what the components [the input and output devices] are — the broad components — fairly soon after you have done the site and system audit. Because you've already identified the limiting factors of the user base, and in this particular case it was drivers who were coming back after 11 hours in the field, very tired, wanting to get back to their wives. The last thing in the world they wanted to do would be to be confronted with a complex, rather annoying system, so you needed to make it as easy as possible. The easiest thing in the world [is] to use single interfaces; finger, screen [a touchscreen].

Tokairo was in a fortunate position, being able to choose the input and output devices. In many situations, however, designers have little control over the hardware. For example, the designer of a web page cannot influence the specification of the computer accessing the page or the input and output devices being used.

As well as simplicity, an important factor in the decision-making was the expertise of the designers.

Caroline: How did you decide upon the input and output devices?

Tim: It was a brainstorming session. It was, "This was what we wanted to achieve," and everybody pooled ideas. . . . The touchscreen was, I think, Hugh's initial input because he'd done something else once in the past with touchscreens, so he knew it would work in that environment.

Paul: I'd say that sort of idea just came from, as Tim was saying . . . cash point PIN machines and other such touchscreen designs that I have seen.

Caroline: How long would it have taken you to come up with that idea? . . . Is that two weeks or 10 minutes?

Paul: Probably more like 10 minutes really.

Taking inspiration from other systems is a useful technique. In this case, they assumed that if their users were familiar with an ATM, they should be able to use a touchscreen kiosk. The eventual kiosk is robust and fits well into the reception area, as you can see in Figure 15.4.

4.3 Developing Prototypes: Communicating Ideas

Developing both high- and low-fidelity prototypes is an essential part of the design process.

Paul: I prototyped it [the screen for the kiosk] in Visual Basic . . . and captured it as an image and put it in the spec so the people at Tankfreight, Hugh and Rachel, etc., had a feel for what we had in mind. So they could say, "Yeah, that's more or less what we had in mind as well." . . . It only takes a few minutes to prototype a screen.

When you are working with client organizations, low-fidelity prototypes of this sort can help to ensure that everyone understands what is being developed. They also

Figure 15.4 The drivers' reception area containing the kiosk.

provide the opportunity to negotiate design decisions. Effectively these designs were the outcome of an informal conceptual design process.

> *Caroline: Did that prototype have any formal evaluation, or was it more people looking at it and saying, "Yes that's what we thought we meant."*

> *Tim: That's about what happened.*

> *Treve: It tends to work that way because you have to rely on your client understanding their business environment, plus your own understanding of the business environment.*

In a business environment, you often need to make compromises. Ideally, they would have asked the drivers to evaluate these designs, but they felt that in this case it could have appeared to reflect a lack of confidence in the client organization.

Tokairo chooses different approaches to prototyping, depending on the circumstances. Sometimes the company uses a whiteboard:

> *Tim: [Talking about another project] There was a big whiteboard in the middle of the development area, so we sketched . . . on the board between us, the ideas of how we could produce this and what it would look like and juggled around with that a few times; and that took half an hour maybe, and when we were all happy that it looked nice and we could actually code it; then that's what we went with.*

Again, the prototype was used as a discussion tool.

4.4 Designing the Screens

Having chosen the input and output devices, Paul decided on the basic screen layout.

Paul: It was working out what needs to be presented to the user, what the user needs to input, basically identifying three areas. Since it's a single-layer window, we split it into three frames.

The approach Paul took focuses on the task requirements. It also creates a consistent appearance for the screen.

The choice of colors was less of an issue, as they were modifiable.

Paul: It's actually user definable; the colors, there [are] only two main colors, the . . . foreground and a background . . . you can actually define . . . within the program. . . . I think I . . . chose . . . one of the company's colors [which] is a type of blue on their logo, so I went with that and it was a simple thing to make it very definable within the program. Basically it left the decision with them to what color [to use], because it would impact within the environment it was being used [in], the light and that sort of thing, so they could actually change it without any problems.

A different approach was taken to the choice of colors for the buttons:

Caroline: How did you choose the colors for the buttons?

Tim: That was actually Rachel's input. The first time she came down to look at Paul's user interface . . . [she said] it would be nice if the enter button could be green like it is on the cash points . . . red for stop, green for go, all those kinds of things.

The choice of font was not an issue either, as it too was modifiable, so they used the default, which they felt was readable anyway. The UI contains very little text, but they did think carefully about the language used. For example, in Figure 15.3(b) the screen contains the instruction "Please verify shift date." The shift date is highlighted because it was entered incorrectly.

Caroline: Why did you use the word "verify" rather than "correct"?

Treve: Verify, yes, that was an interesting one, that one surprised us . . . I perceive [verify] to be [a] quite technical word, but they seemed to be very happy with it — "verify the form," whereas I would say "correct the form" . . .

Caroline: It's just interesting, because . . . you mentioned feeling that "correct" sounded as though they had done something wrong, whereas "verify" sounded a bit more neutral.

Particular words can have a much greater significance than designers realize. In this case, the designers accepted the extra time to learn the unfamiliar word "verify" because it was preferable to using a familiar word that turned out to have negative connotations.

4.5 Designing the Worksheet

The worksheet was designed in parallel with the kiosk.

> *Caroline: Where did you get the idea of the lottery style form from?*

> *Treve: That was once again at that initial meeting. I can't remember who originally came up with the lottery ticket idea. It was around the table.*

> *Tim: I know where it came from. . . . We had some sample forms with us, and one of them was a medical, blood tests results form. . . . You requested the tests you wanted done on the blood, so you had various OMR [optical mark recognition] type tick boxes and you ticked off what you wanted — a sugar test or whatever. While we were talking about the form design, we had examples of other forms in front of us, and that's the one that took the eye because it was one of the easier ones to complete, and it was very similar to a UK lottery ticket; it was like red squares and numbers in the boxes, so we said, "well, that's it, that's like a big lottery ticket, so let's go for a big lottery ticket."*

> *Treve: We needed to find something everyone could use and the only thing we knew that was nationally used — [something] everyone knows how to fill in — was a lottery ticket. So it was something that evolved around the table through conversation, brainstorming. Once we latched onto the idea, it evolved very quickly, literally in five minutes.*

The new worksheet and a lettery ticket are shown in Figure 15.5 and Figure 15.6, respectively.

As with the kiosk, the priorities for the design team were that the form should be easy to use and look familiar. Looking through a number of contrasting examples is a good approach, as it gives you the opportunity to learn from other people's experience.

4.6 Developing Prototypes: Facilitating Evaluation

The early evaluation of screen designs is important.

> *Caroline: Did you test [the screen layout] on the users to see if it would work or did it just seem like a good idea and go with it?*

> *Tim: If you consider Rachel as the users . . . because she represents the implementation team at Tankfreight. Rachel came down and had her input, so [there were] . . . a few changes based on that but it was very much while we were developing the product. . . .*

> *Tim: The drivers didn't see the screen until the project coding was more or less finished.*

Thus, Tokairo used someone with a good knowledge of the users, who took on the role of a user and who in this role criticized the design. Tokairo took a different approach to evaluating the worksheet.

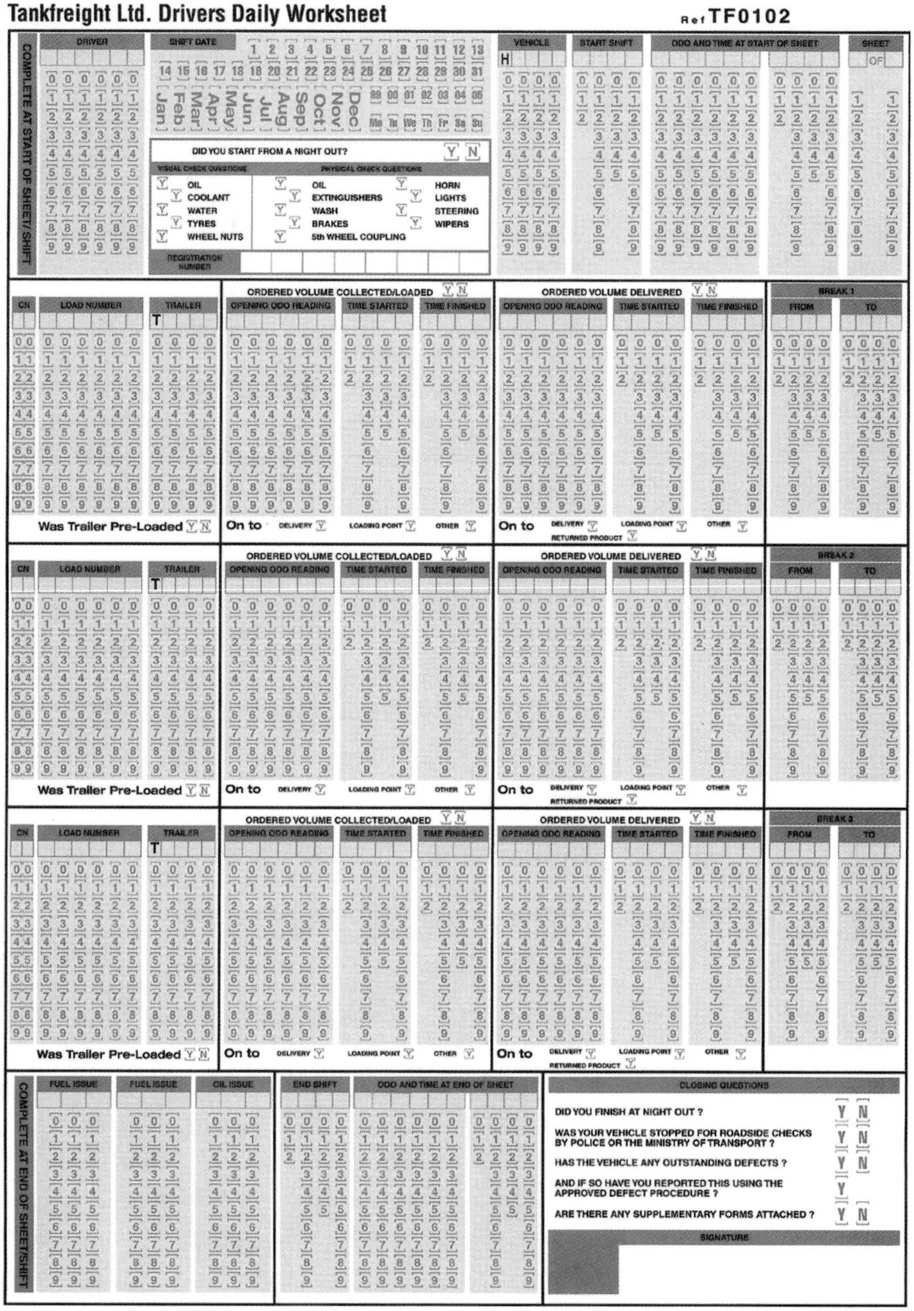

Figure 15.5 The new worksheet uses a lottery ticket metaphor.

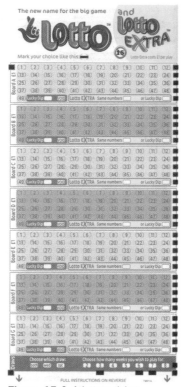

Figure 15.6 A lottery ticket.

Tim: [The drivers] saw a form a long time prior to it going live. We had to know they were capable of completing the form properly.

Treve: The form was altogether a different process . . . when we put that into the field . . . Tankfreight selected the most militant driver area they could find . . . and it went in there for three or four weeks, and they were using those forms, filling them out, but their business process was exactly the same. So there was that process that was going on in parallel to the actual system design and system interface. . . .

Paul: We received those forms as we were developing. It gave us something we could test what we were doing against.

Treve: Real forms from real drivers.

Some minor modifications were made to the forms as a consequence of the evaluation. It had the additional advantage that the recognition software could be tested on actual forms, forms with coffee and oil stains, errors, and so on.

It was possible to ask the drivers to evaluate the forms because filling in a different form did not cause any significant practical difficulties: the drivers already had to complete a form, so it was a minor change. This contrasted with the implications of asking the drivers to evaluate the computer system.

Treve: Drivers' . . . objective in life will be to drive a truck, and to deliver the consignment, and to do as little administration as possible. If you then ask them about a design of a system they want to have minimum involvement in their life, imagine the type of response you are going to get. They are not actually going to be the responses you need. So you need to get to a stage where they have already passed that threshold and they see it as a benefit to them. Immediately they see it as a benefit to them you will get constructive feedback; before that you could potentially have destructive feedback.

It is not possible to use the same approach in every circumstance. As this scenario shows, it is necessary to be flexible and use the approach that is most appropriate, but there is always a cost if you do not involve the users.

Treve: Where a client for whatever reason actually prevents you or doesn't want you to talk to the actual user . . . [and] there may be some very valid reasons for that . . . you will tend to find that you will get more changes during the prototyping, the beta stage, and even [the] prelive stage, which is expensive. Very expensive. That's the difficulty on costing . . . you don't hit the bull's eye.

The beta stage for the kiosk was quite successful.

Treve: Buttons were moved around a bit once it had gone into the field. . . . It was shall we say 70 or 80% there . . . this button a bit too close to this one, so let's move it around.

This success largely resulted from the detailed knowledge of Tokairo's users, their tasks, and the environment, gained from the requirements gathering.

4.7 Two Surprises

However carefully you gather the requirements and carry out the design process, there are likely to be a few surprises. One of the facilities in the kiosk software was its ability to reject forms that had more than a certain number of errors. This was disabled when we visited the Shell Haven installation.

Treve: The reason they don't use it is [because] initially, when it went in, forms were being rejected, because they weren't doing it right. What we must remember here is that this is a two-way, even a three-way process. Just because a company has decided to put a system in, it doesn't mean it is going to be successful. You need to win over the ultimate user, which is the driver, and if you go and antagonize the driver they will ultimately get cheesed off with you and they will block it. If they block a system, it is not going to be successful no matter how good it is. So even though the logic may be there, to throw it out as we saw it . . . from the driver's point of view they didn't want to go and refill the form. That's the reason. . . . They perceive it as a retro step if they are chucked off the system and another driver goes in there and they have to go back. It's like being . . . told off.

Tim: Also, the only reason that feature was in there was to prevent one driver from holding another driver up . . . but that didn't happen in reality . . . they didn't all arrive back at the same time.

Tokairo had not anticipated the attitude of the truck drivers or that there was no need for the facility. It is never possible to anticipate every situation.

The kiosk had an option called global messaging, which could be used for passing messages to all the drivers when they had finished a shift. Figure 15.7 illustrates the screen where the global message would go. As you can see from the photograph, this facility was not being used at Shell Haven.

> *Treve: The global messaging is really just used as and when they need to get some communication out. And there isn't much communication they need to get out, because the drivers tend to talk to the foremen fairly regularly. It's far better to have personalized communication than impersonal communication.*
>
> *Tim: It was probably intended more for the unmanned depots, because we have some depots where there isn't a permanent presence.*

This reinforces the need for flexibility. Installations are likely to have different characteristics.

5   **Summary**

The real test for any requirements-gathering and design process is the usability of the final system.

Figure 15.7 Global messaging.

In this case study, we gave members of the Tokairo team the opportunity to explain the process they went through when they designed the UI for the truck drivers' system. This process had a number of characteristics:

- It was largely informal. This had the advantage that it allowed changes to be made to both the requirements and the design, without a lengthy approval process. Thus, the process was naturally iterative. This informality was more easily achieved because the project was relatively small.
- Most of the decisions were made at meetings involving all the stakeholders, including the truck drivers and truck driver foremen. They often made these decisions very quickly. The knowledge and experience of the participants, plus other artifacts such as example forms, directed the decision making.
- The decisions to do with the UI were not written down, but they were formalized in prototypes.
- The open-plan layout of the Tokairo office and the good relationship between the Tokairo team and the Tankfreight team helped to ensure that the process was collaborative and that all the necessary information was communicated.
- The process was carried out in a reflective manner.

The support desk at Tokairo has received very few queries from Tankfreight. Also they have been asked to install a number of additional kiosks. Thus, the project appears to have been a great success.

16

Designing a graphical user interface (GUI)

See Chapter 10 for more information on metaphors and Chapter 11 for more information on interaction styles.

For a lively discussion of the issues involved in GUI design, see Cooper (1995).

1 Introduction

Most modern software used by people has a graphical user interface (GUI). It is usual for GUIs to blend a variety of interaction styles, including menu selection, form-filling, and direct manipulation. In addition, they allow for the inclusion of metaphors. This results in UIs that represent the important information and commands visually, thus satisfying the principle we presented in Chapter 5: it is easier to recognize something than to recall it.

You almost certainly use a GUI on a regular basis. This may be a version of Microsoft Windows, the Apple Macintosh operating system, or some other application. When we have been using a particular GUI for some time, it is easy to think that all the problems of UI design have been solved, but remember what it is like to start a new GUI software package. You are often faced with rows of apparently meaningless icons and menus containing commands that you do not understand. Although GUIs have many excellent features, they have not solved all the problems of UI design.

In this section, we have assumed that you are familiar with using GUIs, and thus we do not explain how to use them. Most GUIs have a familiar mixture of windows, **dialog boxes**, and tabs to help structure the interaction. They use menus, tool bars, and command buttons, which enable the user to control the interaction. Option buttons, check boxes, list boxes, and text boxes enable the user to enter information. These various building blocks of a GUI are sometimes referred to as **widgets**.

In this chapter, we will consider these issues:

- *How do you choose the correct widget?* For example, you could use a drop-down menu or a number of option buttons. How do you know which one to choose?
- *How do you use the widget effectively?* For example, how should check boxes be laid out on the screen?

The Interface Hall of Shame is no longer updated. You can visit an archive at http://digilander .libero.it/ chiediloapippo/ Engineering/ iarchitect/msha me.htm. You can find more examples of poor GUI design at the web site called This Is Broken at http://broken. typepad.com.

- *How do you combine widgets?* Most windows and dialog boxes contain a number of buttons, menus, and so on. How should these be combined on the screen?

These sections include examples of poor GUI design taken from the Interface Hall of Shame, a web site containing a wide selection of actual examples of poor UI design.

Finally we provide some extended exercises that give you practice analyzing and designing GUIs.

We draw this section together with a progressive example, based around a GUI for a sports center. In this example, we step you through the design of a GUI from the requirements specification and conceptual design to the actual design. This gives you an experience of the complete design process. If you were carrying out this exercise for real, you should involve the users at every stage, using prototypes to check the developing design.

This is not a comprehensive consideration of all the possible widgets and how they can be used, as this would not be possible in the space available. Instead, we have concentrated on some of the most important ones. Box 16.1 lists some sources of detailed advice.

Appendix 1 at the end of Part 3 contains a summary of the design guidelines we consider in this chapter. As with all guidelines, you need to interpret these according to your particular circumstances, following or disregarding them as appropriate. However, you should be able to justify all the decisions that you make.

Box 16.1	**Style Guides for GUIs**

For extremely detailed information on widgets and designing Windows applications, see The Microsoft Windows User Experience, http://msdn. microsoft.com/library/default.asp?url=/library/en-us/dnwue/html/ welcome.asp.

The equivalent information for Mac OS (user interface Aqua), the Apple User Experience Guidelines, are at http://developer.apple.com/documentation/ User Experience/Conceptual/OSXHIGuidelines/index.html.

The Open Source movement has several desktop environments and other GUI initiatives. Visit www.freshmeat.net for a list. One example is GNOME. The Gnome Human Interface Guidelines are at http://developer.gnome.org/ projects/gup/hig/1.0.

For more GUI design guidelines and more detail on how to design GUIs, see Weinschenk *et al.* (1997), Johnson (2000), and Fowler (1998). We drew on these sources extensively for this chapter.

2 The Appearance of Widgets in Different Pieces of Software

Different pieces of software often represent these widgets in slightly different ways. Figure 16.1 shows Windows XP widgets; Figure 16.2 shows a Mac OS dialog box. As you can see, there are both similarities and differences.

EXERCISE 16.1 (Allow 10 minutes)

Consider the differences between the command buttons in Figure 16.1 and those in Figure 16.2. In particular, consider the following:

- The affordance of the buttons
- The use of color
- The shape of the buttons
- The positioning of the buttons
- The wording of the text inside the buttons

DISCUSSION

Mark writes: In Windows XP, the default button (OK, which is the button you would action if you pressed the Enter key) has a dropped-shadow effect created

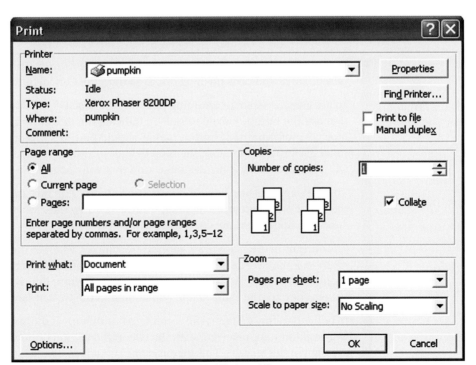

Figure 16.1 Typical dialog box displayed in Windows XP.

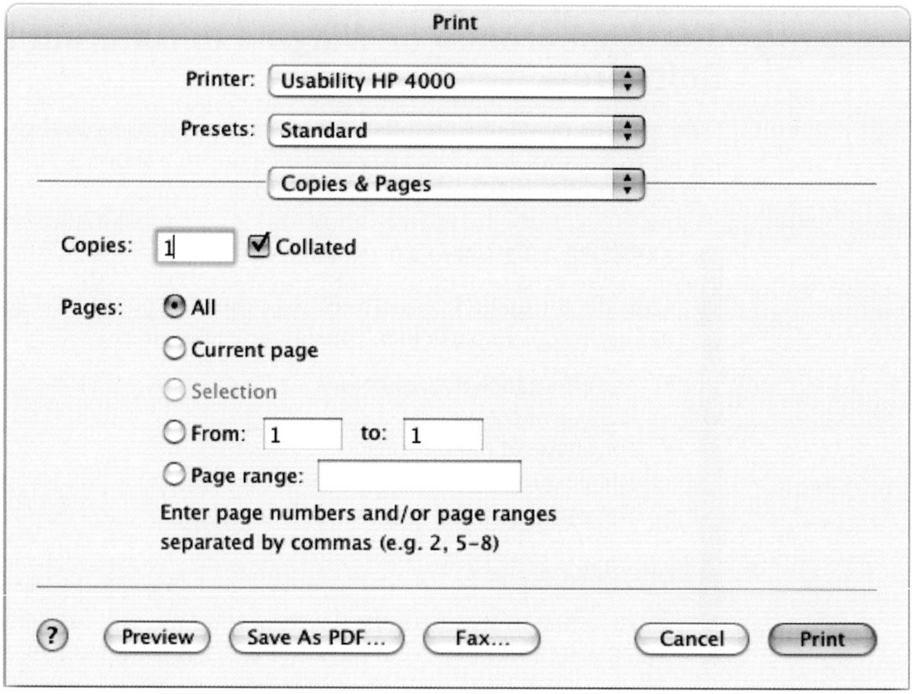

Figure 16.2 A Mac OS dialog box.

by a thicker, dark line to the right and below the button. This makes it looked raised. Thus, it affords pushing, more so than the Cancel button.

To achieve the effect of affording pushing, the Mac OS uses very subtle shading to make the button looked raised. To indicate the default button, color is used. Mac OS prescribes that button names should be verbs that describe the action to be performed, therefore the blue default button is labeled Print rather than OK, which precisely indicates the action that will occur if the button is pressed.

The two approaches have different advantages. For me, the Print button in the Mac OS is more eye-catching, but the shading effect in Windows XP more strongly implies that the OK button can be pressed.

The buttons in the Mac OS are rounded rectangles, whereas the ones in Windows XP have square corners. This does not appear to affect their usability. However, for buttons to appear grouped together, it is important that within an operating system they are the same shape and adhere to the Gestalt law of proximity.

In both operating systems, the command buttons are at the bottom-right corner. However, they are reversed, with the OK on the left in Windows XP and Print on the right in the Mac OS. This inconsistency could result in a lot of mistakes if you move between the operating systems. Which approach is better? It could be argued that the Windows XP approach is better, as we read from left to right and would encounter the OK button before the others. However, it is probably easier to locate the bottom-right corner if you are in a hurry (by allowing your eye to follow the edge of the dialog box). To establish which system is the best, it would be necessary to time how long it takes users to move to the appropriate button for each of the configurations.

Thus, different pieces of software represent the various widgets in slightly different ways, each with it own strengths and weaknesses. However, the most important principle is consistency. For example, the precise position of the OK button is much less important than having the OK button in the same position on every dialog box within a particular piece of software.

3 The Energetic Sports Center

Throughout the remainder of this section on GUIs, we refer to the Energetic Sports Center example. The following is only an outline requirements specification, but it is quite common to have to start designing from vague and abbreviated requirements specifications like this. If you were doing this for real, you would be well advised to go back and find out more. As that would take too long at this point, we will carry on and ask you to make assumptions to fill in the gaps. When you complete the exercises, state the assumptions that you make.

In reality, we would also have detailed information about the limitations of the current UI and the implications for the new design, based on cognitive walkthroughs and other requirements-gathering techniques. For brevity we have not included this information, but it is important to learn from the limitations of the current UI when you are redesigning it.

The task is to redesign the center's system for recording membership data and booking matches.

3.1 Domain

The wider domain is sport, and the particular application domain is the activities available at Energetic and how the sports center handles these. The center offers these activities: toddler's gym (for very young children accompanied by a parent or caregiver), football, a fitness room, women's aerobics, and squash. It has these facilities: the main hall, fitness room, playing field, two squash courts, a bar, and social area. A sketch of the layout is shown in Figure 16.3.

When adults use the facilities, they pay the appropriate charge for the facility plus a day membership fee. Alternatively, they can become a member of the center. It is usually worth becoming a member if you use the sports center more than once each week. The center currently has around 500 members.

The center would like a computer system to record membership details and to book squash matches. If it is successful, the center plans to use it for other bookings in

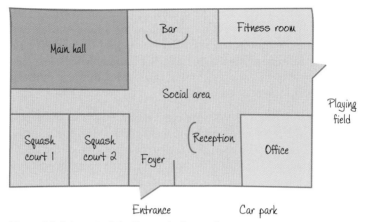

Figure 16.3 Layout of the Energetic Sports Center.

future such as matches and events in the main hall or social area, but these are excluded at the moment.

3.2 Users

In the new system, administrative members of staff will record membership details. Most staff members work part time and rarely stay for more than a few months. There are five part-time staff members and a full-time manager.

The administrative members of staff are mainly mature and have limited knowledge and experience of computing systems. Half a day's training will be available to each one when the computer system is installed. Energetic requires them to speak English fluently. One member of the staff is a wheelchair user and another has arthritis in her hands, which restricts her speed of typing and rules out use of a mouse.

Squash players vary in age from 18 to 70. The level of computer literacy among players varies greatly. At the moment the center does not have any wheelchair users as squash-playing members, but Energetic hopes to encourage the wheelchair basketball players to try the game. Some of the older players are losing some hearing, and many of them have some vision problem such as wearing glasses for reading.

3.3 Main Tasks

▶ Task 1: Adding and Modifying Membership Details

Energetic is a popular sports center, so staff members add or modify membership details at least once each day; it is thus a familiar task. It usually takes about five minutes. Telephone calls often interrupt them.

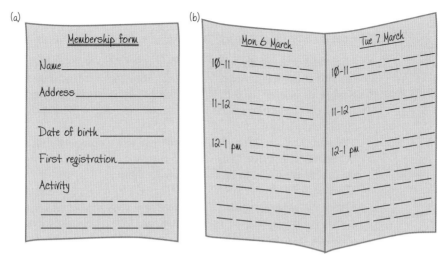

Figure 16.4 Recording details at the Energetic Sports Center.

Membership details are currently recorded using paper forms, as illustrated in Figure 16.4(a). These are stored in a filing cabinet in the office behind the reception desk. Members pay a yearly subscription. This is due on the anniversary of first joining. There are different rates for adults (age 18 and above) and seniors (over 60). Separate arrangements are made for those under 18, depending on the activity.

▶ **Task 2: Booking Squash Matches**

Squash matches are recorded in a diary as illustrated in Figure 16.4(b). This is stored at the reception desk. Bookings are often made over the telephone or after a match has just been played. There are 20 booking slots each day (two courts, each with 10 slots). Members are entitled to book the squash courts seven days ahead. Nonmembers can only book them five days ahead.

In the new system, members can book in person or telephone the center. Players are often in a hurry, as they tend to book their next match on their way out after playing a match. They are well motivated, because if they do not book a court, then the courts may all be fully booked when they want to play their match. In this example, we are not considering how the other activities are booked.

3.4 Environment

The environment is busy and noisy. The bookings diary is kept on a notice board in the reception. The lighting is good. The environment is quite dusty and dirty due to the constant traffic of people through the foyer. There is sufficient room in the social areas for a computer to enable players to book their own squash matches.

3.5 Technology

The center has already made the following decisions about the technology:

- There will be a small network of computers. This will enable the data to be shared.
- Initially there will be two computers. One computer will be at the reception desk. This will be used for both membership details and for booking squash matches. The other will be in the social area and will be only used for booking squash matches.
- The computer at the reception desk will use a conventional screen, mouse, and keyboard. These are well suited to the task. Also, they are cheap and the staff members are likely to be familiar with them.
- The computer in the social area will use a touchscreen mounted in the wall. This was chosen because it is robust and easy to use. There are some practical considerations, such as keeping it clean. The receptionist will be responsible for cleaning it twice each day. Sound output will not be used, as the environment is too noisy.

The center wants the screens to look like the forms that the office staff are used to completing.

3.6 Conceptual Design

The content diagram is based on a number of concrete cases that we have not included; we have deliberately kept the content diagram simple and have limited the task objects to the most important. The less important ones can be added in later as the design progresses.

▶ **Primary task objects: Member, booking.**

▶ **Attributes**

- *Member.* Name, address, other contact details, date of first registration, length of membership, membership number, age, sex, medical conditions, drug allergies, activities interested in.
- *Booking.* Date, court number, name and membership number of person making the booking.

▶ **Actions**

- *Member.* Adding and removing members. Changing the details of a member. Checking a member's record. Creating a master list of all the current members. Searching through the forms to find a particular member. Inserting the form in the correct place. Giving a member a copy of his or her record. Membership renewal.
- *Booking.* Adding a new booking. Canceling a booking.

Figure 16.5 illustrates a section of the corresponding content diagram. It includes the part of the functionality corresponding to the main tasks that have been identified. The main container links to the sequences of containers that correspond to each of the main tasks.

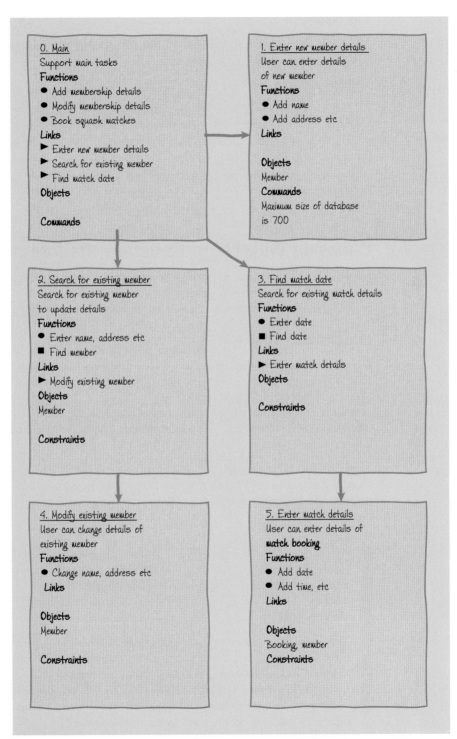

Figure 16.5 A section of the content diagram for the Energetic Sports Center.

▶**Metaphors**

A form on the screen will represent the membership form, and the bookings diary will be represented by a diary metaphor.

▶**Choice of Guidelines**

We have chosen to develop this UI broadly in line with the Microsoft Windows User Experience Guidelines. For consistency, it is often a good idea to follow industry standards if your users are familiar with them. When you design according to a specific choice like this, you will find that the resulting designs are often consistent with industry standards, but not always. Our choices do not necessarily align with our chosen guidelines in every case. The purpose of the example is to give you the opportunity to think through the issues for yourself.

4 Choosing Widgets to Structure the Interaction

Most GUIs are organized using high-level widgets, such as windows, dialog boxes, and tabs. These allow the designer to structure the UI so that it reflects the conceptual design. In this section, we look briefly at each of these widgets.

4.1 Using Primary Windows

A typical primary window contains a frame, title bar, menus, scroll bars, and so on. Primary windows often correspond to the main task objects in the conceptual design. Thus, in an office-style application, we may have one primary window for the word processor and another for the spreadsheet program. In these cases, the corresponding main task objects would be the document being written and the spreadsheet being created.

There are usually only a small number of primary windows in a UI. Each of these usually acts as a base to which the user keeps returning. You sometimes encounter a primary window used as a launch pad. In other words, it allows you to jump to other primary windows.

> **EXERCISE 16.2 (Allow five minutes)**
>
> List the two primary windows needed for the Energetic Sports Center. Sketch an additional launch pad window to choose between these.
>
> **DISCUSSION**
>
> The primary windows will be membership and bookings, each corresponding to one of the main task objects. If we also think of this in terms of the content diagram shown in Figure 16.5, membership corresponds to container four and bookings corresponds to container five. This might seem a little strange, as neither container four nor container five are directly linked to the main container. The reason for this will become clear as the design progresses, but do remember that the content diagram is there *to inform* the UI design. There are

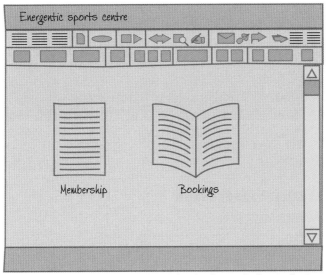

Figure 16.6 The launch pad window for the Energetic Sports Center.

often a number of different ways of creating the final design from a single content diagram. Membership will contain a representation of a membership form, and bookings will contain a representation of a bookings diary.

A possible design for the launch pad is illustrated in Figure 16.6. Selecting either the membership icon or the bookings icon will take the user to the relevant primary window.

4.2 Using Secondary Windows

Secondary windows typically complement primary windows, providing additional functionality and support for the user. There are several different types of secondary windows. Two especially useful types are message boxes and dialog boxes.

▶ Message Boxes

Message boxes, as their name suggests, pass messages to the user. These messages often relate to problems that have arisen or situations that the user needs to deal with urgently. Figure 16.7 contains some examples of message boxes that are *not* helpful for the user:

- The error message in (a) was generated when one of our authors was trying to install Visual Basic. Needless to say, she did not understand it! The programmer presumably wrote it when trying to debug the software.
- The message box in (b) appears from time to time when copying files. It is trying to help the user by offering a predicted time for the copy, but in this case the estimate time is completely incorrect.
- The problem with (c) is that the positive message "No error occurred" is delivered in the format of an error message.

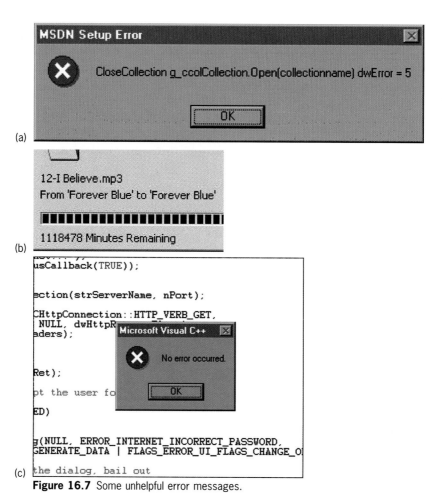

Figure 16.7 Some unhelpful error messages.

These examples show that you need to establish whether a message box is really necessary; if it is, then it has to be worded carefully.

Message boxes are often **modal**, meaning that you have to click on them if you want to continue working. (**Modeless** windows do not impose this constraint.) Modal windows are a valuable way of alerting a user if something requires immediate attention and it is important not to enter any more data. They become annoying if the diagnosis of the situation that is presented to the user does not adequately explain what is going on or why the user's input is necessary. This is one of the reasons message boxes can be so irritating — you do not invoke them, the system does; but you have to respond to them before carrying on. They can also confuse the novice user who does not understand why the system has stopped responding. Otherwise, the choice between modal and modeless windows really depends on the needs of the users and task. Novice users may find modal windows simpler, as their attention is more clearly directed, but expert users may find modal windows unnecessarily restrictive.

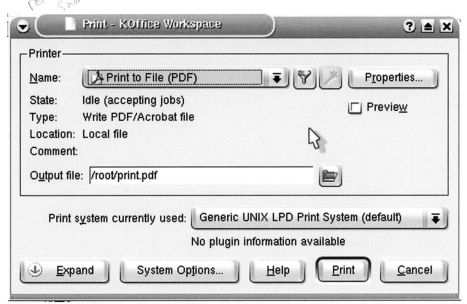

Figure 16.8 Open source print dialog box.

▶ Dialog Boxes

Dialog boxes are invoked by the user. They are often used where additional information is needed to carry out a task. For example, Figure 16.1 is the dialog box that appears when the user wants to print from Microsoft Word. You may be familiar with it or with one of the similar dialog boxes in Figure 16.2 or Figure 16.8. These dialog boxes all ask for similar information: the details about the printer, pages to print, and other options for the printing task.

Dialog boxes can be complex screen entities, containing text fields, command buttons, and so on. Most dialog boxes are modeless, allowing the user to swap to other windows as needed.

Sometimes the user needs to work through a series of dialog boxes in a strict sequence to complete a task, in which case modal dialog boxes will probably be a good idea. A series of modal dialog boxes like this is often called a **wizard**.

EXERCISE 16.3 (Allow 10 minutes)

In the Energetic Sports Center, the membership primary window will display the details of one center member. Which of the other containers associated with members in the content diagram is likely to correspond to a dialog box? What types of information will the user need to enter?

DISCUSSION

When the appropriate membership details are displayed, you can add and modify the details within the main window. Searching through the membership

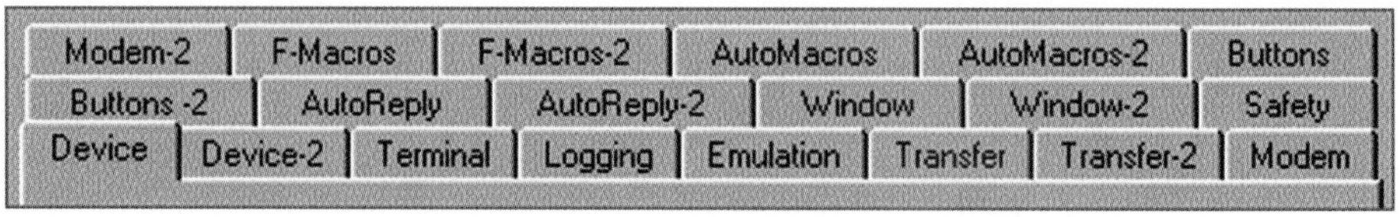

Figure 16.9 Unwise use of tabs. (From www.iarchitect.com/shame.htm, retrieved on September 9, 2000.)

forms is not possible. It will be necessary either to enter a command to step through the forms or, more powerfully, to invoke a dialog box that allows the user to specify the type of search. This dialog box corresponds to container two. Thus, the user may enter the member's name, address, and so forth.

4.3 Using Tabs

Tabs are useful for classifying the properties of a task object represented by a window. They are based on an index card metaphor. For example, if you want to alter the settings on your display, the relevant dialog box may contain a number of tabs: one may allow you to alter the screen saver, another to alter the background, and so on.

However, as Figure 16.9 illustrates, you can have too much of a good thing. In this example, there are three rows of tabs; they change position when one of them is selected. The rows are different lengths and the labels are confusingly organized: why is Modem in a completely different position to Modem-2? Thus, as with all other interface components, tabs need to be used with care. They are not the answer to all problems.

There are a number of issues that you need to consider when you use tabs:

- *Is the information on the different tabs independent?* It should be; otherwise the user is likely to get confused. If you think about the way index cards are used — for storing names and contact details, say — the information is always independent.
- *How many tabs do you need?* As we have shown, too many tabs can make the situation worse. It might be better to use more than one dialog box.
- *Do the tabs need to be completed in a specific order?* If so, this does not fit the metaphor and an alternative approach should be used.

> **EXERCISE 16.4 (Allow 10 minutes)**
>
> In the Energetic Sports Center, the membership primary window will display the details of one center member. How could this information be divided into more than one tab? You should consider the original membership form when you make this decision.
>
> Also, the managers have decided to ask each member which activities particularly interest them. This is mainly for statistical and planning purposes, but also

so that members can be advised to be cautious if they are considering a very active sport when they are unwell. Think about how you will represent the information on the form. For example, will you use only text boxes or a mixture of text boxes and other widgets? This is significant, because a block of option buttons takes up more space than a single text box.

DISCUSSION

One approach might be to divide the information into general details, membership details (when they first joined, length of membership, etc.), medical conditions, and activities. These are all reasonably independent.

However, if the person has a heart condition, then he or she should not play squash; so it does not work perfectly. This design runs the risk of the staff member not noticing the potential danger as the information would be on different tabs.

One way around this would be to automatically gray out the squash option on the activities tab once a heart condition has been indicated on the medical conditions tab. However, this option assumes that the details of any medical conditions are always entered before the activities, which may not be the case.

Using tabs also means that the user may forget to complete one of them. This would be less likely to occur if all the information is on a single dialog box. However, tabs do help to organize the data and can result in less complex screens.

5   Choosing Widgets to Control the Interaction

The user controls the interaction using a variety of GUI widgets, including menus, tool bars, and command buttons. These widgets allow the user to carry out the tasks specified in the conceptual design. In this section, we look briefly at each of these widgets.

5.1 Using Menus

Most GUIs contain a variety of types of menu.

- *Drop-down menus* appear when a menu title on the menu bar or an icon on a tool bar is selected (their existence is sometimes indicated by a down arrow). This is the most common form of menu.
- *Cascading menus* are submenus that appear when the user moves his or her mouse over a menu item that has a triangular arrow beside it. This can result in a number of menus being displayed on the screen at the same time. Cascading menus require the user to have particularly good mouse control.
- *Roll-up menus* are free-standing movable menus. These are often invoked from drop-down menus and can be moved according to need. To save screen space, they can be rolled up (contracted, so that only the menu header is displayed) and rolled down again.

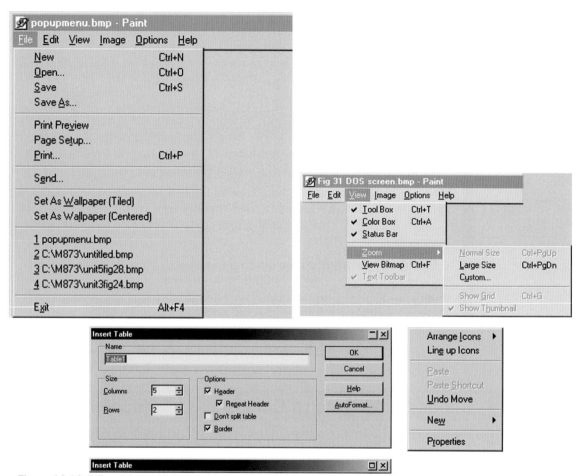

Figure 16.10 Different types of menus.

- *Pop-up menus* are floating menus that are invoked by the user. The position of a pop-up menu on the screen and its precise menu items depend on the cursor position when it is invoked. The menu contains the most common tasks associated with the object at that cursor position. Thus, pop-up menus provide shortcuts for expert users.

Figure 16.10 illustrates these menu types.

A number of issues need to be taken into account when designing menus:

- *How do you name menu items?* If you do not understand the purpose of a menu item, you do not know when to use it. Many of us are now familiar with the Microsoft convention of placing a File menu on the left-hand end of the menu bar and a Help menu at or toward the right-hand end. But have you ever hesitated over which top-level menu heading contains the command you want?

Have you ever wondered why in Microsoft Word you insert a header using the View menu not the Insert menu? And have you ever clicked on a menu because you are not quite sure what commands it contains? All of these are symptoms of the problem of naming menu items.

- *Do the menus allow the users to do what they want to do, but no more?* Programmers may be tempted to design the menu structure around their program, allowing users access to functions that they may never want to use. Or the menus may reflect the functions offered in the program rather than the tasks that a user wants to do.
- *How do you order the menu bar and menu items?* Most users read from left to right and from top to bottom. Thus, you would expect the most frequently used menus to be in the top-left corner, but this is rarely the case. Alternatively, they could be organized so that the one used most widely through the program is on the left, working through to the most specific or detailed on the right.

The important factor is that the user should be able to understand why the menus are positioned as they are. Conventions exist for the ordering of menu items, so you need to decide whether to adopt these or to design your UI from first principles.

One approach to involving the user in the design of the menu structure is known as **card sort**. In this approach, the various functions are put on different cards and the users are asked to group these into a number of piles, each of which will correspond to a menu. It is a simple and quick technique, and it could save you a lot of time in making decisions about how to name and organize your menus.

> ### EXERCISE 16.5 (Allow 10 minutes)
>
> Draw a menu bar and associated drop-down menus for the membership window of the Energetic Sports Center. They should allow the user to perform the following tasks:
>
> - Search for a particular member (corresponding to the link to container two in the content diagram shown in Figure 16.5).
> - Print the details of the displayed member. (This was derived from the "Giving a member a copy of their record" action for the member task object in the conceptual design.)
> - Add a new member (corresponding to the link to container one in the content diagram).
> - Sort the members into a particular order. (This was derived from the "Inserting the form in the correct place" action in the conceptual design — you add a new member and then sort the list.)
> - List, in tabular form, the members in a secondary window. (This was derived from the "Creating a master list of all the current members" task.)
> - Delete an existing member from the membership list.
>
> You should be able to justify your decisions: why you chose the menus you did, how you named the menus and menu items, and how you specified the ordering.

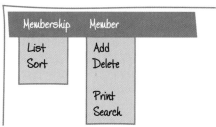

Figure 16.11 Menus and menu items for the Energetic Sports Center.

DISCUSSION

The menus that we designed are illustrated in Figure 16.11. The tasks can be divided into two groups: the first relates to the membership list, the second to individual members. We chose menu titles and item names that the user should be able to understand. Thus, we refer to membership lists rather than database files. We decided to order the menu bar so that the most global menu is at the left end.

We have ordered the menus alphabetically, as they are so short. We have left a gap between Delete and Print in the Membership menu because we want to emphasize that Add and Delete are grouped together.

Do you agree with our choices, or would you do it differently?

5.2 Using Tool Bars

Tool bars complement the menu hierarchy. They contain a range of frequently used commands, represented by icons. The icons are often explained by ToolTips, small pop-up windows that contain the associated menu command. Tool bars enable the experienced user to operate the software quickly. It is common to have a selection of different tool bars each specializing in a different area of the program's functionality. Often these can be made invisible if they are not required.

Tool bars often appear below the menu bar on primary windows. They can also appear in a secondary window, known as a palette window. Palette windows are often used in drawing packages.

One of the key issues for tool bars is which icons to choose. This is a difficult task, and any choices that you make must be user tested. Users often interpret icons in unexpected ways.

Figure 16.12 A selection of icons from Microsoft PowerPoint tool bars.

EXERCISE 16.6 (Allow five minutes)

Look at the icons in the tool bars shown in Figure 16.12 and write down the function that each one invokes.

DISCUSSION

Caroline writes: I found it easy to name the first three from the top left (New, Open, Save). I would have to go back to PowerPoint to find out what the next two are, even though I have used various versions of this program for several years. Then we have a group for print, print preview, and spelling check. . . . Yes, I know what they all do up to the grayed-out little globe next to the table icon. Then I have no idea about the remaining ones on this line.

If you found this exercise was too easy because you knew all the icons, then maybe you should ask a friend or relative who is less familiar with PowerPoint what she or he thinks each one does. The answers might be surprising.

The following list of desirable properties of icons is adapted from Horton (1991):

- *They can easily be distinguished from each other.* As designers, we want to ensure that the user selects the correct icon, even when in a hurry. If the icons are too similar, users can make mistakes.
- *They can easily be recognized and understood.* The users must be familiar with the illustrated object and be able to associate it with the underlying concept.
- *They are visually simple.* An icon should not contain unnecessary detail. For example, a printer icon does not need to include all the buttons and trays.
- *They are informative.* For example, the left- and right-justify icons used in some word processors illustrate how the text will look.
- *They represent concrete objects.* Even if the concept is abstract, it is often better to represent it using a closely associated concrete object. Thus, a house could represent a web home page. The same applies for processes: a disk could represent the process of saving a file.
- *They are easy to perceive.* It is important to choose colors carefully and to avoid too much complexity, or the icon could be difficult to perceive. This is particularly true if the icon is small or the screen resolution is low. How often have you had to peer at an icon in order to work out what it represents?

For more details on icon design, see Horton (1994).

EXERCISE 16.7 (Allow 10 minutes)

Draw a tool bar for the menu hierarchy designed for Exercise 16.5, choosing two of the menu items to be represented on the tool bar. How did you choose the menu items to go on the tool bar? How did you design the icons?

DISCUSSION

Our design is illustrated in Figure 16.13. We chose the commands that we thought were likely to be the most frequent: adding a new member and searching for a member.

- For adding a new member we used a matchstick person with a "+" beside it. This is visually simple and easily recognized. The "+" is associated with addition, so it indicates a new person. The image should be familiar to the user and represent a concrete object. We have simplified the image, so it is easy to perceive.

Figure 16.13 Tool bar for the Energetic Sports Center.

- To search for a member, we used the image of a pair of binoculars. Although binoculars do not directly represent the process of searching, they are closely associated with that process, so they should communicate the correct meaning to the user. In addition, they are widely used for searches in GUIs, so they should be familiar to most users. We have simplified the image so that it is easy to perceive.

Do these images work for you?

5.3 Using Command Buttons

Command buttons are typically used for controlling the operation of dialog boxes. Like tool bars, they have the advantage of always being visible.

There are a number of issues that you need to consider when using command buttons:

- *How will you label them?* It is extremely important that the user should understand what action the button carries out.
- *How will you position them on the screen?* They are often found at the bottom of dialog boxes, but this is not always the case. Also, what order should you put them in? The usual approach is to have the most important buttons at the left end of horizontal lines of buttons and at the top of vertical columns of buttons. In our culture, this reflects the order in which people read.
- *What size should the buttons be?* To visually group the buttons, they should be the same size and shape. Buttons of different width are acceptable if the labels are different lengths and the buttons are in a row.

Figure 16.14 shows the use of two command buttons in a dialog box that appeared after a user unsubscribed from a mailing list. What is wrong? The labeling. It is not at all clear what will happen when the buttons are selected. For example, when Undo is selected, does this mean that the user will be resubscribed to the mailing list? It may mean that the confirmation message will not be sent. (Why does it need to be sent anyway when this message has already been received?) Furthermore, it might cause the dialog box to disappear. However, it seems likely that this is what the Con-

Figure 16.14 Poor use of command buttons. (From www.iarchitect.com/shame.htm, retrieved on September 9, 2000.)

tinue button does. In addition, neither button is highlighted as the default button, and there are no keyboard equivalents.

This type of situation tends to arise if you stick excessively rigidly to the principle of consistency. In the case of these buttons, it seems likely that there were many other dialog boxes with the options "Undo" and "Continue" where those commands were entirely reasonable — but they do not work for this specific message.

EXERCISE 16.8 (Allow 10 minutes)

The membership window of the Energetic Sports Center needs to invoke a "Search for member" dialog box from the relevant menu and tool bar (corresponding to container two in the content diagram shown in Figure 16.5).

We need three command buttons, which should perform the following operations:

- Carry out the search.
- Cancel the search and clear the dialog box from the screen.
- Provide help.

Note: The second and third operations are in a supportive role to the tasks in the conceptual design — there is not a direct correspondence, but they are necessary for the GUI to function correctly.

Draw the section of the dialog box that contains the buttons that carry out these operations. Draw the buttons positioned horizontally. Repeat this task, drawing an alternative dialog box with the buttons positioned vertically.

DISCUSSION

In Figure 16.15(a), the buttons are in a horizontal row at the bottom of the screen. Having them at the bottom seems appropriate, as most users will work their way down the screen, completing the form and then selecting the appropriate button. Even if they intend to cancel the box, the users are likely to scan the contents first.

(a) (b)

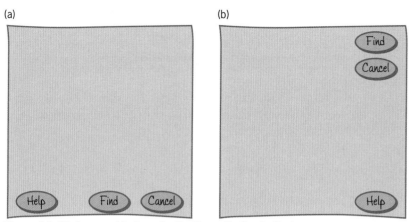

Figure 16.15 Command buttons for the Energetic Sports Center.

There is one button for each outcome. Each button contains a single word, which is intended to be self-explanatory. We used the word Find instead of OK, as we feel it is more self-explanatory, but you may prefer to use OK.

The most frequently used button, Find, is in the right corner, to the left of Cancel. Help is in the left corner at the bottom. This separation emphasizes the fact that this button carries out a different type of function to the others.

The buttons are in a line and are all the same size and shape with the same font. Imagine the usability problems if the buttons had been spread all around the dialog box, each a different size using a different font.

In another approach, shown in Figure 16.15(b), the buttons are down the right-hand side of the screen. We have maintained the order of Find and Cancel, with Find at the top as it is the most frequently used. Help is in the bottom-right corner, again separated from the others.

6 Choosing Widgets to Enter Information

Option buttons, check boxes, list boxes, and text boxes are the basic widgets for enabling users to provide information. It is also possible to build specialist widgets if these ordinary ones are insufficient.

6.1 Using Option Buttons and Check Boxes

We have grouped option buttons and check boxes together, as they perform a similar function and are often confused. Both represent a quick and accurate way of entering information into the computer system. Option buttons (sometimes referred to as radio buttons) are used when the user needs to choose *one* option out of a selection, whereas check boxes are used when the user needs to choose more than one option out of a selection.

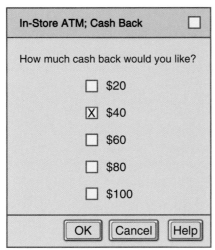

Figure 16.16 Inappropriate use of check boxes. (Adapted from Johnson, 2000.)

We often find examples where the single-option radio buttons have been used for input when more than one choice may be appropriate for the user, or we find examples where only one option is possible but check boxes have been offered. Johnson (2000) described this is as "Blooper 8: Confusing check boxes and radio buttons." Figure 16.16 illustrates one of these. Here, even though the user can only pick one choice of the amount of cash back, check boxes are offered.

There are several questions you need to consider when using option buttons and check boxes:

- *How many options can you reasonably represent in this way?* Clearly, choosing one out of three is likely to be acceptable, even in a small window or dialog box; but would one out of 30 be acceptable?
- *How should the options be grouped and laid out on the screen?* If you put them in a column, vertically, then there will be no ambiguity for the user in picking the answer required — but it takes more space on the screen.
- *How should they be ordered on the screen?* It helps if they are in some sort of order: alphabetic, in order of the most likely answer, or grouped in some other predictable way.
- *How should the options be labeled?* As with menus, the label for the option needs to be something that the user will understand.

For a more detailed discussion of the choice of input widgets, see Miller and Jarrett (2001).

The answers to these questions will depend on the context. The example given in Figure 16.16 offers a selection of numerical amounts, so it makes a lot of sense to offer them in numerical order. Also, most users pick smaller amounts of cash back, so it makes sense to order them from smallest to largest so that the most frequently chosen option is at the top. However, where the design goes wrong is that single option radio buttons should have been used rather than check boxes.

EXERCISE 16.9 (Allow 15 minutes)

We now move on to the detailed design of the membership window for the Energetic Sports Center. It was specified in the conceptual design that the representation should be a form, and in Exercise 16.3 we established that the tabs would contain general details, membership details, medical conditions, and activities. If we look at the list of attributes in the conceptual design, this will include age, sex, and the activities that interest the user. Draw the relevant parts of the general details and activities tabs, showing how options boxes and check boxes can be used to enter this information.

DISCUSSION

Our designs are shown in Figure 16.17. Your design may be quite different, but that is acceptable if you can justify the differences convincingly.

General details tab. As you can see, we decided that age and sex need to be represented by option buttons: the new member can only be one age and one sex at a time. The choice of age ranges is more challenging. We have labeled these in chronological order, so the correct one can be found quickly. The age ranges reflect how the membership is organized: under 18, 18 to 60, over 60. We have grouped the buttons for age and sex into separate blocks. Having the blocks side-by-side will reduce the need for scrolling, but users who are working quickly may forget to select the appropriate age range.

Activities tab. If we assume that new members can register for more than one activity, these activities need to be represented by check boxes. We have put them in alphabetical order, so they can be found easily. They are grouped together in a single column. It will help avoid errors if the check boxes that are not relevant are grayed out. For example, if the potential member is male, the "Women's aerobics" check box could be grayed out (and vice versa, for the situation where the activities tab is completed first).

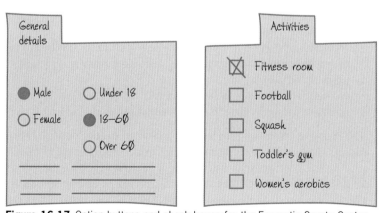

Figure 16.17 Option buttons and check boxes for the Energetic Sports Center.

This design also made us wonder why the sports center does not offer men's aerobics or mixed aerobics. Could it be that the requirements-gathering process overlooked these activities? This often happens in practice: while making your design choices, you spot that something could be missing or unclear in the requirements; this is one of the reasons why user interface design needs to be an iterative process.

6.2 Using List Boxes

If you want to allow the user to choose from a large number of options, then list boxes can be the answer. Some list boxes restrict the user to selecting one option; multiple-selection list boxes allow the user to select more than one option. In addition, some list boxes drop down and others are permanently displayed. Both types are illustrated in Figure 16.18. Drop-down boxes allow the user to select only one option. Some permanently displayed list boxes allow the user to select more than one option using the CTRL key, but unfortunately many users do not know how to do this; if this type of input is desirable, then you may need to add extra instructions near the box that explain how to do it.

There are several questions you need to consider when using list boxes:

- *How many options should be displayed?* Some authors recommend displaying between three and eight options, but sometimes options that are out of sight and need to be scrolled to will never be seen by users.
- *How much space is available?* Is there space for a permanently displayed list box, or should a drop-down list box be used?
- *Are the options likely to change?* If they are, a list box is much more flexible than option buttons or check boxes.
- *Are multiple selections needed?* If so, the list box should allow for this.
- *What default values should be used?* Defaults can speed up the use of the program significantly.

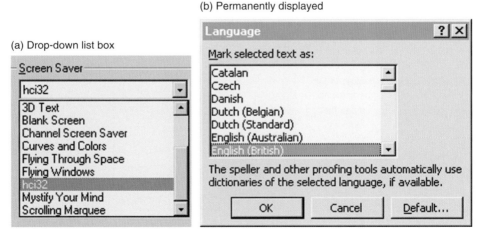

Figure 16.18 Drop-down and permanently displayed list boxes.

List boxes are often combined with text boxes, allowing the users to choose from a list or to type in the option themselves. The text box can also be used for filtering a long list of options.

EXERCISE 16.10 (Allow 15 minutes)

The bookings primary window for the *Energetic* sports center will appear on both the PC in reception and the touchscreen in the social area. It has been established in the conceptual design that this will take the form of a diary metaphor.

In this exercise we concentrate on the design of the touch screen in the social area.

Illustrate how the bookings window may look. The users should be able to make their booking by entering their membership number using a drop-down list box.

Include buttons to allow the users to turn the pages in the booking diary. This will correspond to container three in the content diagram shown in Figure 16.5.

DISCUSSION

Our design is shown in Figure 16.19.

The user chooses the correct day by repeatedly pressing the left or right arrow keys. This could be rather slow, but it is simple and most users play regularly, so only a few presses should be necessary.

We have chosen to display two days on the screen and to make the screen look as similar to a book as possible. If the user is going to enter her membership

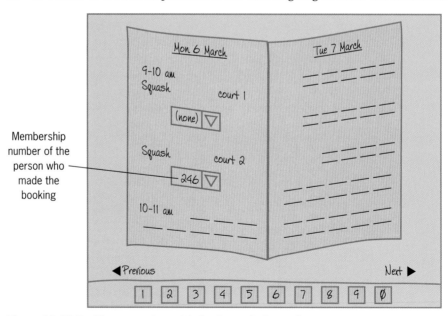

Figure 16.19 Booking a squash court in the Energetic Sports Center.

number, there needs to be an onscreen keypad. We have included this in a line across the bottom in order to avoid using too much space on the screen. It could be argued that we should have used a more standard keypad shape for ease of recognition and speed of use.

Once the user has touched the squash court she is interested in booking, she touches the down arrow key in the combo box and the membership list is displayed. She then starts entering her membership number, and this acts as a filter for the list (scrolling through would be a slow process with so many members). This list contains the name of the member to confirm that the user has entered the correct number. The user can then either type the complete number or select her number from the list. All the buttons would need to be large enough to be selected by finger.

6.3 Using Text Boxes

The text box is the most flexible widget for entering information. If it is not possible to anticipate the user input, or if you do not wish to constrain choice, then a text box will be appropriate.

However, this flexibility can be a disadvantage when the GUI requires standardized information to be entered. For example, if the GUI is a front end for a database, the data will need to be in a standardized form. Searching the database would be difficult if different users specify their sex as "female," "Female," "FEMALE," or just "F."

Text boxes are often used in conjunction with list boxes. The resulting widget is known as a combo box. **Combo boxes** overcome the standardization problem by matching the characters being entered into the text box against the list.

Figure 16.20 illustrates a situation where a text box should have been used. Using the drop-down list boxes would require 18 selections (select the down arrow and select the number, nine times) as opposed to one selection and nine key presses for a text box. Even overwriting the zeros would still require nine selections and nine key presses.

There are several further questions you should consider when using text boxes:

- *What size and shape should the text box be?* The size of the text box should indicate how much information is required. This is true for both the number of lines and the line length. If your program requires the user to enter a name, a single-line text box should be sufficient. However, a multiple-line text box will be needed if you are asking for additional comments.

Figure 16.20 Where a text box is needed. (From www.iarchitect.com/shame.htm, retrieved September 9, 2000.)

- *Do you know how much information the user wants to enter?* If it is not possible to anticipate the quantity of user input, then the text box should be scrollable. If the text box is scrollable, then it should also be multiple-line so that the user can look back over what he or she has written.
- *Will you want to gray out the text box?* Graying out involves altering the background of the text box and the text itself to different shades of gray. In some circumstances, you may want the text box to be grayed out to show that the content of the box cannot be changed. For example, a dialog box for changing a customer's address may include a grayed-out customer name text box. This reassures the user that he is looking at the correct record, but stops him from changing it.

EXERCISE 16.11 (Allow five minutes)

Returning to the membership window for the Energetic Sports Center, which of the following will require a text box, and why? If a text box is not appropriate, which widget would be? If a text box is needed, should it be scrollable?

- Street in the member's address
- Whether or not the member wants to go on the mailing list
- Additional information about the member's medical history

DISCUSSION

- Even a small town would have too many streets for it to be practical to offer them in a list. A text box would be much better.
- Choice of being on or off the mailing list could be represented either by a single check box or two option buttons. The two option buttons would be clearer for the user, but a single check box solution would take up less room. A drop-down list could be used, but it seems a little excessive with only two options.
- Typically, medical conditions would be entered using a number of check boxes, followed by a multiple-line scrollable text box for any unusual conditions or other additional information. The check boxes allow the data to be scanned for particular conditions.

7 Combining GUI Widgets

A user interface is more than an isolated selection of widgets, so in the final section of this chapter we consider some of the issues in combining widgets.

- If you have two possible designs, which is better? Or should you think of a third, different option?
- How would you put together a sequence of screens to complete a task for the user?
- How would you extend your design to incorporate new features?

We have done this by creating some extended exercises and discussions. We think that you will find them more valuable if you try the exercises yourself before reading the discussion, but even just reading them should help to start you thinking through some of the issues.

EXERCISE 16.12 (Allow 15 minutes)

Figure 16.21 illustrates two different designs for a tab box. Design (a) uses a sequence of traffic lights in the bottom-right corner of the dialog box. They are numbered from one to six, each corresponding to one of the tabs. According to the UI user guide, yellow means that some information has been entered on the tab, red means that not all of the information has been entered, and green indicates that all of the information has been entered. Design (b) has an indicator attached to each tab. This indicator can be on or off: "off" shows that the information is complete, whereas "on" shows that more information is required.

1. List three problems with the design in (a). Focus on the tabs, traffic lights, and command buttons, rather than on the text boxes.
2. Explain how these issues are addressed in (b).
3. Draw an alternative design that does not use tabs.

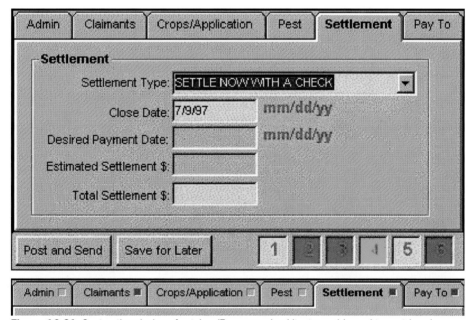

Figure 16.21 Contrasting designs for tabs. (From www.iarchitect.com/shame.htm, retrieved on September 9, 2000.)

DISCUSSION

In design (a), it is not at all clear how you differentiate between "some information" and "not all information." Why would you want to? Either the tab is complete or it is not. Thus, the design is overcomplex. This is especially unfortunate for color-blind users, who may find the colors difficult to distinguish.

The Post and Send button presumably can only be activated once all the tabs have been completed. However, it has not been grayed out. The traffic lights are giving one message, and the button is giving another.

The traffic lights are physically separated from the tabs. Thus, it is not immediately apparent that they are connected in any way. This violates the principle of structure. Once the connection has been made, the traffic lights are numbered, but the tabs are not. This means the user will need to count along to find the correct tab.

Design (b) addresses all of these problems by having an on/off indicator placed on each tab. But could there be a better solution than either (a) or (b)?

We have sketched a design in Figure 16.22 that dispenses with tabs altogether, creating a sequence of dialog boxes, each of which must be completed before continuing to the next one. (The Continue button only becomes active when the box has been completed.) This has the advantage of simplicity: the user does not need to keep moving between cards so the indicators are unnecessary. However, one benefit of tabs is that they provide an overview of the structure of the information being entered. This is lost in our sketched design. Another approach would be to put all the information on to one scrollable form. However, this would result in information not being immediately visible until you had scrolled down the page. You need to consider the context of your design and the users' needs before deciding which approach is best.

Often design is a series of ideas, tests, and compromises like these.

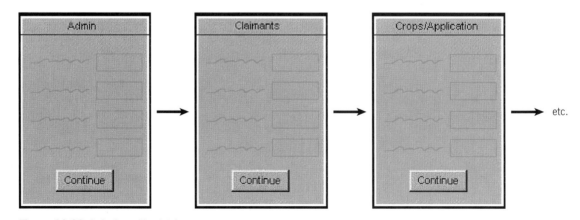

Figure 16.22 A design without tabs.

In the previous exercise, we explored the issues by comparing two alternative designs for the same UI. Our next exercise also looks at two different designs, this time comparing sequences of screens for the same task.

EXERCISE 16.13 (Allow 15 minutes)

Figures 16.23 and 16.24 illustrate two different designs for the dialog box used for configuring a mouse in Microsoft Windows.

We would like you to consider the following points:

1. What has been omitted in the later design? Why do you think this might be?
2. Discuss the wording of the tab labels (buttons, pointers, motion) in the later design. Are they better or worse than those in the earlier design?
3. Compare the approach to setting the double-click speed in the two designs. Which is better?
4. Compare the design of the slider used for adjusting the pointer speed in the two designs.
5. In the earlier design, Figure 16.23(c), there are three option buttons used to specify the button selection. In the later design, Figure 16.24(a), this has been reduced to two and the name has been changed to button configuration. Why?

DISCUSSION

1. Several tabs have been omitted completely. In particular, the Productivity and Visibility tabs in the earlier design — Figure 16.23(d) and (e) — do not exist in the later design (unless they are in a separate part of the Control Panel that we have yet to discover). These tabs contain more unusual options, such as having the mouse pointer disappear when the user is typing. This is the Macintosh standard, but presumably Microsoft established that it was not being used, so the designers simplified the mouse dialog box. The wheel tab is also missing, possibly because the mouse installed does not require it.
2. The names of the tabs in the later design (Figure 16.24) are easier to understand and seem more closely linked to user goals. The tab names Buttons, Pointers, and Motion seem to cover all aspects of the operation of a mouse that the user is likely to want to change. In the earlier design, it would have been difficult for users to anticipate what the StepSavers, Basics, Visibility, Productivity, Wheel, and General tabs actually did.
3. The approach taken in the earlier design (see Figure 16.23(c)) seems more intuitive, as the users have to carry out the task they are specifying (double-clicking on an icon). However, it requires concentration and a steady hand to get it right. In the later design, Figure 16.24(a), the slider position indicates the current setting for the double-click speed. If, after setting the slider and testing the speed, the user finds it is too fast or slow, he or she can then drag

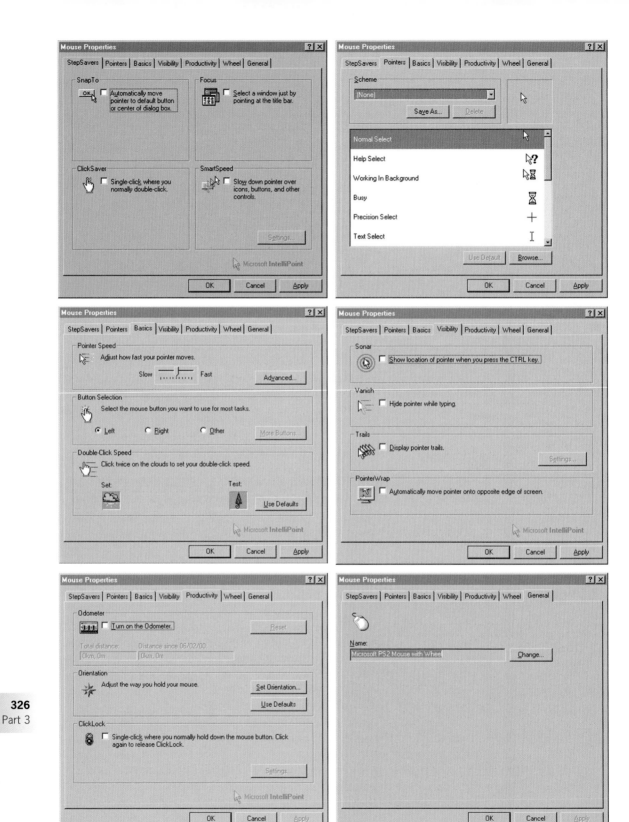

Figure 16.23 Mouse dialog boxes–the earlier design.

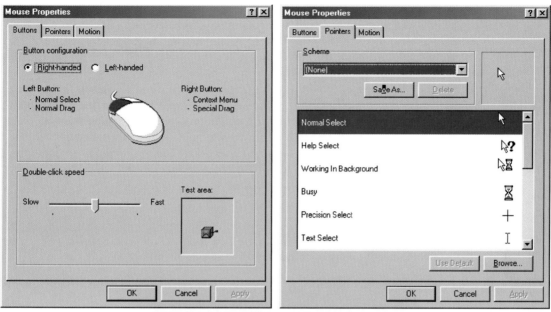

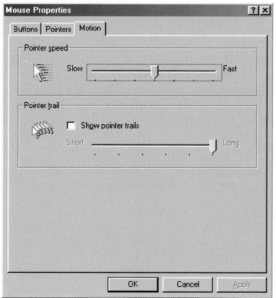

Figure 16.24 Mouse dialog boxes–the later design.

the slider indicator and try again. This is preferable to the earlier design, in which the user would need to start again each time.

4. The slider in the later design, Figure 16.24(c), is longer than in the earlier design, Figure 16.23(c). This means the pointer speed can be set with greater precision. Presumably this better reflects the requirements of the users.

5. Most mice only have two buttons, so the third option button in the earlier design, Figure 16.23(c), will usually be unnecessary. Also, the word "Other" by the third option button is ambiguous — it could mean a third button or options that relate to both buttons. What would happen if there were four buttons? In Figure 16.24(a), the later design focuses on the user, rather than on the mouse, asking about the characteristics of the user. This is a move toward a more user-centered design.

Our final exercise looks at the problem of extending a design to accommodate new requirements. We return to our example. Some time after the software was developed, an additional area of activity was identified for the Energetic Sports Center. This involves the staff taking bookings for functions in the main hall.

This required the UI designer to extend the conceptual design to include a new task object.

▶ **Primary task object:** Event

▶ **Attributes**

Date; name of the organizer; type of event (in recent years, parties, wedding receptions, and theatrical productions have been held in the hall); facilities needed (the hall, social area, and car park are available); whether an alcohol license is needed; start and finish times for the booking; any other information (such as catering requirements); name of the staff member making the booking.

▶ **Actions**

Adding a new booking; changing an existing booking; canceling a booking. A number of containers would need to be added to the content diagram, corresponding to these tasks.

▶ **Metaphors**

An onscreen form will represent the booking form.

It seems appropriate to link this activity to the bookings primary window, illustrated in Figure 16.19. Thus, instead of creating a new primary window, the information will be entered via a dialog box activated by selecting an evening booking button on each page of the diary. This option would only be available on the computer at the reception desk.

> **EXERCISE 16.14 (Allow 20 minutes)**
>
> Draw the dialog box that will collect the necessary information for booking an event, using the design guidelines in Appendix 1 to justify your design decisions.

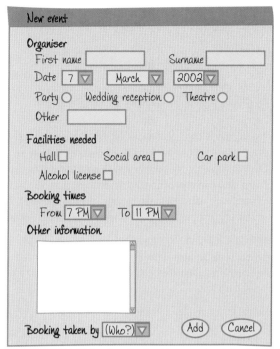

Figure 16.25 Dialog box for booking events at the Energetic Sports Center.

DISCUSSION

The dialog box we designed is illustrated in Figure 16.25.

The surname and first name are entered into one-line text boxes. The names cannot be anticipated, so no other form of widget would be possible.

The day, month, and year are entered using text boxes with drop-down list boxes. The user can therefore either choose the relevant information or type it in. The default date is that of the day jumped from in the bookings diary.

The event can only be of one type, so option buttons are used. In case it is something unusual, there is also a single-line text box.

One or more of the facilities can be requested, so check boxes have been used.

A single check box indicates whether an alcohol license is required. Two radio buttons could have been used, but a single check box is more common in GUIs for yes/no questions.

The bookings times are entered using text boxes with drop-down list boxes. The text box values are set to default times that represent the most frequent "from" and "to" times. The times on the drop-down lists increase in increments of 30 minutes. This is because the charging is for every 30 minutes.

Other information is entered into a multiple-line scrollable text box. This encourages the user to enter as much additional information as is necessary.

The different sections of the dialog box are grouped together and lined up. The hope is that the headings are self-explanatory.

8 Summary

In this chapter, we introduced the key GUI widgets and explained how to choose the most appropriate ones, how to use them effectively, and how to combine them in order to create a GUI. We did this by looking in detail at an extended example based around a sports center. It is important to remember that in an actual design you would carry out an iterative process, probably changing your design prototypes several times and involving the users at all stages in order to check the developing design.

In the next chapter, we look at the web design area. Many web sites contain GUI widgets, so the issues presented in this chapter may also apply to the next.

17

Designing for the web

1 Introduction

Organizations and individuals around the world are developing web sites. The good design of a web site is essential for its success, as a user only needs to select the back button on the browser to leave the site — possibly never to return. Thus, as a designer, you need to create a site that is usable and useful, providing content and functionality that are of value to your users.

In this chapter, we look at five aspects of web design:

- *Design principles for web sites.* These are based around the mnemonic HOME-RUN, which stands for **H**igh quality content, **O**ften updated, **M**inimal download time, **E**ase of use, **R**elevant to user's needs, **U**nique to the online medium, and **N**et-centric corporate culture.
- *Designing web sites.* We consider how to structure a site so that it is easy to navigate; users need to know where they are, where they have been, and where they can go.
- *Designing home pages and interior pages.* We consider the differing requirements of the home page and interior pages.
- *Design issues for web pages.* We look in more detail at a variety of issues, including the layout of web pages and designing for different screens and platforms.
- *Writing the content of web pages.* In particular, we consider the inverted pyramid writing method that is used by journalists.

For more details of HOME-RUN, see Nielsen (2000).

At the time of the dot-com boom around the end of the 1990s/early 2000s, the Web was changing so fast that it seemed almost impossible to offer advice to people who were designing web sites because it might be out of date in a day or two. Now we see a slightly slower pace of change. On e-commerce sites in the United States in 1998, there was little consistency: for example, you would have had to click on "order list" (www.qvc.com) or "shopping cart" (www.amazon.com) or hunt to a lower page (www.gateway.com) in order to see your purchases. Today, all these sites have a "shopping cart" linked directly from the home page — and most users expect to find a shopping cart or shopping basket when they are buying things online. Now that the pace of change is less rapid, we hope that the advice in this chapter will be helpful for some time to come.

As with the section on GUIs, we include a progressive example. This time it is based around the web site for a hotel booking service. This only represents a single pass through the design process. In reality, you would iterate a number of times, involving the users throughout, using prototypes to check the developing design. We also include screen dumps from a variety of web sites. These sites may have been redesigned if you visit them. This does not matter, as it is the design issues that count.

Appendices 2 and 3 contain summaries of the design guidelines we consider in this chapter. Again, as with all guidelines, you need to interpret these according to your particular circumstances, following or disregarding them as appropriate, and you should be able to justify all the decisions that you make.

When we were writing this chapter, we found these sources to be particularly useful:

- Lynch and Horton (1999)
- Nielsen (2000)
- Koyani, Bailey, and Nall (2003)
- IBM Ease of Use guidelines (as of June 2004)
  http://www_3.ibm.com/ibm/easy/eov_ext.nsf/publish/602

2 The Lovely Rooms Hotel Booking Service

The Lovely Rooms hotel booking service is the example we have created for this chapter. As for the Energetic Sports Center, you will find some gaps in the specification and you will need to make assumptions to fill the gaps.

2.1 Domain

The Lovely Rooms hotel booking service specializes in finding rooms in small, privately owned hotels in the East of England (Essex, Suffolk, Norfolk, Cambridge, Hertfordshire, and Bedfordshire). The hotel may be described as a bed and breakfast, an inn, or may be part of a pub, but we will call them all hotels for the moment. This is a semirural, somewhat old-fashioned part of England and the hotels are mostly in traditional buildings. Most of them only have two to five rooms to let, and the hotel owners also do all the work in the hotel themselves including all the cleaning and cooking as well as financial aspects and publicity.

2.2 Users

Lovely Rooms has identified three target groups of users:

- Vacationers planning to visit the East of England from overseas who want to find a uniquely British experience that they cannot get through a standard chain hotel

- UK residents who are visiting the area for an occasion such as a wedding or class reunion and want to take advantage of the lower rates offered by small hotels
- UK business travelers who are bored with the sameness of the big hotels and want the more personal experience offered by a small, privately owned hotel

All users will have a reasonable degree of computer literacy, otherwise they would not be surfing the Internet. However, they may be using the Internet in a relatively unsophisticated way, perhaps simply to find the telephone number of a hotel in the right area.

2.3 Tasks

Lovely Rooms would like the web site to provide various services for customers, including the following:

- Recommend a choice of three hotels geographically nearest to a location specified by the user that have availability for the nights required ("Find a lovely room")
- Offer special rates and discount packages if the hotel chosen has one available ("Special offers")
- Allow the user to book the room either online through Lovely Rooms, or by contacting the hotel's own web site directly ("Online booking").

The exercises in this chapter will focus on the design of the pages presenting the details of hotels that are close enough and have rooms available.

2.4 Environment

Because Lovely Rooms wants to appeal to busy business travelers, the booking service has specified that the site must be easy to use, even if the user is interrupted or in a noisy environment such as a busy open-plan office. Other than that, Lovely Rooms assumes that its users might be in any type of environment: home or office or even another hotel room.

2.5 Technology

Similarly, each user might have a different computer configuration. However, Lovely Rooms is assuming that some users, especially UK residents looking for a bargain, will have relatively low-specification PCs and will be using high-priced UK telephone lines and a slow modem. This means that the web pages should be designed to download as quickly as possible.

2.6 Conceptual Design

The content diagram is based on a number of concrete use cases that are not included. It is only a small part of the conceptual design, focusing on the customer who wants to look at the details of hotels that are available. We have deliberately kept this simple so that the exercises do not take you too long.

▶ **Primary Task Object: Hotel**

▶ **Attributes**

Hotel type (bed and breakfast, purpose-built hotel, converted older property, traditional inn or pub, restaurant with rooms); number of bedrooms; location; special features.

▶ **Actions**

Browse through hotels; search for a hotel near a particular location.

Figure 17.1 illustrates a simplified section of the corresponding content diagram. The main container links to the sequences of containers that correspond to each of the primary tasks.

▶ **Metaphors**

To help users who are not very familiar with the geography of the region, results from a search will be shown on a map as well as in a list.

3 Design Principles for Web Sites

Before we start looking at some more specific guidelines, you should be aware of a number of key principles. We have grouped these according to the HOME-RUN acronym defined in Nielsen (2000).

3.1 High-Quality Content

The content of your site is critical. If you do not provide the information or functionality that your target users want, they may never visit your site again. If your web site sells, say, cars, and it does not include key information such as current prices, availability, optional extras that can be selected, and delivery times, potential car purchasers may be disappointed and shop elsewhere.

3.2 Often Updated

Most sites need to be updated regularly. The frequency of the update will vary according to the nature of the site:

- A news site will probably need to be updated several times each day.
- A site selling washing machines will only need to be updated when there is a price change or a new model is added to the range, making a weekly update sufficient.
- A personal site will be updated when the owner feels that a change is necessary.
- An archival site, such as the records of meetings of a town council, will be added to (when the next meeting is held), but the older pages will need to stay as they are or at least keep the same addresses (URLS).

The importance of the updating process to the users varies according to the site. For example, the content of an online encyclopedia is likely to remain relatively

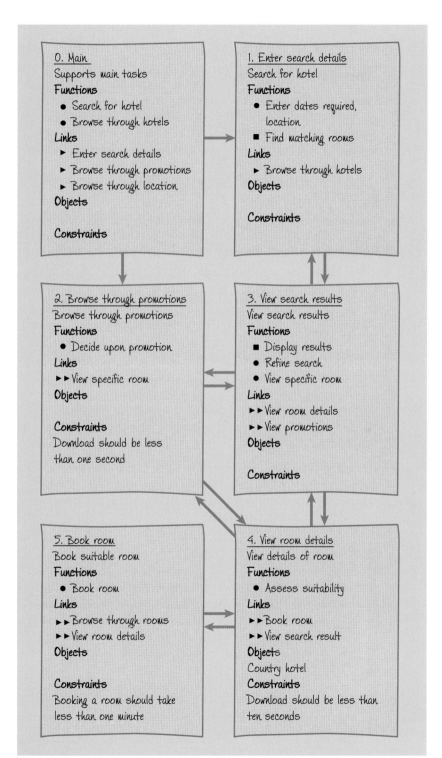

Figure 17.1 A section of the content diagram for the Lovely Rooms hotel booking service.

unchanged, and updates will not be the main reason most users visit the site. In contrast, a news site will be visited because it is up to date.

3.3 Minimal Download Time

We will be talking about download time in more detail later in this chapter. However, most of us have experienced frustration at slow-to-download web pages that contain large and unnecessary graphics or irritating animations. Such sites are likely to be unpopular with users, particularly those using slower dial-up connections or trying to connect from mobile devices.

3.4 Ease of Use

Users need to be able to find the information or services they need quickly and easily.

3.5 Relevant to User's Needs

In addition to having good content, your site must allow the users to carry out the tasks they want to perform. For example, if a user is choosing a car, it should be easy to compare the features of different cars on the same screen. You should be imaginative about the way in which the users will want to use the information on your site.

3.6 Unique to the Online Medium

Why use a web site? Most companies have some expertise in developing publicity leaflets. If this is all you are using your web site for, maybe you should just use a leaflet. Web sites should provide some additional benefits.

3.7 Net-centric Corporate Culture

The company behind the web site needs to put the site first in most aspects of its operation. It is not enough to pay lip service to the technology. With the competitive international environment that currently exists, a good web site could be the difference between success and failure.

> **EXERCISE 17.1 (Allow 10 minutes)**
>
> Suppose that you are designing a web site for a small local group of volunteers who do shopping and other errands for people who cannot easily leave their homes. The volunteers want to offer contact details for new recruits and to have a password-protected area where they can match volunteers with people who need help. Do you think that all the HOME-RUN guidelines apply to this web site, or would you suggest some changes to them?
>
> **DISCUSSION**
>
> *Often updated.* This web site won't be of much use if the contact details and volunteering opportunities are out of date, so the group needs to decide who will maintain it and how often.

Minimal download time. It is likely that some of the volunteers and some of the people that they help will have older computer equipment and possibly dial-up access to the Internet, so speedy download times are important.

Ease of use. If the web site is difficult to use then it won't be popular, so ease of use is very important here.

Relevant to user's needs. Volunteers tend to be forthcoming with their views on things that affect their volunteering, so this is a crucial guideline if you want to keep them happy.

Unique to the online medium. It might be just as easy to create a notice board in a local community center. Maybe the group does not really need a web site? Or perhaps it would work just as well if the group replicates the system it already has on its web site? This guideline may not be all that important in this case.

Net-centric corporate culture. It is important to remember that the purpose of this group is to help other people, not to make money or operate web sites. So this guideline doesn't really apply.

If you are designing a web site or web service for a group, it is well worth reading this article before you begin: "A Group Is Its Own Worst Enemy" (Shirky, 2003).

---

4   Designing Web Sites

We are going to look at three specific areas of designing a web site:

- How the web pages are structured in relation to the tasks the users want to carry out and the natural organization of the information
- How to tell users where they are
- How to help users navigate around the site

4.1 Designing the Web Site Structure

You are probably studying this book in a linear manner: you read a bit, try the associated exercises, read the next bit, and so on. An alternative approach would be to study the book in a nonlinear manner, jumping around the text.

For more information on hypertext, see Nielsen (1990).

The concept of nonlinearity has been implemented in many software systems. It is usually referred to as **hypertext**. Hypertext is a network of nodes (often implemented as separate screens containing text, images, and other screen components) that are linked together. The Web is a hypertext system made up of a huge number of pages that are linked together in a very complex way. This means that you can surf the Web in different ways, visiting sites and then moving on to new ones as you wish.

This approach is extremely flexible, but can be confusing for the user. Some web sites are made up of hundreds of pages. Such sites may have developed over a number of years in a chaotic and unplanned manner. This can make it difficult for users to form a mental model of the site structure; hence, it is easy for them to lose track of where they are and become disoriented. For this reason, it is important for the site to be clearly structured. The most common site structure is some form of hierarchy, with the home page as the root node.

Some corporate web sites are organized around the structure of the organization. This can be useful if you work for the company; thus, it can be suitable for intranets, but it can be confusing for an outsider.

The site structure should always support the tasks that the target users will want to complete. This can be difficult to achieve because, however good your requirements gathering, it is difficult to anticipate every user requirement. For this reason, it is important to make the process of accessing the site as flexible as possible. That is why many web sites, as well as allowing you to follow the links, also allow you to search the site.

When you are designing the structure of a site, it can help to look first at the natural organization of the information. For example, Figure 17.2 represents a fairly standard approach to classifying books. This classification can be useful for structuring a web site to sell books. In fact, you could create a web page for each node in this classification. However, it is often not this simple, as you need to consider the following points.

- *How deep and how wide should the hierarchy be?* As web pages can be slow to download, it is irritating to have to move through too many pages to find the information you want. It is often better to have a structure that is broad rather than deep. If we were to translate every node in Figure 17.2 into a web page, this would produce a deep structure. However, if we were to have a very shallow

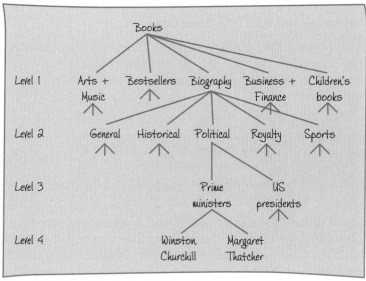

Figure 17.2 Organizing the book information.

structure, with every book linked to from the home page, then the home page would be extremely long. Thus, we need to achieve a compromise.

- *Is it better to divide a block of information into several short pages or leave it as one long page?* The advantage of having a single page is that the user does not need to keep waiting for pages to download. However, the original download will take longer. Longer pages also allow the user to read (or print out) the whole page, which can be more convenient than having to jump around. A general rule of thumb is this: if the web page is less than two ordinary printed pages long, then it is probably better to leave it undivided. In a bookselling web site, it is unlikely that the readers would want the details of a particular book to be spread over several web pages, as these details naturally belong together and the readers may want to print them out.

- *Can several web pages be combined into one larger one?* This is the complement of the previous issue. In a bookselling web site, it would be possible to put the details of several books on a single web page. For example, the details of all the biographies of Winston Churchill could be on a single page, the details of all the biographies of Margaret Thatcher on another, and so on. This would remove the need for one layer in the hierarchy. It would also mean that the reader could browse through all the biographies of a particular person more easily.

- *Does the structure of the site reflect the structure of the tasks the users want to carry out?* For example, a user who just wants to see what is available will probably want to browse, whereas a user who knows what she or he wants will probably want to carry out a search. For browsing, the structure of the data will need to be reflected in the structure of the site, but this is not necessary if the users know precisely what they want. For example, if the users of a bookselling site knew precisely which book they wanted, then it would be possible to just have search facilities on the home page and no explicit hierarchy. In reality, such sites would probably want to cater for both browsers and searchers, so both approaches would be used.

- *How should the site content be grouped?* We have already discussed the natural organization of the site content, but this is not enough. In the bookselling example, as well as pages about books, we will need a page providing information about the company, another set of pages for book reviews, and so on. One way of deciding how to organize these pages in a meaningful way is to use card sort, as described in Chapters 16 and 27.

Figure 17.3 illustrates one way of structuring the pages in a bookselling web site. In Figure 17.3 there is one page for each of the level-one categories from Figure 17.2. These pages contain brief summaries about the level-four categories. These summaries then link to the corresponding detailed descriptions. For example, the biography page would contain a list of all the people whose biographies are available. These details would link to the detailed descriptions of the biographies of the particular person. Thus, the structure in Figure 17.3 omits levels two and three of the book hierarchy. We are assuming that the number of level-four categories is quite small, otherwise the level-one category pages would become very long. If there were

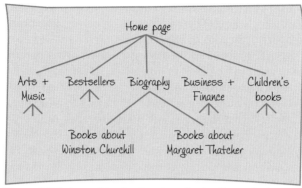

Figure 17.3 A possible structure for a bookselling web site.

lots of level-four categories, then we might do better to keep all the layers shown in Figure 17.2.

It is common to have additional links, such as links that are related by topic within the hierarchy. For example, the Winston Churchill page could be linked to the Margaret Thatcher page, as they were both prime ministers of the United Kingdom. This means that a reader who is generally interested in biographies, but more particularly interested in the biographies of former prime ministers, can browse through them more easily. We have chosen not to illustrate such links, because the structure can quickly become complex and rather confusing. However, you should be aware of the need to have a flexible navigational strategy. It is rarely adequate to only be able to move around the hierarchy level by level.

Developing an information hierarchy, or "information architecture" for a large site is outside the scope of this book. We recommend Rosenfeld and Morville (2002)

The hierarchical structure of web sites often breaks down when the user is booking or purchasing something. At this point it is common for the user to be stepped through a linear sequence of pages that collect all the necessary information. On a bookselling site, these pages typically request information about the delivery address, method of payment, and so on. The same design issues arise here: should all the information be requested on a single web page, or should it be divided into several? In what order should the questions be asked? As ever, the design should reflect the requirements of the user. For example, if the user enters most of the information and then discovers that he does not have the appropriate credit card, he is likely to be very frustrated — it would have been better to warn him about the acceptable cards earlier in the interaction.

EXERCISE 17.2 (Allow 10 minutes)

Sketch an outline hierarchy representing the organization of the hotel information for the Lovely Rooms scenario. Base this information on the details in the requirements specification and the content diagram (containers two, three, four, and five in Figure 17.1).

One of the tasks for the "hotel" task object in the conceptual design for Lovely Rooms is "Find a lovely room." Sketch an outline structure for the web pages in the Lovely Rooms site, which will allow customers to browse through a selection of rooms that are available for their choice of arrival and departure dates. Explain why you have chosen this particular structure and describe briefly what information will be contained at each level.

DISCUSSION

1. The information has been organized into a hierarchy as shown in Figure 17.4.
2. Once you have an information hierarchy, this usually suggests a corresponding structure for your web site. Figure 17.5 illustrates an outline structure for the Lovely Rooms site. This closely parallels the organization of the information. The main change is offering two different views of the results: a map view and a "Distance from your location" view.

The "Hotel details" pages contain information about specific amenities and the location of each hotel. This is an important issue, so it seems sensible to have a separate page for this.

The county pages contain information about the transport network and other facilities relevant to the customers. They also contain information about the main towns. The information is at this level so customers know about the town before moving to the corresponding town page.

The "Hotel details" pages are linked together, so someone considering making a reservation can look at the next hotel in the list of available rooms rather than having to navigate back to the "List of hotels" page (this is not illustrated).

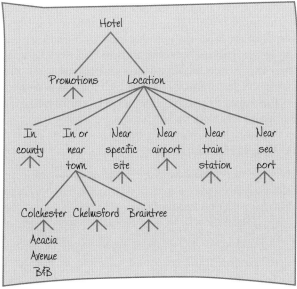

Figure 17.4 The information hierarchy for "Find a lovely room."

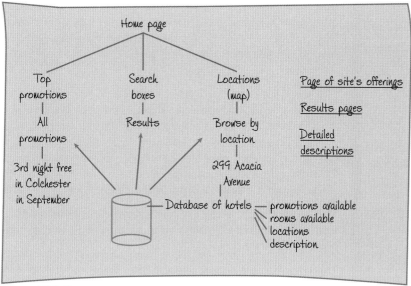

Figure 17.5 The structure of the Lovely Rooms web site.

4.2 Helping the Users Know Where They Are

It is quite common for users to jump directly to a page within a web site without passing through the home page. How are they supposed to know where they are? The answer is that you have to tell them by clearly labeling each page. The most common way of doing this is by including the organization's logo in the top-left corner, along with the name of the site.

Even moving within a web site can be confusing. Have you left the site, moved to a subsite within the same organization but with a different subbrand, or moved to a linked site from another organization? For legal or branding reasons, some organizations have strict rules about how they handle this. For example, some sites insist on opening other sites in new browser windows. Other sites rely on a small disclaimer near to any external links. Some, especially web logs (also known as "blogs"), make no mention of the move to another site but rely on branding of the target site to inform the user about the change.

EXERCISE 17.3 (Allow five minutes)

Think about the three ways we have mentioned for informing users that they have moved away from your site to that of a different organization. What advantages and disadvantages can you think of?

DISCUSSION

We have listed some advantages and disadvantages in Table 17.1. Your list may be different.

Table 17.1 Advantages and Disadvantages of Ways of Informing Users That They Are Leaving Your Site

Technique	Advantages	Disadvantages
Opening a new window	Clearly shows that it is a different site Preserves the user's location in the originating site	User cannot use the Back button to return to the originating site May disorient users who are using accessibility options such as screen readers or enlargers
Putting a disclaimer near the external link	Doesn't mess up use of the Back button Warns users that they are going to the external site but does not force them to locate a new window	Some users may fail to see the disclaimer Text of the disclaimer takes up space onscreen Negative wording of the disclaimer may undermine confidence in the originating site
Relying on branding of the destination site	Minimizes the disturbance to the user: the Back button continues to work and users do not have to locate a new window	Users may not notice that the destination site has new branding or is from a different organization, so they may be confused about where they are

4.3 Helping the Users Navigate around the Site

Three types of link allow the user to navigate around a site: **structural navigation links, associative links**, and "**See Also**" **links**.

- *Structural navigation links.* These form the underlying structure of the site. They point to other web pages within the site.
- *Associative links.* When a page is particularly long, it is common practice to have associative links that connect to fixed places on the page. For example, there may be a contents list at the start of the page, with each list item being an associative link that points to the corresponding section further down the page.
- *"See Also" links.* These point to other web sites. They are often of particular value to users, as they enable them to explore related sites. This can be useful if your site is not quite what the user was looking for. Links of this sort also provide an endorsement for the site being pointed to, so you have to be careful which sites you choose for your "See Also" links: an inappropriate link may reflect badly on your site.

Text is often used to represent links. You should consider the following questions when you use text links:

- *What color should text links be?* At one time, most sites stuck to the convention of saturated blue underlined text like this for links. The color then changed to purple or red after the link had been selected. Now we have learned that web sites that look good are also more trusted and are perceived as easier to use, so many designers use a variety of cues to indicate a clickable link that they consider to fit within the overall impression of the web site. When choosing your colors and styles for links, make sure that your choices are distinctive and consistent so that users can tell where the links are ("Provide consistent clickability cues," Guideline 10.1, www.usability.gov, 2003), and make sure that the link changes in a consistent way once the user has visited it ("Designate used links," Guideline 10.8, www.usability.gov, 2003).
- *How do you make the names of links meaningful to the user?* As with the choice of command names in menus, it is important to make the wording of text links meaningful to the user. For example, one of our team of authors recently visited a museum site that had a link called "Visiting?" in the navigation bar and another link called "What's on?" It was not at all clear what the difference was between these links, nor what might be found by following either of them. It helps if the wording of a text link closely reflects the users' goals. Thus, for the museum site, it turned out that "Visiting?" led to a page with the directions to the museum so a link title like "How to find us" would have been better.

You may wish to consider alternatives to text links:

- *Buttons or selectable graphical images.* The use of buttons is consistent with GUIs, so your users will probably be familiar with them. Selectable graphics can be more of a problem, and research has shown that they have a relatively low success rate. If there is a selectable graphic with text by it, most users will select the text. You also need to consider the needs of visually impaired users who may be using a screen reader: the selectable graphic will be invisible to the screen reader unless it has a text label.
- *Drop-down lists.* With these lists, options are chosen from one or more list boxes and the required page is identified according to these choices. This approach tends to be less usable, as the available options are invisible until the list is selected. Also, unlike text links, the list items do not indicate when the particular page has been viewed previously. This makes it even more difficult for the user to develop a mental model of the site. However, list boxes do take up less space than multiple text links.

Users feel more confident in their use of the web site if they can predict what lies behind a link before choosing it. Here are some factors to think about when picking the text for the link:

- *Should you provide additional information about what the user will find when he or she follows the link?* Figure 17.6 illustrates how small pieces of text can be used to give a flavor of the material that will be found by following the link. This stops users from wasting time jumping to pages that are of no use to them. How often have you followed links with names like "More info" only to be

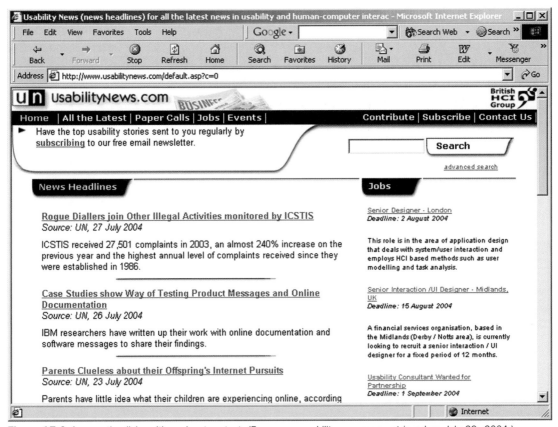

Figure 17.6 Augmenting links with explanatory text. (From www.usabilitynews.com, retrieved on July 29, 2004.)

disappointed? As a designer, you want to ensure that the users' expectations of the pages being linked to are satisfied.

- *Should you use link titles?* These are pop-up boxes that appear when the mouse pointer is over the link. They are particularly useful when there is insufficient room on the page to include additional information. Types of information they can contain include the name of the site being linked to, a summary of what the page contains, how it relates to the present page, and any potential difficulties, such as needing to register at the site.

4.4 Navigation Aids

Links are often combined into **navigation aids**. These provide users with an overview of the site structure and enable them to move around the site. Here are some useful navigation aids:

- *Site map*. Many sites offer a site map showing the site hierarchy condensed onto a single page (for example, Figure 17.7).

Figure 17.7 A typical site map. (From www.latimes.com/services/site/la-about-sitemap.htmlstory, retrieved on July 2, 2004.)

- *Breadcrumb trail.* In a breadcrumb trail, every level in the hierarchy from the top to your current position is listed from left to right. You can see this mechanism across the top of the web page in Figure 17.8, starting with "handbags" and finishing with "fabrics." In this way, it shows you both where you are and where you have come from. Every level is selectable, so you can move around very quickly.
- *Geographical or visual maps.* Links are contained within a visual metaphor. Figure 17.9 illustrates the use of a map to navigate a site; the user finds out about different parts of Ireland by selecting the appropriate part of the map. If you take this approach, it is important to include textual labels that can be read by screen readers, so that the site may be used by the visually impaired. This metaphor can, however, increase the download time for a page.
- *Navigation bars.* Figures 17.7, 17.8, and 17.9 all have variants of **navigation bars**, all of them in the L shape that is currently popular. The bar across the top can

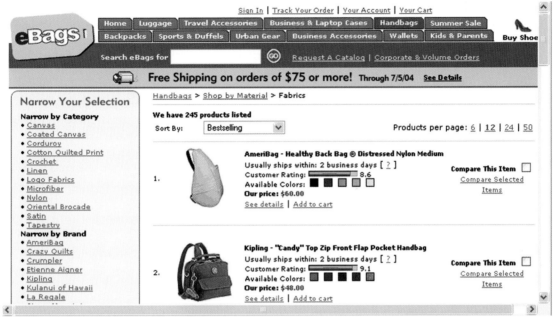

Figure 17.8 An e-commerce site with a typical breadcrumb trail. (From www.ebags.com, retrieved on July 2, 2004.)

Figure 17.9 A geographic map exploits physical geography to organize links. (From www.goireland.com, retrieved on July 2, 2004.)

be shown visually as a simple list (as in Figure 17.7), a single line of tabs (as in Figure 17.9), or even rows of tabs (Figure 17.8). At one point, Amazon.com had several rows of tabs but they turned out to be too confusing, and most sites now try to stick to a single row. The vertical bar is on the left-hand side in all of these examples, but it could be placed at the right if that seems to work better stylistically. Generally, the simpler styles (such as in Figure 17.8 or Figure 17.9) work better than the complicated multipurpose styles such as in Figure 17.7.

- *Drop-down lists.* Some sites with large quantities of links use drop-down lists of associated links to organize them into sets while saving space. There is an example in Figure 17.9, where the relatively long list of Irish counties has been compressed into a single drop-down list. This works best when the links in the list really are parallel, such as the counties, and where users really are likely to only want one of them at a time.

EXERCISE 17.4 (Allow 10 minutes)

Assume the structure of the Lovely Rooms web site illustrated in Figure 17.5. In this exercise, you will design three different navigation aids for moving around the site.

- Sketch a navigation aid that allows the prospective purchaser to skip to the town level in the hierarchy. It should use drop-down lists. This is equivalent to container one in the content diagram and represents the "search for a hotel room in a particular town" task in the conceptual design.
- Sketch a navigation aid that allows the prospective purchaser to choose between the different tasks the web site supports (not just choosing a hotel room — you will need to look at the requirements specification). In particular, discuss the color of the links, whether the links should be textual or graphical, how to make the links meaningful to the user, providing additional information, and using link titles.
- Illustrate a metaphor for the "Hotel details" page.

DISCUSSION

Our designs are illustrated in Figure 17.10.

1. In Figure 17.10(a), there is a search area for specifying the date(s) that the vacationer (user) will want the room. The user can take advantage of a calendar pop-up for easy selection of the arrival and departure dates.
2. In Figure 17.10(b), the site map has an area for the current top promotions and for the room finder, parts of which are shown in parts (a) and (d). "Top promotions" lists the most attractive promotions at the home page, with a link to browse all the available promotions for the East of England.
3. The obvious metaphor for the "Area location" section of the home page would be a map of East Anglia. This is illustrated in Figure 17.10(c). This would give vacationers an idea of the layout of this area of England. The map could also include the major roads and railways to provide some informa-

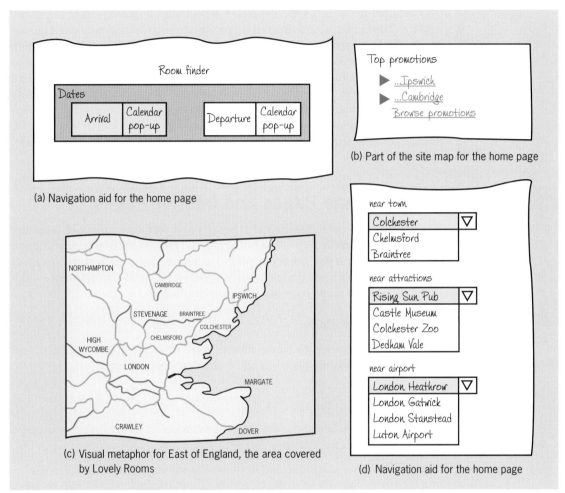

(a) Navigation aid for the home page

(b) Part of the site map for the home page

(c) Visual metaphor for East of England, the area covered by Lovely Rooms

(d) Navigation aid for the home page

Figure 17.10 Navigation aids for the Lovely Rooms web site.

tion about the transport infrastructure. Selecting one of the counties would result in the corresponding county being selected in the county location box (see Figure 17.10(d)). If we had decided not to include the county list box, this map could have been used to jump directly to the town pages instead.

4. In Figure 17.10(d), to find an "ideal" hotel, the location of the hotel can be specified in relation to a number of different criteria. Shown are the list boxes for town, airport, and near attractions; the UI also includes list boxes for choosing the location according to a particular rail station or sea port. Vacationers can even search any location; this enables them to see what hotels are available on the particular dates the user has entered and would also show any available promotions.

The defaults for each of the list boxes reflect the most frequently requested options. The list items are ordered according to frequency of previous choices. The links are in underlined blue text. We decided to follow the usual convention because we wanted to ensure that first-time users would be able to use the site easily. We did not make the links graphical, as we wanted to make the download as fast as possible: some customers may be using slow modems. We are aware that some customers may have language problems, so we have used simple language. Also, the wording of the links has been chosen to be closely related to the user goals. It is necessary to include textual labels that can be read by screen readers.

5 Designing Home Pages and Interior Pages

We are going to look in detail at the two types of pages found on most web sites: the home page and the interior pages. The home page is typically the first page you come to and the one to which you keep returning. The home page usually corresponds to container zero in the content diagram. Interior pages are those that you move on to after you have left the home page but have not left the site.

5.1 Designing the Home Page

Because it sets the scene for the whole site, the most challenging web page to design is the home page. The home page has two main functions:

- It tells the users where they are.
- It tells the users what the site does.

How you achieve these functions varies greatly from site to site. However, most sites include some, or all, of the following items:

- The name or logo of the organization that owns the site. This is usually in the top-left corner. Unless your organization is as well known as Coca Cola or you wish to be obscure for stylistic reasons, it is usually a good idea to include a **tagline**, a few words of text that describe what your organization does.
- The name of the web site. This is usually at the top of the screen. It should also be in the title bar for the browser window.
- A brief introduction to the site.
- Some sort of navigation aid.
- A summary of the latest news, promotions, or changes to the site. This is particularly useful for repeat visitors.
- A summary of the key content for first-time visitors.
- A search facility. This should help experienced web users to find the information they need quickly (and is welcomed by less experienced users if your design fails to get them to their destination quickly).

An important part of telling the users where they are also involves making decisions about the choice of typeface, colors, and page layout.

We have chosen three contrasting home pages, all from web sites owned by the CNN part of AOL Time Warner to illustrate different styles. These are all news sites and are likely to change rapidly, so you may want to look at the sites as they are today and compare them with our screenshots. The first one, Figure 17.11, is the international edition of CNN's web site. The majority of the page is filled with a big variety of links to different categories and types of news stories.

Figure 17.12 is a typical **splash page**, a Welcome page that exists to welcome the visitor and give minimal information about the brand.

Figure 17.13 has a style somewhere between the restrained, rich-link style of Figure 17.11 and the minimalist, splash page style of Figure 17.12. Much of the page is used for big, brand-driven images relating to specific facilities on the site.

Figure 17.11 Contrasting home pages: an international news site. Branding is subdued, and there are many routes away from the home page. (From edition.cnn.com, retrieved on July 3, 2004.)

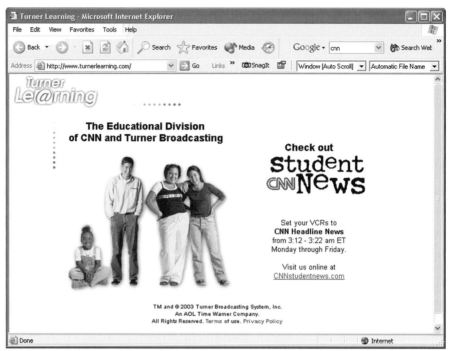

Figure 17.12 Contrasting home pages: a splash page. Almost all of the page is devoted to a strong visual related to the brand. (From www.turnerlearning.com, retrieved on July 3, 2004.)

Figure 17.13 Contrasting home pages: a news site aimed at high school students. Much of the page is about branding and directing the visitor to one specific feature, the "weekly rewind." (From www.cnnstudentnews.cnn.com, retrieved on July 3, 2004.)

Figure 17.14 An interior page. (From edition.cnn.com, retrieved on July 4, 2004.)

Figure 17.15 The same story referred to on a different site. (From cnnstudentnews.cnn.com, retrieved on July 4, 2004.)

EXERCISE 17.5 (Allow 10 minutes)

List the different elements that you anticipate will be on the Lovely Rooms home page. Would you choose a link-rich, restrained style, a minimalist style, a heavily branded style, or something else? You may want to look at some competitive hotel booking sites for inspiration.

DISCUSSION

We suggest the following elements to be on the home page, and same elements that can be safely included:

- The Lovely Rooms logo, plus the tagline "Traditional small hotels."
- As the customers are likely to be goal driven, they will not be interested in the detailed background of the company.
- The navigation aids from Figure 17.10. We decided not to use a general search engine, because visitors want to know what rooms are available on their chosen dates rather than the overall possibilities.
- We have not included a summary of the key content, as this should be apparent from the other elements.
- A list of the latest special promotions with brief descriptions. These will be linked to the detailed descriptions. This facility will be particularly useful for frequent visitors to the site.

5.2 Designing Interior Pages

Interior web pages tend to have slightly different characteristics to the home page. Typically, they contain more content and less introductory and navigational information. It is important that they help to orient the user, so it is still necessary to have information such as the name of the site and the company logo, but these perhaps should be smaller and less intrusive.

You should always include a link to the home page, as this will provide the necessary background information about the site. This is particularly important if the interior page does not contain the site navigation bar. It is also common to contain links to the other pages at the same level in the hierarchy.

Figure 17.14 and Figure 17.15 show two interior web pages, corresponding to the home pages illustrated in Figure 17.11 and Figure 17.13. Both interior pages continue the design of the home page, but they simplify it so that the user can concentrate on the specific topic of the page.

EXERCISE 17.6 (Allow 10 minutes)

List the different elements that you anticipate will be on the Lovely Rooms interior page to provide detailed information about a single hotel.

DISCUSSION

We anticipate that the following elements will be on this interior page:

- The Lovely Rooms logo. This acts as a link to the home page.
- The tagline of the site.
- Details of the particular hotel. This will take up the majority of the page and will look include a photograph of the hotel and a photograph of a typical room at the hotel, with a description of the amenities offered.
- A navigation bar aligned to the navigation bar of the site as a whole.
- Links to the next and previous hotels with availability on the nights chosen. This will allow the user to browse through the hotels.

6 Design Issues for Web Pages

When you are designing web pages, you should remember the principles and guidelines we discussed in earlier chapters, especially Chapters 5 and 9.

There are also a number of additional issues that you need to take into account when designing a web page. We discuss some of the more important ones next.

6.1 Widgets on Web Pages

In Chapter 16, we considered the design of GUIs. Web pages are a form of GUI and increasingly use a similar range of widgets. The issues we introduced in the section on the Lovely Rooms Hotel also need to be considered when you are using widgets on web pages.

6.2 Scrolling

The most important content should be visible without scrolling. Web designers talk about positioning content **above the fold**, a term taken from newspaper design. Broadsheet newspapers are displayed folded in racks, so the stories above the fold are the only ones visible to the potential purchaser. Similarly, the web content above the fold has to sell the site to the visitor. There is a risk that readers will miss content that falls below the fold. Figure 17.16 illustrates a home page that requires scrolling in order to see important information, such as the purpose of the site and the internal links. The text does imply that the user needs to scroll down.

At one time, the phrase "users don't scroll" was frequently quoted as a design guideline, for example, in the 1996 column by Jakob Nielsen located at www.useit.com/alertbox/9606.html. However, since then users have become more adept in using the Web and designers have become more sensitive to the benefits and problems of longer web pages. Recent advice has been more user centered. For example, Koyani, Bailey, and Nall (2003) noted:

> *Guideline: Make page-length decisions that support the primary use of the Web page.*

Figure 17.16 A home page that needs scrolling. (From www.candlemaking.org.uk, retrieved on July 6, 2004.)

See Chapter 13 for more information on writing legible text.

Comments: In general, use shorter pages for homepages and navigation pages, and pages that need to be quickly browsed and/or read online. Use longer pages to (1) facilitate uninterrupted reading, especially on content pages; (2) match the structure of a paper counterpart; (3) simplify page maintenance (fewer Web page files to maintain); and (4) make pages more convenient to download and print.

Scrolling horizontally, across the page, continues to be very unpopular with users as it interrupts the flow of reading on every line. Try to ensure that either the text wraps to the user's screen size or the line length is less than the anticipated screen size. Also, if the line length is more than about 60 characters (eight to twelve words), this will affect the legibility of the text.

6.3 Designing for Different Screens and Platforms

In conventional GUIs, it is possible to control the precise appearance of the screen. This is not possible for web sites. Therefore, it can be difficult to address fully the scrolling issue. For example, the user may be viewing the site using a small screen on a handheld computer, which requires scrolling around extensively in order to find anything. Similarly, a visually impaired user may be using much larger type sizes, which means that both horizontal and vertical scrolling are almost inevitable.

See Lynch and Horton (1999) for more information on calculating image-safe areas.

A partial solution is to ensure that the most important information is at the top-left of the screen. It is also useful to anticipate the typical screen size and resolution. This will enable you to specify an **image-safe area**. This is the area of the web page that you assume will be visible to most users. Even this is not ideal, as those users with the appropriate screens may be viewing the page through a window that is smaller than the maximum screen size.

The site www.alistapart.com often has good articles on designing flexible layouts.

The maximum image-safe area will always be smaller than the size of the screen, because of tool bars, scroll bars, and other components of the browser window. For example, if your users mainly have 640 × 480 pixel screens, then the image-safe area will be 595 pixels (width) by 295 pixels (height).

Figure 17.17 shows an example of what can happen if the important information on the screen does not fit into the image-safe area. In this case, the message "Forget me not!" will be read as "Forget me."

If you like want to maintain many different browsers, then www.thesitewizard.com/webdesign/multiplebrowsers.shtml say how to do it (visited July 5, 2004).

Another approach that is sometimes suggested is to have variants of your site. For example, you may have a variant designed to be accessed by users with handheld computers or mobile telephones, or a text-only variant aimed at people who prefer to avoid the download times associated with graphics or who are using a screen reader. Unfortunately, some organizations have failed to maintain their variant alongside the main version or put promotions and special offers solely on the graphic-laden site, so text-only variants have become somewhat discredited. If you do opt for a variant-site policy, then make sure you put as much effort into maintaining it as the main site — and you may well find that it is less effort to design a single site that works flexibly and accessibly.

You should always try your web site out on different browsers and operating systems in order to see what it really looks like to your users. A variety of commercial services will do this for you so that you do not have to maintain dozens of different

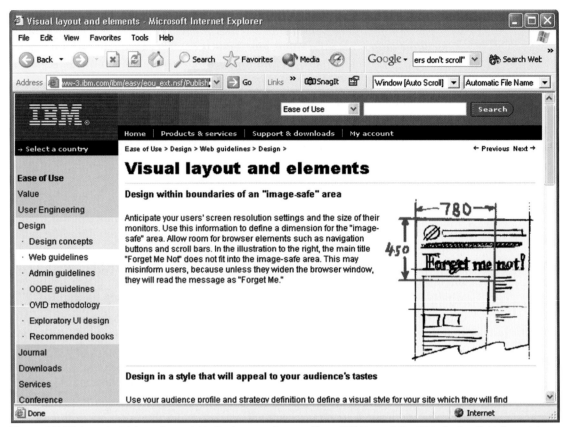

Figure 17.17 Important information outside the image-safe area. (From IBM Ease of Use Web Design Guidelines, taken from http://www-3.ibm.com/ibm/easy/eou_ext.nsf/Publish/602 on July 6, 2004.)

combinations. These services come and go, but one that was flexibly priced and offered free trials in the summer of 2004 was www.browsercam.com.

6.4 Using the Screen Area Effectively

How often have you waited for a page to download only to find that it contains mainly advertisements, menu bars, and white space? White space can be useful for emphasizing the structure of information, and it is quick to download. However, users are interested in the content, so having so little can be frustrating. Ideally the content should represent at least 50% of the screen.

As with all aspects of UI, no design is perfect. It is always necessary to make compromises. However, if the user has downloaded the site to access the content, then he or she expects to see it, so you need to make it worthwhile.

6.5 Improving the Download Time

Web sites are widely used to disseminate images, animations, sound clips, and video clips. Pages also often include Java and other types of code. The inclusion of any of these media will result in a page taking longer to download. Nielsen (2000) recommends that, to avoid the user's concentration being interrupted, web pages need to download in less than one second. He also recommends 10 seconds as a compromise download time, because this is about as long as a user will wait without getting distracted by other thoughts or tasks.

For modem users, a download time of one second or less rarely happens, but it is a realistic target for users who have access from their office, as most offices have much faster Internet connections. Thus, the download time of your page depends on the users who are accessing it. You should aim to make the download time of your site acceptable for your particular users, which may involve making compromises over its content. It is interesting to note that many of the most frequently used web sites are visually simple and fast to download.

The web site in Figure 17.18 uses white space and small images to convey a strongly design-led, artistic impression while keeping the download time short. The one in

Figure 17.18 A website with a lot of white space. (From www.momat.go.jp/english_page/index_e.html, retrieved on July 5, 2004.)

Figure 17.19 is apparently similar in its design, but it takes much longer to download due to the presence of a flash animation and larger images.

When including larger files such as images, flash animations, or sound, you need to ask yourself: Is the benefit worth the extra download time? If not, it might be better to make them smaller or remove them altogether. It may be that the aesthetic effect you want justifies the extra time. Or it may be that the user experience is much better. For example, sound will clearly enhance a site that sells CDs, as it will allow potential purchasers to listen to clips from the CD they are thinking of buying. However, having a continuous backing track to a site that provides information about a local tourist destination is unnecessary and irritating. It is often best to make the download of sound optional. Many users keep the sound switched off; if you use sound on

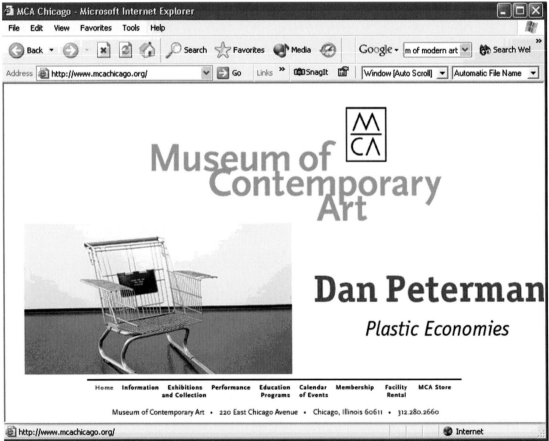

Figure 17.19 Similar web site, much longer download time. (From www.mcachicago.org, retrieved on July 5, 2004.)

your site, it is therefore a good idea to flag this visually, so that the user can opt to switch on the speakers.

If you need to include media that may take some time to download, it is courteous to warn your users, preferably telling them how long the download might take. Your visitor can then make an informed decision about whether to select the link.

As web site managers hope to get repeat visitors, it makes sense to ensure that pages are built up on the screen so that header and navigation information is displayed first. The repeat visitor will then be able to select the required option without needing to wait for the graphics to download. This is also helpful for people using screen readers, as the text will be read before the images are in place.

6.6 Using Style Sheets

It is important for your site to have a consistent visual appearance. One way of achieving this is to use a **style sheet**. Style sheets also allow you to change the appearance of the whole site with relative ease. Thus, if you decide that the typeface used for titles should be changed, you simply alter the style sheet rather than changing every title by hand. A style sheet helps create the visual identity for a site. Style sheets are widely used in books, magazines, and newspapers. How do you know if you are reading the *Washington Post* newspaper? Probably because it looks like the *Post*, rather than like *USA Today* or the *Wall Street Journal*.

The web site www.csszengarden.com has many designs that all appear different but are in fact the same content presented with differing style sheets. In Figure 17.20, we have chosen four examples.

A thoughtfully designed implementation of style sheets has great benefit for some users, especially people with impaired vision, if the design allows the user to override the style sheet with one that is more suitable for their needs. You will undo all your careful work in creating your style sheet if you then apply styles directly within the HTML markup.

6.7 Designing for Accessibility

The Web can provide tremendous benefits, but only if it can be accessed. Designing for accessibility has two parts: working within the appropriate guidelines for accessibility and ensuring that your design process includes users with disabilities. The World Wide Web Consortium's Web Accessibility Initiative describes how to decide whether your web site conforms to their Web Accessibility Content Guidelines at www.w3.org/WAI/eval/Overview.html, and a big selection of tools that help you to do it is listed at www.w3.org/WAI/ER/existingtools.html.

Generally, going back over an existing web site to amend it to conform to appropriate guidelines is a tedious and error-prone approach. Writing it to conform to the guidelines in the first place is much more likely to succeed.

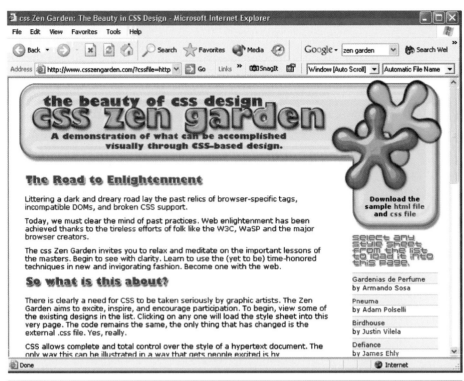

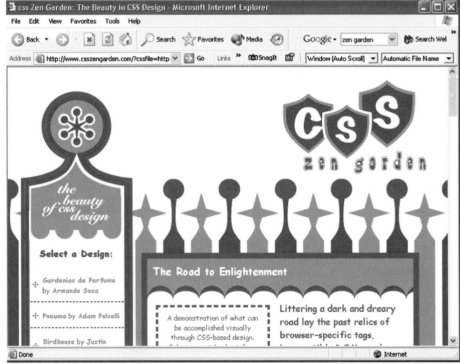

Figure 17.20 Styling with CSS (a) "No Frontiers!" by Michal Mokrzycki; (b) "Snack Bar" by Jay Wiggins Style; (From www.csszengarden.com, visited July 6, 2004.)

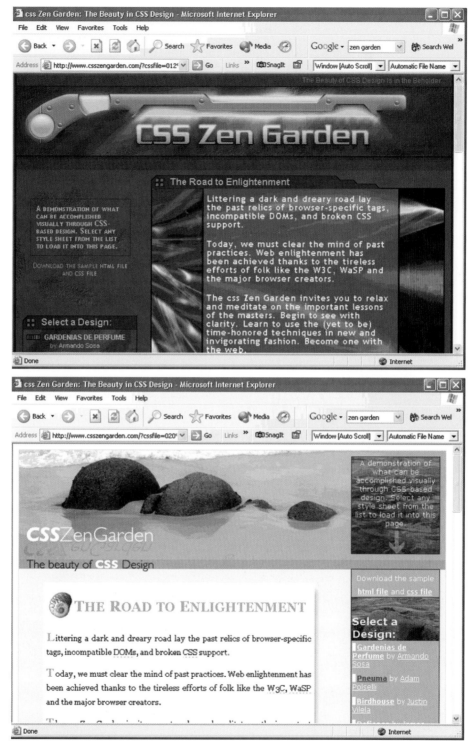

Figure 17.20—(c) "TechnOhm" by Josh Ambrutis (d) "Friendly Beaches" by Sophie G. (From www.csszengarden.com, visited July 6, 2004.)

EXERCISE 17.7 (Allow 15 minutes)

Draw the complete home page for the Lovely Rooms Hotel booking service based on the decisions you have made in response to the previous exercises. Justify your design in terms of the following points:

- The HOME-RUN principles.
- Scrolling.
- The use of white space.
- The download time.
- The page layout, the use of color, sound, images, animation, and video (some of these may not be used).

DISCUSSION

There is a variety of possible designs; ours is illustrated in Figure 17.21. Your design is probably quite different, but this is acceptable so long as you can justify your design according to the guidelines and principles we have explained.

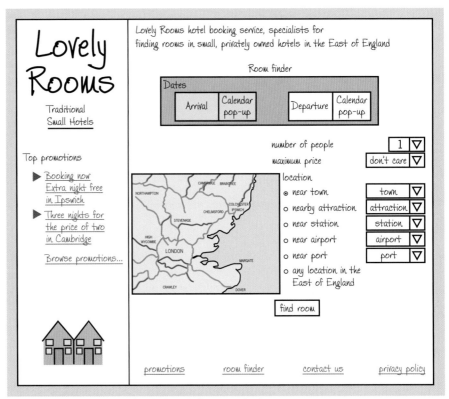

Figure 17.21 Home page for the Lovely Rooms web site.

The background color is white, with black text, which provides maximum contrast. The links are dark blue and underlined. The top promotions are grouped down the left-hand side, and there is a link to browse other promotions not visible. There is a short description of the site's purpose, and the words "Room Finder" are in dark blue and in a larger typeface to clearly indicate the purpose of the site. The navigation aid containing the arrival and departure dates is light blue to make it stand out. A map has been included near the "location" area to show where East of England is.

The home page contains all the usual elements of a home page: the company logo ("Lovely Rooms") in a loopy, swirly font in the top-left corner. The company's tagline, ("Traditional Small Hotels"), is under the logo. The name of the site ("Room Finder") is across the top. All of these, with a short description of the site's purpose, establish the identity of the site.

The "Top Promotions" section is regularly updated. Each promotion is described as succinctly as possible in three lines or less. The description contains key information, such as the location. As the space is limited for the available promotions, there is a link that will allow visitors to browse them all.

Sound, video, and animation have not been included as they would increase the download time without adding significant value to the site. White space emphasizes the structure of the information by separating the different sections of the page.

The compact nature of the screen should mean that scrolling is unnecessary on most screens. To check this, it would be necessary to ensure that the whole screen is within the image-safe area.

This web site represents an appropriate use of the online medium as it provides rapid and up-to-date access to rooms in a specific area, in a way that would be difficult to achieve using conventional approaches.

7 Writing the Content of Web Pages

Even ugly, hard-to-navigate web sites may still be successful if they have good enough content. When you go to see an action film, you may enjoy the explosions and other special effects but, if there is no plot, it soon gets boring. The same applies to web sites: even though they may look impressive, if there is no content of interest to the users, then they will not revisit the site.

It is common for web sites to contain a lot of text. This is partly because text is easy to handle and partly because English-speaking countries tend to be text-based societies. Good writing is good writing irrespective of the medium, but frequently we find that moving text to the Web brings its deficiencies into sharp focus.

See Chapter 13 for more information on writing legible text.

The following guidelines will help you to write good content:

- Keep text to a minimum. You should probably include only about 50% of the text you would include in print form.

- Enable users to scan the text in order to pick out important points.
- Divide long blocks of text into separate sections.

We now look at each of these guidelines in more detail.

7.1 Keep Text to a Minimum

Most users do not enjoy reading long sections of text from the screen. This is largely because screen resolution is much lower than the resolution of paper. In time, this limitation will probably be overcome, but for the moment we find that many people prefer to print out anything that is longer than a couple of screens of text.

For more ideas and an overall process for editing for the Web, see www. editingthatworks. com (a web site designed and maintained by one of our authors).

Thus, when you transfer the information to a web page, aim to reduce the amount of text by about 50%. Perhaps surprisingly, this is often quite easy to achieve:

- Introductions are often difficult to write, and some writers take a long time to get going. Try deleting the introductory paragraphs and see whether they were really necessary.
- Make use of numbered or bulleted lists and tables to organize the information while also removing words.
- Check whether the text actually adds value from the user's point of view. "Marketese" and waffle are especially unpopular on the Web and may reduce the credibility of your web site.

As you are likely to have a range of users, possibly from different countries, it is best to keep the language simple and to avoid jargon. Also, humor does not always cross cultures very well. Generally it is best to keep your content concise and factual. At the very least, you should ensure that your spelling and grammar are correct. Poorly checked web sites can put users off completely, as they imply a lack of professionalism and care.

Journalists are taught an approach to writing called the **inverted pyramid method**. The idea behind this approach is to start by writing a brief conclusion and then slowly add detail. Thus, even if readers skim, they will still get the main points. This also meets the needs of users who are resistant to scrolling down web pages.

7.2 Help Users to Scan

Readers in general tend to scan and skip when they are on the hunt for the material that interests them. One reason for this is that users are often very busy, and there may be other sites that will meet their needs just as well. Thus, users want to establish if your site is the right one for them as quickly as possible. If it takes too long, then they may give up and move on.

The following guidelines will help you write text that can be easily scanned:

- *Use headings and subheadings as appropriate.* These help clarify the structure of the content. It is also useful for visually impaired readers with screen readers.

For example, a site that sells books may have headings that indicate the different categories of books the user might be looking for.

- *Use meaningful headings that explain clearly what is in the section.* For example, a site selling computer-based products should not have a heading like "Other Gizmos" as this is not very clear — gizmos might be computer based, or they might not be. If, say, cell phones and personal organizers are the actual "gizmos" the term represents, then a better heading might be "Cell Phones and Personal Organizers."
- *Include bulleted and numbered lists.* Like this one!
- *Highlight and emphasize important issues and topics.* Links can help with this, as they make the linked words stand out. Avoid underlining normal text; because underlined text often indicates a link, users could become confused.

For more information on how people with visual impairments read web sites, see Theofanos and Redish (2003), also available from www.redish.net/content/papers.html.

The wording of links is very important. It is quite common to see links like this: "For more information on link types **click here**." When you scanned this page, your eyes probably picked out the words 'click here' because they look different. This is not very useful when you are scanning to get an overview of the page content, and it is especially unhelpful if you are using a screen reader to listen to the links, on their own, without the surrounding content. It would be better to write this as "**Link types: more information**." Users can then pick out the phrase "link types" when they scan the page. Putting the most helpful part of the link first ("link types") also helps people using screen readers, as many of them like to listen to just the first part of the link.

7.3 Dividing Long Blocks of Text into Separate Sections

Long blocks of text are difficult to read, so it is better to split such blocks into sections. These may either be on the same page and accessed by associative links or on separate web pages. Splitting text is often done in a rather clumsy way, with pages being linked by buttons that say "Next Page." This is not very helpful, as it means the users still have to read all of the text and wait for pages to download at regular intervals. It also makes it more difficult to move around the text. In this situation, it might be better to have a long page containing associative links. This will have the additional benefit of allowing the users to print out all of the text so they can read it in the bath, on the bus, or wherever they want. A better approach is to split the text into chunks, each relating to a different topic.

> **EXERCISE 17.8 (Allow 15 minutes)**
>
> Rewrite the following property details for the Lovely Rooms web site. Aim to reduce the number of words, and add headers and bullet points as appropriate. Use the inverted pyramid method for the introduction. In addition, suggest what graphics could be used.
>
> This charming small hotel is located on Acacia Avenue, just minutes from the busy town center. The hotel is surrounded by a high hedge and is conveniently

located opposite the Rising Sun public house. There is a large private garden where residents can sit if the weather is fine. The hotel was built in 1926 and has the following amenities: a dining room, a residents' sitting room, and a breakfast room. There are four guest rooms, each with en-suite bathroom including "power shower." We have recently upgraded our telephone system and now offer a modem data point in every room.

DISCUSSION

We came up with the following:

Charming small hotel built in 1926

Location: Acacia Avenue, close to town center, opposite the Rising Sun Public House

Amenities:

- Private, enclosed garden with seating
- Dining room
- Residents' sitting room
- Breakfast room

Guest rooms

- Four rooms with en-suite bathroom including "power shower"
- Modem data point in every room

This cuts the word count by almost 50% and makes the information much easier to scan. There is some loss of detail, but the salient facts remain and it should be possible to download and print more comprehensive details. The inclusion of a map of the location and small photographs of the hotel, garden, and a typical guest room would add clarity.

EXERCISE 17.9 (Allow 15 minutes)

Draw an interior page for the Lovely Rooms web site that describes a particular hotel. This should complement the home page you designed for Exercise 17.7 and include the description of the hotel that you wrote for Exercise 17.8.

Justify the design in terms of the home page design. Why is it different? What trade-offs did you make?

DISCUSSION

Our design is illustrated in Figure 17.22. We have organized the page around the description of the hotel. We have included descriptions of the hotel itself, the accommodations it provides for guests, and the gardens the hotel is set in. Details of nearby attractions are also given.

Pictures accompany some of the descriptions; these are small **thumbnail images**, with an option to enlarge the image.

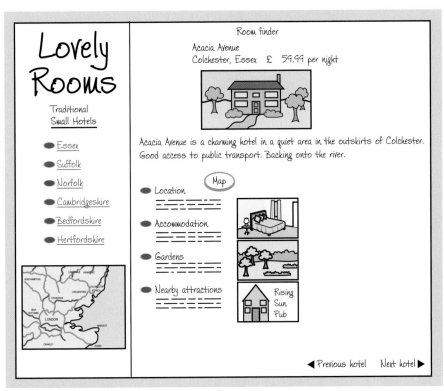

Figure 17.22 An interior page for the Lovely Rooms.

> The price of the room per night is at the top, as this is extremely important to most customers. If the hotel were offering a promotion, this information would be located near to the per-night room price. Next to the location description is a button that users can press to see the hotel's location on a city scale map. There is a location navigation bar with the counties and a map of the East of England down the left-hand side. This would show the area where the hotel might be. We decided to opt for a slightly longer description than in exercise 17.8 because we felt that it worked better with the branding of the site.

8 Summary

In this chapter, we have considered a variety of issues relating to the design of web sites. In particular, we have considered the structure of a site, the design of individual pages, and the writing of content. As an illustration, we have looked in detail at an ongoing example based on a web site for a hotel booking service. It is important to remember that in an actual design, you would carry out an iterative process, probably changing your design prototypes several times and involving the users at all stages in order to check the developing design.

In the next chapter, we look at the design of embedded systems.

18

The design of embedded computer systems

1

Introduction

In earlier chapters, we have referred to a variety of embedded systems. This is an increasingly important design area, and although it has much in common with the design areas that we looked at in Chapters 16 and 17, there are special issues to consider.

Embedded systems include a huge variety of computer systems, ranging from air-traffic control systems and process control systems through washing machines and microwave ovens to personal digital assistants (PDAs), cell phones, and digital cameras. The defining characteristic of these systems is that they are all computer based but do not look like a conventional PC.

The more effective embedded systems also share the following characteristics:

- They are specialist devices, designed to work well for a restricted range of tasks.
- The UI is tailored to meet the meets the needs of the particular users, their tasks, and the environment in which they are working. They are not general purpose interfaces as for a PC UI. This has particular implications for the choice of interaction devices. For example, embedded systems may use small screens, telephone keypads, buttons, levers, and other devices rarely used as part of a PC user interface.
- The design components are well integrated. As the UI is tailor made, the different hardware and software components can be designed to work together well, in terms of both usability and aesthetics.

Classifying such a diverse range of computer systems is difficult but necessary in order to identify the particular design issues. We have already encountered some of the categories, such as consumer appliances and safety critical systems. Other categories, such as specialized business systems (for example, the Prague ticket machine) or process control systems, we have only mentioned briefly or not at all.

In this chapter, we briefly consider safety critical systems and then go into more detail on the design of information appliances (IAs). We have chosen these two types of embedded systems because they have particular design characteristics that separate them from other embedded systems.

2 Types of Embedded System

2.1 Safety Critical Systems

In Chapter 1, we defined safety critical systems as being those in which human or environmental safety is of paramount concern. They therefore include nuclear power stations, aircraft control consoles, air traffic control systems, medical systems, and rail safety systems.

For an excellent analysis of the Three Mile Island incident, see Leveson (1995).

The importance of safety has particular implications for the design process. In Chapter 1, we learned that the control panel for the Three Mile Island nuclear power plant was designed to support more than 1500 alarm conditions. Designing this type of control panel so that it does not confuse the users is extremely difficult. Clearly, there were problems with the design because when the incident occurred, the users had more than 100 alarms to deal with within 10 seconds of the first alarm. In hindsight, it is not surprising that they had problems deciding what to do.

The design process needs to have safety at its center, taking into account the hazards that may arise when the system is in use and how the user can be supported in handling these.

We do not have space to consider safety critical systems in detail. If you want to know more, see Leveson (1995).

Safety critical systems also have to take into account particular types of issues, such as the work often being routine and consequently users finding it difficult to concentrate. If you are a car driver, can you recall ever driving your car for several miles without being aware of exactly where you were or what you were doing? Users who are not concentrating properly may need to handle a hazardous situation unexpectedly. This has implications for the UI design. In particular, any alerts must draw the user's attention quickly and must be easy to interpret and respond to.

As you can see, the design of safety critical systems is a demanding and specialized area.

> **EXERCISE 18.1 (Allow 10 minutes)**
>
> The safety issues in car design, though not as critical as for a nuclear power station or airplane, are still of paramount importance. For the purpose of this exercise, consider cars as a type of safety critical system.
>
> Consider the design of the car instrument panel illustrated in Figure 18.1 in terms of the following points:
>
> - The choice of output devices
> - The use of icons

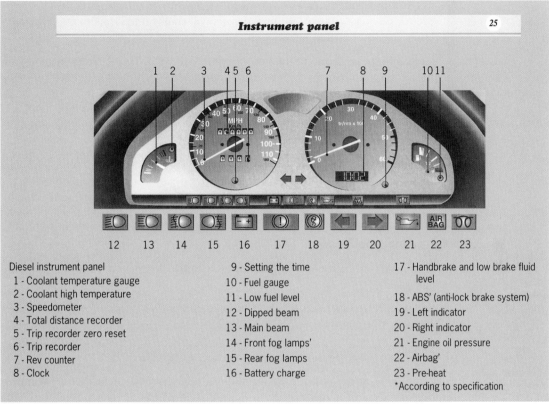

Figure **18.1** The Peugeot 106 instrument panel.

Diesel instrument panel
1 - Coolant temperature gauge
2 - Coolant high temperature
3 - Speedometer
4 - Total distance recorder
5 - Trip recorder zero reset
6 - Trip recorder
7 - Rev counter
8 - Clock

9 - Setting the time
10 - Fuel gauge
11 - Low fuel level
12 - Dipped beam
13 - Main beam
14 - Front fog lamps'
15 - Rear fog lamps
16 - Battery charge

17 - Handbrake and low brake fluid level
18 - ABS' (anti-lock brake system)
19 - Left indicator
20 - Right indicator
21 - Engine oil pressure
22 - Airbag'
23 - Pre-heat
*According to specification

- The use of color
- The use of size, shape, and grouping

For each of these issues, consider the safety implications for the design.

DISCUSSION

The output devices are a mixture of lights and dials and tend to be simple to understand and reliable. However, if a warning light malfunctioned, it could fail to indicate a dangerous situation. Most drivers listen to the sound of the engine, so the reading on the rev counter, 7, will be reinforced by the sound of the engine (or should be, if there are no problems).

There is extensive use of icons. Item 16 looks like a battery (a concrete object), so it can be easily recognized if you know what car batteries look like — some drivers may not. However, 17 requires you to remember its meaning. These icons tend to be standard across most makes of cars, but there are so many icons that it is easy at vital moments to forget what they mean.

The warning lights, such as 16, are all red (not shown in the diagram). Red is standard for this type of light, so most drivers will soon notice if there are any problems. The information lights, such as 13, are green.

The dials are large and in the immediate line of sight. This is because the driver monitors them constantly. It would be possible to confuse the two dials, as they look quite similar. The speedometer is labeled MPH, which helps. The light icons (12 to 15) are grouped together, as are the warning icons. The warning lights are in the driver's line of sight, so they catch his or her attention if there is a problem. These icons are the same size and shape.

As with all safety critical systems, the use of such basic layout techniques can improve safety considerably. For example, positioning the brake-fluid level gauge behind the steering wheel, where it cannot be readily seen, could lead to a serious accident.

2.2 Information Appliances

Norman (1998), in his book *The Invisible Computer*, defines an information appliance as:

> *An appliance specializing in information: knowledge, facts, graphics, images, video or sound. An information appliance is designed to perform a specific activity, such as music, photography, or writing. A distinguishing feature of information appliances is the ability to share information among themselves. (p. 53)*

Norman (1998) developed the information appliance concept further by defining three design principles for them:

> *Simplicity. The complexity of the appliance should be that of the task, not the tool. The technology is invisible.*

> *Versatility. Appliances should be designed to allow and encourage novel, creative interactions.*

> *Pleasurability. Products should be pleasurable, fun, and enjoyable. A joy to use, a joy to own. (modified from p. 67)*

Thus, information appliances (IAs) are computer systems that specialize in processing information. PDAs and pagers are examples of IAs. IAs should allow users to focus on what they are trying to achieve rather than have them struggling to use the technology. For example, an IA that enables the user to compose music should be simple to operate, with the complexity coming from the challenge of writing music. The user should be struggling with musical concepts rather than with the UI. Such a device would also need to be versatile. It should, for instance, enable rhythm lines to be included, specifying different percussion instruments. If this were not possible, it would be inferior to a piece of manuscript paper.

Pleasurability is even more difficult to achieve. It is different to the pride that many technically oriented people feel when they purchase the latest gadget. Pleasurability

For more guidance on designing information appliances in general, see Mohageg and Wagner (2000).

is rather the enjoyment and delight derived from using an information appliance that is well made and fit for purpose. In non-IA terms this might mean a specialist camera for photographing birds or an authoritative and well-bound book for identifying plants in the garden.

Two IAs that are changing especially rapidly are cell phones and personal digital assistants (PDAs), and devices that combine a phone, a PDA, plus possibly a camera, MP3 player, or radio as well. In the previous chapter, we warned you that web sites are a rapidly changing area and we would try to stick to general principles that will help you even as things change. The same applies to IAs, perhaps more so. In this chapter, then, we will discuss some of the issues as we saw them while writing and let you decide whether they continue to apply when you read this.

3 Design Issues for IAs

As embedded systems are so diverse, it is difficult to identify universal design issues. We have therefore chosen to consider in a bit more detail the following design issues of particular interest for those embedded systems that most of us carry and use every day: the information appliances. These design issues are:

- Portability
- General purpose versus special purpose
- Connectedness
- The commercial environment

3.1 Portability

Many IAs are portable. A number of issues arise concerning a portable computer system:

- *How heavy and bulky is it?* If it is too inconvenient to carry, you will probably leave it at home.
- *How robust is it?* A device with a screen can be seriously damaged if you drop it or knock it.
- *How long will the batteries last?* What happens if the batteries fail or need replacing?
- *Will you need to operate the device in a poorly lit or noisy environment?* Using a cell phone in a noisy factory could be problematic if you do not have a headset or a vibrating alarm.
- *Does its operation require steady hands?* Devices with small keys are difficult for people with poor motor control.

The importance of each of these issues depends on the characteristics of the users, the tasks they are carrying out, and the environment in which they are working.

Manufacturers are constantly searching for the products that offer the right functionality compared to weight and portability. For a while, the clamshell-with-

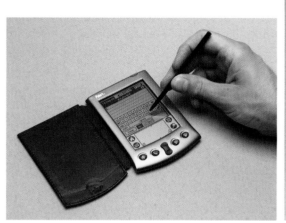

Figure 18.2 Two contrasting personal digital assistants, both being overtaken by composite phone/PDAs.

Figure 18.3 The Treo600 composite cell phone, which is operated using both a keyboard and a stylus.

Figure 18.4 A selection of cell phones from a leading manufacturer. (From www.sonyericsson.com, retrieved July 6, 2004.)

keyboard style of PDA in Figure 18.2(b) looked like a winner — only to be completely edged out of the market by the smaller, stylus-operated style of PDA in Figure 18.2(a). It looks likely that both of these in their turn could be edged out by some sort of composite between a cell phone and the stylus-operated PDA style, taking on the larger screens of the handheld and the superior keyboards of the cell phone, as shown in Figure 18.3.

Meanwhile, cell phones are expanding and contracting. While some of them are becoming more like PDAs, others are shrinking. For example, one leading manufacturer of cell phones listed 18 models for the U.S. market, three of which were not yet available and all of which varied in terms of capabilities, size of screen, and layout of keyboard, as you can see in Figure 18.4. The variety of their phones looks minimal compared to models from another manufacturer, some of which looked more like small flying saucers than phones when they first appeared (see Figure 18.5). Will they become the standard format or will they disappear?

One helpful method for establishing whether a portable device has achieved a good compromise between functionality and portability is to prototype it. Jeff Hawkins, the inventor of the Handspring PDA, used a block of wood to prototype his new

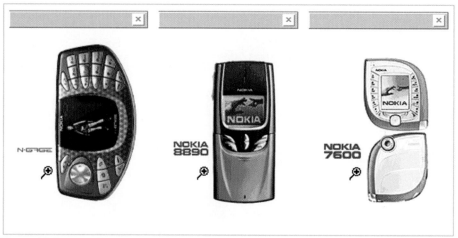

Figure 18.5 In July 2004, the phone in the middle looked ordinary and the ones on the outside looked outlandish. (From www.nokia.com, retrieved July 6, 2004.)

device, and the technique still works well (see Box 18.1). He was designing for himself, whereas now we would ask typical users to work with us by "using" the block of wood, pulling it out wherever they might use the portable device and making notes on what they would do with it.

Hal Shubin of Interaction Design used blocks of wood for the first round of prototyping for a new Dictaphone product (see Figure 18.6). Shubin writes:

> *Because it was a physical device, we started with blocks of wood in our group-design exercise, rather than paper. Team members worked in groups, using stickers and pens to mock up what they thought the device should look like. It was a great way to start the project and understand what everyone had been thinking. The discussion brought out some really good ideas. (Shubin, 2004, www.user.com/p-files/ dictaphone-wood-mic-protos.htm.)*

3.2 General Purpose versus Special Purpose

Traditionally, many information appliances are designed to carry out just one particular task. For example, you cannot play computer games on your digital camera or surf the Web on your digital alarm clock (not yet, anyway!). The Internet Fridge that allowed you to surf while rummaging in the icebox appeared in 2002 — and promptly disappeared again, possibly due to its eye-watering price tag: considerably more than the cost of a luxury refrigerator and a good-quality computer bought separately.

The single-task model has many benefits, as it means that the design can be tailored to the requirements of the particular task. For example, a digital camera is designed to take photographs, so it does not need a keyboard or mouse — a number of special-

| Box 18.1 | **The Philosophy of the Handheld** |

People thought Jeff Hawkins was crazy when they saw him taking notes, checking appointments, and synchronizing a small block of wood with his PC, pretending all the while that the block was a handheld computer.

"If I wanted to check the calendar I'd take it out and press the wooden button," the father of handheld computing told an audience of Palm developers at PalmSource 99. . . .

Hawkins did the same thing when he designed his new Handspring handheld, which has an expansion slot for adding hardware extras like a cell phone.

"I walked around answering phone calls with this block of wood, and of course it didn't do anything," he said. "I did it to see if it worked. I decided it worked pretty well." . . . [Hawkins] said the most important principles are the functionality of the product and the user experience. From there, the product is designed backwards.

Hence, playing make-believe with wooden prototypes to figure out how people will use them.

When designing the original PalmPilot, instead of concentrating on hardware specs like the size of the screen or the speed of the chip, Hawkins instead focused on where to store the pen, where to put the buttons, and the number of steps it would take to open up the datebook.

"To heck with specs," he said. "I don't care about them."

When working out the Palm's handwriting recognition system, Graffiti, Hawkins said he scribbled notes all day on a pad of paper. But he didn't write the letters side by side. Instead he scrawled them one on top of each other — just the way it's done on the Palm — ending up with indecipherable blobs on the page.

"People thought I was crazy," he said. "But I got a feel for how it would work."

From Leander Kahney, 1999, at
www.wired.com/news/technology/0,1282,32010,00.html.

purpose buttons will suffice. Another advantage is that the UI can be made simple, as only a limited range of tasks are permitted. Think how few controls there are on a pager. Furthermore, frequent or particularly important tasks can be allocated to individual buttons. For example, a PDA may have a dedicated button for launching a particular application. This means the task–action mapping is simple.

One disadvantage is that each UI is likely to be quite different. This means there will be a lack of consistency between embedded devices, which can make them more difficult to learn.

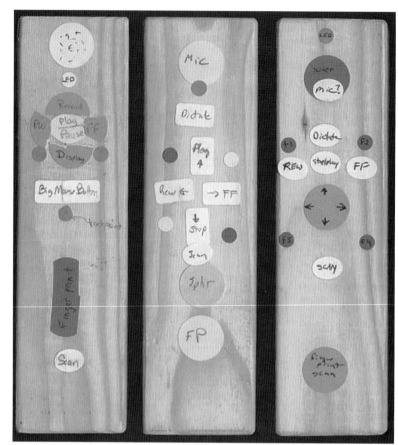

Figure 18.6 Block of wood prototypes for a new Dictaphone product.

On the other hand, if you are using one device, then why not get it to do other things as well? The early 2000s saw the introduction of cell phones with cameras and FM radios built in, at first with considerable compromise in the quality of picture and radio reception. Or if you have a computer with a good-quality display, why not get it to work as a television as well?

EXERCISE 18.2 (Allow 10 minutes)

Here are some examples of multifunction devices. Which of them do you think are successful combinations, and which might be better kept apart? What are your reasons?

- Binoculars that have a digital camera built in (Figure 18.7)
- Sports watch that is also a PDA (Figure 18.8)
- Pen that is also an SD (SanDisk) card reader (Figure 18.9)

Figure 18.7 Binoculars with a digital camera. (From www.binoculars.com, visited July 7, 2004.)

Figure 18.8 Sports watch with PDA. (From www.timex.com, visited July 7, 2004.)

Figure 18.9 Pen with SD card reader. (From www.gizmodo.com, visited July 7, 2004.)

DISCUSSION

Caroline writes: I'm a bit of a gadget nut and I'm willing to try anything, but the binocular/camera combination seems to be a bit too much like the Internet Fridge: two devices put together that would be better apart.

The watch/PDA doesn't attract me either. It looks like it would be heavy to wear and I'd worry about having to recharge it so often that it lost value as a watch.

Although the pen/SD card reader looks odd, I think I'd find it useful as a way of getting data from SD cards into my laptop.

3.3 Connectedness

Another feature of some embedded systems, particularly IAs, is the ability to share information. For example, the addresses and appointments on a PDA can be synchronized with the corresponding data on a PC. Similarly, the video output from a home security system can be uploaded to a web site for viewing in another part of the world.

These ideas are constantly being developed. There have been numerous newspaper articles about futuristic houses, where computers are embedded into different appliances that are networked. This would enable the microwave oven to ask the refrigerator if there are any frozen meals to be cooked, or the washing machine to check that the dryer is empty. Potentially, many household tasks could be made easier or even automated. The vision of the refrigerator ordering more food from the supermarket when it is empty seems to have foundered with the demise of the first generation of the Internet Fridge, but maybe the combination will return.

The ability to communicate with other computer systems can be an important attribute to look for in embedded systems. It is easier to enter data on a desktop computer than a handheld device (Weiss, 2002), so connectedness, and the ability to synchronize data, can help to solve the problem of entering data using only the tiny keyboards of portable devices.

3.4 The Commercial Environment

Thus far we have discussed generic design issues. Another aspect to be considered in the design of embedded systems is the commercial environment. Devices such as PDAs, cell phones, and pagers are increasingly becoming fashion accessories. Many users buy them as much for their appearance as for their functionality. This can be seen particularly in the teenage market, where cell phones of different shapes and colors have appeared. It is likely that these new designs will have an impact on the usability of the devices.

A related issue is the commercial power of added functionality. Customers often buy devices containing a wide variety of functions that might never be used. We have all done it: "You never know — it might come in handy." These additional functions often make a device less usable.

The design of the UI, therefore, is not the only factor that influences customers. In fact, usability can be difficult to assess when looking through shops, catalogs, or e-commerce sites. However, it becomes extremely important once the customer takes the device home and tries to use it. A poor experience will give a bad impression, not only of the device itself, but also of the brand and of the place from which the device was purchased.

---

4   Design Guidelines for Embedded Devices

Weiss (2002) is a practical, hands-on guide to application design for handheld devices such as e-mail pagers, PDAs, and cell phones.

Although we have entitled this section design guidelines for embedded systems, projecting what the guidelines of the future will be is difficult given the changing nature of the technology. Instead, here we will present some guidelines that were available at the time of writing, with the proviso that they may not maintain their relevance for the life of this book. In addition to any manufacturer-specific guidelines you may be following, for the design of embedded systems it is also important to keep in mind the principles of universal design discussed in Chapter 9.

4.1 UI Design Guidelines for Handheld Devices

Handheld devices are those devices used by people on the go (Weiss, 2002). With a strong focus on usability, Weiss has developed the UI design guidelines for handheld devices presented in Table 18.1.

Table 18.1 UI Design Guidelines for Handheld Devices (adapted from Weiss, 2002, pp. 66–70)

Guideline	Description
"Select" versus "Type"	Text entry on a small device can be difficult. Where possible, and where it is appropriate to the application, the user should be offered a selection option rather than be made to enter text. Finding the best solution will require both thought and user testing.
Be consistent	Ensure that the same terminology is used within an application and that the same terminology is used between handheld applications. In the absence of guidelines, try to borrow ideas from applications that have been well designed and have a high degree of usability.
Consistency between platforms	While the same terminology can be used between handheld applications, you will need to think carefully when adapting an application from a desktop to a handheld device. It is not necessarily the case that terminology that works for a desktop will work for the smaller screened handheld device.
Design stability	In the event of, say, a connectivity failure, the system should allow the user to pick up from where he or she left off when the connection is restored. For example, if the user is completing some sort of form and a wireless connection goes down, the data in the fields from previously should not be lost and have to be reentered.
Provide feedback	The system should support the user with feedback regarding what the application is doing. Feedback in relation to, say, the use of an application or navigation within it could be provided via an assigned information key.
Forgiveness	The UI should be tolerant of user errors and provide an Undo function by, where feasible, a specially designated Back key.
Use metaphors	Real-world metaphors in line with the size of the display should be used. For example, while a desktop metaphor would be inappropriate for a cell phone, the use of an address book for storing telephone numbers would be okay.

Table 18.1 UI Design Guidelines for Handheld Devices (adapted from Weiss, 2002, pp. 66–70)—cont'd

Guideline	Description
Clickable graphics should look clickable	If a graphic is clickable, then it should have defined borders and the graphic should have high contrast with the background color. Conversely, graphics that are static should not appear to be clickable.
Use icons to clarify concepts	Icons should be meaningful and representative of the concepts they are meant to convey.

4.2 Guidelines Specific to a Manufacturer

Pearrow (2002) discusses a selection of manufacturers' sites and guidance for wireless devices.

Manufacturers of embedded devices, especially cell phones, are generally eager for the development community to create third-party applications for their products. Once you have identified the device that you wish to target, then look at the developers' section of the manufacturer's web site to see whether they offer guidelines for the user interface.

For example, Nokia offers detailed usability guidelines for its products such as this small section from the guidelines for people developing games for one of their ranges of cell phones:

Navigating in the Phone

Even if game menus are implemented with custom graphics, this does not mean that the interaction style should be custom. On the contrary, the style of interaction should be consistent, even if custom graphics are used. The user should encounter familiar controls in navigation, and custom graphics should have some familiar characteristics. . . .

1. Use the navigation key as a primary control. Users are likely to be very familiar with a five-way navigation key. Users should be allowed to move focus with the navigation key and select items with it. Also, many users are used to conducting default actions with the navigation key.

2. Display soft-key labels in the screen. Users are likely to be very familiar with the concept of soft keys, and this familiarity should not be wasted. Soft-key labels should always be used, even in fullscreen mode. A minimalist solution for a soft-key label is a simple symbol that tells the user which soft key opens the game menu.

3. Use the left soft key as an Options menu, and also as a secondary selection key. The pop-up Options menu is familiar to users. However, it might be a good idea to avoid using pop-up menus. (From Nokia Series 60 Developer Platform 2.0: Usability Guidelines For Symbian C++ Games.)

4.3 Guidelines for Kiosks

Kiosks are systems that deliver information and services to the general public. They are located in public places and deliver particular information according to public need. We will all have met a kiosk at one time or another. It may have been when buying a rail ticket from a ticket machine in a train station. It may have been when we withdrew cash from a cash machine in a shopping mall. Or it may have been when we visited a museum, where information kiosks are sometimes used to describe exhibits.

Everything you have learned about UI design for the different design areas is applicable to the design of kiosks. Kiosks, however, differ from these other systems in that they can and will be used by virtually anyone. They are systems that are approached and used; initially users will have no previous experience of them, and no prior training. Thus, kiosks need to be designed to be error tolerant and easy to learn and to use.

If you find yourself involved in the design and development of a kiosk, we recommend Maguire's review of the UI design guidelines for public information kiosk systems (Maguire, 1998) from www.lboro.ac.uk/eusc/g_design_kiosks.html.

5 Summary

In this chapter, we have presented a very brief look at different embedded systems. We then looked at design issues for information appliances.

As information appliances are rapidly changing, there are very few stable guidelines around to support their design and development. We have presented those guidelines available at the time of writing: UI design guidelines for handheld devices developed by Weiss (2002) and an example of a manufacturer's guidelines from Nokia's web site.

19

Case study on requirements, design, and evaluation: NATS

1 Introduction

The Final Approach Spacing Tool (FAST) is an air traffic management system developed by the research and development group at the United Kingdom National Air Traffic Services (NATS). It is an advisory system for air traffic controllers. Currently, one of the tasks that an air traffic controller performs is to analyze the data from the radar screen and other sources in order to calculate the timings at which the aircraft should turn toward the runway before landing. The controller then communicates these timings to the pilot of the aircraft waiting to land. FAST reduces the controller's workload by calculating these timings and indicating when the aircraft will need to start turning. The high level of air traffic over Europe means that tools such as FAST are becoming increasingly important.

We visited the Air Traffic Management and Development Centre (ATMDC), one of the locations for the NATS research and development group, several times during 2000. This was just before FAST became operational. We met the users and the project team who were involved with developing FAST.

We chose this case study because FAST demonstrates how a big team did user-centered design and development on a small but very important part of an interface.

We have placed it between Parts 3 and 4 because the team iterated between design, as discussed in Part 3, and evaluation, which we are about to cover in Part 4. They also continually reviewed and refined the requirements throughout.

We start by describing the final interface, then we discuss what we learned about how the team developed it.

2 The Final Approach Spacing Tool (FAST)

2.1 National Air Traffic Services

You can find out more about NATS on its web site, www.nats.co.uk.

NATS is a wholly owned subsidiary of the Civil Aviation Authority in the United Kingdom. It provides air traffic control, navigation, and telecommunication services to civil aircraft in the United Kingdom's airspace, over the eastern half of the north Atlantic and at most of Britain's busiest airports.

Operating on a commercial basis, NATS employs around 5000 people, has a turnover of £5000 million (around U.S. $9000 million, or €7500 million), and is recognized as a world leader in the field of air traffic management. It has more than 40 years of experience providing air traffic services in the United Kingdom. In addition, it leads the market in developing new air traffic control systems, equipment, and procedures to make the best use of the airspace and to allow aircraft to use the most efficient routes and altitudes.

The prime objective of NATS is to ensure safe passage for all the aircraft using its services. Air traffic controllers are at the heart of its operation; they operate from airports and from area terminal control centers (ATCCs) at West Drayton, near London's Heathrow Airport, and near the airports at Manchester and Prestwick. London-Heathrow is one of the busiest international airports in the world. London Area Terminal Control Centre (LATCC) at West Drayton, near the airport, handles aircraft flying over England, Wales, and the Isle of Man. LATCC is the busiest control center in Europe. During the year July 1999–June 2000, it handled 1,865,180 aircraft movements.

To enable the airport to maximize the number of aircraft landing on its runways in a given period, the space between any two aircraft needs to be as close to the minimum safe distance as possible, but, of course, not below it. The spacing between aircraft depends in part on when the aircraft turns toward the runway before landing. Controllers calculate the time of this turn and contact the pilot as the time draws near.

A business case was raised by LATCC to develop FAST to advise the controllers when each aircraft should turn toward the runway, helping them to achieve the maximum arrival runway capacity with increased accuracy and consistency.

LATCC, as a customer, was also a stakeholder in FAST. LATCC commissioned FAST and was responsible for financing the project. It actively participated in the evaluation sessions, provided observers, and kept a regular check on the progress of the project.

2.2 Air Traffic Management Systems

Within the airspace, a network of corridors (or roads in the sky) is established. These corridors, or "airways," are usually 10 miles wide and reach a height of around 24,000 feet from a base of between 5000 and 7000 feet. The airspace up to 24,500 feet is the

Figure 19.1 An air traffic controller at work.

lower airspace. The area above 24,500 feet is the upper airspace. Aircraft fly in the airspace under the supervision of air traffic controllers. For each journey pilots are required to file a flight plan to the air traffic control centers; the flight plan contains details such as destination, route, timing, and requested cruise altitude. Figure 19.1 shows an air traffic controller at work.

The programs that deal with the data from the radar about the aircraft, as well as the flight plans, are known as air traffic management systems. The outputs from these systems are presented on the controllers' radar displays, as shown in Figure 19.2. The display is explained in more detail later in this chapter.

2.3 Final Approach Control

Flights pass through several sectors of airspace, where each sector is managed by a different team of controllers. When an aircraft is about to land, a specific team of controllers at the area terminal control center takes over. One of the most important tasks for these controllers, and the task we will concentrate on in this case study, is final approach control, which involves guiding aircraft into the most efficient order for landing. FAST is an air traffic management system that assists with this task.

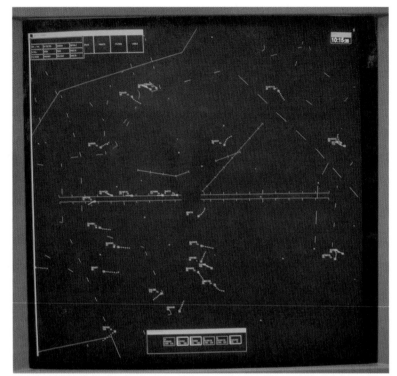

Figure 19.2 The radar display. You do not need to understand the details of this figure. It is here to give you a general impression of the radar display.

The aircraft waiting to land on Heathrow's runways are arranged in four holding stacks, as shown in the Figure 19.3. While an aircraft is in a stack, it flies a specified holding circuit until the intermediate controller (the controller who has been given this particular task), instructs it to leave the stack in the correct order for joining the landing sequence. A controller referred to as the final director then takes over and controls the aircraft through the final approach before handing it over to a controller at the airport for landing.

The final director combines the aircraft into a single sequence for landing. This involves determining the times of the aircraft turns based on the information on the radar screen and on data such as the speed and direction of the wind. The final director advises each pilot when to turn to get the aircraft in the right sequence and to achieve as close to the maximum arrival runway capacity as possible.

The spacing of aircraft can be a complex process. A critical issue is the wake vortex, which is the air turbulence behind an aircraft: the larger the aircraft, the larger the wake vortex. Consequently, if a large aircraft is in front of a smaller aircraft in the landing sequence, the space between them needs to be greater so that the wake vortex does not engulf the smaller aircraft. A larger aircraft is not as vulnerable, so it could be closer. This means that to optimize the spacing between the aircraft, it tends

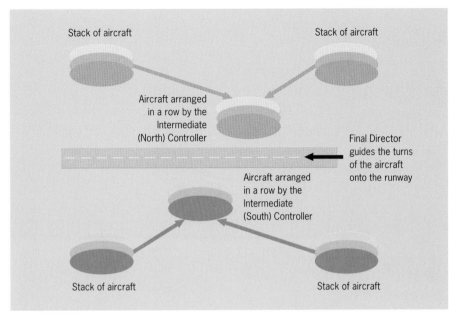

Figure 19.3 The final approach to the runway.

to be better to group them according to size. It also means that it is particularly important for an aircraft not to turn onto the runway too soon. FAST is designed to help the final director inform a pilot when to turn an aircraft to maximize the use of the runway.

Another task-related issue, which is mentioned in the transcripts in the section titled "The Design and Evaluation of the User Interface," presented later in the chapter, is that with the present system, controllers are supplied with flight strips that are placed in colored holders. Each strip corresponds to an aircraft, its color corresponding to the aircraft's size. The strips act as a visual reminder, indicating the aircrafts flying within a sector at a particular time. They are placed beside the radar monitor.

2.4 The FAST User Interface

There are two main parts to the FAST user interface: improvements to the existing radar display that shows the aircraft in the airspace and a new touch panel. The parallel lines in the center of the screen in Figure 19.2 show the runways the aircraft are approaching, and the marks above and below the runways correspond to the aircraft. An interesting aspect of the whole FAST development is the amount of care and investment that was put into creating a system that outputs a very small, but important, extra piece of information on this complex display.

One of the improvements is the landing sequence shown at the bottom of the screen and enlarged in Figure 19.4(a). Each of the boxes contains the details of an aircraft that is about to land. Another improvement is the countdown to turning illustrated

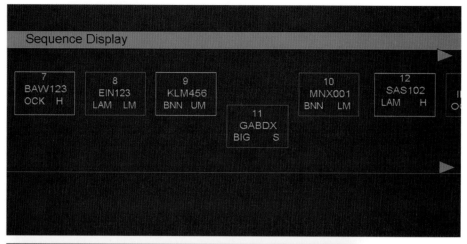

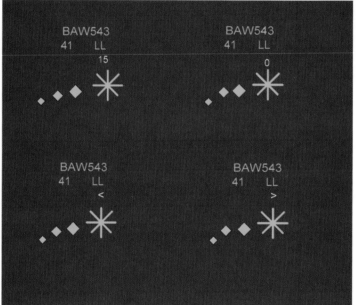

Figure 19.4 Improvements to the radar display. The FAST introduced the small white characters 15, 0, <, >.

in Figure 19.4(b). In this figure, the star and associated diamonds are an enlargement of the marks corresponding to aircraft in Figure 19.2. The star corresponds to the aircraft and the diamonds to the aircraft's previous positions. The flight number is also shown — in this figure the flight number is BAW543.

It is difficult to illustrate this in a still image, but a white number appears 15 seconds before an aircraft needs to make its final turn onto the runway. The number counts down from 15 to zero for the first turn toward the runway, then a white chevron

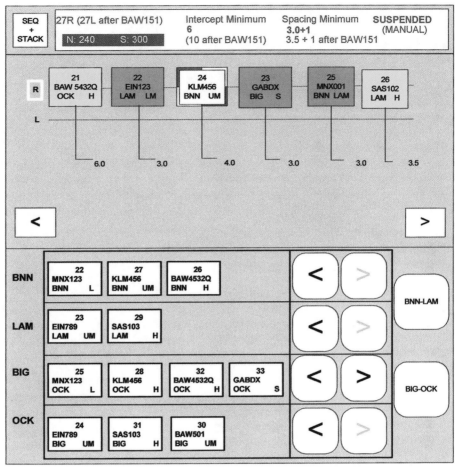

Figure 19.5 The FAST touch panel.

⟨ or ⟩ appears for an additional 15 seconds, indicating the direction in which the aircraft needs to make its second turn to line up with the runway. After 7.5 seconds, the chevron starts to flash, emphasizing that the maneuver needs to be made imminently. It is this small white number that forms the output from FAST.

The touch panel shown in Figure 19.5 is the second part of the user interface. Strategic data such as the weather conditions, visibility, the speed and direction of the wind, and the minimum spacing required between the aircraft are all fed into FAST through this panel. The intermediate controllers use the touch panel to make changes in the input data to FAST. The final director concentrates on interpreting the data on the radar screen and instructing the pilots about their final approach and landing.

You do not need to understand the details of Figure 19.5. It is here to give you a general impression of the FAST touch panel.

3 How the Team Developed FAST

3.1 NATS Research and Development

Research and development at NATS employs about 250 people, including scientists, human factors specialists, development engineers, and support staff. Controllers are also involved in the research projects, bringing with them extensive domain knowledge.

The main aim of improving and developing air traffic management systems is to ensure the safety of air traffic by keeping the workload of controllers within acceptable bounds. Some air traffic management systems carry out bookkeeping tasks currently undertaken by controllers. Others display information to controllers in more meaningful ways, so that the controllers can focus on their main decision-making tasks. Reducing the workload of the controllers should also increase the number of aircraft per hour they can safely handle.

3.2 The Human Factors Unit

The human element in air traffic control — the controllers — is the most complex and critical element of all. The human factors unit analyzes the work the controllers carry out and the environment in which they work to help project teams establish how best to design air traffic management systems that support them.

The human factors unit is concerned with all the aspects of the controllers' involvement with technology. These aspects range from the design of workstations to measuring the controllers' workloads, analyzing the cognitive tasks required of the controllers, understanding how the controllers make decisions, and exploring the probability of human errors. In particular, it evaluates new air traffic management systems to ensure they meet the needs of the controllers.

3.3 The FAST Project Team

The core FAST project team consisted of five members: a project manager, a requirements engineer, a software developer, an algorithm developer, and a human factors practitioner. Other people joined the team for short periods to provide specialist support.

"Human factors practitioners" are user interface specialists who have qualifications in human factors (or ergonomics).

All the core members of the project team participated in the meetings that took place throughout FAST's development life cycle. The active involvement of the human factors specialist with the software developers meant that from the start, usability activities were undertaken in parallel with the software development. The complex underlying algorithms and the user interface were designed, developed, and evaluated in parallel. We met Colin Smith, the project manager, Alyson Evans, the usability practitioner, Margaret McKeever, the software developer, and Richard Harrison, one of the air traffic controllers who actively participated in the design and evaluation process.

In the next two sections, we discuss the user-centered design and evaluation of FAST. We have included extracts from our conversations with the project team.

4 Requirements Gathering

4.1 The Domain, Users, Environment, and Usability Requirements

▶ **The Air Traffic Controllers and LATCC**

The users of FAST are air traffic controllers. They typically range from 23 to 50 years old and undergo an 18-month training course. About 20% of them are women, and more women are joining the air traffic services every year. The controllers are organized in a hierarchy that reflects their roles and experience, watch manager being the most senior, followed by senior controller, and finally controller.

Air traffic controllers earn good salaries and are well motivated. They generally have a strong team spirit and a good sense of humor. This is important, as controllers work collaboratively, sharing information in a potentially stressful environment.

▶ **The Tasks Carried Out by Air Traffic Controllers Using FAST**

We described the specific task that FAST helps with in the previous section. The development team had to understand the final approach task as well as its relationship with all the other tasks undertaken by controllers.

▶ **The Air Traffic Control Room**

The controllers work in large air traffic control operations rooms. They interact with large radar displays and other air traffic control equipment. A lot of communication takes place within a control room, sometimes creating a noisy working environment. This communication takes a number of forms. The watch managers communicate information and decisions to the controllers by telephone and face to face.

Each controller is generally responsible for one sector at one time. As each aircraft passes from one sector to another and, therefore, from one controller to another, the controllers discuss the situation and occasionally look at each other's displays while making decisions. The controllers have headphones with microphones and speak to the pilots via the radio.

Controllers normally work an eight-hour shift. To avoid mental overload and fatigue, they take frequent breaks, leaving the air traffic control room to relax. As a consequence, each controller seldom works for more than one and a half hours at a stretch. The control rooms are generally well lit and air conditioned.

▶ **Usability Requirements**

When we visited ATMDC, we inquired in particular about usability requirements.

Alyson: *One [usability requirement] was that it should not increase the controller's workload, and if possible reduce the controller's workload. Another usability requirement which I suppose I would have imposed on it and I have tested for is that it should not be a system which would induce controllers to make errors in their inputs . . . it's just that input on the touch panel . . . should be possible in a simple fashion, and the potential for errors to be made should be reduced, and indeed we have done that.*

These requirements are of particular importance in a safety critical environment, because any increase in the workload of the air traffic controllers could lead to stress and fatigue, which could threaten the safety of aircraft. Similarly, the entry of incorrect data could cause mistakes.

4.2 How the Project Team Gathered the User Requirements

To help in gathering requirements, The FAST project team visited LATCC and observed the controllers performing their tasks. They also interviewed controllers, both individually and in groups, and had many informal discussions.

Alyson: At the start of the design process, task analysis was carried out at Heathrow, which meant a number of visits up to the operations room itself. Once there, we usually sat in and watched the controllers actually carrying out their job of work. Following that [we went] somewhere and discussed with them, in some detail, precisely what it was that they were doing in controlling the aircraft.

In this book, we decided to use cognitive walkthrough as our task analysis technique (see Chapter 4) rather than HTA. For more information on HTA, see Preece et al., (1994) or Dix et al. (2004).

Based on what they observed, the project team used hierarchical task analysis (HTA) to analyze the controller's tasks. This involves breaking the tasks into a hierarchy of actions.

Alyson: Based on interviews and observation, we performed HTA. I think the air traffic control tasks can easily be broken down in a hierarchical manner, it's easy to do. If you asked Richard now "what do you do?" he'd perhaps give you six statements of what he did, and then it's very easy to say "Okay, break that first statement down for me." . . . I think it fits, perhaps, the way controllers see their job anyway. You know, there are distinct phases to any controller's piece of work, and in each of those distinct phases there are subtasks . . . people give you a broad, high-level description of what they do and . . . [you] ask them to break it down. [HTA] is a very simple process to go through, to get a lot of detail.

They used their observations and analysis to help create the requirements specification, which was refined throughout FAST's development life cycle. The team reviewed and discussed the requirements specification with controllers at regular intervals. This helped the team to validate the requirements and also to gain a better understanding of the controllers' tasks. As the project progressed, the changes in the requirements became minimal as the requirements became increasingly stable.

5 The Design and Evaluation of the User Interface

The FAST project team made the decision to follow an iterative, user-centered design approach.

> Alyson: *A user-centered design approach is essential within air traffic control, because it is crucial that the controllers have a system that is tailored to fit within the tasks that they have to do within their environment. They're well able to explain to us where information should be located, how that information should be highlighted, and how they want to use that information . . . and because they were so closely involved in this design process they were able to feed into the process, regularly over the years that the process took, so that it ensured the design was something that they were happy to work with.*

The involvement of a large number of controllers was not easy, particularly as they mostly worked full time and were all based at LATCC, more than an hour's drive from ATMDC.

> Alyson: *The way it works down here, because of the seasonal nature of the traffic levels, [is that] we are told "the trials basically have to happen in winter." So we're given a date . . . and we're told the trial must happen . . . and so the software has to be ready at that point.*

We asked how many controllers were involved in the development process.

> Richard: *There's been a number of controllers involved over the period of the development. I think there's about two of us who've seen the project through from the beginning to the end, and then, during those years . . . various controllers have come along and gone, so there's been at least 10.*

This flexible approach meant that various viewpoints were brought to the project at different times, but there was still continuity, represented by the two controllers who stayed with the project. Thus, even for an important project such as FAST, a fairly small number of users were able to make a significant difference to the usability of the final UI.

As the controllers are highly trained and experienced, their involvement was important, not only so that the project could take advantage of their professional skills and domain knowledge, but also so that they would accept the new UI once it was complete.

> Richard: *Well, when I first got involved with FAST . . . when it was first mooted about having this help for the final director, I thought, "Why are we doing this? We don't need this." I mean controllers are professional people, they're very proud of what they do, and at the end of the day they can provide very accurate and consistent spacing. And I couldn't see for the life of me why we needed a tool to help us do a job which we're doing, as far as I could see, very well anyway.*

Also, users can sometimes feel challenged by, uncertain about, and even threatened by the introduction of new technology.

> Richard: *Controllers do not like change . . . most people don't like change, but controllers don't like any change whatsoever. So it's important that we came down here [ATMDC], and we tried everything out and developed it the best way that we*

possibly could [so that it would] be acceptable at the end of the day to the controllers actually using it.

Once the controllers became involved and started to notice the benefits of the new system, they become committed to its design and development.

Richard: *I think [that] over the number of trials we've done, various benefits have come out of it which weren't first envisaged. When the final director was controlling the aircraft onto the final approach, to get the spacing, none of us realized how much work and effort we were actually putting into it to achieve that. With FAST, I noticed that you weren't so tired, you felt much more relaxed and at ease doing it, and came away from the session being a little bit more relaxed and less tired.*

Alyson summarized the importance of following a user-centered design approach.

Alyson: *It's been essential. We really wouldn't have the product that we've got, I don't think, if we hadn't [followed a user-centered design approach]. Our progress would have been a lot slower . . . and I don't think we'd have had a product that would have worked as effectively as FAST currently does. It just wouldn't have been possible.*

5.1 Design by Prototyping

NATS has developed a comprehensive design and evaluation methodology for air traffic management systems; it was applied throughout FAST's development life cycle. Each evaluation of FAST involved determining the usability of the user interface, measuring the controllers' workloads, exploring situations that might cause human error, and measuring performance. This involved developing a number of increasingly complex prototypes. At each stage, the design team both observed the users interacting with the prototype and inspected the prototype for usability problems.

▶ Low-Fidelity Prototyping

After gathering the requirements, the team used paper prototypes to start developing their ideas for the physical design.

Alyson: *Some low-fidelity prototypes were put together, and a user group of controllers was assembled. They were presented with the different possible designs and asked for opinions, and [their comments were] incorporated into the design. It's a matter of having structured walkthrough sessions with them, based around some paper prototypes, and really taking their feedback, recording that at the time, and then going away and reconstructing another prototype to take back to them for further discussion at a later stage. [The paper] prototyping phase lasted for a number of months, until the controllers had an interface that they felt was worth mocking up on a higher-fidelity prototype.*

The selected paper prototypes were then emulated using Microsoft PowerPoint. These prototypes took the form of screen mockups, with a small amount of animation, such as the countdown sequence. They were evaluated by the controllers. We wondered how the controllers felt about the limited functionality of the prototype.

> Richard: *Well, obviously it would have been nice to . . . see something . . . better but at the end of the day, [using] PowerPoint to start with was fine.*

The low-fidelity prototyping helped the team to identify the main usability problems without investing too much effort in programming or creating a realistic physical environment.

▶ **High-Fidelity Prototyping**

Next the prototypes were developed in C++. These prototypes were written so they would be easy to alter. Often, the project team held workshops with the controllers in the morning, modified the design based on that feedback immediately, and were ready to have their next workshop with controllers in the afternoon. It was a process of rapid prototyping — designing a prototype, evaluating it, and changing its design within a short period.

The next step was to start the operational development of FAST. This often involves discarding all or part of the prototypes that have been built.

> Margaret: *The touch panel and the radar display were thrown away because they weren't compatible with the operational system. The FAST server software itself wasn't thrown away; it was adapted and remodeled and reworked in a more formal way . . . suitable for operational software. But basically most of the code was reused, because the underlying algorithms had been proved in the trials, so we used those. The code was restructured to be more efficient in an operational environment.*

Thus, the underlying algorithms, which were developed alongside the UI, were kept, but the UI designs needed to be recreated. This may seem like unnecessary additional work, but developing the initial UI designs in a form that can be easily modified saves time overall.

The final step was to evaluate the UI in a realistic environment. Throughout these evaluations, the team was improving the design in response to the controllers' comments, until a stage came when a consensus on the design was reached.

> Alyson: *I remember that trial . . . when . . . controllers had to sit back in [their] chairs and say "Yes, this is really coming together now."*

Once the evaluations had been successfully conducted in the current systems operations room, FAST was evaluated at LATCC, where it had been planned to install FAST when it became operational. In the next two sections, we look in more detail at the project team's experience of observing the users, inspecting the UI, analyzing the evaluation data, and communicating its findings to the customers.

5.2 Preparing to Evaluate

▶ Writing the Evaluation Plan

We will go into
more detail
about doing
evaluations in
Part 4.

Before the evaluation process began, the project team wrote an evaluation plan. This plan described the different stages at which evaluations would be conducted, what would be the objectives of each evaluation, and how they would be conducted.

However carefully you write your plan, you always need to allow for the unexpected.

> Alyson: *The major milestones are planned right at the very beginning of the project, but then it's a case of, well, what happens after the first trial? Do we want to progress this? In that case, we do [the] next round of planning. It depends what improvements you want to have, what the next phase is going to be, how long it's going to take, . . . how many controllers you want, whether you want a full-blown trial again. Or we have . . . sort of mini trials, where we invite just three or four controllers down, for two days perhaps, just to try out a certain aspect again.*

It is important to plan for changes, otherwise you may run out of time or money.

▶ Choosing the Users

The project team made an effort to involve controllers who were representative. The customer (LATCC) assisted the team in this effort.

> Alyson: *I think the customer did look to try and get a mix of people who they thought would be positive and actually negative toward the system, so that we had people coming to test it from . . . a range of attitudes, in order that the system would eventually be more acceptable to a broader range of controllers . . . we had some trainees and some experienced controllers. Another aspect was [that] the tool [FAST] was felt perhaps [to] be of benefit during training, so they also wanted some . . . trainees as well, as well as a range of experts.*

Notice that LATCC made sure that all types of controllers were represented, not just those who might be positive about the system.

▶ Creating the Correct Physical Environment

The early evaluations, using low-fidelity prototypes, were carried out in an office environment. A more realistic environment was possible for the later evaluations, which used high-fidelity prototypes. These were conducted in the current systems operations room at ATMDC (Figure 19.6). This room is set up as an air traffic control room, which enables air traffic management systems and procedures that are being developed or changed to be evaluated safely in a realistic environment. The room has 18 workstations, each with a Siemens Plessey 40 cm color raster scan display. These displays are integrated into standard air traffic control systems equipment, including real-time flight strip printing, automated stack departure times, and both static and dynamic electronic information display services.

> Margaret: *Someone had to basically sit down and write a plan and say, "This is what a Heathrow suite looks like" — the position of the strips, the telephone panel, where*

Figure 19.6 The current systems operations room.

the RT plugs in, things like that. Also for FAST we had the touch panel. In fact, one of the major issues was exactly where we positioned the touch panel within the suite. So part of the design was that it had to be flexible; so that if we wanted to move the touch panel from one physical location to another, then we could do that . . . and, because the [room] is in constant use . . . for lots of different projects, you have a limited time scale when . . . the engineers can get in and physically rip it apart and reconstruct it for the next trial.

This shows it is important to anticipate how you may need to modify a physical environment during an evaluation.

▶ **Planning the Evaluation Sessions**

The air traffic varies throughout the day, so it was essential to simulate the most important variations.

Richard: *We have a major peak at six o'clock in the morning that goes . . . right the way through until about 10 o'clock, and we get a slight lull, and another peak at around 11 o'clock. Then it eases off again until about five [or] half past five, and then it can continue peaking until about nine o'clock at night, or perhaps beyond sometimes.*

Alyson: *So we replicated all those different . . . examples, but we just didn't replicate them at the same time of day . . . the controllers might have been controlling traffic, for example, which was representative of six o'clock in the afternoon, in fact at nine o'clock in the morning during the trial.*

This detailed knowledge was presumably elicited during the requirements-gathering process or during discussions with the controllers involved with the design and evaluation process.

5.3 Observing the Controllers

During the evaluation sessions, the appropriateness of the advice from FAST, the timing of this advice, and its usefulness to the controllers were all checked. The project team did this by observing the controllers when they were using the various prototypes. The sessions were recorded on videotape.

> Alyson: *A usability specialist [and] another team member . . . sit behind a controller for the duration of an exercise, which is generally about an hour, and try not to speak to the controller too much as [he is] working, but note any . . . negative comments that the controller might make about what [he is] doing, noting positive comments, generally trying to spot any difficulties or problems that seem to arise as the controller is actually using the tool . . . the controllers were so involved with the project from the start [that] they were prepared to give the feedback anyway and that, as Richard said, they would tell you if something wasn't right anyway. You wouldn't have to coax them.*

For more information on observing users, see Part 4.

This shows that having a good relationship with your users can make them more forthcoming, so your approach to evaluation can be less formal. It also meant that the controllers did not feel uncomfortable about being observed.

▶ Debriefing Sessions

After some of the evaluation sessions, one or more team members conducted a debriefing session with the controllers. These conversations were often audio recorded.

> Alyson: *The observation notes can then be used as the basis for debriefs that we also do with controllers, usually about three times during a two-week trial. We carry out debriefs . . . with the group of controllers . . . and just talk about their responses to the system, what their major problems are . . . likes and dislikes . . . anything that they feel really desperately might need to be changed before they even continue working with the system. That's at the start. At the end of the trial, we're looking for a more formal response on the HCI design and on the overall usability and performance of the system as a whole. It's semistructured really. There are usually a certain number of questions that [a] particular individual would want to ask; [the] requirements team will be there asking questions, [the] usability people will be asking questions, [the] project manager will be asking questions, but we are open to any comments the controllers want to make.*

Debriefing sessions of this sort are opportunities for the users to give you an immediate response to the design, but it is important to identify the questions that you want answered.

▶ Questionnaires

At the end of some evaluation sessions, the project team gave the controllers a questionnaire to complete. This was designed to elicit the controllers' reactions to the prototype. We wondered why they had used questionnaires in addition to the debriefing sessions.

Alyson: We use [questionnaires] to complement the debriefs that we do, which can be dominated by perhaps more verbal individuals or stronger personalities, and one of the reasons that we do questionnaires is to enable every individual to have an equal say . . . putting [forward] their views on the system.

The questionnaire covered all aspects of FAST: usability, performance, and workload.

Alyson: We derived a questionnaire here, specifically for the purpose of evaluating FAST — you know, all the factors that we considered to be relevant were included . . . we don't use [a] standard questionnaire for each trial because the objectives of each trial will change.

The team designed various questionnaires as the project progressed, because the questions to which they needed answers changed. They covered a wide range of issues.

Alyson: Questions on the quality of the advisories, on the controller's views on how spacing was affected by FAST. Questions on the final director's workload, which aspects of FAST most affected any time pressure they were under, which aspects of FAST were most effective, the level of mental demand they felt, physical demand . . . usage of the FAST advice. How often did they actually take notice of the advice? Questions about the parameters surrounding the advice. Is the 15-second countdown suitable? If it's not suitable can they suggest alternatives? Questions about the HCI: whether that was actually acceptable, whether it was clear. And then the touch panel: what information they were referring to on the touch panel, or how easy it was to access the information. If there was any information that wasn't easily accessible . . . whether they made inputs, how often they made inputs, whether they thought making inputs increased their workload.

We asked about the detailed design of the questionnaire and about the balance of open and closed questions.

Alyson: We actually have tended toward using scales more. I suppose that's more recently though, for ease of controllers answering the question, because there have often been a lot of questions to get through . . . actually there was often a scale response with a box for comments afterward. So it was a mix of . . . scales with a sort of open comment aspect to it from what I remember. I don't think there were many open questions.

This highlights the difficulty that often users do not like completing questionnaires, so there is a balance to be struck between eliciting detailed written comments and using standardized scales. When combined with debriefing sessions, the importance of open questions is reduced.

For more information on a SUMI questionnaire, see Chapter 23.

The team also used the Software Usability Measurement Inventory (SUMI) questionnaire. This is a standardized questionnaire that is available commercially and measures users' perceptions of a user interface.

Alyson: The controllers' response to the system in terms of general usability was measured using a SUMI questionnaire, which looks at learnability, efficiency, control, helpfulness, and how likeable the system is. It has a number of different aspects of usability incorporated into it as separate scales, and the controllers [completed] that questionnaire at different phases during the evaluations that we carried out. We saw in the first trial low scores; in our second major trial we saw that the scores had improved somewhat, and throughout the development process we were able to see the SUMI scores increasing, as the feedback from the controllers was incorporated into the design. So at the final evaluation the SUMI scores really were quite high and . . . indicated that the technology was really state of the art.

By using questionnaires that contain scales, it is possible to demonstrate to the managers within an organization that the usability of a UI is improving. Figure 19.7 shows how the scores from the SUMI questionnaires improved as the UI improved.

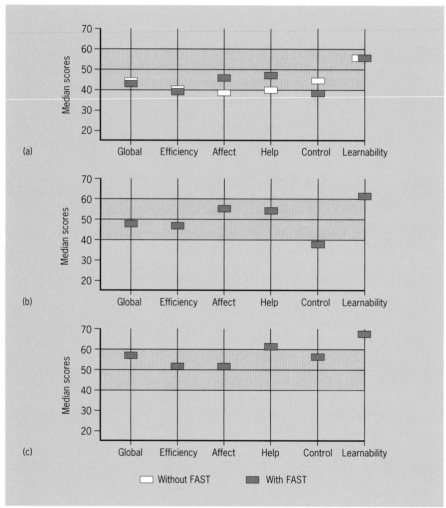

Figure 19.7 The results of the SUMI questionnaire. The scores improve from earlier (a) through to final (c).

In one of the early evaluations, the controllers' opinions were compared during final approach with and without FAST. As Figure 19.7(a) shows, the controllers liked FAST (affect) and found it helpful. However, they felt less in control while using FAST.

FAST's usability improved as the prototypes reflected improvements suggested by the evaluations, as the generally higher scores in Figure 19.7(b) demonstrate. Figure 19.7(c) shows the result of one of the final evaluations of FAST. All six usability factors are higher than in Figure 19.7(a).

▶ Workload Assessment Tool

The team ran evaluation sessions both with and without FAST, to determine its effect on the controllers' workloads. The team used a tool designed in-house called the individual self-assessment tool (ISA) to measure a controller's workload. This tool was designed to have minimal impact on the user's performance and workload.

> Alyson: [The ISA uses] a five-point scale of workload, going from low through to excessive . . . and it translates into a push button panel that the controllers have on the control suite when they do trials here. We ask them to . . . make an input every two minutes, using that push button selection, and they're actually prompted to do that, with the little LED lights. We have a printout then for every trial exercise that they do of the progress of their workload over two-minute periods. So when we compare the new system runs with the base-line runs, which are the current system, we can actually see what the difference in workload is.

This type of technology is useful for collecting quantitative data about the workload of the controllers. This data can then be used alongside the data from the SUMI questionnaire to demonstrate how the UI has improved.

▶ Some Changes Resulting from Having Observed the Controllers

Several features of the user interface design were redesigned or added in response to the controllers' feedback during the evaluations of FAST. In Figure 19.4(b), we illustrated the countdown number next to the label of the flight that is waiting to make the final turn onto the runway. Originally, the chevron that then appeared remained steady. During the development process, the controllers identified an improvement to this representation.

> Richard: We didn't know what we wanted to start with, but . . . people came up with ideas. We decided that with the chevron — which came up as a steady chevron for 15 seconds — we didn't know where we were in the 15-second countdown. So we decided that at, 7.5 seconds, it would start to flash.

As this example shows, users often come up with ideas that you may not have thought of yourself. The controllers also proposed the landing sequence bar shown in Figure 19.4(a). This was not envisaged in the original design and is now one of the features most liked by the controllers.

5.4 Inspecting the User Interface

For more information on inspecting user interfaces, see Part 4.

As well as observing the users, the project team inspected the user interface (the team uses the term "predictive evaluation") to help anticipate and avoid problems with the design. However, inspections alone are insufficient.

> Alyson: *Heuristic or predictive evaluation and trial-based [user-based] evaluation, complement each other. If we'd used only heuristic evaluation, we wouldn't have had the response from the real individuals [who] are going to be affected by the system; as a usability assessor, I could have sat there and said, "Yes it's not going to affect memory load, yes the design is consistent, . . . yes the dialogue is simple." But I'm not a user. I wouldn't have really known what it was like to use it for real. With an environment that is [as] safety critical as air traffic control, it is absolutely essential that the users see the system as well.*

Inspecting a UI can save time, because it helps you to anticipate problems that may become apparent only after a number of evaluation sessions when you are observing users.

> Alyson: *There was [a problem] . . . with the layout of information, where we . . . had two separate dialogues that were adjacent to each other on the touch panel, which looked very similar, and could actually be confused by the controllers. So we decided to make those more distinct by making them different colors, and, in fact, in one of the evaluations . . . we had the controller actually make the mistake of inputting into the wrong dialogue. We waited probably three or four trials before we actually saw the controller making that error. If you use predictive evaluation, then you actually systematically address that potential in the system, without having to wait for people to make those errors, which [they] may never do during a trial.*

The project team used two main types of inspection: a variant of the cognitive walk-through that they call "task analysis" and a guideline review.

▶ Predicting the Likelihood of Errors

NATS has an in-house methodology for assessing human reliability, which predicts how likely users are to make errors.

> Alyson: *What you're required to start off with is a task analysis of how the user will actually use the piece of equipment, which was easy to put together for FAST. And then you look at that task analysis, using a flowchart of questions based on stages of human information processing, which gets the assessor to consider whether . . . a user is likely to have any memory load problems that will make them do certain things, whether the layout of the information could potentially be confusing in visual detection, whether any aspect of the system could cause a controller to make a judgment error.*

This approach is similar to cognitive walkthroughs, where the usability practitioner has to step through the task and keep asking the same three questions: Is the correct answer sufficiently evident to the user? Will the user connect the description of the correct action with what she or he was trying to do? On the basis of the system's response to the chosen action, will the user know if she or he has made a right or wrong choice?

▶ **Guideline Review**

The human factors unit has developed a customized set of human–computer interaction (HCI) design guidelines for air traffic control systems. This customized style guide is based on the various guidelines in the HCI literature, the ISO standards, and some guidelines specific to air traffic services that have been developed by the Federal Aviation Authority in the United States. FAST was evaluated against this customized style guide.

> Alyson: *I have a set of HCI design guidelines, which takes account of ISO 9241 and also the BSI 7179 I think, and any software that we develop here is now audited using those guidelines. They also include a lot of other HCI design guidelines. It's an assembly of guidelines that we've put together for systems in ATC [air traffic control] anyway. So those are a guide to all our systems now, so that we can comply with those standards.*

We were interested in establishing how rigidly they applied these guidelines.

> Alyson: *There are certain standards that you have to be fairly rigid about. You know — if you can't see a letter because it's too small then you have to increase the size of it, and increasing it to the recommended size is going to solve your problem. But there are other guidelines, especially if they don't come from those international standards, that we are a lot more flexible about. We use them as guidance rather than as . . . directive. If [we are] . . . deciding on a color to use for a highlight, we use a guideline that came from the Federal Aviation Authority in America, which [has] done some research on colors within ATC displays. They recommend that magenta or cyan are the best colors to use for . . . attracting controllers' attention. But we will take on board feedback from controllers on their views on recommended colors, and if there is evidence that another color would work better, then we will try that.*

▶ **A Change Resulting from Having Inspected the User Interface**

The design was modified as a consequence of inspecting the UI.

> Richard: *The aircraft are divided up into weight categories . . . you have to provide different amounts of spacing behind each aircraft to take into account the wake vortex. So at West Drayton [LATCC] we have colored strip holders that indicate which category these aircraft fall into. So we have something like a [Boeing] 747 [which is a yellow strip]. So we've used that yellow [in] FAST, as the background [for 747s on] the sequence display [and] on the touch panel as well . . . so that sort of thing's been carried on from reality into the new development.*

This choice of color satisfies the consistency design principle we introduced in Chapter 9, enabling the controllers to use their knowledge of the existing system to understand the new one.

5.5 Analyzing and Interpreting the Evaluation Data

For more
information on
analysing
evaluation data,
see Part 4.

The project team did not perform any complex statistical analysis on the evaluation data. Instead, they used a more informal approach.

> Alyson: *It's a matter of looking for consensus. You can't really do statistical analysis on output from five people . . . the main analysis we did . . . was actually asking the controllers, "Is this advice accurate, is it what you can use?" If it wasn't, we would then look at all the logs (we do actually record all the events in the simulator), and perhaps . . . try different versions of the software to see if we can improve the advice.*

Thus, in most cases the team elicited the controllers' responses through the observation sessions, debriefings, and questionnaires and then used them to guide the analysis of the logs, but analyzing the logs is not always necessary for FAST.

> Alyson: *We take a pragmatic approach to analysis . . . we do what we need to do to feel confident that we know what the controllers' response is. We don't do extremely detailed analysis if we don't really feel that we need to.*

Pragmatism of this sort can save a lot of time. The main purpose of analysis is to help you understand the weaknesses of the design and how to overcome them. You will want to achieve this understanding as quickly and easily as possible.

5.6 Communicating the Findings to the Customer

For more
information on
communicating
your findings
to other
stakeholders,
see Part 5.

The evaluation results need to be communicated to all the stakeholders, in particular the customers. One way of achieving this is to involve all the stakeholders in the evaluation process. For example, if the customers are involved, they will gain a clear understanding of the changes required to satisfy the users' requirements.

> Alyson: *The customers are very much like the users, well, from our perspective anyway . . . they get involved right from the very beginning, and we are very fortunate that we [have] very friendly customers . . . they're very supportive of what we're doing . . . and they're very helpful, because they're ex-controllers themselves, so they have knowledge of the system.*

The FAST team also wrote regular evaluation reports. They sent copies of these to all the stakeholders to inform them about the status of the project.

> Alyson: *It goes to the customer, so they can see . . . precisely how the system that's being developed for them is coming along. It also . . . provides information to the development team . . . precisely what they need to address in the next iteration of the design cycle.*

This inclusive approach meant that when they needed more resources for research and to buy new hardware, the customer understood the issues and was willing to help.

> Alyson: *[The touch panel] hardware . . . wasn't acceptable to the controllers . . . the customer decided that there would have to be some significant effort put into*

finding a touch panel that was suitable, and the system couldn't have gone opera-
tional unless we had found one. The main thing that the customer had to get
involved with was approving the funds . . . to get a new touch panel. The role they
played in facilitating the . . . transportation of the system from the development
process to the actual operational environment was significant.

6   Summary

FAST has been developed in a thoughtful, rigorous, and professional manner. During
our conversations with the project team, we identified some characteristics of their
approach:

- Air traffic controllers were actively involved with FAST's design and evaluation
  from early in the project and throughout its development. They felt that FAST
  had been designed in consultation with them rather than imposed on them.
  Their feedback was encouraged during the evaluation sessions, and changes
  were made to the design to suit their requirements.
- The team created a succession of increasingly complex prototypes. This allowed
  them to make most changes early in the design process, when they were easy to
  make, because it only involved changing a paper prototype or a screen created
  using PowerPoint.
- The team chose a range of complementary techniques for their evaluations,
  combining both observations of the users and inspections of the UI. The main
  source of evaluation data was feedback from the controllers during the
  observations and debriefing sessions.
- Effective communication among all the stakeholders is vital for the success of
  any project. LATCC, the customer, had a pivotal role, and the project team
  achieved good communication with it by encouraging its representatives to be
  actively involved throughout the project. This enabled the project team and the
  LATCC representatives to develop a shared understanding of the controllers'
  requirements and their expectations of FAST.

Appendix 1

GUI design guidelines

General	It is often best to follow accepted conventions if your users are familiar with these.
	Most users read from left to right and from top to bottom. You should order widgets to reflect this.
	Follow the layout, text, color, and image guidelines explained in Part 4.
Primary windows	To identify primary windows, start by looking at the main task objects in the conceptual design.
	A launch pad window can be a useful way to organize primary windows.
Secondary windows	Message boxes should be worded so that the user understands the message. Avoid unnecessary jargon.
	Avoid using unnecessary message boxes.
	Use modal secondary windows if the situation requires immediate attention and it is important not to enter any further data.
	Use dialog boxes if additional information is required to carry out a task.
Tabs	The information on different tabs should be independent.
	Avoid using too many tabs.
	Tabs should not be used for sequential steps, as this does not fit the metaphor.
Menus	Menu items should be named so that their name indicates their purpose.
	The menu structure should be organized around the needs of the users rather than around the underlying software. Card sort can help achieve this.
Toolbars	ToolTips can help the user to understand the meaning of icons.
	Design icons that users can easily recognize and understand.

Design icons that are visually simple.
Design icons that are informative.
Design icons that can be easily distinguished.
Design icons that represent concrete objects.
Design icons that are easy to perceive.

Command buttons	Commands should be worded so that they clearly indicate the action that the button carries out. Place command buttons along the bottom of dialog boxes or up the right-hand side. The buttons on a dialog box should be the same size and shape. Different-width buttons are acceptable if the labels are different lengths and the buttons are in a row.
Option buttons and check boxes	Use option buttons when the user needs to choose *one* option from a selection. Use check boxes when the user needs to choose more than one option from a selection. Limit the number of options or check boxes on the screen according to the amount of space available.
List boxes	Use list boxes when there are a large number of options. Use a list box, rather than option buttons or check boxes, if the options are likely to change. Use a drop-down list where there is only limited space. Combine the list box with a text box if appropriate.
Text boxes	Use a text box if it is not possible to anticipate the user input. Do not use a text box without a list box if the GUI requires standardized information. The size of the text box should indicate how much information is required. The text box should be scrollable if it is not possible to anticipate the quantity of user input. If the text box is scrollable, ensure that sufficient lines are visible to give sufficient context for the person entering the text. Gray-out the text box if you want to show that, in a particular context, the content of the box cannot be changed.

Appendix 2
Principles and guidelines for web site design

Design Principles

HOME-RUN (Nielsen, 2000). This acronym describes the characteristics of a good web site.

High-quality content

Often updated

Minimal download time

Ease of use

Relevant to user's needs

Unique to the online medium

Net-centric corporate culture

Design Guidelines

General	Follow the layout, text, color, and image guidelines explained in Part 4.
The structure of the site	Take into account the natural organization of the information.
	Reflect the structure of the tasks the users want to carry out.
	Make the structure intuitive to your users. Card sort can help achieve this.
	Have a structure that is broad rather than deep.
	Create a flexible navigational structure.
	One or more of the pages are likely to correspond to the main task objects in the conceptual design.

Helping the users know where they are	Include the name of the web site on every page. Include the company name and logo on every page. Create a consistent visual appearance for the site.
Helping the users navigate around the site	Only use "See Also" links to sites whose contents you wish to endorse. Text links should change color once they have been selected. Text links should be worded so that they reflect the users' goals. Avoid using selectable graphics for links. Drop-down list boxes take up less space than text links, but the options do not change color after the selected page has been accessed. Provide additional information to explain what is on the linked-to page. Use link titles to explain what is on the linked-to page.
Site maps	Breadcrumb trails can be useful for deep hierarchies. If you use a visual metaphor, include textual labels that can be read by screen readers. Visual metaphors can make the page slow to download. Always include a link to the home page.
Designing the home page	The home page should tell the users where they are. The home page should tell the users what the site does. The home page usually contains the name and logo of the company that owns the site, the name of the web site, a brief introduction to the site, a summary of the key content for first time visitors, and a search facility.
Designing interior pages	Interior pages usually contain more content and less introductory and navigational information than home pages.
Scrolling	The most important content should be visible without scrolling. All links should be visible without scrolling. Users will scroll down if they think it will help them accomplish their task. Shorter pages are better for home pages, for documents intended to be read online, and for pages that contain large graphics or other components that increase the download time.

	Longer pages are better when the content needs to be regularly updated and where documents are intended to be printed out and read. Avoid horizontal scrolling.
Designing for different screens and platforms	Specify an image-safe area. Try out your web site on different browsers and operating systems.
Using the screen area effectively	Maximize the content on the page. White space can be useful for emphasizing the structure of the information and is quick to download.
Improving the download time	The download time should be acceptable for your users. Only include images, animation, sound, and video if they are needed. Warn the user if a page is going to be slow to download; indicate the file size. Make downloading of additional media, such as sound and video files, optional. Warn the users if they need to have their speakers switched on. Ensure the page is built up on the screen so that the header and navigation information appear first.
Using style sheets	Use style sheets to create a consistent visual appearance.
Widgets on web pages	See the GUI guidelines in Appendix 1.
Designing for accessibility	Ensure that your site is accessible to as many different types of users as possible. See the guidelines in Appendix 3.
Writing for the Web	Keep text to a minimum. Keep the language simple and avoid jargon. Be concise and factual. Check your spelling and grammar. Use the inverted pyramid method.
Making visual scanning	Use headings and subheadings. Use meaningful headings. Include bulleted and numbered lists. Highlight and emphasize important issues and topics. Do not use underlined text, except for links. Use color in text links to emphasize important concepts.
Dividing long blocks of text into separate sections	Divide long pieces of text into chunks, with each chunk relating to a different topic.

Appendix 3
Web sites for users with disabilities

The following guidelines are adapted from Head (1999):

- Individual pages of a site should have a consistent and simple layout so that users with visual impairments or blind users using screen readers can more quickly navigate through a page and find the information they are trying to locate.
- Important information should be placed at the top of the page since screen readers, commonly used by blind users, read from left to right and from top to bottom.
- Backgrounds should be kept simple, with enough contrast so that users with low vision, color blindness, or black and white monitors can read the visual clues.
- Buttons should be large, easy targets so that users with physical and mobility disabilities can select them easily from the screen.
- Functional features—buttons, scroll bars, navigational bars—should be identified as working functions rather than images.
- A site should not use hard coding. Application colors, graphical attributes, volume, font sizes and styles should be adjustable by the user based on individual needs. When a font adjustment is made by a user, the page layout should automatically resize to match.
- Blinking or constantly changing text elements should not be used, so that users with visual impairments, learning disabilities, or recurring headaches are not challenged. (Blinking tags have been known to crash screen readers.)
- All images should have descriptive alternative text (ALT tags) and, if possible, captions so that users who are visually impaired or blind and are using a screen reader know what exists on a page.
- Image maps should include menu alternatives, so that users who are visually impaired or blind can access embedded links.
- Video and audio segments should include closed captions so that users with hearing impairments and those who are using a screen reader (which may monopolize the system's sound card) have alternative methods for accessing the information. The page should inform users that closed captioning is available, and it should include instructions for use.

- Links should have fully descriptive headings so that users using screen readers get the full context of the link's meaning. Sites that use "Click here" are of little use because they do not impart any information for decision making.
- Tables, frames, and columns should be used sparingly, if at all, because the majority of screen readers that read from left to right will not distinguish separate cells of information in the translation.
- Plug-ins and Java applets should be used very sparingly, if at all.
- A dividing character between links that occur consecutively should be used, so that a screen reader can distinguish between different links. Ideally, links should be separated by more than just a new line.
- Sentences, headers, and list items should end with punctuation, so that screen readers can signal the shift to the user. (Screen readers do not recognize bullets or physical separation.)
- Pages that include forms should ensure that the forms can be downloaded and mailed or e-mailed later in case the user needs hands-on assistance with filling out the form.

4

Evaluation

1 Overview

The aims of the evaluation part of this book are:

- To help you understand the rationale for conducting usability evaluations of user interface (UI) designs and the factors that guide these evaluations
- To introduce the activities involved in conducting usability evaluations
- To equip you with a toolbox of techniques that you can apply in different ways to conduct evaluations to improve the usability of your UI designs
- To guide you through your first usability evaluation

We do this by guiding you through the main activities necessary for any evaluation and considering the major questions that you will need to address. To help with this effort, we use, as an extended example, the Global Warming interface developed for a distance learning introductory science course.

2 What You Will Find in the Chapters

We begin in Chapter 20 by discussing the reasons for evaluating UI designs. We then discuss the evaluation process and the activities involved in undertaking evaluations, and we show that the process of evaluation is iterative in nature. In this chapter we also describe the Global Warming UI — our running example for this part of the book. In Chapter 21, we look at the evaluation strategy, making the key choices about why you are evaluating: deciding on the overall purpose, determining the type of data you need to collected, and addressing any constraints that you might be operating under. Chapter 22 gets into the detail of planning, the who, what, where, and when: who you should recruit as participants, what you will ask them to do, where to do the evaluation, and when to do it.

Chapter 23 then considers methods of data collection, including some of the types of technology available and also the low-technology methods such as writing paper notes. Chapter 24 is the final planning chapter. We think about the roles that different members of the evaluation team will undertake, we prepare an evaluation script, and we discuss the importance of running a pilot test. It's then up to you to run your evaluation and get as much data as you can.

By Chapter 25, we have collected lots of data from the evaluation, so the time has come to decide how to analyze the data and turn them into findings. We mention briefly how to document and present those findings. (We come back to communicating the results from usability evaluation in more detail in Part 5.) User observation is the evaluation technique that is most widely used by usability practitioners, but there are other techniques that can be useful in different circumstances. In Chapter 26 we present one of these: heuristic inspection. There are many other variations of user observation and heuristic inspection. In Chapter 27, we draw comparisons between these two techniques and explain the *elements* of evaluation, a way of thinking about evaluations that allows you to tailor them for different circumstances. The chapter goes on to describe the elements of evaluation: *observe*, *listen*, *compare*, and *measure*. Finally in Chapter 27, we go into more detail about the variations of the evaluations, and describe how you might do more comprehensive evaluations or combine different techniques to explore different aspects of the user experience with the UI.

Evaluation is fascinating and not difficult, but you do have to think carefully about the choices you make and what is most appropriate for your system. Often, we learn the most from evaluations that turn out to be nothing like we expected. You may, like us, come to view evaluation as one of the most interesting and rewarding parts of creating UIs.

3 Learning Outcomes

After studying Part 4, you will be able to:

- Form an evaluation strategy and create an evaluation plan for evaluating a UI design
- Choose the evaluation techniques and elements that meet the needs of your interface design project
- Prepare for your first evaluation session by creating an evaluation strategy and plan
- Conduct your first evaluation session
- Analyze the evaluation data obtained from applying the evaluation techniques using qualitative and quantitative methods
- Interpret the analyzed data and make recommendations to improve the usability of UI designs
- Conduct the two main techniques in different ways by varying the methods of collecting the evaluation data

4 Theoretical Influences

This section draws from experimental psychology, ethnography, and usability engineering, and it reinforces some concepts that you learned in Parts 1 and 2 of this book. It also draws on the practical evaluation experience of our authors and other usability practitioners.

20

Why evaluate the usability of user interface designs?

1   Introduction

Many times before in this book, we have referred to the importance of evaluation in user interface (UI) design — in Part 1, for example, where we described how evaluation is part of the star life cycle. Perhaps you had the opportunity to try some evaluations while gathering requirements.

Whitelock (1998) reports on the original Global Warming evaluation.

Now we change focus from evaluation for determining requirements to evaluation for assessing the usability of UI designs. To illustrate the process of evaluation, we chose a real prototype user interface (called here Global Warming), which was evaluated before this book was written. Part 4 broadly reflects the experiences of the Global Warming developers, but it is not a historical account. It is an example created for teaching purposes that reflects some elements of the original work.

As we talk about the Global Warming example, we will invite you to choose a user interface that you want to evaluate — and to plan, conduct, and analyze the data from your evaluation alongside the one we describe. We will refer to your choice as "your system" throughout Part 4.

2   Why Evaluate the Usability of User Interface Designs?

In Chapter 1, you saw that users interact with a computer system through the user interface, and that for users, the user interface is the system. Evaluating the user interface design helps us to understand the user experience with the system and, where there are difficulties, to find ways of improving it.

2.1 Does the Interface Meet the Usability Requirements?

If you have been involved in the design and development of the UI, then you will have access to any usability requirements that have been specified and your

Box 20.1	**Terminology**

If you read further about evaluation, you will find that different authors use a variety of terms. Here are the ones that we prefer and some of the alternatives:

- A **usability evaluation**, or just an **evaluation**, is the complete test of the UI. An evaluation may consist of one or more evaluation meetings or sessions. Each individual **evaluation session** will last for about an hour or so, and each involves testing the prototype(s) with one participant. You may also see evaluation referred to as **usability testing**, **user testing**, or user try-out or inspection.
- The **participant** is the person who interacts with or inspects the UI to give feedback about its usability. A participant is usually, but not always, a user of the UI. Some authors use the term "subject," but we prefer to think of the UI as the subject of the test and the participant as helping us to test the UI.
- An **observer** observes the participant and makes notes of the participant's comments and any usability problems.
- The **facilitator** manages the evaluation, explains the aims of evaluation to the participant, and describes how the evaluation will be conducted. The facilitator also answers any queries that the participant may have during the session.
- The **evaluator** is the person who plans an evaluation, analyzes the data, and reports on its findings. Often the evaluator also takes on the role of the facilitator and sometimes acts as observer as well. Other terms you will see for evaluator include "**test monitor**," "**tester**," and "**interviewer**." There are some other roles within an evaluation that we explain in more detail in Chapter 24.
- **Evaluation data** is the information obtained during an evaluation session. There are usually several types of data, including the participant's comments, the observers' and facilitators' notes and comments, and possibly audio or video recordings.

evaluation will be a way of exploring whether or not your system meets those requirements.

We discussed the definition of usability in detail in Chapter 6. To reiterate, Quesenbery (2003) describes these dimensions of usability:

- *Effective.* The completeness and accuracy with which users achieve their goals.
- *Efficient.* The speed (with accuracy) with which users can complete their tasks.
- *Engaging.* The degree to which the tone and style of the interface makes the product pleasant or satisfying to use.
- *Error tolerant.* How well the design prevents errors or helps with recovery from those that do occur.
- *Easy to learn.* How well the product supports both initial orientation and deepening understanding of its capabilities.

Therefore, a purpose of evaluation is to assess whether the UI design is effective, efficient, engaging, error tolerant, and easy to learn and, if it is not, to identify the problems that are affecting its usability so they may be improved upon.

As the dimensions of usability emphasize the goals of the users, evaluations often focus on the goals and tasks of the users by asking users to attempt tasks with the interface. If possible, the evaluation also considers the users' environment — either by setting the evaluation in the actual environment of system use or by simulating it where appropriate.

2.2 Exploring Other Concerns in Evaluations

Sometimes you do not know what the usability requirements were for the UI. You may be trying to establish what the requirements are, or you may be working with a partly designed or existing system where you do not have access to the original team. So another purpose of evaluation is to explore particular areas of concern in relation to the usability for the UI (Dumas and Redish, 1999). For example:

425
Part 4

- You might want to investigate why users are unable to complete particular tasks very easily.
- You might be concerned about whether the UI that has been developed for novice users is acceptable to experienced users.
- You might like to find out if the users like a particular design feature.

So if you do not have access to, or do not know, what usability requirements have been defined for a system, that is okay. Instead, use your concerns as a basis for defining some qualitative or quantitative usability requirements that you can use as a starting point for the evaluation. We will explain how to do this in Chapter 21.

3 Users, Tasks, Environment, and Domain

Understanding the users, tasks, environment, and domain is just as important for evaluation as it is for design.

To put our example in context, here is a brief description of the users, tasks, environment, and domain for Global Warming.

3.1 Our Running Example: Global Warming

The Global Warming program is part of the multimedia materials for a Level 1 distance learning course, S103 Discovering Science, offered by the Open University in the United Kingdom. The course S103 introduces students to the academic disciplines of biology, chemistry, earth sciences, and physics. The Global Warming program complements written course notes, videotapes, home experiment kits, and face-to-face tutorials. The Global Warming developers had to create the underlying software including some complex mathematical models, but we will concentrate on the user interface.

▶ **The Users for S103**

Level 1 courses from the Open University take most of a year to study (February to October). Anyone can apply to do these courses; no academic or other qualifications are needed. They are designed both to teach the subject and to develop study skills, so that by the end of the year successful students will have reached a standard of work in the subject area similar to that achieved by the end of the first year of a full-time, undergraduate degree.

Some S103 students will have qualifications from high school or even a degree in another subject. For example, some people decide to change careers later in life. If one's new direction includes the need for a qualification in science, then S103 is a good way to begin.

Nearly all S103 students have busy lives away from their studying. The majority have full-time jobs. Most of those who do not have paying full-time jobs have caring or family responsibilities that take as much time, or more, than full-time jobs. Some students have retired and are pursuing an interest in science that they did not have time for during their working lives. A small number of students are of working age and taking a career break to study. Due to the flexible distance learning nature of the Open University, its students include people who could not attend a conventional university — for example, because they have health problems, are on military assignments, or are in prison.

▶ Users' Tasks and the Global Warming UI

The Global Warming UI is one of the interactive learning programs on the S103 course CD-ROM. S103 students learn about the relationship between varying climatic factors and global warming, and about using a mathematical model to predict natural events. The S103 course team wanted their students to have "a motivating learning experience" (Whitelock, 1998).

▶ The Domain for the Global Warming UI

S103 students are expected to possess some enthusiasm for studying and a basic command of mathematics, but no other background knowledge: no knowledge of computers, modeling, or the scientific concepts behind Global Warming. The system is used alongside paper-based distance learning materials, but students can choose to study the CD-ROM activities at any time during the course, so there is no guarantee that they will have completed the paper-based materials by the time they encounter the CD-ROM.

▶ The Environment for the Global Warming UI

Although students can study anywhere, most S103 students study at home or while traveling between home and work. It is a common sight to see Open University students studying their paper-based materials on commuter trains. When working on the CD-ROM exercises, they are more likely to be at home, possibly using a computer that is shared with other members of the household. Thus they may be in a noisy environment, with partners and family members vying for their attention — or the computer! Some S103 students may have a family member or friend who is knowledgeable about computers who will help them, but many will not. They all have a tutor, and telephone, or Internet access to the Open University's computer help service, but response to a query may not be immediate.

> **EXERCISE 20.1 (Allow five minutes)**
>
> Is the environment described here similar to the environment in which you are reading this book? Would you be suitable as a participant for an evaluation of Global Warming? Who would make a suitable participant?
>
> **DISCUSSION**
>
> We do not know your personal circumstances, of course, so you will have to compare your answer with this discussion. Most people who read a book like this one are knowledgeable about computers. You are likely to have graduated from high school or have equivalent secondary school qualifications, probably including some background in science and mathematics. It is therefore likely that you are more scientifically aware, more confident about studying, and more adept with computers than most users of Global Warming.
>
> You could still be a participant in the Global Warming evaluation, but the designers would need to be cautious about applying the information gained from your experience to their user group as a whole.
>
> A suitable participant for the evaluation is someone who:
>
> * Has just started, or is just about to start, a distance learning degree
> * Is studying science or plans to do so
> * Has no scientific or computer background

427
Part 4

3.2 Description of the Global Warming User Interface

Many areas of the Global Warming program were not explored (and did not work properly, or even at all) in this preliminary version. For example, the navigation between sections was sometimes inconsistent and sometimes nonexistent.

The model starts with Figure 20.1. When the user clicks on the "Global mean surface temperature" button, he or she moves into a welcoming voiceover with a sequence of pictures of different seasons. One of these is shown in Figure 20.2. This sequence proceeds automatically and finishes with the first navigation screen (Figure 20.3).

> **EXERCISE 20.2 (Allow five minutes)**
>
> Consider Figure 20.3 from the point of view of the principles of visibility, affordance, and feedback. Can you see any areas where improvements might be possible?
>
> **DISCUSSION**
>
> Your list may be different, but we noticed these points:

Figure 20.1 The early version of the opening screen from Global Warming.

Figure 20.2 Winter picture from welcome sequence of Global Warming.

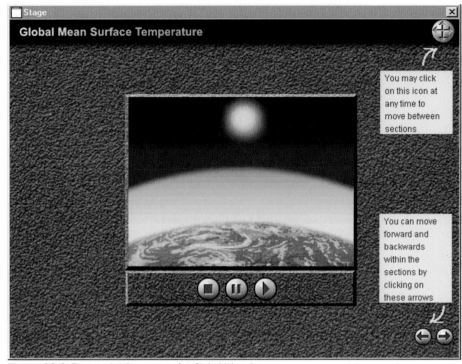

Figure 20.3 First navigation screen for Global Warming.

- There are six icons that have an affordance for clicking.
- The visibility of three icons is improved by having explanations on a yellow background that explain exactly what these icons do.
- The three icons in the center under the image may be familiar to users from other contexts as they are often used on video or tape recorders. However, the visibility would be better if they had explanations like the other three icons.
- From a static picture, we cannot tell if the system has good feedback.

Even from this short inspection, we have a range of evaluation data: some aspects of the interface are quite good and should be preserved, some aspects could be better, and some things we do not yet know and more evaluation work is needed. This is typical of evaluations in general.

Moving forward, the user gets a screen that contains explanations of each of the seven factors that form the basis of this particular model of Global Warming (see Figure 20.4 and Figure 20.5). You may spot some problems with this early prototype: for example, in Figure 20.4 some of the text runs into the description area and is hidden beneath the spiral notebook.

To explore the model, users are expected to change a factor on the screen in Figure 20.6. Users predict the effect on the model and then run the model to check their

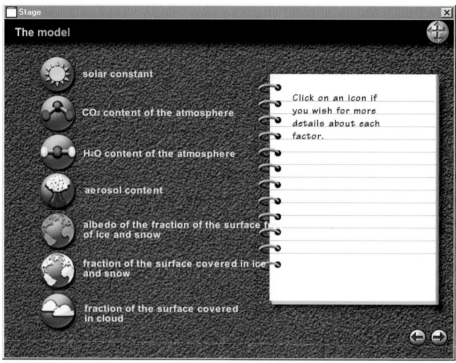

Figure 20.4 Explanation of each factor in the model.

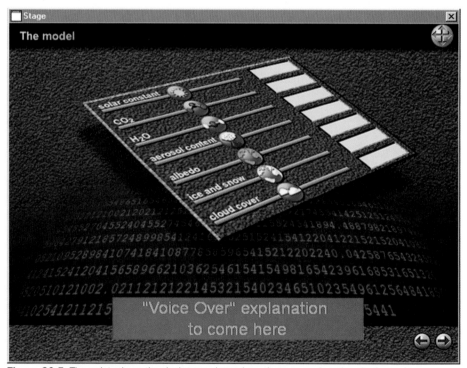

Figure 20.5 The point where the designers planned a voiceover explanation. In the early prototype, they simply put a note to explain what they intended.

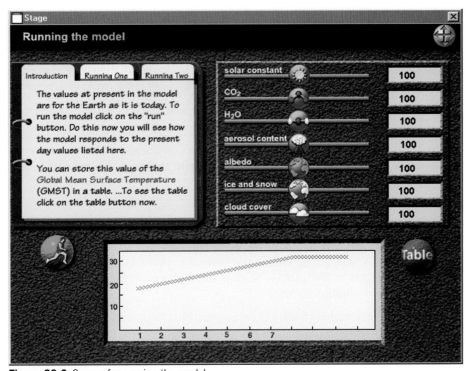

Figure 20.6 Screen for running the model.

prediction. The image of a running man becomes an animated running figure when the user clicks on the button and the model starts to process. The graph is blank to start with. As the model proceeds, the red line appears on the graph.

EXERCISE 20.3 (Allow five minutes)

Consider the use of metaphor in Figure 20.6. Do you think the metaphors used are appropriate when thinking about the likely users of this interface?

DISCUSSION

Several metaphors are used in this screen:

- A tabbed section in the top-left quarter of the screen describes the use of the model.
- Slider bars with globes can be used to adjust factors in the model.
- The use of a graph illustrates the effect of factors.
- A button with a picture of a running man starts the model.

The tabbed metaphor is close to the real-world idea of tab dividers in a file and is likely to be familiar to everyone.

> At first glance, it's not at all clear what the slider bars do or why you would want to interact with them, especially as the icons are in the middle of the bars, but the values next to them are set to 100. Does this mean 100%?
>
> If you're from an engineering background, then the use of a graph to show results is probably familiar. For the target users, it may need some further explanation.
>
> We'll find out more about the user reaction to the image of the running man later in Part 4, Chapter 25.

At this point, and before we move into doing the activities for evaluation later in this part, you might want to think about the users, tasks, domain, and environment for your system.

4   The Activities of Usability Evaluations

A typical approach to the process of usability evaluation is shown in Figure 20.7. As shown, the process models the evaluation of a prototype UI design using a single evaluation technique.

If you think back to the case study in Chapter 19, you will recall that sometimes evaluation is much more complex than this, combining or alternating several techniques. However, for the moment we will assume that:

- We are evaluating our system using a single technique.
- The overall purpose of the evaluation is to incorporate feedback into the UI design.
- We have a definition of the usability requirements.

Working from the usability requirements, we start the evaluation process by formulating an **evaluation strategy**. Your evaluation strategy describes what you want to achieve by conducting the evaluation session(s) and what constraints you have (time, money, and so on). Deciding on the evaluation strategy will help you to generate an **evaluation plan** for how and when the evaluation session(s) will be conducted. This will be the focus of Chapter 21.

The next activity involves setting up and conducting one or more usability evaluation sessions during which evaluation data are collected. Each session generally involves a single participant working alone. This will be the focus of Chapters 22, 23, and 24.

After the session, the evaluation data are analyzed and interpreted. **Data analysis**, or just **analysis** is the process of collating and summarizing the data collected and identifying any **usability problems**. **Data interpretation** of the analyzed data, or just **interpretation**, involves finding the causes of the usability problems, creating a set of recommendations for resolving them, and documenting the results and recommendations in an evaluation report. This will be the focus of Chapter 25. Although Figure 20.7 shows analysis followed by interpretation, it would be wrong to get the

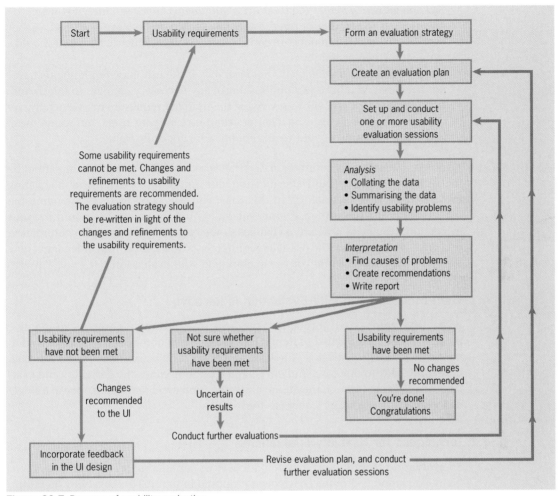

Figure 20.7 Process of usability evaluation.

idea that you do one and then the other — they are usually undertaken simultaneously rather than as two distinct steps. So when you identify usability problems (analysis), you should at the same time be thinking of the causes for the usability problems (interpretation) and considering changes that would be required to overcome the usability problems (recommendations).

As Figure 20.7 shows, after the evaluation results have been interpreted and the results documented, one of three situations could result:

- *The usability requirements have been met.* If the usability requirements have been met and there are no usability problems with the prototype, then you have achieved what you set out to do in this phase of design. Well done.

- *You are not sure whether the usability requirements have been met.* If you are uncertain as to whether or not the usability requirements have been met because the evaluation data are contradictory or inconclusive, then you should conduct further evaluations.
- *The usability requirements have not been met.* If the usability requirements have not been met, you have two options: make any necessary changes to the UI and evaluate again, or go back to reviewing the usability requirements. Generally, changing the UI will result in a better experience for your users, but sometimes you learn that some of your requirements were not quite right.

After an evaluation, it is common to find that some usability requirements cannot be met as stated in the usability specification, due, for example, to constraints relating to time, money, or technology. In this case, you will need to revise or refine the requirements and recommence your evaluation from the beginning, reforming your evaluation strategy to reflect the changes to the requirements. It is also common to find out a lot about what the usability requirements ought to be, and indeed that may be one of the concerns that you are exploring in your evaluation.

4.1 The Process of Usability Evaluation Is Iterative

As we have emphasized throughout the book, user interface design is an iterative process. Just as you needed to iterate for requirements and design, you also need to iterate the evaluation itself, as shown in Figure 20.7. If this sounds time consuming, then think back to our case study in Chapter 19: sometimes the designers and evaluators were going through the design and evaluation cycle more than once in a single day, even gathering requirements as they went.

4.2 Techniques for Usability Evaluations

An **evaluation technique** is a systematic way of conducting an evaluation session. Many evaluation techniques have been proposed in the HCI and usability literature.

▶ User Observations

Most usability practitioners agree that the single most valuable evaluation technique is to observe a participant attempting a realistic task on your system. Because this technique is so valuable, many authorities refer to it simply as "user testing" or "usability evaluation" without further distinction in the terms. We want to discuss variations as well as this primary technique, so we call it **user observation**. During a user observation, the evaluator makes notes of the participant's comments and opinions on the usability of the prototype user interface and interaction designs. The participant is either a prospective user of the system (that is, a real user) or a representative of one of the user groups that were identified during requirements gathering. Because of its importance, we will spend most of Part 4 on user observation.

▶ **Inspections of the User Interface**

With an **inspection of the user interface**, also called **heuristic inspection** or just **inspection**, the participant (or inspector) is usually a domain expert or usability expert. The object is for the inspector to evaluate or inspect the user interface to check that it conforms with, say, a set of design guidelines, design principles, or with particular **usability standards** such as ISO 9241.

Inspections rely on the ability of the inspectors to predict the kind of usability problems that users will experience if the UI fails to conform to the design guidelines or principles against which it is being tested. You will learn more about inspections in Chapter 26.

▶ **Other Evaluation Techniques**

Constraints on UI development vary. There may be particular skills in the project team, special demands due to the task, restrictions in access to users, and many other variables that make some aspects of user observation or inspection either impractical or inappropriate. For this reason, usability practitioners and academics have devised many other evaluation techniques. Our view is that most of these can be regarded as variations of user observation or inspection. We describe this view and how to derive variations in Chapter 27 at the end of Part 4.

435

Part 4

5 | What Happens in a User Observation Evaluation Session?

User observation is not difficult to do, but you will get better results if you think carefully about every aspect of it and prepare appropriately. So here is an outline of what happens in a typical user observation when a participant arrives to help you to evaluate your system.

You start by welcoming the participant and explaining the purpose of your evaluation and their role within it. You check that the participant is happy to continue and ask for the participant's consent to your planned use of the data you obtain.

If you are testing a commercial product before it is released, you may need to ask the participant to promise not to divulge anything learned about the product during the evaluation. If you are testing an early prototype or partly developed system with defects, then you may need to ask the participant to avoid certain parts of it.

You then proceed to the main part of the session: asking the participant to complete one or more tasks using your system while you observe and record what you see.

Once the tasks are complete (or your time is up), you can ask for the participant's views on the experience in another interview or ask the participant to complete a post-test questionnaire.

The session closes with your final thanks, possibly including a payment or other reward (known as the incentive).

Table 20.1 takes a brief look at some of the choices and other preparations that you will make. you want to ask the participant about?

Table 20.1 Preparing for a User Observation

Item in a user observation	Your strategic choices
You start by welcoming the participant and explaining the purpose of your evaluation and the participant's role within it. You check that the participant is happy to continue and ask for his or her consent to your planned use of the data you obtain.	What is the purpose of the evaluation? Which users to choose? Where will you do the evaluation? What data do you need to collect?
If you are testing a commercial product before it is released, you may need to ask the participant to promise not to divulge anything learned about the product during the evaluation. If you are testing an early prototype or partly developed system with defects, then you may need to ask the participant to avoid certain parts of it.	What product, system, or prototype are you testing?
You then proceed to the main part of the session: asking the participant to complete one or more tasks using your system while you observe and record what you see.	What tasks will you ask the participants to try?
Once the tasks are complete (or your time is up), you can ask for the participant's views on the experience in another interview or you can ask the participant to complete a posttest questionnaire. The session closes with your final thanks, possibly including a payment or other reward (known as the incentive).	Are there any specific concerns or questions that

6 Summary

This chapter has set the scene for Part 4 on evaluation by explaining why we should evaluate the usability of user interface designs, which is to establish whether the interface meets the usability requirements or to explore other concerns. We outlined the users, tasks, environment, and domain for our Global Warming running example and gave a brief description of its interface. We then started to look at the activities of usability evaluations and two key techniques: user observations and inspections.

We now have a set of strategic choices:

- What is the purpose of the evaluation?
- Which users will you choose?
- Where will you do the evaluation?
- What data do you need to collect?
- What product, system, or prototype are you testing?
- What tasks will you ask the participants to try?
- Are there any specific concerns or questions that you want to ask the participant about?

In the next chapter, we will go into more detail about making those choices to create an evaluation strategy.

21

Deciding on what you need to evaluate: the strategy

1   Introduction

At the end of the previous chapter, we identified some important questions that you need to answer in order to set up and conduct an evaluation:

- What is the purpose of the evaluation? Are there any specific concerns or questions that you want to ask the participant about? Are there any usability requirements to explore?
- What data do you need to collect?
- What product, system, or prototype are you testing?
- What constraints do you have?
- Which users will you choose?
- What tasks will you ask the participants to try?
- Where will you do the evaluation?

We found Dumas and Redish (1999), Hix and Hartson (1993), Karat (1988), Mayhew (1999), Rubin (1994), Snyder (2003), and Wixon and Wilson (1997) very useful when writing this chapter.

In this chapter, we will discuss the first four of these questions: the purpose of the evaluation and exploring specific concerns or usability requirements, the data you need to collect, your choices about what you are testing, and any constraints you may have. Your evaluation strategy will be formed by answering these questions.

In the next chapter, we will look at which users to choose, the tasks you will ask them to try, and where to do the evaluation. We will also discuss practical considerations for evaluation, such as how much time to allow, and when to do the evaluation. Your evaluation plan will be formed by answering these questions.

2   Creating an Evaluation Strategy

2.1 What Is the Purpose of This Evaluation?

In Chapter 20, we mentioned two key purposes of evaluation: establishing whether a system meets its usability requirements and exploring concerns.

If you do not have access to the usability requirements for the system you are evaluating or if none are available, then you should try to define some yourself. You saw in Part 2 that there are two types of usability requirement: qualitative and quantitative. We review them here.

▶ Qualitative Usability Requirements

Qualitative usability requirements describe desired features for the usability of the UI. They can be subjective and are not always easy to measure or quantify. Here are two examples:

- Railway clerks work in extremely noisy environments, so any warning messages to them should be visually distinct and highlighted on the screens.
- The users on an e-shopping site should be able to order an item easily and without assistance.

Even though the qualitative requirements are clearly stated, it may be difficult to determine whether they have been met in the final design, or to use them directly as acceptance criteria for the system in the same way that quantitative usability requirements can be used. For example, what do we mean by "visually distinct" or "easily"?

▶ Quantitative Usability Requirements/Usability Metrics

Usability requirements are quantitative when explicit measures, such as percentages, timings, or numbers are specified. These are referred to as **usability metrics**. Here are three examples:

- It should be possible for the users to load any page of a web site in 10 seconds using a 56K modem. This quantification of a requirement helps in validating the prototype.
- It should take no more than two minutes for an experienced user (one who has domain knowledge and has undergone the prescribed level of training when the new system is introduced) to enter a customer's details in the hotel's database.
- At least four out of five novices using the product must rate it as "easy to use" or "very easy to use" on a five-point scale where the points are "very easy to use," "easy to use," "neither easy nor difficult to use," "difficult to use," and "very difficult to use."

In these examples, note that not only have particular measurements (or metrics) been specified (the page loading time, the transaction time, and the satisfaction rating), but the type of user (novice and expert) has also been considered. This level of specificity is necessary with usability metrics if the interface is to be evaluated against them.

Although we have said that it may be difficult to determine whether qualitative usability requirements have been met in the final design, the third example just presented shows that it is possible to convert a qualitative usability requirement — in this case, satisfaction — into something measurable, which can be used as acceptance criteria.

Usability metrics can be assigned levels that can be assessed and validated during evaluation. For example, Whiteside *et al.* (1988) suggest using the levels: *current* (now), *best case, planned*, and *worst case*. Box 21.1 shows an example of how these levels are set for usability metrics.

Assigning levels to metrics helps to guide the iterative process of evaluation. In the example in Box 21.1, if you achieve the planned level of three minutes during evaluation, you have met the metric and can move on to the next level of design. Given fewer constraints and more resources (time, money, and fast technology), you might even be able to achieve the best case of two minutes. However, if the measurements taken during evaluation indicate that the time taken to perform the task is five minutes (worse than the current level and worse than the worst case level), then the new design would be unacceptable, and further design and evaluation would be required for the design to achieve the planned (or even best) level of performance.

As the results of evaluation can be checked (or *validated*) against the specified usability metrics, they are often used as acceptance criteria by the customers and other stakeholders for the system.

▶ **Prioritizing Usability Requirements and Concerns**

Usability requirements can be prioritized for design and evaluation. Knowledge about the domain, the users, their tasks, the environment, and any constraints regarding costs, budgets, timescales, and technology will help you to determine which usability requirements are most important to the success of the system. These requirements should then be given a higher priority for design in comparison to other requirements.

Box 21.1	**Setting Levels to a Usability Metric That Can Be Validated during Evaluations**

If the user takes four minutes to perform a task with the current system, then four minutes is the *current* level of performance.

When you are designing a new system, it might be appropriate to aim for improving this time. So with the new system, your plan is to, say, achieve two minutes as the task time. This would be the *best case* level of performance. This is what you *would like* to achieve.

However, in the first version of the new system, you probably would aim for three minutes. This is the *planned* level of performance.

A *worst case* level would be the lowest acceptable level of user performance rather than the worst that can happen. Here the worst case level would be a time slightly shorter than the current level of four minutes.

One way of helping stakeholders to think about and prioritize requirements is to get them to assign values to the five dimensions of usability, the Five Es, which we discussed in Chapter 6 (see Figure 21.1).

Table 21.1 Comparison of Usability Requirements for Two Web Sites (adapted from Quesenbery, 2003)

Usability dimension	Requirements for the exhibition subsite	Requirements for the overall museum web site
Effective	The content of the site must be effective in communicating the exhibition material. Questions about the artist and the museum exhibit must be easily answered.	The site must include content that answers users' questions in an easy-to-find location.
Efficient	This is not a primary concern. People browsing photographs are more interested in in the richness of the experience than in how quickly they can move around the site. However, the size of the images might be a problem, and long downloads need to be avoided.	Attention spans are relatively short. The site structure must be straightforward and direct to minimize navigation time. Writing should be concise and easily scanned.
Engaging	The site needs to be engaging in several ways: to encourage those unfamiliar with the artist to stay and explore, to provide new and interesting information for researchers, and to create a compelling experience in its own right as an exhibition.	For the users, the site provides their first impression of what the museum is like. The degree to which the site can delight the visitor (and by extension convince them to visit the actual museum) is a measure of success.
Error tolerant	Any content errors are unacceptable.	Errors are not acceptable in any form, especially those caused by a failure to meet user expectations.
Easy to learn	One of the goals of the site is to encourage discovery. It must therefore invite exploration.	Users do not expect to have to learn to use an information site.

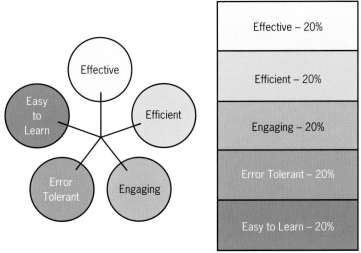

Figure 21.1 The five dimensions describe different aspects of usability. This diagram shows them in balance. (From Quesenbery, 2003.)

Some stakeholders, especially in financial institutions, like the idea of "spending" a total of one hundred dollars on the five dimensions, spending a minimum of five dollars and a maximum of eighty dollars on any single dimension. Some people seem to find dollars easier or more interesting to work with than percentages. This idea comes from Scott McDaniel (personal communication).

Quesenbery (2003) describes an example of contrasting priorities for two products: an online photography exhibition and a museum web site:

> *To accompany an exhibition, a photography museum created a web site with samples of the images, information about the artist and about the exhibition. The museum wanted to both attract more visitors and to provide a long-term educational site. The primary target users were: tourists looking for exhibitions, people already interested in the artist, and casual visitors linking from the museum site for additional information.*

> *The museum also has a general web site, with information about their exhibits, educational programs, awards, and other activities. The user groups for the larger site are more diverse than those for the exhibit, including the same tourists, [but also] people shopping in the museum store, job seekers and art world colleagues keeping up with the institution. All of these users are seeking information about the museum, though the details [of what they are looking for] might be different. (pp. 90–92)*

The usability requirements, in terms of the Five Es, for each of these two web sites are described in Table 21.1. The narrative explanation shows that there are some important differences in the requirements, but it does not easily convey how big the differences might be in terms of stakeholders' priorities.

Asking stakeholders to assign numeric proportions, out of 100%, to each of the Five Es helps to create a common focus and understanding. They must assign at least five percent to each dimension, as users will expect a minimum level of performance on every dimension even if it is a lesser priority (see Figures 21.2 and 21.3).

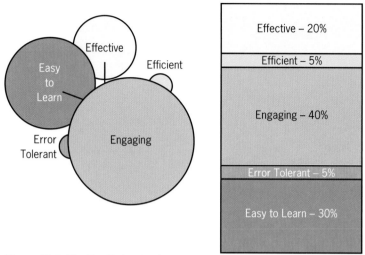

Figure 21.2 The Five Es for the Online Museum Exhibition: Here we see the high priority placed on "Engaging." (From Quesenbery, 2003.)

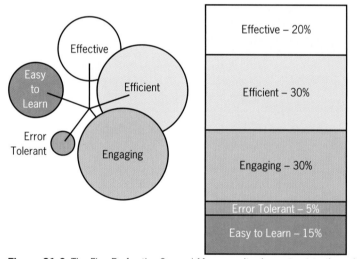

Figure 21.3 The Five Es for the General Museum site. In contrast to the exhibition, the museum site has more balanced usability requirements. (From Quesenbery, 2003.)

2.2 What Type of Data Do I Want to Collect?

As part of your evaluation strategy, you must identify the type of evaluation data that will help you explore the usability requirements (see Table 21.2). Two types of data are obtained during evaluations: quantitative and qualitative.

- **Quantitative data** are any type of numeric data derived from taking measurements. For instance, if during evaluation, you are recording

Table 21.2 Evaluation Data for the Dimensions of Usability

Dimension	Possible quantitative data to collect	Possible qualitative data to collect
Effective	Whether the task was completed accurately or not	User's views of whether the task was finished correctly or not
Efficient	Counting clicks/keystrokes or elapsed time on realistic tasks Analysis of navigational paths to see how often users made good choices	User's views of whether the task was easy or difficult
Engaging	Numeric measures of satisfaction	User satisfaction surveys or qualitative interviews to gauge user acceptance and attitudes toward the user interface
Easy to learn	Number of "false starts" — use of incorrect functions or routes Time spent in incorrect routes Time spent by a novice to complete a task compared to time spent by an experienced user to complete a task	Novice users' reports about their level of confidence in using the interface
Error tolerant	Level of accuracy achieved in the task compared to time spent in false starts	Users reports of a feeling of confidence in the interface even if they make mistakes

measurements such as the time taken by the participant to complete a task or the time spent by the participant on referring to the documentation, then you get quantitative data.

• *Qualitative data* are any data without a numeric content. For example, subjective descriptions of the difficulties that participants faced while interacting with the UI or users' stated likes or dislikes of UI features are qualitative data.

2.3 What Am I Evaluating?

The third question that guides the evaluation strategy concerns whatever it is that is being evaluated — that is, is it a low-fidelity prototype such as a storyboard or a content diagram or is it a high-fidelity interactive software prototype?

For low-fidelity prototypes, your evaluation might be limited to asking participants about the proposed navigation, choice of colors, and so on in order to validate your understanding of their requirements. Low-fidelity prototypes can help with validating qualitative requirements and other usability concerns, but they are less useful for collecting quantitative data or for validating usability metrics.

If, on the other hand, the prototype is a high-fidelity one with some interactivity involved, your evaluation could be more detailed. You could take measurements to obtain quantitative data to validate the usability metrics.

In either case, if the prototype supports one or more user tasks, then you could ask the participant to perform a task using the prototype and then determine the percentage of the task that could be completed. Alternatively, you could time how long a user takes to complete the task or the amount of time spent using online help.

For a thorough explanation of the best way to explore usability requirements and concerns using paper prototypes, see Snyder (2003).

2.4 What Constraints Do I Have?

Finally, and most important, while formulating an evaluation strategy, you should consider your constraints. What you would like to do will be affected by the constraints within which you have to work such as:

- Money
- Timescales
- Availability of usability equipment
- Availability of participants and the costs of recruiting them
- Availability of evaluators

For example, if your budget is small, you may have to undertake a smaller-scale study than you would like to. Or if the time schedules of your project are extremely tight, you might have to use evaluation techniques that take less time to apply. Fortunately, some of the quickest techniques are also the most valuable in helping you to find out about your user interface.

You will also need to think about human resources. Designing and evaluating a user interface and taking it through several iterations is likely to require commitment and involvement from members of the design team and other stakeholders.

In practice, we often find that we know a lot about the constraints (Figure 21.4) but the other parts of the evaluation strategy are harder to define.

2.5 Documenting the Evaluation Strategy

When answering the questions and formulating your evaluation strategy, it will help you and other team members if you record your decisions detailing what it is you want to do in order to validate the usability requirements, and why. This document need not be long or complicated: a short note to the members of the team is likely to be sufficient, and we will give an example from the Global Warming UI at the end of the next section.

Figure 21.4 "We know a lot about the constraints."

3   The Global Warming UI: The Evaluation Strategy

We will now go through the process of forming an evaluation strategy for Global Warming, with some ideas to help you decide on the strategy for your evaluation.

At the time we join them, the Global Warming developers already had a working prototype of parts of the interface, but the prototype contained some gaps and defects. For example, the mathematical model had not been completed on time, but the software production schedule still had to proceed. The developers wanted to be sure that when the model was slotted in, the students would be able to navigate through the UI. They also had these statements from stakeholders about the requirements for the system:

Learning requirements	It has to work as a teaching tool for conveying the important concepts of global warming and as a way of introducing students unfamiliar with mathematical concepts to the idea of a mathematical model.
Satisfaction requirements	Using the Global Warming program must be an enjoyable learning experience.
Navigation requirements	It has to be easy to install, navigate, and use, even for people with no computer experience.

Notice that stakeholders will use their own language and that their ideas about requirements do not always line up neatly with what we need to know as user interface designers. In the case of the Global Warming UI, the stakeholders are thinking about "learning" in the sense of grasping the underlying scientific concepts rather than the idea of "easy to learn" in the Five Es, which is about whether the UI itself is easy to learn. We can probably see that if the UI is hard to learn, students will be using up some mental capacity on learning to use the UI rather than concentrating on the scientific concepts, so we probably need to identify "easy to learn" as a priority.

EXERCISE 21.1 (20 minutes)

Suppose that the Global Warming team has called you in as a consultant. The team has sent you the few details of the interface that you have just read and now wants your help in choosing an evaluation strategy. You will be attending a meeting with the team shortly. You need to formulate an evaluation strategy by answering the following questions:

- Why am I evaluating? Which concerns or usability requirements am I exploring?
- What type of data do I want to collect?
- What am I evaluating?
- What constraints do I have?

What strategy suggestions can you make, and what questions would you ask of the team?

DISCUSSION

Caroline writes: This probably seems like an unfair exercise, but it is not unusual for user interface designers and evaluators to have to start to construct an evaluation from this level of detail. Table 21.3 contains my initial answers.

You will see that even with this small amount of information we can start to form an evaluation strategy. Also, in answering the four questions, we are already working on some of the following preparation activities:

- Noticing that we may have to guide our users carefully around any gaps in the design, so we will need to have a set of tasks that avoids the problem areas.
- Looking for some ways of getting quantitative data as well as qualitative.
- Thinking about the equipment we will need.
- Looking back at our user profile—the user needs to help guide our recruitment and selection of tasks.

3.1 Deciding What to Test

Throughout this book, we have emphasized the importance of an iterative approach to UI design. You should evaluate systems at all stages of development: early prototypes, UIs nearing delivery, newly installed systems, or even mature systems that are being replaced after years of use. However, sometimes the problems of working around defects or gaps in early versions can make it tempting to wait until you have

Table 21.3 Forming an Evaluation Strategy for Global Warming

Question I need to answer	Information I have	First ideas about evaluation choices	Questions to ask the designers/other stakeholders
Why am I evaluating?	Designers want to find out if the UI navigation ideas will work, and they have some learning and satisfaction requirements to think about.	Should I try to get them to restate their requirements in terms of the Five Es? Perhaps we would do better to think about concerns.	Do the designers have just one prototype, or do they have another design that they want to compare with it? What parts of the UI will be available? Can we construct task descriptions that are sensible but limited to the available areas?
Which concerns or usability requirements am I exploring?	The designers have thought about the domain, users, task, and environment. They have some qualitative usability requirements.	Usability metrics are not yet available. Suggest that we use the first round of evaluation to formulate some metrics.	Have the designers thought about measuring "easy to navigate," "easy to install," "easy to use," "enjoyable experience", and "conveying important concepts"?
What type of data do I want to collect?	If I am guiding the users around the gaps in the UI, I will be unable to take any timings for performing tasks, as the extra help will mess up the task time.	Need to concentrate on qualitative data: comments, opinions.	Check that the designers will be happy with qualitative data, such as opinions, at this stage.
What am I evaluating?	Prototype with some gaps and defects.	May have to use a specific computer.	Is this prototype confined to a particular computer, or could it be installed anywhere?
What constraints do I have?	We do not have much information here. Should be reasonably easy to find appropriate students as users.	It may be awkward designing tasks when parts of the system are missing. Must remember to check carefully that they will work.	Is there any budget to offer a financial incentive to users? Do the developers have ideas about recruitment? Do we need to plan to involve other stakeholders? Does the team have access to video equipment or money to buy it?

a better or nearly finished system to test. The problem is that this limits your options: the later you test, the harder it is to change the interface, the harder it is to refine usability requirements, and the fewer opportunities exist for further testing if something goes badly in your first test.

> **EVALUATION TIP 1**
> Test early, test often

The Global Warming developers had a prototype and a window in the project while the mathematical model was developed. Also, in a small team they felt committed to acting on their findings, so they did not need to involve other stakeholders. Their decision became less "what to test" than "how to make the most of our testing opportunity." However, they felt that the gaps in the prototype would make it difficult to evaluate the learning requirements or to test the installation process, so they decided to look mainly at the navigation and satisfaction requirements in their first evaluation.

3.2 Do You Have to Work within Any Constraints?

The Global Warming developers were new to evaluation but otherwise had few constraints. They even had access to video equipment, a topic we will return to in more detail in Chapter 23.

Most of us have resources that are limited in some way, and therefore we have to make our choices according to what we can do rather than what we would like to do.

3.3 Writing Up Your Evaluation Strategy for the Global Warming Evaluation

Even if your evaluation is purely for your own purposes, it is good practice to record your decisions for your strategy in some way. If you are working with other people, then you might choose to document your strategy as minutes from a meeting, an e-mail circulated among your team, or a formal statement in a report: the format does not matter, but making sure that other team members are clear on what you plan to do is important.

Box 21.2 contains the notes for the Global Warming evaluation strategy.

> **EXERCISE 21.2 (Five minutes)**
>
> Review the Global Warming evaluation strategy. Can you suggest any improvements?
>
> **DISCUSSION**
>
> Although finding out about navigation should be helpful to the team, the designers should not lose sight of the learning requirements for this UI because these are likely to be the most important ones for this interface. They could start work on efficiency, effectiveness, and satisfaction metrics, perhaps by asking users how long they would expect to spend on this activity and whether they enjoy the parts that are currently available.

Box 21.2	**Evaluation Strategy for Global Warming**	
Purpose of the evaluation	We want to find out whether our UI navigation ideas will work for students in our user profile.	
Specific concerns to ask users about	We want to know whether the participants think that this will be an enjoyable learning experience.	
Data to collect	Participants' comments on the interface as they use it.	
Prototype that we are testing	Prototype user interface to Global Warming. The underlying mathematical model will not be available and will not be assessed.	
Constraints	Team are new to evaluation.	

The designers have not made notes about any constraints, so that may make the next stage of planning a bit harder. These notes on the strategy are enough to remind a small team about its choices, but a justification for a manager might need more detail about why the team made these choices.

4 Summary

In this chapter, we thought about some of the important choices we need to make in evaluation:

- What is the purpose of this evaluation?
- What type of data do I want to collect?
- What am I evaluating?
- What constraints do I have?

The evaluation strategy is formed by answering these questions.

In the next chapter, we focus on considerations for the evaluation plan: choosing your users, creating a timetable, preparing task descriptions, and deciding where to do the evaluation.

22

Planning who, what, when, and where

1 Introduction

In Chapter 21, we made some of the major choices about our evaluation to create an evaluation strategy: deciding on the purpose, the type of data to collect, the system, and looking at any constraints.

In this chapter, we consider choosing your users, creating a timetable, preparing task descriptions, and deciding where to do the evaluation. These choices will form the evaluation plan.

2 Choosing Your Users

For a system where the typical users are likely to use the system on their own, each evaluation session usually has a single participant using the system on his or her own. To get a variety of views, the session is repeated with further participants. Perhaps surprisingly, usability practitioners find that they learn so much from the first few participants that about five participants are often enough.

Selecting your participants is important. Ideally, each participant will be a real user, though it is sometimes helpful to bring in a representative user (based on the user profile) or a usability or domain expert instead. Selecting participants completely at random is unlikely to be the best choice (see Figure 22.1).

We found Barnum (2002), Dumas and Redish (1999), Mayhew (1999), and Rubin (1994) extremely useful in writing this chapter.

EXERCISE 22.1 (Allow five minutes)

Why might it be advantageous to involve a usability expert in evaluation?

DISCUSSION

Usability experts are trained to understand usability issues and how to solve them, so they may be able to identify common mistakes more quickly than real

Figure 22.1 Selecting participants completely at random is unlikely to be the best choice.

users. However, the overall aim is to ensure that real users can use the system, not that usability experts approve of it.

The other factor that determines the choice of participants is availability. Sometimes you may need the help of external agencies to recruit representative users or to hire a usability expert. These external services can be expensive, and they will usually require you to give a financial incentive to the participants.

Here are some points to consider when choosing your participants for the evaluation:

- Who is a real user, and when is it acceptable to have someone else do your testing?
- Should you have one participant at a time, or would it be better for them to work in pairs?
- How many participants do you need?

2.1 Who Is a Real User?

Table 22.1 has some examples of participants for evaluating an early prototype. Notice that in one case the choice of users is narrower than the actual real users,

Table 22.1 Examples of Participants for Evaluating an Early Prototype

Type of system	Actual users of system	Participants in user observation for evaluating an early prototype
Public information kiosk for tourist information	Full range of the general public, including tourists who do not speak English	Actual users, but all of whom speak English for the first round so that it is easier for us to communicate with them. This should allow us to fix the most obvious errors, and we can get some non-English-speaking users for the second round.
Safety critical system for monitoring a car assembly line	Plant supervisors with considerable experience of the job	Actual users, because the domain knowledge of the actual users is so important.
Web site offering bereavement counseling	People who have recently been bereaved	User representatives, bereavement counselors, or people who were bereaved some time ago.

and in another it would be better to choose a different user group than the actual users.

Your aim in recruiting participants is to find users who reflect the different skills, domain knowledge, and system experience of the users you described during requirements gathering. Often, you have to recruit whoever is available and then ask about their backgrounds and skills. Even if you got the sample you aimed for, you should consider whether the participants in your evaluation are typical users, because there is usually a certain amount of variability between users.

> **EXERCISE 22.2 (Allow five minutes)**
>
> You are evaluating a web site for French students visiting the United States. Consider the following three participants:
>
> - A student from a French university, who happens to be American
> - A French student who lived in the United States as a child and is now visiting the country again
> - A recent graduate of a French university, visiting the United States for the first time
>
> Should you give equal weight to all their views or pay more attention to one participant?

> **DISCUSSION**
>
> Although the recent graduate is not currently a student, and therefore falls outside the strict definition of the user profile, we would usually give more weight to that person's opinion than the first two participants. The first two participants would know much more about the United States than a typical user.

2.2 Users Working Alone or in Pairs

User observation is usually based on a single user working alone, because most current computer systems are intended for such users. However, sometimes you should consider recruiting users to work as a pair. Consider the following situations:

- The users usually work cooperatively. For example, some very small businesses still ask staff to share a computer.
- Cultural constraints make it difficult for users to be critical of an interface to someone in authority. For example, some Japanese usability practitioners find that pairs of users working together find it easier to discuss the interface objectively with each other than with an evaluator because of the politeness in Japanese culture. Snyder (2003), who does nearly all of her testing with American participants, uses this as her routine approach, as she finds that participants chat to each other more easily than to a facilitator.
- You observe that your users prefer to work in pairs. For example, when one of us was testing business administration products intended for self-employed builders working as single-person businesses, we found that it was often the case that the builder was a married man and his wife helped him by doing the business administration. So it worked best if both of them came along to the test.

There are also times when you should consider recruiting a helper or user advocate to work alongside the participant, for example:

- If the users are children, think about whether you are likely to need a parent, teacher, or other responsible adult who is known to the child to be present during the evaluation
- If the participant speaks a language other than English, you will need an interpreter. Some practitioners consider it acceptable to run usability tests in a foreign language if you are reasonably fluent in that language. Others consider that if you are not a native speaker of the language, you are likely to miss nuances in the participants' reactions and therefore bias the test.
- If your participant has a speech impairment or a learning or cognitive disability that affects speech or understanding, then you may have difficulty understanding his or her comments or explaining what you want the participant to do. You may want to recruit a helper or ask the participant to bring a helper or interpreter.

For advice about usability testing with children, see Hanna, Risden, and Alexander (1997), available at www.microsoft.com/usability/UEPostings/p9-hanna.pdf.

Sign languages such as American Sign Language or British Sign Language are also different from English, and you will definitely need an interpreter unless you happen to be a signer yourself.

> **Evaluation Tip 2** *Speak to the participant, not the interpreter*
> When working with any advocate, helper, or interpreter, make sure that you address your remarks to the participant, not to the intermediary.

2.3 Number of Participants

You are likely to need only a few users, particularly if you are doing an evaluation at an early stage in the development of your interface. If one participant spots the problem in Figure 22.2, how many more participants do you need to tell you about the problem? If no other participant notices the problem, would you ignore it or put it on the list of defects for consideration?

You are testing to find problems and do something about them, so it becomes frustrating when participant after participant finds the same problems. Usability practitioners tend to do many rapid evaluation/redesign cycles with very few users each time, particularly when the interface needs a lot of work. Box 22.1 has a usability practitioner's comments on recruiting users.

It is important to realize that a failure to find problems does not imply that the interface is usable. If you have one or two participants and they do not find any problems, then you cannot conclude that your interface is acceptable for users in general. All you know is that these users with these tasks found that your interface worked. Try again, aiming to recruit a different sort of user (maybe a novice rather than an experienced user or vice versa). It can also help if you ask users to attempt a different set of tasks.

The number of participants required for a usability test has been a topic of lively discussion (for example, see Bevan *et al.*, 2003). Our view is that you should start with five, and then test with more participants if you have more time and resources available and feel that the data gathered so far are insufficient for helping you to decide what to do next.

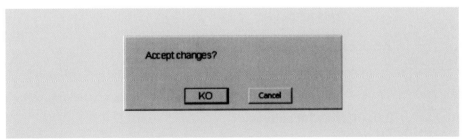

Figure 22.2 How many users do you need? (Adapted from a figure © Caroline Jarrett, used with permission.)

Box 22.1	**Recruiting Five Users: Comments from a Practitioner**

If the user profile is reasonably homogeneous, then I aim to recruit five users. I find that about one person in five fails to turn up: they forget, or have a work or family crisis, or simply change their mind. Also, about one person in five seems to be outside my user profile due to some misunderstanding in the recruitment process: someone failed to ask the right questions, or the participant did not quite understand. That leaves me with about three users who are right in the target area, and this seems to be enough in practice to get a flavor for the variety of user experiences.

If I have two really contrasting user groups, then I aim for five users from both groups.

Sometimes the first user points out so many problems that the client wants to stop the test right there to work on them. It really is worth persisting with a few more users: they do add extra information. But if you have five or more users trying the same task on the same interface, you will keep coming across the same problems and it gets harder and harder to be truly interested and surprised when you are getting the same information from each one.

From Caroline Jarrett, 2001, private communication; used with permission.

2.4 Recruiting Extra Participants

If time and budget allow, some practitioners recommend recruiting spare or "floating" participants who will take the place of anyone who fails to turn up. As Weiss (2002) notes:

Always overrecruit. Research participants are human, and things come up that require cancellation, and worse, sometimes participants just do not show up. Either recruit two respondents for each one-person time slot, or recruit floaters who will cover two consecutive time slots. Be prepared, and have reading material on hand for floaters who might not be interviewed. We recruit nine respondents for six [user observations].

2.5 Ideas for Participants

Table 22.2 contains some ideas for participants and lists some advantages and disadvantages of each type of participant.

2.6 Offering Incentives

It is usual to offer some sort of thanks to the participants for their time and trouble. In a very informal setting, such as asking a colleague, then just saying "thank you" may be sufficient. However, if the evaluation is even slightly more formal, then

Table 22.2 Ideas for Participants

Type of person	Advantages	Disadvantages
Work colleagues familiar with your system	Should be possible to choose users who are sympathetic	May be too close to the designer's viewpoint and too unlike a typical user
Work colleagues unfamiliar with your system, for example from a different type of job (sales, customer support, secretarial staff, training)	Should be possible to choose users who are sympathetic Should be possible to choose users similar to your typical user groups	May need extra persuasion to give up time to your project May be more familiar with your system than a typical user
Family members or friends who do a different type of work than yourself	Likely to be helpful and sympathetic Could be a good choice if your system is for the general public	May intend to help you by being overly positive about your system May not have the right domain knowledge if your system is for a specific domain
Real users	Best option for appropriate feedback Should be possible to find users representing the right level of experience (novice/ intermediate/expert/ occasional user) Should be possible to find users with the right domain knowledge	If you are unable to make changes, they could be disappointed May need extra persuasion to give up time to your project May need to obtain permission to approach these users from your manager/your user's manager/ other people such as account managers or sales staff
User advocates or helpers on their own, such as people who work with charities or nonprofit organizations that support your target user group	Will help you to decide whether your evaluation and system are appropriate for your target user groups	May inadvertently misrepresent user views

prepare a letter recording your thanks, and confirm the confidentiality of the evaluation and the use you will make of the data. If the participants come from a work setting (such as a colleague), then it is sometimes even more acceptable to send an extra thank-you letter to their managers. Make sure that you have the appropriate management permissions for the time that the participants will spend on your evaluation.

A suggested code of conduct from the Usability Professionals' Association (Ballman, 2001) mentioned the following:

> *Participants should ordinarily be compensated for their participation except in instances where their employer forbids such compensation, or where compensation could bias the data collected.*

If at all possible, you should pay participants if they have out-of-pocket expenses, such as for travel, if they are students or otherwise on a low income, or if they might lose income because of being away from work. If the evaluation is part of your work, you should try to arrange some payment or reward. If a market research organization recruits for you, then the organization will tell you how much is necessary. If you are working on a product that your participants would like to own, then giving them a sample could be an appropriate incentive. Table 22.3 lists some other examples.

Even for professional work, participants do not always expect an incentive. It is nice though to offer a token gift, such as a potted plant, but consider whether it will be awkward for the participant to carry away (see Figure 22.3). If you plan to offer food, such as chocolates, or drink, such as a bottle of wine, then be extra careful about the culture and views of your organization and your participants. For example, a bottle

Table 22.3 Examples of Incentives

Evaluation	Incentive
E-commerce web site	Credit to be used for buying something from the site as part of the test
University administrative web site	Mug with the university logo
Field study of users in a large government organization	Box of chocolates big enough to share among the work team, plus individual letters to each user and her or his manager
Forms filled in by accountants as part of their ordinary work	Corporate pen

Figure 22.3 Consider whether your incentive will be awkward for your participant to carry away.

of wine is generally acceptable in the United Kingdom or Australia but frequently unacceptable in the United States.

EXERCISE 22.3 (Allow 10 minutes)

Decide whether to offer a financial or other incentive for your first evaluation, and draft a letter of thanks.

DISCUSSION

Caroline writes: I never needed to offer any incentive for my evaluations when I was a student myself, as participants liked the idea of helping me with my academic work. I found that participants appreciated a letter afterward expressing my thanks. One student that I taught offered the incentive of buying a lunchtime sandwich for a colleague who helped by evaluating his prototype.

2.7 Recruiting Screeners and Pretest Questionnaires

If you need to be sure that your participants fit a particular user profile, then it may be helpful to create a **recruitment screener**, a list of questions to ask each potential participant to assess whether or not the person will be suitable. If you have enough money in your budget to have your recruitment done by a recruitment agency, then the agency will definitely require a screener, and may charge you extra for writing one.

When the participant arrives, you may want to repeat the questions in the screener to make sure that the person really does fit the required profile. You may also want to ask extra questions that are directly related to the domain of the user interface. For example, for the Global Warmng UI, it was important to know whether participants had knowledge of science in general and the science of global warming in particular. Questions that you ask at the beginning of the evaluation are usually called a **pretest questionnaire**. They are tricky to design and to administer, because first we say to a participant, "Don't worry, we're not testing you," but then we ask a load of questions that may seem exactly like a test.

2.8 Choosing Users for Global Warming

The Global Warming designers decided to recruit experienced computer users because they thought that such users would not be intimidated by the need to avoid the defects in the prototype. They also reasoned that if people with some computer experience had any difficulty with their interface, then their target users who did not have computer experience would certainly have problems as well. Because the course was aimed at distance learning students, they did not have any actual students on campus, but there was a convenient pool of hundreds of computer users among the academics and administrators on campus. The designers got an agreement to call for participants using the university e-mail system. With such a large number from which to recruit and an interesting product to test, they felt that no incentive was necessary. They planned to have more tests with authentic distance learning students when they had enough of the interface in place to test their learning and satisfaction requirements (see Table 22.4).

> **EXERCISE 22.4 (Allow five minutes)**
>
> Do you agree with the choice of users for Global Warming? Can you see any dangers in the designers' strategy?
>
> **DISCUSSION**
>
> Experienced computer users are not typical users for this system. The designers may have to revise their ideas extensively when they see typical users working with the interface. However, as the Global Warming designers are new to evaluation, it may help them to feel more confident to practice first with experienced colleagues.

Table 22.4 Participant Summary for First Round of Global Warming Evaluation

Number of participants	Ten, working alone
Participant profile	Experienced computer users from a mixture of university departments but without scientific backgrounds
Incentive for participant	Volunteer out of interest only
Evaluation time	Maximum of one hour for each participant

3   Creating a Timetable

There are two components to consider when drawing up a timetable for the evaluation:

1. How long do you need for each evaluation session?
2. How much time will the whole evaluation process take?

3.1 Decide the Duration of the Evaluation Session

If possible, you should aim for the each evaluation session to last for somewhere between 30 and 90 minutes, allowing time for greeting the participant and explanations before the tasks and for finishing up with your final questions. Longer sessions can tire the participants and evaluators, thus making the evaluation less effective. On the other hand, it takes time to welcome the participant and explain what will happen, so it can seem strange if the session is less than 30 minutes. If your session needs to last longer than 60 minutes, you should consider whether to plan a refreshment and comfort break part way through.

> **Evaluation Tip 3**   *Make sure the participants know to ask for a break if feeling tired or for any other reason*

You also need to allow some time between participants so that you can tidy up, so a timetable for a typical day might be something like Table 22.5. Notice that we start at 8:30 a.m. and finish sometime after 6:30 p.m. — a long day.

3.2 Create an Evaluation Timetable

Once you have worked out the details of the session days, you can plan your overall evaluation timetable. Once you have seen the detail you could decide to adopt a gentler schedule for the sessions than the one in Table 22.5 and instead plan to have

Table 22.5 Example of Timings for a Day's Evaluation Session

Time	Participant	Activity
8:30 a.m.		Make sure everything is in place for first participant
9 a.m.	First participant	
10:30 a.m.		Tidying-up time
11 a.m.	Second participant	
12:30 p.m.		Tidying-up time and lunch break
1 p.m.	Third participant	
2:30 p.m.		Tidying-up time
3 p.m.	Fourth participant	
4:30 p.m.		Tidying-up time
5 p.m.	Final, fifth participant	
6:30 p.m.		Tidy up and finish

five sessions in two eight-hour days, with each one yielding an hour's worth of notes from watching participants plus an assortment of other data.

We'll go into more detail about the collection and analysis of the data in Chapters 23 and 25, but for now we will make a rough guess and estimate that it will take two hours to analyze the data from each participant, so we have 10 hours of analysis.

After that, we'll probably want to create some sort of report or presentation for a meeting. We'll go into this in more detail in Chapters 25 and 28, but for now we will estimate that creating the report takes an additional 10 hours and that we are going to present it at a meeting.

Therefore, if we want to finish up with a report on Friday, we have an evaluation week that looks like the example shown in Table 22.6. Working backward, by the time we get to the evaluation sessions we must have created our strategy, done the detailed planning, prepared the evaluation, and recruited the participants. Generally, it is best to recruit participants about one to two weeks in advance of the evaluation. If you recruit them too far in advance, there is more chance that their plans may change or they might simply forget. If you try to recruit them too close to the evaluation sessions, it is much harder because they are already busy. To keep things simple, we will allow two weeks. This results in an overall timetable of about four weeks (see Table 22.7) — but the level of activity within those weeks is uneven, with weeks one and four being the really busy ones.

Table 22.6 Timetable for a Week of Evaluation and Reporting

Monday	8 hours	Evaluation sessions
Tuesday	8 hours	Evaluation sessions
Wednesday	8 hours	First part of analysis
Thursday	2 hours 6 hours	Finish analysis Start to write report
Friday	4 hours	Finish report
	4 hours	Prepare and present at meeting

Table 22.7 Overall Evaluation Timetable

Week 1	Create evaluation strategy Decide who to recruit Start preparing evaluation materials Run pilot test
Week 2	Recruit participants
Week 3	Finalize evaluation materials
Week 4	Evaluation week as in Table 22.6

> **EXERCISE 22.5 (Allow 10 minutes)**
>
> Draw up an overall timetable for your evaluation. Decide how long you need with each participant, determine how many participants you will need, and estimate how long your analysis will take you. Then work back to determine when you should start.
>
> **DISCUSSION**
>
> Your timetable may look similar to the one in Table 22.7, or perhaps not. We have sometimes had to turn around an evaluation in less than two days overall, for a particularly rushed project. On other occasions, we have allowed a lot longer because we knew that the participants were especially hard to find or we had the luxury of knowing that we were going to do an evaluation some time in advance.

> *Evaluation Tip 4*   *Draw up a timetable early*
> Your evaluation is likely to depend on other people. You will need to recruit your participants and give them some notice of when they are needed. You may have to coordinate with developers or book time on specific equipment. The sooner you create an outline timetable, the easier it will be to keep track of when you need to do things. It is better to have an estimated timetable that you can adjust as things become clearer than to try to muddle through without one.

4   Preparing Task Descriptions

You have already met task scenarios in Chapter 4. If you have written the task scenarios in plain language that will be appropriate for your participants, then you can use them as they are; but usually they are simplified somewhat for evaluation, in which case, we call them **task descriptions**. Task descriptions represent the tasks the participant will perform while interacting with the prototype during the evaluation. As part of the planning for evaluation, you will need to decide which tasks you will administer and how many you will want to evaluate; it would not be feasible to evaluate all the tasks and all the paths of user–system interaction even for an only moderately complex system.

Some authors use the term "task scenarios" where we use "task descriptions."

The complexity of the individual task descriptions and the amount of time you have allocated for the evaluation sessions will have an influence on the number of tasks you choose. The functionality provided by the system or prototype will also influence which tasks you choose. Here is a list of the different kinds of tasks (from Hix and Hartson, 1993) that you might consider:

- Core tasks that are frequently performed by the users
- Tasks that are very important to the users or to the business
- Tasks that have some new design features or functionality added
- Critical tasks, even though they may not be frequently used
- A task that you feel has to be validated with the users for greater clarity and understanding of the design team

- Any design features that will be highlighted in marketing efforts
- Tasks that the use scenarios were based on, which you used for developing the content diagram during conceptual design of the user interface

For your evaluations we recommend that you choose tasks that help you in validating the usability requirements or that focus on any particular design features or usability concerns you want to assess.

> **EXERCISE 22.6 (Allow five minutes)**
>
> Think of a web site that you have worked on or visited recently. Assume that you have been asked to evaluate it. Write a brief task description for one of the types of tasks from the preceding list.
>
> **DISCUSSION**
>
> We were involved in the evaluation of a gardening web site. The aim of the evaluation session was to determine whether the users found the site's search mechanism easy to use and whether the search engine gave effective results.
>
> The participant's task for the evaluation was to search for information on setting up and maintaining a new lawn in the home page of the web site. We created the following task description: "Assume that you have moved to a new home and would like to cultivate a new lawn for your backyard. Since you want to do this yourself, you are using this web site to find information about how you can sow the lawn and maintain it."

4.1 Task Cards

A "task card" is simply a card with the task description on it. We find it is convenient to use ordinary index cards (13 cm by 7.5 cm/five inches by three inches) like the one in Figure 22.4. Notice that this task card needs a supplementary card with details for subscription form. Task cards are convenient if you want to vary the order of tasks for each participant when some tasks might be easier or harder depending on the order you do them in. We often choose a simple task for the first one, then shuffle the remainder like playing cards.

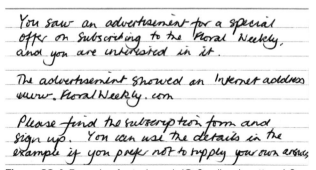

Figure 22.4 Example of a task card. (© Caroline Jarrett and Gerry Gaffney, used with permission.)

> ***Evaluation Tip 5*** *Make a task card for each evaluation rask description creating your task descriptions*

4.2 Task Descriptions for Global Warming

Because they only had part of the system available, the Global Warming designers were limited in the tasks they could choose to evaluate. They also particularly wanted to test the navigational aspects of the system. So they chose a single, general task, "Please use this system as if you were a student in this science course." However, to ensure that they got plenty of comments they decided to use the cognitive questions from the cognitive walkthrough in Chapter 4 as a way to prompt the participants and to ensure that they got as many comments as possible on each part of the interface.

We will describe these cognitive questions in more detail in Chapter 23.

They decided that, as they only had one task but many questions, they would incorporate the questions in their evaluation script and omit the task cards.

> **EXERCISE 22.7 (Allow five minutes)**
>
> Do you agree with the Global Warming decision to omit task cards?
>
> **DISCUSSION**
>
> *Caroline writes:* I would prefer them to make a task card, even if the designers only have one task for the evaluation. They could add the cognitive questions to it. The task card gives both the participant and the evaluator a clear, easy-to-reference description of what they are both trying to do.

We will go into more detail about writing an evaluation script in Chapter 24.

You may feel that controlling the participants' tasks is too restrictive or that it is hard to anticipate the tasks that participants would wish to undertake with the system. You can solve this problem by making your tasks very general, you can allow or encourage the participants to create their own tasks as they use your interface, or you can have a mixture. Table 22.8 presents some of the options.

5   Where Will You Do the Evaluation?

Evaluations that are undertaken in the user's own environment are called **field studies**. Evaluations conducted at a place somewhere else are known as **controlled studies**.

5.1 Field Studies

The benefit of a field study is that you can gather data about the environment within which the users work as well as about your system. For example, you might observe that the participant is being constantly interrupted by other colleagues' queries. Based on this knowledge, in the next phase of design you might plan to incorporate reminders and status messages that would help the user resume her or his tasks after interruptions.

Table 22.8 Controlling the Participant's Tasks

Type of control	Advantages	Disadvantages	Example system
All tasks designed by the evaluator.	Good when the interface has a clearly defined purpose. Better control over the evaluation. Ensures that the participant tests the part of the interface you are interested in. Makes it easy to compare results from different participants. If you have experts rather than real users, it can help the experts understand the user domain.	Little opportunity to find out what participants expect in the interface, unless they have particularly strong ideas and are willing to express them.	Embedded system, such as a burglar alarm or washing machine. Application with a specific purpose, such as time recording.
Start participants with one or more tasks suggested by the evaluator. Ask participants to add their own tasks as they work with the interface.	Good when the users are guaranteed to get some training or where there are at least a few highly predictable tasks. Should create a good start to the evaluation. Your task sets the scene for the type of tasks you want to test. Can find out whether the interface encourages exploration and learning. At least some comparison possible between participants.	May restrict participants to tasks that are similar to the type of tasks you suggest. Might miss important but infrequent tasks. Might miss combinations of tasks (e.g., dealing with one customer when another interrupts).	E-mail program, where you could assume that everyone wants to send an e-mail and read an incoming e-mail; but some users may want more sophisticated features or have particular expectations of the interface.

Table 22.8 Controlling the Participant's Tasks—cont'd

Type of control	Advantages	Disadvantages	Example system
Offer participants a choice between their own tasks or a suggested list. Ask or encourage participants to suggest new tasks as they work with the interface.	Good when some participants may have ideas but others are not that interested in the interface. Ensures that all participants have some tasks to attempt with the interface. Good when you need to gather ideas about what participants might want from the interface.	Can make it difficult or impossible to compare results between participants. Can make the evaluation unpredictable: the interface may simply not support the participant's chosen tasks.	Web site offering advice on a topic where some participants are likely to be knowledgeable but others may have no idea about the topic or experience with it.
Ask participants to suggest their own tasks. Encourage participants to suggest new tasks as they work with the interface.	Good when learnability of the interface is crucial or when you want to see whether the interface supports exploration. Can be a way to explore participants' expectations of the interface. Sometimes useful for investigating existing systems to generate ideas for new systems.	Can be nerve-wracking, albeit interesting, for the evaluator if the participant sets off on a task that you have not designed for at all. Likely to be very difficult to compare results between participants.	Web site designed to sell products and you want to see whether the participant understands the range and types of products on offer.

A limitation of field studies is that they can be cumbersome to arrange and set up. In addition, they may not be as effective as one would anticipate if there are situations where a participant is called away from the evaluation session. Sometimes there are other reasons why it may not be possible to undertake evaluations in the users' work environment. For example, the participant's manager may object to releasing personnel for evaluations in the workplace or the workplace may be unsuitable for visitors.

5.2 Controlled Studies

Evaluations conducted at a place other than the user's work environment are known as controlled studies. A controlled study can be informal or formal. An informal setting could be space in your office or at your home, or even a meeting room at a hotel or at the user's workplace. Figure 22.5 shows a room layout for an informal controlled study.

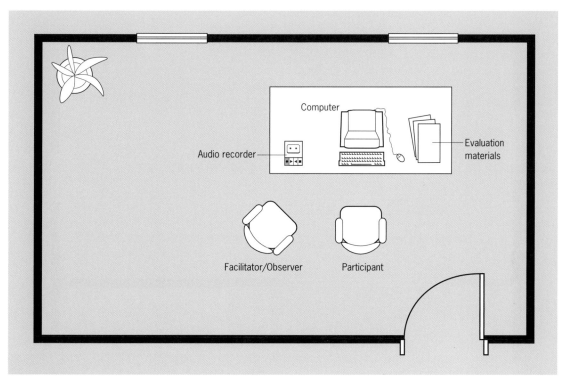

Figure 22.5 A room layout for an informal controlled study.

The STC Usability SIG web site maintains an up-to- date selection of advice on building a usability lab, lab equipment vendors, and labs for hire at www.stcsig.org/ usability/topics/ usability-labs.html.

In situations where it is impractical to carry out an evaluation in the user's real environment, controlled studies may be the only way to undertake an evaluation. To make the controlled study more realistic, the evaluation sessions should closely simulate the user's actual work environment. For instance, in the evaluation of a system that is being designed for a safety critical environment, simulation rooms containing the same equipment, furniture, lighting conditions, and background noise as the actual work environment would be used.

Many systems are designed for use in an ordinary office environment, so evaluating them in an ordinary office environment is entirely sensible. Generally, it is easier for the participant to concentrate if the room is clean and tidy and without excessive distractions. As one of the greatest distractions is other people in the room, many usability evaluations are done in usability laboratories that offer a separate room for observers. A typical setup is shown in Figure 22.6.

5.3 The Setting for the Global Warming Evaluation

The Global Warming team decided to ask the users to come to the team (controlled study) rather than going to the users (field study).

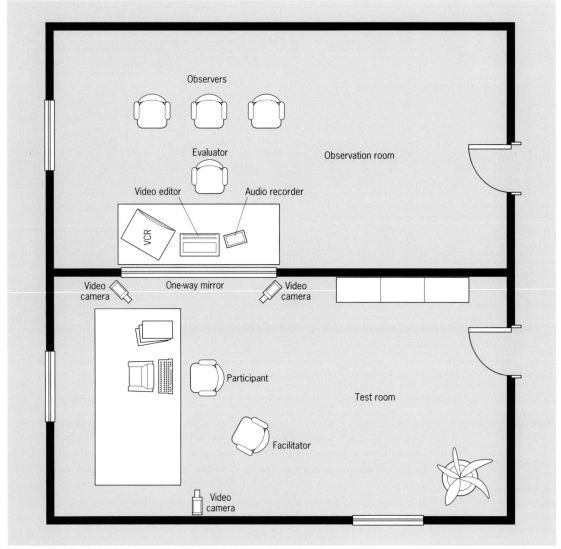

Figure 22.6 Typical setup for a controlled study in a usability laboratory.

EXERCISE 22.8 (Allow five minutes)

Do you agree with their decision to opt for a controlled study?

DISCUSSION

The Global Warming UI is an early prototype with several areas missing. The user environment is reasonably familiar: most people study at home, and most of us know that homes vary in their suitability as study locations. Therefore, as learning about the user environment is not a high priority and as the prototype is not really suitable for delivery to a user's computer, we agree with the Global Warming team's decision to opt for a controlled study.

5.4 Arranging Usability Evaluation Sessions

Whether you are planning to conduct a field study or a controlled study, it is important to make all the necessary arrangements. You might like to include in your evaluation plan a checklist that details all the necessary tasks for making the arrangements. Your checklist should include the following items:

- Scheduling suitable dates and times for the evaluation sessions
- Planning travel and reserving any usability equipment required for the session if you are undertaking a field study
- Reserving a room if you are undertaking an informal controlled study
- Booking a usability laboratory if you are undertaking a formal controlled study
- Informing all the evaluators and participants concerned with the arrangement details

5.5 The Arrangements for the Global Warming Evaluation

EXERCISE 22.9 (Allow five minutes)

Do you agree with their choices? Would you suggest anything else to think about?

DISCUSSION

We would like to check that the team's own computer had a similar specification to that of a typical user's computer, as often developers have higher specification machines (bigger screens, faster processors, etc.).

The users may be worried if they encounter a defect. Try to remember to include an instruction about defects in the introductory materials, perhaps something like: "This is an early prototype, and there are a few places where it does not work. Please point the mouse to where you want to click next and then check with me before doing the actual clicking. Don't worry if you forget: you can't damage anything, but I may need to spend a couple of minutes restarting the software."

6 | Summary

At the end of Chapter 20, we listed the main choices to be made for your evaluation:

- What is the purpose of the evaluation?
- Which users will you choose?

Box 22.2	**The Evaluation Plan for Global Warming**

Memo: To all team members

Subject: Evaluation plan

We are all set for our first evaluation next Wednesday. Here are the key details:

We will use the small meeting room from 9 a.m. to 7:30 p.m. Please avoid this room unless you have a role in the evaluation.

The sessions will start at 9:30 a.m., 11:30 a.m., 1:30 p.m., 3:30 p.m., and 5:30 p.m. We have allowed 15 minutes for greeting the participant including explaining the purpose of the test and giving participants the opportunity to ask any questions. We have allowed 1 hour for working on the tasks and 15 minutes for the final interview and thanks.

There is a 30-minute interval after each participant leaves to allow for tidying up the materials and resetting the prototype.

Participants will arrive at the main reception area, and our receptionist has agreed to look after them until their scheduled time.

We have a spare participant who has kindly agreed to be a substitute if any of the main participants are unable to come at the last minute.

We will test version 1.2 of the prototype using the laptop computer. Please note that any changes after version 1.2 will not be part of this evaluation.

We have decided not to use video or audio recording equipment for this evaluation.

This will be a long day, but we hope to learn a lot about the system from these participants. If you would like to hear about our findings, please attend the analysis and debriefing meeting on Thursday at 1 p.m.

- Where will you do the evaluation?
- What data do you need to collect?
- What product, system, or prototype are you testing?
- What tasks will you ask the participants to try?
- Are there any specific concerns or questions that you want to ask the participant about?

Now that we have completed Chapters 21 and 22, we have done most of the planning arising from those choices. There remains just one area that we need to think about in detail — collecting the data, which we will do in the next chapter.

23

Deciding how to collect data

1   Introduction: Preparing to Collect Evaluation Data

All your preparations are aiming for the same thing: to obtain as much useful data as possible from your evaluation. In this chapter, we go into more detail about how to capture data, and in Chapter 25, we consider how to analyze what you have collected.

When you developed your evaluation strategy in Chapter 21, we discussed deciding what qualitative and quantitative data you need to collect by considering the usability requirements and metrics that you established when gathering requirements. For example, if you need to establish the time required for a task, then some way of timing the evaluation is necessary.

Very broadly, you get quantitative data from timing and logging actions — that is, watching and measuring what the participants do — and you get qualitative data from listening to what the participants say about what they are doing, what they thought about it, and how that compared with their expectations.

In this chapter, we start with timing and logging and then move on to listening to and keeping notes on what the participants say. All this may seem a bit low tech to you, so we will look at some of the technologies that are available for recording evaluations — and their limitations.

> **EXERCISE 23.1 (Allow 15 minutes)**
>
> The Global Warming developers' evaluation strategy contained the following remarks on usability requirements and metrics: "We want to get some ideas for a metric on 'Easy to navigate.' Metrics for the other usability requirements are a lower priority at this stage." What data should they try to collect?
>
> **DISCUSSION**
>
> "Easy to navigate" could be looked at the other way: What might show that something is difficult to navigate? The team could count the number of times a user chooses to click on an incorrect interface element, or the number of incorrect screens that the user sees before finding the correct one. Alternatively, the team

could log all the user's actions during the evaluation and then assign them as correct and incorrect during the data analysis stage.

Although at this stage, the designers are less interested in metrics for other usability requirements, they may as well use the opportunity of having participants around to ask them a few questions such as whether or not the interface is enjoyable to use.

2   Timing and Logging Actions

If you are planning to validate time-related usability metrics such as the time taken to complete a task, you will need a clock, watch, or stopwatch for recording the time during the session. The advantage of a stopwatch is that you can stop it if there is a break, such as the participant discussing the task with the facilitator. The disadvantage is that if the equipment operator happens to be the same person as the facilitator, it is easy to forget to restart the stopwatch again after the break.

If the tasks involved are at all complex, then you may want to log more than start time and stop time. For example, did the participant go to the Help option or spend time searching through menus? One simple way of keeping track of events is to note the time of each comment or significant user action as well as the comment or action itself. If you are technically inclined, it is fairly easy to set up a spreadsheet that adds a time stamp to each line of comment that you type in.

2.1 Automatic Logging of Keystrokes and Mouse Clicks

You may think, why should I write all this stuff down when a computer could record it for me? Indeed there are products available that can help. These generally come from one of these traditions:

- Products intended to keep track of user actions to check that they are doing the work they are supposed to do and not trying to breach security
- Products intended to capture sequences of user actions for use in demonstrations or help
- Web-based products that aim to capture the number of visits to the various pages on a web site and possibly the routes through the site (the "clickstream")

Irrespective of the tradition that it came from, any of these can be useful for evaluations. For example, if efficiency is an important usability requirement, then a security-type product that will count every keystroke for you will save a lot of tedious note taking. If easy-to-learn on a web site is important, then an analysis of the clickstream will help you to see where the participant went wrong.

One general problem with many of these products is that there is no provision for aligning notes or comments from the participant with the log of actions. This means that you are likely to have some laborious work to do, linking together the data from the log of actions and your notes about what the participant was saying at the time.

2.2 Specialist Logging Software for Usability Evaluations

To help meet the needs of practitioners, some commercial companies offer more complex logging and tracking software. These products vary considerably in cost: one product shown in Figure 23.1 is offered as freeware, others can cost up to tens of thousands of dollars depending on the features offered and the level of integration with other equipment such as video. The advantage of the specialist loggers is that they allow you to make notes that are tied to the time of specific user actions.

2.3 Choosing a Logging Product

Before you invest time or money in any of these products, it is worth mentioning that many usability practitioners consider that they are unnecessary. They prefer to rely on a typed or written record of the session, possibly supplemented by audio or video recording — a topic we will return to later in this chapter.

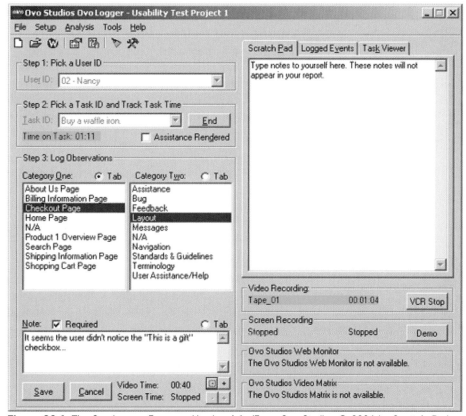

There is a list of usability equipment suppliers on the STC Usability SIG web site at www.stcsig.org/ usability/topics/ usabilty-labs.html.

Figure 23.1 The Ovo Logger Freeware Version 4.1. (From Ovo Studios © 2004 by Scott A. Butler, used with permission.)

3   **Think-Aloud and Offering Help**

If you want to find out why participants are making their various choices while interacting with the interface, you will need to ask them about it. One way of doing this is to encourage the participants to talk about what they are trying to do during the evaluation. The evaluation data obtained while thinking aloud are called **think-aloud protocols**, or sometimes **talk-aloud protocols** or **verbal protocols** (Hix and Hartson, 1993).

If you can persuade your participant to think aloud, you are likely to learn a great deal about your UI and the usability defects the participant is facing. There are other advantages:

- You get immediate feedback on the way the participant is thinking about the interface and any problems or surprises.
- Because the participants are continuously explaining what is happening, thinking aloud can help them to focus and concentrate during the evaluation session.

There are, though, some disadvantages:

- Some participants can find thinking aloud unnatural and distracting.
- Thinking aloud can slow the participant's thought processes. This could have an effect on task performance. Because the participants are performing the task with greater concentration and at a slower pace while thinking aloud, they are less likely to commit errors as when working in their usual environments.
- Sometimes it can become very exhausting for the user to verbalize thought processes for the duration of the evaluation session.

Usually you learn the most from user observation if you let the participant explore the interface without offering any help. If the user is struggling with a particular task, you might prompt with questions such as "What were you trying to do?" or "What did you expect to happen when you clicked on that icon?" or "How would you like to perform that action?" However, if the performance time of the user is being recorded, then you should avoid interrupting, as it will invalidate the quantitative data you are aiming to collect.

Exactly how much to intervene with questions is sometimes a matter of fine judgment. Too much, and you upset the participant's concentration. Too little, and you can fail to find out what you need from the evaluation. One usability practitioner (Anderson, 2004) had these thoughts on the problem:

> *One form of interaction we all have experience with is getting a user to talk. Non-directive, open-ended questions such as "What are you thinking?" "Is that what you expected?" or "What just happened?" seem to work best here. More directive interjections like "Are you confused?" or "Were you trying to copy the file?" run the risk of interpreting behavior and, thus, possibly influencing it. They should be avoided.*

A particularly good method to keep users talking involves "active listening." This limits interaction more to echoing what the user just said and lots of "uh-huhs." The former is particularly useful if what the user said was incomplete ("This isn't what . . .") or vague ("Wow!").

Personally, I also do all I can at the beginning of the test to address the unusual situation that users find themselves in (and which, I believe, contributes to their being silent). I directly address the oddness of the environment, the unfamiliarity of thinking out loud, and of my sitting there but not participating. Telling users that the system, and not them, is the "subject" of the test helps too. Treating the user as more of a partner in the study is even more beneficial.

A final necessary interaction is to elicit specific issues. Though we design our tests to lead the user to these issues as part of a real task, human behavior is unpredictable, and users don't always end up where we think they will. Note, though, that this kind of interaction is much less straightforward and much more prone to bias.

3.1 Using Cognitive Walkthrough Questions

In Chapter 4, we described a cognitive walkthrough, looking at whether a user is likely to recognize what to do with an interface and make appropriate decisions. These cognitive walkthrough questions can be an interesting way of prompting the participant. We have adapted them slightly in Table 23.1 to language that seems appropriate to us for an evaluation. You might want to change them some more, perhaps thinking about Anderson's ideas as you do so.

Table 23.1 Cognitive Walkthrough Questions Adapted for an Evaluation

Question	Technical description of question	Question to ask in an evaluation
Question 1	How does the user know what to do next? Is the correct action sufficiently evident to the user (i.e., can he or she recognize it) or does the user have to recall what to do from memory?	Is there anything there that tells you what to do next?
Question 2	Will the user connect the description of the correct action with what he or she is trying to do?	Is there a choice on screen that lines up with what you want to do? If so, which one?
Question 3	On the basis of the system's response to the chosen action, will the user know if he or she has made a right or wrong choice?	Now that you've tried it, has it done what you wanted it to do?

4 │ Taking Notes When Observing Users

Note taking, including the participant's comments and your observations, is the most effective means of capturing your observations. For example, suppose the participant needs to find the menu item Options. He or she might say, "I'm not sure which menu to look in for the Options item." You might observe that the participant is searching for the menu item in the wrong menu. You would record both the participant's comment and your observation.

If you can predict what the participant should do for each task, then you can write these predictions out in advance and use them as the basis of a form (such as the one suggested in Figure 23.2) for collecting and recording the data. Instead of writing by hand, you may prefer to record the data on a portable computer, but be aware that any keystrokes or mouse sounds may be distracting for the user.

> **Evaluation Tip 6**   *Have plenty of paper for note taking*
> Even if you create a data collection form or opt for a technological method of taking notes, make sure you have plenty of paper as a backup. Unexpected events are common in evaluations, and you would not want to miss anything.

5 │ Conducting Post-Session Discussions

After the session, you will probably want to ask the participant further questions about the experience. Frequently, the participant also wants to comment on the interface and may need some reassurance. Participants often blame themselves for any problems they have met.

If you have carried out an evaluation session without interrupting the participants or asking them to think aloud, it is then often helpful to review the audio/video recordings and ask them about their thoughts and actions. This will give the participants an opportunity to reflect on their interaction with the prototype and give you feedback. Rerunning the events of the evaluation and asking the participant to comment is called a **retrospective protocol** (Hix and Hartson, 1993). A general discussion after an evaluation session about what has happened is called a **post-session interview** or a **debrief**.

Both think-aloud and retrospective protocols are useful for evaluation, subject to the following points:

- If you are recording time during the sessions the retrospective protocol does not affect or interfere with the task performance of the user or in the collection of timing data. Thus, retrospective protocols are useful when you are collecting quantitative data for the usability metrics. Think-aloud protocols are useful in situations where you are collecting qualitative data.

Task Description No:		Session Date:
Evaluator's Name:		Session Start Time:
User's Name:		Session End Time:
Actions involved in the task description	User's remarks	Observer's comments

This column could be filled with the actions before the session

Make sure the cells are quite big to allow for plenty of notes

Figure 23.2 Data collection form for user-observation.

- Analyzing think-aloud data during an evaluation session can force the evaluator to make assumptions about what the participant was really thinking or trying to do. In a retrospective protocol, an evaluator can discover from the participants what they were thinking without having to guess or infer, although care must be taken when interpreting the data as some users may rationalize their behavior when giving a retrospective account of their actions.
- Think-aloud protocols are more immediate. The participant forgets a lot of the detail by the end of the evaluation session and often, once a participant has solved a problem posed by the interface, it is difficult for him or her to recall why he or she had the problem in the first place. Think-aloud protocols therefore usually give richer qualitative data.
- Some people find thinking aloud difficult. It can be hard to concentrate on a difficult task and also talk about what you are doing. A retrospective protocol may be your only option if the participant stops talking while trying to solve problems.

An intermediate approach can combine the best of the think-aloud and retrospective protocols by breaking the task description into smaller chunks of five or 10 minutes task time and allowing the participant to do each part in his or her own time while thinking aloud. Then after each chunk, ask the participant to go back and replay his or her thoughts while giving a retrospective protocol.

6 Questionnaires

Questionnaires have several advantages for collecting data from the evaluation:

- The questions you want to ask are all written on the questionnaire, so there is less chance of forgetting to ask something.
- The participants all see the same question, so there is more possibility of comparing answers from different participants.
- You may be able to collect some quantitative data, such as "Three of the four participants said the interface was easy to navigate."

Questionnaires also have disadvantages:

- They are difficult to design well enough to stand alone as your sole data-gathering technique. Even apparently straightforward, factual questions can be ambiguous. "Did this system meet your expectations?" might receive a yes answer from someone who expected it to work badly, and it did. Someone who expected it to work well, and it did, would also answer yes. So we would have two yes answers: one referring to a bad opinion, another referring to a good opinion.
- You have to predict the topics that your users will want to tell you about. This can be just as hard as predicting how they will use your system.
- The closed questions that are easy to analyze (for example, "Please rate how easy it is to navigate") give you little information about why the users have answered in the way they have.

For more information on questionnaire design, see Dillman (2000) or Oppenheim (1992).

Questionnaire designers always strongly recommend that you start the process of creating a questionnaire by interviewing potential respondents on the topics of the questionnaire. This gives you the opportunity to discover what other points your users wish to make and to find out whether the users have interpreted your questions in the way you meant.

> **Evaluation Tip 7** *if you use a questionnaire, then always interview as well, in order to probe the answers to the questions*
> After the participant fills in the questionnaire, use it as the basis for an interview so that you have an opportunity to explore the reasons why the participant chose the answers.

The NATS case study in Chapter 19 included the use of a SUMI questionnaire as part of evaluation.

Fortunately, several questionnaires are available that are designed for use as part of a usability evaluation. Some of them are free or available for academic or personal use without further charge. Two of the best known and most thoroughly validated are the Software Usability Measurement Inventory (SUMI; see Box 23.1) and the Website Analysis and MeasureMent Inventory (WAMMI). SUMI and WAMMI require payment, but you may consider this fee to be worthwhile to get the benefits of the statistical basis and long history of these questionnaires. Both of them are available in a range of European languages as well as in U.S. and U.K. English.

The SUMI questionnaire is discussed in detail in Kirakowski and Corbett (1993).

Tullis and Stetson (2004) compared five questionnaires for assessing the usability of a web site: one that they had used for several years in their own lab and the four

483
Part 4

| Box 23.1 | SUMI |

One example of a measurement questionnaire is **SUMI (the Software Usability Measurement Inventory)**. SUMI is a 50-item questionnaire in which all 50 items involve rating statements with three options: agree, undecided, or disagree. The statements explore the following attributes:

Learnability. For example, "I will never learn all the features of this software."

Helpfulness. For example, "The instructions and prompts are helpful."

Control. For example, "I sometimes don't know what to do next with this system."

Efficiency. For example, "If the software stops, it is not easy to get back to what I was doing."

Affect (the user's emotional response to the system). For example, "I would recommend this software to a colleague."

SUMI has an associated software package that calculates a score for each of these attributes and compares the interface being evaluated with computer systems in general.

Table 23.2 Four Questionnaires for Usability

Questionnaire	Reference	Available at/information available from
System Usability Scale (SUS)	Brooke (1996)	www.cee.hw.ac.uk/~ph/sus.html
Questionnaire for User Interface Satisfaction (QUIS)	Chin, Diehl, and Norman (1988)	www.lap.umd.edu/QUIS/index.html
Computer System Usability Questionnaire (CSUQ)	Lewis (1995)	www.acm.org/~perlman/question.cgi? form=CSUQ
An adaptation of Microsoft's Product Reaction Cards	Benedek and Miner (2002)	www.microsoft.com/usability/UEPostings/ ProductReactionCards.doc

Other questionnaires are listed at www.acm.org/ ~perlman/ question.html.

questionnaires listed in Table 23.2. Tullis and Stetson concluded that the System Usability Scale (SUS) gave the most reliable results. It was also the simplest of the questionnaires that they studied. But if you plan to use one of these questionnaires in your evaluation, think carefully about whether you should adapt it to ensure that it is meaningful to your participants and asks questions that are meaningful for your system. Tullis and Stetson modified all four of the questionnaires that they studied.

7 Using Technologies to Help with Recording

7.1 Video and Audio Recording

You will learn more about the way to communicate the evaluation results to the design team and other stakeholders in Chapter 28.

Video recording the evaluation session can help you review it to find out exactly where the user faced problems and where the user could comfortably proceed with the task. The video recording also serves as backup if any observations or notes were missed during evaluation. At the end of the session, when you present the evaluation results to the rest of the designers or to the management, video clips can be useful for convincing them about the severity of the usability defects.

With affordable, good-quality camcorders and video cameras readily available, video recording has become attainable for almost everyone, either by purchasing a camcorder or by borrowing one from a kindly friend or family member. If you have a flat-screen monitor or laptop computer, you can point the camera at the computer and record everything that the participant does. Doing the same thing with a CRT monitor is possible, but you are likely to get nasty banding effects that make it hard to view the recording afterward.

If you have a little more equipment available, Whitney Quesenbery (private communication, 2004) suggests that you can capture the participant as well as the screen they are interacting with by doing this:

- Use a laptop as the main computer for your evaluation.
- Attach an external monitor, keyboard, and mouse.
- Set the laptop at right angles to the participant.
- Ask the participant to use the external monitor, keyboard, and mouse.
- Point your video camera at the laptop screen and the participant.

A schematic is presented in Figure 23.3.

If video equipment is not available, audio recording on its own can be useful. It is easy to set up and is often considered less intrusive than video recording. Although audio recording does not capture the visual aspects of the session, the oral exchanges that take place can be a valuable source of data. However, it is often difficult to relate the recording to what the user and system are doing.

7.2 Eye-Tracking Equipment

Although you can tell a lot about where a user is looking, there is always the suspicion that you are missing some eye movements or misinterpreting them. Eye-tracking systems aim to record exactly where a user is looking, and they can distinguish between glancing at something and fixing on it.

Some of the earlier eye-tracking equipment was difficult to set up and intrusive for the user, as you can see in Figure 23.4. More recent equipment looks much like an ordinary flat-screen monitor (see Figure 23.5).

By analyzing the data from the eye-tracking it is possible to determine where a participant is looking during the evaluation; or by taking data from several participants, it is possible to work out what the most frequently viewed parts of the screen might be. Figure 23.6 shows one such map.

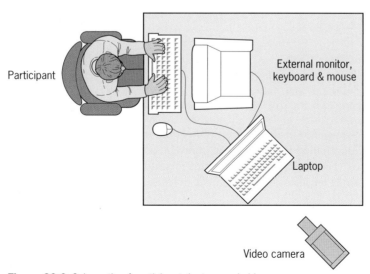

Figure 23.3 Schematic of participant, laptop, and video camera.

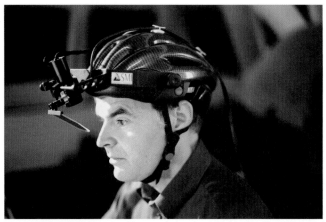

Figure 23.4 Early eye-tracking equipment was intrusive for the participant.

Figure 23.5 Recent eye-tracking equipment looks like a modified flat-screen monitor.

However, few usability practitioners use eye-tracking equipment unless their organization happens to specialize in it. The cost of the equipment is still high, and there are occasionally a few difficulties in setting it up if the participant wears glasses or contact lenses or has certain eye defects.

7.3 Practitioner's Choice of Technology

One colleague said:

> *I have all sorts of video equipment. I usually work with other people who are acting as observers and taking notes. Even so, I still write paper notes of my own all the time. Taking notes has three benefits.*

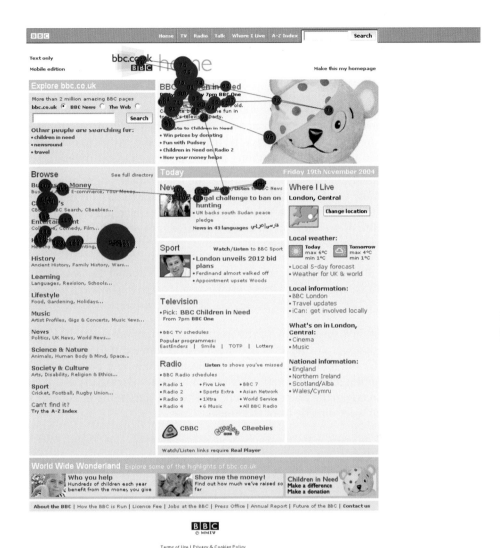

Figure 23.6 Eye fixations of participants looking at and discussing an information page. Bigger spots means longer fixations.

> *First, it shows the participants that you are paying close attention to their experiences and comments, and helps you to focus so that you can write the notes.*
>
> *Second, you have a paper backup in case any of your equipment fails.*
>
> *Third, looking away occasionally to write notes reminds you to glance at your watch and your script, to check that you are on time and doing all you should be doing.*

and another said:

> *I have had experience of the video not being turned on or pointing at the wrong place. Also, the video does not always pick up the screen, the keyboard, and the user's*

face at the same time. Transcription of the comments from video is very time consuming. Your own notes will focus on the highlights.

▶ **What to Do If a Participant Does Not Agree to Be Recorded**

The user always has the right to request that the video or other recording device is switched off. If you mention the recording when you recruit, you will find that it is most unusual for the user to object when he or she arrives. If it does happen, do not worry about it. Simply ask the user if he or she wishes to continue with paper notes, then turn off the equipment, and proceed with paper notes.

Equally, the user may ask to stop the test at some point, or you may run out of time before you have finished the tasks. Offer your thanks for the comments so far (even if they were minimal) and stop the test. The user still has the right to the incentive, if one is on offer, because the incentive is to reward the user for turning up not for "being a good participant".

> **Evaluation Tip 8**   *Your participant is more important than your test*
> Do not worry if you have to stop or cut short a test, or switch to paper notes because a participant is unhappy. You can always test another day with a different participant.

Perhaps surprisingly, many usability practitioners prefer not to use video or audio recording, or they may use them only if they wish to show the recording to clients later on. Analyzing video and audio recordings can be cumbersome and time consuming, and you need to make careful notes during the test so that you can jump directly to the point in the recording when something interesting happened. So why not work directly from the notes?

> **Evaluation Tip 9**   *Don't rely on equipment to observe for you*
> Even though there are many types of technology to help you watch users, the best user interface designers learn to use their own eyes and watch for evidence of problems.

Almost without exception, the person who has agreed to participate in your test wants to be helpful. Therefore, if you are unsure of your skills as an observer, ask your participant to contribute by describing what is going on (thinking aloud). One of our authors remembers the following incident:

> *My eyesight is not the greatest. In one evaluation, I had to sit at an angle to the screen and the light was dim. My participant had stopped working and seemed puzzled but said nothing. I genuinely could not see what he was looking at, so I said, "I'm sorry, I can't see that screen at all well. Please tell me what it is saying to you." The participant suddenly seemed to catch on to the idea of commenting. Since then, I have often used that approach, even if it has been a little bit untruthful because I can read the screen easily.*

> **Evaluation Tip 10**   *One way to prompt your users is to ask for their help*
> "I'm sorry, I can't see that screen at all well. Please tell me what it is saying to you."

8 | The Global Warming Choices for Data Collection

The Global Warming team wanted to find out whether the system was easy to navigate and whether it prompted a good learning experience. The designers decided to count the number of screens visited and the number of incorrect navigation choices made, but their main focus was on what the participants said about what they saw. They decided to use cognitive walkthrough questions (similar to those in Table 23.1). They also devised a pretest questionnaire because they thought it was especially important to find out about (1) the participants' level of expertise on computers and (2) the participants' background knowledge of the science of global warming.

9 | Summary

In this chapter, we looked at ways of collecting evaluation data, including preparing forms or questionnaires and using a variety of technologies such as timing or logging actions, video or audio equipment, eye-tracking equipment, and keyboard or click-stream logging. We also mentioned that most practitioners opt for the simplest possible technologies where they can, generally reserving video for occasions on which they will need to create video reports.

24

Final preparations for the evaluation

1 Introduction

At the end of Chapter 20, we gave an outline of a user observation and the strategic choices that are needed. We looked at some of the strategic choices in Chapter 21, and we went on to do the planning to implement those choices in Chapters 22 and 23. Now we have to complete the preparations identified in Table 24.1.

1.1 Evaluation Materials for Global Warming

For comparison, we have compiled the Global Warming team's decisions in Table 24.2.

2 Roles for Evaluators

For an evaluation session, you may be the sole person involved and therefore have to do everything. If other members of the team are also participating in the evaluation, several roles are available, and you can assign different roles to different people.

2.1 Facilitator

A good facilitator is the key to a good evaluation session. If the participants feel comfortable and welcomed, then they are more likely to relax and comment constructively on the interface. Snyder (2003) calls this the "flight attendant" role for the facilitator: looking after the well-being of the participant.

The second job for the facilitator is to try to keep the participant talking about what is going on. Snyder calls this the "sportscaster" role. It is definitely subordinate to the flight attendant role, but is especially valuable for the purposes of data collection.

The third job for the facilitator is to ensure that the purpose of the evaluation is fulfilled, the correct questions are asked, and that the questions are phrased in an objective manner. Snyder calls this the "scientist" role. It is also subordinate to the flight

Table 24.1 Final Preparations for the Evaluation

What happens in a user observation	Your strategic choices	Preparations that may be needed
You start by welcoming the participant and explaining the purpose of your evaluation and their role within it. Check that the participant is happy to continue, and ask for their consent on your planned use of the data you obtain.	What is the purpose of the evaluation? Which users will you choose? Where will you do the evaluation? What data do you need to collect?	Book the location Recruit participants Assign roles for evaluators Prepare briefings for evaluators Create evaluation script Create consent form Create pretest interview plan or questionnaire
If you are testing a commercial product before it is released, you may need to ask the participant to promise not to divulge anything they learn about the product during the evaluation. If you are testing an early prototype or partly developed system with defects, then you may need to ask the participant to avoid certain parts of it.	What product, system or prototype are you testing?	Create nondisclosure form Prepare the system or prototype Check that you can do the tasks with the system or prototype
You then proceed to the main part of the session: asking the participant to complete one or more tasks using your system, while you observe and record what you see.	What tasks will you ask the participant to try?	Create task descriptions Create data collection form Prepare technologies for data collection Create forms for data analysis and interpretation
Once the tasks are complete (or your time is up), you can ask the participant for their views on the experience in another interview or by asking them to complete a posttest questionnaire. The session closes with your final thanks for their help, possibly including an incentive.	Are there any specific concerns or questions that you want to ask the participant about?	Create posttest interview plan or questionnaire Obtain incentives

Table 24.2 Final Preparations for Global Warming

Preparations that may be needed	Is it needed for the Global Warming evaluation?
Book the location?	Yes. We need to book the conference room.
Assign roles for evaluators?	Yes. We have several team members, and each person needs to know what she or he has to do.
Brief the evaluators?	No. All members of the team have been involved in preparing the evaluation strategy and evaluation plan, so no further briefing is necessary.
Create evaluation script?	Yes. A short script is needed that describes the purpose of the evaluation, what the participants will do, and the data to be collected.
Create consent form?	No. We will use the standard university form.
Create a pretest interview plan or questionnaire?	Yes. We want to ask about level of computer experience and background knowledge of the science of global warming.
Recruit participants?	Yes.
Create a nondisclosure form?	No. There is nothing proprietary or confidential in this system.
Prepare the system or protoype?	Not necessary. We already have the prototype.
Check that you can do the tasks with the system or prototype?	Not at this stage. We will do this during the pilot test.
Create task descriptions?	Not necessary. We have a single task and will include it in the overall script.

Table 24.2 Final Preparations for Global Warming—cont'd

Preparations that may be needed	Is it needed for the Global Warming evaluation?
Create data collection form?	No. We have done this already.
Prepare technologies for data collection?	No. We have decided to use paper data collection forms.
Create forms for data analysis and interpretation?	No. We have done this already.
Create a posttest interview plan or questionnaire?	Possibly. Are there any overall questions that we would like to ask participants?
Obtain incentives?	Yes. We need to prepare a thank-you letter for each participant.

attendant role, but it is especially valuable for the validity and usefulness of the data that you collect.

2.2 Note-Taker

Someone needs to make a record of what is happening in the evaluation, a role that we call **note-taker**.

2.3 Equipment Operator

If you have video or other recording equipment, then it helps to have someone on hand who is comfortable setting the equipment up and solving any problems that arise. If you are using a high-fidelity prototype or the actual system, you may need to arrange to have the system reset to its initial or unvisited state between participants.

2.4 Observer

Observing a usability evaluation is an excellent way to help stakeholders understand the importance of user-centered design, a topic we will return to in Chapters 28 and 29.

> *Usability testing is often the first or only time that many designers, developers, writers, and managers see actual users working with their site. Usability testing is a dose of reality that many need to see (www.usability.gov/methods/who_else.html, visited July 17, 2004).*

Gaffney (2001) suggests these rules for briefing observers. He uses the term "test administrator" where we say "facilitator":

Introduction

Usability testing can be very stressful for participants. Having observers present can add to this stress. Participants may be nervous and uncomfortable. Therefore please follow these guidelines.

Respect

At all times, we must treat participants with respect.

- *Be quiet. Keep noise levels to a minimum to avoid disrupting the test.*
- *Do not discuss participants' personal attributes. It is inappropriate to discuss participants in any way that is not directly related to the work we are carrying out.*
- *Do not include participant names in any notes you make.*
- *Refrain from joking and laughing, as this may be misinterpreted as being directed at the test participant.*
- *The test administrator is in charge of the visit. At any stage the administrator may request that any observer leave the area. If this happens, please comply immediately and without discussion.*

Wait for the results

You may see behavior that suggests particular design elements do not work well.

However, please refrain from making design changes until all the participants have been seen and the data analyzed.

2.5 Meeter and Greeter

A **meeter and greeter** is the person who meets the participants when they arrive for the evaluation. The meeter and greeter is generally responsible for all the domestic arrangements such as:

- Ensuring that the participant has access to the toilets if necessary
- Offering refreshments if appropriate
- Keeping the participant entertained if the evaluations are running late or the participant arrives early

2.6 Recruiter

The **recruiter** is the person or organization who finds the participants for the evaluation and who gets permission to go to the participant's home or work environment if this is a field study.

2.7 The Lone Evaluator

If you are doing it all by yourself, then you may want to make the evaluation sessions a little longer and allow extra time between sessions to keep yourself organized.

3 Creating an Evaluation Script

One way of making sure that you pick the right level of questioning and introduce each task accurately is to write an **evaluation script** (also called a **test script** or **discussion guide**). Opinion varies among usability practitioners about whether or not to stick closely to an evaluation script at all times. For example, Clifford Anderson (Anderson, 2004) and Gerry Gaffney (Gaffney, 2003a) are both clear on the view that you should always have a formal script. Anderson notes:

> *I am famous for my extremely detailed test scripts. These typically include the scenario I will give the user and detailed steps for the correct and any logical alternate paths (whether correct or incorrect). The scripts also include possible interactions and interventions for each step. Though no test will ever go so neatly as my test scripts, thinking ahead what you are going to say in this manner can help ensure that each user will hear the same open-ended, non-directive questions.*

Gaffney says:

> *You should read a formal script to each participant in order to ensure that all participants receive the same information.*

> *Avoid the temptation to run usability testing without a script — it is very easy to give too much or too little information without one.*

But Snyder (2003) takes a different point of view when talking about testing paper prototypes:

> ***Wean yourself from scripts.*** *In a script, you write down everything you will say to the users and read it to them at the proper time. Scripts are useful in usability testing when it's important to control all the interactions you have with the users. For example, if you were testing two competing software packages, you'd want your introductions of them to use equally neutral wording. But in paper prototype testing, it's unlikely that you need this degree of scientific rigor — when an interface is rapidly changing, a detailed script can become more trouble to maintain than it's worth. . . . Although scripts are okay when you're starting, as soon as you gain confidence in usability test facilitation, I recommend that you pare them down into checklists.*

Our view is that an evaluation script is essential when you do your first evaluation, and beneficial for quite a few evaluations after that. Our objective as evaluators is that our participants should leave the evaluation session feeling no worse than when they arrived, and better if possible. You have many steps to cover, and it is easy to forget something that might be important to your participant. Although reading from a script may seem artificial, we find that the benefit of thoroughness outweighs the formality.

> **Evaluation Tip 11**   *Your first duty in the evaluation is to look after your participant*
> You will learn a lot from the evaluation if you allow the participants to solve problems
> without your help. It can even be acceptable for the participants to become annoyed
> with the UI or even mildly upset by it. However, watch out and make sure that the
> needs of your participants take priority over your desire to learn about the UI.

3.1 An Example of an Evaluation Script

Table 24.3 is an example of a typical script. We have added an extra column showing
how the sentences in the script align with the stages in the evaluation. The evaluator
reads from the script, apart from the *instructions in italics.*

3.2 Using a Script for the Global Warming Evaluation

At first, the designers elected not to use a formal script in their first round of evaluation. Their participants were all colleagues from the same university, albeit from

Table 24.3 An Evaluation Script for a Web Site Evaluation

First, thank you for coming here today. I have a script here that I'll read to you. This may seem very formal, but it ensures that all participants receive the same information. *Pause/offer opportunity for questions after each paragraph*	Welcome the participant.
The purpose of today's activity is to test a web site that has been developed for Project X. We want to find out whether the web site works well for people who are not familiar with the project. Based on what we learn, we will advise the developers on how to improve it. I am going to ask you to try some tasks. We want to find out if the site makes them easy or difficult. It's important to emphasize that we are not testing your abilities in any way. We will be finished in about an hour. I will be taking notes all the time, and I will ask you to complete a short questionnaire about yourself. I will also ask for your comments. The information you give us is confidential, and your name will not be stored with this information.	Brief the participant.
Can you please read this consent form, and sign it if you agree. The wording is a bit formal, so you are welcome to ask me about anything that is not completely clear. *Give the participant the consent form, and allow time for him or her to read and sign it.* Thank you.	Obtain consent.

Table 24.3 An Evaluation Script for a Web Site Evaluation—cont'd

Before we start, I would like to ask you to complete a brief questionnaire about yourself. Once again, let me point out that your name is not stored with this information. *Give the participant the questionnaire, and allow time for him or her to complete it.* Thank you.	Pretest the questionnaire.
We will now move on to the tasks. For each task, I will give you a card that has the task written on it. I would appreciate it if you can give me a running commentary on what you are doing, because I cannot see the screen very easily from where I am sitting. You may find that the web site makes it difficult to do a task. If you get stuck because of this, that's fine. Just let me know, and we will skip that task and move on. If you want to take a break at any stage, let me know and we can do so.	Offer training or explain the task.
Are you ready to begin? *Administer each task in turn by offering the task card to the participant.* *Take notes of participant comments and your observations.* That completes the tasks. It has been really helpful to know that some of them have been a bit difficult. That will give the developers some ideas about what to do to improve the site.	During the session, observe the participant and record your observations.
I would now like to ask you some general questions about the web site. *Work through the post-session interview.*	Begin the post-session questionnaire or interview.
That completes the session. Thank you for giving your time today. *Escort participant from test area.*	Offer final thanks.
Collect notes and any other materials from observers, if any, and tidy the test area. Reset the computer/web site to ensure that the visited links are cleared and temporary data in cookies are deleted.	If data collection forms have been used, collect them from all involved.

different work areas, so they felt confident that they could be informal but appropriately polite and respectful of the time and trouble being taken by the participants. Instead, they created the following short checklist to use during the evaluation:

- Welcome participant.
- Explain the evaluation and confidentiality.
- Administer a pretest questionnaire.
- Administer the task and ask cognitive questions.
- Conduct an exit interview.
- Thank the participant.

EXERCISE 24.1 (Allow five minutes)

Review the Global Warming checklist. Does it cover all the important points? What improvements would you suggest?

DISCUSSION

The Global Warming designers found out almost nothing about the participants, so there is a risk that they will be unable to determine the differences between their participants and their target user profile. There is no explicit step to obtain consent to the evaluation. It may be overlooked.

The designers appear to hope that participants will understand the tasks without any explanation. A participant might be unsure about what to do.

They have not said what they mean by "cognitive questions," and they may forget them during the evaluation.

4   Forms to Use When Asking for Permission to Record

You need the agreement of the participant to take part in the evaluation, and you may also need their permission to record the evaluation. Burmeister (2000) has listed 10 principles relating to informed consent in usability testing:

2.1.1 Minimal risk (P1)

Usability testing should not expose participants to more than minimal risk. Though it is unlikely that a usability test will expose participants to physical harm, psychological or sociological risks do arise. If it is not possible to abide by the principle of minimal risk, then the usability engineer should endeavor to eliminate the risk or consider not doing the test.

2.1.2 Information (P2)

Informed consent implies information is supplied to participants. Information . . . can be summarized as: the procedures you will follow; the purpose of the test; any risks to the participant; the opportunity to ask questions; and, the opportunity to withdraw at any time.

2.1.3 Comprehension (P3)

The facilitator needs to ensure that each participant understands what is involved in the test. This must be done in a manner that is clear. It must also be done so as to completely cover the information on the form. The procedure for obtaining consent should not be rushed, nor made to seem unimportant. . . . Clearly one possible outcome of applying this principle is that the person involved may choose not to participate. However, not to permit such opportunities may adversely affect their ability to make an informed choice . . .

2.1.4 Voluntariness (P4)

. . . Coercion and undue influence should be absent when the person is asked to give their consent to participate in the test. Undue pressure might come in a number of subtle ways that one needs to be wary of. For instance, if you are in a position of authority over the participant such as employer to employee or teacher to student. Another subtle form of coercion is involved when participants receive payment for their participation. In the case of the latter it may be prudent to make the payment upfront, prior to the test. That way the participant will not feel pressured to have to stay to the end of the test (see P5 about the right to leave the test at any time). . . .

2.1.5 Participant's rights (P5)

Countries vary as to their recognition of human rights. Even where there is general agreement, definitions of those rights and interpretations of how they apply vary. Participants should have the right to be informed as to what their rights are. . . .

2.1.6 Nondisclosure (P6)

When the product is under development or in any way confidential, participants need to be informed that they cannot talk about the product or their opinions of it. . . .

2.1.7 Confidentiality (P7)

Confidentiality is different from the participant's right to privacy; it refers to how data about the participants will be stored [and used]. . . . laws concerning privacy and confidentiality vary greatly. The legalities must be investigated in the context of where the test is taking place.

2.1.8 Waivers (P8)

Permission needs to be obtained from participants to use materials such as questionnaires, audio and video recordings (and their transcripts). In many countries they have the right to refuse to give waivers. Participants should be given the option . . . of having the data used for the [immediate] purposes of the test, or of also having it used in a wider context. If the latter, then the consent form should state in what further ways the data will be used, so that an informed decision can be taken by the participant. Such permission should state the purposes for which the material will be used. Several usability engineers the author corresponded with in researching the material for this paper gave anecdotal stories of near court cases and in one case an out of court settlement where material obtained during a usability test was subsequently used in very different settings; such as sales promotion of the product and for training purposes. . . .

2.1.9 Legalese (P9)

. . . It is too tempting to have legal departments draft the consent form. Just as software engineering terminology and legal jargon can hinder the signing of forms, so in usability testing such language does not make for rapport building prior to the start of a usability test. Sensitive use on non-legal jargon should be made so that comprehension (P3) on the part of the participant is possible.

2.1.10 Expectations (P10)

Globalization and related issues to do with international differences in cultural and ethnicity lead to the notion of expectations. Each social grouping has its own means of resolving issues of power and hierarchy, turn taking, how interactions between people proceed, who can interrupt and contradict. There are expected behaviors. There are accepted behaviors. Cultures interact through expectations. . . . Misunderstandings arise due to differences in work practices and social class systems.

501
Part 4

Burmeister (2000) points out that some of these principles are more important than others:

So which of these principles are mandatory and which are discretionary? Informed consent is about protecting the rights of all parties involved in a usability test. The first 5 principles are concerned with the rights of participants, the next 4 are concerned with the rights of the company that has organized the testing to take place. The last applies to both. On an international scale, all these principles are in the "discretionary" category, none are "mandatory." Given the heterogeneous nature of people involved in remote testing in particular, this is an inescapable reality. Yet in most Western societies, at least those that might be described as representing the European Anglo Celtic view, the first 4 principles fall into the "mandatory" category. That is, despite the differences in legal requirements, all these societies have value systems similar to each other.

Bearing all that in mind, decide whether you need to prepare a consent form for your evaluation or whether you prefer to cover the points listed in your evaluation script and just obtain the participant's verbal permission. Signing a form feels more formal and may add to the overall stress of the evaluation but may be essential if you have to obtain agreement from a legal department.

4.1 Nondisclosure Agreements

If your system is proprietary or confidential in any way, you may need to ask participants to make some type of agreement to keep what they learn in the evaluation to themselves. These are usually known as **nondisclosure agreements** (NDAs). Generally, organizations that require NDAs also have legal departments with strong views as to how they should be worded. If possible, try to make sure that the NDA is worded in plain language and that you can both understand it and explain it to your participants. Box 24.1 presents an example of a combined nondisclosure agreement and consent form.

Box 24.1	**An Example of a Consent Form**

Understanding Your Participation

Please read this page carefully.

Xerox Corporation is asking you to participate in evaluating a new product. By participating in this evaluation, you will help us improve this and other Xerox products.

We will observe you and record information about how you work with the product. We may also ask you to fill out questionnaires and answer interview questions.

We will videotape all or some of the interview and your work. By signing this form, you give your permission to Xerox to use your voice, verbal statements, and videotaped pictures for the purposes of evaluating the product and showing the results of these evaluations. We will not use your full name.

You will be working with a product that is still being developed. Any information you acquire about this product is confidential and proprietary and is being disclosed to you only so that you can participate in the evaluation. By signing this form, you agree not to talk about this product to anyone. You may tell them that you helped to evaluate new software.

If you need a break, just tell us.

You may withdraw from this evaluation at any time.

If you have any questions, you may ask now or at any time.

If you agree with these terms, please indicate your agreement by signing here:

Please print your name

_____

Signature

_____

Date

_____

From www.stcsig.org/usability, retrieved July 17, 2004.

5 The Pilot Test

Before any actual evaluation sessions are conducted, you should run a **pilot test** as a way of evaluating your evaluation session and to help ensure that it will work. It is a process of debugging or testing the evaluation material, the planned time schedule, the suitability of the task descriptions, and the running of the session.

5.1 Participants for Your Pilot Test

You can choose a participant for your pilot test in the same way as for your actual evaluation. However, in the pilot test it is less important that the participant is completely representative of your target user group and more important that you feel confident about practicing with him or her. Your aim in the pilot test is to make sure that all the details of the evaluation are in place.

5.2 Design and Assemble the Test Environment

Try to do your pilot test in the same place as your evaluation or in a place that is as similar as possible. Assemble all the items you need:

- Computer equipment and prototype, or your paper prototype. Keep a note of the version you use.
- Your evaluation script and other materials.
- Any other props or artifacts you need, such as paper and pens for the participant.
- The incentives, if you are offering any.
- If you are using video or other recording equipment, then make sure you practice assembling it all for the pilot test. As you put it together, make a list of each item. There is nothing more aggravating than forgetting some vital part of your equipment.

5.3 Run the Pilot Test

Run the pilot participant through the evaluation procedure and all supporting materials. The session should be conducted in the same way as the actual evaluation session. Ideally, the evaluator(s) who will conduct the actual evaluation session should participate in the pilot test. They should observe, take notes, and facilitate the pilot test, just as they would do in the actual session. For example, they should consider the following questions:

The importance of pilot testing questionnaires and interview questions was discussed in Chapter 2.

- Is the prototype functioning as required for the session?
- Is the introductory material clear enough to the evaluator(s) and the participant?
- Are the observation and data-collection procedures working?
- Are the evaluator(s) aware of their roles and responsibilities for the evaluation session?
- Can the task descriptions be accomplished within the planned session time?

While observing the pilot participant, make a note of where the evaluation materials and procedures may need to be improved before conducting the actual usability evaluation sessions.

It is often helpful to analyze and interpret the data that you get from the pilot test. This often points out that an important facet of the evaluation has been overlooked and that some essential data, which you need to validate certain usability requirements, has not been collected.

If you are short of time, then you might consider skipping the pilot test.

> **Evaluation Tip 12**   *Always try to do a pilot test*
> Whenever we skip the pilot test, we find that the first participant becomes the pilot test instead because some details of our plans are wrong. Then we hurriedly have to try to change our scripts and evaluation materials before the second participant.

If you do omit the pilot test, you will find that you forget to design some details of the tasks or examples, discover that some item of equipment is missing, realize that your interview plan omits a topic of great importance to the participant, or find that your prototype does not work as you intended. Doing a pilot test is much simpler than trying to get all these details correct for your first participant.

> **Evaluation Tip 13**   *If you can, do the pilot test before finalizing recruitment*
> You may have to delay your evaluation because you need an extra pilot test, or you may need longer with each participant because your tasks take longer than expected.

Often, the pilot test itself reveals many problems in the UI. You may want to start redesigning immediately, but it is probably best to restrain yourself to the bare minimum that will let the evaluation happen. If the changes are extensive, then it is probably best to plan another pilot test.

6   Summary

In this chapter, we discussed the final preparations for evaluation:

- Assigning roles to team members (or adjusting the plan to allow extra time if you are a lone evaluator)
- Creating an evaluation script
- Deciding whether you need forms for consent and for nondisclosure
- Running a pilot test

Once you have completed your pilot test, all that remains is to make any amendments to your materials, recruit the participants, and run the evaluation.

25

Analysis and interpretation of user observation evaluation data

1   Introduction: How to Analyze and Interpret Data from Your Evaluation

An evaluation session generates a large amount of data. After the session, you will have at least some, if not all, of the following data items:

- Background data about the participant
- Notes made by the evaluator(s)
- Audio or video recordings
- Completed data collection forms
- Quantitative data on times, errors, and other usability metrics
- Quantitative (and possibly qualitative) data from pre- and post-session questionnaires
- Retrospective protocols
- A list of any usability problems identified during observations

The process of analysis is concerned with turning the evaluation data collected into information from which you can make decisions. We will describe three steps in the analysis of evaluation:

- Collating the data
- Summarizing the data
- Reviewing the data to identify any usability problems

2   Collating the Data

There can be a surprisingly large quantity of pieces of paper after each evaluation session (see Figure 25.1): your own notes, test materials, notes made by the participant, perhaps printed outputs, and (often) observer's notes. You may also want to

Figure 25.1 There can be a surprisingly large quantity of pieces of paper after an evaluation.

back up data entered by the participant. If you are testing a web site, you could take screen shots or back up the log to show the participant's visited links before you reset the site for the next participant.

Paper forms are convenient if you want to record the results of discussing your findings in a debriefing meeting. If you have responses on questionnaires, then a database might be a good way to collate them. User observations usually produce so much qualitative data that it is worth typing it up in some way. A usability practitioner provided the following quote:

> *I collect and number the notes and other forms from each participant immediately — between participants. I keep each set separately in a plastic wallet that is large enough to hold any videotape or backup as well. Then I try to type up the notes by the end of the next day at the latest. Even a week later it can be difficult to remember what I meant. But all I try to do is type up the raw notes. There is no need to do all the analysis at this stage, and usually I find that it is easier to make sense of the data if I do all the typing up first, then all the analysis together separately. That way, themes emerge more easily and I do not get side-tracked by one participant's experiences. It helps me to ensure that I have considered all the data before moving to recommendations.*

Other practitioners have other methods for writing up notes. Some use index cards, with a point of interest on each; some use a spreadsheet, with an entry for each point of interest; others use a word processor, typing each comment.

Whatever method you choose, be sure to include a reference back to the original participant so that you can identify which participant inspired which comment. You should also be careful to note the difference between what a participant said and what you happened to notice. It is perfectly acceptable for you to form your own opinions about the UI as you watch someone work on it, but you would not want to inadvertently quote your opinion as that of a user.

3 Summarizing the Data

Summarizing the data involves extracting key comments from the collated data. It may also involve performing simple mathematical calculations (to compute averages of times spent on tasks and so on). For example, suppose your usability requirement was to validate the usability metric "Time spent to recover from an error," whose planned level is 30 seconds. During the evaluation session, you will record the start time of the task and the end time. You then subtract the start time from the end time to calculate the time spent on the task by the participant. That wasn't too hard, was it?

As the number of participants in most evaluations is small, complex statistical analysis is not applicable (Dray and Siegel, 1999), so we have not included details or methods for the statistical analysis of evaluation data.

4 Reviewing the Data to Identify Usability Problems

A key purpose of evaluation is to decide whether the interface has met the usability requirements and, if it has not, what to do about it. This entails reviewing the summarized evaluation data. If a review of the data shows that the usability requirements have been met, then no further analysis or interpretation of the data is required. If, however, incidents are revealed where, say, the participant has made an error, could not complete the task description, was unsure what to do next, or had to ask for or look up further information, these incidents should be compiled into a list of usability problems. Usability problems are also referred to as usability defects in the literature; from this point on, we will adopt the term "usability defect."

A **usability defect** is a usability problem in the user interface. Usability defects can lead to confusion, error, delay, or outright failure to complete some task on the part of the user. They make the UI, and hence the system, less usable for its target users. To help you identify usability defects, we have listed some of their characteristics in Box 25.1 (adapted from Chauncey Wilson, personal communication, 2001).

Box 25.1	**Characteristics of Usability Defects**

A usability defect has one or more of the following characteristics:

- It irritates or confuses the user.
- It makes a system hard to install, learn, or use.
- It causes mental overload of the user. (For example, the user may have to think a lot as the required action or feedback from the system may not be obvious or sufficient.)
- It causes poor user performance.
- It violates design standards or guidelines.
- It reduces trust or credibility of the system.
- It tends to cause repeated errors.
- It could make the system hard to market.

The usability defects identified from the summarized data can be recorded onto data analysis forms. We have suggested a template data analysis form for user observation in Table 25.1. Some sample data have been entered into the table for illustrative purposes.

5 | Working with Quantitative Data

Quantitative data are more eye catching for the readers of your evaluation report and are often regarded as more objective than qualitative data. If you have clearly defined

Table 25.1 Data Analysis Form for User Observation

Task Scenario No: 1 Evaluator's Name: John Participant: Beth		Session Date: February 25 Session Start Time: 9:30 a.m. Session End Time: 10:20 a.m.
Source of evaluation data (video clips, audio clips, participant's verbal protocols, observer's notes, retrospective protocols, etc.)	Usability defect description	Evaluator's comments
Verbal protocol	The user did not select the right menu item (Options) to initiate the task.	The user was not sure which menu the menu item Options was in.
Video	—	—

usability metrics, then reporting is relatively simple as you can compare the results you got with the results you wanted. If you have not taken measurements during the evaluation, the qualitative data can still yield some numbers; for example, three out of five participants have made similar comments on some feature of the UI. Be particularly careful to avoid statistical language such as "significant result" unless you have enough data to undertake a statistical analysis that will support your claims.

There are three groups of methods for summarizing quantitative data:

- Tabulations, charts, and rankings that provide a visual representation of your data.
- **Descriptive statistics** such as mean, median, and mode that describe the data you have obtained.
- **Inferential statistics** such as tests of statistical significance that give the probability that a claim arising from your data can be applied to your user population as a whole.

(Clegg, 1983) is a good introduction to statistics. (Huff, 1991) explains how to use statistics appropriately.

In most evaluations, we look for information to help us decide what to do next with the UI, and small frequent tests are more helpful than a single, large-scale technique. We therefore usually opt for small numbers of participants in most usability evaluations. However, these small samples do not support the mathematics of most inferential statistics. For example, usually you need a random sample of 50 to 100 users as a minimum before calculating significance. If you are contemplating large-scale quantitative techniques such as administering a questionnaire to a big group of users, then we suggest that you refer to one of the standard works on the topic.

Mathematically, you can use descriptive statistics on any sample size. For example, it is mathematically correct to take a task time of five seconds for one user, six seconds for the second user, and 55 seconds for the third, then calculate the average (mean) task time as $(5 + 6 + 55) / 3 = 22$ seconds. From a mathematical point of view, including this average in your usability report does not claim anything for the likely task time for the user population as a whole. However, many readers of usability reports either do not have statistical training or are too busy to challenge your figures. They will assume that any descriptive statistics apply to the user population. If you include descriptive statistics in your report then consider whether they can or should apply to the user population. Is it likely that your users are all rather similar? Or might there be subgroups with very different profiles? Also, think about the conclusions that your readers might draw from the descriptive statistics.

Tabular and visual representations of your data can provide a break from the narrative of your report and highlight the relevant material. For example, Box 25.2, Table 25.2, and Figure 25.2 all have the same data. Which do you find easiest to understand?

Box 25.2   **Example of Task Times**

The task time for participant one (experienced) was five seconds. Participant two (experienced) took six seconds. The third participant was a novice and took 55 seconds. The target for task time is four seconds.

Table 25.2 Example Data from an Evaluation

Participant	Experience level	Task time
Participant 1	Experienced	5 seconds
Participant 2	Experienced	6 seconds
Participant 3	Novice	55 seconds
Target		4 seconds

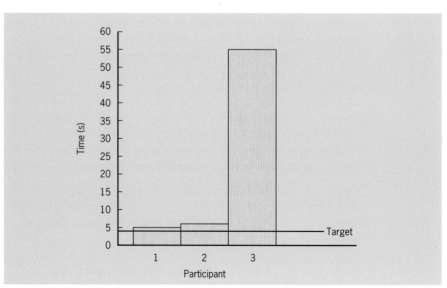

Figure 25.2 Example data from an evaluation.

EXERCISE 25.1 (Allow five minutes)

An evaluation gets the results shown in Table 25.2. Which of the following assertions would be appropriate for the report?

1. 67% of participants were within 50% of target task time.
2. The average task time was over 20 seconds, more than five times greater than target.
3. Although the two experienced participants were within a couple of seconds of our target task time (four seconds), our single novice took 55 seconds, which is far outside the target.

DISCUSSION

All these statements are mathematically correct. However, statement one says nothing about the exceptional participant and might give the impression of a larger sample size than three. Statement two highlights an average dominated by the single very long task time. We prefer statement three, which points out the problem but also explains that it arose from only one measurement.

6 Working with Qualitative Data

Quantitative data can show you that a defect exists, and perhaps the extent of its impact, but often it is qualitative data that give you the insights into the cause of the problem and what to do about it. For example, did a task take too long because the system response time was excessive or because the user found the interface confusing and chose incorrect options?

6.1 An Example of Data from Global Warming

One participant in a Global Warming evaluation provides a good example of the usefulness of qualitative data. He worked happily on the screen in Figure 25.3, clicking on the different icons and reading the explanations that appeared on the Notebook page. Then he clicked on the "Move forward" arrow in the bottom right-hand corner and got to the screen in Figure 25.4. There is a section from the evaluation notes in Figure 25.5.

The middle of the screen shows a tilted view of the slide bars with round "factors" icons on them. The participant tried to click on these factors icons before going to the correct choice: the round button with an arrow in the bottom right-hand corner. This is a clear failure of "Easy to navigate," but do we know why?

EXERCISE 25.2 (Allow five minutes)

Review Figures 25.3 and 25.4 to find the usability defect that caused the participant to make a mistake.

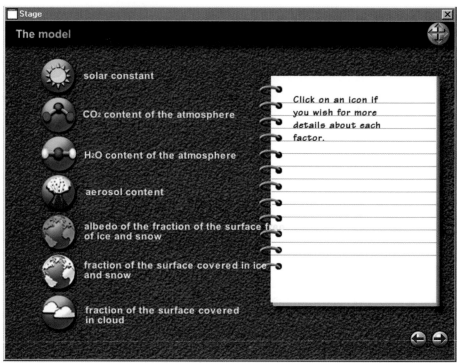

Figure 25.3 Explanation of each factor in the model.

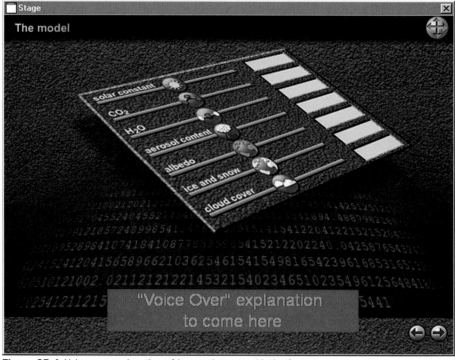

Figure 25.4 Voiceover explanation of how to interact with the factors.

Script	User's remarks
When screen appears, ask: Do you know what to do next? Do you recognize what to do, or did you have to recall what to do? What are you trying to do? *Ask user to take action*	*I have to skip on from that Nothing happens when I click on these icons. I presume I'll have to click on the go forward button.*

Figure 25.5 A section of notes from a Global Warming participant.

DISCUSSION

In Figure 25.3, the factor icons have an affordance for clicking and an instruction to click on an icon if you wish to know more. For example, clicking on the sun icon results in an explanation of the solar constant.

Figure 25.4 shows the same icons, with a reduced affordance for clicking because they are on a sloped image. It seems that the reduction in affordance was not enough to tell the participant that he should not click on these icons.

6.2 Making Decisions with Qualitative Data

Working with qualitative data is a process of making decisions that start with thinking about what to note in the evaluation (collecting the data), continues through the collation and review process, and then influences your summary (analysis and interpretation).

Those decisions need to be made in the light of the following factors:

- *The differences between the participants in your evaluation and the real users.* For example, your test participants might have more experience of the system than real users, or they might lack specialist domain knowledge.
- *The differences between your test environment and the users' environment.* For example, you may have had to stop the test while you solved a configuration problem in the system, or the room where you conducted the test might be much quieter or noisier than the users' environment.

The same decisions apply to the data from your pilot test. It is even more likely that your pilot participant is different from your real users, so you need to be more cautious about drawing conclusions from the pilot data. The actual process of examining your qualitative data to identify usability defects depends very much on your user interface and on what happened in your evaluation. In practice, it is usually quite easy to spot the important problems and find causes for them.

EXERCISE 25.3 (Allow 20 minutes)

Table 25.3 has a selection of collated data relating to the first task for Global Warming. Review the comments, and draw up a list of usability defects. What priority would you give them?

Table 25.3 A Selection of Collated Data from the Global Warming Evaluation

Participant	Screen	Remark
A	Intro	The pictures were nice.
A	Intro	The voice told me about changing temperature of the world using a model.
A	Intro	The model doesn't mean anything to me.
A	Intro	I don't know how I'm going to use the model.
A	Explanation	The icons look as if they mean stop, pause, and play [left to right].
A	Factors	It looks like a notebook page but there's no way to write on it.
B	Intro	These are nice [points to pictures].
B	Intro	I like having a voice — it's like having a tutor in the room with me.
B	Model	Why does the graph start in the middle?
C	Intro	The voice is okay, it did something sensible.
C	Explanation	I'll click on the Play icon that looks like a video recorder.
C	How to use the model	Nothing happens when I click on these icons.
C	Model	I can't see why all these units go to 100. I'm sure I just read about some different ranges in the explanation.
C	Model	I'll have to click on Run — oh, he's running; I'm baffled.

DISCUSSION

There are various ways of grouping comments or observed problems:

- Chronological order — that is, which problem happens first?
- Severity of the defect — that is, which problem is the most important?
- The part of the UI that needs to be changed — for example, if the content and the navigation are the responsibility of different teams
- Whether or not you are sure that you know the cause of the comment or problem
- The level of difficulty of fixing the defect or changing that area of the UI

We found one overall problem and three pages that need changes:

- Overall: "Model" is not clearly explained: what it is or how to use it.
- Factors: The "Notebook" graphic gives the impression to one user that you can write on it.
- How to use the model: It has a misleading graphic.
- Model: The running man graphic did not help the participant. The page needs better axes in the graph and units on the factors.

We also noticed that the participants commented on two favorable areas.

- Two participants liked the pictures and the idea of a voice as explanation.
- The stop, pause, and play icons are successful.

You may choose a different categorization or make the points in another way. Notice that we recorded the positive remarks as well as the defects. When you design the next version of the UI, you usually want to preserve good aspects of it as well as solving problems.

It often helps to speed up the work of reviewing your qualitative data if you establish a **coding scheme**. A coding scheme is any method of assigning a group, number, or label to an item of data. For example, you might look first for all the data about icons, then for everything about the meaning of labels, then for remarks about navigation. Some practitioners establish their coding schemes in advance, perhaps from a list of heuristics or from an inspection of the UI. Others derive a scheme from the pilot test. However, evaluations frequently surprise even the most experienced practitioner, and it is quite usual to find that the coding scheme needs to be modified somewhat when you start interpreting the data.

It is also typical to find that some of the data are inconclusive, cannot be retrieved, or have been badly written down. If your only data from an evaluation were derived from a video recording and the tape cannot be read, you have a disaster — which is why we place so much emphasis on taking paper notes of some kind along with any electronic data collection.

Generally, your chances of deciphering what a comment meant (whether from bad writing or clumsy phrasing) are much better if you do the analysis promptly and preferably within a day of the evaluation sessions.

7 Interpretation of User-Observation Data

Once you have analyzed your data — for example, by grouping them according to a coding scheme — your final step is interpretation: deciding what caused the defects that you have identified and recommending what to do about them. In Table 25.4, we suggest a template for gathering defects and interpretations. Again, some sample data have been entered into the table for the purposes of illustration. For the example task, because the defect is related to the first action of the task and the task cannot be accomplished until the user chooses the right menu item, we have assigned a **severity rating** of "High." Notice that this form carefully preserves the distinction between our observations and our comments on them.

Some practitioners prefer to gather the defects and the good points about the interface on a single form, whereas others prefer to deal with all the defects and all the good points in two separate passes. Choose whichever method you prefer.

7.1 Assigning Severities

We discuss the choice of severity scale in more detail in Chapter 28.

The process of summarizing the data usually makes it obvious which problems require the most urgent attention. In our form in Table 25.4, we have included a column for assigning a severity to each defect.

Bearing in mind our comments about statistics, one important point to remember is that the weighting given to each participant's results depends very much on comparison with your overall user profile.

Table 25.4 Data Interpretation Form for User Observations

Task Scenario No. 1 Evaluator's Name: John		Session Date: February 25 Session Start Time: 9:30 a.m. Session End Time: 10:20 a.m.	
Usability observation	Evaluator's comments	Cause of the usability defect, if there is one	Severity rating
The user did not select the right menu item (Options) to initiate the task.	The user was not sure which menu item Options was in.	The menu name is inappropriate, as it does not relate to the required action.	High
—	—	—	—

> **Evaluation Tip 14** *With small samples of users, you have to interpret each user's results according to your user profile*

In the data example in Table 25.2, we had one novice participant and two experienced participants. If this data came from evaluating a UI designed mainly for experienced users, we might choose to concentrate on shaving a further one or two seconds off their task time. If novices are more important, then the excessive task time for the novice has a much higher priority.

7.2 Recommending Changes

Some authorities stop here, taking the view that it is the responsibility of the development team to decide what to change in the interface. For example, the Common Industry Format for summative evaluation does not include a section for recommendations, taking the view that deciding what to do is a separate process when undertaking a summative evaluation:

> *Stakeholders can use the usability data to help make informed decisions concerning the release of software products or the procurement of such products. (http://zing.ncsl.nist.gov/iusr/documents/whatistheCIF.html)*

If your task is to improve the interface as well as to establish whether it meets the requirements, then you are likely to need to work out what to do next: recommending changes.

So we suggest a template in Table 25.5 to record the recommendations. In the table, the "Status" column indicates what is being planned for the recommended change — when the usability defect will be rectified, if it has been deferred, or if it is being ignored for the time being.

517
Part 4

Table 25.5 Recommendations Form

Participant	Usability defect description	Cause of the usability defect	Severity rating	Recommended solution	Status
Beth	The user did not select the right menu item (Options) to initiate the task.	The menu name is inappropriate, as it does not relate to the required action.	High	The menu name should be changed to "Group."	Make change in next revision.
Mary	—	—	—	—	

> **EXERCISE 25.4 (Allow five minutes)**
>
> Look back at the data in Table 25.2. If the UI is designed mainly for novice users, what action would you recommend?
>
> **DISCUSSION**
>
> Although the task time for the novice participant is well outside target, we would also bear in mind that there was only one participant. We would consider both reviewing the qualitative data, to see if there is any explanation for the much longer task time, and running a further evaluation with some more novice users.

It is hard to be specific about interpretation of results. Fortunately, you will find that many problems have obvious solutions, particularly if this is an exploratory evaluation of an early prototype.

Evaluations are full of surprises. You will find defects in parts of the interface that you thought would work well, and conversely you may find that users are completely comfortable with something that you personally find irritating or never expected to work. Equally frequently, you will find that during the analysis of the results you simply do not have the data to provide an answer. Questions get overlooked, or users have conflicting opinions. Finally, the experience of working with real users can entirely change your perception of their tasks and environment, and the domain of the user interface.

Your recommendations, therefore, are likely to contain a mixture of several points:

- Successes to build on
- Defects to fix
- Possible defects or successes that are not proven — not enough evidence to decide either way (these require further evaluation)
- Areas of the user interface that were not tested (no evidence) (these also require further evaluation)
- Changes to usability and other requirements

> **EXERCISE 25.5 (Allow 10 minutes)**
>
> Review the defect list that you drew up for Exercise 25.3. What changes would you recommend to the Global Warming team for this part of the interface?
>
> **DISCUSSION**
>
> Here is our list:
>
> - Ensure that "model" is clearly explained: what it is and how to use it.
> - Make the navigation elements in the right-hand corners of the screen more prominent, and consider an introductory tutorial on basic navigation for novice users.
> - Replace the running man graphic with a simple Run button.

8   Writing the Evaluation Report

Generally, you need to write up what you have done in an evaluation:

* To act as a record of what you did
* To communicate the findings to other stakeholders

The style and contents of the report depend very much on who you are writing for and why: a topic we will return to in more detail in Chapter 28. Meanwhile we will give you an example of a typical report created for an academic journal.

8.1 An Academic Report on Global Warming

The original Global Warming software was evaluated three times. Box 25.3 contains an extract from one report.

Box 25.3   **Extract from an Academic Paper on the Global Warming Evaluations**

Abstract

The Open University [OU] has undertaken the production of a suite of multi-media teaching materials for inclusion in its forthcoming science foundation course. Two of these packages (*Global Warming and Cooling* and *An Element on the Move*) have recently been tested and some interesting general issues have emerged from these empirical studies. The formative testing of each piece of software was individually tailored to the respective designers' requirements. Since these packages were not at the same stage of development, the evaluations were constructed to answer very different questions and to satisfy different production needs. The question the designers of the *Global Warming* software wanted answered was: "Is the generic shell usable/easy to navigate through?" This needed an answer because the mathematical model of global warming had not been completed on time but the software production schedule still had to proceed. Hence the designers needed to know that when the model was slotted in the students would be able to work with the current structure of the program.

2.0 Background

The multimedia materials for this Science Foundation course consisted of 26 programs. This first year course introduces students to the academic disciplines of Biology, Chemistry, Earth Sciences and Physics and so programs were developed for each of these subject domains. The software was designed not to stand alone but to complement written course notes, video tapes, home experiments and face to face tutorials.

The aims of the program production teams were to: —

- Exploit the media to produce pedagogical materials that could not be made in any other way
- To produce a program with easy communication channels to
  i) the software itself via the interface
  ii) the domain knowledge via the structure and presentation of the program
- To provide students with high levels of interactivity
- To sustain students with a motivating learning experience

In order to test whether the programs would meet the above aims a framework for the developmental testing of the software was devised. A three phased approach was recommended and accepted by the Science Team. This meant that prototypes which contained generic features could be tested at a very early stage and that the developers would aim, with these early programs, to actually make prototypes to be tested quickly at the beginning of the software's life cycle. This was known as the Primary Formative Testing Phase. The subjects for this phase would not need to be Open University students but people who were more "competent" computer users. We wanted to see if average computer users could navigate through a section and understand a particular teaching strategy without then having to investigate all the details of the subject matter. This would mean the testing could take place more quickly and easily with subjects who could be found on campus.

The Secondary Formative Testing Phase was aimed to test the usability and learning potential of the software. It would take place later in the developmental cycle and would use typical Open University students with some science background. Pre- to post-test learning measures would indicate the degree of learning that took place with the software. Testing the time taken to work through the programs was an important objective for this phase. It was agreed that the Open University students would be paid a small fee when they came to the University to test the software.

The Tertiary Testing Phase would include the final testing with pairs of Open University students working together with the software. In this way the talk generated around the tasks would indicate how clearly the tasks were constructed and how well the students understood the teaching objectives of the program. [The framework is summarized in the table presented here.]

3.0 Framework for Formative Developmental Testing

3.1 The Testing Cycle

. . . The aim of the testing here was to evaluate some generic features, therefore all the pieces of the program did not have to be in place. In fact the aim of this evaluation study was to provide the developers with feedback about general usability issues, the interface and subjects' ease of navigation around the system . . .

3.2 Subjects

. . . Generic features were tested with "experienced users" who did not have scientific background knowledge and could easily be found to fill the tight testing schedule. . . . In order to understand if certain generic structures worked, "experienced users" were found (mean age = 32.6 years +5). These consisted of ten subjects who worked alone with the software and had already used computers for at least five years and had some experience of multimedia software. The reason these types of subjects were selected was that if these experts could not understand the pedagogical approach and use the interface satisfactorily, then the novice learners would have extreme difficulty too. Also these subjects were confident users and could criticise the software using a "cognitive walk through" methodology.

Evaluation type	Aims	Subjects
Primary Phase	Test design and generic features	Competent computer users
Secondary Phase	Test usability and learning potential of product	OU students with science background
Tertiary Phase	Test usability and whole learning experience	Pairs of OU students with science background

Framework for the Developmental Testing of the Multimedia Materials Produced for the Science Foundation Course

3.3 Data Collection Instruments

. . . In order to understand the students' background knowledge, they were given two questionnaires to complete which were about their computer experience and also a pre-test about the subject area which was going to be investigated. The pre-test was made up of eight to ten questions which addressed the main teaching objectives of the software . . .

4.0 Evaluation Findings

. . . The *Global Warming* program introduced the students to a climatic model of the factors that change the earth's temperature. These variables which include the solar constant, levels of carbon dioxide and water vapour, aerosol content, cloud cover, ice and snow cover and albedo could all be changed by the student who could then explore these factors' sensitivities, understand the effects of coupling between factors by again manipulating them and finally, to gain an appreciation of the variation of global warming with latitude and season.

There is a large cognitive overhead for the students using this software and they have to be guided through a number of tasks. It was, therefore, important to test the screen layout, interface and pedagogical approach very early in the developmental cycle and this was achieved by testing a prototype without the mathematical model being in place.

The "cognitive walk through" technique worked well here. Subjects said when they arrived at a stumbling block *"I don't know what to do here."* The main difficulty experienced was when tabs instead of buttons suddenly appeared on the interface. The functionality of the tabs was lost on the subjects. A general finding here is not to mix these two different interface elements. Subjects liked the audio linkage between sections and the use of audio to convey task instructions. One subject enthusiastically mentioned that, *"this feels like I have a tutor in the room with me — helping me."* Other findings suggest that any graphical output of data should sit close to the data table. The simulation run button did not need an icon of an athlete literally running; however, the strategy of predict, look and explain was a good one when using the simulation . . .

Conclusions

The two formative testing approaches proved to be effective evaluation techniques for two separate pieces of software. This was because the multimedia programs were in different phases of their developmental cycle. On the one hand, usability of a generic shell was the primary aim of the testing and experienced users, who could be found at short notice, were an important factor to the success of this evaluation. The ability of the subjects to confidently describe their experience became critical data in this instance.

Extracted from Whitelock (1998).

EXERCISE 25.6 (Allow 15 minutes)

Review the extract from the academic report in Box 23.3. Which aspects of the evaluation are the main focus of the report?

DISCUSSION

This academic paper has a few examples of the particular findings, but it is mostly interested in conveying the value of the techniques used in the overall

Formative evaluation will be discussed in Chapter 27.

development. It expects the reader to be familiar with the specialist terminology of user interface design and development, such as "formative evaluation."

8.2 Should You Describe Your Method?

If you are writing a report for an academic audience, it is essential to include a full description of the method you used. An academic reader is likely to want to decide whether your findings are supported by the method and may want to replicate your work.

If you are writing for a business audience, then you will need to weigh up their desire for a complete record of your activities and the time that they have to read the report. Some organizations like to see full descriptions, similar to those expected by an academic audience. Others prefer to concentrate on the results, with the detailed method relegated to an appendix or even a line such as "Details of the method are available on request."

8.3 Describing Your Results

"Description" does not need to be confined to words. Your report will be more interesting to read if you include screenshots, pictures, or other illustrations of the interface with which the user was working.

Jarrett (2004a) gives two alternative views of the same piece of an evaluation report:

We know that long chunks of writing can look boring, and we joke about "ordeal by bullet points" when we're in a presentation. But how often have we been guilty of the same sins in our reports?

Here are two ways to present the same information. First, as a block of text:

> *It seems off-putting to be "welcomed" with the phrase "Your location is not set." This seems somewhat accusing rather than giving me encouragement to delve further. The long list of partner names is off-putting. It's important to see what the site is covering but this presentation makes it a blur. This information would be better presented in a bulleted list. The three prompts have equal visual weight and it is not clear whether you have to enter one or all of them. The prompts and headings are hard to read (orange on white). The three prompts are the same color as the headings so give an impression of being headings rather than guiding data entry. The primary functionality for search is "below the fold" at 800×600. Text requires horizontal scrolling at 800×600. The black line is dominant on the page. (p. 3)*

Indigestible, right? Now look at the screenshot [in Figure 25.6]. I preferred it, and I hope that you do too.

9   Summary

In this chapter, we discussed how to collate evaluation data, analyze it, interpret it, and record recommendations. We introduced the concept of a severity rating for a usability defect: assigning severity ratings to usability defects helps in making decisions about the optimal allocation of resources to resolve them. Severity ratings, therefore, help to prioritize the recommended changes in tackling the usability defects. Finally, we started to think about how to present your findings. We will return to this topic in more detail in Chapter 28, but first we will look at some other types of evaluation.

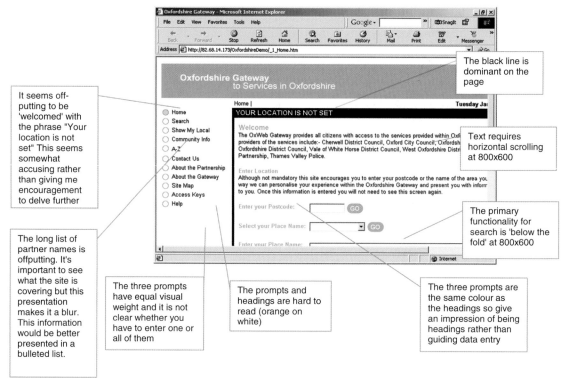

Figure 25.6 Findings presented with a screenshot. From Jarrett (2004a).

26

Inspections of the user interface

1 Introduction

Although user observation gives you a huge amount of insight into how users think about the user interface, it can be time consuming to recruit participants and observe them only to find that a large number of basic problems in the user interface could have been avoided if the designers had followed good practice in design. Undertaking an inspection of the user interface before (but *not* instead of) user observation can be beneficial to your evaluation.

The contents of this section have been particularly influenced by the following sources: Virzi (1997), Nielsen (1994), and Nielsen (1993).

"Inspection of the user interface" is a generic name for a set of techniques that involve **inspectors** examining the user interface to check whether it complies with a set of design principles known as **heuristics**. In this chapter, we describe the **heuristic inspection** technique (also known as **heuristic evaluation**). Heuristic inspection was chosen as it is one of the most popular and well-researched inspection techniques for evaluation (Molich and Nielsen, 1990).

2 Creating the Evaluation Plan for Heuristic Inspection

2.1 Choosing the Heuristics

In Chapter 9, we offered a selection of guidelines for user interface design and then in Chapters 16, 17, and 18, we referred to further sets of guidelines. Your first task in planning a heuristic inspection is to decide which set of guidelines or heuristics you will use. If your organization has established a specific style guide, then that is one obvious choice. The advantage of using heuristics that you have used for design is that you can establish whether they have been applied consistently. Otherwise, the advantage of using a different set is that you get a fresh eye on the interface and may spot problems that would otherwise be overlooked.

One set of heuristics often used in inspections is the set proposed by Nielsen (1993), which we have included as Table 26.1.

Table 26.1 Nielsen's Heuristics (1993)

Heuristic	Description
Visibility of system status	The system should always keep users informed about what is going on, through appropriate feedback within reasonable time.
Match between system and the real world	The system should speak the users' language, with words, phrases, and concepts familiar to the user, rather than system-oriented terms. Follow real-world conventions, making information appear in a natural and logical order.
User control and freedom	Users often choose system functions by mistake and will need a clearly marked "emergency exit" to leave the unwanted state without having to go through an extended dialogue. Supports undo and redo.
Consistency and standards	Users should not have to wonder whether different words, situations, or actions mean the same thing. Follow platform conventions.
Error prevention	Even better than a good error message is a careful design that prevents a problem from occurring in the first place.
Recognition rather than recall	Make objects, actions, and options visible. The user should not have to remember information from one part of the dialogue to another. Instructions or use of the system should be visible or easily retrievable whenever appropriate.
Flexibility and efficiency of use	Accelerators — unseen by the novice user — may often speed up the interaction for the expert user such that the system can cater to both inexperienced and experienced users. Allow users to tailor frequent actions.
Aesthetic and minimalist design	Dialogues should not contain information that is irrelevant or rarely needed. Every extra unit of information in a dialogue competes with the relevant units of information and diminishes their relative visibility.

Table 26.1 Nielsen's Heuristics (1993)—cont'd

Heuristic	Description
Help users recognize, diagnose, and recover from errors	Error messages should be expressed in plain language (no codes), precisely indicating the problem, and constructively suggesting a solution.
Help and documentation	Even though it is better if the system can be used without documentation, it may be necessary to provide help and documentation. Any such information should be easy to search, focus on the user's task, list concrete steps to be carried out, and not be too large.

We found that the humorous article in Box 26.1 helped us to understand how these heuristics might be applied.

Box 26.1	**A Heuristic Evaluation of the Usability of Infants**

For your consideration . . .

Results from a heuristic evaluation of infants and their user interface, based on direct observational evidence and Jakob Nielsen's list of 10 heuristics from www.useit.com. All ratings from 1 to 10, with 1 being worst and 10 being best.

Visibility of System Status **6**. While it is easy enough to determine when the infant is sleeping and eating, rude noises do not consistently accompany the other primary occupation of infants. Further, infants can multitask, occasionally performing all three major activities at the same time.

Match between System and the Real World **3**. The infant does not conform to normal industry standards of night and day, and its natural language interface is woefully underdeveloped, leading to the error message problems cited below.

User Control and Freedom **2**. The infant's users have only marginal control over its state. While they can ensure the availability of food, diapers, and warmth, it is not often clear how to move the infant from an unfavorable state back to one in which it is content. When the default choice (data input) doesn't work, user frustration grows quickly.

Consistency and Standards **7**. Most infants have similar requirements and error messages, and the same troubleshooting procedures work for a variety of infants. Cuteness is also an infant standard, ensuring that users continue to put up with the many user interface difficulties.

Error Prevention **5**. Keeping the infant fed, dry, and warm prevents a number of errors. Homeostasis is, however, a fleeting goal, and the infant requires almost constant attention if the user is to detect errors quickly and reliably. All bets are off if the infant suffers from the colic bug or a virus.

Recognition Rather Than Recall **7**. The various parts of the infant generally match those of the user, though at a prototype level. The users, therefore, already have in place a mental model of the infant's objects. The data input and output ports are easily identifiable with a minimum of observation.

Flexibility and Efficacy of Use **2**. Use of the infant causes the user to conform to a fairly rigid schedule, and there are no known shortcuts for feeding, sleeping, and diaper buffer changing. Avoid buffer overflows at all costs, and beware of core dumps! While macros would be incredibly useful, infants do not come equipped with them. Macro programming can usually begin once the infant attains toddler status.

Aesthetic and Minimalist Design **5**. As mentioned earlier, infants have a great deal of cuteness, and so they score well on aesthetic ratings. Balancing this, however, is the fact that the information they provide is rather too minimal. Infants interact with the user by eating, generating an error message, or struggling during buffer updates.

Help Users Recognize, Diagnose, and Recover from Errors **1**. Infants have only a single error message, which they use for every error. The user, therefore, is left to diagnose each error with relatively little information. The user must remember previous infant states to see if input is required, and the user must also independently check other routine parameters. Note the error message is not the same as a General Protection Fault. That is what resulted in the infant in the first place.

Help and Documentation **1**. While some user training is available from experts, infants come with effectively no documentation. If users seek out documentation, they must sift through a great deal of conflicting literature to discover that there are very few universal conventions with regard to infant use.

Mean score 3.9

This user has been up since 3:30 this morning (perhaps you can tell), and still has three to five months to go (he hopes) before stringing together 8 hours of uninterrupted sleep.

McDaniel (1999, p. 44): This article was originally published in STC Intercom.

2.2 The Inspectors

Instead of recruiting a real or representative user to be your participant, you need to find one or more inspectors. Ideally, an inspector is an expert in HCI and the domain of the system. These skills are rarely available in one person. It is also difficult for anyone, no matter how expert, to give equal attention to a variety of heuristics and domain knowledge. It is therefore more usual to find two or more inspectors with different backgrounds. Box 26.2 presents some ideas.

3   Conducting a Heuristic Inspection

Because you know who the inspectors are, you usually do not need to ask them any questions about their background. Because the inspectors fill in the defect reports immediately, there is usually no need to record the session — there is little insight to be gained from watching a video of someone alternating between looking at a screen and filling in a form! However, you may want to record it if the inspector is verbalizing his or her thoughts while undertaking the inspection. If you want to record the inspection for later review, you will need to obtain permission from your inspector(s).

If your inspectors are domain or HCI experts, then they are unlikely to need any training before the session. If you have less experienced inspectors, it may be worthwhile to run through the heuristics with them and perhaps start with a practice screen so that everyone is clear about how you want the heuristics to be interpreted for your system.

3.1 Task Descriptions

You can prepare task descriptions just as you would for a user observation. The inspector then steps through the interface, reviewing both the task description and the list of heuristics, such as those shown in Table 26.1, at each step. This may make

---

Box 26.2	**Choosing Inspectors for Heuristic Evaluations**

- Usability experts — people experienced in conducting evaluations.
- Domain experts — people with knowledge of the domain. (This may include users or user representatives.)
- Designers with extensive design experience.
- Developers without any formal usability training but who are keen to explore the usability defects that users might experience.
- Nonexperts — people who are neither system domain experts nor usability experts, although they may be experts in their own particular domains. Nonexperts could be friends, colleagues, or family members who understand what you are doing and are willing to inspect the user interface to provide feedback.

it easier to predict what users might do, but it has the disadvantage of missing out on those parts of the interface that are not involved in the particular task.

Alternatively you might try to check each screen or sequence in the interface against the whole list of heuristics. It helps if you plan the sequence in advance, so that each inspector is looking at the same screen at the same time while undertaking the inspection.

3.2 The Location of the Evaluation Session

Generally, heuristic inspections are undertaken as controlled studies in informal settings that need have no resemblance to the users' environments. For example, Figure 26.1 shows a usability expert, Paul Buckley, from a big UK telecommunications company, British Telecom (BT), doing a heuristic inspection in the BT usability laboratory.

3.3 Collecting Evaluation Data

In Table 26.2, we have suggested a template for the collection of data during a heuristic inspection. You can see a similar form on the clipboard on the expert's lap in Figure 26.1. Note that there is a column for recording the usability defects. This is because the inspectors will identify most of the usability defects as they walk through the interface during the evaluation session. This is different from the data collection form for user observation, where the usability defects are identified during the analysis of the data.

If more than one inspector is involved in the inspection, then each inspector should be encouraged to complete an individual data-collection form. Completing individual forms is useful at the time of specifying the severity ratings, because each individual inspector may want to specify her or his own severity ratings for the usability defects based on her or his own experience and opinions. Encourage the inspectors

Figure 26.1 Heuristic inspection of a BT user interface.

Table 26.2 Data Collection and Analysis Form for Heuristic Inspection

Task Scenario No.: 1 Evaluator's Name: John Inspector's Name: George		Session Date: February 25 Session Start Time: 9:30 a.m. Session End Time: 10:20 a.m.	
Location in the task description	Heuristic violated	Usability defect description	Inspector's comments regarding the usability defect
New e-mail message arrives in the mailbox	*Visibility of system status*	*The user is not informed about the arrival of a new e-mail.*	*The user would like to be alerted when a new message arrives.*
—	—	—	—

to be as specific as possible in linking the usability defects to the heuristics. This helps the inspectors concentrate on the heuristics to be checked.

4 | Analysis of Heuristic Inspection Data

The analysis of your data follows the same process as for user observation. In theory, collating and summarizing data from a heuristic inspection is a relatively simple matter of gathering together the forms that the inspectors have used. However, because inspectors do not always have the same opinion, you may want to get the inspectors to review each other's forms and discuss any differences between them, perhaps going back over the interface collectively to resolve any disagreements.

5 | Interpretation of Heuristic Inspection Data

We will discuss severity ratings in more detail in Chapter 28.

The interpretation of your data follows the same process as for user observation. In Table 26.3, we have suggested a template for the interpretation of data during a heuristic inspection. When you produce your recommendations, you may want to invite the inspectors back to review your recommendations or the whole of your report to check that they agree with your interpretation.

6 | Benefits and Limitations of Heuristic Evaluations

In general, there are several benefits to conducting heuristic evaluations and inspections:

Table 26.3 Interpretation Form for Heuristic Evaluation

Task Scenario No.: 1 Evaluator: John Inspector's Name: George		Review Meeting Date:	
Usability defect	**Inspector's comments regarding the usability defect**	**Severity rating**	**Recommendations**
The user is not informed about the arrival of a new e-mail message.	*The user would like to be alerted when a new message arrives.*	High	*Add sound or a visual indicator that alerts the user when a new e-mail message arrives.*

- Inspections can sometimes be less expensive than user observation, especially if you have to recruit and pay participants for the latter.
- During an inspection, inspectors more often than not suggest solutions to the usability defects that they identify.
- It can be annoying to discover a large number of obvious errors during a user-observation evaluation session. Inspecting the UI first can help to reveal these defects.

There are, however, some limitations to conducting heuristic evaluations and inspections:

- As usability inspections often do not involve real or representative users, it is easy to make mistakes in the prediction of what actual users will do with the UI. However, real users can find the heuristics difficult to understand and the atmosphere of an inspection session to be unrealistic, thus limiting the data obtained.
- Inspectors often differ from real users in the importance they attach to a defect. For example, they may miss something they think is unimportant that will trip up real users, or they may be overly concerned about something that in fact only slightly affects the real users.
- Inspectors may have their own preferences, biases, and views toward the design of user interfaces or interaction design, which in turn may bias the evaluation data.
- The evaluation data from inspection is highly dependent on the skills and experiences of the inspectors. Sometimes, the inspectors may have insufficient task and domain knowledge. This can affect the validity of the evaluation data as some domain- or task-specific usability defects might be missed during an inspection.

7 Variations of Usability Inspection

7.1 Participatory Heuristic Evaluations

If instead of human–computer interaction (HCI) or domain experts you recruit users as your inspectors, then the technique becomes a *participatory heuristic evaluation* (Muller *et al.*, 1998). Muller and his colleagues created an adaptation of Nielsen's list of heuristics in order to make it them accessible to users who are not HCI experts (see Table 26.4).

7.2 Guideline Reviews

Guideline reviews are inspections that use a set of design guidelines, such as a corporate style guide, instead of one of the sets of heuristics we have included here.

> **EXERCISE 26.1 (Allow 10 minutes)**
>
> Figure 26.2 shows the home page of a gardening web site. In Chapter 17, you considered the design guideline for the home page of the web site. The guidelines included the following points:

Table 26.4 Heuristics in Participatory Heuristic Evaluation (from Muller *et al.*, 1998, pp. 16–17)

System status

1. *System status*. The system keeps users informed about what is going on through appropriate feedback within a reasonable time.

User control and freedom

2. *Task sequencing*. Users can select and sequence tasks (when appropriate), rather than the system taking control of the users' actions. Wizards are available but are optional and under user control.
3. *Emergency exits*. Users can
   - easily find emergency exits if they choose system functions by mistake (emergency exits allow the user to leave the unwanted state without having to go through an extended dialog)
   - make their own decisions (with clear information and feedback) regarding the costs of exiting current work
   - access undo and redo operations
4. *Flexibility and efficiency of use*. Accelerators are available to experts but are unseen by the novice. Users are able to tailor frequent actions. Alternative means of access and operation are available for users who differ from the average user (e.g., in physical or cognitive ability, culture, language, etc.).

Table 26.4 Heuristics in Participatory Heuristic Evaluation (from Muller *et al.*, 1998, pp. 16–17)—cont'd

Consistency and relevancy

5. *Match between system and the real world.* The system speaks the users' language, with words, phrases, and concepts familiar to the user rather than system-oriented terms. Messages are based on the users' real world, making information appear in a natural and logical order.
6. *Consistency and standards.* Each word, phrase, or image in the design is used consistently, with a single meaning. Each interface object or computer operation is always referred to using the same consistent word, phrase, or image. Follow the conventions of the delivery system or platform.
7. *Recognition rather than recall.* Objects, actions, and options are visible. The user does not have to remember information from one part of the dialogue to another. Instructions for use of the system are visible or easily retrievable whenever appropriate.
8. *Aesthetic and minimalist design.* Dialogs do not contain information that is irrelevant or rarely needed (extra information in a dialogue competes with the relevant units of information and diminishes their relative visibility).
9. *Help and documentation.* The system is intuitive and can be used for the most common tasks without documentation. Where needed, documentation is easy to search, supports a user task, lists concrete steps to be carried out, and is sized appropriately to the users' task. Large documents are supplemented with multiple means of finding their contents (tables of contents, indexes, searches, and so on).

Error recognition and recovery

10. *Help users recognize, diagnose, and recover from errors.* Error messages precisely indicate the problem and constructively suggest a solution. They are expressed in plain (users') language (no codes). Users are not blamed for the error.
11. *Error prevention.* Even better than good error messages is a careful design that prevents a problem from occurring in the first place. Users' "errors" are anticipated, and the system treats the "error" as either a valid input or an ambiguous input to be clarified.

Task and work support

12. *Skills.* The system supports, extends, supplements, or enhances the user's skills, background knowledge, and expertise. The system does not replace them. Wizards support, extend, or execute decisions made by users.
13. *Pleasurable and respectful interaction with the user.* The user's interactions with the system enhance the quality of her experience. The user is treated with respect. The design reflects the user's professional role, personal identity, or intention. The design is aesthetically pleasing — with an appropriate balance of artistic as well as functional value.
14. *Quality work.* The system supports the user in delivering quality work to his clients (if appropriate). Attributes of quality work include timeliness, accuracy, aesthetic appeal, and appropriate levels of completeness.
15. *Privacy.* The system helps the user to protect personal or private information — that belonging to the user or to the user's clients.

Figure 26.2 Home page of www.canadiangardening.com (taken December 24, 2004).

- The home page usually contains the name and logo of the company who owns the site, and the name of the web site.
- The home page should tell the users what the site does.
- The home page should have a search facility.
- The home page usually contains a brief introduction to the site.

Highlight four UI features of the home page in Figure 26.2 that you feel either conform or do not conform to these guidelines.

DISCUSSION

We came up with the following:

- The home page of this web site has the name and logo of the organization, but the advertisement along the top might be mistaken for the logo at a first glance.
- The home page is a bit mixed in the messages that it gives out concerning what it is for. The site places a lot of emphasis on advertisements for the gardening magazine and subscriber services, but these are somewhat undermined by the large picture of a cake in the advertisement and the culinary prize in the competition.
- There is a search facility, and it is quite prominently placed.
- The tagline is "Canada's favourite gardening magazine" which clearly explains this site's role as a support for the printed publication.

7.3 Standards Inspections

In Chapters 1, 6, and 9, we discussed usability standards such as ISO 9241.

A standards inspection uses a standard such as ISO 9241 as the reference rather than a set of heuristics.

Table 26.5 presents part of a sample data collection form (an applicability and adherence checklist) for evaluating a design with respect to part 12 of the ISO 9241 standard, which relates to the presentation of information.

Standards are written in a formal manner for practitioners, rather than being accessible for users. If you need to do a standards inspection, then you really should consider bringing in an expert who is familiar with the standard and its language as one of your inspectors. If that is impractical, then allow extra time during your preparation for becoming thoroughly familiar with it yourself.

A usability standard such as ISO 9241 is generalized to cater to a wide variety of user interfaces, so there may be some guidelines in the standard that are not applicable for the prototype you are evaluating (hence, the second column in Table 26.5 to record the applicability). The next column is for recording the adherence/nonadherence of the interface feature to the particular guideline of the standard. The inspector records his or her comments in the last column.

7.4 Cognitive Walkthrough

Cognitive walkthrough is a technique for exploring a user's mental processes while performing particular task(s) with a UI. In Chapter 4 we used cognitive walkthrough

Table 26.5 Applicability and Adherence Checklist Used in Standards Inspection

Recommendations (an example from ISO 9241, part 12)	Applicability		Adherence		Evaluator's comments
	Yes	No	Pass	Fail	
Labels	✓		✓		*The label names are meaningful.*
Labeling fields, items, icons and graphs					
Fields, items, icons, and graphs are labeled unless their meaning is obvious and can be understood clearly by the intended users.					

for gathering requirements. For evaluation, a cognitive walkthrough may be used to assess the usability of a user interface design by examining whether a user can select the appropriate action at the interface for each step in the task. This can sound quite simple, and is, but you can gain a lot of information by using the cognitive walkthrough technique for evaluation.

7.5 Peer Reviews

A peer review is an evaluation where a colleague, rather than an HCI or domain expert, reviews your interface. Early in the life cycle of designing and evaluating user interfaces, a simple approach is to ask someone to have a look at it. A peer review can be as informal as asking, "What do you think of this?" or you could go through the full process of a heuristic inspection. A degree of formality — such as booking a meeting; thinking carefully about which set of heuristics, standards, or guidelines you want to use; and taking notes — will help to ensure that you learn the most from the evaluation.

8   Summary

For more information on standards inspection, guideline reviews, and other inspections, see Nielsen and Mack (1994).

In this chapter, we discussed how heuristic evaluation, one of the most widely applied inspection techniques, is conducted, and we considered the benefits and limitations of conducting inspections for evaluations. The procedure for conducting a heuristic evaluation can be applied to any other inspection, such as evaluating the user interface against a set of standards or guidelines or a customized style guide.

27

Variations and more complex evaluations

1 Introduction

The selection of an appropriate evaluation technique depends on two key factors: the context in which you are working and the objective of your evaluation. The two techniques we have discussed so far, user observation and heuristic inspection, have the same overall objective, namely to establish whether the system is usable. Although there are similarities in the way you prepare and conduct the evaluation, the two techniques do have some differences.

2 A Comparison of User Observation and Heuristic Inspection

In a user observation, you ask the participant to attempt tasks with the interface and to comment from his or her own point of view. In a heuristic inspection, you ask the inspectors to consider each heuristic individually and to justify any defects they find by identifying which heuristic has been broken. Heuristic inspections do not yield evaluation data from the perspective of a user, as users or user representatives are not always involved. Inspections, therefore, complement user observation.

In a user observation, the evaluator observes what the participant does. In a heuristic inspection, inspectors observe themselves — noticing where typical users might look and trying to predict what a typical user might do.

In a user observation, you usually ask the participant to describe his or her thoughts in a think-aloud or retrospective protocol. In heuristic inspections, the inspectors asks themselves questions such as "Is this a simple and natural dialogue?"

Finally, in user observation, the key measurements are often effectiveness (can the user do this task?) and efficiency (how long does it take?). In heuristic inspection, the key measurement is "How many violations of heuristics are there in this UI?"

Because inspection can often help take care of most of the obvious usability defects, a user observation undertaken after an inspection will help identify the less obvious problems that only a user can spot. This will make the user involvement during user observation more effective and useful and help focus on problems from a user's perspective. Thus, the two techniques should be viewed as complementary to evaluation. Later in this chapter we will discuss combining techniques for multiple evaluation sessions. Meanwhile, we are going to look into these similarities and differences, and find ways to change them so as to tailor evaluations for different contexts and purposes.

3 | Observe, Listen, Compare, Measure: The Elements of Evaluation

Evaluation techniques generally combine some variation of each of these areas of focus, which we refer to as **elements**.

The concept of elements of evaluation is based on work by Denise Whitelock.

- **Observe**. Most evaluations include some type of observation: observing the user during user observation or the inspectors keeping track of their own actions while inspecting the user interface.
- **Compare**. We are often comparing the UI with some standard of excellence or good practice such as the list of usability requirements or our innate sense of what makes a good interface.
- **Listen**. In many evaluations, we learn from what users and inspectors have to say about the usability of user interface design. Listening can be informal, such as simply asking someone's opinions and listening to what the person has to say, or more formal, such as listening closely to the audio and video recordings, or indirect, such as reading responses to a questionnaire.
- **Measure**. While performing evaluations, we not only want to know whether the user interface design is good or bad, but also how good or how bad it is. How good or how bad implies having some numbers or measures in the evaluation data. Measuring implies obtaining quantitative data during evaluations to validate the usability requirements. For example, if you aim to validate the usability metric "the time taken by the user to complete a task" using the prototype, or the "the number of errors made" in an evaluation session, then you will collect this data by taking measurements.

A comparison of these elements for the two techniques we have looked at in detail is shown in Table 27.1.

In earlier chapters, we looked at some of the different options for various parts of the evaluation. Table 27.2 brings these together from the point of view of the elements of evaluation.

It is possible to vary one or more of the four elements of user observation and heuristic inspection to create further techniques for evaluation. Some of the possible variations are shown in Figure 27.1. For evaluation, each variant technique (though it has its own name) is undertaken in a similar way to its parent technique. We discussed the variations of usability inspections in Chapter 26.

Table 27.1 Evaluation Element Choices for User Observation and Heuristic Inspection

Element	User-observation choices	Heuristic inspection choices
Observe	Evaluator observes the participants	Inspectors observe themselves
Compare	Participant's personal standard of a good interface	List of heuristics
Listen	Think-aloud or retrospective protocol	Inspectors ask themselves the questions posed by the heuristics
Measure	Timing tasks Obtaining satisfaction ratings	Number of times heuristics are violated

4 Combining the Elements for Evaluation

The elements of evaluation discussed here can be considered to be the ingredients of an evaluation technique, just as flour, sugar, eggs, and water are the ingredients for making a cake. In Table 27.1 we presented the element choices for user observation and heuristic evaluation. By varying the combination of the elements and the choices you make for each element, you can tailor the two main techniques.

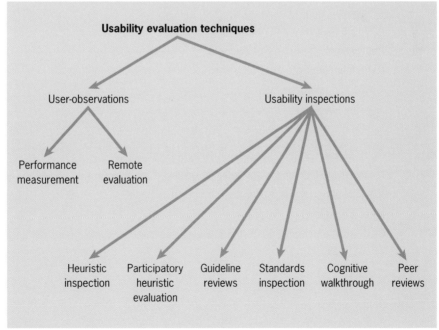

Figure 27.1 Variations of the two main techniques: user observation and inspection.

Table 27.2 The Various Evaluation Elements as Part of a Technique in an Evaluation Session

Element	Available choices
Observe	Direct observation of participants by being next to them and watching them
	Indirect observation of participants:
	Video recordings
	View the participant through a one-way mirror in a laboratory
	Use eye-tracking equipment to show precisely where the participant is looking
	Use software — directly or over the Internet — to replicate the user's screen on another computer, so that you can see the changes to the screen at the same time as the user sees them
	Rely on the participants observing themselves and recalling what they did in a retrospective protocol
Compare	User's personal concept of what constitutes a good interface
	Heuristics
	Design principles
	Design guidelines
	Usability standards
	Customized style guide
Listen	Think-aloud protocols
	Asking cognitive walkthrough questions
	Post-session interviews or debriefs
	Retrospective protocols
	Asking the user's opinions
	Questionnaires
Measure	Post-session questionnaires (to measure satisfaction)
	Measure whether or not the interface allowed the user to complete the task successfully
	Measure time taken to do a task
	Measure metrics

Looking again at Table 27.1, let us take, for example, the technique of heuristic evaluation and see how the elements of evaluation can be varied by picking some of the different choices available from Table 27.2.

- *Observe.* Supposing you want to get a lot of information very quickly from the inspectors in a heuristic inspection. You could vary the observe element by arranging for each inspector to have an assigned observer instead of relying on the inspectors to observe themselves. As the inspector reviews the interface and considers each heuristic, the observer would watch what the inspector does and take notes. The advantage is that the inspector does not have to break off from thinking about the interface to make notes.
- *Listen.* You could vary the listen element by audio recording the session as the inspector thinks aloud and then have a post-session discussion with the inspector about the usability of the UI.
- *Compare.* In Chapter 26, we talked about varying the standard of comparison by using a style guide or set of guidelines instead of using a set of heuristics.
- *Measure.* As well as asking the inspectors to record violations of heuristics, you could ask them to record how many mouse clicks or keyboard actions are required to complete typical tasks.

Box 27.1 shows how the elements can be combined for planning an evaluation session for user observation.

Box 27.1	**Integrating Elements in User Observation**

Suppose our aim is to obtain data for the usability metric "time taken to complete a task." Using Table 27.1, we thought of the following ways of combining the elements in an evaluation session of user observation:

Observe. We would video-record the session. This will indicate the path the user followed through the screens of the prototype while undertaking the task described in the task description. In addition, we would observe the user interacting with the prototype — taking care to ensure that the user is not interrupted so that the timed data are not invalidated.

Listen. Because the time for completing the task description will be recorded, we would discourage the user from thinking aloud. Instead, we would have a post-session discussion with the user, which would include a retrospective protocol while reviewing video clips.

Compare. At the end of the session, we would ask the user whether this seems to be a good system; but we would vary the element by also asking questions based around Nielsen's heuristics or other design guidelines so that there are a variety of ways of judging the system.

Measure. We would use a stopwatch to measure the time the user takes to complete the tasks.

EXERCISE 27.1 (Allow five minutes)

You have been asked to evaluate the software of the time-management system in your organization. Many users have complained that it takes a lot of time to enter the week record (time spent on different activities during a week). Your objective is to investigate the current system for its usability defects. You have decided to conduct a user observation. What choices will you make for the four evaluation elements?

DISCUSSION

Debbie writes:

Observe. I would ask a colleague to perform the task of entering a week record into the system, observing as the person does so.

Measure. My aim is to determine the time it takes for my colleague to enter a week record into the system. This would give me an idea of the current level of performance. I would use a stopwatch during the evaluation session.

Listen. I would prefer to ask the colleague to think aloud during the task, but this might conflict with the time measurement; so instead I will ask my colleague to replay the task in a retrospective protocol.

Compare. I think we would have a more productive discussion about whether this is a good system if we have some guidelines to think about. So I shall explain the principles of visibility, affordance, and feedback, and we will decide together whether or not we feel that the interface conforms to those principles.

5 Varying Other Aspects of the Evaluation

When the system is used by its eventual users, they will be doing actual tasks in their own environment and domain. In evaluation, we may vary these aspects. For example, we can vary the participants either by having inspectors rather than real users participate; or we can employ task descriptions rather than using real tasks. Evaluation is a compromise between our desire to predict whether the UI will work in real life and the problems of simulating some aspects of real life. Table 27.3 illustrates the ranges along which these aspects of evaluation lie.

A typical heuristic evaluation is closer to simulation (that is, the right-hand side of the ranges) in all aspects. However, you can make other choices. For example, rather than the inspectors simply answering the comparison questions by filling in the data-collection forms, you could ask them to think aloud while comparing the UI to the heuristics to try to gather more comprehensive information about any problems they are experiencing with the UI.

Table 27.3 Reality or Simulation in Evaluation

Range available in evaluation		
Aspect	Real life	Simulation
Users	Actual users← – – – – – – – – →User representatives/experts	
Tasks	Actual tasks← – – – – – – – – →Task descriptions	
User environment	Real environment (field study)← – – →Controlled environment	
Real domain of knowledge	Actual users with anticipated training← – – – – – – →People without domain knowledge	

EXERCISE 27.2 (Allow five minutes)

Look at the variable aspects of evaluation detailed in Table 27.3. Decide which choices you would need to make for the users, tasks, environment, and the amount of domain knowledge when undertaking a user observation. Is a typical user observation closer to real life or to simulation?

DISCUSSION

A typical user observation is close to real life (that is, to the left-hand side of the ranges) in all aspects, and this is what gives it so much value. However, you can make other choices.

For example, you could ask an HCI expert to act as the participant in a user observation. Although the HCI expert will usually lack domain knowledge, an HCI expert is likely to have a more developed notion of what makes a good interface and is also likely to be good at thinking aloud.

Often, because the available range of participants is confined to friends and family, students ask people without domain knowledge to act as participants in their first evaluations.

In Chapter 26, we looked at inspections of the user interface and discussed some variants of them. Guideline reviews, standards inspections, and cognitive walkthroughs are all inspections that vary the compare element.

Peer reviews and participatory heuristic evaluations differ from heuristic inspections in two ways:

- By including nonexperts as the reviewers
- By varying the compare element accordingly

Notice that including a user rather than an expert as the reviewer in a heuristic inspection does not turn that inspection into a user observation because the type of task the user will do is driven by the comparison with the list of heuristics. Similarly, asking an expert to act as participant in a user observation does not turn the user observation into a heuristic inspection.

6   Variations of User Observations

Some people are reluctant to try user-observation for various reasons. We have included some of these problems in Table 27.4 with some suggestions for solving them.

Krug (2000) wrote this about recruiting users for testing web sites:

> When people decide to test, they often spend a lot of time trying to recruit uers who they think will precisely reflect their target audience — for instance, male account-ants between the ages of 25 and 40 with one to three years of computer experience who have recently purchased expensive shoes.

> The best-kept secret of usability testing is the extent to which it doesn't much matter who you test.

> For most sites, all you really need are people who have used the Web enough to know the basics.

> If you can afford to hire someone to recruit the participants for you and it won't reduce the number of rounds of testing that you do, then by all means be as specific as you want. But if finding the ideal user means you're going to do fewer tests, I recommend a different approach:

Take anyone you can get (within limits) and grade on a curve.

> In other words, try to find users who reflect your audience, but don't get hung up about it. Instead, try to make allowances for the differences between the people you get and your audience. (pp. 147–148)

6.1 Remote Moderated Testing

What do you do if geography or other considerations make it impossible for you to travel to the participants or for them to come to you? Web technologies make it possible for the participant to use your system or prototype while taking part in a telephone call or video conference with you. Safire (2003) coined the term "remote moderated testing" to describe a user observation that takes place with the participant and facilitator in different locations.

There are several ways of collecting data in remote evaluations:

Table 27.4 Problems with User Observation and Suggestions for Solving Them

Problem	Suggestion
Real tasks cannot be used because the data is too sensitive or there is too much risk of damaging something.	Create simulated tasks that are as close to reality as possible — for example, by preparing a test database.
There is only a paper prototype at the moment.	Change the compare element from users personal concept of what is a good interface to the "cognitive questions" from cognitive walkthrough. That is, ask users to explain what they would do next at each step, rather than asking them to attempt an actual task. Then ask them how it went.
Several designers need to watch this user, but it will be too intimidating.	Change the observe element to using video, so that several people can either watch on a remote link or view the tapes later.
There may be obvious errors in the product. Users need to see a product that conforms to principles of good design.	Do the observation anyway. The users may give you some pointers about what is really important to them. Also, it is often easier to get users to comment on a product that has a couple of obvious errors or does not look too finished. If you think your design may be very poor, consider heuristic inspection first or consider a pilot test with some users who will not be worried by errors — perhaps colleagues from another development team.
It is difficult to find real users.	Your system will be used by real users eventually, so it is worth persisting in trying to find some. For example, if you find even one real user, then you could ask that person to help you recruit more. Meanwhile, and being very careful not to be complacent about what you find, try testing with anyone who is even slightly like a real user.

- *Remote-control evaluation.* The user's and evaluator's workstations are connected via the Internet and special software applications are installed on both machines. The evaluator can view (and videotape) the user's interaction in real time on the user's workstation and listen/communicate with the user during evaluation, as is done in traditional evaluations. Alternatively, the evaluator can have the usage data collected automatically by other specialized software installed on the user's workstation.

- *Video conferencing.* A remote evaluator can view the user's interaction with the system via video-conferencing equipment and also can listen/communicate with the user simultaneously by telephone.
- *Instrumented remote evaluation.* Data loggers are installed on the user's workstation to collect usage data, which is then packaged and sent over the Internet to the evaluators for analysis.
- *Remote questionnaire.* Questionnaires are sent to the remote users. The completed questionnaires can be sent over the network to the evaluators. If, for example, a web site has to be evaluated, then the URL could be sent to the remote users. The users could fill in an online questionnaire to send their feedback.

The advantage of remote moderated evaluations are that they overcome the problem of getting into the same room as the participant. The disadvantages are:

- A lot of technology is involved, and there are many opportunities for some element of it to go wrong, such as the web conferencing program fighting with the participant's firewall software.
- It is harder to get the participant started and you are relying on what the participant says much more than in a face-to-face evaluation, so if the participant does not understand something or does not like to think aloud, then it may be a difficult experience.

There is a web site about remote moderated usability testing at http:// msafire.home. mindspring.com /links.htm.

You must be even more meticulous in your preparation than in a face-to-face evaluation, and a pilot test is invaluable. Make sure that you try all the different technologies involved in your pilot and that your pilot participant tries all the materials such as any instructions required to download software or log into a conference system.

Once you have overcome the difficulties, Tullis *et al.* (2002) found that remote moderated testing is likely to give you data that is approximately as useful, although not necessarily the same, as the data from a conventional user observation.

6.2 Performance Measurement Evaluations

A performance measurement evaluation is a user observation that is particularly strict about the listen and measure elements. It aims to compare the performance of two different versions of the interface or to compare one version against a set of defined performance metrics. So that it is possible to compare results across different participants, the introductory material, question sequence, and tasks have to be the same for each. This confines your choices for the listen element to those that are reproducible between participants.

> **EXERCISE 27.3 (Allow five minutes)**
>
> Which listen choices from Table 27.2 are appropriate for a performance measurement evaluation?

> **DISCUSSION**
>
> Anything that disrupts the participant during the task might affect the measurements, so think-aloud protocols are not suitable. A retrospective protocol where the participant is asked to relay his or her thoughts after all the timings have been done would be appropriate, as might a post-session interview or questionnaire.

7 Obtaining Opinions and Ideas

What if you want to get users' views and opinions, but it is too early to ask them to undertake specific tasks? What if no product exists at all? Is there anything you can do? Maybe you do not yet know what the overall purpose of the system will be, and you want to get some opinions and ideas about it.

7.1 Focus Groups

For more information on focus groups used for product ideas or advertising research, see Gordon (1999).

In a focus group, about eight people led by a moderator discuss something. This could be an idea, some stimulus material such as a storyboard or mockups of an interface, or a tangible product. Focus groups are used extensively in getting user reactions to new product ideas, such as a new cereal or cookie, and in exploring user reaction to advertising or marketing campaigns. Focus groups work best when a skilled moderator gets the groups to react to and bounce off each others' opinions. They are helpful in user interface design when no product yet exists and your main aim is to find out what users' needs and hopes might be.

7.2 Card Sorting

We mentioned cart sorting in part 3.

In contrast to focus groups, where the skill of the moderator has a major effect on the value of the information obtained, card sorting is one of the simplest of techniques involving users. The technique is outlined in Box 27.2 and is an excellent way of finding out how users might categorize and group concepts or terminology applied in a user interface.

8 Evaluations without People

In the previous section, we looked at ways of exploring usability with people when no product yet exists. In this section, we look at ways of exploring usability without people. If you try a usability inpsection, you will quickly begin to wonder whether computers could do some of the checking for you. And indeed they can.

8.1 Accessibility Checkers and HTML Validators

One group of products that is especially helpful is the accessibility checkers/HTML validators. The best known of these products is Bobby, a commercial service that you can try for free at http://bobby.watchfire.com/bobby/html/en/index.jsp. The check-

| Box 27.2 | **Card Sorting** |

Card sorting is a technique for exploring how people group items, so that you can develop structures that maximize the probability of users being able to find items. Card sorting:

- Is easy and cheap to conduct
- Enables you to understand how real people are likely to group items
- Identifies items that are likely to be difficult to categorize and find
- Identifies terminology that is likely to be misunderstood

When Is Card Sorting Appropriate?

Card sorting is appropriate when you have identified items that you need to categorize.

Card sorting is particularly useful for defining web site structures.

How Is Card Sorting Conducted?

Card sorting can be conducted in a variety of circumstances using various means: one on one, during workshops, by mail, or electronically. The following is the basic process:

- Names of items to be categorized are printed on individual cards. Cards should be large enough to accommodate the names in a font that participants can read easily when spread out on a desk or table — at least 14 point.
- Participants are asked to group items in a way that makes sense to them.
- Participants may also be asked to name the resulting groups.
- Once all participants have completed the exercise, enter the data in a spreadsheet, and examine the groupings. There will be general agreement about many items, and these groupings will be fairly apparent. For example, all participants may group "Technical Support" with "Complaints" and "Product Assistance."
- You can use cluster analysis to get a pictorial representation of the resultant groupings. An easy way to do this is using IBM's EZSort program (free from www-3.ibm.com/ibm/easy/eou_ext.nsf/Publish/410).

Pay special attention to items about which a consensus does not exist. Would renaming the item improve the situation, or does it need to be included in more than one category?

From Gaffney (2003b).

The STC AccessAbility SIG maintains a list of current accessibility validators at www.stcsig.org/sn/internet.shtm l#VALID.

ers examine the source of your web site and look for violations of guidelines. Bobby offers a choice of guidelines to use: Web Content Accessibility Guidelines 1.0 or the U.S. Section 508 Guidelines, as discussed in Chapter 9. Other products will check that your HTML is valid, good practice in general and helpful for screen readers and other technologies that rely on valid HTML to work. For example, the W3C Consortium has

The W3C Consortium's CSS checker is at http://jigsaw.w3 .org/css-validator.

a free facility that will check whether your Cascading Style Sheets (CSS) conform to W3C recommendations.

The limitation of the automated checkers is that they cannot interpret what they find. For example, they can report whether or not an image has an ALT tag defined for it but they cannot report whether the text in the ALT tag will help a user to understand the page. Like any inspection method, these checkers should be supplemented with user-observation of real users.

8.2 Usability Checkers

Usability checkers work in a similar way to accessibility checkers. They inspect the source of the web site but are comparing what they find to usability guidelines rather than accessibility guidelines. Usability checkers are especially helpful when they can be configured to keep watch on your web site continuously, monitoring for problems such as downtime or broken links. Like accessibility checkers, they suffer from the problem that they can only report on mechanical violations of guidelines, such as broken links, but not on conceptual problems, such as a link title not being meaningful to the user.

8.3 Hybrid Methods

The STC Usability SIG maintains a list of current remote usability checkers and other remote tools at www.stcsig.org/ usability/topics/ remote-evaluation.html.

To overcome the limitations of automated checking, some providers of online checking services have developed hybrid methods that offer a mixture of automated checking and user input. These may be elaborate surveys that include some usage of the system, or they may track what users do as well as what they say they did and thought about it. For example, Vividence (www.vividence.com) generally asks users to attempt typical tasks while a downloaded program runs in the background "observing" what they do. The automated data collection is supplemented by a post-test questionnaire.

Hybrid methods can be a good way of getting feedback relatively quickly from a large sample of users of web sites. They tend to be more expensive than usability testing, and they are harder to administrate.

9 | Different Purposes of Evaluations

In most of Part 4, we have assumed that your main reason for evaluating is to get ideas about how to improve the user interface while you are developing it. Evaluations that seek to find as many usability problems as possible are called diagnostic. Measurement evaluations can be done at any stage during or after development, and their aim is, as the name implies, to measure the extent to which a system has met its usability requirements or to measure some aspect of the user experience.

Evaluations that are part of a continuing development process are called **formative evaluations**. **Summative evaluations**, on the other hand, aim to establish whether or not a system has met its usability requirements and are usually done when it is complete.

Rubin (1994) classifies evaluation into four types: exploratory, validation, assessment, and comparison. Each evaluation type has a different purpose and is applied at a different time (or times) in the design life cycle.

9.1 Exploratory Evaluations

Exploratory evaluations are conducted early in development, often with low-fidelity prototypes. They are often very informal, based on discussions with typical users sometimes including establishing the tasks that users may want to undertake. They serve several purposes:

- To explore the user interface design features of the prototype
- To gather feedback on preliminary designs
- To verify the assumptions held about the real users, which you will have compiled in the user profile

The evaluation data obtained from an exploratory session is usually qualitative and helps to both establish and validate qualitative usability requirements. Exploratory evaluations are both formative and diagnostic.

Exploratory evaluations are relatively easy to set up because the claims we are making are relative, not absolute. That is, our purpose is to say, "In this evaluation, we learned something about the user interface that will be useful to us."

9.2 Validation Evaluation

Validation evaluations are conducted toward the end of the development cycle or once the system is in use. Their purpose is to verify that the system meets a predetermined usability standard or benchmark prior. They may also be undertaken to assess how all the components of the system — such as the documentation, help, any online tutorials, and any other software/hardware integrated with the system — work together. Validation evaluations usually concentrate on measurement and are usually summative rather than formative.

Validation evaluations generally seek to make claims that are absolute — that is, that this interface definitely does or does not meet specific levels of performance. This takes them out of the relatively relaxed realm of the exploratory evaluation where learning anything is good into the much more controlled area where experimental design starts to become important. To support claims such as "this interface meets these requirements," we have to (as a minimum):

- Establish a hypothesis, the testable claim or assertion that we are evaluating
- Establish a null hypothesis, the possibility that the claim will not be met
- Decide what sample size will support our assertions
- Ensure that our participants are a random sample drawn from the appropriate user population

All of these are part of experimental design, an important subject in its own right that requires a textbook of its own.

We suggest that you start with Coolican (1996) to learn about experimental design.

For the purposes of this book, we ask you to bear in mind that we have been aiming at exploratory, diagnostic evaluations for formative purposes, so be careful not to make assertions that cannot be supported by the data.

9.3 Assessment Evaluation

Assessment evaluations are carried out in an early or midway stage in the design life cycle, after the feedback from the exploratory sessions has been incorporated into the designs and the conceptual model has been created. By this point in development, you should have a good understanding of users' tasks, and an assessment evaluation is conducted using task descriptions to determine whether the users' tasks are supported and what usability problems they find in the design. Even though the work of establishing requirements should be complete by this stage, you will frequently find out plenty of detailed points where the requirements need to be refined and occasionally you discover that the requirements need to be completely revisited. Assessment evaluations are also usually formative and diagnostic, but they may also be used to start to establish measures of the level of usability such as whether or not the UI is likely to meet its targets for best-case and worst-case task times. Therefore measurement starts to become important.

Some authorities in the field recommend that assessment evaluations are done with the same level of rigor in experimental design that is appropriate for a validation evaluation. We feel that our methods will support some measurement, which is why we discussed the evaluation element "measure."

9.4 Comparison Evaluation

Comparison evaluations can be performed at any stage of the life cycle. You might perform a comparison evaluation early in the life cycle to compare two designs with different interaction styles. Further along in the life cycle, you might like to compare the efficiency of two alternative designs. In comparison evaluations, care must be taken to maintain consistency across the evaluation sessions, for example, time must be measured in a similar way, and the same task description must be used for the sessions that are being compared.

Evaluation is usually a better way of choosing between two competing design ideas than general preference or sheer chance, but once we get into comparison evaluations, we have to consider statistical significance and whether or not the differences we observed between the two approaches are due to sampling, the way we tested, chance, or actual important differences. Nielsen (1993) puts it like this:

> *Statistical significance is basically an indication of the probability that one is not making the wrong conclusion (e.g., a claim that a certain result is significant at the $p < .05$ level indicates that there is a 5% probability that it is false). Consider the problem of choosing between two [products]. If no information is available, you*

might as well choose by tossing a coin, and you will have a 50% probability of choosing the best interface. If a small amount of user testing has been done, you may find that [version] A is better than [version] B at the 20% level of significance. Even though 20% is considered "not significant," your tests have actually improved your chance of choosing the best [product] from 50/50 to 4-to-1, meaning that you would be foolish not to take the data into account when choosing. Furthermore, even though there remains a 20% probability that A is not better than B, it is very unlikely that it would be much worse than B. Most of the 20% accounts for cases where the two are equal or where B is slightly better than A, meaning that it would almost never be a really bad decision to choose A. In other words, even tests that are not statistically significant are well worth doing since they will improve the quality of decisions substantially. (p. 166)

If you need to undertake a comparison evaluation, then carefully think through what you need to esablish from it. Do you need to make an absolute assertion that interface A is better than B? If so, you are straying into experimental design again and should consult an appropriate textbook. Do you simply need to find out all you can about A and all you can about B and then use that information as part of your process of deciding what to do next? If so, then the techniques you have learned in this book should help you. Jarrett (2004b) put it like this:

Designing comparative evaluations

It was one of those calls that is simultaneously good news and bad news. "We'd like you to do an evaluation for us. We have two designs here and we want to know which one is better."

The good news: Well, I'm a consultant so phone calls offering work are always good, right?

The bad news: comparative evaluations. Ugh. So I thought I'd at least make use of the pain by writing a few notes on them here.

IS A BETTER THAN B?

The first challenge of a comparative evaluation is that the client wants a nice clear answer: A is better than B. Or perhaps: B is better than A. The problem is that the actual answer is usually more complicated. Parts of A are better than parts of B. Parts of B are better than parts of A. Some bits of A are horrible. Some bits of B, usually but not always different ones, are also horrible. There's probably an approach C that is better than A or B, and the final answer is probably D: a bit of C, plus some of the good points from A and from B. It's not exactly a nice clean story, is it?

"BETWEEN SUBJECTS" or "WITHIN SUBJECTS"

I don't like to use the term "subject" for the participant in a test, because my view is that the system is the subject not the person. But here we need to turn to the design of psychological experiments where the subject of the experiment is the person. If you have two designs to test, are you going to get the same participants to test both designs ("within subjects") or are you going to do two rounds of testing: one group of participants gets A, and another gets B ("between subjects")?

The problem with "within subjects" design is that nearly all systems have some learning effects. If you ask the participants to try the same or similar tasks with both systems then they learn about the task with the first system and can't unlearn that knowledge before they try the second system. If they try different tasks with each system then are they really comparing like with like? I've known participants who had a hard time with the task on A so they were adamant that they preferred B even though it was downright horrible to do the task with B. And we also get into much larger sample sizes because we have to vary the order of presentation of systems so that one group of participants get A then B and an equal group gets B then A.

The problem with "between subjects" design is that you can't ask the participants which they preferred. And surely that is one of the main reasons why we're doing an evaluation anyway, to establish preference? So we end up in the murky world of inferential statistics: trying to figure out what the population as a whole might prefer on the basis of the two samples from that population who tried these two interfaces. And now we're into the issues of random sampling and statistical tests that require much larger sample sizes than we normally use in usability testing.

MINIMAL OR RADICAL DIFFERENCES?

My third recurring problem with comparative evaluation is the "identical twins" problem. The client knows these babies and sees all the subtle and, to them, important differences that they want to explore. The participants see them as identical twins: both products look pretty much the same. For example, we were looking at three different versions of a form that is much hated by the general public. The client could see all sorts of really, really major differences between them. The participants just saw the form they loathed.

SOME TIPS

If you do have to undertake a comparative evaluation, maybe these tips will help:

1. Prepare your client for a complicated answer that picks elements from the different approaches.

2. Be prepared to undertake far more tests. You'll probably need at least three times the number of participants you usually work with rather than just twice the number.

3. Dust off your statistics books. You really do need to think about what assertions are supported by your sample size.

4. Try to make sure that the differences you are exploring really do seem like differences to your participants.

10 Undertaking More Comprehensive Evaluations

To present the basic principles of each of the evaluation activities and for the sake of simplicity, up to now we have discussed the evaluation of a prototype user interface design using a single technique. We also indicated that where the evaluation involves more than one session, each would be undertaken using the same technique. Although often you may choose to evaluate designs through the single technique of user observation, in reality there is sometimes a need to evaluate a prototype UI design using a combination of complementary techniques — for example, you might start with a heuristic evaluation followed by a user observation.

Another example: if you are evaluating low-fidelity prototypes early in the design life cycle and are trying to discover whether the menu commands are obvious for a particular task, then you could just conduct a cognitive walkthrough with real users. However, prior to undertaking the cognitive walkthrough, you may have decided that it would useful to perform peer reviews.

The disadvantage of combining techniques is that you have to plan and conduct two evaluations. If you are using more than one technique, you should try to choose techniques that complement each other. For example, some of the combinations could be undertaking cognitive walkthroughs followed by user observation, or conducting heuristic evaluations, then participatory heuristic evaluations, followed by user observation. The choice of techniques depends on:

- *The state of the interface.* For example, if you wanted to measure performance, you would not be able to do this if only low-fidelity prototypes were available.
- *The stage of the life cycle.* Techniques such as peer reviews are most effective if they are applied early on in the life cycle, while user observations can be used throughout the design life cycle.
- *Any constraints.* Shortages of time, money, technology, or human resources will influence what you can do.

Table 27.5 lists the techniques and the stages of the life cycle when they can be applied.

11 Summary

We started this chapter by comparing user observation and heuristic inspection. From that, we derived four elements of evaluation: observe, listen, compare, and measure. We explained how these elements could be combined in different ways to produce variations of the evaluation methods.

We then went on to discuss variations of other aspects of evaluation such as remote moderated testing, where the participant is in a different geographic location, and performance measurement evaluations, where the purpose is to measure what happens.

Table 27.5 Choosing Evaluation Techniques

Technique	State of the prototype	Stage of the life cycle at which the technique can be applied
User observation for qualitative feedback	Both low- and high-fidelity prototypes: paper prototype, screen printouts from a drawing package, or interactive (working) software prototype	Can be conducted throughout the life cycle
User observation for collecting usability metrics	High-fidelity prototypes: only with an advanced version of the interactive (working) software prototype	Can be conducted only when an advanced prototype is available to facilitate measurements
Inspection (e.g., heuristic evaluation, peer reviews, participatory heuristic evaluation, standards inspections, and guideline reviews)	Both low- and high-fidelity prototypes: paper prototype, screen printouts from a drawing package, or an interactive (working) software prototype	Inspections can be conducted throughout the life cycle, but if applied early on in the life cycle the user interface should be sufficiently developed to enable a useful inspection
Cognitive walkthrough	Both low- and high-fidelity prototypes: the prototype of the user interface design should support navigation through a task description	Can be conducted from early on in the life cycle when tasks have been simulated in the prototype

We briefly discussed some other techniques to use where a system does not yet exist, such as focus groups, card sorting, or where a large sample size is important, such as automated checking.

In most of Part 4, we have assumed that your purpose in evaluation was finding problems with an interface with a view to doing something about it. However, there are other possible purposes of evaluations, and we discussed validation, assessment, and comparison evaluations to give you a flavor of the possibilities. The chapter, and this part of the book, ended with a discussion of more complex evaluations where you use more than one technique.

5

Persuasion

1 Overview

Many of us work, or plan to work in the future, in organizations. It is as important to convince your colleagues of the need to make changes to the UI so as to decide what those changes might be. This final part is about the challenges of winning and maintaining support for the changes you wish to make. When we say, "your project" or "your system," we mean a user interface that you have worked on or are trying to improve.

If you are a one-person organization, a student, or simply designing outside of the conventional organizational structures, then you may feel at first that this part is less relevant to you. We suggest that when we say, "your organization," you think in terms of any organization that you know — ideally one that might be affected in some way by your user interface design. Even those of us who are not working within organizations often have to encounter them: perhaps as current or prospective clients, employers, or suppliers. We hope that the ideas we offer here about persuading organizations may prove helpful now, and in the future.

2 What You Will Find in the Chapters

Chapter 28 covers two areas: making use of your findings, and identifying who is affected by the change. We hope that you have decided that it is important for a UI to be usable. Having completed an evaluation and found some good and some bad features of a UI, you now need to make use of your findings. That is, you now need to communicate your findings to those in your organization whose support you need in order to make the necessary changes. What happens when you suggest that your organization adopt user-centered design? We show you how to find out who would be affected by the changes you are proposing, how to assess the usability maturity of an organization, and how this information can help you to choose the communication activities to undertake in order to convince your colleagues.

In Chapter 29 we look at ways of justifying user-centered design, and discuss what to do when you need to bid for resources to undertake the techniques you have learned in this course.

The book finishes with Chapter 30, where we point out some of the key learning points we have covered.

3 Learning Outcomes

After studying Part 5, you will be able to:

- Choose the best way of communicating the results of your UI design activity
- Prepare an evaluation report that maximizes the likelihood of obtaining action on the recommendations

- Identify the groups within your organization who will be affected by your project
- Choose methods for winning support for user-centered activities that are appropriate for your organization

4   Theoretical Influences

The content is based around management theory and the experience of usability practitioners.

5   Finally

When you have finished this part, you have finished the book. We hope that you have enjoyed studying user interface design and evaluation and will have the opportunity to use the skills you have developed.

28

Communicating and using your findings

1 Introduction

The previous chapters of this book have discussed the theory of user-centered UI design and evaluation, and you have had opportunities to try various practical techniques in exercises. Now we step back to ask: Why are you doing this? How can you convince your organization that the principles of usability are worth applying? How can you make best use of the knowledge you have gained about your system and about best practice?

We will be using the terms "your organization" and "your project" throughout this chapter. If you do not happen to be in an organization at the moment, or if your own work does not involve developing interfaces for users, then we suggest that you pick an example that interests you to think about — perhaps one that is included elsewhere in this book. Please interpret "your project" and "your organization" accordingly.

This chapter has two main sections:

Making use of your findings. By this stage in the course, we hope you have decided that usability is important. You have done your evaluation and discovered some good things and some bad things about your interface. What next? Should you communicate your findings, and if so, to whom? How will you continue to improve the usability of the next version of your user interface?

Who is affected by the changes? What happens when your manager asks you to "do usability"? Will all your colleagues fall into line and enthusiastically adopt your new approaches? Here, you will learn how to find out who is affected by the changes to working practices that you are proposing, how to assess the **usability maturity** of an organization, and how this can help you to choose appropriate communication activities.

Figure 28.1 Usability is more than a façade that you stick on the front of your interface.

2 Making Use of Your Findings

In a typical evaluation, you learn a lot about your interface. Some aspects of the interface will be successful, and you will want to keep those aspects just as they are. Other parts will not have met the needs of your users. If you are a single-person organization, or if you have complete control over the product you are developing, then you can go ahead and deal with the problems you found. But most of us work in more complex organizations where we have to consider many different factors. We have to work with other people to make changes.

2.1 Using Your Results

When organizations first start doing usability evaluation, there is a tendency to think that they can stick a bit of usability onto their UI by doing some evaluation near the end of the project, as in Figure 28.1. You do not achieve a usable interface by investigating users' needs or by finding problems. You achieve a usable interface by designing to meet users' needs and by fixing problems.

This section is about making use of your findings. Those findings may have come from the evaluation activity or, thinking back to investigation and requirements activities, they may be about meeting user needs or communicating user needs to other people.

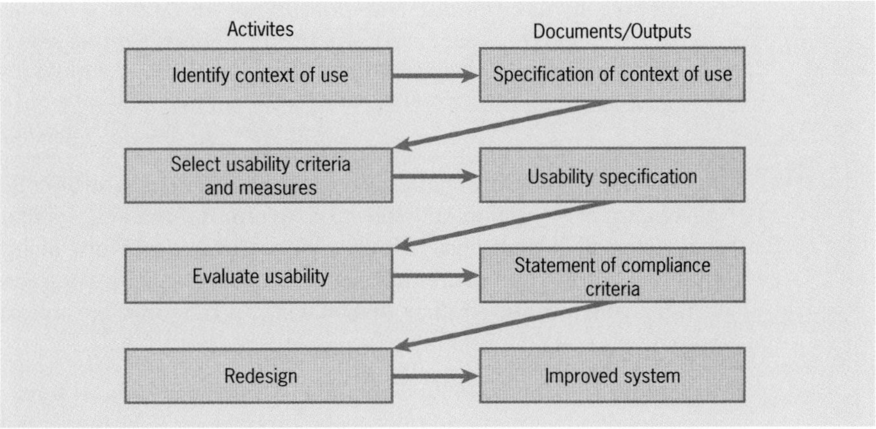

Figure 28.2 Usability activities and associated documents. (Adapted from ISO 9241:11, 1998.)

Figure 28.2 emphasizes the point that there is more to do after your evaluation. Notice that you have to *redesign* (and rebuild) before you get to the *improved* stage. In between, there is this mysterious activity, *statement of compliance criteria*.

In many environments you will be expected to create a report on your activities. Usually, that report will include statements of areas where your interface achieved what you wanted for your users and areas where it failed to meet the requirements. This report is a "statement of compliance criteria."

Reports and formal statements have their place, but these documents will have no effect until someone reads them and decides to act on them. In the next section, we will discuss how to write reports that achieve action. We will also look at some of the other ways of communicating what you find.

2.2 Communicating the Results

▶ Involvement and Interpretation

We asked a selection of usability practitioners how they conveyed the message about the need for changes to an interface after an evaluation. They all said that the most effective method was to get the developers involved.

If you have been evaluating your own interface, you too may have been surprised (possibly even embarrassed) by the experience of watching your users have difficulties with your interface — difficulties that you might never have anticipated. In a perfect world, the developers themselves conduct their evaluations, learn what the users feel about the product, and go away with a clear understanding of what they need to do to make the product work. However, the skills of programming, design, and working with users do not always coexist happily in one person. Another practitioner put it like this:

I'm no good as evaluator. They have to put me behind a one-way mirror. If I'm in the room with the user I can't stop myself — I just want to say "Do it like this. Why can't you see how it works?" I have to get somebody else to do the evaluation. Then I go and do the work.

Anonymous personal communication

In addition, in some organizations it is impractical to take colleagues away from development or support activities to go to remote sites and watch users work. So how can you achieve that sense of involvement without everyone being there at the same time? How can you ensure that the direct experience of your actual users is at the core of your product, rather than having to rely on what management (theirs or yours) tells you about them?

Beyer and Holtzblatt (1998) describe the **interpretation session**. After a visit to see users working with an interface, each interviewer — and we think it works equally well with an observer from an evaluation — has a meeting with all the other developers and explains what happened. Everyone at the session can throw in ideas, comments, and suggestions. This allows the experience of one interviewer, or one observer, to be shared quickly. It can even be more effective than everyone doing interviews themselves, because the discussion of the observations and suggestions that arise from them is immediately shared with the whole team.

Beyer and Holtzblatt (1998) explain it as follows:

It's not enough for the members of the design team to understand the customers they visited and talked to individually. If the team is to agree on what to deliver, all members of the design team need to understand every customer as though they had been there. They need to build an understanding of all the customers and how they work that is shared by the whole team. A team develops this understanding through conversation and mutual inquiry into the meaning of the facts about the customer's work. In this way the different members of the design team can learn each other's perspective, the unique focus each person brings to the problem. They can probe each other's understanding, learning from and teaching each other what to see. When one thinks another is wrong, they can look at concrete instances to see how the different perspectives reveal different issues in customer data. (p. 125)

▶ Highlights and Summaries

If you have a product that works well on the whole, or if your product in use has long periods when users apparently do nothing but think, then it may be more efficient for one person, or a small team, to do the evaluation and prepare **highlights** for your colleagues. This is one of the advantages of video or audio recording, or screen capture. You can go back over your recordings, cutting out the bits that do not give you any new information and condensing the interesting material for your reports (see Box 28.1).

<table>
<tr><td>**Box 28.1**</td><td>**Edited Highlights**</td></tr>
</table>

We did an evaluation where users had to type large quantities of data from paper forms into computers. This was highly repetitive work, and problems only occurred at comparatively long intervals. We decided to video the evaluation, and then assigned one patient person to the task of counting the problems, identifying what caused them, and preparing a list of highlights for the rest of the team.

This saved time for the other team members, who only had to allow enough time to view the highlights. We were then able to produce a video of the most important learning points and use it to communicate the results to senior managers. The counts of problems also helped us to understand the relative importance of the problems we saw.

Anonymous personal communication.

One of the reviewers for the course on which this book is based wrote the following paragraph:

I have found that an "edited highlights" video can work wonders. Often, developers have their work priorities set by marketing or product managers, and these managers can be very sensitive to user needs. Using video highlights with them can place usability improvements high up the software development priority list (although you have to be careful not to alienate the developers by being regarded as "going behind their backs").

▶ **Reports, Requirements, and Recommendations**

Quite often, there is no escape: you have to write reports. Many organizations need to record that the work was done and to circulate its results among those who might need to know about it. A report becomes the expected method of achieving these aims.

Often, these reports become thick documents, written in a highly formal style, printed in small fonts and with very few pictures or diagrams to aid the reader. Reading them is rarely enjoyable (see Figure 28.3).

It helps if you think of your report as a product that has users of its own. Who is the report for? What do they want to get out of your report (their goals)? How can you meet those needs?

Here are some ideas for making your reports more useful:

- *Try issuing **snapshot reports***. Harrison and Melton (1999) called them "**road runner**" **reports**. These are one-page summaries of a single day's highlight results. If you can keep it short, the developer or manager who needs to read it

Figure 28.3 "I've finished the usability report for you."

is more likely to be able to cope with the message. You can always offer a telephone number or e-mail address in case someone wants to ask for more information. As Harrison and Melton noted:

> *There are several advantages to delivering a quick report with some of the highlights of the usability evaluation's findings. First, the teams you support will appreciate the timely turnaround. Second, a quick turnaround method keeps the products teams interested. We consider these short, engaging and popular reports an appetizer to the full report. (p. 14)*

- *Try putting your methods and detailed results in an appendix.* Perhaps make the appendix an optional extra. Cutting the thickness of the report will make it seem more approachable.
- *Include a management summary of the main messages from the reports.* Keep your management summary to a single page, and include it before the table of contents. If you are lucky, the busy reader will be so excited and interested by your single page that she or he will want to read more.
- *Make sure that each of your findings is clearly expressed as a recommendation for action.* If your reader has to do the interpretation, not only will it take longer to read the report but also there is a serious risk that your reader's interpretation will be different from your own.
- *Consider making your reports into a presentation instead.* Having to boil down the messages to a 20-minute set of slides will help you to discover the most

important points. You can always have the reports to hand out once you create enthusiasm for reading them.

▶ Severity Scales and Priorities

Typically, your requirements, design, and evaluation activities will discover a long list of problems and opportunities for improvement. Furthermore, you will find these out at a very inconvenient time in your project. One way of guaranteeing a lack of interest in the user interface design problems is to demand that they are all fixed at the exact moment in the project when management is demanding that it is delivered by yesterday.

In Chapter 25, you learned about assigning severity levels to the problems you discover. The use of a severity scale or method of assigning priorities that is well understood in your organization can be more effective than writing reports. Many organizations have their own categorization schemes for defects, system problems, or bugs, and you will need to work with the way your organization does this — or might do it in the future. We introduced one such classification scheme in Chapter 25. To give you some other ideas, we asked several usability practitioners in a variety of organizations about their use of severity scales. Boxes 28.3 to 28.6 contain examples.

Box 28.2

Example of a Severity Scale from Rolf Mohlich

We use the following categories in our usability test reports:

1. Disaster.

- The user is unable to continue without human intervention (support, colleague, etc.).
- The user expresses strong dissatisfaction with the irrational or totally unreasonable behavior of the program.
- There is a critical difference between what the program does and what the user thinks the program does.

We require that 25% of our test participants encounter a disaster before we accept it as such.

2. Serious problem. The user is delayed significantly but is able to continue on his own.

3. Cosmetic problem. The user hesitates for a short moment.

This is the first dimension (the seriousness of the problem).

The second dimension is how difficult the problem is to fix.

The third dimension is frequency of occurrence.

All these dimensions are important when making the political decision on what problems should be corrected.

From Rolf Mohlich, Dialog Design, Denmark; personal communication, used with permission.

| Box 28.3 | **Example of a Severity Scale from Julianne Chatelain** |

This is what my group actually does. It is binary. If it is close to ship date, there are "problems we have absolutely gotta fix" and "all others."

At Trellix we call the first group thumb-in-the-eye problems (and there's a gesture, probably not safe to internationalize, that goes with the name). The idea is that the customers are *trying* to use the product, but get poked in the eye by this problem or feature badly enough to make them stop dead [quit using it]. We discuss with a cross-functional team "whether it's a thumb," and if enough of us think it's a thumb, then we fix it. And now you have provoked me to define exactly what we mean. . . .

The user testing we do while the product is essentially code-frozen and in Quality Assurance (QA) is now called thumb-in-the-eye testing, and yes we do usually find at least one thumb. Most of the thumbs appear where pieces arrive at the last

minute and either were never before used together or were not implemented like our pretested prototype, or both.

From Julianne Chatelain, Trellix, United States; personal communication, used with permission.

Elizabeth Buie added the following observation to Julianne's ideas:

Then there's the very most important kind of usability problem — the kind that could result in physical damage to the external environment, especially the injury or death of a person (think of medical systems and air traffic control). I'd call this even more severe than a thumb in the eye.

From Elizabeth Buie, Computer Sciences Corporation, United States; personal communication, used with permission.

It helps considerably if you have usability requirements as part of your overall project requirements. Meeting usability requirements then simply becomes a delivery issue like anything else, and negotiating the priority of usability requirements gets the same attention as those from other areas such as marketing or legal.

3 | Who Is Affected by the Changes?

In your project or organization, who will be affected by the changes that are needed to deliver usable interfaces? If you change your methods or discover a lot of new data and requirements, then you may affect other people. Resistance to the changes may pop up unexpectedly — or be predictable. How can you persuade those who resist to work with you?

| Box 28.4 | **Example of a Severity Scale from Lars Jensen** |

When categorizing, we don't differentiate between usability problems and other kinds of software problems (we find the distinction serves no useful purpose, and just wastes time and creates bad feeling while people argue about it).

We use just two categories, which tend to have a rough correlation, but there are plenty of exceptions in either direction. (Note the cunningly named field values, for proper alphabetical sorting!)

Severity.
How bad is it, just in the context of operating the software?
Crash Program stops functioning (whether it was a real crash or a graceful shutdown).
Major Substantial areas of functionality are unavailable, or there is an unacceptable cosmetic problem.
Medium Something is not working, but a workaround is possible.
Minor Something is not working, but a pretty easy, obvious workaround is possible.
Nuisance Noticeable problem, but usage is not likely to be affected. Usually cosmetic.

Priority How badly do we want to fix it?
Critical Fix for the next internal release if possible; will not release externally without a fix.
High Fix for the next release if possible.
Inter-mediate Fix when feasible.
Low Fix is desirable but not necessary.
Very low Fix is unlikely soon, but we do not want to forget about it.

We have separate fields for QA priority, so their opinion gets preserved, and development priority, which is what engineers actually work from and which tends to take more issues into account (such as the cost/complexity of the proposed fix).

The severity tends not to change once it is assigned. The development priority tends to change as we approach freeze/release dates and as we learn about what a fix involves, or about who is affected (e.g., a minor problem that affects a large customer might be bumped up to high priority).

From Lars Jensen, iMarket Inc, United States; personal communication, used with permission.

| Box 28.5 | **Example of a Severity Scale from Avi Harel** |

Our approach is to classify usability problems by business goals. Here are some typical **business goals**:

1. Market penetration of a new product — product acceptance by novice users.
2. Long-term credibility — product acceptance by experienced users.
3. User productivity — user task performance (time measurements include error recovery).
4. Development schedule — save programmers' time that may be wasted chasing phantom bugs.
5. Training costs — reduce the time required for training new users.
6. Help Desk costs — reduce the time required to track the product operation.
7. Prevent accidents — identify instances of "almost accidents."

A business goal is associated with one of the following usability types:

1. Apparent usability is about aspects of which users or observers are aware, such as learnability and user satisfaction.
2. Continuous usability is about long-term aspects of which the users typically are not aware, such as those that affect the user performance.
3. Critical usability is about aspects that observers practically cannot trace, such as those that affect the user reliability.

Once you identify your business goal, you might be able to decide which of the usability types is relevant to your product.

From Avi Harel, Ergolight, Israel; personal communication, used with permission.

In this section, we will think about who is involved, and their level of usability maturity. Then in Chapter 29, we will go on to think about how to win support for usability activities based on the level of usability maturity.

3.1 Who Is Involved in Your Project?

In Chapter 3, we mentioned stakeholders in the user interface. Projects have stakeholders in the same way that UIs have stakeholders. Even if you are a single-person organization, your project might affect your family and friends, your customers or clients, and your suppliers or other contacts.

▶ **Example: The At Home Catalog**

We have chosen an imaginary example to use for exercises in Chapters 28 and 29: At Home, a typical business (see Figure 28.4). It produces a selection of consumer prod-

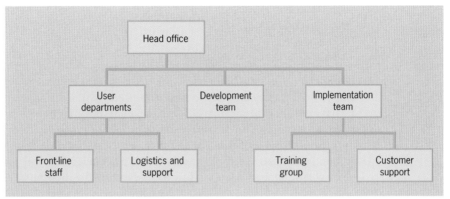

Figure 28.4 An organization chart for At Home.

ucts, currently listed in a paper catalog and now to be listed on a web site as well. Front-line staff take telephone orders for products, which are dispatched by mail to the customers. For simplicity, we will ignore the way in which products are selected for inclusion in the catalog and purchased to fulfill current and future orders.

Historically, there has been a high turnover of front-line staff: this is one of the reasons for developing the web site. A small team of trainers recruits and trains the front-line staff. Finally, there is a customer support department that looks after complaints and returns. For historical reasons, these are located in the organization alongside the trainers in the implementation team.

The At Home head office has decided to implement a web site. Some orders will now be placed directly through the Web; other customers will find what they want on the Web but will prefer to talk to a person when placing their order. There is a new development team, reporting directly to the head office.

EXERCISE 28.1 (Allow five minutes)

Who are the stakeholders in the At Home web site project?

DISCUSSION

Perhaps you will agree with us that all the groups — front-line staff, trainers, and support — are stakeholders in the project. The primary group of users is the customers of the firm. Some of the internal stakeholders will also be users of the web site.

▶ **The Influence of Stakeholders on Your Project**

Unless you consider the implications of the new way of working for the stakeholders who are affected by the changes, you will find that you encounter all sorts of opposition to your efforts to be user centered. There are four types of stakeholder:

- Beneficiaries
- Decision makers
- Gatekeepers
- Workers

A **beneficiary** is a stakeholder who stands to benefit by the project or whose life is going to be made easier. In the web site example, the management plans that the external customers of the organization will benefit. Other beneficiaries are the shareholders or owners of the organization, who will see a better return on their investments through the profits made by the new service. The managers at the head office who commissioned the project will also be beneficiaries if the project is successful — they will be seen to have made a good decision for their business.

A **decision maker** decides what to do in the project. Decision makers are not necessarily limited to the managers in charge of the development staff. If you need to obtain resources from elsewhere in the organization in order to run your project effectively, then the people who control those resources are decision makers in your project. Looking back to our web site example, if you needed to get data from support staff about the type of calls they were getting from customers, then decision makers would need to release that data to you. It may seem surprising that there is a decision to be made in this example, but logs of activity within a department are a powerful management tool. It is quite common for managers to be defensive or protective about releasing details to people elsewhere in the organization.

A **gatekeeper** controls access to other groups. The usual example of a gatekeeper is the secretary of a senior manager. The secretary does not make decisions but, by controlling whom the manager sees, has a powerful influence over the decision-making process. Gatekeepers can appear in unexpected places. In our web site example, the managers of the front-line staff might be gatekeepers if you wanted front-line staff to be participants in the usability activity. Other gatekeepers might be the owners of the customer mailing list.

A **worker** is a stakeholder whose workload will be affected, and usually increase, because of the changes brought about by a project or because he or she has the extra work of learning a new process. A worker might simply be worried that his or her workload *might* increase; perception is more important in this analysis than actual workload. Even if you are asking someone to do something that will save the person time, he or she may worry about the extra time needed to learn the new method or approach.

In the At Home web site example, the front-line staff, logistics staff, trainers, and support staff all count as workers. They may be as worried by the threat of changed work or of losing their jobs as by the possibility of extra work.

> **EXERCISE 28.2 (Allow 10 minutes)**
>
> Consider again the groups affected by your own project. Can you identify the gatekeepers, beneficiaries, decision makers, and workers in those groups?

DISCUSSION

We usually find it easier to identify the beneficiaries and workers than the decision makers and gatekeepers. But the decision makers and gatekeepers are crucial for persuasion activities. They can also help you to win over the workers.

3.2 Choosing Ways to Communicate the Results

Earlier in this chapter, we thought about how best to communicate the results from a usability activity. You learned about four groups of methods:

1.   Involvement and interpretation
2.   Highlights and snapshots
3.   Reports and recommendations
4.   Severity scales and priorities

Table 28.1 presents a summary of the communication techniques and the four groups of stakeholders affected by the project. We have identified the following techniques:

• Techniques we think are the most appropriate for each group
• Techniques we think could be appropriate, but we suggest you use them with caution
• Techniques that seem to us to be not recommended for this group

You may decide that your organization is different, and so our suggestions may not work so well for your circumstances. Table 28.1 is aimed at getting you to think about the choices you make and their impact on the groups in your project.

Table 28.2 lists stages in a usability activity, a communication activity that is possible at each stage, and whether we considered that the activity is suitable for each of the groups. A usability activity could be an evaluation or an activity earlier in the life cycle such as a site visit to find out about users' needs.

We can see from Table 28.2 that, by the time a report is issued, it is not a surprise to any group. The workers have seen what the important findings are, the gatekeepers have been kept in touch, and the decision makers have agreed to the priorities and understand what the findings mean in terms of priorities.

EXERCISE 28.3 (Allow 10 minutes)

Consider the stakeholders in your project. Do you agree with our views in Table 28.2 about the communication activities at each stage of the usability activity? For example, do your gatekeepers want to be kept informed about key findings or would they see it as an unwelcome addition to their workload?

DISCUSSION

One point that you may find surprising is our recommendation to restrict involvement in the report to the beneficiaries. We are not suggesting that the

Table 28.1 Summary of Communication Techniques and the Four Groups of Methods

	The technique is not recommended	Use with caution	The technique is appropriate	
	Involvement and interpretation	Highlights and snapshots	Reports and recommendations	Severity scales and priorities
Beneficiaries	Likely to be participants. Not the main audience for the outcomes.	May want to see them, but not the main audience.	Likely to read the reports; best to get to endorse them recommendations.	Sets priorities and severities according to needs of beneficiaries.
Decision makers	Unlikely to have time for these methods.	May want to see them, but not the first choice of method.	May review the recommendations if asked to decide.	Helps the decision maker decide what to do.
Gatekeepers	Unlikely to have time for these methods.	Helps to give background without taking too much time.	May want to see evidence of types of activity.	The gatekeeper is not the decision maker, so involving a gatekeeper in setting priorities just adds complication.
Workers	Might be the only way to explain why they have to change their working practices.	Likely to be the best route to involvement and interpretation.	Better to get them to help create the recommendations rather than expecting communication by report to win them over.	May regard these as an imposition and try to fight them.

Table 28.2 Stages in a Usability Activity and Communication Activities

Stage of activity	Communication activity	Beneficiaries	Decision makers	Gatekeepers	Workers
Planning	Decide requirement, set priorities	✓	✓		
Throughout the activity	Involvement	✓			One or two
As findings emerge (perhaps daily)	Create snapshots			✓	✓
While extracting the findings and analyzing the data	Interpretation				✓
Collate key findings	Highlights			✓	✓
Consider relative importance of findings	Severity levels and priorities	✓			✓
Product request for action	Severity levels and priorities		✓	✓	
Write report	Report and recommendations	✓			

other groups should be refused access to the report, just that it may be more effective for them to see the report as a record of decisions that have already been made than as a communication channel for the results of your usability activity.

▶ Pugh's Principles of Organizations

Designing and evaluating a user interface in a user-centered way creates two sets of changes for many organizations:

- The changes created by the project for which the user interface is needed
- The changes of approach from traditional to user-centered methods

Both sets of changes are likely to be easier if you understand the complexity of the stakeholders and the impact that different activities may have on them. Pugh (1978) offered four principles for understanding organizational change:

Principal one. Organizations are organisms. They are not mechanisms which can be taken apart and reassembled differently as required. They can be changed, but the change must be approached carefully with the implications for various group-ings thought out and the participants convinced of the worthwhileness from their point of view. They must be given time to understand the change proposals, and to "digest" the changes after they have been made. Do not make changes too frequently. They are too hard to digest and will become dysfunctional or cosmetic.

Principle two. Organizations are occupational and political systems as well as rational resource allocation ones. Each reaction to a change proposal must be inter-preted not only in terms of the rational arguments of what is best for the firm (which are the ones that are used). The reactions must also be understood in relation to the occupational system (how it affects the ways of working, number of jobs, career prospects, motivation, of the particular person or group whose arguments are being heard) and the political system (how it affects the power, status, prestige of the group).

Principle three. All members of an organization operate simultaneously in all three systems — the rational, the occupational and the political ones. Do not make the mistake of becoming cynical and thinking that the occupational and political aspects are all that matter, and that rational arguments are merely rationalizations to defend a particular position. The arguments by which the Personnel Manager, for example, resists a diminution in the department's functions will be real ones, even though they will inevitably be suffused with occupational and political considerations.

Principle four. Change is most likely to be acceptable and effective in those people or departments who are basically successful in their tasks but are experiencing tension or failure in some particular part of their work. They will have the two basic ingredients of confidence in their ability and motivation to change. The next most likely to change are the successful. They will have the confidence that must be invested in developing the motivation. Least likely to understand and accept change are the unsuccessful. They will attempt to protect themselves by rigidity. (pp. 109–110)

From Pugh's principles we learn that change, in this case creating a user interface using a user-centered approach, is a two-way matter. If you are changing your design methods to take account of the users, then you are also asking the users to change. If you are part of a development team or are in a wider organization, then other parts of the organization are also affected by your change of approach.

Consider once again the At Home web site example. The manager who has commis-sioned the new site appears in the development department. "I've just been looking at a big competitor's web site, and it's horrible to use. I've heard about usability — and I want us to do usability on our new site."

EXERCISE 28.4 (Allow five minutes)

Suppose that you are the developer whose manager has just issued the instruction to "do usability." You have been trying to get a more user-centered approach to developing the At Home web site. What would you do first?

DISCUSSION

Before you rush back to Part 2 and start gathering your requirements, remember that not only do you want to build a usable interface but also that this project will be a change for your stakeholders. As you make your plans, you should also think about who will be affected by your project. How big a change will it be for the groups involved? Is anyone likely to resist your attempts to be user centered? Will they want to be part of the activities you plan, or will you need to persuade them?

EXERCISE 28.5 (Allow 10 minutes)

Think about each group of stakeholders in the At Home web site. Why might they help you with usability activities and implementing the system? Are there any reasons why they might be worried about this change?

For example, we thought that the front-line staff might want to help because they will have to deal with calls from customers who have bits of information from the web site. They might be worried by the change because they could see the web site as taking away their jobs — customers will order electronically. The other stakeholder groups are developers, logistics, trainers, customer support, and the head office.

DISCUSSION

Caroline writes: Perhaps I was feeling negative the day I thought about this problem, but I could see many reasons why these groups might be worried by the change. Some of the arguments would be rational and would be likely to come out into the open: more work, the need to acquire new skills, and so on. Some would be deeper fears and might be felt rather than expressed: worries about losing their jobs, uncertainty over whether they can acquire new skills. Note that it is quite common for a single group of people to have two opposite worries at the same time: having more work to do and having less work to do, so there are redundancies.

I could also think of some reasons why they might be enthusiastic about the project and want to help you. For example, the customer support people might expect fewer complaints, and the head office started the project and wants it to be successful. Sometimes you find a usability champion — someone who is already committed to user-centered techniques and is eager to see them used.

▶ Expressed, Felt, and Normative Needs

In Chapter 3, you learned about expressed, felt, and normative needs. Expressed needs are what people say they want. Felt needs are what they feel they want, but they do not want to express them or do not realize that they ought to. Normative needs are what someone other than users thinks the users might need. Usually, each of the stakeholder groups will have a different set of needs.

EXERCISE 28.6 (Allow 10 minutes)

During a meeting to plan the At Home web site, the head of the customer support department is being very negative about the proposed usability activities. He says, "I don't know why you want to involve customers. You should hear the calls they make to us — they are all idiots. It was the same for the last big change. We didn't have the staff to cope. And I certainly can't allow you to have any of my team's time for evaluating the prototype; they are far too busy."

Think about the expressed, felt, and normative needs of the head of the customer support group. How can Pugh's principles help us to understand the objections and possibly find some ways around them?

DISCUSSION

The head of the customer support department is expressing a need to minimize the time his staff spend away from the job. The head of this department may not realize that only a few hours will be necessary, involving only one person at a time, and you can plan the activities for times when fewer calls are received. There may also be worries that the customer support team is seen as failing to keep up with the demands on them. If you can make the customer support department seem more successful, then the department head is less likely to resist change (principle four).

There may also be a felt need to make involving the customer support staff a priority, rather than the less coping customers who form the majority of their work. Or it could be that the customer support team is resentful because effort is going into this new project rather than the existing systems that cause them difficulties. Or the team members may even be worried that they will lose their jobs because customers will not need so much support any more, so the department head could be defending the interests of an occupational group (principle two). You may need to provide some reassurance through political routes, such as showing future budgets with an increase rather than a decrease in the customer support team, so that the change seems less threatening (principle three).

Finally, even if the head of department's fears are groundless, it is important to take them seriously and allow time to adjust and to influence the project. Otherwise resistance can become a rigid refusal to work with the project (principles one and four).

3.3 Is Your Organization User Centered?

If your organization is already quite user centered, then choosing and using a user-centered design technique is not asking a great deal of yourself or your colleagues. If these ideas are new, then you have a lot more persuading to do. Read the description in Box 28.6 of the four stages of acceptance described by Ehrlich and Rohn (1994).

Box 28.6	**Four Stages of Acceptance**

The following four stages of acceptance affect the cost–benefit ratio of performing usability engineering:

Stage One: Skepticism

This stage typifies organizations that have never been involved with UCD [user-centered design]. UCD is viewed with some skepticism because it is unclear what benefits it will bring. They fear that inclusion of usability testing will lengthen their product development cycle, causing them to miss their market window. They are very focused on the product features and its development schedule and are less concerned with the usability of the product. Meeting schedule deadlines gets rewarded over quality, user input, or collaboration with other groups . . .

Stage Two: Curiosity

As organizations move beyond skepticism, they start to become curious about what UCD can offer. They recognize that their products need help and that they might not have the expertise (or perhaps the time) to devote to improving their product's usability. However, they do not quite understand what UI designers or usability engineers do and need some convincing before they are willing to commit money and resources. This group may be open-minded about UCD, but needs to be educated about UI design and usability engineering . . .

Stage Three: Acceptance

The organization understands and relies on the involvement of one or more UCD people on the team [who are] there from the beginning. Their role and expertise are well understood and appreciated as an important part of product development. There is a high degree of communication among members of the group.

Stage Four: Partnership

In this organization, the team is a seamless entity with a clear product vision and purpose, a high level of communication, and a deeply held commitment to providing products that are not only more usable but more useful. A lot of time is spent by everyone getting customer input early in the process and often throughout development. (pp. 76–78)

From Ehrlich and Rohn (1994).

> ### ▶ Usability Maturity

Ehrlich and Rohn described four stages of acceptance:

Stage One: Skepticism
Stage Two: Curiosity
Stage Three: Acceptance
Stage Four: Partnership

We call these stages "usability maturity," which avoids the awkward phrase "the acceptance stage of acceptance." Ehrlich and Rohn's model provides an informal introduction to the ideas of usability maturity. We find that it gives us a quick method of gaining insights into choosing and justifying usability activities, and we will go on to describe these in more detail in the next section.

Since Ehrlich and Rohn developed their model, the idea of usability maturity has been developed in more detail in the INUSE usability maturity model. The INUSE model provides a six-step scale from level X (unrecognized) to level E (institutionalized). It is based on the idea that organizations at a low level of usability maturity will not understand the benefits of a fully user-centered approach to user interface design. As Earthy (1998) noted:

> *The level of human-centeredness of an organization provides information about how best to communicate with an organization about human-centered issues. An organization with a low rating is unlikely to be able to conceive of the processes necessary to bring about the highest levels of maturity. However, they will be able to understand the benefits of the next level of maturity and will be able to see how to extend what they do now in order to improve or move up a level. (pp. 11)*

> ### ▶ Assessing Your Organization's Usability Maturity

The EUSC/INUSE web site at www.lboro.ac.uk /eusc/index_r_ assurance.html has more information on the INUSE usability maturity model. There you will also find a more comprehensive set of questions to ask to assess the level of maturity of an organization.

The INUSE model has a formal framework of questions that allows you or an auditor to assess the level of maturity of an organization. A typical question is as follows (Earthy, 1998):

A. Problem recognition attribute

Does your organization understand that there is a need to improve the usability of your products or services?

Answer: Not at all, partly, fully.

The INUSE model aligns closely with the user-centered design standard: ISO 13407, "Human-centered design for interactive systems." It also allows organizations to assess their usability maturity as part of an overall assessment in terms of ISO/IEC TR 15504-1:1998, "Information technology — software process assessment."

The Ehrlich and Rohn model is sufficient to give you a quick indication of the likely level of usability maturity of your organization (or part of it). If you would like a structured approach to the diagnosis of usability maturity or need to provide evidence of usability maturity, then it is worth pursuing the more detailed approaches in the ISO standards and the INUSE model.

Most of the people and organizations that we come in contact with are at the earlier stages of usability maturity. We hope that by this point in studying this book, you too are at least at stage two (curiosity) and maybe you have even moved to stage three (acceptance).

4 Summary

In this chapter, we have described how to make use of and report your findings from evaluation. We have also discussed who in an organization will be affected by the changes needed to deliver usable interfaces. We have also discussed usability maturity and how to assess the usability maturity of an organization.

In the next chapter, we will think about ways to choose arguments for justifying user-centered techniques — according to the stages of usability maturity — which will help you to win and maintain support for user-centered design.

29

Winning and maintaining support for user-centered design

1 Introduction

If you work alone, have complete control over the interface you are designing, and will be using it yourself, then you will not need to win or maintain support for usability activities and you may find this chapter is not relevant to you. However, most of us have to work with other people, and the interfaces we are trying to design or improve are not just for ourselves — so persuading others to accept what we want them to do is likely to be important. In this chapter, we will use the phrase "your organization" to mean an organization that you are working with or working for. If that does not apply to you, then we suggest that you think instead of an organization that you have encountered in the past or that you might want to work for in the future.

In Chapter 28, you learned about four stages in usability maturity: skepticism, curiosity, acceptance, and partnership. If you are lucky enough to work in an organization at the partnership stage, then you will already have backing for your usability activities. Most of us need a selection of different arguments for winning and maintaining support for user-centered design (UCD). We have grouped them according to the stages of usability maturity.

In practice, you may find that an argument from a different level in the model suits your organization better, or is more suitable for the current stage in your project's development, or just seems more attractive. Often, different stakeholders are at different levels. When you make your choice, bear in mind that expressed needs may be different from felt needs, and that Pugh's principles may push you in the direction of a different set of choices.

2   "Skepticism" Arguments: Finding Out about Usability

In Chapter 1, you learned the ISO 9241:11 definition of usability. It refers to user satisfaction. One way of helping your organization realize that it may need to improve its user interfaces is to find out whether the users are happy with the product. In Part 4, we emphasized user observation as an important method of learning about the usability of your product, and we suggested some other techniques and variations on them. Often, the person new to UI techniques tries one or more of them and discovers that there is a major problem with some part of the interface — or even the whole system. There is a great temptation to rush back to the design team with your findings, which proclaim (in person or in writing): "Our users hate our product because it is horrible to use. You have to do something about it."

> **EXERCISE 29.1 (Allow five minutes)**
>
> Picture yourself as the designer who hears or reads the previous remark. What might your reaction be?
>
> **DISCUSSION**
>
> Occasionally a generous and empathetic designer will say, "Oh no! We must do all we can to fix it." But more typical reactions include the following:
>
> Anger: "What right have you got to criticize me?"
>
> Defensive: "We're doing our best for these people, we can't do any more."
>
> Denial: "Well I don't think so. Why are you saying that?"
>
> Dismissive: "They must be stupid if they use it like that."
>
> Surprise: "They weren't supposed to use it like that!"
>
> Upset: "How can you be so horrible to me when you know I've worked so hard on this?"

If your organization is at the "skepticism" stage, then you are more likely to meet these negative reactions than positive ones. By portraying the designer's efforts as unsuccessful, you are likely to provoke resistance and denial. Recall Pugh's (1978) fourth principle.

> *Change is most likely to be acceptable and effective in those people or departments who are basically successful in their tasks but are experiencing tension or failure in some particular part of their work. They will have the two basic ingredients of confidence in their ability and motivation to change. The next most likely to change are the successful. They will have the confidence that must be invested in developing the motivation. Least likely to understand and accept change are the unsuccessful. They will attempt to protect themselves by rigidity. (p. 110)*

As a user interface designer, you may find yourself involved in three different types of usability project:

- The project or subproject of running a usability activity such as an evaluation and getting action on the findings.
- The overall project of developing a user interface.
- The underlying project of persuading your team or organization to become more user centered. As Boddy and Buchanan (1992) note:

Projects begin in a loose and unstructured way. Someone has an idea, sees a possibility, observes an opportunity for improvement. Through a process of trying the idea on colleagues, discussing how it might work, lobbying for support, an identifiable project comes into being. (pp. 73–74)

If your organization is at the skepticism stage, it is likely that stakeholders in your project have priorities that are different from yours and that do not yet fit comfortably with user-centered interface design. According to Boddy and Buchanan (1992):

The areas concerned probably report to a different senior manager and have their own priorities and interest. They may be indifferent to the project or strongly opposed to it, especially if it conflicts with personal ambitions. They may also be under pressure from other changes taking place in the business — and can only cope with so much. Project managers need to spend time and effort anticipating what they need from other areas, and securing their ownership and support. (p. 89)

Boddy and Buchanan are talking about project managers, but it applies equally to the process of managing your project — any of the three types of usability projects we mentioned.

2.1 Organizational Goals That May Conflict with Usability

Grudin (1991) has a selection of "goals that shape interfaces when users' voices are not heard":

SOFTWARE DEVELOPMENT GOALS:

Certain constraints that can affect the interface are particularly familiar because they force tradeoffs or compromises in other aspects of software development. These competing goals are often the greatest impediment to usability. Because most developers are all too aware of them, I mention them and then focus on the more subtle problems that often escape notice. The relative lack of attention by no means suggests relative lack of importance. (p. 166)

Grudin mentions goals such as minimizing memory and processor use, producing modular code, and producing reliable, maintainable, and secure software. He also mentions the cognitive capabilities that we all share as humans, such as

our inability to forget. . . . If we could put out of mind what we know about how a computer works or how we use it, we could better imagine how someone else less

knowledgeable or with a different job will experience it. But this we cannot do.
(p. 167)

We have already covered this problem, of the designer or software developer under-standing the user's reactions to the system, earlier in this book. But Grudin reminds us that the designer has another intellectually challenging task: understanding and working with the complexity of the software or system design itself. These create business goals for the design:

- An architecture that is easy for the designers to understand while working on it
- A consistent design from the point of view of its implementation
- A simple design

Grudin (1991) used the following example:

Another desktop metaphor example illustrates the trade-off between simplicity and a potentially useful complexity. Many systems represent all directories (collections of documents or other files) by folder icons. Some systems add complexity by also providing cabinet icons and cabinet drawer icons. Like the folder icons, these cor-respond to directories, essentially indistinguishable to the system (e.g., one can place a cabinet inside a folder just as easily as the other way around). Does having three different representations for directories complicate things? The complexity is intro-duced to provide a methodical way to organize directories hierarchically. Strictly to help users manage their files, the designers added a distinction that is not required by the system. Having used both systems, I feel that in this case the designers wisely overcame the attraction of simplicity (although opinions vary). (p. 172)

In Part 3 we discussed some of the problems that can result from the use of metaphor.

Sometimes in our role as user interface designers, we forget that other developers are also people and want to do well in their jobs. They have career goals that may align with or be different from organizational goals. Grudin mentions career goals such as wanting to stay current in their technical skills, wanting to protect their own area of responsibilities, and wanting to express themselves.

Recall Pugh's (1978) first principle.

Principal one. Organizations are organisms. They are not mechanisms which can be taken apart and reassembled differently as required. They can be changed, but the change must be approached carefully with the implications for various group-ings thought out and the participants convinced of the worthwhileness from their point of view. (p. 172)

If you are interested in managing teams, decision making, or competing in the marketplace, then we recommend following up Grudin's original article.

Grudin points out that the usability concerns may cause difficulties in organizing the team and communicating within it. Grudin gives the example of moving a menu item to a lower level in a hierarchy, which is where the user needs it, perhaps making the design look unbalanced or messy on paper. It could also mean that a developer's work becomes apparently subordinate to some other function. Maybe someone who has thought of herself or himself as working on one menu area now has to mentally (or physically) move groups to work within another area. The problem can be worse if a lower-status group (such as the help authors) suggest a change to a higher-status group (such as the system architects).

3 "Skepticism" Arguments: Creating Curiosity

Despite all these objections, it is possible to overcome skepticism and create curiosity within your organization. We will explain three strategies for overcoming skepticism:

- Start small.
- Find a champion.
- Be an objective voice.

3.1 Start Small

Even if you have a grand plan for several major iterations through investigation and analysis, design, and evaluation, it is often easier to get agreement for a small first step.

- By starting small, you run less risk of your usability activity being seen as a threat.
- You may not need to ask for a public commitment of resources. Asking for 10 minutes of someone's time is a lot easier than asking for several days or weeks.
- You are more likely to be able to use informal contacts and methods of working.

Here is an example. One of us had a student who ran his very first evaluation with a user who happened to have a shared interest outside work — they had become friends. He planned an evaluation of a paper prototype to take about half an hour. The evaluation took place during lunch, with the incentive of a sandwich. This meant that there was no need to go through elaborate requests for taking the user away from his work. Even this small initial evaluation gave the student immediate feedback: a couple of the design ideas were poor, some looked promising but needed further work, and one was likely to be welcomed by the users. Thus,

- The student had an opportunity to practice evaluation in a nonthreatening environment. He was able to improve his interview plan. He also found that he could get through more tasks than he expected in half an hour.
- He was able to report back to the development team what the user had said. There was no need to give precise details of the venue or incentive.

There was also a benefit for more formal evaluations later: the user had some understanding of the evaluation process, and when asked again to release a colleague for another evaluation, he was happy to give permission.

The low-key approach of trying small-scale activities helps to disseminate the message to the stakeholders quietly — and allows you to find out what support you need from them.

3.2 Find a Champion

In our discussion of the At Home web site stakeholders in Chapter 28, we thought about how some stakeholders might see usability activities as a threat but others might welcome them. A **usability champion** is a stakeholder who helps a usability activity by providing resources or other backing.

Mayhew (1999) describes how a powerful individual can become a usability champion — sometimes without being initially all that interested in usability ideas. She uses the terms "Usability Engineering" and "Usability Lifecycle" for her user-centered approach to development.

> *Sometimes a single individual plays the role of change agent. This individual may be at any management level, from a project leader who decides to hire a usability expert onto his or her project team, to a vice president of research and development who decides to make usability a part of his or her organizational territory. In this case, it is the vision of a single individual that motivates change, and it is that individual's raw organizational power that accomplishes change. . . . one client organization had a powerful vice president who seized upon Usability Engineering as a way to expand his organizational turf. . . . In another client organization, a project manager saw a career opportunity in introducing and implementing the Usability Lifecycle approach. (p. 142)*

If you want a good short book about usability to help convince a potential usability champion, try Krug (2000).

Your champion could be someone in your own group or department, or from elsewhere. For example, a marketing person might become interested because she sees your product losing market share to another product that has better usability, or the support manager may be getting an excessive number of calls that are traced to usability problems.

3.3 Be an Objective Voice

Our third suggestion is to offer a usability activity as a way of getting an objective solution if there are disagreements about the best way to proceed within an interface development project. As Grudin's examples demonstrate, there are many different pressures on developers. These pressures can escalate into conflicts over what to do. A usability activity — investigating the users' needs or testing a prototype of each proposed design — provides an outside, objective voice that can allow the parties to the dispute to break out of an entrenched position and resolve their differences.

EXERCISE 29.2 (Allow five minutes)

Look back to the At Home web site example discussed in Chapter 28. Which of the three strategies for overcoming skepticism is appropriate for this organization?

DISCUSSION

In Exercise 28.1, we looked at the stakeholders who might be affected by the At Home web site project. One of the stakeholders is the manager, mentioned in Exercise 28.4, who commissioned the web site. He has read an article about usability and seems enthusiastic about it. He could be a usability champion for the usability activities.

4 | "Curiosity" Arguments: Moving toward Acceptance

Let us suppose that your organization has already got to the curiosity stage of usability maturity. Perhaps you found a champion or ran a usability activity then successfully communicated the results and got action on the findings. The next challenge is to move from isolated activities toward a coherent program of user interface design and evaluation as described in the earlier units of this course. At this stage of usability maturity, more resources are required and you are likely to need to justify your requests. As Bias (1994) notes:

> Good usability of computer products is not a luxury; customers are unequivocal in their call for more usable products. Most executives are aware of this. Still, the usability engineer labors in an area where all the related disciplines have long established metrics for quantifying their costs and benefits. Lines of code, person-months, problem tracking reports, bugs per thousand lines of code, and system test scenarios are just a handful of the many quantitative tools that measure effort and quality — tools that engineers and computer scientists deal with so facilely. It is this milieu that the usability engineer enters, admonishing that the product must be made "more usable."

> And this works fine as long as development time and money are not tight and the product manager acknowledges the value of usability engineering. But if time is tight, money is constrained, the product manager is not sold on the value of usability engineering, or even if this product manager is simply being economical, the usability engineer is likely to hear one of the following questions in response:

> How much more usable must the product be?

> How will we know if our product is more usable?

> What will qualify as "usable enough"?

> How much will it cost me to make it more usable?

> How much additional revenue will this added usability yield? (p. 4)

EXERCISE 29.3 (Allow 15 minutes)

In an earlier exercise, you thought about making suggestions about "doing usability" for the At Home web site. Now suppose that the finance manager has heard about the iterative design process that you have suggested to the development team. Think back to Part 2 (where you learned about requirements), Part 3 (where we discussed work reengineering), and Part 4 (where we went through the theory of evaluation). Which areas of theory might help to justify your activities to a finance manager?

DISCUSSION

Chapter 6 describes usability requirements, including quantitative targets. These would help to answer the question "What will qualify as usable enough?"

> The theory of work reengineering, discussed in Chapter 8, will help you to establish how much it costs to do the work now and how much the new processes are likely to cost.
>
> Chapter 27 explains how to vary user observations by changing the *measure* element so that they become performance measurement evaluations with quantitative outputs.

A technique is **cost justified** if the savings achieved by using the technique are greater than its expense. By this point you should have plenty of ideas about the usability techniques you would want to use on a project and how much they are likely to cost. Where can you find the savings?

4.1 Cost of Staff Time and Accuracy

In many service businesses, a major cost is staff time. This could be time per customer call, time per sale, or time that a member of staff is being kept from some other work.

Returning once more to the At Home example, the business offers a free phone telephone support line to its customers. The cost of the telephone support staff is a pure cost to the business. If a customer rings up to consider an order, then the time to access the order information is costing the business money in three ways: the cost of the staff, the cost of the telephone call, and the possible risk of lost business if the customer gets tired of waiting and goes elsewhere.

Requirements based on staff time and the degree of success in use of the system are useful in two ways:

- Finding out what the targets should be is a good way of justifying investigation activities.
- Finding out whether the UI is likely to cause or prevent lost time due to errors and work arounds can have a big impact on the overall success or failure of the system.

> **EXERCISE 29.4 (Allow 15 minutes)**
>
> Your manager wants to do an evaluation activity to find out whether your new system is meeting its usability requirements for staff time. Which evaluation techniques would you recommend?
>
> **DISCUSSION**
>
> For example, you could do the following:
>
> - Observe staff members using the system and record the times they take to do typical activities.
> - Compare the time taken with the targets in the usability requirements.

Suppose your target is that it should take X minutes of staff time to work each item. If your observed time is $Y\%$ greater than your target, then your cost justification is

Box 29.1	**Usability in a Government System**

One large government system had poor usability. The users were given function groups based on different roles. To deal with a typical set of business tasks, users constantly had to swap roles. The performance measurement (based on the system statistics) showed that the computer was spending 10% of its processing time dealing with role swap requests. Arranging the function groups in a way that suited the work and avoided role swap requests meant that the government was able to avoid the purchase of several hundreds of thousands of dollars of extra computing power.

$$\text{Expected cost} = (\text{Cost per minute of staff time}) \times (\text{Number of items}) \times \text{X}$$
$$\text{Actual cost} = \frac{(\text{Cost per minute of staff time}) \times (\text{Number of items}) \times \text{X}(100 + \text{y})}{100}$$

A cost justification based on staff time works best in the following circumstances:

- You have a high cost per minute of staff time.
- There is a large number of work items.
- The observed time is much greater than the target time.

4.2 Performance Measurement: Computer Time

For some types of computer system, where a large server is involved or where computer time is an issue, it may be possible to justify usability activities by looking at the computer performance issues. When calculating the size of computer needed to support hundreds or thousands of transactions, the performance specialists assume that each person is choosing the correct transaction for the business task in hand. However, if you can demonstrate that the typical user is making and correcting mistakes or choosing the wrong transaction, then this upsets the performance calculations. This can provide a powerful cost-driven argument for usability changes. See the example in Box 29.1.

4.3 Costs of Learning and Training

Perhaps the biggest implementation risk, if your organization produces packaged products, is the risk that the buyer cannot make it work right from the start. The initial experience — the out-of-the-box experience — can establish the entire attitude of the user to the product (see Figure 29.1). Perhaps you can think of a software package you installed that has never worked or some gadget you bought on a wave of enthusiasm that failed to live up to the promise on the package. Maybe you returned it, went to a competitor, lost interest in products of that type — or persisted with it, but complained to your friends and colleagues about it. Any of these outcomes would have an effect on the revenues of the product maker. These products can simply fail in the market place because no one considered the initial learning experience.

Figure 29.1 The out-of-the-box experience can establish the entire attitude of the user to the product.

Some of the consumer movements, such as the Consumers Association in the UK (publishers of *Which?* magazine, a product comparison and investigation monthly similar to *Consumer Reports* in the United States), have been assessing the usability of packaged products for many years. This trend is beginning to migrate to the assessment of computer products. For example, the UK *PC Magazine* explicitly assesses usability for each product it reviews. If your products fall into this category, then you will probably find it easy to justify observational techniques. The most important criterion in your usability requirements is likely to be learnability.

Perhaps your product has nothing to do with the consumer market. Do not assume that the out-of-the-box experience is irrelevant to you. For example, users are notoriously impatient with help systems, web sites providing information, and product tutorials. You may be able to think of other systems or subsystems where learnability is crucial.

Box 29.2	**Training Costs for a Government System**

Some years ago, more than 25,000 staff had to be trained on the large government system mentioned in Box 29.1. Each trainee's time cost the organization about 15 cents per minute. Asking staff to spend half a day (about four hours) on training meant $4 \times 60 = 240$ minutes were spent by each trainee. At 15 cents per minute, that is $36 per person. This does not sound expensive until you remember that more than 25,000 staff needed training: $25,000 \times \$36 = \$900,000$. Saving even half a day of training had a big financial impact.

However, some products have to be learned because they support sophisticated tasks. In other cases, you may want to compromise learnability and have less satisfied users initially, because you have built the product to be extremely efficient for experienced users.

4.4 Continuing Support Costs

Supposing that your user struggles on through that initial out-of-the-box experience. What happens when that user gets to the next round of problems?

You may offer training, telephone support, or even onsite support. The costs of these remedies can be considerable, as the example in Box 29.2 shows. Even if your system has fewer users than the example in Box 29.1, it can still be worth investigating how long your users should be spending learning to use the system. During the time that users spend training, they will not be able to fulfill their normal duties and, unless there are a lot of them, customer service may suffer.

There can also be hidden costs of training. Simply doing less training is not necessarily the answer. Most users learn a little during their formal training program and then learn a lot more as they try to use the system in their everyday work. When you did the investigation activities in Chapters 3 and 4, you probably found that when users have a problem they do not usually ask for more training. Quite likely they do not even call the support line. What they mostly do is turn to the most convenient and sympathetic people around and ask them how to solve the problem. Now you have one problem causing two people to lose time — or else they muddle through, being less efficient than they could be.

4.5 Cost of Support

Help lines can be a fruitful source of ideas for justifying usability activities. The people who deal with user calls develop a deep knowledge of exactly what is wrong with your products. Also, many organizations offer a free help line or subsidize its cost, so if you can cut down on calls to the help line, then you are justifying your expenditure on usability activities. To establish the possible savings from cost of support, consider the following points:

- Set targets for each type of call and how long you expect them to take.
- Investigate the number and length of calls.
- Organize the calls by type of problem encountered.
- Compare the number of calls you receive with the targets you expect.

Your potential cost saving is the estimated number of support calls that will be avoided multiplied by the average length of a support call and the cost per minute of providing the support.

However, here is a cautionary tale. A usability practitioner sent me the description in Box 29.3 of the full range of problems she found when making use of data from support calls. The story about the muffin was true.

4.6 Cost of Maintenance and Change

Most large, or continuing, systems have a backlog of change requests and defects to fix. Working on the backlog is rarely the most glamorous job in the organization, and there is often a lot of pressure to keep up releases and deliver them quickly. If you can deliver a system that meets users' needs from the start, then you will cut down the change requests. Development staff can be released to work on new projects.

Here is how to establish the possible savings from maintenance and change:

- Find out how many change requests relating to user requirements were raised on a similar or typical previous project for your organization.
- Estimate how many could have been avoided by taking a more user-centered approach. At first, it is probably best to be very conservative in your estimate — perhaps taking the view that 10% of change requests could have been avoided.
- Find out the average cost of a change request. In some organizations, this is quite easy because each request has a cost or manpower estimate attached to it. If your organization does not maintain those figures, you may have to gather some estimates from colleagues or do some yourself.

Your potential cost saving is the estimated number of change requests that will be avoided multiplied by the average cost of a change request.

4.7 Cost Justification Is Not the Whole Story

Although your management will often ask for a cost justification, which is a rational justification, Pugh's principles explain that the rational explanation is not the only one that counts. We also have to consider the management's political and occupational reactions to your proposal. As Boddy and Buchanan (1992) note:

> *Creating a convincing vision of the change is crucial. People expect change to be disruptive — so they need to be convinced the pain will be worth it . . . [you need to] work with senior management to create and sell that vision, to give the change a legitimacy which encourages others to support it. Top management setting out con-*

Box 29.3	**Usability Problems Logged by a Support Center**

It depends . . . on the quality of data collected by your customer service group. In one situation, we set up categories in the call-tracking system and tried to measure the number of calls on a specific problem, time spent on certain types of problems, and so on, but found the data a little shaky. For our specific product and customer base, we found things like:

A customer might call with several problems. If the support rep logged them all separately, it inflated that rep's call statistics. If they didn't, we couldn't get at all of the problems. It was a flaw in the logging system.

It's essential to track the number of customers as well as the number of raw calls. We had one customer who called every single morning to be walked through a simple (really!) daily procedure. That's a lot of calls. But it didn't mean that our customers were actually having trouble with the procedure.

It can be difficult to determine how long it took to resolve a problem. Suppose a customer is on the phone for one hour. A complex problem? A talkative customer? Support rep put the customer on hold while she went down to the cafeteria for a muffin? Hard to say.

Or suppose a customer calls many times over several weeks. A complex problem? The customer has really high staff turnover? Problem takes two minutes to solve once the customer remembers her password? (Actually, the latter situation will tend to be recorded in increasingly colorful terms in the call notes.)

Once we realized that the statistics were mushy, we started reading the call notes in detail. Some really long calls would be logged as "walked customer through fixing network problem." Period. Others would be recorded in exquisite detail, with attachments, screen captures, etc. We learned a lot from these notes, both about our customers and our customer service staff. . . .

So yes, really interesting and useful information came from examining the customer service traffic, but not in the way we initially expected it. A lot of good information came from just talking to the customer service group and occasionally from just hanging around outside their cubicles eavesdropping on their frustration level.

Personal communication, usability practitioner in the United States.
(Permission to quote anonymously.)

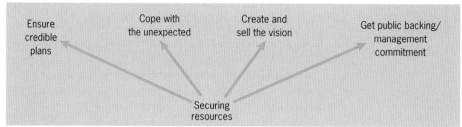

Figure 29.2 Managing up: Four ways of securing resources. (Adapted from Boddy and Buchanan, 1992.)

> *vincing reasons for the change and associated turmoil provides a powerful incentive for others to give it their support. (p. 76)*

Although management frequently likes to have the plans expressed in cost justification terms, the *process* of gaining their support is often the important outcome. Once their support is in place, then you have a powerful ally in the process of negotiating the realization of the plan with other groups (see Figure 29.2).

You are likely to need the following:

- *A credible plan.* Your plan needs to include the activities you propose, the justification of costs and other resources, and the reports or other deliverables that you will produce.
- *An analysis of any risks.* How will you cope with the unexpected? What is the impact on other stakeholders? If something goes wrong, do you have a contingency plan?
- *Support from other groups.* If stakeholders' first contact with your plans is in a formal document, they may see this as extra work rather than an opportunity. You may need to lobby them ahead of time by "creating and selling the vision" of what your activities will achieve for them.
- *Public backing.* Often, you need management to support you by making your activities a political priority as well as by giving you the budget and other resources that you ask for in your plan.

EXERCISE 29.5 (Allow 15 minutes)

As a member of the At Home web site development team, you found a usability champion and your organization is now at the curiosity stage of usability maturity. Your champion wants you to justify a full program of user-centered design activities starting with requirements investigation and continuing through design of at least two rounds of prototypes. You also want to evaluate your ideas and prototypes with users at every stage. You recall that the manager of the customer support department reacted badly to your suggestions about involving users, but you need staff from the customer support department to test the parts of the system that they will use. How can you obtain these resources?

DISCUSSION

Boddy and Buchanan suggest that you need a plan that is credible — to the manager of the customer support department as well as to the other stakeholders. A cost justification that looks at cost of support might increase the credibility of the plan, and the manager of the customer support department might even be willing to help you with the justification. Even though your organization as a whole is at the curiosity stage, this key stakeholder is still skeptical, so it might be worth planning a small initial activity to build curiosity about usability. The public backing from your champion might help persuade the difficult manager to release one or two staff members for a small activity. You'll also need to think about risks: if you fail to convince the difficult manager, what impact will that have on your overall program of activities? Could you delay involving users from the customer support department until other departments have been involved, perhaps spreading some enthusiasm and creating the vision of the benefits of usability?

5   "Acceptance" Arguments: Maintaining Momentum

Your first round of user interface design has been a success: the users are pleased that the system is improving; the development team agreed to make some changes; management has offered to support your next activity. What can possibly go wrong?

5.1 Be Sensitive to the Stage of the Project

It often happens that you want to put a "good" version of the product in front of the users in the evaluation so that they are not distracted or disconcerted by defects or crashes. However, this can mean that the evaluation happens so near to the ship date, or the go-live date, that there is no time to make changes. By then, the requirements are frozen and the cost of change is high. Also, nearly all projects slip, so there is greater political risk in making changes as the promised delivery date draws near. Figure 29.3 illustrates the general case: the scale will depend on your particular project.

You can see from Figure 29.3 that earlier, smaller evaluations during the development phase are likely to have a better chance of success. As Ehrlich and Rohn (1994) note:

> *"Short and Sweet" vs. Comprehensive Evaluations. An area that has a significant effect on the cost-benefit ratio is selecting the appropriate method for the need. For instance, if the product team has two days to make a decision on a particular design detail, planning and implementing a comprehensive lab observation with 12 participants whose profiles match the target customers' will not help them. Performing a "short and sweet" evaluation with a handful of participants and producing results within the product team's time frame will help them. (p. 99)*

However, if you *only* do short and sweet evaluations, you may be missing the big picture. Perhaps that single dialog box is more usable, but overall the system is not going to meet the users' goals. It is great to get a lot of requests to do quick

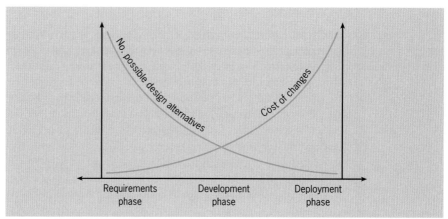

Figure 29.3 The number of possible designs decreases as the cost to make changes increases. (From Ehrlich and Rohn, 1994.)

evaluations on particular points, but from time to time stand back and ask, "Should we be looking at the whole system here?"

5.2 Balance Delivery and Usability

It is also important to remember that a clear, simple, and easy-to-use interface will still be seen as unusable if it is in front of an inaccurate, slow, buggy, or unreliable system. If a user interface change means alterations to several underlying modules, then the development manager may resist that change because of the risk that alterations in many places may introduce defects. The person in charge of a project frequently has to juggle the management of changes. According to Mayhew and Bias (1994):

> [E]ven the most convincing cost-benefit analysis can fall on deaf ears if crucial organizational incentives are not in place.

> For example, software managers are typically held accountable for staying within planned budgets and schedules and for providing agreed-upon functionality. Their incentives — performance reviews, salaries and promotions — are tied to these deliverables. Software managers are not typically held accountable for such things as user productivity (in an internal development organization) or sales (in a vendor company). Other organizations (user groups and sales and marketing staff, respectively) are held accountable for these things, in spite of the fact that it is the user interface to the software that largely determines these outcomes.

> For example, interface design often seems to be driven by the need for ease of implementation (that is, by what is easiest to implement from a technical point of view and easiest to manage from an organizational point of view) rather than by an analysis of user tasks and requirements. This is because ease of implementation helps a project to stay within budget and schedule constraints.

. . . the development manager is held accountable for budget and schedule goals and is not held accountable for usability. (p. 292)

If you look back at Figure 29.3, you will see that the cost of change is lowest early in the requirements phase, as plans are being made and objectives agreed on. This is why Chapter 1 emphasizes the need for early usability activities. If you can get the big picture correct at the start, then you can do your short and sweet evaluations later, with confidence that your iterations are tuning up the finer details.

5.3 Manage User Expectations

Initially, your users are likely to be pleased that you are asking their opinions and taking notice of them. However, do not get over-enthusiastic and promise more than you can deliver.

- The developers may not agree with your requests, for many reasons.
- It may not be technically possible to implement what you have designed.
- Other people who are affected by the change may block it.

It is best to under-promise and then over-deliver.

5.4 Do Not Become Stuck on One Technique

Rosenbaum, Rohn, and Hamburg (2000) carried out a survey of usability practitioners and user interface designers to rate the usability methods and organizational approaches that they considered to be the most effective for achieving strategic usability — moving from single activities to a user-centered approach to systems design and development. The three top methods were all varieties of usability testing: testing in a lab (number one), usability testing without a lab or outside a lab (number two), and usability testing with a portable lab (number three). We agree that usability testing is an important technique, and that is why this book has devoted most of Part 4 to it.

The pitfall is that stakeholders can become so impressed with the results of usability testing that they think that "doing usability" *means* doing testing.

6   "Partnership": The Benefits

We have spent much of this chapter and Chapter 28 discussing organizations where usability is not yet a primary concern in user interface design: communicating the results of usability activities, overcoming objections to user-centered design, and helping your organization move to a greater level of usability maturity. If your organization is already at the partnership stage, then you may have found some of this irrelevant. Understanding users and their needs and involving them in testing throughout the life cycle are likely to be natural parts of your development life cycle, as shown in Figure 29.4.

Most of us work in or with organizations that are not yet at the partnership stage. The final message of this chapter and this book is to keep working toward partnership.

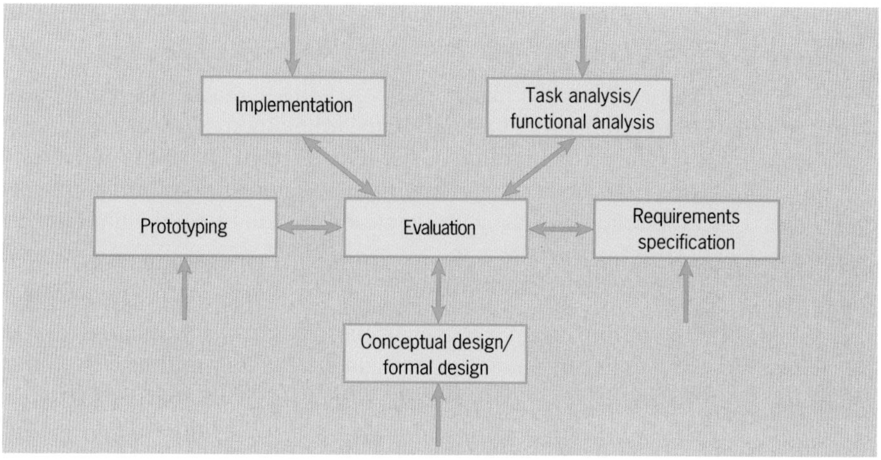

Figure 29.4 The star life cycle. (From Hix and Hartson, 1993.)

Involving users in user interface design is worth the effort. Each iteration around the life cycle gets easier, and you will find that delivering user interfaces that really work well for their users is tremendously rewarding.

7 Summary

This chapter, in conjunction with Chapter 28, has been about establishing user-centered approaches within your organization. We introduced ways to win and maintain support for user-centered design. These include starting small, finding a usability champion, and using usability activities as an objective voice. We went on to look at ways of cost-justifying usability activities, and we finished by considering ways of maintaining momentum and the importance of keeping a focus on the users throughout the development life cycle. The information presented in this chapter builds on and extends the information presented in Chapter 28 — how to make the best use of your findings, who is affected by the changes they bring about, and how to win support for usability activities.

30
Summary

We have now reached the end of this book. At the beginning we stated our aims, which were to communicate to, and impress upon you, the reader, that

- UI development should be user centered.
- Developing a UI should be an iterative process; it requires repeated prototyping and evaluation, as well as close collaboration with users and other stakeholders.
- A UI is an ensemble of elements. It is necessary to look at the relationship among these elements in order to understand the whole.

We hope that this viewpoint has come across. As presented, these points mostly describe the theoretical perspective of the book. The book, however, has also taken a very practical go-and-do-it-now approach (remember all those exercises?), so by now you will have gained a range of skills that you can apply to user interface design and evaluation.

We realize, though, that we have presented our theoretical viewpoint and our practical how-to-do-usability guidance in a great number of pages. So in this chapter we felt it would be useful to reiterate the most important points to take away from this book.

1. User-centered system design focuses on people, their work, their work environments, and how technology can best be deployed and designed to support them.

Therefore, you *must* involve real users throughout the life cycle — in requirements, in design, in evaluation — at all stages. You need to discover, first hand, who the actual real users are, what they want to do with the system, and where they undertake their work. Armed with this knowledge you will then be in a position to arrive at an optimal solution — in terms of UI look and feel, input and output devices, and so on — that should meet the need of the users and support them in what they want or need to do with the system.

2. Prototyping is an appropriate way to communicate design information to users, and crucially to facilitate their input in the iterative design/development process.

We would highly recommend, in particular, the use of low-fidelity (paper) prototypes, which include such things as screen mockups, sketches, storyboards, and even content diagrams. They can be used throughout the design life cycle to get reactions to designs, test ideas (say, for example, in relation to the meaningfulness of icons or commands), and communicate the physical design to users. Although they have a few limitations, as described in Chapter 6, on the plus side they are one of the quickest and cheapest ways to test your design — iteratively — with users. As they are easily changeable, they work well in rapid test-revise-retest cycles of evaluation, with real users, at any stage of the design life cycle.

Furthermore, one of our evaluation tips in Chapter 21 was *test early, test often*. Low-fidelity prototypes support this approach. We are not advocating that there is no place for high-fidelity prototypes; however, we are saying that as high-fidelity prototypes are based on software, they can take a bit of time to develop and can be far less easy to change than paper prototypes.

3.   Evaluation isn't hard — it mainly requires thinking through and planning.

In this book, we have equipped you with the theoretical underpinnings for conducting evaluations. We have outlined the evaluation process and then looked at each of the activities in the evaluation process. We have presented two evaluation techniques in detail — user observations and inspections — and demonstrated how you can tailor the method of each technique by varying the way the elements of *observe*, *listen*, *compare*, and *measure* are combined. And we showed that evaluations are iterative in nature. More practically, we have presented a flexible, hands-on procedure for undertaking evaluations, which you should be able to apply easily. We have also provided a selection of evaluation tips that we hope you will find helpful.

4.   You can, and should, endeavor to win and maintain support for user-centered design.

In this book, we have discussed approaches that can be used to communicate your findings in order to influence others to incorporate the iterative cycles of design, development, and evaluation of UIs in their development life cycle and to win support for usability activities. If you have been convinced by the aims and messages of this book, then we hope that you, too, will become a spokesperson for taking an iterative, user-centered approach to user interface design and evaluation.

Glossary

Above the fold A term taken from newspaper design, which describes the uppermost half of the front page where the most eye-catching stories are placed. For web design, this is the part of the web page that can be seen without scrolling.

Accessibility An approach which ensures that a **UI** is designed to be usable by the widest group of people possible, especially by **users** with physical, visual, or hearing disabilities, and who may be using support tools or assistive technologies to use the UI.

Action An individual operation or step that needs to be undertaken as part of a **task**, which in turn is an activity undertaken, or believed to be required to achieve a **goal**. Actions, as part of tasks, are performed at a very specific and detailed level. For example, for the task of typing the word "the," three actions are required: typing the letter *t*, typing the letter *h*, and typing the letter *e*.

Affordance An aspect of an object that makes it obvious how the object could be used. For example, a panel on a door signals "push" to open the door, while a vertical handle indicates "pull" to open it. In **HCI** usage, this term has been modified from its original use by the perceptual psychologist J. J. Gibson.

Analogue data Data that have an infinite number of steps or increments. Temperature is an example of analogue data. Analogue data, which is handled by **continuous input devices**, is common in sounds, movements, and images. Computers are designed to cope with **digital data** and so can find analogue data difficult to handle.

Analysis The activity of examining data to make sense of it. For **requirements gathering**, analysis involves examining the information gathered so it may be translated into design requirements. For example, if the **users** of an application for learning math concepts will be children under 10 years of age, then it is necessary to design the **user interface** for the manual skills and computing abilities of the under 10s. This includes, among other things, easily understood terminology or picture icons, colorful and attractive screens, easy navigational structures, and perhaps music, sound, or a spoken narrative to guide the children using the application.

For **evaluation**, analysis involves collating and summarizing the **evaluation data** collected and identifying any **usability problems** so recommendations can be made as to how they may be rectified.

Anthropomorphic An **interaction style** that aims to interact with **users** in the same way that humans interact with each other. Examples include natural language interfaces and interfaces that recognize gestures, facial expressions, or eye movements.

Artifact An object produced through human workmanship rather than occurring naturally; an object or aid which helps in the performance of **tasks**. In **HCI**, artifact is sometimes used to refer to the **computer system** being developed.

Assessment evaluation Evaluations carried out at an early or midway stage in the design life cycle, after the feedback from the exploratory sessions has been incorporated into the designs and the **conceptual design** has been created. An assessment evaluation is conducted using **task descriptions** in order to validate that the understanding of the requirements is correct and to determine whether the **users'** **tasks** are supported. Assessment evaluations are undertaken to identify **usability problems**.

Associative link A type of **link** that links one part of a web page to another part. Associative links can often be found in contents lists at the top of a long page; selecting one causes the browser to jump to the selected section. Other types of link found on web sites include **<u>See also links</u>** and **structural navigation links**.

Attitude The opinion or view engendered in users by a **computer system**. Where computer systems are usable (that is, easy to learn and easy to use), their attitudes will be positive.

Beneficiary A **stakeholder** who stands to benefit from a project.

Business goal A business goal is something an organization wants to achieve. The organization may see development or change of a **computer system** as important to meeting the business goal.

Card sort A technique for structuring information such as menus that involves writing the various concepts onto different cards and asking the **users** to group these into a number of piles, each of which will correspond to a menu.

Cathode ray tube (CRT) The technology behind the conventional desktop visual display unit (VDU).

Class An abstraction of a group of **primary task objects**. For example, in the digital library, *resource* is an abstraction of a *book*, *CD-ROM*, *video*, or *journal*. In other words, it contains the attributes that are common to all of these objects, such as title, author, and year of publication.

Classic life cycle A predominantly sequential life cycle model where each phase of the software life cycle is completely satisfied before the next begins.

Closed question A question in which the respondent is asked to select an answer from a predetermined set of alternative replies.

Closure One of the **Gestalt** laws, which says we tend to see an incomplete element as complete — that is, we ignore missing information and fill in the gap.

Cocktail party phenomenon A phenomenon identified in cognitive psychology that describes the way in which we are able to interact within noisy environments, such as cocktail parties, by focusing on a single conversation and picking out parts of other conversations as they interest us. This is relevant to **UI design**, as **users** need to be encouraged to focus on the important information on the screen, to be distracted only by vital information such as error messages.

Coding scheme A method of assigning a group, number, or label to an item of data. Establishing a coding scheme, either in advance or after the **evaluation data** have been collected, often speeds up the work of reviewing **qualitative data** obtained from an evaluation.

Cognitive task analysis Cognitive task analysis techniques, or cognitive modeling techniques as they are often referred to in the **HCI** literature, assess and model the amount of mental effort expended by a **user** while performing **tasks**. In undertaking tasks, designers recognize that some of the **actions** required to accomplish them will be physical (for example, key presses or moving pointers) and some will be mental. This mental effort can be in terms of mental processing, in terms of making decisions, or in terms of the knowledge used in performing a task. The **cognitive walkthrough** is a cognitive task analysis technique.

Cognitive walkthrough A technique for exploring a user's mental processes while he or she performs particular **task(s)** with a **user interface**. For **requirements gathering**, a cognitive walkthrough may be used as a technique for **task analysis**. For **evaluation**, a cognitive walkthrough may be used to assess the **usability** of a **user interface design** by examining whether a **user** can select the appropriate **action** at the interface for each step in the task.

Color saturation The chromatic purity of a color.

Combo box A text box used in conjunction with a list box. A combo box is a type of widget used in **graphical user interfaces**.

Command line An **interaction style** providing a means of directly instructing the **computer system**, using function keys on your keyboard (F1, F8, etc.), single characters, abbreviations, or whole-word commands. The **user** enters commands onto a command line to obtain access to system functions.

Commercial style guides A commercial **style guide** is a set of **design principles**, **design guidelines**, and **design rules** used to specify the look of all the software produced for a particular platform, for example Microsoft Windows, Apple Macintosh, or Unix.

607

Compare element The **element of evaluation** that focuses on comparing the **UI** with some standard of excellence or good practice. Some comparators are the user's personal standard of a good UI, **heuristics**, **design principles**, **design guidelines**, and **usability standards**.

Comparison evaluation Evaluations that can be performed at any stage of the life cycle to compare different or competing designs. With comparison evaluations, care must be taken to maintain consistency across the evaluation sessions; for example, time must be measured in a similar way, using the same **task description** for the sessions that are being compared.

Computer system The combination of hardware and software components that receive input from and communicate output to a **user** in order to support the user's performance of a **task**. Examples include PCs, domestic appliances (for example, a microwave oven or a VCR), and handheld devices (for example, a mobile phone or a **personal digital assistant**). Many of these devices make use of **embedded computer systems**.

Computer-based prototyping See **high-fidelity prototyping**.

Concatenation An approach to speech generation that employs a computer to store digital recordings of real human speech and then combine them to construct sentences as required.

Conceptual design The process of representing the underlying structure of a new **UI**. In particular, the relationships between the different parts of the UI and initial decisions about what functions the different parts will support and the data they will need to contain. The output of conceptual design is a **content diagram**.

Concrete use case A detailed description of a **task**. A concrete use case is similar to a task scenario, but it is not personalized and so describes the use of a **system** at a slightly more generic level. Also see **essential use case** and **task scenario**.

Conditions of interaction Conditions that determine the navigational flow between **containers** in a **content diagram**.

Consistency A **design principle**. Consistency in appearance, placement, and behavior within the UI makes a system easy to learn and remember. Other **design principles** are **affordance**, **feedback**, **visibility**, **simplicity**, **structure**, and **tolerance**.

Constraints Factors that may influence choices in design. For example, having to adhere to a particular **system** configuration (e.g., older or slower technology) or a particular system platform may place limits on what you can achieve for a particular design. For **evaluation**, constraints refer to factors that influence the type of evaluation you are able to undertake, for example, time, money, access to equipment, or the availability of **users**.

Containers An abstract representation of a part of the user's work and the functions that are required to do that part of the work. The content of containers is informed by the associated **primary task objects** and their attributes. A container is part of a **content diagram**.

Content diagram A low-fidelity prototype that takes the form of a network of **containers** and **links**, representing the organization and structure of the **UI** from the designer's perspective. The content diagram results from the process of **conceptual design**.

Continuity   One of the **Gestalt** laws, which says we tend to group items together as one single entity when they follow smoothly from one another, rather than as two single items, which they may in fact be.

Continuous input devices   Devices designed to handle **analogue data**. A mouse is an example of a continuous input device. These are different to **discrete input devices**, which handle **digital data**. Continuous input devices are divided into **direct pointing devices** and **indirect pointing devices**.

Controlled studies   An **evaluation** conducted at a place other than the user's work environment is known as a controlled study. A controlled study can be *informal* or *formal*. An informal setting could be space at home, in an office, or even in a meeting room at the user's workplace. A formal study is usually undertaken in a usability laboratory.

Cost-justify   The process of showing that an activity will produce sufficient cost savings or other benefits to justify its expense.

Customized style guides   A customized **style guide** is a set of **design principles**, **design guidelines**, and **design rules** compiled specifically for use in relation to a particular **UI** development.

Data analysis   See **analysis**.

Data interpretation   See **interpretation**.

Dataflow diagram (DFD)   A structured analysis technique for representing diagrammatically the way in which data moves through a system and is transformed. An important feature of DFDs is that they represent computer systems as a hierarchy of functions — that is, they model the functional requirements. Whereas DFDs depict information flow, they do not show relationships between data; this is usually done in an **entity–relationship diagram**.

Debrief   See **post-session interview**.

Decision maker   A **stakeholder** who makes decisions about what to do in a project.

Descriptive statistics   A way of summarizing **quantitative data** using factors such as the mean, median, and mode.

Design area   A class of **UI** that has particular design requirements. Examples of design areas are **graphical user interfaces (GUIs)**, web sites, and **embedded computer systems**.

Design components   A **UI** is made up of hardware and software design components. Hardware design components are the input and output devices (the collective term for which is **interaction devices**). Software design components are the aspects of the **UI** generated by the computer system, such as text, color, images, moving images, and sound.

Design guidelines Specific information about how to design a usable **UI**. An example of a design guideline is "Use drop-down list boxes to save space." They are less prescriptive than **design rules**, allowing the designer to choose whether and how to apply them. They are more specific than **design principles**.

Design principles High-level generic information for designing usable **UI**s. "Be consistent" is an example of a design principle. They need to be interpreted by the designer according to the **requirements** of the particular UI. **Design rules** and **design guidelines** are more specific than design principles.

Design rationale A documented explanation (be it paper or electronic) of why an **artifact** has been designed the way that it has — that is, the reasoning behind a design.

Design rules Low-level, highly specific instructions that can be followed with the minimum of interpretation or translation by the designer. Because they are so specific, they are only applicable in relation to a particular system platform; for example, in **commercial style guides** such as the *Apple Human Interface Guidelines for the Macintosh*. You will also find company-specific house or corporate style guides; however, these are often considered to be commercially sensitive and are not freely available. Also see **design principles**.

Designer's model The designer's understanding of a system. This includes both the functional and structural aspects of the system — both how to operate it and how it works. The designer's model is communicated to the user through the **system image**.

Diagnostic evaluation An **evaluation** that takes place primarily to find any **usability** problems that might exist in a system. Diagnostic evaluations are usually **formative**. Methods used for a diagnostic evaluation are **user observation**, **interviews**, and the **cognitive walkthrough**.

Dialog box A secondary window displayed by an application. Dialog boxes are used where additional information is needed from **users** to carry out a **task** or to inform users of the system's state.

Digital data Data that have a finite number of states, steps, or increments. The state of a light switch is an example of digital data: it can be on or off. Numbers and letters are also digital data, as they can be represented by binary digits. **Discrete input devices** handle digital data; **analogue data**, on the other hand, generally requires the use of **continuous input devices**.

Direct manipulation (DM) An **interaction style** that allows a **user** to manipulate the **UI** in a way that is analogous to the way he or she manipulates objects in space.

Direct pointing devices Input devices that allow the **user** to point directly at the object she or he is interested in. Examples include the **touchscreen**, the light pen, and the stylus (as used in **pen systems**). Direct pointing devices tend to be more intuitive to use than **indirect pointing devices**.

Discrete input devices   Input devices designed to handle **digital data**. A keyboard is an example of a discrete input device, being made up of a number of keys, each of which can be in one of two states: pressed or not pressed. **Continuous input devices** are used for handling **analogue data**.

Discussion guide   See **evaluation script**.

Displacement joystick   A **joystick** whose lever can be moved in two dimensions. Moving the lever in a particular direction causes the cursor to move and to continue moving in that direction.

Domain   An area of expertise and knowledge in some real-world activity. The domain provides the underlying concepts and meanings (or semantics) for the **computer system**. Some examples of domains are graphic design, stock trading, and travel. A domain consists of concepts that highlight its important aspects. Stock, bond, trade, and commission schedule are some of the important concepts for stock trading. Flight, reservation, and airport are some of the important concepts for air travel.

Domain analysis   The activity of gathering information about a **domain**.

Domain models   Models that contain a subset of the total expert knowledge of the whole **domain**. They describe the information and concepts relevant to a particular **computer system** under development.

Double link   In a **content diagram**, a double link (►►) indicates that the work in a second **container** needs the context of the first container and that the **user** will will switch back and forth between the two containers to perform the **task**. An example is when you are working in a Word document and you invoke the spell checker.

Effectiveness   In relation to **usability**, effectiveness is the accuracy and completeness with which specified **users** can achieve specified **goals** in particular environments.

Efficiency   In relation to **usability**, efficiency is defined as the resources expended in relation to the accuracy and completeness of the **goals** achieved.

Element of evaluation   The specific area of focus for an **evaluation technique**. There are four elements of evaluation: **observe**, **compare**, **listen**, and **measure**.

Embedded computer systems   An intrinsic part of many devices or appliances. They perform valuable functions without the **user** necessarily being aware of the underlying computer technology. The technology is invisible to the user. For example, **personal digital assistants**, watches, microwave ovens, bread makers, and cell/mobile phones all contain computers, but users are not required to know about the existence of these computers. **Information appliances** are embedded computer systems that process information. Also see **computer system**.

Entity–relationship diagram (ERD)   A structured analysis technique for describing and representing diagrammatically data and the relationships between data in a **computer system**. ERDs model the data requirements and focus on the structure of the data rather than on the processing of the data. A **dataflow diagram** is used to show the way these data are processed.

Environment The set of circumstances or conditions in which a **user** works. These include the **physical environment**, the **organizational environment**, the **social environment**, and the **user support environment**.

Essential use case A very-high level description of a **task**. Essential use cases are simple and general descriptions of **tasks** containing no assumptions about the type of **UI** or technology to be used. They focus more on what a **user** would like to do (the user's intentions or purpose when using a **computer system**) and what the system's responsibilities need to be than on how these will be achieved. Also see **concrete use case** and **task scenario**.

Evaluation The complete test of the **UI**. A process through which information about the **usability** of a system is gathered in order to improve the **system** (known as **formative evaluation**) or to assess a completed **interface** (known as **summative evaluation**). An evaluation may aim to find as many problems as possible (known as **diagnostic evaluation**) or it may aim to measure some aspect of the usability of the interface (known as **measurement evaluation**). Formative evaluations are usually diagnostic, and summative evaluations are usually measurement.

Evaluation data The information obtained during an **evaluation session**. There will be several items of data, including the **participant's** comments, the **observers'** and **facilitators'** notes and comments, and possibly audio or video recordings.

Evaluation plan A description of how and when the **evaluation session(s)** will be conducted. It is based on the **evaluation strategy**.

Evaluation script A description of the detailed steps for an **evaluation**. It should include the chosen sequence of events for the evaluation, but may also include any logical alternate paths (whether correct or incorrect) **users** might take. Evaluation scripts should also include the possible interactions and interventions for each step of the script.

Evaluation session One individual test of a **prototype UI design** with one participant.

Evaluation strategy The overall description of what an **evaluator** wants to achieve by conducting the **evaluation session(s)** and the **constraints** for the **evaluation** (time, money, etc.). It is based on the **usability requirements** for the **computer system**. Deciding on the evaluation strategy and what to investigate will help in the formation of the **evaluation plan**.

Evaluation technique A procedure for collecting relevant data about the operation and **usability** of a **computer system**.

Evaluator The person who plans and conducts an **evaluation**.

Exploratory evaluation An **evaluation** conducted early in the life cycle with **low-fidelity prototypes** to explore the **UI design** features and gather feedback about features of the preliminary designs. Exploratory evaluations are almost always **formative**, because their purpose is to provide insights for the further development of the interface, and they are also almost always **diagnostic**, aiming to find as many problems or ideas for improvement as possible. The **evaluation data** obtained from an exploratory session are usually **qualitative data** and help to validate qualitative **usability requirements**.

Expressed need What people *say* they want. An expressed need may or may not be the same as a **felt need** — that is, sometimes they are identical, but other times the expressed need may be a subset of the felt needs; for example, "Well, I thought all word processors can justify text so I didn't ask for it explicitly."

Facilitator An **evaluator** role: the evaluator who manages the **evaluation** and explains the aims of evaluation to the **participant** and how it will be conducted. The facilitator also answers any queries that the participant may have during the session. One evaluator can act as both facilitator and **observer**, or alternatively two or more evaluators could perform these roles.

Feedback Information sent back to the **user** to confirm what action has been done or what result has been accomplished. Feedback can be visual (e.g., text on a display, flashing alert messages), auditory (e.g., beeps, bells, or other noises like key clicks as you press keys on a keypad or keyboard), or tactile (e.g., a button can be felt to move as it is pressed).

Felt need What people *feel* they want, which they identify themselves. Often a felt need may be latent or not particularly obvious because people may not know or understand what a **computer system** may be able to offer them; thus, they may not realize they have a need in the first place. An **expressed need** is what people *say* they want.

Field studies **Evaluations** that are undertaken in the **user's** own work **environment**. The benefit of a field study is that you can gather data about the environment within which the users work as well as about your **system**.

Figure ground segregation One of the **Gestalt** laws, which says that while we see particular groupings of objects (for example, **proximity**), we also see objects against a ground. That is, when a figure has two or more distinct areas, we can usually see part of it as a figure and the rest of it as background — especially where edges are present or boundaries exist between areas in relation to brightness, color, or texture.

Flexibility The extent to which a system can accommodate changes to the **tasks** and **environments** beyond those first specified.

613

Flexible interview An **interview** in which the **interviewer** is free to explore the opinions of the interviewee. A **structured interview** is different in that it consists of set questions.

Font A particular font is made up of two components: the **typeface** and the type size, which may be within a range such as eight point to 72 point.

Formative evaluation An **evaluation** that takes place before the final implementation of a **computer system** in order to influence its development. Examples of formative evaluation methods are **user observation**, **interviews**, and the **cognitive walkthrough**. A formative evaluation that happens at an early stage of development may also be referred to as **exploratory evaluation**. Most formative evaluations are **diagnostic** — that is, they aim to find as many ideas for improvement as possible. In contrast, **summative evaluation** aims to provide a statement of the level of **usability** achieved by a system, and it is usually done when development of the system (or part of the system) is complete.

Form-fill An **interaction style** that allows the **user** to enter information via a form on the screen.

Frame Frames are a structuring device used to partition a **UI** into sections. Frames are used in a **GUI** to group together all the related information and controls needed for a set of related tasks. Web pages are commonly partitioned into frames, which can be accessed and controlled independently; some web designers like them, others do not.

Full prototype A **prototype** that contains the full functionality of the final system but with reduced performance.

Functional model A user's **mental model**, which consists of "how to use it" knowledge about a device. For example, a functional model of a digital watch will consist of information about how to set the time, use the stopwatch, or turn on the back light in dark conditions, but it will contain little information about the circuitry of the watch. Also see **structural model**.

Gatekeeper A **stakeholder** who owns access to another group or to resources.

Gestalt psychology A school of thought that says our ability to interpret the meaning of scenes and objects is based on innate laws of spatial organization. This is important for the way in which screens are laid out. Also see **closure**, **continuity**, **figure-ground segregation**, **proximity**, **similarity**, and **symmetry**.

Goal A goal is something to be achieved, but it does not always precisely indicate what to do. Examples of goals are "travel to work," "get something to eat," "watch a tennis match," and "send a letter." Goals, **task(s)**, and **action(s)** create a hierarchy. Actions make up tasks, and tasks make up goals.

Graphics tablet An **indirect pointing device**. It is a flat panel placed near the screen. The user moves a stylus or finger across the tablet, and the motion is reflected by the movement of a cursor on the screen.

Graphical user interface (GUI) A **UI design area**. GUIs represent the majority of information in a visual form, often using **widgets** such as buttons and **combo boxes**.

Head-mounted display (HMD) An output device. It is a helmet or a pair of spectacles that contains one or more screens that are positioned in front of the eyes.

HMDs allow the users to feel part of a **virtual world** created by the software and are thus often used in **virtual reality systems**.

Head-up displays Output devices. A head-up display is a specialized form of projection system often used in aircraft cockpits, where key information is projected onto the front window of the aircraft. This means that the pilot does not need to keep looking down at the cockpit control system.

Heuristic evaluation See **heuristic inspection**.

Heuristic inspection An **evaluation** in which the **participants** (usually referred to as **inspectors**) inspect the **UI design** to check whether it conforms to a standard set of **heuristics**.

Heuristics A set of **design principles**, that focuses on key usability issues of concern.

High-fidelity prototyping An approach to **prototyping** that utilizes software packages such as Visual Basic and PowerPoint to construct prototypes of the **user interface** to the **system** under development; a high-fidelity prototype thus has a **look and feel** that is close to the finished product. A different approach is that of **low-fidelity prototyping**, which uses paper prototypes.

Highlight A short excerpt from an **evaluation** activity that illustrates an important part of the user experience.

Human–action cycle A psychological model proposed by Norman (1988) that describes the steps **users** take when they interact with **computer systems**. In particular, the cycle shows the way in which users perform **actions** and **tasks** in order to achieve their **goals**.

Human–computer interaction (HCI) The study of how humans interact with computer systems.

Hypertext A nonlinear approach to organizing information in a **computer system**. **Users** are not compelled to read the information in order; rather, they can jump around according to their particular interests and preferences. Web sites use hypertext, and, indeed, the World Wide Web is a massive hypertext system.

Image-safe area The area of the web page that the designer assumes will be visible to most **users**. To calculate the image-safe area, you need to anticipate the typical screen size and resolution.

Indirect pointing devices Input devices that are physically remote from the object to which they are pointing. Examples include the mouse, the **trackball**, the **joystick**, and the **graphics tablet**. They are different from **direct pointing devices**, which allow the user to point directly at an object.

Inferential statistics Tests of statistical significance, which give the probability that a claim arising from **quantitative data** can be applied to a **user** population as a whole.

Information appliances **Embedded computer systems** that process information. They are designed to perform a particular **task** and are able to communicate with other information appliances. A digital camera is an example of an information appliance. **Pleasurability**, **versatility**, and **simplicity** are important **design principles** for information appliances.

Inspection An **evaluation technique** that involves evaluating or inspecting a **user interface** to check that it conforms with a set of **design guidelines**, **design principles**, or particular **usability standards** such as **ISO 9241**. The **participant** (usually referred to as an **inspector**) is often a **domain** expert or **usability** expert, rather than a real or representative **user**.

Inspection of the user interface See **inspection**.

Inspector An **HCI** expert or **domain** expert who undertakes the **inspection** of the **UI**.

Interaction The two-way communication between **user** and **system**. The user interacts with the **system** via an input interaction device, and the **system** responds by presenting the output on an output interaction device.

Interaction devices The collective term for input and output devices, which are also known as the hardware **design components**.

Interaction style A generic term that includes the different ways in which **users** interact with **computer systems**. Examples of interaction styles are **command line**, **menu selection**, **form-fill**, **direct manipulation**, and **anthropomorphic**.

Interactive computer system See **computer system**.

Interface See **user interface**.

Interpretation The process of finding the causes of **usability problems** in the analyzed data, creating a set of recommendations for resolving them, and documenting the results and recommendations in an evaluation report.

Interpretation session A session where one developer, or team member, replays a **usability** activity for other team members so that they can share the experience and insights gained.

Interviewer See **evaluator**.

Interviews An **evaluation** technique that involves questioning **users** to obtain their opinions about the **usability** of a **prototype** or the implemented **system**.

Intrinsic brightness The brightness of a color. This concept is related to **color saturation**.

Inverted pyramid method An approach to writing the textual content of web pages. You start by writing a brief conclusion and then slowly add detail. Thus, even if the reader does not read the whole section, she or he will still have the main point. This is a method commonly used by journalists.

Iris recognition   A method whereby a computer system identifies a **user** based on the user's iris (the colored part of the eye). This is useful where security is an important issue, such as accessing restricted areas or withdrawing money from an ATM.

ISO 9241   A **user interface standard** that contains guidelines for the software and hardware ergonomics aspects of the use of visual display terminals (VDTs). It covers issues such as the requirements for displays, guidance on the working environment, and the use of icons and menus.

Isometric joystick   A **joystick** whose lever can be moved in two dimensions. Isometric joysticks work in a similar way to **displacement joysticks**, but their lever is rigid and the pressure on the lever is translated into the necessary movement.

Iterative design   An approach to **user interface design** and development that involves cycling through one or more of the activities a number of times, perhaps as the result of a greater understanding of the requirements brought about by **evaluation** and **userability testing**. For example, the requirements for a **computer system** cannot be captured completely from the **requirements-gathering** activities alone; a further understanding and definition of the requirements will follow from **prototyping** and the testing of those prototypes with real **users**.

Job analysis   The examination of what individual workers do in their jobs on a daily or weekly basis. The analysis is across different workers with different responsibilities and is at a low level of detail.

Joystick   A lever mounted in a fixed base. Moving the lever in a particular direction causes the cursor to move in that direction. Joysticks are a type of **continuous input device**. Also see **displacement joystick** and **isometric joystick**.

Knowledge in the head   Information that is stored in the user's memory, accumulated through experience. When interacting with a computer, the **user** combines this with **knowledge in the world**.

Knowledge in the world   Information in the environment. In user–computer interaction, this includes the information provided by the **interface**, in particular concerning the current system state. When interacting with a computer, the **user** combines this with **knowledge in the head**.

Learnability   The time and effort required to reach a specified level of user performance (also described as "ease of learning").

Light pen   A penlike device or stylus that is attached to a computer and can be used to point at areas of a **cathode ray tube** screen. A **direct pointing device**.

Likert scale   A selection of statements, each similar to a semantic differential, that when analyzed together portray a user's altitude.

Link   As found in web pages. There are three types of links. An **associative link** takes the browser to a different part of the same page. A **structural navigation link** takes the browser to a different page within the same site. A "**See Also**" **link** takes the browser to a different site.

Links are also used in a **content diagram** to indicate the direction of flow between **containers**. Also see **single link** and **double link**.

Liquid crystal display (LCD)   A type of computer screen. The screen is flat and is often a shade of gray or blue. LCD screens have the advantages of being light and requiring a low operating voltage. Thus, they are ideal for handheld and portable devices.

Listen element   The **element of evaluation** that focuses on listening to and learning from what **users** and **inspectors** have to say about the **usability** of a **user interface design** (or the usability of user interface designs). Listening can be informal, such as simply asking others their opinions and listening to what they say, or more formal, such as listening closely to audio and video recordings.

Look and feel   Common name for the overall **interface** style of an application.

Low-fidelity prototyping   An approach to **prototyping** that concentrates on the structure and appearance of a **computer system**. It involves using paper, pens, sticky notes, and so on to create sketches, screen mockups, and storyboards of the **user interface** of the **system** under development. A good low-fidelity prototype should be capable of being updated in moments. A different approach is that of **high-fidelity prototyping**.

Macro   A set of commands that can be called by a name to be executed in one go; they are useful for combining commands that are to be performed in a strict sequence. Macros are sometimes used in **command line** interfaces.

Main container   The **container** that represents the first thing a **user** encounters and that will be central to the user's work. In a **GUI**, this might be a launch pad window that contains icons corresponding to the main tasks that can be carried out. The main container is part of the **content diagram**.

Measure element   The **element of evaluation** that helps you to assign a number to the **usability** of the **user interface design**. Measuring implies obtaining **quantitative data** during evaluations to validate the **usability requirements**.

Measurement evaluation   Aims to measure some aspect of the **usability** of a system. Laboratory experiments are one method of measurement evaluation. **Validation evaluations** that aim to establish whether a system has met some specified level are almost always measurement evaluations. **Summative** evaluations that aim to determine the level of **usability** of a **system** are also almost always **measurement evaluations**. Often, a **diagnostic evaluation** will have taken place before a measurement evaluation.

Meeter and greeter   An **evaluator** role. An evaluator who meets the **participants** when they arrive for the evaluation. The meeter and greeter is generally responsible for all the domestic arrangements.

Mental model   A mental representation that people use to organize their experience about themselves, others, the environment, and the things with which they interact. People use their mental models to make associations between the information (words, pictures, sounds, smells) they are learning and the information they already know. Mental models can provide predictive and explanatory power for understanding experiences. Other forms related to **user interface design** include **user's model** and **designer's model**.

Menu   A screen or **widget** that has options from which the **user** can choose.

Menu selection   An **interaction style** in which the **user** selects from a number of prespecified options.

Metaphor   The metaphorical use of words on the screen, static images and icons, and interactive graphics, such as the calculator that comes with Windows. These elements are used metaphorically when the designer deliberately draws on the user's existing knowledge in order to enable the **user** to formulate an accurate **mental model** of the **UI**. Metaphors are often used in **direct manipulation** interfaces.

Modal   Message boxes are often modal. This means they require input from the **user** before they can continue working. This is in contrast to **modeless** message boxes.

Modeless   Modeless message boxes do not require input from the **user** before they can continue working. This is in contrast to **modal** message boxes.

Navigation aid   A section of a website that provides provides **users** with an overview of a site's structure and enables them to move around the site. Examples of navigation aids include site maps, breadcrumb trails, and **navigation bars**.

Navigation bar   An area of a web page that contains **structural navigation links** designed to enable the **user** to navigate around the web site. It is often found down the left-hand side or across the top of the screen.

Nondisclosure agreement (NDA)   A legal agreement used in confidential or commercially sensitive situations. In signing an NDA, the **participant** agrees not to disclose the confidential information that has been viewed during an **evaluation**.

Normative needs   The professional's view of what is needed for a **system** under development. This may or may not result in a system that meets the **users'** needs.

Note-taker   An **evaluator** role. An evaluator who records what is happening in the **evaluation**.

Observe element   The **element of evaluation** that focuses on observing the **user** or **participant** during user observation, or watching the **inspectors** inspecting the **user interface**, to help you identify the difficulties they are facing in using the interface.

Observer   An **evaluator** role. An **evaluator** who observes the **participant** during an **evaluation session** and makes notes of the participant's comments and any **usability problems**. One evaluator can act as both **facilitator** and observer, or alternatively two or more evaluators could perform these roles.

Open question   A question in which the respondent is free to provide his or her own reply.

Organizational environment   The structure, working practices, and culture of the company for which a **computer system** is being developed or within which a computer system is in place. The organizational environment includes, for example, working hours, work practices, management attitudes, organizational aims, performance monitoring, and performance feedback. Other environments to consider include the **physical environment** and the **social environment**.

Paper-based prototyping   See **low-fidelity prototyping**.

Participant   The person who interacts with or **inspects** the **UI** to give feedback about its **usability**. A participant is usually, but not always, a real **user** of the UI.

Pen system   A combination of **touchscreen** and stylus. A stylus is a **direct pointing device** that, unlike a **light pen**, is detached from the computer. As with a light pen, the **user** is required to touch the screen using the stylus. Handheld devices such as **personal digital assistants** are often pen systems.

Persona   A description of a **user** and what he or she wishes to do when using a **system**. Personas are not real; rather they are imaginary examples of the real users they represent.

Personal digital assistants (PDAS)   Handheld computer systems designed to help with the everyday aspects of life, such as keeping a diary, maintaining an address book, and making notes. The functionality of such devices is developing rapidly, with some containing modems, acting as pagers, and so on. These devices are a type of **embedded computer system**.

Physical design   The process of combining **design components** in order to best satisfy **usability requirements**. The **content diagram** informs this process.

Physical environment   The physical aspects of the area within which a **computer system** will be used. This involves a consideration of the workspace, lighting, temperature, and noise levels where the system is to be used. Any dangers in the environment that affect how **users** will work are also considered here — for example, hazards in the workplace that may require protective clothing or that make working difficult. Other environments to consider include the **organizational environment** and the **social environment**.

Pilot test A trial-run **evaluation** undertaken before attempting the main evaluation. A pilot test is a way of evaluating your **evaluation session**, to help ensure that it will work. It is a process of debugging or testing the evaluation material, the planned time schedule, the suitability of the **task descriptions**, and the running of the evaluation session.

Pixels An abbreviation for picture element. Screen **resolution** is defined in terms of the number of pixels per unit area; the larger this number, the higher the resolution.

Pleasurability A term that relates to an **information appliance**. Part of the definition of an information appliance is that it should be pleasurable to use and own, in the way that a good-quality car or motorcycle may be pleasurable to own and use (drive).

Post-session interview A general discussion of what happened during an **evaluation**. Post-session interviews may also be referred to as a **debrief**.

Pretest questionnaire Questions that are asked, either via an **interview** or paper questionnaire, at the beginning of an **evaluation**.

Primary task objects The units of information, or data, with which the **users** interact in order to carry out their **tasks**. They are high-level objects, central to the tasks the user will be carrying out. Primary task objects have attributes and actions that can be performed on them. They are used to inform the choice and content of **containers** within **content diagrams**. Primary task objects are often referred to simply as **task objects**.

Primary users People or groups of people who use a **computer system** directly, usually referred to as users. See **user** and **stakeholder**.

Prototype (noun) An experimental incomplete design of an application used for testing design ideas. There are various prototypes, depending on whether a **high-fidelity prototyping** or **low-fidelity prototyping** approach has been used.

Prototyping The creation or construction of a version of a **system** that (1) may be functionally incomplete, (2) may not cover the whole scope of the system, or (3) may lack the performance of the final system. Different kinds of prototyping include **low-fidelity prototyping** and **high-fidelity prototyping**.

Proximity One of the **Gestalt** laws, which says that elements that are close together appear to belong together in a group.

Qualitative data Any data without a numeric content. For example, statements of **usability problems**, or subjective descriptions of the difficulties that **participants** faced while interacting with the **UI**, are qualitative data.

Quantitative data Any type of numeric data. For instance, if during **evaluation** you are recording measurements such as the time taken by the **participant** to complete a **task** or the time spent by the participant referring to documentation, then you are collecting quantitative data.

Recoverability   The ability of the **users** to recover from their mistakes in their interaction with the system and hence accomplish their **goals**. This is an aspect of **tolerance**.

Recruiter   An **evaluator** role. A recruiter is a person or organization who finds the **participants** for the **evaluation** and who obtains permission to go to the participant's home or work environment if this is a **field study**.

Recruitment screener   A script or sequence of questions that is used to prompt someone who is recruiting participants for a **usability evaluation**.

Requirements   The global term used to refer to the **requirements elicitation**, **requirements gathering**, and **requirements specification** phase of **user interface design**.

Requirements elicitation   The activity of finding out from **users**, **stakeholders**, and previous system documents what the system requirements are. This includes gathering information about the application **domain** of the **computer system**, the problem to be solved, and the needs of the users and stakeholders. Among others, the techniques used for requirements elicitation include **interviews**, brainstorming, observing users, and surveying users and stakeholders to discover their views. Also see **requirements gathering** and **requirements specification**.

Requirements gathering   Also called requirements analysis. The process of finding out what a client (or customer) requires from a software system. The activities here focus on investigations and analyses of the **domain(s)**, **user(s)**, **task(s)**, and **environment(s)** within which the **system** will be used. Other steps in discovering what is needed from the design are **requirements elicitation** and **requirements specification**.

Requirements specification   The deliverable document produced following **requirements elicitation/gathering**. It attempts to describe, as formally as possible, what the **system** should do from the point of view of the **user**, although in practice this is a dynamic document that is subject to change throughout the design and development life cycle. In different organizations, this document may be called, among other names, the requirements document, the functional specification, the systems requirements specification, or the software requirements specification.

Resolution   The fineness of detail that can be produced for images, sounds, and other **analogue data**. The higher the resolution, the clearer the representation and the larger the file.

Retrospective protocol   The evaluation data obtained when a **participant** reviews the audio or video recordings of her or his **evaluation session** and comments on what her or his thoughts and actions were during the evaluation session.

Road runner report   See **snapshot report**.

Satisfaction   In relation to **usability**, satisfaction is the comfort and acceptability of the work system to its **users** and other people affected by its use.

Secondary users   People or groups of people who are not **primary users** but who are affected or influenced in some way by the **computer system** or who can affect or influence its development. Secondary users can have a direct or indirect influence on the system requirements. Secondary users may include, among others, senior managers, business analysts, system analysts, project managers, application developers, interface designers, marketing and sales representatives, trainers, and customer support staff. If the computer system is intended for use at home, the secondary users may include friends or relatives of the **primary user** or visitors to the home.

"See Also" link   A type of **link** that links one web site to another. They are often of particular value to the **user**, as they enable the user to explore related sites. Other links found on web sites include **associative links** and **structural navigation links**.

Semantic differential   An attitude scale that requires respondents to rate an item using a scale with bipolar adjectives at each end (e.g., easy/difficult).

Severity rating   A measure given to a **usability defect** to indicate the criticality of its impact on the **usability** of the **user interface design**.

Similarity   One of the **Gestalt** laws, which says that similar elements, for example, elements of the same shape or color, tend to be grouped together.

Simplicity   A **design principle**. It is important to keep the **UI** as simple as possible. Designers are encouraged to use **actions**, icons, words, and UI controls that are natural to the users. Simplicity is an important design principle for **information appliances**. Other design principles are **affordance**, **feedback**, **visibility**, **consistency**, **structure**, and **tolerance**.

Single link   In a **content diagram**, a single link (▸) indicates that the user moves to another **container**, which then becomes the focus of the user's activity.

Snapshot report   A one-page summary of a single day's **highlight** results from a **usability** activity. Also known as "**road runner**" report.

Social environment   The local aspects of a workplace that affect the way in which a **user** works. Aspects to be considered are, for example: Do workers work alone, or is there dependency between workers to complete particular **tasks**? Are workers under pressure to perform tasks quickly and accurately? Do people who share information for tasks work in the same location, or are they scattered around in different parts of the building? Other types of environment to consider include the **organizational environment** and the **physical environment**.

623

Speech recognition   A method whereby a **computer system** is able to recognize the words a **user** speaks. This is useful in a variety of situations, including those in which the user is disabled.

Splash page   A web page introducing a web site that often contains a photograph or the company logo and name, but little else. The **user** then has to download the home page.

Stakeholder   Every **primary user** and every **secondary user** for a computer system. Also see **users** and **secondary users**.

State transition diagram   A graphic structure indicating possible states of a **system** and transitions from one state to another.

Stereoscopic displays   **Head-mounted displays** where there are two screens, one in front of each eye. The two images represent slightly different perspectives on the object and together they combine to create the illusion of three dimensions. This can be useful for **virtual reality** applications.

Structural model   A user's **mental model** that consists of "how it works" knowledge about a device. For example, a structural model of a digital watch will consist of information about the circuitry of the watch and the microprocessor contained within it. Structural models allow the user to reason about and to predict the object's behavior in novel situations. Also see **functional model**.

Structural navigation link   A type of **link** that points to other pages within the same web site. A Home button is an example of a structural navigation link. Other types of link found on web sites include **associative links** and **"See Also" links**.

Structure   A **design principle**. It is important to organize the **UI** in a meaningful and useful way. Features that **users** think of as related should appear together on the user interface, or at least they should be clearly and closely associated. Other **design principles** are **affordance**, **feedback**, **visibility**, **consistency**, **simplicity**, and **tolerance**.

Structured interview   An **interview** in which all the questions are predetermined and there is little scope for exploring the individual's opinions. Alternatively, a **flexible interview** allows more opportunity to gain the interviewee's opinions.

Style guide   A group of **design principles** and **design rules** used to specify the **look and feel** of all the software produced by a software house.

Style sheet   A method for maintaining a consistent **look and feel** for a web site. It allows the appearance of the whole site to be changed relatively easily. For example, if you decide that the **font** you have used for titles needs changing, you simply alter the style sheet, rather than changing every title individually.

SUMI (The software usability measurement inventory)   SUMI is a 50-item questionnaire in which all 50 items are rating statements with three options: agree, undecided, or disagree. The statements explore the following attributes of the **user interface**: **learnability**, helpfulness, control, **efficiency**, and affect.

Summative evaluation An **evaluation** that aims to establish the level of **usability** achieved by a **system**. Summative evaluations usually take place when a system, or a substantial part of it, has completed development. Summative evaluations are also often **validation evaluations** — that is, they aim to establish not only the level of usability but also whether that level has met the **usability requirements**. Because summative evaluations aim to establish the level of usability, they are often referred to as **measurement evaluations** in the **HCI** literature. Often, a **formative evaluation** will have taken place earlier in the development of the system.

Symmetry One of the **Gestalt** laws, which says that we tend to see objects bounded by symmetrical or balanced borders as coherent figures.

System See **computer system**.

System image The UI, supporting documentation, training, and so on. The purpose of the system image is to communicate the **designer's model** to the **user** so that the user can create an accurate **mental model** of the system.

Tagline A few words of text included on a web site to describe what that web site does.

Talk-aloud protocols See **think-aloud protocols**.

Task An activity undertaken, or believed to be necessary, to achieve a **goal**. For example, a goal could be "Managing e-mail correspondence." Some of the tasks aiming to fulfill this goal would be "Read new mail," "Write a new message," "Forward Debbie's mail to Caroline," and so on. Also see **action**.

Task allocation The process of deciding which activities are to be carried out by humans and which by computers. This is part of **work reengineering**.

Task analysis (TA) The process of examining the way people perform their **tasks**. It involves looking in depth at the tasks and **actions** a person undertakes, along with the knowledge needed to perform the task(s) and reach **a goal**. Also see **cognitive task analysis**.

Task description A description of the **task** to be carried out by the **user** during a **user-observation** session.

Task objects See **primary task objects**.

Task scenario A narrative description of a **task**, describing the current use of a **computer system**. Task scenarios are very detailed and they describe, step by step, the procedures a **user** follows to complete a task, as well as the features and behavior of the computer system with which the user interacted while undertaking the task. Also see **concrete use case**, **essential use case**, and **use scenario**.

Task–action mapping The number of **actions** required to complete a **task**. Frequent tasks should require as few actions as possible. Where this is the case, the task–action mapping is good.

Technological convergence   The tendency for different technologies to merge. For example, many mobile telephones can be used for accessing the Web as well as for making telephone calls. This means that the various **design areas** are increasingly overlapping.

Test script   See **evaluation script**.

Test monitor   See **evaluator**.

Tester   See **evaluator**.

Think-aloud protocols   The evaluation data obtained when a **participant** is encouraged to talk about what he is trying to do, why he is having a problem, what he expected to happen that did not, what he wishes had happened, and so on, during an evaluation. Think-aloud protocols may also be referred to as **talk-aloud protocols** or **verbal protocols**.

Throughput   The number of **tasks** accomplished by experienced **users**, the speed of task execution, and the errors made (also described as "ease of use").

Thumbnail image   A small image displayed on web pages that the **user** can choose to select in order to download a larger version of the image. This reduces the initial download time.

Tolerance   A **design principle**. The **UI** should be designed to minimize the number of **user** errors and facilitate recovery from errors. Other design principles are **affordance**, **feedback**, **visibility**, **simplicity**, **structure**, and **consistency**.

Touchscreen   A **direct pointing device**. It allows the **user** to point at the area of the screen she or he is interested in.

Trackball   A ball within a fixed socket that a **user** can rotate in any direction to move a cursor on a computer screen. Trackballs are often incorporated into games consoles and notebook computers. A type of **indirect pointing device**.

Typeface   A component of the **font**, for example, Times New Roman or Arial. There are two main types of typeface: serif and sans serif. The serif is the finishing stroke at the end of the letter.

Ubiquitous computing   Where the **UI** of computer-based devices is invisible to the **user**, just as it already is for many conventional devices such as food mixers and gas cookers.

Usability   The extent to which a product can be used by specified **users** to achieve a specified **goal** with **effectiveness**, **efficiency**, and **satisfaction** in a specified context of use (**ISO 9241**:11 definition).

Usability champion   A person within an organization who is already committed to user-centered techniques and who is eager to see them used in the development of a **system** or product.

Usability defect   A difficulty in using the **user interface design** that affects the **user's satisfaction** and the system's **effectiveness** and **efficiency**. Usability defects can lead to confusion, error, delay, or outright failure to complete some **task** on the part of the user. They make the **user interface**, and hence the **system**, less usable for its target users.

Usability evaluation   See **evaluation**.

Usability maturity   The degree to which the importance of **user-centered design** is accepted by an organization, team, or individual.

Usability metrics   Performance measures of the **usability** of a system. For example, in processing sales orders, a metric might be that "At least eight out of 10 sales clerks should be able to complete the steps involved in a sales order in one minute or less."

Usability problem   See **usability defect**.

Usability requirements   The desired qualitative or quantitative usability goals for a computer system. Qualitative usability requirements can be subjective and are not easily measurable; for example, the **user** should be satisfied using the system. Quantitative usability requirements (or **usability metrics**) can be measured; for example, the time taken to complete a particular **task**.

Usability specification   A specification detailing qualitative and quantitative requirement levels of **usability** for a **system**.

Usability standards   A series of generally stated instructions for **user interface design**. They are usually imposed in some formal way or are published by a government body. The United Kingdom's national standards organization is the British Standards Institution (BSI), whereas international standards are set by the International Standards Organization (ISO). Standards may also be defined by professional bodies, such as the British Computer Society (BCS).

Usability testing   Determines whether a **system** meets a predetermined, quantifiable level of **usability** for specific types of **users** carrying out specific **tasks**. Also see **evaluation**.

Use scenario   A narrative description of a **task** at a very detailed level. It differs from a **task scenario** in that it describes the anticipated use of the **computer system** under development. Use scenarios are based on the specified requirements and are used to envision what the future computer system will be like for the **user**.

User   Anyone who uses a computer **system**. In this book, we reserve the term "user" for those who use an **interface** directly (often referred to as **primary users**).

User interface (UI)   That part of the **computer system** with which a **user** interacts in order to undertake his or her **tasks** and achieve his or her **goals**. An interface is thus the bridge between the world of the computer system and the world of the user. It is the means by which the computer system reveals itself to the users and behaves in relation to their needs. The style of the interface is known as its **look and feel**.

User interface design The activity of establishing the mechanisms for **interaction** between a **system** and its **user**. To assist **UI** designers, the activities involved in **UI design** and development may be framed by, for example, the STAR life cycle.

User interface standards See **usability standards**.

User support environment The type of support in use of the **system** which has been provided to the **users** of the system. These would include the provision of manuals for reference, training, and the availability of guidance from colleagues and expert users of the system.

User testing See **evaluation**.

User-centered design (UCD) An approach to **user interface design** and development that views the knowledge about the intended **users** of a **system** as a central concern, including, for example, knowledge about users' abilities and needs, their **task(s)**, and the **environment(s)** within which they work. These users would also be actively involved in the design process.

User observation An **evaluation technique** that involves observing a **participant** interacting with a **prototype**. The **evaluator's** role is to make notes of the participant's comments and opinions on the **usability** of the **prototype user interface** and **interaction** designs. The participant is either a prospective **user** of the system (that is, a real user) or a representative of one of the user groups that were identified and profiled during **requirements gathering**.

User's model A **mental model** consisting of the set of relationships that a **user** perceives to exist among elements of any situation. Users develop mental models through experiences in the real world, including experiences with **computer systems**. Based on the relationships in the model, a user develops expectations from any system that she or he interacts with.

Validation evaluation An **evaluation** conducted toward the end of the life cycle to verify that the **system** meets a predetermined **usability standard** or benchmark prior to its release. These evaluations may also be undertaken to assess how all the components of the system — such as the documentation, help, online tutorials, or any other software/hardware integrated with the system — work together. Validation evaluations are usually both **summative** and **measurement** evaluations.

Verbal protocols See **think-aloud protocols**.

Versatility An **information appliance** should be designed so it encourages the **user** to interact in a novel and creative way.

Virtual reality system Hardware and software that allows the creation and exploration of a **virtual world**. An aircraft simulator is an example of a virtual reality system.

Virtual world   An artificial world that exists purely within a **computer system**. The **user** becomes immersed in the virtual world, possibly carrying out actions that correspond to a real task such as test-driving a racing car. To access a virtual world, **virtual reality** hardware and software is needed.

Visibility   The properties of an object that make it obvious to **users** what the object is used for. For example, the steering wheel of a car is perhaps visible, but not the headlight dipswitch.

White space   An area of the **computer screen** that does not contain any other software components — it is blank. White space is very useful for emphasizing the **structure** of the layout.

Widget   An interface component — for example, a check box, a command button, or a **menu**. It is often associated with a **graphical user interface**.

Wizard   A series of **modal** dialog boxes provided in a strict sequence to assist the **user** in completing a **task**.

Work reengineering   Deciding how a new UI should support the users as they carry out their tasks, An important part of work reengineering is **task allocation**.

Worker   A **stakeholder** whose workload may increase because of a project or who perceives that it may increase.

Workflow analysis   The examination of how overall work **goals** are achieved within an organization. For many work goals, several people will be working together; thus the focus would be on aspects such as how workers communicate and how they coordinate their work with others' to get the job done. Also see **job analysis**.

References

Anderson, C. (2004). *How Much Interaction Is Too Much?* Available from www.stcsig.org/usability/newsletter/0404-howmuchinteraction.html.

Baber, C. (1997). *Beyond the Desktop: Designing and Using Interaction Devices.* Computers and People Series. London: Academic Press.

Ballman, D. (2001). "It's time for a usability code of ethical conduct." In Branaghan, R. J. (Ed.), *Design for People by People: Essays on Usability.* Chicago: Usability Professionals' Association.

Barnum, C. (2002). *Usability Testing and Research.* New York: Pearson Education.

Bell, J., and Hardiman, R. J. (1989). "The third role: The naturalistic knowledge engineer." In Diaper, D. (Ed.), *Knowledge Elicitation: Principles, Techniques, and Applications* (Chapter 2, pp. 49–85). Chichester: Ellis Horwood.

Benedek, J., and Miner, T. (2002). *Measuring Desirability: New Methods for Evaluating Desirability in a Usability Lab Setting.* Usability Professionals Association Conference, July 2002, Orlando, FL.

Bennett, J. (1984). "Managing to meet usability requirements." In Bennett, J., Case, D., Sandelin, J., and Smith, M. (Eds.), *Visual Display Terminals: Usability Issues and Health Concerns.* Englewood Cliffs, NJ: Prentice-Hall.

Bentley, R., Hughes, J. A., Randall, D., Rodden, T., Sawyer, P., Sommerville, I., and Shapiro, D. (1992). "Ethnographically-informed system design for air traffic control." In Turner, J., and Kraut, R. (Eds.), *CSCW'92 Conference Proceedings* (pp. 123–129). New York: ACM Press.

Benway, J. P., and Lane, D. M. (1998). "Banner blindness: Web searchers often miss 'obvious' links" (available from www.internettg.org/newsletter/dec98/banner_blindness.html).

Berry, D. M., and Lawrence, B. (1998). "Requirements engineering." *IEEE Software*, vol. 15, no. 2, 26–29.

Bevan, N., Barnum, C., Cockton, G., Nielsen, J., Spool, J., and Wixon, D. (2003) Panel: "The 'magic number 5': Is it enough for web testing?" *CHI '03* extended abstracts (pp. 698–699). Ft Lauderdale, FL.

Beyer, H., and Holtzblatt, K. (1998). *Contextual Design: Defining Customer-Centred Systems.* San Francisco, CA: Morgan Kaufmann.

Bias, R. G. (1994). "Wherefore cost justification of usability: Pay me now or pay me later — but how much?" In Bias, R. G., and Mayhew, D. J. (Eds.), *Cost-Justifying Usability* (pp. 3–8). Boston: Academic Press.

Boddy, D., and Buchanan, D. (1992). *Take the Lead: Interpersonal Skills for Project Managers.* Hemel Hempstead: Prentice Hall.

British Standards Institution (BSI) (1998). *BS EN 1S0 9241-11:1998. Ergonomic Requirements for Office Work with Visual Display Terminals (VDTs). Part 11: Guidance on Usability.* London: BSI.

Brooke, J. (1996). "SUS: A quick and dirty usability scale." In Jordan, P. W., Thomas, B., Weerdmeester, B. A., and McClelland, I. L. (Eds.), *Usability Evaluation in Industry.* London: Taylor & Francis (also see www.cee.hw.ac.uk/~ph/sus.html).

Brookes, M. J. (1982). "Human factors in the design and operation of reactor safety systems." In Sills, D. L., Wolf, C. P., and Shelanski, V. B. (Eds.), *Accident at Three Mile Island: The Human Dimensions* (pp. 155–60). Boulder, CO: Westview Press.

BSI (British Standards Institution). (1998). *BS EN ISO 9241-11:1998. Ergonomic Requirements for Office Work with Visual Display Terminals (VDTs). Part 11: Guidance on Usability.* London: BSI.

Burmeister, O. K. (2000). "Usability testing: Revisiting informed consent procedures for testing internet sites." Selected papers from the *Second Australian Institute Conference on Computer Ethics.* Canberra, Australia.

Chapanis, A. (1996). *Human Factors in Systems Engineering.* New York: Wiley.

Cherry, E. C. (1953). "Some experiments on the recognition of speech with one or two ears." *Journal of the Acoustical Society of America*, vol. 25, no. 5, 975–979.

Chin, J. P., Diehl, V. A., and Norman, K. (1988). "Development of an instrument measuring user satisfaction of the human–computer interface." *Proceedings of ACM CHI '88*, (pp. 213–218). Washington, DC.

Clegg, F. (1983). *Simple Statistics.* Cambridge: Cambridge University Press.

Compaq Computer Limited, UK and Ireland. (1999). "Rage against the Machine" (available at www.mori.com/polls/1999/rage.shtml).

Constantine L. L., and Lockwood, L. A. D. (1999). *Software for Use: A Practical Guide to the Models and Methods of Usage-Centred Design.* New York: ACM Press.

Coolican, H. (1996). *Introduction to Research Methods and Statistics in Psychology.* London: Arnold Publishers.

Cooper, A. (1995). *About Face: The Essentials of User Interface Design.* New York: Programmers Press.

Cooper, A. (1999). *The Inmates Are Running the Asylum.* New York: SAMS.

Czaja, S. J. (1997). "Computer technology and the older adult." In Helander, M. G., Landauer, T. K., and Prabhu, P. K. (Eds.), *Handbook of Human–Computer Interaction* (2nd ed., pp. 797–812). Amsterdam: Elsevier Science.

Dallenbach, K. M. (1951). "A picture puzzle with a new principle of concealment." *American Journal of Psychology*, vol. 64, no. 3, 431.

Dillman, D. A. (2000). *Mail and Internet Surveys: The Tailored Design Method.* New York: Wiley.

Dix, A., Finlay, J., Abowd, G., and Beale, R. (2004). *Human–Computer Interaction* (3rd ed.). Harlow: Pearson Education.

Dray, S. M., and Siegel, D. A. (1999). "Penny-wise, pound-wise: Making smart trade-offs in planning usability studies." *Interactions*, vol. 6, no. 3, 25–30.

Dumas, J. S., and Redish, J. C. (1999). *A Practical Guide to Usability Testing* (rev. ed.). Exeter: Intellect.

Earthy, J. (1998). *INUSE D5.1.4s* "Usability Maturity Model: Human Centeredness Scale." Lloyd's Register and the European Commission. Available forn www.usability/strco/trump/resources

Ehrlich, K., and Rohn, J. A. (1994). "Cost justification of usability engineering: A vendor's perspective." In Bias, R. G., and Mayhew, D. J. (Eds.), *Cost-Justifying Usability* (pp. 73–110). Boston: Academic Press.

Erikson, T. D. (1990). "Working with interface metaphors." In Laurel, B. (Ed.), *The Art of Human–Computer Interface Design* (pp. 65–73). Reading, MA: Addison-Wesley.

Eyewitness Travel Guide (2004). *Amsterdam* (pp. 120–121). London: Dorling Kindersley.

Fowler, S. (1998). *GUI Design Handbook.* New York: McGraw-Hill.

Gaffney, G. (2001). "Rules for Briefing Observers." Available from www.infodesign.com.au/ftp/ObserverGuidelines.pdf.

Gaffney, G. (2003a). Usability Testing Materials. Available from www.infodesign.com.au/usabilityresources/evaluation/usabilitytestingmaterials.asp.

Gaffney, G. (2003b). "What Is Cardsorting?" Available from www.infodesign.com.au/usabilityresources/design/cardsorting.asp.

Gordon, W. (1999). *Good Thinking: A Guide to Qualitative Research.* World Advertising Research Center. Henley-on-Thames, Oxfordshire.

Götz, V. (1998). *Color and Type for the Screen.* Berlin: RotoVision (in collaboration with Grey Press).

Gould, J. D., and Lewis, C. (1985). "Designing for usability: Key principles and what designers think." *Communications of the ACM*, vol. 28, pp. 300–311.

Greenberg, S. (1996). "Teaching human–computer interaction to programmers." *Interactions*, vol. 3, no. 4, 62–76.

633

Grudin, J. (1991). "Systematic sources of sub-optimal interface design in large product development organizations." *Human–Computer Interaction*, vol. 6, 147–196.

Hackos, J. T., and Redish, J. C. (1998). *User and Task Analysis for Interface Design.* New York: Wiley.

Hanna, L., Risden, K., and Alexander, K. (1997). "Guidelines for usability testing with children." *Interactions*, vol. 4, no. 5, 9–14.

Harrison, C., and Melton, S. (1999). "Are your product teams reading your usability reports?" *Common Ground (Journal of the Usability Professionals Association)*, vol. 9, no. 1, p. 14.

Hartley, J. (1994). *Designing Instructional Text* (3rd ed.). London: Kogan Page.

Head, A. J. (1999) *Design Wise: A Guide for Evaluating the Interface Design of Information Resoures.* New Jersey: Cyber Age Books.

Hix, D., and Hartson, H. R. (1993). *Developing User Interfaces: Ensuring Usability Through Product & Process.* New York: Wiley.

Horton, W. (1991). *The Icon Book: Visual Symbols for Computer Systems and Documentation.* New York: Wiley.

Horton, W. (1994). *Illustrating Computer Documentation.* New York: Wiley.

Huff, D. (1991). *How to Lie with Statistics.* London: Penguin.

IBM Systems (1991). *IBM Systems Application Architecture: Common User Access (CUA) Guide to User Interface Design.* IBM Document SC34-4289-00.

ISO (International Organization for Standardisation). (1997). *13407 Human-centered design processes for interactive systems.* Draft International Standard ISO/DIS 13407.

Jarrett, C. (2004a). "Better Reports: How to Communicate the Results of Usability Testing." *Proceedings of the 51st Annual Conference of the Society for Technical Communication.* Baltimore, MD.

Jarrett, C. (2004b). "Designing Comparative Evaluations." Available from www.usabilitynews.com, retrieved August 2004.

Johnson, J. (2000). *GUI Bloopers: Don'ts and Do's for Software Developers and Web Designers.* San Francisco: Morgan Kaufmann.

Johnson, P. (1992). *Human–Computer Interaction: Psychology, Task Analysis and Software Engineering.* Maidenhead, Berkshire, UK: McGraw-Hill.

Karat, J. (1988). "Software evaluation methodologies." In Helander, M., Landauer, T. K., and Prabhu, P. (Eds.), *Handbook of Human–Computer Interaction* (pp. 891–903). Amsterdam: Elsevier Science.

Kirakowski, J., and Corbett, M. (1993). "The software usability measurement inventory." *British Journal of Educational Technology*, vol. 24, no. 3, 210–212.

Koffka, K. (1935). *Principles of Gestalt Psychology.* New York: Harcourt Brace.

Köhler, W. (1947). *Gestalt Psychology.* Princeton, NJ: Princeton University Press.

Kotonya, G., and Sommerville, I. (1998). *Requirements Engineering: Processes and Techniques.* Chichester: Wiley.

Koyani, S. J., Bailey, R. W., and Nall, J. R. (2003). *Research-based web design and usability guidelines.* Communication Technologies branch, Office of Communications, National Cancer Institute, http://usability.gov/pdfs/guidelines_book.pdf, visited July 6, 2004.

Krug, S. (2000). *Don't Make Me Think! A Commonsense Approach to Web Usability.* Indianapolis, IN: Que Publishing.

LC Technologies, (2000). *Information Leaflet.* From LC Technologies, 94555 Silver King Court, Fairfax, VA 22031-4713 (www.eyegaze.com).

Leveson, N. (1995). *Safeware: System Safety and Computers.* New York: Addison-Wesley.

Lewis, J. (1995). "IBM Computer Usability Satisfaction Questionnaires: Psychometric Evaluation and Instructions for Use." *International Journal of Human-Computer Interaction*, vol. 7, no. 1, 57–78.

Lynch, P. J., and Horton, S. (1999). *Web Style Guide: Basic Design Principles for Creating Websites.* New Haven, CT: Yale University Press.

Macaulay, L. (1995). *Human–Computer Interaction for Software Designers.* London: International Thomson Computer Press.

Maguire, M. (1998). *A Review of User-Interface Design Guidelines for Public Information Kiosk Systems.* HUSAT Research Institute, The Elms, Elms Grove, Loughborough, Leicester, UK. September 1998. Available from www.lboro.ac.uk/eusc/g_design_kiosks.html.

Marchant, G., and Robinson, J. (1999). "Is knowing the tax code all it takes to be a tax expert? On the development of legal expertise." In Sternberg, R. J., and Horvath, J. A. (Eds.), *Tacit Knowledge in Professional Practice: Researcher and Practitioner Perspectives.* Mahwah, NJ: Lawrence Erlbaum Associates.

Mayhew, D. (1999). *The Usability Engineering Lifecycle: A Practitioner's Handbook for User Interface Design.* San Francisco: Morgan Kaufmann.

Mayhew, D., and Bias, R. G. (1994). "Organizational inhibitors and facilitators." In Bias, R. G., and Mayhew, D. J. (Eds.), *Cost-Justifying Usability.* (pp. 287–318). Boston: Academic Press.

McDaniel, S. (1999). "A Heuristic Evaluation of the Usability of Infants." *STC Intercom*, vol. 46, no. 9, 44.

635

McGown, A., Green, G., and Rogers, P. A. (1998). "Visible ideas: Information patterns of conceptual sketch activity." *Design Studies*, vol. 19, no. 4, 431–453.

Michaelis, P. R., and Wiggins, R. H. (1982). "A human factors engineer's introduction to speech synthesisers." In Badre, A., and Shneiderman, B. (Eds.), *Directions in Human–Computer Interaction* (pp. 149–178). Norwood, NJ: Ablex. Cited in Shneiderman, 1998.

Miller, S. J., and Jarrett, C. (2001). "Should I use a dropdown? Four Steps for Choosing Form Elements on the Web." Available from www.formsthatwork.com.

Mohageg, M. F., and Wagner, A. (2000). "Design considerations for information appliances." In Bergman, E. (Ed.), *Information Appliances and Beyond.* San Francisco: Morgan Kaufmann.

Molich, R., and Nielsen, J. (1990). "Improving a human–computer dialogue." *Communications of the ACM*, vol. 33, 338–348.

Muller, M. J., Matheson, L., Page, C., and Gallup, R. (1998). "Participatory heuristic evaluation." *Interactions*, vol. 5, no. 5, 13–18.

National Statistics (2004). *Living in Britain. Results from the 2002 General Household Survey.* HMSO London. Also available from www.statistics.gov.uk/downloads/theme_compendia/lib2002.pdf), retrieved June 2004.

Neale, D. C., and Carroll, J. M. (1997). "The role of metaphors in user interface design." In Helander, M. G., Landauer, T. K., and Prabhu, P. K. (Eds.), *Handbook of Human–Computer Interaction* (pp. 441–462). Amsterdam: Elsevier Science.

Newman, W., and Lamming, M. G. (1995). *Interactive System Design.* New York: Addison-Wesley.

Nielsen, J. (1990). *Hypertext and Hypermedia.* Boston: Academic Press.

Nielsen, J. (1993). *Usability Engineering.* New York: Academic Press.

Nielsen, J. (1994). "Heuristic evaluation." In Nielsen, J., and Mack, R. L. (Eds.), *Usability Inspection Methods* (pp. 25–62). New York: Wiley.

Nielsen, J. (2000). *Designing Web Usability: The Practice of Simplicity.* Indianapolis, IN: New Riders Press.

Nielsen, J., and Mack, R. (Eds.). (1994). *Usability Inspection Methods.* New York: Wiley.

Norman, D. (1998). *The Invisible Computer.* Boston: MIT Press.

Norman, D. A. (1987). "Some observations on mental models." In Baecker, R. M., and Buxton, W. A. S. (Eds.), *Readings in Human–Computer Interaction: A Multidisciplinary Approach* (pp. 241–244). San Mateo, CA: Morgan Kaufmann.

Norman, D. A. (1988). *The Design of Everyday Things.* New York: Doubleday/Currency Ed. Previously published as *The Psychology of Everyday Things.* New York: Basic Books.

Norman, D. A. (1993). *Turn Signals Are the Facial Expressions of Automobiles.* New York: Perseus.

Norman, D. A., and Draper, S. W. (1986). *User Centered System Design.* Hillsdale, NJ: Lawrence Erlbaum Associates.

Oppenheim, A. N. (1999). *Questionnaire Design, Interviewing and Attitude Measurement.* London: Continuum International Publishing Group.

Pagendarm, M., and Schaumburg, H. (2001). "Why are users banner-blind? The impact of navigation style on the perception of web banners." *Journal of Digital Information*, vol. 2. Available from http://jodi.ecs.soton.ac.uk/Artlcles/v02/i0l/Pagendarm.

Partridge, C. (1999). "Communication breakdown." *The Times*, July 7.

Pearrow, M. (2002). *The Wireless Web Usability Handbook.* Hingham, MA: Charles River Media.

Pickering, J. (1981). Figure 9, Unit 5 Perception, DS262, Introduction to Psychology. The Open University.

Preece, J., Rogers, Y., Sharp, H., Benyon, D., Holland, S., and Carey, T. (1994). *Human–Computer Interaction.* Wokingham: Addison-Wesley.

Pruitt, J., and Adlin, T. (in press). *Personas and User Archetypes: A Field Guide for Interaction Designers.* San Francisco: Morgan Kaufmann.

Pruitt, J., and Grudin, J. (2003). "Personas: Practice and theory." *Designing for User Experiences. Proceedings of the 2003 Conference on Designing for User Experiences* (pp. 1–15). New York: ACM Press. Also available from http://research.microsoft.com/research/coet/Grudin/Personas/Pruitt-Grudin.pdf, June 2004.

Pugh, D. (1978). "Understanding and managing organisational change." In Mabey, C., and Mayon-White, B., *Managing Change.* Milton Keynes: The Open University.

Quesenbery, W. (2003). "The Five Dimensions of Usability." In Albers, M. J., and Mazur, B. (Eds.), *Content and Complexity: Information Design in Technical Communication.* Mahwah, NJ: Lawrence Erlbaum Associates.

Rieman, J., Lewis, C., Young, R. M., and Polson, P. G. (1994). " 'Why is a raven like a writing desk?': Lessons in interface consistency and analogical reasoning from two cognitive architectures." In Adelson, B., Dumais, S., and Olson, J. (Eds.), *Human Factors in Computing Systems. Proceedings of CHI '94.* New York: ACM Press.

Rivlin, C., Lewis, R., and Davies Cooper, R. (Eds.). (1990). *Guidelines for Screen Design.* Oxford: Blackwell Scientific.

Roberts, D., Berry, D., Isensee, S., and Mullaly, J. (1997). "Developing software using OVID." *IEEE Software*, vol. 14, no. 4, 51–57.

Rogers, Y., Rutherford, A., and Bibby, P. (Eds.). (1992). *Models in the Mind: Theory, Perspective and Application.* London: Academic Press.

637

Rosenbaum, S., Rohn, J. A., and Hamburg, J. (2000). "A Toolkit for Strategic Usability." *Proceedings of CHI 2000.* New York: ACM Press.

Rosenfeld, L., and Morville, P. (2002). *Information Architecture for the World Wide Web: Designing Large Scale Websites.* Sebastofol, CA: O'Reilly & Associates.

Rubin, J. (1994). *Handbook of Usability Testing: How to Plan, Design, and Conduct Effective Tests.* New York: Wiley.

Rudd, J., Stern, K. R., and Isensee, S. (1996). "Low vs. high-fidelity prototyping debate." *Interactions,* (January, pp. 76–85).

Safire, M. (2003). "Remote moderated usability: What, why, and how." *12th Annual Usability Professionals Association Conference.* Phoenix, AZ.

Selfridge, O. G. (1955). "Pattern recognition and modern computers." In *Proceedings of the Western Joint Computer Conference.* New York: IEEE.

Shackel B. (1990). "Human factors and usability." In Preece, J., and Keller, L. (Eds.), *Human–Computer Interaction: Selected Readings.* Hemel Hempstead: Prentice Hall.

Shirky, C. (2003). "A group is its own worst enemy." A speech given at *ETech: The O'Reilly Emerging Technology Conference* Santa Clara CA, April 22–25, 2003. Available from www.shirky.com/writings/group_enemy.html.

Shneiderman, B. (1995). "A taxonomy with rule base for the selection of interaction styles." In Baecker, R. M., Grudin, J., Buxton, W. A. S., and Greenberg, S. (Eds.), *Readings in Human–Computer Interaction: Toward the Year 2000* (pp. 401–410). San Francisco: Morgan Kaufmann.

Shneiderman, B. (1998). *Designing the User Interface: Strategies for Effective Human Computer Interaction* (3rd ed.). Reading, MA: Addison-Wesley-Longman.

Snyder, C. (2003). *Paper Prototyping: The Fast and Easy Way to Design and Refine User Interfaces.* San Francisco: Morgan Kaufmann.

Sommerville, I. (1992). *Software Engineering.* (4th ed.). Wokingham: Addison-Wesley.

Sommerville, I. (1995). *Software Engineering* (5th ed.). Harlow: Addison-Wesley.

St. Julien, T. U., and Shaw, C. D. (2003). "Firefighter Command Training Virtual Environment." In *Richard Tapia Celebration of Diversity in Computing. Proceedings of the 2003 Conference on Diversity in Computing* (pp. 30–33). Atlanta, GA.

Sternberg, R. J., and Horvath, J. A. (Eds.), (1999). *Tacit Knowledge in Professional Practice: Researcher and Practitioner Perspectives.* Mahwah, NJ: Lawrence Erlbaum Associates.

Stone, D. K. (2001). *"An investigation into support for early human–computer interaction design activities,"* Ph.D. thesis. The Open University Milton Keynes, UK.

Suwa, M., and Tversky, B. (1996). "What architects see in their sketches: Implications for design tools." In *Human Factors in Computing Systems, CHI '96 Conference Companion* (pp. 191–192). New York: ACM Press.

Tepper, A. (1993). "Future assessment by metaphors." *Behaviour and Information Technology*, vol. 12, 336–345.

Theofanos, M. F., and Redish, J. C. (2003). "Bridging the gap: Between accessibility and usability." *Interactions*, vol. 10, no. 6, 36–51, November/December. Author's version available from www.redish.net/content/papers.html.

Tufte, E. R. (1990). *Envisioning Information.* Cheshire, CT: Graphic Press.

Tullis, T., Fleischman, S., McNulty, M., Cianchette, C., and Bergel, M. (2002). "An empirical comparison of lab and remote usability testing of web sites." *Usability Professionals Association Conference*, July 2002. Orlando, FL.

Tullis, T. S. (1988). "Screen design." In Helander, M. G. (Ed.). *Handbook of Human–Computer Interaction* (pp. 377–411). Amsterdam. North-Holland.

Tullis, T. S., and Stetson, J. N. (2004). "A comparison of questionnaires for assessing website usability." *Usability Professional Association Conference.*

Tyldesley, D. A. (1988). "Employing usability engineering in the development of office products." *Computer Journal*, vol. 31, no. 5, 431–436.

U.S. Census Bureau. (2001). "Home Computers and Internet Use in the United States: August 2000, Special Studies," Issued September 2001. Available at www.census.gov/prod/2001pubs/p23-207.pdf, June 2004.

Virzi, R. A. (1997). "Usability inspection methods." In Helander, M., Landauer, T. K., and Prabhu, P. (Eds.), *Handbook of Human–Computer Interaction* (2nd ed., pp. 705–715). Amsterdam: Elsevier Science.

Weinschenk, S., Jamar, P., and Yeo, S. C. (1997). *GUI Design Essentials.* New York: Wiley.

Weiss, S. (2002). *Handheld Usability.* Chichester: Wiley.

Welbank, M. (1990). "An overview of knowledge acquisition methods." *Interacting with Computers*, vol. 2, no. 1, 83–91.

Wharton, C., Rieman, J., Lewis, C., and Polson, P. (1993). "The cognitive walkthrough method: A practitioner's guide." In Nielsen, J., and Mack, R. L. (Eds.), *Usability Inspection Methods.* New York: Wiley.

Whitelock, D. (1998). "Matching measure for measure? A route through the formative testing of multimedia science software." In Olver, M. (Ed.), *Innovation in the Evaluation of Learning Technology*. London: University of North London.

Whiteside, J., Bennett, J., and Holtzblatt, K. (1988). "Usability engineering: Our experience and evolution." In Helander, M. (Ed.), *Handbook of Human–Computer Interaction* (pp. 791–817). Amsterdam: North-Holland.

Wilson, F., and Clarke, A. (1993). "Evaluating design rationalisations." In Byerley, P. F., Barnard, P. J., and May, J. (Eds.), *Computers, Communication and Usability: Design Issues, Research and Methods for Integrated Services* (pp. 379–411). Amsterdam: North-Holland.

Wilson, S., Bekker, M., Johnson, H., and Johnson, P. (1996). "Costs and benefits of user involvement in design: Practitioners' views." In Sasse, M. A., Cunningham., R. J., and Winder, R. L. (Eds.), *People and Computers XI. Proceedings of HCI '96* (pp. 221–240).

Wixon, D., and Wilson, C. (1997). "The usability engineering framework for product design and evaluation." In Helander, M., Landauer, T. K., and Prabhu, P. (Eds.), *Handbook of Human–Computer Interaction* (2nd ed., pp. 653–688). Amsterdam: Elsevier Science.

Young, R. R. (2003). *The Requirements Engineering Handbook.* Norwood, MA: Artech House.

Index

M

Macro, 207, 618
Mail merging, storyboard of, 118–119
Main container, 155, 618
  for digital library system, 155–156
Maintenance costs, 596
Management summary, of usability results, 568
Managers, as users, 18, 50, 130
Manipulation
  direct. *See* Direct manipulation (DM).
  with music clips, 267
Manual dexterity, pointing device choice based on, 230–231, 235–236
Maps
  effective use of, 260
  for web site navigation, 345–347
Marketese, 366
Marketing
  prototype as tool for, 120
  through images, 260
Marketing personnel, as users, 18, 50
Marshaling signals, emphasizing with color, 256–257
Mean, of quantitative data, 509
Measure element, 540–541, 604, 618
  combining for evaluation, 541–544
Measurement criteria, for usability, 104–106
Measurement evaluation, 23, 618
Media, web site download time and, 358–361
Median, of quantitative data, 509
Medical applications, sound devices for, 266
Meeter and greeter, 495, 619
Membrane keyboards, 228
Memory
  as design principle, 90, 95–96, 617
  in interaction styles, 207, 209, 213, 219
Mental models, 77, 619
  characteristics of, 78–79
  enabled by user interface, 197–199

direct manipulation, 214
form-fill, 210–211
structural *vs.* functional, 80–82
utility of, 82–83, 191, 194
Menu bar, 99, 162
  ordering of, 311
Menu items, naming of, 311, 325
Menus and menu selection, 619
  as interface, 120, 208–210, 619
    advantages and disadvantages of, 217, 235
    guidelines for designing, 209, 274
  in conceptual design, 144–145, 148, 162
  in graphical user interfaces, 309–312, 411
    issues to consider, 310–311
    types of, 309–310
  in handheld devices, 384–385
Message boxes
  in conceptual designs, 144, 154
  in graphical user interfaces, 305–306, 314
  types of, 619
Metaphors, 200, 619
  as word processing context, 200–201, 214, 219
  benefits of, 200
  choosing suitable, 203–204
  form-fill interface as, 211
  in Energetic Sports Center design, 304, 328
  in Global Warming program, 431
  in handheld devices, 384
  in Tokairo case study, 289–291
  problems with, 201–203
  site map, 156, 174
  tabs as, 308–309
  users' experience and, 202–204
Metrics, usability, 104, 627
  evaluation strategy based on, 440–441
  example specifications from, 104, 106–107
  measurement criteria for, 104–106
  selection of appropriate, 106, 120
  time-related, 476

Microwaves
  embedded computers in, 5, 22, 371, 382
  mental model of, 83
Minimal risk, informed consent and, 499
Minimalist design, heuristic inspection of, 526, 528, 534
Mobile phones. *See* Cell phones.
Modal dialog boxes, 307
Modal message box, 306–307, 619
Mode, of quantitative data, 509
Modeless message box, 306, 619
Modeling, scientific, in Global Warming program, 427–432
Monochrome design, 255
Motivation
  as user characteristic, 38, 40–41
  in ATM customer profiles, 44–48
  through images, 260, 264
  video clips for, 266
Mouse
  accuracy of, 235, 237
  as input device, 4, 213, 224, 230
  dialog boxes combined with, 325–327
Mouse clicks, automatic logging of, 476
Movement, animation illustration of, 264
Moving images
  animation as, 264
  as software component, 247, 264–265
  video clips as, 265–266
Multifunction devices, embedded computers in, 375–378, 380–382
Multimedia products, Section 508 standards for, 181–183
Multimedia teaching application, 30
Multimedia user interfaces, ISO standards for, 166
Multiple selections, for list boxes, 319–320